READINGS IN DEVIANT BEHAVIOR

READINGS IN DEVIANT BEHAVIOR

SIXTH EDITION

ALEX THIO
Ohio University

THOMAS C. CALHOUN
Jackson State University

ADDRAIN CONYERS
The College at Brockport, State University of New York

Allyn & Bacon

Boston • New York • San Francisco
Mexico City • Montreal • Toronto • London • Madrid • Munich • Paris
Hong Kong • Singapore • Tokyo • Cape Town • Sydney

Publisher: Karen Hanson
Editorial Assistant: Courtney Shea
Senior Marketing Manager: Kelly May
Senior Production Administrator: Karen Mason
Manufacturing Buyer: Debbie Rossi
Cover Administrator: Joel Gendron
Editorial Production Service: Modern Graphics, Inc.
Electronic Composition: Modern Graphics, Inc.

Library of Congress Cataloging-in-Publication Data

Readings in deviant behavior / [edited by] Alex Thio, Thomas C. Calhoun, Addrain Conyers. — 6th ed.
p. cm.
Includes bibliographical references and index.
ISBN-13: 978-0-205-69557-7 (alk. paper)
ISBN-10: 0-205-69557-4 (alk. paper)
1. Deviant behavior. I. Thio, Alex. II. Calhoun, Thomas C. III. Conyers, Addrain.

HM811.R4 2010
302.5'42—dc22

2008053803

8 2019

Allyn & Bacon
is an imprint of

PEARSON

www.pearson highered.com

ISBN 10: 0-205-69557-4
ISBN 13: 978-0-205-69557-7

Contents

PART FOUR
PHYSICAL VIOLENCE 57

PART FIVE
INTIMATE VIOLENCE 89

PART SIX
SELF-DESTRUCTIVE DEVIANCE 115

PART TEN
INTERNET DEVIANCE 237

PART ELEVEN
PRIVILEGED DEVIANCE 271

PART TWELVE
UNDERPRIVILEGED DEVIANCE 295

PREFACE

In this sixth edition of *Readings in Deviant Behavior*, the following articles are new:

"What Drives the Libyan Suicide Bombers in Iraq?"
"'Hey, Don't Blame Me . . . Blame the Booze'"
"Damn, It Feels Good to be a Gangsta: Selling Drugs on Campus"
"Show Me the Money: Online Mistresses and Slaves"
"Cyberbullying: Offenders and Victims"
"The Good Thing about Workplace Deviance"
"What It's Like to be Known as a Sex Offender"
"Responses to Workplace Bullying "
"Eating for Two: How Pregnant Women Neutralize Nutritional Deviance'"

These articles, along with most of the others in this edition, reflect the current trend in the sociology of deviance. The inclusion of many more studies on noncriminal deviance—such as lesbianism, personal bankruptcy, online dating, exotic dancing, and binge drinking—represents a significant shift from criminal deviance, such as murder, robbery, and rape. Some of the noncriminal deviances, such as the proliferation of cyberdeviance, have only recently emerged on the scene; others, such as binge drinking and corporate corruption, have been around for a long time but have only recently become the subject of research by sociologists. On the theoretical front, there is a change in emphasis from the positivist perspective to the constructionist one. In research methodology, there is greater use of ethnography at the expense of the traditional use of surveys. All these new developments are showcased in the current edition of this reader.

Like its previous editions, this anthology offers comprehensive coverage. As its editors, we decided against taking a single theoretical approach when selecting articles. Instead, we present a great variety of readings that represent the full range of deviance sociology. We believe that students should be exposed to different theories of deviance. Students should also know different kinds of data collected with different research methodologies.

This reader covers all the major theories in deviance sociology, from classic ones such as Merton's strain theory and Becker's labeling theory, to modern ones such as shaming, phenomenological, and feminist theories. In addition, this anthology encompasses a wide spectrum of deviant behaviors. There are articles about deviances that have long attracted sociological attention, such as homicide, suicide, drug abuse, and mental disorders. There are also articles on deviances that in recent years have leapt into public and sociological consciousness, such as suicide bombing, sex tourism, binge drinking, and Internet deviance. Analyses of these subjects rely on data from theory-informed research that runs the gamut from surveys to ethnographic studies. All these analyses are multidisciplinary, coming not only from sociologists but also from scholars and researchers in other fields. They all effectively reflect what the sociology of deviance is like today: diverse, wide-ranging, and exciting.

This is a user-friendly reader, put together with students in mind. The articles are not only authoritative, but also interesting. Many were chosen from a variety of books and journals. Some were solicited from sociologists and researchers. Most important, unique to this reader, most of these articles have been carefully edited for clarity, conciseness, and forcefulness. Students will therefore find them easy and enjoyable to read while learning what deviance is all about.

ACKNOWLEDGMENTS

We want to thank our colleagues who specifically wrote for this reader. Our deep gratitude also goes to all those writers whose published works are presented here. Further deserving our thanks are the many reviewers who have greatly contributed to preparation of a truly useful and student-oriented reader. For contributing to the current edition our thanks go to William Beaver, Robert Morris University; Brian Lawton, Sam Houston State University; and Timothy O'Boyle, Kutztown University.

Introduction

What is deviant behavior? Why ask what it is? Doesn't everybody know it has to do with weirdos and perverts? Not at all. There is, in fact, a great deal of disagreement among people about what they consider deviant. In a classic study, sociologist Jerry Simmons asked a sample of the general public who they thought was deviant. They mentioned 252 different kinds of people as deviants, including homosexuals, prostitutes, alcoholics, drug addicts, murderers, the mentally ill, communists, atheists, liars, Democrats, reckless drivers, self-pitiers, the retired, career women, divorcées, Christians, suburbanites, movie stars, perpetual bridge players, prudes, pacifists, psychiatrists, priests, liberals, conservatives, junior executives, girls who wear makeup, smart-aleck students, and know-it-all professors. If you are surprised that some of these people are considered deviant, your surprise simply adds to the fact that a good deal of disagreement exists among the public about what deviant behavior is.

There is a similar lack of consensus among sociologists. We could say that the study of deviant behavior is probably the most "deviant" of all the subjects in sociology. Sociologists disagree more about the definition of deviant behavior than they do on any other subject.

CONFLICTING DEFINITIONS

Some sociologists simply say that deviance is a violation of any social rule, but others argue that deviance involves more than rule violation—it also has the quality of provoking disapproval, anger, or indignation. Some advocate a broader definition, arguing that a person can be a deviant without violating any rule or doing something that rubs others the wrong way. According to this argument, individuals who are afflicted with some unfortunate condition for which they cannot be held responsible are deviant. Examples include psychotics, paraplegics, the mentally challenged, and other people with physical or mental disabilities. These people are considered deviant because they are disvalued by society. In contrast, some sociologists contend that deviance does not have to be negative. To these sociologists, deviance can be positive, such as being a genius, reformer, creative artist, or glamorous celebrity. Other sociologists disagree, considering "positive deviance" to be an oxymoron—a contradiction in terms (Heckert and Heckert, 2002).

All of these sociologists apparently assume that, whether it is a positive or a negative, disturbing, or disvalued behavior, deviance is real in and of itself. The logic behind this assumption is that if it is not real in the first place, it cannot be considered positive, negative, disturbing, or disvalued. Other sociologists disagree, arguing that deviance does not have to be real behavior for it to be labeled deviant. People can be falsely accused of being criminal, erroneously diagnosed as mentally ill, stereotyped as dangerous because of their skin color, and so on. Conversely, committing a deviant act does not necessarily make a person a deviant, especially when the act is kept secret. It is, therefore, the label *deviant*—a mental construction or image of an act as deviant, rather than the act itself—that makes an individual deviant.

Some sociologists go beyond the notion of labeling to define deviance by stressing the importance of power. They observe that relatively powerful people are capable of avoiding the fate suffered by the powerless—being falsely, erroneously, or unjustly labeled deviant. The key reason is that the powerful, either by themselves or through influencing public opinion or both, hold more power for labeling others' behavior as deviant. Understandably, sociologists who hold this view define deviance as any act considered by the powerful at a given time and place to be a violation of some social rule.

From this welter of conflicting definitions, we can nonetheless discern the influence of two opposing perspectives: positivism and social constructionism. The positivist perspective is associated with the sciences, such as physics, chemistry, or biology. It influences how scientists see and study their subject. In contrast, the constructionist perspective has more to do with the humanities, such as art, language, or philosophy. It affects how scholars in these fields see and study their subject. These two perspectives can be found in sociology; some sociologists are more influenced by the positivist perspective and others by the constructionist. Positivist sociologists tend to define deviance in one way, whereas constructionist sociologists pursue another way. The two perspectives further influence the use of certain theories and methodologies for producing knowledge about deviant behavior. The conflicting definitions that we have discussed can be couched in terms of these two perspectives. The definitions that focus on deviance as rule-breaking behavior are essentially positivist, whereas those that center on labeling and power are constructionist. Let us delve more deeply into the meanings and implications of these two conflicting perspectives.

CONFLICTING PERSPECTIVES

The knowledge about deviance basically consists of answers to three questions: (1) What to study? (2) How to study it? (3) What does the result of the study mean? The first question deals with the subject of study, the second has to do with the method of study, and the third concerns the data-based theory about the subject. Positivism and constructionism provide conflicting answers to each question.

Subject: What to Study?

Positivism suggests that we study deviance or deviants. The reason deals with the positivist's absolutist definition of deviance. According to this definition, deviance is absolutely or intrinsically real in that it possesses some qualities that distinguish it from conventionality. Similarly, deviants are thought to have certain attributes that make them different from conventional individuals. By contrast, social constructionism suggests that we study law enforcers and other such people who are influenced by society to construct an image of certain others as deviants and then label them as such, or how the process of such labeling takes place and affects the labeled. This is because the constructionist assumes the relativist stance in defining deviance as a socially constructed label imposed on some behavior. Such a definition can be said to be relativist by implying that the deviancy of a behavior is relative to—dependent on—the socially constructed negative reaction to the behavior.

Absolutism: Deviance as Absolutely Real. Around the turn of the twentieth century, criminologists believed that criminals possessed certain biological traits that were absent in noncriminals. Those biological traits included defective genes, bumps on the head, a long lower jaw, a scanty beard, an unattractive face, and a tough body build. Because all these traits are inherited, people were believed to be criminals simply because they were born criminals. If they were born criminals, they would always be criminals. As the saying goes, "If you've had it, you've had it." No matter where they might go—

they could go anywhere in the world—they would still be criminals.

Then the criminologists shifted their attention from biological to psychological traits. Criminals were thought to have certain mental characteristics that noncriminals did not have. More specifically, criminals were believed to be feeble-minded, psychotic, neurotic, psychopathic, or otherwise mentally disturbed. Like biological traits, these mental characteristics were seen as inherent in individual criminals. Also, like biological traits, mental characteristics would stay with the criminals, no matter where they went. Again, because of these psychological traits, criminals would always remain criminals.

Today's positivist sociologists, however, have largely abandoned the use of biological and psychological traits to differentiate criminals from noncriminals. They recognize the important role of social factors in determining a person's status as a criminal. Such status does not remain the same across time and space; instead, it changes in different periods and with different societies. A polygamist may be a criminal in Western society but a law-abider in Moslem countries. A person who sees things invisible to others may be a psychotic in Western society but may become a spiritual leader among some South Pacific tribes. Nevertheless, positivist sociologists still largely regard deviance as intrinsically real. Countering the relativist notion of deviance as basically a social construction in the form of a label imposed on an act, positivist Travis Hirschi (1973) argues: "The person may not have committed a 'deviant' act, but he did (in many cases) do something. And it is just possible that what he did was a result of things that had happened to him in the past; it is also possible that the past in some inscrutable way remains with him and that if he were left alone he would do it again." Moreover, countering the relativist notion of mental illness as a label imputed to some people's behavior, positivist Gwynn Nettler (1974) explicitly voices his absolutist stance: "Some people are more crazy than others; we can tell the difference; and calling lunacy a name does not cause it." These positivist sociologists seem to say that just as a rose by any other name would smell as sweet, so deviance by any other label is just as real.

Relativism: Deviance as a Label. Social constructionists hold the relativist view that deviant behavior by itself does not have any intrinsic characteristics unless it is thought to have those characteristics. The so-called intrinsically deviant characteristics do not come from the behavior itself; they originate instead from some people's minds. To put it simply, an act appears deviant only because some people think it so. As Howard Becker (1963) says, "Deviant behavior is behavior that people so label." Therefore, no deviant label, no deviant behavior. The existence of deviance depends on the label. Deviance, then, is a mental construct (an idea, thought, or image) expressed in the form of a label.

Because they effectively consider deviance unreal, constructionists understandably stay away from studying it. They are more interested in the questions of whether and why a given act is defined by society as deviant. This leads to studying people who label others as deviant—such as the police and other law-enforcing agents. If constructionists study so-called deviants, they do so by focusing on the nature of labeling and its consequences.

In studying law-enforcing agents, constructionists have found a huge lack of consensus on whether a certain person should be treated as a criminal. The police often disagree among themselves about whether a suspect should be arrested, and judges often disagree about whether those arrested should be convicted or acquitted. In addition, because laws vary from one state to another, the same type of behavior may be defined as criminal in one state but not in another. Prostitution, for example, is legal in Nevada but not in other states. There is, then, a relativity principle in deviant behavior; behavior gets defined as deviant relative to a given norm, standard of behavior, or the way people react to it. If it is not related to the norm or to the reaction of other people, a given behavior is in itself meaningless—it is impossible to say whether it is deviant or conforming. Constructionists strongly emphasize this relativistic view, according to which, deviance, like beauty, is in the eye of the beholder.

Method: How to Study It?

Positivism suggests that we use objective methods such as survey, experiment, or detached observation. The subject is treated like an object, forced, for example, to answer the same questions as presented to everybody else with the same value-free, emotionless demeanor. This is because positivists define deviance as a largely objective fact, namely, a publicly observable, outward aspect of human behavior. By contrast, social constructionism suggests that we study individuals with more subjective methods, such as ethnography, participant observation, or open-ended, in-depth interviews. With these methods, subjects are treated as unique, whole persons and are encouraged to freely express their feelings in any way they want. This is because constructionists define deviance as a mostly personal experience—a hidden, inner aspect of human behavior.

Objectivism: Deviance as an Objective Fact. By focusing on the outward aspect of deviance, positivists assume that sociologists can be as objective in studying deviance as natural scientists can be in studying physical phenomena. The trick is to treat deviants as if they are objects, like those studied by natural scientists. Nonetheless, positivist sociologists cannot help being aware of the basic difference between their subject, human beings, and that of natural scientists, plants, animals, and inanimate objects. As human beings themselves, positivist sociologists must have certain feelings about their subject. However, they try to control their personal biases by forcing themselves not to pass moral judgment on deviant behavior or share the deviant person's feelings. Instead, they try to concentrate on the subject matter as it outwardly appears. Further, these sociologists have tried hard to follow the scientific rule that all their ideas about deviant behavior should be subject to public scrutiny. This means that other sociologists should be able to check out the ideas to see whether they are supported by facts.

Such a drive to achieve scientific objectivity has produced substantial knowledge about deviant behavior. No longer popular today are such value-loaded and subjective notions as maladjustment, moral failing, debauchery, demoralization, sickness, pathology, and abnormality. Replacing these outdated notions are such value-free and objective concepts as innovation, retreatism, ritualism, rebellion, culture conflict, subcultural behavior, white-collar crime, norm violation, learned behavior, and reinforced behavior.

To demonstrate the objective reality of these concepts, positivist sociologists have used official reports and statistics, clinical reports, surveys of self-reported behavior, and surveys of victimization. Positivists recognize the unfortunate fact that the sample of deviants in the studies—especially in official statistics—does not accurately represent the entire population of deviants. Nevertheless, positivists believe that the quality of information obtained by these methods can be improved and refined. In the meantime, they consider the data, though inadequate, useful for revealing at least some aspect of the totality of deviant behavior.

Subjectivism: Deviance as a Personal Experience. To social constructionists, the supposedly deviant behavior is a personal experience and the supposedly deviant person is a conscious, feeling, thinking, and reflective subject. Constructionists insist that there is a world of difference between humans (as active subjects) and nonhuman beings and things (as passive objects). Humans feel and reflect, but animals, plants, things, and the others do not. It is proper and useful for natural scientists to assume and then study nature as an object, because this study can produce objective knowledge for controlling the natural world. It may also be useful for social scientists to assume and then study humans as objects, because it may produce objective knowledge for controlling humans. However, this violates the constructionist's humanist values and sensibilities.

Constructionists are opposed to the control of humans; instead, they advocate the protection and expansion of human worth, dignity, and freedom. One result of this humanist ideology is the observation that so-called objective knowledge about human behavior is inevitably superficial whenever it is used to control people. In order for the former white racist government in South Africa to control blacks, for example, it needed only the superficial knowledge that blacks were identifiable and separable from whites. However, to achieve the humanist goal of protecting and expanding blacks' human worth, dignity, and freedom, a deeper understanding of blacks is needed. This understanding requires appreciating and empathizing with them, experiencing what they experience as blacks, and seeing blacks' lives and the world around them from their perspective. We must look at the black experience from the inside as a participant rather than from the outside as a spectator. In a word, we must adopt the internal, subjective view instead of the external, objective one.

The same principle, according to constructionists, should hold for understanding deviants and their deviant behavior. Constructionists contrast this subjective approach with the positivists' objective one. To constructionists, positivists treat deviance as if it were an immoral, unpleasant, or repulsive phenomenon that should be controlled, corrected, or eliminated. In consequence, positivists have used the objective approach by staying aloof from deviants, studying the external aspects of their deviant behavior and relying on a set of preconceived ideas to guide their study. The result is a collection of surface facts about deviants, such as their poverty, lack of schooling, poor self-image, and low aspirations. All this may be used to control and eliminate deviance, but it does not tell us, in Howard Becker's (1963) words, "what a deviant does in his daily round of activity, and what he thinks about himself, society, and his activities." To understand the life of a deviant, constructionists believe, we need to use the relatively subjective approach, which requires our appreciation for and empathy with the deviant. The aim of this subjective approach, according to David Matza (1969), "is to comprehend and to illuminate the subject's view and to interpret the world as it appears to him."

As a result of their subjective and empathetic approach, constructionists often present an image of deviants as basically the same as conventional people. People who are deaf, for example, are the same as those who hear in being able to communicate and live a normal life. They should, therefore, be respected rather than pitied. This implies that so-called deviant behavior, because it is like so-called conventional behavior, should not be controlled, cured, or eradicated by society.

Theory: What Does It Mean?

Positivism suggests that we use etiological, causal, or explanatory theories to make sense of what research has found out about deviant behavior, because positivists favor the determinist view that deviance is determined by forces beyond the individual's control. By contrast, constructionism suggests that we go for largely noncausal, descriptive, or analytical theories. Such theories provide detailed analyses of the subjective, experiential world of deviance. Constructionists feel at home with these analyses because they regard most deviance as a voluntary act, an expression of free will.

Determinism: Deviance as "Determined" Behavior. Overly enthusiastic about the prospect of turning their discipline into a science, early sociologists argued that, like animals, plants, and material objects that natural scientists study, humans do not have any free will. The reason is that acknowledgment of free will would contradict the scientific principle of determinism. If a killer is thought to will, cause, or determine a murderous act, then it does not make sense to say that the murderous act is caused by such things as the individual's physical characteristics, mental condition, family background, or some social experience. Therefore, in defending their scientific principle of determinism, the early sociologists maintained their denial of free will. However, today's positivist sociologists assume that humans do possess free will. Still, this assumption, they argue, does not undermine the scientific principle of determinism. No matter how much a person exercises free will by making choices and decisions, the choices and decisions do not simply happen but are determined by some causes. If a woman chooses to kill her husband rather than continue to live with him, she certainly has free will or freedom of choice so long as nobody forces her to do what she does. However, some factor may determine the woman's choice of one alternative over another, or the way she exercises her free will. One such factor, as research has suggested, may be a long history of abuse at the hands of her husband. Thus, according to today's positivists, there is no inconsistency between freedom and causality.

Although they allow for human freedom of choice, positivists do not use it to explain why people behave in a certain way. They will not, for example, explain why the woman kills by saying "because she chooses to kill." This is no explanation at all, because the idea of choice can also be used to explain why another woman does not kill her husband—by saying "because she chooses not to." According to positivists, killing and not killing (or, more generally, deviant and conventional behavior), being two contrary phenomena, cannot be explained by the same thing, such as choice. The idea of choice simply cannot explain the difference between deviance and conventionality; it cannot explain why one man chooses to kill when another chooses not to kill. Therefore, although positivists do believe in human choice, they will not attribute deviance to human choice. They will instead explain deviance by using such concepts as wife abuse, broken homes, unhappy homes, lower-class background, economic deprivation, social disorganization, rapid social change, differential association, differential reinforcement, and lack of social control. Any one of these causes of deviance can be used to illustrate what positivists consider a real explanation of deviance, because, for example, wife abuse is more likely to cause a woman to kill her husband than not. Etiological theories essentially point out factors like those as the causes of deviance.

Voluntarism: Deviance as a Voluntary Act. To social constructionists, the supposedly deviant behavior is a voluntary act or an expression of human volition, will, or choice. Constructionists take this stance because they are disturbed by what they claim to be the dehumanizing implication of the positivist view of deviant behavior. The positivist view is said to imply that a human being is like "a robot, a senseless and purposeless machine reacting to every fortuitous change in the external and internal environment." Constructionists emphasize that human beings, because they possess free will and choice-making ability, determine or cause their own behavior.

To support this voluntarist assumption, constructionists tend to analyze how social control agencies define some people as deviant and carry out the sanctions against them. Such analyses often accent, as Edwin Lemert (1972) has observed, "the arbitrariness of official action, stereotyped decision-making in bureaucratic contexts, bias in the administration of law, and the general preemptive nature of society's controls over deviants." All this conveys the strong impression that control agents, being in positions of power, exercise their free will by actively, intentionally, and purposefully controlling the "deviants."

Constructionists also analyze people who have been labeled deviant. The "deviants" are not presented as if they are robots, passively and senselessly developing a poor self-image as conventional society expects. Instead, they are described as actively seeking positive meanings in their deviant activities. In Jack Katz's (1988) analysis, murderers see themselves as morally superior to their victims. The killing is said to give the murderers the self-righteous feeling of defending their dignity and respectability because their victims have unjustly humiliated them by taunting or insulting them. Katz also portrays robbers as feeling themselves morally superior to their victims—regarding their victims as fools or suckers who deserve to be robbed. If robbers want to hold up somebody on the street, they first ask a potential victim for the time, for directions, for a cigarette light, or for change. Each of these requests is intended to determine whether the person is a fool. The request for the time, for example, gives the robber the opportunity to know whether the prospective victim has an expensive watch. Complying with the request, then, is taken to establish the person as a fool and hence the right victim.

SUMMARY AND CONCLUSION

Each of the positivist and social constructionist perspectives consists of three related assumptions, and each assumption suggests a strategy for contributing to the sociology of deviance. For the positivist perspective, the first is the absolutist assumption that deviant behavior is absolutely real. This suggests that we study deviance or deviants. Second is the objectivist assumption that deviant behavior is an objective, publicly observable fact. This suggests that we use objective research methods such as survey, experiment, or detached observation. Third is the determinist assumption that deviance is determined or caused by certain social forces. This suggests that we use causal theories to make sense of research data. With the social constructionist perspective, the first assumption is that deviant behavior is basically a label, mental construct, or social construction. This suggests that we study law enforcers and other labelers, the process of labeling, and the consequences of labeling. The second assumption is that the supposedly deviant behavior is a personal experience. This suggests that we use less objective research methods such as ethnography, participant observation, or open-ended, in-depth interviews. The third assumption is that the so-called deviance is a voluntary, self-willed act. This suggests that we develop noncausal, descriptive theories. (See Table I.1 for a quick review.)

The diverse definitions, theories, methodologies, and data we have discussed reflect many different aspects of deviant behavior. Although they appear to conflict, they actually complement each other. They may be compared with the different views of a house. From the front, the house has a door, windows, and a chimney on top. From the back, it has a door and a chimney on top but fewer windows. From the side, it has no doors, but it has windows and a chimney on top. From the top, it has no doors or windows, but a chimney in the

Table I.1 A Summary of Two Perspectives

POSITIVIST PERSPECTIVE	CONSTRUCTIONIST PERSPECTIVE
Absolutism Deviance is absolutely, intrinsically real; hence, deviance or deviants are the subject of study.	*Relativism* Deviance is a label, a social construction; hence, labelers, labeling, and the impacts of labeling are the subject of study.
Objectivism Deviance is an objective, observable fact; hence, objective research methods are used.	*Subjectivism* Deviance is a personal experience; hence, subjective research methods are used.
Determinism Deviance is a determined behavior, a product of causation; hence, casual, explanatory theory is developed.	*Voluntarism* Deviance is a voluntary act, an expression of free will; hence, noncausal, descriptive theory is developed.

middle. It is the same house, but it looks different, depending on one's position. Taking in the different views on the house ensures a fuller knowledge of what the house actually looks like. Similarly, knowing the different views on deviant behavior ensures a fuller understanding of deviance. This reader is intended to make that possible.

REFERENCES

Becker, Howard S. 1963. *Outsiders: Studies in the Sociology of Deviance.* New York: Free Press.

Heckert, Alex, and Druann Maria Heckert. 2002. "A New Typology of Deviance: Integrating Normative and Reactivist Definitions of Deviance." *Deviant Behavior* 23:449–479.

Hirschi, Travis. 1973. "Procedural Rules and the Study of Deviant Behavior." *Social Problems* 21:166–171.

Katz, Jack. 1988. *Seductions of Crime: Moral and Sensual Attractions in Doing Evil.* New York: Basic Books.

Lemert, Edwin M. 1972. *Human Deviance, Social Problems, and Social Control*, 2d ed. Englewood Cliffs, NJ: Prentice Hall.

Matza, David. 1969. *Becoming Deviant.* Englewood Cliffs, NJ: Prentice Hall.

Nettler, Gwynn. 1974. "On Telling Who's Crazy." *American Sociological Review*, 39:893–894.

PART ONE

DEFINING DEVIANCE

Bonnie Pitzer, a middle-school student, was taking a vocabulary test. When she drew a blank on the word "desolated," she did not panic, but instead quietly searched the Internet for the definition. Was she cheating? If she was, her behavior may be regarded as deviant. In today's Internet age, however, a growing number of educators, including Bonnie's teacher, do not consider her behavior to be cheating or deviant. To them, intelligent online surfing and analysis are more important than rote memorization. To her teacher, Bonnie aced the test not only because she knew how to surf the Internet for the meaning of a word, but also because she was able to use the word in a sentence. As her teacher explains, "I want the kids to be able to apply the meaning, not to be able to memorize it." But many other teachers would regard Bonnie as deviant for cheating on her test.[1]

There is, in fact, a great deal of disagreement among people as to what they consider deviant. If you ask a variety of people who they think is deviant, they will likely mention many different kinds of people, including prostitutes, alcoholics, drug users, murderers, the mentally ill, atheists, liars, Democrats, Republicans, reckless drivers, movie stars, smart-aleck students, know-it-all professors, and so on. To you, some of these people are not deviant at all, but to others they are. Given this disagreement, who determines what constitutes deviance? This question, in effect, asks how sociologists go about defining what deviance is. Here are two related articles that deal with this subject. In the first article, "Images of Deviance," Stephen Pfohl presents the sociological view on why some people are seen and treated as deviant. In the second article, "Defining Deviancy Down," Daniel Patrick Moynihan discusses how our society today no longer sees many harmful behaviors as deviant. In Moynihan's words, many people define deviancy down by accepting or tolerating a large amount of it as normal, but more conservative Americans define deviance up by demonizing it, condemning it, or advocating a harsh penalty for it.

[1]Ellen Gamerman, "Legalized Cheating." *Wall Street Journal*, January 21, 2006, pp. 1, 8.

CHAPTER 1

IMAGES OF DEVIANCE

STEPHEN PFOHL

The scene is a crowded church during the American Civil War. "It was a time of great and exalting excitement. The country was up in arms, the war was on, in every breast burned the holy fire of patriotism." So says Mark Twain in his short and searing parable—*The War Prayer*. Amidst the clamor of beating drums, marching bands, and toy pistols popping, Twain describes an emotional church service. A passionate minister stirs the gallant hearts of eager volunteers; bronzed returning heroes; and their families, friends, and neighbors. The inspired congregation await their minister's every word.

And with one impulse the house rose, with glowing eyes and beating hearts, and poured out that tremendous invocation—

> God the all-terrible!
> Thou who ordainest,
> Thunder thy clarion
> and lightning thy sword!

Then came the "long" prayer. None could remember the like of it for passionate pleading and moving and beautiful language. The burden of its supplication was that an ever-merciful and benignant Father of us all would watch over our noble young soldiers and aid, comfort, and encourage them in their patriotic work; bless them, shield them in the day of battle and the hour of peril, bear them in His mighty hand, make them strong and confident, invincible in the bloody onset; help them to crush the foe, grant to them and to their flag and country imperishable honor and glory.

Wars come and go. Words vary. Nonetheless, the essential message of this sermon remains alarmingly the same: "God is on our side." Before continuing with Twain's story, I ask you to consider a more contemporary version of this age-old narrative—the 1991 Gulf War between Iraq and the United States–led coalition of "New World Order" forces demanding an Iraqi withdrawal from Kuwait. Claiming it to be its moral imperative to repel an act of international aggression, the United States pictured Iraqi President Saddam Hussein as a Hitler-like character bent on world domination. Iraq in turn cited contradictions in the U.S. position (its long-term support for Israeli occupation of Palestinian territories, for example) as evidence of both U.S. hypocrisy and what Iraq alleged to be the true motives for the attack on Iraq—namely, "American" efforts to police the price of oil. Each side in this conflict represented the other as evil, treacherous, and power-mongering. Each side claimed to be righteous and blessed by God. This is typical of societies engaged in war.

Returning to Twain's story, what is untypical about this thoughtful tale is what happens next. It is not only untypical, but "deviant." After the minister completes his moving prayer, an "unnaturally pale," aged stranger enters the church. He is adorned with long hair and dressed in a full-length robe. The stranger motions the startled

Source: Stephen Pfohl, *Images of Deviance and Social Control*, 2nd ed. (New York: McGraw-Hill, 1994), pp. 1–6. Reprinted with permission.

minister aside and informs the shocked parishioners that he is a messenger from Almighty God. He tells the congregation that God has heard their prayer and will grant it, but only after they consider the full import of their request. In rephrasing the original sermon the mysterious messenger reveals a more troubling side to the congregation's prayer. When they ask blessing for themselves they are, at the same time, praying for the merciless destruction of other humans (their enemies). In direct and graphic language the old man portrays the unspoken implications of their request, as follows:

> help us to tear their soldiers to bloody shreds with our shells;
>
> help us to cover their smiling fields with the pale forms of their patriotic dead;
>
> help us to draw the thunder of the guns with shrieks of their wounded, writhing in pain;
>
> help us to lay waste their humble homes with a hurricane of fire;
>
> help us to wring the hearts of their unoffending widows to unavailing grief;
>
> help us to turn them out roofless with their little children to wander unbefriended the wastes of their desolated land.

The strange old man continues—talking about blighting their lives, bringing tears, and staining the snow with blood. He completes his war prayer with a statement about the humble and contrite hearts of those who ask God's blessings. The congregation pauses in silence. He asks if they still desire what they have prayed for. "Ye have prayed it; if ye still desire it, speak! The messenger of the Most High waits." We are now at the final page of Twain's book. The congregation's response is simple and abrupt. As suggested previously, the old stranger was clearly a social deviant. In Twain's words: "It was believed afterward that the man was a lunatic, because there was no sense in what he said."

The stranger in *The War Prayer* directly threatens the normal, healthy, patriotic, and blood-lusting beliefs of the embattled congregation. Yet it is with ease that they contain and control this threat. They do not have to take seriously the chilling implications of his sermon. Their religious and patriotic senses are protected from his disturbing assault. Why? The reason is as simple as their response. They believe that he is a lunatic. They believe that he is a deviant. By classifying the old man as a deviant they need not listen to him. The congregation's beliefs are protected, even strengthened. The lunatic's beliefs are safely controlled. *The War Prayer* is thus a story of how some people imagine other people to be "deviant" and thereby protect or isolate themselves from those whom they fear and from that which challenges the way in which "normal" social life is organized. It is a story of how people convince themselves of what is normal by condemning those who disagree. It is a story of both deviance and social control. . . .

The story of deviance and social control is a battle story. It is a story of the battle to control the ways people think, feel, and behave. It is a story of winners and losers and of the strategies people use in struggles with one another. Winners in the battle to control "deviant acts" are crowned with a halo of goodness, acceptability, normality. Losers are viewed as living outside the boundaries of social life as it ought to be, outside the "common sense" of society itself. They may be seen by others as evil, sleazy, dirty, dangerous, sick, immoral, crazy, or just plain deviant. They may even come to see themselves in such negative imagery, to see themselves as deviants.

Deviants are only one part of the story of deviance and social control. Deviants never exist except in relation to those who attempt to control them. Deviants exist only in opposition to those whom they threaten and those who have enough power to control against such threats. The outcome of the battle of deviance and social control is this. Winners obtain the privilege of organizing social life as they see fit. Losers are trapped within the vision of others. They are labeled deviant and subjected to an array of current social control practices. Depending upon the controlling wisdom at a particular moment in history, deviants may be executed, brutally beaten, fined, shamed, incarcerated, drugged, hospitalized, or even treated to heavy doses of tender loving care. But first and foremost they are prohibited from passing as normal women or men. They are branded with the image of being deviant.

When we think of losers in the battle to control acceptable images of social life, it may seem natural to think of juvenile gang members, serial killers, illegal drug users, homosexuals, and burglars. Indeed, common sense may tell us that such people are simply deviant. But where does this common sense come from? How do we come to know that certain actions or certain people are deviant, while others are "normal"? Do people categorized as deviants really behave in a more dangerous fashion than others? Some people think so. Is this true?

Think of the so-called deviants mentioned above. Are their actions truly more harmful than the actions of people not labeled as deviants? In many cases the answer is no. Consider the juvenile gang. In recent years the organized drug dealing and violent activities of gangs have terrorized people living in poverty-stricken and racially segregated urban neighborhoods. Gang-related deviance has also been the focal point for sensational media stories and for social control policies ranging from selective "stop-and-search" police tactics to the building of new prisons and (in Los Angeles) even the criminalization of alleged gang members' parents.

But what about the people most responsible for the oppressive inner-city conditions that lie at the root of many gang-related activities? What about the "gangs" of bankers whose illegal redlining of mortgage loans blocks the investment of money in inner-city neighborhoods? What about the "gangs" of corporate executives whose greed for short-term profits has led to the "off-shoring" of industrial jobs to "underdeveloped" countries where labor is cheap and more easily exploitable? Aren't the actions of such respectable people as costly as, if less visible than, the activities of most inner-city gangs? Yet, there is an important difference: unlike gangs of elite deviants, inner-city youths have little or no real access to dominant institutions in which contemporary power is concentrated.

A related question may be posed concerning serial killers. The violence of serial killers haunts our nightly news broadcasts. Indeed, the seemingly random character of serial killings—although they are most commonly directed against women and children—instills a deep and alarming sense of dread within society as a whole. Nevertheless, the sporadic violence of serial murderers, no matter how fearful, is incomparable in terms of both scope and number to the much less publicized "serial killings" perpetrated by U.S.-supported *death squads* in countries such as El Salvador and Guatemala. The targets of such death squads are typically people who dare to speak out in the name of social justice. From 1980 to 1991, for instance, approximately 75,000 Salvadoran civilians were secretly killed or made to "disappear" by paramilitary executioners. Why is it that such systematic murders are rarely acknowledged as true serial killings? Why, moreover, do such cold-blooded killings provoke so little U.S. public outrage in comparison to the attention given to the isolated violence of individual murderers, such as Ted Bundy or Jeffrey Dahmer? Is it because the people who authorize them are respectable persons, sometimes even publicly elected officials? Is it because, though we feel vulnerable to other serial killers, we ourselves—at least those of us who are white, male, North American, and economically privileged to live at a distance from the violence that historically envelops the daily lives of others—feel protected from death squads?

Similar questions might be raised about drug users. When we speak of the abuse of drugs, why do we often think only of the "controlled substances" that some people use as a means of achieving psychic escape, altered consciousness, and/or bodily pleasure? True, we as individuals and as a society may pay a heavy price for the abuse of such drugs as cocaine and heroin. But what about other—legal—substances that many of us are "on" much of the time? Some of these drugs are even more dangerous than their illicit counterparts. In addition to alcohol, tobacco, chemical food additives, and meat from animals that have been fed antibiotics and hormones, our society openly promotes the use of prescription and over-the-counter drugs for everything from losing weight, curing acne, and overcoming anxiety to building strong bodies, fighting depression, and alleviating allergies caused by industrial pollution. Certainly many of these substances have their salutary effects and may help us adjust to the world in which we live. However, even legal substances can be abused; they too can be dangerous. The effects can be direct, jeopardizing an individual's health or fostering addiction, or they can be indirect and more insidious. For example, consider the role drugs play in creating and sustaining our excessively image-conscious, age-conscious environment and in promoting our tendency to avoid dealing with personal conflicts and everyday problems in a thoughtful and responsible manner. Also—not to belabor the issue—just think of what we are doing to our planet, to our future, with our use of pesticides, fertilizers, and other industrial products and by-products. To raise such concerns is not to claim that legal drugs are more dangerous than illegal drugs, but simply to suggest that what is officially labeled illegal or deviant often has more to do with what society economically values than with whether the thing is physically harmful per se.

Further consider the actions of sexist heterosexuals. Such persons may routinely mix various forms of sexual harassment with manipulative patriarchal power and an intolerance of alternative forms of sexual intimacy. Despite the harm these heterosexist individuals cause, they are far less likely to be labeled deviant than are gay, lesbian, or bisexual lovers who caress one another with affection. The same goes for corporate criminals, such as the executives . . . implicated in the savings and loan scandal. The stealthy acts of such white-collar criminals have cost the U.S. public as much as $500 billion. Yet the elite deviance of the upper echelon of rule breakers is commonly less feared than are the street crimes of ordinary burglars and robbers.

From the preceding examples it should be evident that many forms of labeled deviance are not more costly to society than the behaviors of people who are less likely to be labeled deviant. Why? The answer . . . is that labeled deviants are viewed as such because they threaten the control of people who have enough power to shape the way society imagines the boundary between good and bad, normal and pathological, acceptable and deviant. This is the crux of the effort to understand the battle between deviance and social control. Deviance is always the flip side of the coin used to maintain social control.

REVIEW QUESTIONS

1. Explain what the author means when he says, "Deviants never exist except in relation to those who attempt to control them."
2. Why did the congregation dismiss what the "strange old man" had to say?
3. Using Pfohl as your frame of reference, how does one become a "winner" or a "loser"?

CHAPTER 2

DEFINING DEVIANCY DOWN

DANIEL PATRICK MOYNIHAN

In one of the founding texts of sociology, *The Rules of Sociological Method* (1895), Emile Durkheim set it down that "crime is normal." "It is," he wrote, "completely impossible for any society entirely free of it to exist." By defining what is deviant, we are enabled to know what is not, and hence to live by shared standards.

The matter was pretty much left at that until seventy years later when, in 1965, Kai T. Erikson published *Wayward Puritans*, a study of "crime rates" in the Massachusetts Bay Colony. The plan behind the book, as Erikson put it, was "to test [Durkheim's] notion that the number of deviant offenders a community can afford to recognize is likely to remain stable over time." The notion proved out very well indeed. Despite occasional crime waves, as when itinerant Quakers refused to take off their hats in the presence of magistrates, the amount of deviance in this corner of seventeenth-century New England fitted nicely with the supply of stocks and whipping posts. Erikson remarks:

> *The agencies of control often seem to define their job as that of keeping deviance within bounds rather than that of obliterating it altogether. Many judges, for example, assume that severe punishments are a greater deterrent to crime than moderate ones, and so it is important to note that many of them are apt to impose harder penalties when crime seems to be on the increase and more lenient ones when it does not, almost as if the power of the bench were being used to keep the crime rate from getting out of hand.... Hence "the number of deviant offenders a community* can afford *to recognize is likely to remain stable over time." [My emphasis]*

Social scientists are said to be on the lookout for poor fellows getting a bum rap. But here is a theory that clearly implies that there are circumstances in which society will choose *not* to notice behavior that would be otherwise controlled, or disapproved, or even punished.

It appears to me that this is in fact what we in the United States have been doing of late. I proffer the thesis that, over the past generation, since the time Erikson wrote, the amount of deviant behavior in American society has increased beyond the levels the community can "afford to recognize" and that, accordingly, we have been redefining deviancy so as to exempt much conduct previously stigmatized, and also quietly raising the "normal" level in categories where behavior is now abnormal by any earlier standard....

[In today's normalization of deviance] we are dealing with the popular psychological notion of "denial." In 1965, having reached the conclusion that there would be a dramatic increase in single-parent families, I reached the further conclusion that this would in turn lead to a dramatic increase in crime. In an article in *America*, I wrote:

> *From the wild Irish slums of the 19th century Eastern seaboard to the riot-torn suburbs of Los Angeles, there is one unmistakable lesson in American history: a community that allows a large number of young men to grow up in broken*

Source: Daniel Patrick Moynihan, "Defining Deviancy Down," *The American Scholar*, vol. 62, no. 1 (Winter 1993), pp. 17–30.

> *families, dominated by women, never acquiring any stable relationship to male authority, never acquiring any set of rational expectations about the future—that community asks for and gets chaos. Crime, violence, unrest, unrestrained lashing out at the whole social structure—that is not only to be expected; it is very near to inevitable.*

The inevitable, as we now know, has come to pass, but here again our response is curiously passive. Crime is a more or less continuous subject of political pronouncement, and from time to time it will be at or near the top of opinion polls as a matter of public concern. But it never gets much further than that. In the words spoken from the bench, Judge Edwin Torres of the New York State Supreme Court, Twelfth Judicial District, described how "the slaughter of the innocent marches unabated: subway riders, bodega owners, cab drivers, babies; in laundromats, at cash machines, on elevators, in hallways." In personal communication, he writes: "This numbness, this near narcoleptic state can diminish the human condition to the level of combat infantrymen, who, in protracted campaigns, can eat their battlefield rations seated on the bodies of the fallen, friend and foe alike. A society that loses its sense of outrage is doomed to extinction." There is no expectation that this will change, nor any efficacious public insistence that it do so. The crime level has been *normalized.*

Consider the St. Valentine's Day Massacre. In 1929 in Chicago during Prohibition, four gangsters killed seven gangsters on February 14. The nation was shocked. The event became legend. It merits not one but two entries in the *World Book Encyclopedia.* I leave it to others to judge, but it would appear that the society in the 1920s was simply not willing to put up with this degree of deviancy. In the end, the Constitution was amended, and Prohibition, which lay behind so much gangster violence, ended.

In recent years, again in the context of illegal traffic in controlled substances, this form of murder has returned. But it has done so at a level that induces denial. James Q. Wilson comments that Los Angeles has the equivalent of a St. Valentine's Day Massacre every weekend. Even the most ghastly reenactments of such human slaughter produce only moderate responses. On the morning after the close of the Democratic National Convention in New York City in July, there was such an account in the second section of the *New York Times.* It was not a big story; bottom of the page, but with a headline that got your attention. "3 Slain in Bronx Apartment, but a Baby is Saved." A subhead continued: "A mother's last act was to hide her little girl under the bed." The article described a drug execution; the now-routine blindfolds made from duct tape; a man and a woman and a teenager involved. "Each had been shot once in the head." The police had found them a day later. They also found, under a bed, a three-month-old baby, dehydrated but alive. A lieutenant remarked of the mother, "In her last dying act she protected her baby. She probably knew she was going to die, so she stuffed the baby where she knew it would be safe." But the matter was left there. The police would do their best. But the event passed quickly; forgotten by the next day, it will never make *World Book.*

Nor is it likely that any great heed will be paid to an uncanny reenactment of the Prohibition drama a few months later, also in the Bronx. The *Times* story, page B3, reported:

9 Men Posing as Police Are Indicted in 3 Murders

DRUG DEALERS WERE KIDNAPPED FOR RANSOM

The *Daily News* story, same day, page 17, made it *four* murders, adding nice details about torture techniques. The gang members posed as federal Drug Enforcement Administration agents, real badges and all. The victims were drug dealers, whose families were uneasy about calling the police. Ransom seems generally to have been set in the $650,000 range. Some paid. Some got it in the back of the head. So it goes.

Yet, violent killings, often random, go on unabated. Peaks continue to attract some notice. But these are peaks above "average" levels that thirty years ago would have been thought epidemic . . .

A Kai Erikson of the future will surely need to know that the Department of Justice in 1990 found that Americans reported only about 38 percent of all crimes and 48 percent of violent crimes. This, too, can be seen as a means of *normalizing* crime. In much the same way, the vocabulary of crime reporting can be seen to move toward the normal-seeming. A teacher is shot on her way to class. The *Times* subhead reads: "Struck in the Shoulder in the Year's First Shooting Inside a School." First of the season . . .

The hope—if there be such—of this essay has been twofold. It is, first, to suggest that the Durkheim constant, as I put it, is maintained by a dynamic process which adjusts upwards and *downwards*. Liberals have traditionally been alert for upward redefining that does injustice to individuals. Conservatives have been correspondingly sensitive to downward redefining that weakens societal standards. Might it not help if we could all agree that there is a dynamic at work here? It is not revealed truth, nor yet a scientifically derived formula. It is simply a pattern we observe in ourselves. Nor is it rigid. There may once have been an unchanging supply of jail cells which more or less determined the number of prisoners. No longer. We are building new prisons at a prodigious rate. Similarly, the executioner is back. There is something of a competition in Congress to think up new offenses for which the death penalty is seen the only available deterrent. Possibly also modes of execution, as in "fry the kingpins." Even so, we are getting used to a lot of behavior that is not good for us.

As noted earlier, Durkheim states that there is "nothing desirable" about pain . . . Pain, even so, is an indispensable warning signal. But societies under stress, much like individuals, will turn to pain killers of various kinds that end up concealing real damage. There is surely nothing desirable about *this*. If our analysis wins general acceptance, if, for example, more of us came to share Judge Torres's genuine alarm at "the trivialization of the lunatic crime rate" in his city (and mine), we might surprise ourselves how well we respond to the manifest decline of the American civic order. Might.

REVIEW QUESTIONS

1. Defend this statement: "we have been redefining deviancy so as to exempt much conduct previously stigmatized . . ."
2. What are the themes of this article?
3. Since the St. Valentine's Day Massacre, what types of activities have become crimes? Why?

PART TWO

POSITIVIST THEORIES

Soon after 7:00 A.M. on April 16, 2007, the campus police at Virginia Tech University found two students in a dormitory who had been shot to death. About two hours later, the killer, a Virginia Tech senior, went to the school's engineering building. First he chained all the entrance doors shut. Then he headed to a German class and peered in as if he was looking for somebody. He left but soon returned. Quiet and purposeful, he shot the teacher in the head and methodically went around the room and took out the students one by one, pumping at least three bullets into each victim. He then went to three other rooms to carry out the massacre in the same way. After he killed 32 people, he committed suicide by shooting himself in the temple.[1]

What caused Cho Seung-Hui to perpetrate these horrendous acts? Various causes were reported in the media, but the most commonly mentioned ones were his mental illness and the easy availability of guns in the United States. Such a focus on the causes of deviant behavior, like Cho's killing spree and suicide, characterizes positivist theories of deviance. There are many positivist, causal theories of deviance. The most well-known examples are shown in the four articles in this part. In the first, "Strain Theory," Robert Merton explains how a lack of opportunity to achieve success pressures individuals toward deviance. In the second article, "Differential Association Theory," Edwin Sutherland and Donald Cressey attribute deviance to an excess of deviant associations over conventional associations. In the third selection, "Control Theory," Travis Hirschi blames deviance on a lack of control in the individual's life. In the final piece, "Shaming Theory," John Braithwaite shows how disintegrative shaming causes deviance to flourish.

[1]Nancy Gibbs, "Darkness Falls: One Troubled Student Rains Down Death on a Quiet Campus." *Time*, April 30, 2007, pp. 37–53.

CHAPTER 3

STRAIN THEORY

ROBERT K. MERTON

The framework set out in this essay is designed to provide one systematic approach to the analysis of social and cultural sources of deviant behavior. Our primary aim is to discover how some *social structures exert a definite pressure upon certain persons in the society to engage in nonconforming rather than conforming conduct.* If we can locate groups peculiarly subject to such pressures, we should expect to find fairly high rates of deviant behavior in these groups, not because the human beings comprising them are compounded of distinctive biological tendencies but because they are responding normally to the social situation in which they find themselves. Our perspective is sociological. We look at variations in the *rates* of deviant behavior, not at its incidence. Should our quest be at all successful, some forms of deviant behavior will be found to be as psychologically normal as conformist behavior, and the equation of deviation and psychological abnormality will be put in question.

PATTERNS OF CULTURAL GOALS AND INSTITUTIONAL NORMS

Among the several elements of social and cultural structures, two are of immediate importance. These are analytically separable although they merge in concrete situations. The first consists of culturally defined goals, purposes and interests, held out as legitimate objectives for all or for diversely located members of the society. The goals are more or less integrated—the degree is a question of empirical fact—and roughly ordered in some hierarchy of value. Involving various degrees of sentiment and significance, the prevailing goals comprise a frame of aspirational reference. They are the things "worth striving for." They are a basic, though not the exclusive, component of what Linton has called "designs for group living." And though some, not all, of these cultural goals are directly related to the biological drives of man, they are not determined by them.

A second element of the cultural structure defines, regulates, and controls the acceptable modes of reaching out for these goals. Every social group invariably couples its cultural objectives with regulations, rooted in the mores or institutions, of allowable procedures for moving toward these objectives. These regulatory norms are not necessarily identical with technical or efficiency norms. Many procedures which from the standpoint of particular individuals would be most efficient in securing desired values—the exercise of force, fraud, power—are ruled out of the institutional area of permitted conduct. At times, the disallowed procedures include some which would be efficient for the group itself—for example, historic taboos on vivisection, on medical experimentation, on the sociological analysis of "sacred" norms—since the criterion of acceptability is not technical efficiency but value-laden

Source: Reprinted with permission of The Free Press, a Division of Simon and Schuster Adult Publishing Group, from *Social Theory and Social Structure* by Robert K. Merton.

sentiments (supported by most members of the group or by those able to promote these sentiments through the composite use of power and propaganda). In all instances, the choice of expedients for striving toward cultural goals is limited by institutionalized norms.

We shall be primarily concerned with the first—a society in which there is an exceptionally strong emphasis upon specific goals without a corresponding emphasis upon institutional procedures. If it is not to be misunderstood, this statement must be elaborated. No society lacks norms governing conduct. But societies do differ in the degree to which the folkways, mores and institutional controls are effectively integrated with the goals which stand high in the hierarchy of cultural values. The culture may be such as to lead individuals to center their emotional convictions upon the complex of culturally acclaimed ends, with far less emotional support for prescribed methods of reaching out for these ends. With such differential emphases upon goals and institutional procedures, the latter may be so vitiated by the stress on goals as to have the behavior of many individuals limited only by considerations of technical expediency. In this context, the sole significant question becomes: Which of the available procedures is most efficient in netting the culturally approved value? The technically most effective procedure, whether culturally legitimate or not, becomes typically preferred to institutionally prescribed conduct. As this process of attenuation continues, the society becomes unstable and there develops what Durkheim called "anomie" (or normlessness).

The working of this process eventuating in anomie can be easily glimpsed in a series of familiar and instructive, though perhaps trivial, episodes. Thus, in competitive athletics, when the aim of victory is shorn of its institutional trappings and success becomes construed as "winning the game" rather than "winning under the rules of the game," a premium is implicitly set upon the use of illegitimate but technically efficient means. The star of the opposing football team is surreptitiously slugged; the wrestler incapacitates his opponent through ingenious but illicit techniques; university alumni covertly subsidize "students" whose talents are confined to the athletic field. The emphasis on the goal has so attenuated the satisfactions deriving from sheer participation in the competitive activity that only a successful outcome provides gratification. Through the same process, tension generated by the desire to win in a poker game is relieved by successfully dealing one's self four aces or, when the cult of success has truly flowered, by sagaciously shuffling the cards in a game of solitaire. The faint twinge of uneasiness in the last instance and the surreptitious nature of public delicts indicate clearly that the institutional rules of the game are *known* to those who evade them. But cultural (or idiosyncratic) exaggeration of the success-goal leads men to withdraw emotional support from the rules.

This process is of course not restricted to the realm of competitive sport, which has simply provided us with microcosmic images of the social macrocosm. The process whereby exaltation of the end generates a literal *demoralization*, that is, a de-institutionalization, of the means occurs in many groups where the two components of the social structure are not highly integrated.

Contemporary American culture appears to approximate the polar type in which great emphasis upon certain success-goals occurs without equivalent emphasis upon institutional means. It would of course be fanciful to assert that accumulated wealth stands alone as a symbol of success, just as it would be fanciful to deny that Americans assign it a place high in their scale of values. In some large measure, money has been consecrated as a value in itself, over and above its expenditure for articles of consumption or its use for the enhancement of power. "Money" is peculiarly well adapted to become a symbol of prestige. As Simmel emphasized, money is highly abstract and impersonal. However acquired, fraudulently or institutionally, it can be used to purchase the same goods and services. The anonymity of an urban society, in conjunction with these peculiarities of money, permits wealth, the sources of which may be unknown to the community in which the plutocrat lives or, if known, to become purified in the course of time, to serve as a symbol of high status. Moreover, in the American Dream there is no final stopping point. The measure of "monetary success" is conveniently indefinite and relative. At each income level, as H. F. Clark found, Americans want just about 25 percent more (but of course this "just a bit more" continues to operate once it is obtained). In this flux of shifting standards, there is no stable resting point, or rather, it is the point which manages always to be "just ahead." An observer of a community in which annual salaries in six figures are not uncommon reports the anguished words of one victim of the American Dream: "In this town, I'm snubbed socially because I only get a thousand a week. That hurts."

To say that the goal of monetary success is entrenched in American culture is only to say that Americans are bombarded on every side by precepts which affirm the right or, often, the duty of retaining the goal even in the face of repeated frustration. Prestigeful representatives of the society reinforce the cultural emphasis. The family, the school and the workplace—the major agencies shaping the personality structure and goal formation of Americans—join to provide the intensive disciplining required if an individual is to retain intact a goal that remains elusively beyond reach, if he is to be motivated by the promise of a gratification which is not redeemed. As we shall presently see, parents serve as a transmission belt for the values and goals of the groups of which they are a part—above all, of their social class or of the class with which they identify themselves. And the schools are of course the official agency for the passing on of the prevailing values, with a large proportion of the textbooks used in city schools implying or stating explicitly "that education leads to intelligence and consequently to job and money success." Central to this process of disciplining people to maintain their unfulfilled aspirations are the cultural prototypes of success, the living documents testifying that the American Dream can be realized if one but has the requisite abilities.

Coupled with this positive emphasis upon the obligation to maintain lofty goals is a correlative emphasis upon the penalizing of those who draw in their ambitions. Americans are admonished "not to be a quitter" for in the dictionary of American culture, as in the lexicon of youth, "there is no such word as 'fail.' " The cultural manifesto is clear: one must not quit, must not cease striving, must not lessen his goals, for "not failure, but low aim, is crime."

Thus the culture enjoins the acceptance of three cultural axioms: First, all should strive for the same lofty goals since these are open to all; second, present seeming failure is but a way-station to ultimate success; and third, genuine failure consists only in the lessening or withdrawal of ambition.

In rough psychological paraphrase, these axioms represent, first a symbolic secondary reinforcement of incentive; second, curbing the threatened extinction of a response through an associated stimulus; third, increasing the motive strength to evoke continued responses despite the continued absence of reward.

In sociological paraphrase, these axioms represent, first, the deflection of criticism of the social structure onto one's self among those so situated in the society that they do not have full and equal access to opportunity; second, the preservation of a structure of social power by having individuals in the lower social strata identify themselves, not with their compeers, but with those at the top (whom they will ultimately join); and third, providing pressures for conformity with the cultural dictates of unslackened ambition by the threat of less than full membership in the society for those who fail to conform.

It is in these terms and through these processes that contemporary American culture continues to be characterized by a heavy emphasis on wealth as a basic symbol of success, without a corresponding emphasis upon the legitimate avenues on which to march toward this goal. How do individuals living in this cultural context respond? And how do our observations bear upon the doctrine that deviant behavior typically derives from biological impulses breaking through the restraints imposed by culture? What, in short, are the consequences for the behavior of people variously situated in a social structure of a culture in which the emphasis on dominant success goals has become increasingly separated from an equivalent emphasis on institutionalized procedures for seeking these goals?

TYPES OF INDIVIDUAL ADAPTATION

Turning from these culture patterns, we now examine types of adaptation by individuals within the culture-bearing society. Though our focus is still the cultural and social genesis of varying rates and types of deviant behavior, our perspective shifts from the plane of patterns of cultural values to the plane of types of adaptation to these values among those occupying different positions in the social structure.

We here consider five types of adaptation, as these are schematically set out in the following table, where (+) signifies "acceptance," (−) signifies "rejection," and (±) signifies "rejection of prevailing values and substitution of new values."

A Typology of Modes of Individual Adaptation

MODES OF ADAPTATION	CULTURE GOALS	INSTITUTIONALIZED MEANS
I. Conformity	+	+
II. Innovation	+	−
III. Ritualism	−	+
IV. Retreatism	−	−
V. Rebellion	±	±

I. Conformity

To the extent that a society is stable, adaptation type I—conformity to both cultural goals and institutionalized means—is the most common and widely diffused. Were this not so, the stability and continuity of the society could not be maintained. . . .

II. Innovation

Great cultural emphasis upon the success-goal invites this mode of adaptation through the use of institutionally proscribed but often effective means of attaining at least the simulacra of success—wealth and power. This response occurs when the individual has assimilated the cultural emphasis upon the goal without equally internalizing the institutional norms governing ways and means for its attainment. . . .

It appears from our analysis that the greatest pressures toward deviation are exerted upon the lower strata. Cases in point permit us to detect the sociological mechanisms involved in producing these pressures. Several researches have shown that specialized areas of vice and crime constitute a "normal" response to a situation where the cultural emphasis upon pecuniary success has been absorbed, but where there is little access to conventional and legitimate means for becoming successful. The occupational opportunities of people in these areas are largely confined to manual labor and the lesser white-collar jobs. Given the American stigmatization of manual labor *which has been found to hold rather uniformly in all social classes*, and the absence of realistic opportunities for advancement beyond this level, the result is a marked tendency toward deviant behavior. The status of unskilled labor and the consequent low income cannot readily compete *in terms of established standards of worth* with the promises of power and high income from organized vice, rackets and crime.

For our purposes, these situations exhibit two salient features. First, incentives for success are provided by the established values of the culture and second, the avenues available for moving toward this goal are largely limited by the class structure to those of deviant behavior. It is the *combination* of the cultural emphasis and the social structure which produces intense pressure for deviation . . . .

III. Ritualism

The ritualistic type of adaptation can be readily identified. It involves the abandoning or scaling down of the lofty cultural goals of great pecuniary success and rapid social mobility to the point where one's aspirations can be satisfied. But though one rejects the cultural obligation to attempt "to get ahead in the world," though one draws in one's horizons, one continues to abide almost compulsively by institutional norms. . . .

We should expect this type of adaptation to be fairly frequent in a society which makes one's social status largely dependent upon one's achievements. For, as has so often been observed, this ceaseless competitive struggle produces acute status anxiety. One device for allaying these anxieties is to lower one's level of aspiration—permanently. Fear produces inaction, or, more accurately, routinized action.

The syndrome of the social ritualist is both familiar and instructive. His implicit life-philosophy finds expression in a series of cultural clichés: "I'm not sticking my neck out," "I'm playing it safe," "I'm satisfied with what I've got," "Don't aim high and you won't be disappointed." The theme threaded through these attitudes is that high ambitions invite frustration and danger whereas lower aspirations produce satisfaction and security. It is the perspective of the frightened employee, the zealously conformist bureaucrat in the teller's cage of the private banking enterprise, or in the front office of the public works enterprise.

IV. Retreatism

Just as Adaptation I (conformity) remains the most frequent, Adaptation IV (the rejection of cultural goals and institutional means) is probably the least common. People who adapt (or maladapt) in this fashion are, strictly speaking, *in* the society but not *of* it. Sociologically these constitute the true aliens. Not sharing the common frame of values, they can be included as members of the *society* (in distinction from the *population*) only in a fictional sense.

In this category fall some of the adaptive activities of psychotics, autists, pariahs, outcasts, vagrants, vagabonds, tramps, chronic drunkards and drug addicts. They have relinquished culturally prescribed goals and their behavior does not accord with institutional norms. The competitive order is maintained but the frustrated and handicapped individual who cannot cope with this order drops out. Defeatism, quietism and resignation are manifested in escape mechanisms which ultimately lead him to "escape" from the requirements of the society. It is thus an expedient which arises from continued failure to near the goal by legitimate measures and from an inability to use the illegitimate route because of internalized prohibitions.

V. Rebellion

This adaptation leads men outside the environing social structure to envisage and seek to bring into being a new, that is to say, a greatly modified social structure. It presupposes alienation from reigning goals and standards. These come to be regarded as purely arbitrary. And the arbitrary is precisely that which can neither exact allegiance nor possess legitimacy, for it might as well be otherwise. In our society, organized movements for rebellion apparently aim to introduce a social structure in which the cultural standards of success would be sharply modified and provision would be made for a closer correspondence between merit, effort and reward.

THE STRAIN TOWARD ANOMIE

The social structure we have examined produces a strain toward anomie and deviant behavior. The pressure of such a social order is upon outdoing one's competitors. So long as the sentiments supporting this competitive system are distributed throughout the entire range of activities and are not confined to the final result of "success," the choice of means will remain largely within the ambit of institutional control. When, however, the cultural emphasis shifts from the satisfactions deriving from competition itself to almost exclusive concern with the outcome, the resultant stress makes for the breakdown of the regulatory structure.

REVIEW QUESTIONS

1. Identify a situation in which an individual could use two of Merton's modes of adaptation simultaneously.
2. What are at least two weaknesses of this theory?
3. Identify and discuss at least three professions that you believe refute the basic assumptions of this article.

CHAPTER 4

DIFFERENTIAL ASSOCIATION THEORY

EDWIN H. SUTHERLAND
DONALD R. CRESSEY

The following statements refer to the process by which a particular person comes to engage in criminal behavior.

1. Criminal behavior is learned. Negatively, this means that criminal behavior is not inherited, as such; also, the person who is not already trained in crime does not invent criminal behavior, just as a person does not make mechanical inventions unless he has had training in mechanics.

2. Criminal behavior is learned in interaction with other persons in a process of communication. This communication is verbal in many respects but includes also "the communication of gestures."

3. The principal part of the learning of criminal behavior occurs within intimate personal groups. Negatively, this means that the impersonal agencies of communication, such as movies and newspapers, play a relatively unimportant part in the genesis of criminal behavior.

4. When criminal behavior is learned, the learning includes (a) techniques of committing the crime, which are sometimes very complicated, sometimes very simple; and (b) the specific direction of motives, drives, rationalizations, and attitudes.

5. The specific direction of motives and drives is learned from definitions of the legal codes as favorable or unfavorable. In some societies an individual is surrounded by persons who invariably define the legal codes as rules to be observed, while in others he is surrounded by persons whose definitions are favorable to the violation of the legal codes. In our American society these definitions are almost always mixed, with the consequence that we have culture conflict in relation to the legal codes.

6. A person becomes delinquent because of an excess of definitions favorable to violation of law over definitions unfavorable to violation of law. This is the principle of differential association. It refers to both criminal and anticriminal associations and has to do with counteracting forces. When persons become criminal, they do so because of contacts with criminal patterns and also because of isolation from anticriminal patterns. Any person inevitably assimilates the surrounding culture unless other patterns are in conflict; a Southerner does not pronounce r *because other Southerners do not pronounce* r. *Negatively, this proposition of differential association means that associations which are neutral so far as crime is concerned have little or no effect on the genesis of criminal behavior. Much of the experience of a person is neutral in this sense, for example, learning to brush one's teeth. This behavior has no negative or positive effect on criminal behavior except as it may be related to associations which are concerned with the legal codes. This neutral behavior is important especially as an occupier of the time of a child so that he is not in contact*

Source: Edwin H. Sutherland and Donald R. Cressey, *Criminology*, 9th ed. (Philadelphia, PA: Lippincott, 1977), pp. 75–77.

with criminal behavior during the time he is so engaged in the neutral behavior.

7. *Differential associations may vary in frequency, duration, priority, and intensity. This means that associations with criminal behavior and also associations with anticriminal behavior vary in those respects. "Frequency" and "duration" as modalities of associations are obvious and need no explanation. "Priority" is assumed to be important in the sense that lawful behavior developed in early childhood may persist throughout life, and also that delinquent behavior developed in early childhood may persist throughout life. This tendency, however, has not been adequately demonstrated, and priority seems to be important principally through its selective influence. "Intensity" is not precisely defined, but it has to do with such things as the prestige of the source of a criminal or anticriminal pattern and with emotional reactions related to the associations. In a precise description of the criminal behavior of a person, these modalities would be rated in quantitative form and a mathematical ratio reached. A formula in this sense has not been developed, and the development of such a formula would be extremely difficult.*

8. *The process of learning criminal behavior by association with criminal and anticriminal patterns involves all of the mechanisms that are involved in any other learning. Negatively, this means that the learning of criminal behavior is not restricted to the process of imitation. A person who is seduced, for instance, learns criminal behavior by association, but this process would not ordinarily be described as imitation.*

9. *While criminal behavior is an expression of general needs and values, it is not explained by those general needs and values, since noncriminal behavior is an expression of the same needs and values. Thieves generally steal in order to secure money, but likewise honest laborers work in order to secure money. The attempts by many scholars to explain criminal behavior by general drives and values, such as the happiness principle, striving for social status, the money motive, or frustration, have been, and must continue to be, futile, since they explain lawful behavior as completely as they explain criminal behavior. They are similar to respiration, which is necessary for any behavior, but which does not differentiate criminal from noncriminal behavior.*

It is not necessary, at this level of explanation, to explain why a person has the associations he has; this certainly involves a complex of many things. In an area where the delinquency rate is high, a boy who is sociable, gregarious, active, and athletic is very likely to come in contact with the other boys in the neighborhood, learn delinquent behavior patterns from them, and become a criminal; in the same neighborhood the psychopathic boy who is isolated, introverted, and inert may remain at home, not become acquainted with the other boys in the neighborhood, and not become delinquent. In another situation, the sociable, athletic, aggressive boy may become a member of a scout troop and not become involved in delinquent behavior. The person's associations are determined in a general context of social organization. A child is ordinarily reared in a family; the place of residence of the family is determined largely by family income; and the delinquency rate is in many respects related to the rental value of the houses. Many other aspects of social organization affect the kinds of associations a person has.

The preceding explanation of criminal behavior purports to explain the criminal and noncriminal behavior of individual persons. It is possible to state sociological theories of criminal behavior which explain the criminality of a community, nation, or other group. The problem, when thus stated, is to account for variations in crime rates and involves a comparison of the crime rates of various groups or the crime rates of a particular group at different times. . . . The explanation of a crime rate must be consistent with the explanation of the criminal behavior of the person, since the crime rate is a summary statement of the number of persons in the group who commit crimes and the frequency with which they commit crimes. One of the best explanations of crime rates from this point of view is that a high crime rate is due to *social disorganization*. The term social disorganization is not entirely satisfactory, and it seems preferable to substitute for it the term *differential social organization*. The postulate on which this theory is based, regardless of the name, is that crime is rooted in the social organization and is an expression of that social organization. A group may be organized for criminal behavior or organized against criminal behavior. Most communities are organized for both criminal and anticriminal behavior, and, in that sense the crime rate is an expression of the differential group organization. Differential group organization as an explanation of variations in crime rates is consistent with the differential association theory of the processes by which persons become criminals.

REVIEW QUESTIONS

1. Using differential association theory, explain how a person could become a drug user, a prostitute, or an insurance con man.
2. What is the basic premise of differential association theory?
3. Can you use this theory to explain embezzlement? Defend your answer.

CHAPTER 5

CONTROL THEORY

TRAVIS HIRSCHI

Control theories assume that delinquent acts result when an individual's bond to society is weak or broken. . . . [Elements of the bond are as follows.]

ATTACHMENT

It can be argued that all of the characteristics attributed to the psychopath follow from, are effects of, his lack of attachment to others. To say that to lack attachment to others is to be free from moral restraints is to use lack of attachment to explain the guiltlessness of the psychopath, the fact that he apparently has no conscience or superego. In this view, lack of attachment to others is not merely a symptom of psychopathy, it is psychopathy; lack of conscience is just another way of saying the same thing; and the violation of norms is (or may be) a consequence.

For that matter, given that man is an animal, "impulsivity" and "aggressiveness" can also be seen as natural consequences of freedom from moral restraints. However, since the view of man as endowed with natural propensities and capacities like other animals is peculiarly unpalatable to sociologists, we need not fall back on such a view to explain the amoral man's aggressiveness. The process of becoming alienated from others often involves or is based on active interpersonal conflict. Such conflict could easily supply a reservoir of socially derived hostility sufficient to account for the aggressiveness of those whose attachments to others have been weakened.

Durkheim said it many years ago: "We are moral beings to the extent that we are social beings." This may be interpreted to mean that we are moral beings to the extent that we have "internalized the norms" of society. But what does it mean to say that a person has internalized the norms of society? The norms of society are by definition shared by the members of society. To violate a norm is, therefore, to act contrary to the wishes and expectations of other people. If a person does not care about the wishes and expectations of other people—that is, if he is insensitive to the opinion of others—then he is to that extent not bound by the norms. He is free to deviate.

The essence of internalization of norms, conscience, or superego thus lies in the attachment of the individual to others. This view has several advantages over the concept of internalization. For one, explanations of deviant behavior based on attachment do not beg the question, since the extent to which a person is attached to others can be measured independently of his deviant behavior. Furthermore, change or variation in behavior is explainable in a way that it is not when notions of interaction or superego are used. For example, the divorced man is more likely after divorce to commit a number of deviant acts, such as suicide or forgery. If we explain these acts by reference to the super-ego (or internal control), we are forced

Source: Reprinted from Travis Hirschi, *Causes of Delinquency* (Berkeley: University of California Press, 1969), pp. 16–26, by permission of the author.

to say that the man "lost his conscience" when he got a divorce; and, of course, if he remarries, we have to conclude that he gets his conscience back. . . .

COMMITMENT

"Of all passions, that which inclineth men least to break the laws, is fear. Nay, excepting some generous natures, it is the only thing, when there is the appearance of profit or pleasure by breaking the laws, that makes men keep them." Few would deny that men on occasion obey the rules simply from fear of the consequences. This rational component in conformity we label commitment. What does it mean to say that a person is committed to conformity? . . . [It means] that the person invests time, energy, himself, in a certain line of activity—say, getting an education, building up a business, acquiring a reputation for virtue. When or whenever he considers deviant behavior, he must consider the costs of this deviant behavior, the risk he runs of losing the investment he has made in conventional behavior.

If attachment to others is the sociological counterpart of the superego or conscience, commitment is the counterpart of the ego or common sense. To the person committed to conventional lines of action, risking one to ten years in prison for a ten-dollar holdup is stupidity, because to the committed person the costs and risks obviously exceed ten dollars in value. (To the psychoanalyst, such an act exhibits failure to be governed by the "reality-principle.") In the sociological control theory, it can be and is generally assumed that the decision to commit a criminal act may well be rationally determined—that the actor's decision was not irrational given the risks and costs he faces. . . .

INVOLVEMENT

Many persons undoubtedly owe a life of virtue to a lack of opportunity to do otherwise. Time and energy are inherently limited: "Not that I would not, if I could, be both handsome and fat and well dressed, and a great athlete, and make a million a year, be a wit, a bon vivant, and a lady killer, as well as a philosopher, a philanthropist, a statesman, warrior, and African explorer, as well as a 'tone-poet' and saint. But the thing is simply impossible." The things that William James here says he would like to be or do are all, I suppose, within the realm of conventionality, but if he were to include illicit actions he would still have to eliminate some of them as simply impossible.

Involvement or engrossment in conventional activities is thus often part of a control theory. The assumption, widely shared, is that a person may be simply too busy doing conventional things to find time to engage in deviant behavior. The person involved in conventional activities is tied to appointments, deadlines, working hours, plans, and the like, so the opportunity to commit deviant acts rarely arises. To the extent that he is engrossed in conventional activities, he cannot even think about deviant acts, let alone act out his inclinations. . . .

BELIEF

The control theory assumes the existence of a common value system within the society or group whose norms are being violated. If the deviant is committed to a value system different from that of conventional society, there is, within the context of the theory, nothing to explain. The question is, "Why does a man violate the rules in which he believes?" It is not, "Why do men differ in their beliefs about what constitutes good and desirable conduct?" The person is assumed to have been socialized (perhaps imperfectly) into the group whose rules he is violating; deviance is not a question of one group imposing its rules on the members of another group. In other words, we not only assume the deviant has believed the rules, we assume he believes the rules even as he violates them.

How can a person believe it is wrong to steal at the same time he is stealing? In the strain theory, this is not a difficult problem. (In fact, the strain theory was devised specifically to deal with this question.) The motivation to deviance adduced by the strain theorist is so strong that we can well understand the deviant act even assuming the deviator believes strongly that it is wrong. However, given the control theory's assumptions about motivation, if both the deviant and the non-deviant believe the deviant act is wrong, how do we account for the fact that one commits it and the other does not?

Control theories have taken two approaches to this problem. In one approach, beliefs are treated as mere words that mean little or nothing. . . . The second approach argues that the deviant rationalizes his behavior so that he can at once violate the rule and maintain his belief in it. . . . We assume, however, that there is variation in the extent to which people believe they should obey the rules of society, and, furthermore, that the less a person believes he should obey the rules, the more likely he is to violate them.

REVIEW QUESTIONS

1. Using control theory as a frame of reference, explain why a city would implement a program that includes midnight football and other recreational programs; a kitchen where an entire family can work together with other families preparing a meal; and a short simple movie, which plays while people are eating, whose theme reinforces some positive aspect of American life, such as respecting others' property and treating all people with dignity and respect.
2. What is the difference between control theory and differential association theory?
3. Can control theory be used to explain prostitution? Defend your answer.

CHAPTER 6

SHAMING THEORY

JOHN BRAITHWAITE

Cultural commitments to shaming are the key to controlling all types of crime. However, for all types of crime, shaming runs the risk of counterproductivity when it shades into stigmatization.

The crucial distinction is between shaming that is reintegrative and shaming that is disintegrative (stigmatization). Reintegrative shaming means that expressions of community disapproval, which may range from mild rebuke to degradation ceremonies, are followed by gestures of reacceptance into the community of law-abiding citizens. These gestures of reacceptance will vary from a simple smile expressing forgiveness and love to quite formal ceremonies to decertify the offender as deviant. Disintegrative shaming (stigmatization), in contrast, divides the community by creating a class of outcasts. Much effort is directed at labeling deviance, while little attention is paid to delabeling, to signifying forgiveness and reintegration, to ensuring that the deviance label is applied to the behavior rather than the person, and that this is done under the assumption that the disapproved behavior is transient, performed by an essentially good person. . . .

The best place to see reintegrative shaming at work is in loving families. . . . Family life teaches us that shaming and punishment are possible while maintaining bonds of respect. Two hypotheses are suggested: first, families are the most effective agents of social control in most societies partly because of this characteristic; second, those families that are disintegrative rather than reintegrative in their punishment processes, that have not learnt the trick of punishing within a continuum of love, are the families that fail at socializing their children.

KEY CONCEPTS

Interdependency is a condition of individuals. It means the extent to which individuals participate in networks wherein they are dependent on others to achieve valued ends and others are dependent on them. We could describe an individual as in a state of interdependency even if the individuals who are dependent on him are different from the individuals on whom he is dependent. Interdependency is approximately equivalent to the social bonding, attachment and commitment of control theory.

Communitarianism is a condition of societies. In communitarian societies individuals are densely enmeshed in interdependencies which have the special qualities of mutual help and trust. The interdependencies have symbolic significance in the culture of group loyalties which take precedence over individual interests. The interdependencies also have symbolic significance as attachments which invoke personal obligation to others in a community of concern, rather than simply interdependencies of convenience as between a bank and a small depositor. A communitarian culture rejects any pejorative connotation of dependency as threatening individual autonomy.

Source: John Braithwaite, *Crime, Shame, and Reintegration* (New York: Cambridge University Press, 1989), pp. 55–56. Reprinted with permission.

Communitarian cultures resist interpretations of dependency as weakness and emphasize the need for mutuality of obligation in interdependency (to be both dependent and dependable). The Japanese are said to be socialized not only to *amaeru* (to be succored by others) but also to *amayakasu* (to be nurturing to others).

Shaming means all social processes of expressing disapproval which have the intention or effect of invoking remorse in the person being shamed and/or condemnation by others who become aware of the shaming. When associated with appropriate symbols, formal punishment often shames. But societies vary enormously in the extent to which formal punishment is associated with shaming or in the extent to which the social meaning of punishment is no more than to inflict pain to tip reward-cost calculations in favor of certain outcomes. Shaming, unlike purely deterrent punishment, sets out to moralize with the offender to communicate reasons for the evil of her actions. Most shaming is neither associated with formal punishment nor perpetrated by the state, though both shaming by the state and shaming with punishment are important types of shaming. Most shaming is by individuals within interdependent communities of concern.

Reintegrative shaming is shaming which is followed by efforts to reintegrate the offender back into the community of law-abiding or respectable citizens through words or gestures of forgiveness or ceremonies to decertify the offender as deviant. Shaming and reintegration do not occur simultaneously but sequentially, with reintegration occurring before deviance becomes a master status. It is shaming which labels the act as evil while striving to preserve the identity of the offender as essentially good. It is directed at signifying evil deeds rather than evil persons in the Christian tradition of "hate the sin and love the sinner." Specific disapproval is expressed within relationships characterized by general social approval; shaming criminal behavior is complemented by ongoing social rewarding of alternative behavior patterns. Reintegrative shaming is not necessarily weak; it can be cruel, even vicious. It is not distinguished from stigmatization by its potency, but by (a) a finite rather than open-ended duration which is terminated by forgiveness; and by (b) efforts to maintain bonds of love or respect throughout the finite period of suffering shame.

Stigmatization is disintegrative shaming in which no effort is made to reconcile the offender with the community. The offender is outcast, her deviance is allowed to become a master status, degradation ceremonies are not followed by ceremonies to decertify deviance.

Criminal subcultures are sets of rationalizations and conduct norms which cluster together to support criminal behavior. The clustering is usually facilitated by subcultural groups which provide systematic social support for crime in any of a number of ways—supplying members with criminal opportunities, criminal values, attitudes which weaken conventional values of law-abidingness, or techniques of neutralizing conventional values.

SHORT SUMMARY OF THE THEORY

The following might serve as the briefest possible summary of the theory. A variety of life circumstances increase the chances that individuals will be in situations of greater interdependency, the most important being age (under 15 and over 25), being married, female, employed, and having high employment and educational aspirations. Interdependent persons are more susceptible to shaming. More important, societies in which individuals are subject to extensive interdependencies are more likely to be communitarian, and shaming is much more widespread and potent in communitarian societies. Urbanization and high residential mobility are societal characteristics which undermine communitarianism.

The shaming produced by interdependency and communitarianism can be either of two types—shaming that becomes stigmatization or shaming that is followed by reintegration. The shaming engendered is more likely to become reintegrative in societies that are communitarian.

In societies where shaming does become reintegrative, low crime rates are the result because disapproval is dispensed without eliciting a rejection of the disapprovers, so that the potentialities for future disapproval are not dismantled. . . .

Shaming that is stigmatizing, in contrast, makes criminal subcultures more attractive because these are in some sense subcultures which reject the rejectors. Thus, when shaming is allowed to become stigmatization for want of reintegrative gestures or ceremonies which decertify deviance, the deviant is both attracted to criminal subcultures and cut off from other interdependencies (with family, neighbors, church, etc.). Participation in subcultural groups supplies criminal role models, training in techniques of crime and techniques of neutralizing crime or other forms of social support that make choices to engage in crime more attractive. Thus, to the extent that shaming is of the stigmatizing rather than the reintegrative sort, and that criminal subcultures are widespread and accessible in the society, higher crime rates will be the result. While societies characterized by high levels of stigmatization will have higher crime rates than societies characterized by reintegrative shaming, the former will have higher or lower crime rates than societies with little shaming at all depending largely on the availability of criminal subcultures.

Yet a high level of stigmatization in the society is one of the very factors that encourages criminal subculture formation by creating populations of outcasts with no stake in conformity, no chance of self-esteem within the terms of conventional society—individuals in search of an alternative culture that allows them self-esteem. A communitarian culture, on the other hand, nurtures deviants within a network of attachments to conventional society, thus inhibiting the widespread outcasting that is the stuff of subculture formation.

REVIEW QUESTIONS

1. There has been a tremendous amount of media coverage of the behavior of some Catholic priests and their interaction with children. Given the coverage, do you think reintegrative or disintegrative shaming should be applied? Defend your answer.
2. What is the value of having a communitarian culture as it relates to the treatment of deviants in a given society? Explain your response in detail.
3. What type of shaming identified in the article works best with white-collar criminals? Justify your answer.

PART THREE

CONSTRUCTIONIST THEORIES

Abortion has been legal since 1973, but it is getting harder to get one. Consider Lisa, a 22-year-old unmarried woman who works in a restaurant. Several months ago she was pregnant and decided to have an abortion. But the abortion provider that was located 15 minutes from her home had just closed down. Only four doctors who performed abortions were left in the entire state of Missouri. The closest one to Lisa's hometown was at the Planned Parenthood clinic in St. Louis, an eight-hour roundtrip. Having no car, Lisa not only had to ask a friend to drive her, but also had to miss two days of work. She had to take the long trip again two weeks later for a follow-up exam that lasted five minutes. Her total expenditure, which included the clinic's bill, the abortion drug, gasoline, food, and incidentals, was more than $600. "It was all very frustrating," she said a month after her abortion. "I only recently paid back everyone I borrowed money from."[1]

Besides Missouri, many other states have also made it more difficult to get an abortion. Not only have they created a hostile environment that has led to the closing of many abortion clinics, they have also imposed legal restrictions on abortion, such as requiring pre-abortion counseling, a waiting period, and parental consent or notification. In effect, they treat abortion as a deviant act. So do positivist sociologists. However, to constructionist sociologists, abortion is not a deviant act; it is only deviant as a mental construction, as a figment of human imagination. Thus, constructionists have developed theories about how people impute the notion of "deviance" to behaviors such as abortion and what consequence this has for themselves and for others.

In this part of our reader, we present various constructionist theories. In the first article, "Labeling Theory," Howard Becker shows how the meaning of deviance derives not from the act a person commits, but from society's labeling of an act as deviant. In the second selection, "Phenomenological Theory," Jack Katz provides a tour into the experiential world of deviants, revealing how they feel about their so-called deviant activities. In the third reading, "Conflict Theory," Richard Quinney describes what he calls "the social reality of crime." The reality is said to comprise the meanings of criminal laws, enforcement of these laws, their violations by relatively powerless people, and the dominant class's crime ideology that supports the enforcement of laws against lower-class criminals. In the fourth article, "Feminist Theory," Kathleen Daly discusses how societal views of women make them differ from men in lawbreaking.

[1]Karen Tumulty, "Abortion: Where the Real Action Is . . ." *Time*, January 30, 2006, pp. 50–53.

CHAPTER 7

LABELING THEORY

HOWARD S. BECKER

A sociological view . . . defines deviance as the infraction of some agreed-upon rule. It then goes on to ask who breaks rules, and to search for the factors in their personalities and life situations that might account for the infractions. This assumes that those who have broken a rule constitute a homogeneous category, because they have committed the same deviant act.

Such an assumption seems to me to ignore the central fact about deviance: it is created by society. I do not mean this in the way it is ordinarily understood, in which the causes of deviance are located in the social situation of the deviant or in "social factors" which prompt his action. I mean, rather, that *social groups create deviance by making the rules whose infraction constitutes deviance*, and by applying those rules to particular people and labeling them as outsiders. From this point of view, deviance is not a quality of the act the person commits, but rather a consequence of the application by others of rules and sanctions to an "offender." The deviant is one to whom that label has successfully been applied; deviant behavior is behavior that people so label.

Since deviance is, among other things, a consequence of the responses of others to a person's act, students of deviance cannot assume that they are dealing with a homogeneous category when they study people who have been labeled deviant. That is, they cannot assume that these people have actually committed a deviant act or broken some rule, because the process of labeling may not be infallible; some people may be labeled deviant who in fact have not broken a rule. Furthermore, they cannot assume that the category of those labeled deviant will contain all those who actually have broken a rule, for many offenders may escape apprehension and thus fail to be included in the population of "deviants" they study. Insofar as the category lacks homogeneity and fails to include all the cases that belong in it, one cannot reasonably expect to find common factors of personality or life situation that will account for the supposed deviance.

What, then, do people who have been labeled deviant have in common? At the least, they share the label and the experience of being labeled as outsiders. I will begin my analysis with this basic similarity and view deviance as the product of a transaction that takes place between some social group and one who is viewed by that group as a rule-breaker. I will be less concerned with the personal and social characteristics of deviants than with the process by which they come to be thought of as outsiders and their reactions to that judgment.

The point is that the response of other people has to be regarded as problematic. Just because one has committed an infraction of a rule does not mean that others will respond as though this had

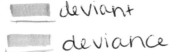

deviant

deviance

happened. (Conversely, just because one has not violated a rule does not mean that he may not be treated, in some circumstances, as though he had.)

The degree to which other people will respond to a given act as deviant varies greatly. Several kinds of variation seem worth noting. First of all, there is variation over time. A person believed to have committed a given "deviant" act may at one time be responded to much more leniently than he would be at some other time. The occurrence of "drives" against various kinds of deviance illustrates this clearly. At various times, enforcement officials may decide to make an all-out attack on some particular kind of deviance, such as gambling, drug addiction, or homosexuality. It is obviously much more dangerous to engage in one of these activities when a drive is on than at any other time. (In a very interesting study of crime news in Colorado newspapers, Davis found that the amount of crime reported in Colorado newspapers showed very little association with actual changes in the amount of crime taking place in Colorado. And, further, that peoples' estimate of how much increase there had been in crime in Colorado was associated with the increase in the amount of crime news but not with any increase in the amount of crime.)

The degree to which an act will be treated as deviant depends also on who commits the act and who feels he has been harmed by it. Rules tend to be applied more to some persons than others. Studies of juvenile delinquency make the point clearly. Boys from middle-class areas do not get as far in the legal process when they are apprehended as do boys from slum areas. The middle-class boy is less likely, when picked up by the police, to be taken to the station; less likely when taken to the station to be booked; and it is extremely unlikely that he will be convicted and sentenced. This variation occurs even though the original infraction of the rule is the same in the two cases.

Why repeat these commonplace observations? Because, taken together, they support the proposition that deviance is not a simple quality, present in some kinds of behavior and absent in others. Rather, it is the product of a process which involves responses of other people to the behavior. The same behavior may be an infraction of the rules at one time and not at another; may be an infraction when committed by one person, but not when committed by another; some rules are broken with impunity, others are not. In short, whether a given act is deviant or not depends in part on the nature of the act (that is, whether or not it violates some rule) and in part on what other people do about it.

Some people may object that this is merely a terminological quibble, that one can, after all, define terms any way he wants to and that if some people want to speak of rule-breaking behavior as *deviant* without reference to the reactions of others they are free to do so. This, of course, is true. Yet it might be worthwhile to refer to such behavior as *rule-breaking behavior* and reserve the term *deviant* for those labeled as deviant by some segment of society. I do not insist that this usage be followed. But it should be clear that insofar as a scientist uses "deviant" to refer to any rule-breaking behavior and takes as his subject of study only those who have been *labeled* deviant, he will be hampered by the disparities between the two categories.

If we take as the object of our attention behavior which comes to be labeled as deviant, we must recognize that we cannot know whether a given act will be categorized as deviant until the response of others has occurred. Deviance is not a quality that lies in behavior itself, but in the interaction between the person who commits an act and those who respond to it. . . .

In any case, being caught and branded as deviant has important consequences for one's further social participation and self-image. The most important consequence is a drastic change in the individual's public identity. Committing the improper act and being publicly caught at it place him in a new status. He has been revealed as a different kind of person from the kind he was supposed to be. He is labeled a "fairy," "dope fiend," "nut," or "lunatic," and treated accordingly. . . .

To be labeled a criminal one need only commit a single criminal offense, and this is all the term formally refers to. Yet the word carries a number of connotations specifying auxiliary traits characteristic of anyone bearing the label. A man who has been convicted of housebreaking and thereby labeled criminal is presumed to be a person likely to break into other houses; the police, in rounding up known offenders for investigation after a crime has been committed, operate on this premise. Further, he is considered likely to commit other kinds of crimes as well, because he has shown himself to be a person without "respect for the law." Thus, apprehension for one deviant act exposes a person to the likelihood that he will be regarded as deviant or undesirable in other respects. . . .

Treating a person as though he were generally rather than specifically deviant produces a self-fulfilling prophecy. It sets in motion several mechanisms which conspire to shape the person in the image people have of him. In the first place, one tends to be cut off, after being identified as deviant, from participation in more conventional groups, even though the specific consequences of the particular deviant activity might never of themselves have caused the isolation had there not also been the public knowledge and reaction to it. . . . Though the effects of opiate drugs may not impair one's working ability, to be known as an addict will probably lead to losing one's job. In such cases, the individual finds it difficult to conform to other rules which he had no intention or desire to break, and perforce finds himself deviant in these areas as well. The drug addict finds himself forced into other illegitimate kinds of activity, such as robbery and theft, by the refusal of respectable employers to have him around.

When the deviant is caught, he is treated in accordance with the popular diagnosis of why he is that way, and the treatment itself may likewise produce increasing deviance. The drug addict, popularly considered to be a weak-willed individual who cannot forego the indecent pleasures afforded him by opiates, is treated repressively. He is forbidden to use drugs. Since he cannot get drugs legally, he must get them illegally. This forces the market underground and pushes the price of drugs up far beyond the current legitimate market price into a bracket that few can afford on an ordinary salary. Hence the treatment of the addict's deviance places him in a position where it will probably be necessary to resort to deceit and crime in order to support his habit. The behavior is a consequence of the public reaction to the deviance rather than a consequence of the inherent qualities of the deviant act.

REVIEW QUESTIONS

1. Mary, a college freshman, has gained a reputation for being loose and easy, willing to have sex with just about anyone, although in reality she is a virgin. How would a labeling theorist like Becker explain this situation?
2. People break the law all the time, yet not all are defined as deviant. After reading Becker's article, explain how this can be so.
3. According to the article, in what ways might labeling of deviance encourage further deviance?

CHAPTER 8

PHENOMENOLOGICAL THEORY

JACK KATZ

The study of crime has been preoccupied with a search for background forces, usually defects in the offenders' psychological backgrounds or social environments, to the neglect of the positive, often wonderful attractions within the lived experience of criminality. The novelty of this [theory] is its focus on the seductive qualities of crimes: those aspects in the foreground of criminality that make its various forms sensible, even sensually compelling, ways of being.

The social science literature contains only scattered evidence of what it means, feels, sounds, tastes, or looks like to commit a particular crime. Readers of research on homicide and assault do not hear the slaps and curses, see the pushes and shoves, or feel the humiliation and rage that may build toward the attack, sometimes persisting after the victim's death. How adolescents manage to make the shoplifting or vandalism of cheap and commonplace things a thrilling experience has not been intriguing to many students of delinquency. Researchers of adolescent gangs have never grasped why their subjects so often stubbornly refuse to accept the outsider's insistence that they wear the "gang" label. The description of "cold-blooded, senseless murders" has been left to writers outside the social sciences. Neither academic methods nor academic theories seem to be able to grasp why such killers may have been courteous to their victims just moments before the killing, why they often wait until they have dominated victims in sealed-off environments before coldly executing them, or how it makes sense to them to kill when only petty cash is at stake. Sociological and psychological studies of robbery rarely focus on the *distinctive* attractions of robbery, even though research has now clearly documented that alternative forms of criminality are available and familiar to many career robbers. In sum, only rarely have sociologists taken up the challenge of explaining the qualities of deviant experience.

The statistical and correlational findings of positivist criminology provide the following irritations to inquiry: (1) whatever the validity of the hereditary, psychological, and social-ecological conditions of crime, many of those in the supposedly causal categories do not commit the crime at issue, (2) many who do commit the crime do not fit the causal categories, and (3) and what is most provocative, many who do fit the background categories and later commit the predicted crime go for long stretches without committing the crimes to which theory directs them. Why are people who were not determined to commit a crime one moment determined to do so the next?

I propose that empirical research turn the direction of inquiry around to focus initially on the foreground, rather than the background of crime. Let us for once make it our first priority to understand the qualities of experience that distinguish different forms of criminality. . . .

Source: Jack Katz, *Seductions of Crime* (New York: Basic Books, 1988), pp. 3–5, 8–10.

A sense of being determined by the environment, of being pushed away from one line of action and pulled toward another, is natural to everyday, routine human experience. We are always moving away from and toward different objects of consciousness, taking account of this and ignoring that, and moving in one direction or the other between the extremes of involvement and boredom. In this constant movement of consciousness, we do not perceive that we are controlling the movement. Instead, to one degree or another, we are always being seduced and repelled by the world. "This is fascinating (interesting, beautiful, sexy, dull, ugly, disgusting)," we know (without having to say), as if the thing itself possessed the designated quality independent of us and somehow controlled our understanding of it. Indeed, the very nature of mundane being is emotional; attention is feeling, and consciousness is sensual.

Only rarely do we actually experience ourselves as subjects directing our conduct. How often, when you speak, do you actually sense that you are choosing the words you utter? As the words come out, they reveal the thought behind them even to the speaker whose lips gave them shape. Similarly, we talk, walk, and write in a sense of natural competence governed by moods of determinism. We rest our subjectivity on rhythmic sensibilities, feelings for directions, and visions of unfolding patterns, allowing esthetics to guide us. Self-reflexive postures, in which one creates a distance between the self and the world and pointedly directs the self into the world, occur typically in an exceptional mood of recognizing a malapropism, after a misstep, or at the slip of the pen. With a slight shock, we recognize that it was not the things in themselves but our perspective that temporarily gave things outside of us the power to seduce or repel.

Among the forms of crime, the range of sensual dynamics runs from enticements that may draw a person into shoplifting to furies that can compel him to murder. If, as social researchers, we are to be able to explain more variation in criminality than background correlations allow, it appears that we must respect these sensual dynamics and honor them as authentic. . . .

Approaching criminality from the inside, social research takes as its subject the morally exceptional conduct that the persons themselves regard as criminally sanctionable in official eyes. Since there is an enormous variety of criminal phenomena, how can one demarcate and set up for explanation a limited number of subjectively homogeneous offenses? I suggest that a seemingly simple question be asked persistently in detailed application to the facts of criminal experience: What are people trying to do when they commit a crime?

The resulting topics will not necessarily follow official crime categories. Crimes, as defined in statutes, surveys of citizens, and police records, take definitional shape from the interests of victims and from practical problems of detection and punishment, not necessarily from the experience of those committing the crimes. But if one begins with rough conventional or folk categories, such as hot-blooded murder, gang violence, adolescent property crime, commercial robbery, and "senseless" and "cold-blooded" murder, and refines the concepts to fit homogeneous forms of experience, one can arrive at a significant range of criminal projects: committing righteous slaughter, mobilizing the spirit of a street elite, constructing sneaky thrills, persisting in the practice of stickup as a hardman, and embodying primordial evil.

By way of explanation, I will propose for each type of crime a different set of individually necessary and jointly sufficient conditions, each set containing (1) a path of action—distinctive practical requirements for successfully committing the crime, (2) a line of interpretation—unique ways of understanding how one is and will be seen by others, and (3) an emotional process and compulsions that have special dynamics. Raising the spirit of criminality requires practical attention to a mode of executing action, symbolic creativity in defining the situation, and esthetic finesse in recognizing and elaborating on the sensual possibilities.

vocab

Central to all these experiences in deviance is a member of the family of moral emotions: humiliation, righteousness, arrogance, ridicule, cynicism, defilement, and vengeance. In each, the attraction that proves to be most fundamentally compelling is that of overcoming a personal challenge to moral—not to material—existence. For the impassioned killer, the challenge is to escape a situation that has come to seem otherwise inexorably humiliating. Unable to sense how he or she can move with self-respect from the current situation, now, to any mundane-time relationship that might be reengaged, then, the would-be killer leaps at the possibility of embodying, through the practice of "righteous" slaughter, some eternal, universal form of the Good.

For many adolescents, shoplifting and vandalism offer the attractions of a thrilling melodrama about the self as seen from within and from without. Quite apart from what is taken, they may regard "getting away with it" as a thrilling demonstration of personal competence, especially if it is accomplished under the eyes of adults.

Specifically "bad" forms of criminality are essentially addressed to a moral challenge experienced in a spatial metaphor. Whether by intimidating others' efforts to take him into their worlds ("Who you lookin' at?") or by treating artificial geographic boundaries as sacred and defending local "turf" with relentless "heart," "badasses" and *barrio* warriors celebrate an indifference to modern society's expectation that a person should demonstrate a sensibility to reshape himself as he moves from here to there.

To make a habit of doing stickups, I will argue, one must become a "hardman." It is only smart to avoid injuring victims unnecessarily, but if one becomes too calculating about the application of violence, the inherent uncertainties of face-to-face interaction in robberies will be emotionally forbidding. Beneath the surface, there may be, to paraphrase Nietzsche, a ball of snakes in chaotic struggle. But the stickup man denies any uncertainty and any possibility of change with a personal style that ubiquitously negates social pressures toward a malleable self.

Perhaps the ultimate criminal project is mounted by men who culminate a social life organized around the symbolism of deviance with a cold-blooded, "senseless" murder. Mimicking the ways of primordial gods as they kill, they proudly appear to the world as astonishingly evil. Through a killing only superficially justified by the context of robbery, they emerge from a dizzying alternation between affiliation with the great symbolic powers of deviant identity and a nagging disease that conformity means cowardice.

Overall, my objective is to demonstrate that a theory of moral self-transcendence can make comprehensible the minutia of experiential details in the phenomenal foreground, as well as explain the general conditions that are most commonly found in the social backgrounds of these forms of criminality.

REVIEW QUESTIONS

1. Do you support Katz's contention that we should focus on the foreground rather than the background of crime? If yes, why? If no, why not?
2. Katz argues that participation in some forms of behavior, most notably shoplifting and vandalism, can be seductive to the individual. How does he arrive at this conclusion?
3. Do you agree with Katz's three requirements for a criminal experience to occur? Why or why not?

Chapter 9

CONFLICT THEORY

RICHARD QUINNEY

A theory that helps us begin to examine the legal order critically is the one I call the social reality of crime. Applying this theory, we think of crime as it is affected by the dynamics that mold the society's social, economic, and political structure. First, we recognize how criminal law fits into capitalist society. The legal order gives reality to the crime problem in the United States. Everything that makes up crime's social reality, including the application of criminal law, the behavior patterns of those who are defined as criminal, and the construction of an ideology of crime, is related to the established legal order. The social reality of crime is constructed on conflict in our society. The theory of the social reality of crime is formulated as follows.

I. The Official Definition of Crime: *Crime as a legal definition of human conduct is created by agents of the dominant class in a politically organized society.*

The essential starting point is a definition of crime that itself is based on the legal definition. Crime, as *officially* determined, is a *definition* of behavior that is conferred on some people by those in power. Agents of the law (such as legislators, police, prosecutors, and judges) are responsible for formulating and administering criminal law. Upon *formulation* and *application* of these definitions of crime, persons and behaviors become criminal.

Crime, according to this first proposition, is not inherent in behavior, but is a judgment made by some about the actions and characteristics of others. This proposition allows us to focus on the formulation and administration of the criminal law as it applies to the behaviors that become defined as criminal. Crime is seen as a result of the class-dynamic process that culminates in defining persons and behaviors as criminal. It follows, then, that the greater the number of definitions of crime that are formulated and applied, the greater the amount of crime.

II. Formulating Definitions of Crime: *Definitions of crime are composed of behaviors that conflict with the interests of the dominant class.*

Definitions of crime are formulated according to the interests of those who have the power to translate their interests into public policy. Those definitions are ultimately incorporated into the criminal law. Furthermore, definitions of crime in a society change as the interests of the dominant class change. In other words, those who are able to have their interests represented in public policy regulate the formulation of definitions of crime.

The powerful interests are reflected not only in the definitions of crime and the kinds of penal sanctions attached to them, but also in the *legal policies* on handling those defined as criminals. Procedural rules are created for enforcing and administering the criminal law. Policies are also established on programs for treating and punishing the criminally defined and programs for controlling and preventing crime. From the initial definitions of crime to the subsequent procedures,

Source: Richard Quinney, *Criminology* (Boston: Little, Brown, 1975), pp. 37–41.

social reality
offical crime
other
form crime

correctional and penal programs, and policies for controlling and preventing crime, those who have the power regulate the behavior of those without power.

III. Applying Definitions of Crime: *Definitions of crime are applied by the class that has the power to shape the enforcement and administration of criminal law.*

The dominant interests intervene in all the stages at which definitions of crime are created. Because class interests cannot be effectively protected merely by formulating criminal law, the law must be enforced and administered. The interests of the powerful, therefore, also operate where the definitions of crime reach the *application* stage. As Vold has argued, crime is "political behavior and the criminal becomes in fact a member of a 'minority group' without sufficient public support to dominate the control of the police power of the state." Those whose interests conflict with the ones represented in the law must either change their behavior or possibly find it defined as criminal.

The probability that definitions of crime will be applied varies according to how much the behaviors of the powerless conflict with the interests of those in power. Law enforcement efforts and judicial activity are likely to increase when the interests of the dominant class are threatened. Fluctuations and variations in applying definitions of crime reflect shifts in class relations.

Obviously, the criminal law is not applied directly by those in power; its enforcement and administration are delegated to authorized *legal agents*. Because the groups responsible for creating the definitions of crime are physically separated from the groups that have the authority to enforce and administer law, local conditions determine how the definitions will be applied. In particular, communities vary in their expectations of law enforcement and the administration of justice. The application of definitions is also influenced by the visibility of offenses in a community and by the public's norms about reporting possible violations. And especially important in enforcing and administering the criminal law are the legal agents' occupational organization and ideology.

The probability that these definitions will be applied depends on the actions of the legal agents who have the authority to enforce and administer the law. A definition of crime is applied depending on their evaluation. Turk has argued that during "criminalization," a criminal label may be affixed to people because of real or fancied attributes: "Indeed, a person is evaluated, either favorably or unfavorably, not because he does something, or even because he is something, but because others react to their perceptions of him as offensive or inoffensive." Evaluation by the definers is affected by the way in which the suspect handles the situation, but ultimately the legal agents' evaluations and subsequent decisions are the crucial factors in determining the criminality of human acts. As legal agents evaluate more behaviors and persons as worthy of being defined as crimes, the probability that definitions of crime will be applied grows.

IV. How Behavior Patterns Develop in Relation to Definitions of Crime: *Behavior patterns are structured in relation to definitions of crime, and within this context people engage in actions that have relative probabilities of being defined as criminal.*

Although behavior varies, all behaviors are similar in that they represent patterns within the society. All persons—whether they create definitions of crime or are the objects of these definitions—act in reference to *normative systems* learned in relative social and cultural settings. Because it is not the quality of the behavior but the action taken against the behavior that gives it the character of criminality, that which is defined as criminal is relative to the behavior patterns of the class that formulates and applies definitions. Consequently, people whose behavior patterns are not represented when the definitions of crime are formulated and applied are more likely to act in ways that will be defined as criminal than those who formulate and apply the definitions.

Once behavior patterns become established with some regularity within the segments of society, individuals have a framework for creating *personal action patterns*. These continually develop for each person as he moves from one experience to another. Specific action patterns give behavior an individual substance in relation to the definitions of crime.

People construct their own patterns of action in participating with others. It follows, then, that the probability that persons will develop action patterns with a high potential for being defined as criminal depends on (1) structured opportunities, (2) learning experiences, (3) interpersonal associations and identifications, and (4) self-conceptions. Throughout the experiences, each person creates a conception of self as a human social being. Thus prepared, he behaves according to the anticipated consequences of his actions.

In the experiences shared by the definers of crime and the criminally defined, personal-action patterns develop among the latter because they are so defined. After they have had continued experience in being defined as criminal, they learn to manipulate the application of criminal definitions.

Furthermore, those who have been defined as criminal begin to conceive of themselves as criminal. As they adjust to the definitions imposed upon them, they learn to play the criminal role. As a result of others' reactions, therefore, people may develop personal action patterns that increase the likelihood of their being defined as criminal in the future. That is, increased experience with definitions of crime increases the probability of their developing actions that may be subsequently defined as criminal.

Thus, both the definers of crime and the criminally defined are involved in reciprocal action patterns. The personal-action patterns of both the definers and the defined are shaped by their common, continued, and related experiences. The fate of each is bound to that of the other.

V. CONSTRUCTING AN IDEOLOGY OF CRIME: *An ideology of crime is constructed and diffused by the dominant class to secure its hegemony.*

This ideology is created in the kinds of ideas people are exposed to, the manner in which they select information to fit the world they are shaping, and their way of interpreting this information. People behave in reference to the *social meanings* they attach to their experiences.

Among the conceptions that develop in a society are those relating to what people regard as crime. The concept of crime must of course be accompanied by ideas about the nature of crime. Images develop about the relevance of crime, the offender's characteristics, the appropriate reaction to crime, and the relation of crime to the social order. These conceptions are constructed by communication, and, in fact, an ideology of crime depends on the portrayal of crime in all personal and mass communication. This ideology is thus diffused throughout the society.

One of the most concrete ways by which an ideology of crime is formed and transmitted is the official investigation of crime. The President's Commission on Law Enforcement and Administration of Justice is the best contemporary example of the state's role in shaping an ideology of crime. Not only are we as citizens more aware of crime today because of the President's Commission, but official policy on crime has been established in a crime bill, the Omnibus Crime Control and Safe Streets Act of 1968. The crime bill, itself a reaction to the growing fears of class conflict in American society, creates an image of a severe crime problem and, in so doing, threatens to negate some of our basic constitutional guarantees in the name of controlling crime.

Consequently, the conceptions that are most critical in actually formulating and applying the definitions of crime are those held by the dominant class. These conceptions are certain to be incorporated into the social reality of crime. The more the government acts in reference to crime, the more probable it is that definitions of crime will be created and that behavior patterns will develop in opposition to those definitions. The formulation of definitions of crime, their application, and the development of behavior patterns in relation to the definitions, are thus joined in full circle by the construction of an ideological hegemony toward crime.

VI. CONSTRUCTING THE SOCIAL REALITY OF CRIME: *The social reality of crime is constructed by the formulation and application of definitions of crime, the development of behavior patterns in relation to these definitions, and the construction of an ideology of crime.*

The first five propositions are collected here into a final composition proposition. The theory of the social reality of crime, accordingly, postulates creating a series of phenomena that increase the probability of crime. The result, holistically, is the social reality of crime.

Because the first proposition of the theory is a definition and the sixth is a composite, the body of the theory consists of the four middle propositions. These form a model of crime's social reality. The model, as diagrammed, relates the proposition units into a theoretical system (Figure 9.1). Each unit is related to the others. The theory is thus a system of interacting developmental propositions. The phenomena denoted in the propositions and their relationships culminate in what is regarded as the amount and character of crime at any time—that is, in the social reality of crime.

The theory of the social reality of crime as I have formulated it is inspired by a change that is occurring in our view of the world. This change, pervading all levels of society, pertains to the world that we all construct and from which, at the same time, we pretend to separate ourselves in our human experiences. For the study of crime, a revision in thought has directed attention to the criminal process: All relevant phenomena contribute to creating definitions of crime, development of behaviors by those involved in criminal-defining situations, and constructing an ideology of crime. The result is the social reality of crime that is constantly being constructed in society.

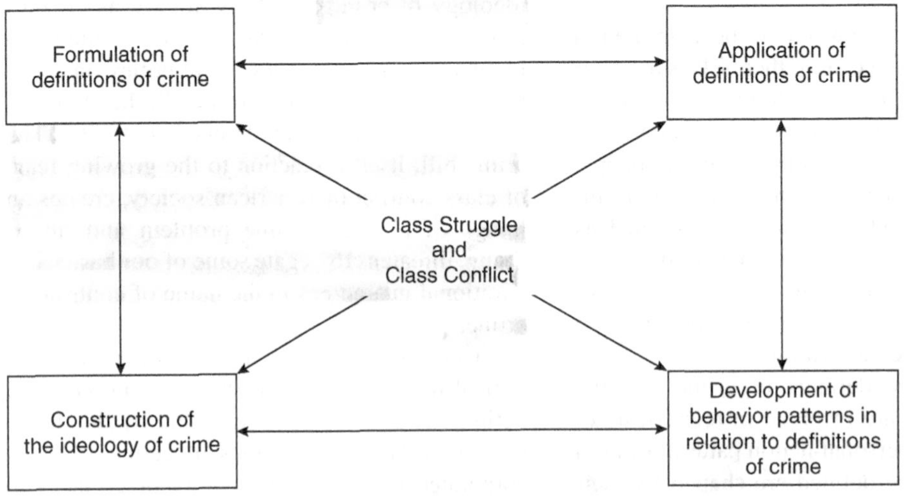

FIGURE 9.1 The Social Reality of Crime

REVIEW QUESTIONS

1. Identify one type of behavior that can be explained by using conflict theory.
2. How might you argue, from a conflict perspective, that changes in marijuana laws are not a reflection of the opinions of the average American but a reflection of the views of those with the capacity to make laws?
3. Do you agree with the assumptions of Quinney's theory? Cite examples to support your stance.

CHAPTER 10

FEMINIST THEORY

KATHLEEN DALY

The [feminist] research literature on women and gender differences in lawbreaking can be divided into two categories. The first is concerned with aggregate patterns and trends from a variety of data sources, and the second addresses the qualities of offenses committed and the life worlds of lawbreakers.

PATTERNS AND TRENDS [OF LAWBREAKING]

First, self-report studies of lawbreaking show higher rates of prevalence (committing an offense) and incidence (number of times) for boys than girls. From the Denver Youth Survey (1976–1980), boys' prevalence rates were higher than girls' for eighteen of twenty offenses. Girls' prevalence rates were slightly higher for "running away from home" and "hitting a parent" (Chesney-Lind and Shelden 1992; Tripplet and Myers 1995). In general, as offense seriousness increases, the gender gap widens in measures of prevalence and incidence. A 1988–1991 survey of self-reported crime by Denver youths in "high-risk" neighborhoods (Esbensen and Huizinga 1993) found higher prevalence rates for nongang boys than nongang girls for street crime, drug sales, and "serious offenses" but not for minor offenses or alcohol or drug use. (Incidence rates were also higher for the boys than the girls for street crime, drug sales, and alcohol use.) Not surprisingly, for both groups, prevalence rates were greater for those boys and girls who were involved in gangs, and especially so for the girls. This "gang effect" in enhancing crime involvement was stronger, however, for the boys than for the girls in reported incidence rates.

Second, arrest data show larger gender ratios of lawbreaking than self-report studies, although a similar structure of offending is apparent. Specifically, gender gaps in lawbreaking are largest for the more serious offenses (such as violent offenses) and smaller for minor forms of property offenses. The structure of offenses for which men and women are arrested is similar: the most typical are substance abuse offenses (alcohol or drug-related) and larceny-theft (Steffensmeier and Allan 1996).

Third, trend data for arrests from 1960 to 1990 show that the female share of all arrests rose from 10 to 20 percent; these shifts are evident for younger (under eighteen) and older women. For both age-groups, increases were greatest for larceny-theft; for older women, increases were also apparent for fraud and forgery (Steffensmeier 1993). For the thirty-year period, Darrell Steffensmeier (1993) sees a shift in the offenses for which both men and women are arrested: today a larger share are arrested for driving under the influence, larceny-theft, and drug law viola-

Source: Kathleen Daly, "Gender, Crime, and Criminology," in Michael Tonry (ed.), *The Handbook of Crime and Punishment* (New York: Oxford University Press, 1998), pp. 85–108.

tions, with a comparatively smaller share arrested for public drunkenness and disorderly conduct. Trends from the National Crime Victimization Survey (1975–1990) for the perceived sex of offenders in robbery, simple and aggravated assault, burglary, and motor vehicle theft show that the female share has remained the same over time (Steffensmeier and Allan 1996).

Fourth, arrest data suggest that in societies and groups where there are high male arrest rates, there are high female arrest rates; where there are low male rates, there are low female rates. Over time, male and female arrest rates will rise and fall in parallel fashion, suggesting roughly similar responses to broader socioeconomic and legal forces (Steffensmeier and Allan 1996). With such a pattern, we would expect that the profile of men and women accused, prosecuted, and imprisoned for crime would have a similar class- and race-based structure. And indeed the profile is similar: compared with their proportions in the general population, criminalized men and women are more likely to be economically marginalized and to be members of racial/ethnic minority groups; they are less likely to have completed high school.

Fifth, gender differences in arrest rates cannot be understood apart from race, ethnicity, and class. Analyses of victimization, self-report, and arrest data show major racial differences in the likelihood of involvement in crime, especially in violent offenses. For example, arrest rates for black, white, and Hispanic women for three violent offenses in New York City during 1987–1990 show significant differences: 1,670 per 100,000 for black women compared with 503 and 126, respectively, for Hispanic and white women (Sommers and Baskin 1992). These racial/ethnic differences may be explained, in part, by where the women lived: those who lived in high-poverty neighborhoods had the highest arrest rates for violent crime compared with those who lived in low- or moderate-poverty areas. Substantially higher proportions of arrested black women lived in high-poverty neighborhoods (69 percent) than did arrested Hispanic or white women (20 and 11 percent, respectively; Sommers and Baskin 1992).

QUALITIES OF OFFENSES AND LIFE WORLDS OF OFFENDERS

First, female involvement in gangs is more varied than earlier research (from the 1940s to the 1960s) had revealed. . . . In surveys of gangs, estimates of female involvement range from 10 to 38 percent (Miller 1996). Esbensen and Huizinga (1993) say that their survey-based estimate—girls or women constitute 25 percent of gang members—is consistent with the gender composition of gangs in other research on urban areas in the late 1980s. But saying that you are "in" a gang and that you participate in criminal activities may not mean the same thing for male and female gang members. Esbensen and Huizinga (1993) found that offending rates were twice as high for gang boys as for gang girls across a range of delinquent acts; the differences were greatest for serious forms of delinquency. It should be emphasized that even in "high-risk" areas in Denver, recent surveys suggest that the percentage of youths reporting gang membership is small, ranging from 3 to 7 percent (Esbensen and Huizinga 1993).

Second, little is known about women's involvement or gender differences in white-collar crime. Beginning with Edwin Sutherland ([1949] 1983), researchers have assumed that the white-collar offender is male (e.g., Mann, Wheeler, and Sarat 1980), a not unreasonable assumption when one examines the profile of those convicted of white-collar crime (Daly 1989). For those offenses considered to be "real" forms of white-collar lawbreaking (i.e., committed by those in occupational positions of power, such as antitrust violations and securities fraud), an analysis of federal court convictions in the late 1970s shows the female share of convictions to be very low (0.5 to 2 percent). The female share of convictions for bank embezzlement was higher (45 percent); but when the specific job that convicted embezzlers held was examined, few women were bank officers or managers (7 percent), whereas just over half of the men were (Daly 1989).

An obvious explanation for gender differences in white-collar crime is to say that there are fewer workplace opportunities for women to engage in such crime. Less obvious but better explanations focus on the gendered structure of opportunities. Such explanations draw linkages between men's sexism toward women in the "upperworld" and "underworld" that may serve to exclude women from men's crime groups (Messerschmidt 1993; Steffensmeier 1983). They may also include attention to gender-based variability in motive, the size of the crime group, and offense roles that would defy a simple "workplace opportunities" argument (Daly 1989). Analyses of drug markets suggest that "opportunities" are circumscribed by particular masculine qualities thought necessary for selling and distributing drugs (Maher and Daly 1996). Gang research reveals that women themselves ratify gender hierarchies and female devaluation, even as they claim to be the equals of men (Miller 1996). Elucidating the *gendered* [emphasis added] structures of illegitimate and workplace opportunities for crime will prove a more fruitful strategy than one which makes the glib assumption that "men and women will behave in like manner when occupying similar positions in the social structure" (Simon and Landis 1991). Indeed, this assumption cannot be sustained in explaining the lawbreaking of poor or marginalized men and women, as we have already seen. Why would we ever assume that gender divisions are less salient for more affluent men and women or those in the paid labor force?

Third, women's roles in offenses are varied. In their review of the literature, Leanne Alarid and colleagues (1996) found that in eleven of nineteen studies, women played minor or secondary roles. Alarid et al. also interviewed 104 young women (average age, twenty years) in boot camp, asking them what part they played in the crime for which they were incarcerated. They found that 15 percent of the women said they acted alone, whereas identical proportions of about 42 percent each said they had primary (or equal) and secondary roles. When the women acted with others, two sources of variability in their offense roles were noted: the woman's race-ethnicity and the offense she committed. A somewhat higher proportion of African-American (48 percent) and Hispanic women (45 percent) played primary or equal offense roles, compared with Anglo women (36 percent). Women were more likely to play primary or equal roles (56 percent) for drug offenses than for property (36 percent) or violent (31 percent) offenses. The women were asked who influenced them to become involved in crime during the past year. While just over half of the Anglo and Hispanic women said they were "influenced by men," only 20 percent of the African-American women said they were influenced by men. But when the women were asked whether they acted as a "leader or a follower when with [their] friends," a similar proportion of both Anglo (38 percent) and African-American (33 percent) women said they were followers. My interpretation of these data is that a larger portion of African-American women are influenced by other African-American women to become involved in crime than are Anglo women, whose deviant pathways appear to be related more to men's influences. Such Anglo and African-American differences were also found in Lisa Maher's (1995) research on New York City women's initiation into drug use.

Fourth, research on gender, offense contexts, and motives is most developed for homicide (see reviews by Ogle, Maier-Katkin, and Bernard 1995; Wilson and Daly 1992). From this research we find that women represent a small share (about 10–12 percent) of homicide arrests. They are more likely to kill intimates (spouses or partners) than are men, who are more likely to kill acquaintances or strangers. The victims of women's homicides are more likely to have initiated the violence than are the victims of men's homicides. Women's homicides generally occur in their own or the victim's residence, while men's homicides occur more frequently outside residential settings. The situational and relational differences in men's and women's homicides can be explained, in part, by the fact that fewer women's homicides occur in the course of robberies, burglaries, or rapes. Ogle, Maier-Katkin, and Bernard report that the "consistency of the pattern of homicides by women, as well as the differences from the patterns of homicides by men, suggests the need for a separate theoretical explanation of female homicide" (1995). I am not persuaded that homicide requires a separate theory from, say, aggravated or simple assault. More important, it is not clear that homicide patterns for women are "consistent" when one considers data from other countries. Margo Wilson and Martin Daly (1992, p. 191) show that U.S. women (especially black women) are far more likely to kill male spouses or cohabitants than are women in Canada, England and Wales, Scotland, Australia, or other countries. They argue against a simple "underclass" or "black" explanation for this pattern and instead suggest a focus on structured and situational sources of marital conflict: the social and economic devaluation of minority group men, which [increases] the men's desire to coerce female partners; residential and kin patterns, which may empower some women to retaliate; and the incidence of step-relationships, which may increase the frequency with which women need to defend their children.

Fifth, girls' and women's pathways to lawbreaking are many and varied. Drawing from U.S. and non-U.S. studies, I identified what I termed the "leading feminist scenario" of women's lawbreaking, that of street women (Daly 1994). These women may have run from abusive households to the street, or they may have been attracted to the "fast money" of a deviant lifestyle. Once on the street, young women engage in petty hustles or prostitution. Life on the street may lead to drug use and addiction, which may lead to more frequent lawbreaking to support a drug habit.

Interview studies by Arnold (1990), Chesney-Lind and Shelden (1992), and Gilfus (1992) have centered attention on girls' sexual and physical victimization while growing up, their efforts to escape abuse and violence, and the consequent "criminalizing of girls' survival" (Chesney-Lind 1989) on the streets. Eleanor Miller (1986) identified several routes for Milwaukee street women: those running away from home to the streets, and those whose households were connected to the streets via "domestic networks." In my analysis of the biographies of forty women prosecuted in the New Haven felony court, I found that street women characterized about a third of my sample. As frequent was a second group I termed "harmed and harming women." These women had chaotic and difficult experiences growing up, with violent or "out of control" behavior evinced in childhood or adolescence. Other groups of New Haven women had associates who used or sold drugs (drug-connected women, about 15 percent) or were fending off and fighting abusive partners (battered women, about 10 percent; Daly 1994).

EXPLAINING PATTERNS OF LAWBREAKING

A decade ago, Meda Chesney-Lind and I identified two related, though distinct, theoretical problems for . . . the study of women, gender, and crime. They are the gender ratio problem (why are men more likely involved in or arrested for crime than women?) and the generalizability problem (do theories of crime based on boys' or men's lives apply to girls or women?; Daly and Chesney-Lind 1988). For most nonfeminist scholars, interest remains in addressing the gender ratio problem, with the working assumption that a "gender-neutral" theory is preferable. Here we see a clash in theoretical objectives.

On the one hand, Darrell Steffensmeier and Emilie Allan (1996) suggest that "the traditional gender-neutral theories [derived from male samples] provide reasonable explanations of less serious forms of [crime]" for men and women. Such thinking is common in nonfeminist and liberal feminist analyses of gender and crime (e.g., Smith and Paternoster 1987; Simon and Landis 1991). On the other hand, feminist scholars, including myself, find it illogical to say that traditional theories derived from male samples are gender-neutral. Traditional theories are more appropriately labeled *male-specific*, not gender-neutral. Such theories may, of course, be relevant to girls and women: we would expect that elements of social control, learning, labeling, and opportunity would be applicable in a general sense. However, even if particular elements are applicable, they may not be applicable in the same ways or to the same degree. Likewise, elements from theories developed from all-female samples may be applicable to boys and men, but not necessarily in the same ways or to the same degree.

We should abandon the concept of, and the quest for, gender-neutral criminological theories. Instead, we should use terms that better describe the theoretical enterprise: to identify variables, factors, or conceptual elements that have similar and different influences on lawbreaking for boys/men and girls/women. This is just one potential focus of theoretical work; there are others, as follows.

Gender ratio of crime. What is the nature of, and what explains the "gender gap" in, lawbreaking and arrests for crime? What is the nature of, and what explains variation in, the kinds of offenses that girls/women and boys/men get involved with (or arrested for), in terms of both prevalence and incidence? What is the nature of, and what explains gender-based variation in, arrest rates across nations, including developed and developing countries?

Gendered crime. What are the contexts and qualities of boys'/men's and girls'/women's illegal acts? What is the social organization of specific offenses (e.g., drug dealing, prostitution, and credit frauds)?

Gendered pathways to lawbreaking. What is the nature of, and what explains the character of, girls'/women's and boys'/men's pathways to lawbreaking? What brings people to the street, to use illegal drugs, to become involved in workplace crime, or to be arrested and prosecuted for crime? How do boys/men and girls/women move in and out of foster homes, conventional work, jails and prisons, hospitals, and halfway houses?

Gendered lives. How does gender organize the ways in which men and women survive, take care of themselves and their children, and find shelter and food? How does gender structure thinkable courses of action and identities?

Researchers may address these thematics with a focus on class, racial-ethnic, age, regional, or other sources of variability. Or they may decide to analyze one particular group, such as black women. Using Don Gibbons's (1994) categories, the gender ratio of crime and gendered crime address "the rates question," gendered crime and gendered pathways attend to questions of "why they did it," and gendered lives examines general life course trajectories that may or may not include lawbreaking. . . . Nonfeminist inquiries on gender and crime are principally focused on the gender ratio and gendered crime problems; they attempt to measure rates of involvement in crime/delinquency and to explain [gender] "gaps" in such involvement. Scholars in this tradition may draw from a nascent understanding of feminist theories, but their guiding metaphors and concepts come largely from [traditional] criminology. By comparison, feminist inquiries on gender and crime are principally focused on demonstrating the ways in which the social organization of gender shapes women's and men's lives on the streets and in neighborhoods, workplaces, and households. [Feminist] research tends to focus on gendered crime, gendered pathways, and gendered lives.

REFERENCES

Alarid, Leanne Fiftal, James W. Marquart, Veliner S. Burston Jr., Francis T. Cullen, and Steven J. Cuvelier. 1996. "Women's Roles in Serious Offenses: A Study of Adult Felons." *Justice Quarterly* 13:431–454.

Arnold, Regina. 1990. "Processes of Victimization and

Criminalization of Black Women." *Social Justice* 17:153–166.

Chesney-Lind, Meda. 1989. "Girls' Crime and Woman's Place: Toward a Feminist Model of Female Delinquency." *Crime and Delinquency* 35:5–29.

Chesney-Lind, Meda, and Randall G. Shelden. 1992. *Girls, Delinquency, and Juvenile Justice.* Pacific Grove, Calif.: Brooks/Cole.

Daly, Kathleen. 1989. "Gender and Varieties of White-Collar Crime." *Criminology* 27:769–794.

———. 1994. *Gender, Crime, and Punishment.* New Haven, Conn.: Yale University Press.

Daly, Kathleen, and Meda Chesney-Lind. 1988. "Feminism and Criminology." *Justice Quarterly* 5:497–538.

Esbensen, Finn-Aage, and David Huizinga. 1993. "Gangs, Drugs, and Delinquency in a Survey of Urban Youth." *Criminology* 31:565–587.

Gibbons, Don C. 1994. *Talking about Crime and Criminals: Problems and Issues in Theory Development in Criminology.* Englewood Cliffs, N.J.: Prentice-Hall.

Gilfus, Mary E. 1992. "From Victims to Survivors to Offenders: Women's Routes of Entry and Immersion into Street Crime." *Women and Criminal Justice* 4:63–89.

Maher, Lisa. 1995. "In the Name of Love: Women and Initiation to Illicit Drugs." In *Gender and Crime*, edited by R. Emerson Dobash, Russell P. Dobash, and Lesley Noakes. Cardiff: University of Wales Press.

Maher, Lisa, and Kathleen Daly. 1996. "Women in the Street-Level Drug Economy: Continuity or Change?" *Criminology* 34:465–491.

Mann, Kenneth, Stanton Wheeler, and Austin Sarat. 1980. "Sentencing the White-Collar Offender." *American Criminal Law Review* 17:479–500.

Messerschmidt, James W. 1993. *Masculinities and Crime: Critique and Reconceptualization of Theory.* Lanham, Md.: Rowman and Littlefield.

Miller, Eleanor. 1986. *Street Woman.* Philadelphia: Temple University Press.

Miller, Jody. 1996. "Female Gang Involvement in a Midwestern City: Correlates, Nature, and Meanings." Ph.D. diss., University of Southern California, Department of Sociology.

Ogle, Robbin, Daniel Maher-Katkin, and Thomas J. Bernard. 1995. "A Theory of Homicidal Behavior among Women." *Criminology* 33:173–193.

Simon, Rita, and Jean Landis. 1991. *The Crimes Women Commit, the Punishments They Receive.* Lexington, Mass.: Lexington Books.

Smith, Douglas A., and Raymond Paternoster. 1987. "The Gender Gap in Theories of Deviance: Issues and Evidence." *Journal of Research in Crime and Delinquency* 24:140–172.

Sommers, Ira, and Deborah Baskin. 1992. "Sex, Race, Age, and Violent Offending." *Violence and Victims* 7:191–201.

Steffensmeier, Darrell. 1983. "Organization Properties and Sex-Segregation in the Underworld: Building a Sociological Theory of Sex Differences in Crime." *Social Forces* 61:1010–1032.

———. 1993. "National Trends in Female Arrests, 1960–1990: Assessment and Recommendations for Research." *Journal of Quantitative Criminology* 9:411–441.

Steffensmeier, Darrell, and Emilie Allan. 1996. "Gender and Crime: Toward a Gendered Theory of Female Offending." *Annual Review of Sociology* 22:459–487.

Sutherland, Edwin H. [1949] 1983. *White Collar Crime: The Uncut Version.* New Haven, Conn.: Yale University Press.

Tripplet, Ruth, and Laura B. Myers. 1995. "Evaluating Contextual Patterns of Delinquency: Gender-Based Differences." *Justice Quarterly* 12:59–84.

Wilson, Margo, and Martin Daly. 1992. "Who Kills Whom in Spouse Killings? On the Exceptional Sex Ratio of Spousal Homicides in the United States." *Criminology* 30:189–215.

REVIEW QUESTIONS

1. What are the patterns and trends of the gender differences in lawbreaking? How would you explain these differences?
2. What is the distinctive nature of the offenses committed by females?
3. What does "criminalizing girls' survival" mean?

PART FOUR

PHYSICAL VIOLENCE

In 2008, Abu Dhaim, a 25-year-old Palestinian, filled a cardboard television box with a semiautomatic rifle, two pistols, and an abundance of ammunition. He then called his 17-year-old girlfriend and discussed their plan to go shopping the next day in Jerusalem. They were going to get married soon and hoped to honeymoon in Turkey. After hanging up the phone, Abu Dhaim drove to a Jewish seminary in Jerusalem and went into a library, where he then killed 8 students and wounded 10 before he himself was shot dead. His girlfriend was totally surprised. She could not have imagined him as a suicide terrorist; she had known him to be cheerful and gentle, and he was from a relatively wealthy and well-educated family.[1]

Actually, Abu Dhaim fits the typical profile of a suicide terrorist. Many suicide terrorists come from families with money and education. But are suicide terrorists psychologically abnormal? Possible answers can be found in the first article, "What Drives the Libyan Suicide Bombers in Iraq?" What about serial murderers? Are they mentally ill or sociopathic? In the second article, "Serial Murder: Popular Myths and Empirical Realities," by James Alan Fox and Jack Levin, the authors present some surprising facts about the shocking crime of serial murder. Other forms of violence are examined in the third and fourth articles. In the third article, "What Triggers School Shootings?" Michael Kimmel and Matthew Mahler explain what kind of student is likely to engage in school violence and why. In the fourth article, " 'I Hope Someone Murders Your Mother!': Extreme Support for the Death Penalty," Margaret Vandiver, David Giacopassi, and Peter Gathje discuss the nature of and reasons for the extreme support for capital punishment.

[1]Tim McGirk, "Israel's Secret War," *Time*, March 24, 2008, pp. 30–31.

Chapter 11

WHAT DRIVES THE LIBYAN SUICIDE BOMBERS IN IRAQ?

KEVIN PERAINO

Even before he vanished, Abd al-Salam Bin-Ali was an easy young man to miss. Pale, lanky and blind in one eye, the unobtrusive 20-year-old didn't leave much of an impression in Darnah, his hometown in eastern Libya. In school he had studied to become a veterinarian, but after graduation he couldn't find a job. "The economic situation was terrible," recalls his older brother, Abd al-Hamid. "He was looking for work every day." Sometimes Abd al-Salam would set up a folding table in Darnah's Old City and hawk cheap perfumes.

Unmarried, with few prospects, he still lived with his mother. At home, for distraction, he would sprawl in front of the family television and watch "Lion of the Desert," the 1981 epic of Libyan resistance fighters starring Anthony Quinn. Abd al-Salam had seen it over and over. As the war in Iraq dragged on, he also tuned in to Al-Jazeera. Nobody in the family had supported the American invasion, but Abd al-Salam was particularly affected by the bloody images he saw on the Arabic cable news channel. He sometimes teased his mother that he wanted to run away to fight the Americans. Before she could protest too much, he always backed down. "No, no, no—don't worry, Mom," he would say with a laugh. "I'll get married instead." His older brother wasn't so confident. "I was sure he would go," Abd al-Hamid recalls. "He was always talking about it." Abd al-Salam was also growing more devout. According to his brother, he spent most of his time at the mosque.

Then one day in late September 2006, Abd al-Salam simply disappeared. "Where is he?" his anxious mother asked when he didn't show up for dinner. His brother reassured her that Abd al-Salam had gone to Benghazi (in Libya), perhaps to buy perfumes, but Abd al-Hamid didn't believe his own story. The younger boy had probably hitched a ride to Cairo (in Egypt), and then flown on to Damascus (in Syria). He later crossed the border into Iraq with $100 cash in his pocket, and joined a cadre of insurgents led by a coordinator he knew as "Hamad." Shortly after Abd al-Salam disappeared, the telephone rang in Darnah. "I'm in Ramadi," the voice on the other end said. "I'm in Iraq."

Late last year American soldiers raided an insurgent headquarters in the northern Iraqi town of Sinjar. Inside they found a document—perhaps an application form that Abd al-Salam had filled out on his way into the country—on the letterhead of the "Mujahedin Shura Council." The document listed little beyond Abd al-Salam's birthday, his brother's phone number and his hometown. Yet as they analyzed the papers, American investigators were struck by one thing. Of the 606 militants

Source: Kevin Peraino, "Destination Martyrdom," *Newsweek*, April 28, 2008, pp. 24–30.

cataloged in the Sinjar records, almost 19 percent had come to Iraq from Libya. Previous intelligence estimates had always held that the bulk of Iraq's foreign fighters come from Saudi Arabia. Indeed, the largest number of militants in the Sinjar records—244 of them—were Saudi nationals. But in per capita terms, Libyans represented a much higher percentage. Perhaps the most startling detail: of 112 Libyan fighters named in the papers, an astoundingly large number—52—had come from a single town of 50,000 people along the Mediterranean coast, called Darnah.

Earlier this month I traveled to Darnah to try to figure out why it was contributing such a large portion of its young men to fight the Americans in Iraq. A stunning natural landscape surrounds the town, nestled in the shadow of rust-colored limestone bluffs that overlook the sparkling Mediterranean. Yet the city's corniche is lined with a dreary procession of crumbling concrete tenements coated in a patina of chipped pastel paint. Libya's economy is dominated by the oil and gas sector, which accounts for 90 percent of the country's revenues, but little of that wealth has ever trickled down to Libya's eastern province. Government officials in Tripoli acknowledge in private conversations that the east has long been neglected. The discrepancy is a truth too obvious for Darnah residents to deny, even given the hazards of speaking openly in President Muammar Kaddafi's police state. "What have we gotten from this government?" asks Abd al-Hamid bin-Ali. One telling detail in the Sinjar documents: of the Libyans who listed their "work" in Iraq, more than 85 percent volunteered for suicide missions—a significantly larger fraction than any other country but Morocco.

Still, economic desperation alone doesn't fully explain the readiness of Darnah's young men to join the insurgents in Iraq. There are tens of millions of impoverished Muslims in the world, but only a handful—perhaps a few hundred at any given time—travel to Iraq to fight. There is little consensus about what ultimately motivates them, what changes someone from a disgruntled viewer of cable news into a suicide killer. "That's the big mystery," says Brian Fishman, a West Point counterterrorism expert who has extensively analyzed the Sinjar records. "The dynamics are very, very local." There are some common denominators. In their interviews with *Newsweek*, family members of the local recruits spoke of young men with bleak lives in search of redemption. Far from being universally motivated by one global ideology, the jihadist recruits often seem to have been driven by personal factors like psychological trauma, sibling rivalry and sexual longing.

Darnah's militants do have one other thing in common: an almost obsessive devotion to their town's place in history. Greek and Roman ruins, the detritus of occupations in the ancient past, dot the wheat and barley fields along Libya's coastal plain. The United States left its own lasting mark on the town's collective memory during the Barbary Wars of the early 1800s. Darnah became a key battlefield in America's first overseas military expedition, when 500 American Marines and local mercenaries marched across the desert from Egypt to assault the town. (The ensuing Battle of Darnah inspired the "shores of Tripoli" line in the current Marine Hymn.)

But it was another country a century later that seared the ideal of armed resistance into the town's psyche. In 1911, Italy landed warships in Darnah's port, the beginning of a ruthless colonial presence that would last through the Mussolini era until the Axis powers were defeated in World War II. Local resistance to the occupation was strongest in the rocky hills near Darnah, but even there it was ultimately crushed. From its dust, a homegrown tradition of Islamic martyrdom emerged.

The local mythology is so pervasive that it guides even the town's most senior officials. On my second day in Darnah, I stopped by the office of Saddik Afdel, the co-chairman of the town's People's Committee—the Libyan equivalent of a mayor. A gentle sea breeze wafted in from an open window behind Afdel's desk. At first he denied that his town was sending a significant number of its young men to Iraq. "We don't know exactly the number," he told me. "Here in Darnah, not more than 10." I showed him the stack of documents, some of which include small photos of the fighters, and the chairman grew quiet. "We have no idea about that," he began, speaking through an interpreter. "They have no reason to go." He took a drag on his cigarette. "Look, this is a huge number," he eventually conceded. "If this number is true, it's very bad. It's bad for politics. But it's not bad for Muslims to do their duty. America said that this war is for freedom. And it's not. What we see on Al-Jazeera is not what we've been told by the Americans. I can't stop them from going. What we've been taught by the Qur'an is jihad." When I asked about the town's history of rebellious militants, Afdel couldn't suppress a grin. "Those are the people who used to stand up and fight for their land," he told me. "We have to remember them."

TO THE SHORES OF TRIPOLI

Most Americans today think of the Barbary Pirates only as a stray detail from a long-ago history exam. But to the Founding Fathers they were the scourge of the seas. The former North American colonies, newly liberated, needed the Mediterranean's shipping lanes to export their tobacco, sugar and other commodities to the Middle East. Having given up the protection of the British Empire's powerful fleet, American ships were falling victim to pirates from modern-day Morocco, Algeria and Libya. Kidnappings were frequent. Fair-skinned women were particularly prized captives, and were added to North African harems. The cycle of kidnappings and ransoms took a harsh toll on the young American nation.

The politicians argued about whether to confront or appease the enemy until President Thomas Jefferson finally ordered American warships into battle in 1801. Things began badly: the USS *Philadelphia* and its crew were captured; the frigate was anchored in Tripoli's harbor as a trophy, and Jefferson intensified American attacks. Stephen Decatur, in 1804 a relatively unknown U.S. naval officer, led a now legendary nighttime mission to assault the *Philadelphia* in the harbor, burning it into the sea. From the east, Gen. William Eaton marched his forces overland across the desert from Alexandria, Egypt, to Darnah in 1805. As described in Michael Oren's history *Power, Faith, and Fantasy*, Eaton rode to the gate of Darnah's Old City and demanded the town's surrender. The local governor replied: "My head or yours." Eaton took the city.

Today there are relics and reminders of the battle all over town. One of the first things a visitor sees on the road into Darnah is a set of four giant yellow concrete numerals advertising the 1805 Resort. One popular eatery on the corniche is the Philadelphia Fast Food restaurant. Libyan schools teach the capture of the *Philadelphia* as a great national victory, although there was no independent nation of Libya at the time; it was a semiautonomous regency of the Ottoman Empire. Fathi Abd al-Moula, who teaches history to 10-year-olds in a small town outside Darnah, says he draws simple pictures of the *Philadelphia* for his classes. His students are too young to remember names like Eaton and Decatur, he explains, but they are old enough to see the battles as a source of national pride. "Libya was the first country to take on America," says Essam al-Hamal, who works at another Philadelphia Fast Food restaurant in Tripoli, where a mast said to be from the American ship is displayed to this day atop the Red Fortress. Libyans refer to the conflict as "the First Libyan–American War."

Nowhere is Darnah's past more present than in the basement headquarters of a local club known as the Hyena Society. It was my first stop upon arrival in Darnah. The group's 200-or-so members include a slightly incongruous collection of aging history buffs, along with a number of younger adventure seekers. The clubhouse is filled with historical artifacts and curios, including stuffed cobras, Ottoman-era carbines and Bedouin tents. The society's president, Muhammad al-Hinid, a wiry and eccentric 76-year-old who wears aviator sunglasses indoors, walked me past an enormous model of the USS *Argus*, one of the supply ships that met and resupplied Eaton's

Army on the march to Darnah. The Barbary Wars are important to Darnah's history, Hinid told me. Still, he added, the Italian occupation left deeper scars on the town. "The Italian war is much more important," Hinid said.

Even by the ugly standards of early-20th-century colonial powers, Italy's domination of its southern neighbor was mind-numbingly brutal. According to one Libyan census, the native population dropped from 1.2 million in 1912 to 825,000 in 1933. "The bulk of the population drop was the direct result of Italian policy," says Ronald Bruce St. John, a widely respected scholar of Libya who says Italy's tools of oppression included concentration camps, deliberate starvation and "mass execution that bordered on genocide." Reading exercises for children in Libyan schools included phrases like "I am happy to be subject to the Italian government" and "The Duce loves children very much, even Arab children."

A strong local resistance emerged, primarily in the rocky hills of eastern Libya. The hero of the insurgency was a charismatic, white-robed Muslim holy warrior named Omar al-Mukhtar. The Lion of the Desert was a disciple of the Senussis, a secretive and deeply conservative order of Islamic ascetics. The order's founder had traveled extensively in Saudi Arabia, where he mingled with members of the puritanical Wahhabi sect in the mid-1880s. By Omar al-Mukhtar's day, the Senussis had honed a strict, yet almost evangelical, variety of Islam that spread quickly through eastern Libya, gaining adherents partly by offering social services like schools and access to wells. For 20 years, Mukhtar harassed the Italian forces with his small band of guerrillas, but the Italians finally captured him in 1931, as they infiltrated and destroyed the Senussi networks.

Today the cult of Omar al-Mukhtar is visible everywhere in Darnah: on posters, billboards, stickers on car windshields. His face may be more ubiquitous even than President Kaddafi's. Bootleg copies of "Lion of the Desert" are brisk sellers in local marketplaces. At the Hyena Society, Hinid showed me a portrait of Mukhtar. He said he painted it on the night of Saddam Hussein's execution. Hinid had watched the hanging on Al-Jazeera. The sad eyes in his painting of Mukhtar, Hinid explained, are actually Saddam's. It isn't difficult to see how the Iraqi dictator might provide Darnah residents with a modern-day stand-in for their martyred hero. "We all love [Saddam] here," Hinid told me.

"EVERYTHING BUT THE GIRL"

Both Saddam and Mukhtar are revered figures at the Hassan Mosque, a spare, whitewashed structure with green pastel trim in the center of Darnah's Old City. A poster of Omar al-Mukhtar, faded and tattered, is affixed to the front door. Anuri al-Hasadi, the mosque's muezzin, was just arriving for afternoon prayers when I stopped by. Dressed in a gray pin-striped dishdasha and sporting a walrus mustache, the 60-year-old had the air of a Dickens character. We sat down on folding chairs in the mosque's lobby, and I asked the muezzin what he thought of the Iraq War. He tried to brush off the question, reluctant to wade into politics—but then he erupted. "Oil! Oil!" he cried. "America needs oil. It's America's fault. You think they came here to buy fruit? They came for the oil!" He declined to say at first whether he thought it was OK for Libyans to travel to Iraq to fight. At last he said he did not approve. The assertion was a little hard to believe after his "oil" outburst. I asked about one of his relatives, an 18-year-old named Ashraf al-Hasadi. According to the Sinjar documents, the young man left Darnah last year for Iraq. The muezzin denied knowing the boy. Then somewhat under his breath, he said softly in Arabic: "He was just a kid."

Ashraf al-Hasadi worked just around the corner from the Hassan Mosque, at his family's spice shop on the Old City's bustling main artery. Tall and clean-shaven, but a little chubby, the youngest of four brothers was also "the quietest of the family," said his brother Bakr, who was working the cash register at the shop when I stopped by. Big sacks of candy, dates and a spice known as baharat were stacked on shelves behind him. Bakr looked a little wary when I first arrived, but he invited me inside and offered a cup of tea. I asked him to tell me what he could about Ashraf.

Bakr explained that he had lately been urging his brother to get married. At 18 years old, Ashraf was still a bachelor, and young to wed. Because a wedding ceremony is expensive and Darnah is relatively poor, most men in town don't end up marrying until at least their late 20s. Still, the spice shop provided the Hasadis with a steady income, and Ashraf was considerably better positioned than most of his friends. After his mother died in 2006, it was up to his brothers to set him up. Ashraf already had a job, a car and an apartment—all the prerequisites. Even so, his brothers worried that the young man was a little tightly wound, sensitive and severe at the same time. He recoiled at the images of Iraq that he saw on Al-Jazeera. "He never watched movies," Bakr recalled. "It was only the news." After work, Ashraf liked to whip his black Hyundai around the tight warrens of Darnah's Old City. To his brothers' dismay, he showed little interest in marriage. "He had everything," his brother Abdelkhader said with a laugh, "except for the girl."

Instead, Ashraf was spending more and more time at the mosque. Darnah is a religious town; several times a day, the shops in the Old City's main street roll down and lock their front doors as the mosques fill for prayers. Even so, Ashraf became "too religious," says his brother Sufian—"seriously religious. He lived at the mosque." One day in the summer of 2007, Ashraf went to see his brothers and told them he was leaving on a trip with a friend. The others didn't make much of the conversation, they said. Then, about a week later, the phone rang. Ashraf got quickly to the point: he was in Iraq. "And that was the last phone call he made to his family," brother Sufian says. The Hasadis fear the worst, but say they don't know for sure whether their brother is dead or alive. I asked them whether they thought Ashraf would ever come home. "God knows," Bakr said. "A lot of them go and come back. Some stay six months, some two years." Then there are the ones who volunteer for suicide missions.

The Hasadi family's flourishing businesses—they own a chain of the spice and candy shops on the same street—make them something of an oddity in run-down Darnah. Their story is just one example of how difficult it is to generalize about the motivations of foreign fighters. Still, there is no doubt that economic misery and its social consequences have scarred Darnah's young people. Many of Tripoli's prostitutes have come to the city from eastern Libya; in some cases they are their families' sole breadwinners. Tripolitan men joke—crudely but revealingly—that they patronize prostitutes from the eastern half of the country as a form of wealth redistribution. For young men in Darnah, unemployment means almost certain bachelorhood—a dismal state in a society as sexually conservative as Darnah's. In a male-dominated community, the predicament of prolonged celibacy also carries an acute social stigma.

That fate may be just what 28-year-old Abdelhakim Okaly feared when he slipped out of Darnah to Iraq last spring. When I called Abdelhakim's father, Mustafa, earlier this month, the elder Okaly at first refused to talk, and then quietly asked if I could tell him where Abdelhakim was. We made an appointment to meet in a parking lot behind a nearby mosque. When Mustafa pulled up, he looped his beat-up station wagon in a wide circle around my car, and then invited me to his house. The Okaly residence, a hardscrabble concrete apartment block abutting the seashore, was significantly more modest than others I had visited in Darnah. As Mustafa's wiry 20-year-old son Awad brought in a tray of cookies and guava juice, the father's eyes began to fill with tears. Later he told me that when he had first spotted me—an obvious outsider—he thought perhaps I had brought back his son.

Mustafa explained he had long feared that Abdelhakim would try to leave for Iraq. Like nearly everyone I talked to in Darnah, his son was deeply affected by the carnage he saw on Al-Jazeera and CNN. The Abu Ghraib scandal angered Abdelhakim, but "what broke his heart was Fallujah," Mustafa said, referring to the crackdown on the restive, mostly Sunni city in the fall of 2004. "Do you agree with this?" Abdelhakim asked his father. "I'm going." Mustafa went so far as to drive down to the local emigration office and ask it to withhold Abdelhakim's permission to travel. But the young man, who had once worked as a cabdriver in Darnah, somehow managed to sneak out of town.

When I asked whether Abdelhakim was married, everyone in the room laughed. "The older one's not even married yet," a brother said with a chuckle. Then their father chimed in. "Well, Abdelhakim's still getting no salary," he grumbled, in something of a scolding manner. "How will he get married now?" And then, almost as if he was trying to convince himself: "He's a grown-up, he'll do what he wants to do." As we talked, the father almost seemed to be trying to teach his other sons a lesson. He said he was particularly concerned about the younger boy, Awad, the one who had brought in the juice. "This one's got no passport," the father said, throwing a glance at Awad. "But he'd like to go." Then he widened his eyes. "One's enough," he concluded.

Awad, who was sitting on the floor in a corner of the room, insisted that he wasn't going anywhere. But then he went on: "If you did want to go, you would keep it a secret. If I was planning to go, I wouldn't tell anybody." It was easy to see why Awad's father was keeping an eye on his youngest son, who displayed a mischievous wit. When I asked whether his brother Abdelhakim had any previous military training, Awad replied, "No training at all. He didn't even have muscles." When I asked Awad what his brother looked like, Mustafa Okaly's youngest child stared at me and then shot back: "He looked like you."

The Okalys said they haven't heard from Abdelhakim for more than a year, nor have they received a call telling them that he has been killed. Before I left, Mustafa made me an offer. He must have seen me as something of a conduit to a distant American world he had little access to. The desperate father leaned in close and insisted, a little conspiratorially, that he would give me a camel if I could find some way to bring his son home.

"IT'S ONLY ME NOW"

The answer to "Why Darnah?" is found, then, in an explosive mix of *desperation*, *pride* and *religious fervor*. These factors, present individually in many parts of the Islamic world, are found collectively here, on the shores of northern Libya. The town's crisis is a serious headache for Libya's diplomats. Libya was supposed to be one of the few triumphs in the Bush administration's War on Terror. In the 1980s and '90s, President Kaddafi was the face of state-sponsored terrorism, denounced by Ronald Reagan as the "Mad Dog of the Middle East." His regime was accused of involvement in the 1988 bombing of Pan Am Flight 103, which killed 270 people, as well as the 1986 bombing in a Berlin discotheque that killed two American servicemen. America retaliated by bombing Tripoli. Yet in 2003, desperate to free Libya from economic sanctions, Kaddafi's government agreed to halt its WMD programs. Three years later the State Department finally removed Libya from its list of terrorist states. The White House trumpeted the news as proof that the invasion of Iraq was scaring America's enemies all over the Mideast.

Despite the Sinjar revelations, few U.S. officials believe that Kaddafi is sending fighters to Iraq. A wave of jihadists returning to Libya from Iraq with new skills would be at least as big a nightmare for him as it is for Americans. The territory around Darnah has long been a locus of Islamist opposition to Kaddafi's regime. In the mid-1990s his security services cracked down hard on militants in Darnah, calling in helicopter gunships to suppress local rebels calling themselves the Libyan Islamic Fighting Group (LIFG).

The town seems calm enough now, but there are still plenty of checkpoints manned by uniformed police. When asked about the LIFG, most residents fall silent, even those who are happy to endorse sending local recruits to Iraq.

The Sinjar documents indicate that the Iraq insurgents had several local coordinators working in Darnah. There are few clues to how the young men were recruited, but after they signed up they were often sent to Iraq in small groups rather than singly. The Darnah pipeline passed through Egypt and Syria, where local coordinators arranged to have the enlistees smuggled across the border into Iraq. But the most recent records date only to last August, and it's an open question whether the pipeline is still flowing. Some analysts say the local Islamists disagree among themselves about whether the real jihad is in Iraq or at home in Libya.

But the old network may be renewing its strength. Late last month a prominent member of the regime's domestic spy agency was assassinated in Darnah, according to a Western diplomat in Tripoli. The diplomat says the murdered Libyan was a notoriously cruel interrogator and had made many enemies, so he wasn't necessarily killed by Islamists. "He was widely known and disliked because he was such an a—hole," says the diplomat.

Kaddafi seems to recognize that he has problems in Darnah. As oil prices have risen, the regime has tried to improve life in eastern Libya. On the main road into Darnah, the government has begun constructing some 2,000 apartments intended to house roughly 13,000 local residents by the end of 2009. The units, known as the Valley Apartments, are so far largely unoccupied, but the plan is to provide free housing to young families and singles. But earlier this year Kaddafi announced that he wanted to experiment with privatizing social services, a sharp departure from his socialist roots. "What he's advocating is something akin to radical libertarianism," says a Western diplomat in Tripoli, asking not to be identified discussing the regime's plans. The short-term result is likely to be hard times for many Libyans, even with oil above $100 a barrel.

In the wake of the Sinjar revelations, U.S. officials have put gentle pressure on Libya. In November a delegation led by Gen. Dell Daily, a senior counterterrorism specialist currently assigned to the State Department, traveled to Tripoli to meet with senior Libyan officials. Told of the documents, the Libyans at first denied the phenomenon, but eventually acknowledged the problem after the Americans presented the evidence. American officials say they're mostly pleased with the cooperation they've gotten from Libyan authorities, and are encouraged by more recent figures out of Iraq that seem to indicate that the flow of fighters may have slowed in recent months. In the meantime, other American analysts are searching for innovative ways to stem the flow, regardless of what the Libyans choose to do. The U.S. counterterrorism expert Brian Fishman says the insurgents often hire common smugglers who care only about profit to move fighters into Iraq. He says it would be smart to try co-opting those smugglers rather than fighting them. "Frankly, we should be trying to buy some of them," says Fishman.

At home in Darnah, Abd al-Hamid bin-Ali says he doesn't know exactly how his brother managed to join up with the insurgents. Abd al-Salam rarely used the Internet, he says, and didn't have any connections with LIFG militants. Shortly after Abd al-Salam's first call home, the young recruit called again from Ramadi to say he was on his way to an "operation." When the phone rang four days later, Abd al-Hamid didn't recognize the voice on the other end of the line. "Abd al-Salam is a martyr," the caller said.

Abd al-Hamid says he has come to terms with the loss of his brother. "When he was killed, I was really very happy," he says, frowning and wringing his hands. "In my opinion he was right to go. He was right to go. We see people getting killed for nothing. I used to think about going myself." Now Abd al-Hamid is the family's sole support. "I can't go now," he says quietly. "It's only me now." He glances up at an oversize portrait of his younger brother the martyr, hanging in the living room. Abd al-Salam's one blind eye stares back. The awkward younger brother has finally found his own place in his drab hometown: in a gold frame, behind a pane of glass, nailed to the wall.

REVIEW QUESTIONS

1. How do history, religion, and economics influence Libyans to become suicide bombers in Iraq?
2. What theory in the sociology of deviance can best explain why the Libyans become suicide bombers?
3. What could have stopped the Libyans from going to Iraq to participate in suicide bombings?

CHAPTER 12

SERIAL MURDER: POPULAR MYTHS AND EMPIRICAL REALITIES

JAMES ALAN FOX
JACK LEVIN

Since the early 1980s, Americans have become more aware of and concerned about a particularly dangerous class of murderers, known as serial killers. Characterized by the tendency to kill repeatedly (at least three or four victims) and often with increasing brutality, serial killers stalk their victims, one at a time, for weeks, months, or years, generally not stopping until they are caught.

The term *serial killer* was first used in the early 1980s (see Jenkins, 1994), although the phenomenon of repeat killing existed, of course, throughout recorded history. In the late 1800s, for example, Hermann Webster Mudgett (*aka* H. H. Holmes) murdered dozens of attractive young women in his Chicago "house of death," and the infamous Jack the Ripper stalked the streets of London, killing five prostitutes. Prior to the 1980s, repeat killers such as Mudgett and Jack the Ripper were generally described as mass murderers. The need for a special classification for repeat killers was later recognized because of the important differences between multiple murderers who kill simultaneously and those who kill serially (Levin & Fox, 1985). *Mass killers*—those who slaughter their victims in one event—tend to target people they know (e.g., family members or coworkers), often for the sake of revenge, using an efficient weapon of mass destruction (e.g., a high-powered firearm). As we shall describe below, serial murderers are different in all these respects, typically killing total strangers with their hands to achieve a sense of power and control over others.

A rising concern with serial killing has spawned a number of media presentations, resulting in the perpetrators of this type of murder becoming a regular staple of U.S. popular culture. A steady diet of television and movie productions could lead viewers to believe that serial killing is a common type of homicide. An increasing interest in serial homicide, however, has not been limited solely to the lay public. During the past two decades, the number, as well as the mix, of scholars devoting their attention to this crime has dramatically changed. Until the early 1980s, the literature exploring aspects of multiple homicide consisted almost exclusively of bizarre and atypical case studies contributed by forensic psychiatrists pertaining to their court-assigned clients. More recently, there has been a significant shift toward social scientists examining the cultural and

Authors' Note: We contributed equally to this work: the order of authorship was determined alphabetically. We wish to acknowledge the able assistance of Stephanie Flagg.

Source: M. Dwayne Smith and Margaret A. Zahn (eds.), *Homicide: A Sourcebook of Social Research* (Thousand Oaks, CA: Sage, 1999), pp. 167–175. © 1999 by Sage Publications, Inc. Reprinted by permission of Sage Publications Inc.

social forces underlying the late 20th-century rise in serial murder as well as law enforcement operatives developing research-based investigative tools for tracking and apprehending serial offenders.

Despite the shift in disciplinary focus, some basic assumptions of psychiatry appear to remain strong in the public mind. In particular, it is widely believed that the serial killer acts as a result of some individual pathology produced by traumatic childhood experiences. At the same time, a developing law enforcement perspective holds that the serial killer is a nomadic, sexual sadist who operates with a strict pattern to victim selection and crime scene behavior; this model has also contributed to myopic thinking in responding to serial murder. Unfortunately, these assumptions from both psychiatry and law enforcement may have retarded the development of new and more effective approaches to understanding this phenomenon. In an attempt to present a more balanced view, this chapter examines (serially, of course) several myths about serial killing/killers, some long-standing and others of recent origin, that have been embraced more on faith than on hard evidence.

MYTH 1: THERE IS AN EPIDEMIC OF SERIAL MURDER IN THE UNITED STATES

Although interest in serial murder has unquestionably grown, the same may not necessarily be true for the incidence of this crime itself. Curiously enough, there may actually be more scholars studying serial murder than there are offenders committing it. Regrettably, it is virtually impossible to measure with any degree of precision the prevalence of serial murder today, or even less so to trace its long-term trends. One thing for certain, however, is that the problem is nowhere near epidemic proportions (Jenkins, 1994). . . .

The lack of any hard evidence concerning the prevalence of serial homicide has not prevented speculation within both academic and law enforcement fields. The "serial killer panic of 1983–85," as it has been described by Jenkins (1988), was fueled by some outrageous and unsupportable statistics promulgated by the U.S. Department of Justice to buttress its claim that the extent of serial murder was on the rise. Apparently, some government officials reasoned that because the number of unsolved homicides had surged from several hundred per year in the early 1960s to several thousand per year in the 1980s, the aggregate body count produced by serial killers could be as high as 5,000 annually (Fox & Levin, 1985). Unfortunately, this gross exaggeration was endorsed in some academic publications as well (see Egger, 1984; Holmes & DeBurger, 1988).

More sober thinking on the prevalence issue has occurred in recent years (Egger, 1990, 1998; Holmes & Holmes, 1998). Although still subject to the methodological limitations noted above in the identification of serial crimes, Hickey has attempted the most exhaustive measurement of the prevalence and trends in serial murder. In contrast to the Justice Department's estimate of thousands of victims annually, Hickey enumerated only 2,526 to 3,860 victims slain by 399 serial killers between 1800 and 1995. Moreover, between 1975 and 1995, the highest levels in the two centuries, Hickey identified only 153 perpetrators and as many as 1,400 victims, for an average annual tally of far less than 100 victims. Although Hickey's data collection strategy obviously ignored undetected cases, the extent of the problem is likely less than 1% of homicides in the country. Of course, that as much as 1% of the nation's murder problem can potentially be traced to but a few dozen individuals reminds us of the extreme deadliness of their predatory behavior.

MYTH 2: SERIAL KILLERS ARE UNUSUAL IN APPEARANCE AND LIFESTYLE

As typically portrayed, television and cinematic versions of serial killers are either sinister-appearing creatures of the night or brilliant-but-evil master criminals. In reality, however, most tend to fit neither of these descriptions. Serial killers are generally White males in their late 20s or 30s who span a broad range of human qualities including appearance and intelligence.

Some serial killers are high school dropouts, and others might indeed be regarded as unappealing by conventional standards. At the same time, a few actually possess brilliance, charm, and attractiveness. Most serial killers, however, are fairly average, at least to the casual observer. In short, they are "extraordinarily ordinary"; ironically, part of the secret of their success is that they do not stand out in a crowd or attract negative attention to themselves. Instead, many of them look and act much like "the boy next door"; they hold full-time jobs, are married or involved in some other stable relationship, and are members of various local community groups. The one trait that tends to separate prolific serial killers from the norm is that they are exceptionally skillful in their presentation of self so that they appear beyond suspicion. This is part of the reason why they are so difficult to apprehend (Levin & Fox, 1985).

A related misconception is that serial killers, lacking stable employment or family responsibilities, are full-time predators who roam far and wide, often crossing state and regional boundaries in their quest for victims. Evidence to the contrary notwithstanding, serial killers have frequently been characterized as nomads whose compulsion to kill carries them hundreds of thousands of miles a year as they drift from state to state and region to region leaving scores of victims in their wake. This may be true of a few well-known and well-traveled individuals, but not for the vast majority of serial killers (Levin & Fox, 1985). According to Hickey (1997), only about a third of the serial killers in his database crossed state lines in their murder sprees. John Wayne Gacy, for example, killed all of his 33 young male victims at his Des Plaines, Illinois, home, conveniently burying most of them there as well. Gacy had a job, friends, and family but secretly killed on a part-time, opportunistic basis.

MYTH 3: SERIAL KILLERS ARE ALL INSANE

What makes serial killers so enigmatic—so irrational to many casual observers—is that they generally kill not for love, money, or revenge but for the fun of it. That is, they delight in the thrill, the sexual satisfaction, or the dominance that they achieve as they squeeze the last breath of life from their victims. At a purely superficial level, killing for the sake of pleasure seems nothing less than "crazy."

The basis for the serial killer's pursuit of pleasure is found in a strong tendency toward sexual sadism and an interest reflected in detailed fantasies of domination. Serial killers tie up their victims to watch them squirm and torture their victims to hear them scream. They rape, mutilate, sodomize, and degrade their victims to feel powerful, dominant, and superior.

Many individuals may have fantasies about torture and murder but are able to restrain themselves from ever translating their sadistic dreams into reality. Those who do not contain their urges to kill repeatedly for no apparent motive are assumed to suffer from some extreme form of mental illness. Indeed, some serial killers have clearly been driven by psychosis, such as Herbert Mullen of Santa Cruz, California, who killed 13 people during a 4-month period to avert an earthquake—at least that is what the voices commanded him to do (the voices also ordered him to burn his penis with a cigarette).

In either a legal or a medical sense, however, most serial killers are not insane or psychotic (see Levin & Fox, 1985; Leyton, 1986). They know right from wrong, know exactly what they are doing, and can control their desire to kill—but choose not to. They are more cruel than crazy. Their crimes may be sickening, but their minds are not necessarily sick. Most apparently do not suffer from hallucinations, a profound thought disorder, or major depression. Indeed, those assailants who are deeply confused or disoriented are generally not capable of the level of planning and organization necessary to conceal their identity from the authorities and, therefore, do not amass a large victim count.

Many serial killers seem instead to possess a personality disorder known as sociopathy (or antisocial personality). They lack a conscience, are remorseless, and care exclusively for their own needs and desires. Other people are regarded merely as tools to be manipulated for the purpose of maximizing their personal pleasure. Thus, if given to perverse sexual fantasy, sociopaths simply feel uninhibited by societal rules or by conscience from literally chasing their dreams in any way necessary for their fulfillment. . . .

MYTH 4: ALL SERIAL KILLERS ARE SOCIOPATHS

Although many serial killers tend to be sociopaths, totally lacking in concern for their victims, some actually do have a conscience but are able to neutralize or negate their feelings of remorse by rationalizing their behavior. They feel as though they are doing something good for society, or at least nothing that bad.

Milwaukee's cannibalistic killer, Jeffrey Dahmer, for example, actually viewed his crimes as a sign of love and affection. He told Tracy Edwards, a victim who managed to escape, that if he played his cards right, he too could give his heart to Jeff. Dahmer meant it quite literally, of course, but according to Edwards, he said it affectionately, not threateningly.

The powerful psychological process of *dehumanization* allows many serial killers to slaughter scores of innocent people by viewing them as worthless and therefore expendable. To the dehumanizer, prostitutes are seen as mere sex machines, gays are AIDS carriers, nursing home patients are vegetables, and homeless alcoholics are nothing more than human trash.

In a process related to this concept of dehumanization, many serial killers compartmentalize the world into two groups—those whom they care about versus everyone else. "Hillside Strangler" Kenneth Bianchi, for example, could be kind and loving to his wife and child as well as to his mother and friends yet be vicious and cruel to those he considered meaningless. He and his cousin started with prostitutes, but later, when they grew comfortable with killing, branched out to middle-class targets.

MYTH 5: SERIAL KILLERS ARE INSPIRED BY PORNOGRAPHY

Could Theodore Bundy have been right in his death row claim that pornography turned him into a vicious killer, or was he just making excuses to deflect blame? It should be no surprise that the vast majority of serial killers do have a keen interest in pornography, particularly sadistic magazines and films (Ressler, Burgess, & Douglas, 1988). Sadism is the source of their greatest pleasure, and so, of course, they experience it vicariously in their spare time, when not on the prowl themselves. That is, a preoccupation with pornography is a reflection, not the cause, of their own sexual desires. At most, pornography may reinforce sadistic impulses, but it cannot create them.

There is experimental evidence that frequent and prolonged exposure to violent pornography tends to desensitize "normal" men to the plight of victims of sexual abuse (Malamuth & Donnerstein, 1984). In the case of serial killers, however, it takes much more than pornography to create such an extreme and vicious personality.

MYTH 6: SERIAL KILLERS ARE PRODUCTS OF BAD CHILDHOODS

Whenever the case of an infamous serial killer is uncovered, journalists and behavioral scientists alike tend to search for clues in the killer's childhood that might explain the seemingly senseless or excessively brutal murders. Many writers have emphasized, for example, Theodore Bundy's concerns about being illegitimate, and biographers of Hillside Strangler Kenneth Bianchi capitalized on his having been adopted. . . .

It is true that the biographies of most serial killers reveal significant physical and psychological trauma at an early age. For example, based on in-depth interviews with 36 incarcerated murderers, Ressler et al. (1988) found evidence of psychological abuse (e.g., public humiliation) in 23 cases and physical trauma in 13 cases. Hickey (1997) reported that among a group of 62 male serial killers, 48% had been rejected as children by a parent or some other important person in their lives. Of course, these same types of experiences can be found in the biographies of many "normal" people as well. More specifically, although useful for characterizing the backgrounds of serial killers, the findings presented by Ressler et al. and Hickey lack a comparison group drawn from nonoffending populations for which the same operational definitions of trauma have been applied. Therefore, it is impossible to conclude that serial killers have suffered as children to any greater extent than others. . . .

Some neurologists and a growing number of psychiatrists suggest that serial killers have incurred serious injury to the limbic region of the brain resulting from severe or repeated head trauma, generally during childhood. As an example, psychiatrist Dorothy Lewis and neurologist Jonathan Pincus, along with other colleagues (1986), examined 15 murderers on Florida's death row and found that all showed signs of neurological irregularities. In addition, psychologist Joel Norris (1988) reported excessive spinal fluid found in the brain scan of serial killer Henry Lee Lucas. Norris argued that this abnormality reflected the possible damage caused by an earlier blow or a series of blows to Lucas's head.

It is critical that we place in some perspective the many case studies that have been used in an attempt to connect extreme violence to neurological impairment. Absent from the case study approach is any indication of the prevalence of individuals who did not act violently despite a history of trauma. Indeed, if head trauma were as strong a contributor to serial murder as some suggest, then we would have many times more of these killers than we actually do.

It is also important to recognize that neurological impairment must occur in combination with a host of environmental conditions to place an individual at risk for extreme acts of brutality. Dorothy Lewis cautions, "The neuropsychiatric problems alone don't make you violent. Probably the environmental factors in and of themselves don't make you a violent person. But when you put them together, you create a very dangerous character" ("Serial Killers," 1992). Similarly, Ressler asserts that no single childhood problem indicates future criminality: "There are a whole lot of conditions that have to be met" for violence to be predictable (quoted in Meddis, 1987, p. 3A). Head trauma and abuse, therefore, may be important risk factors, but they are neither necessary nor sufficient to make someone a serial killer. Rather, they are part of a long list of circumstances—including adoption, shyness, disfigurement, speech impediments, learning and physical disabilities, abandonment, death of a parent, academic and athletic inadequacies—that may make a child feel frustrated and rejected enough to predispose, but not predestine, him or her toward extreme violence.

Because so much emphasis has been placed on early childhood, developmental factors in making the transition into adulthood and middle age are often overlooked. Serial killers tend to be in their late 20s and 30s, if not older, when they first show outward signs of murderous behavior. If only early childhood and biological predisposition were involved, why do they not begin killing as adolescents or young adults? Many individuals suffer as children, but only some of them continue to experience profound disappointment and detachment regarding family, friends, and work. For example, Danny Rolling, who murdered several college students in Gainesville, Florida, may have had a childhood filled with frustration and abuse, but his eight-victim murder spree did not commence until he was 36 years old. After experiencing a painful divorce, he drifted from job to job, from state to state, from prison to prison, and finally from murder to murder (Fox & Levin, 1996).

MYTH 7: SERIAL KILLERS CAN BE IDENTIFIED IN ADVANCE

Predicting dangerousness, particularly in an extreme form such as serial homicide, has been an elusive goal for those investigators who have attempted it. For example, Lewis, Lovely, Yeager, and Femina (1989) suggest that the interaction of neurological/psychiatric impairment and a history of abuse predicts violent crime, better even than previous violence itself. Unfortunately, this conclusion was based on retrospective "postdiction" with a sample of serious offenders, rather than a prospective attempt to predict violence within a general cross section.

It is often said that "hindsight is 20/20." This is especially true for serial murder. Following the apprehension of a serial killer, we often hear mixed reports that "he seemed like a nice guy, but there was something about him that wasn't quite right." Of course, there is often something about most people that may not seem "quite right." When such a person is exposed to be a serial murderer, however, we tend to focus on those warning signs in character and biography that were previously ignored. Even the stench emanating from Jeffrey Dahmer's apartment, which he had convincingly explained to the neighbors as the odor of spoiled meat from his broken freezer, was unexceptional until after the fact.

The methodological problems in predicting violence in advance are well known. For a category of violence as rare as serial murder, however, the low base rate and consequent false-positive dilemma are overwhelming. Simply put, there are thousands of White males in their late 20s or 30s who thirst for power, are sadistic, and lack strong internal controls; most emphatically, however, the vast majority of them will never kill anyone.

MYTH 8: ALL SERIAL KILLERS ARE SEXUAL SADISTS

Serial killers who rape, torture, sodomize, and mutilate their victims attract an inordinate amount of attention from the press, the public, and professionals as well. Although they may be the most fascinating type of serial killer, they are hardly the only type.

Expanding their analysis beyond the sexual sadist, Holmes and DeBurger (1988) were among the first to assemble a motivational typology of serial killing, classifying serial murderers into four broad categories: visionary (e.g., voices from God), mission-oriented (e.g., ridding the world of evil), hedonistic (e.g., killing for pleasure), and power/control-oriented (e.g., killing for dominance). Holmes and DeBurger further divided the hedonistic type into three subtypes: lust, thrill, and comfort (see also Holmes & Holmes, 1998). . . .

Modifying the Holmes–DeBurger framework, we suggest that serial murders can be reclassified into three categories, each with two subtypes:

1. **Thrill**
   - **a.** Sexual sadism
   - **b.** Dominance
2. **Mission**
   - **a.** Reformist
   - **b.** Visionary
3. **Expedience**
   - **a.** Profit
   - **b.** Protection

Most serial killings can be classified as thrill motivated, and the *sexual sadist* is the most common of all. In addition, a growing number of murders committed by hospital caretakers have been exposed in recent years; although not sexual in motivation, these acts of murder are perpetrated for the sake of *dominance* nevertheless.

A less common form of serial killing consists of mission-oriented killers who murder to further a cause. Through killing, the *reformist* attempts to rid the world of filth and evil, such as by killing prostitutes, gays, or homeless persons. Most self-proclaimed reformists are also motivated by thrill seeking but try to rationalize their murderous behavior. For example, Donald Harvey, who worked as an orderly in Cincinnati-area hospitals, confessed to killing 80 or more patients through the years. Although he was termed a mercy killer, Harvey actually enjoyed the dominance he achieved by playing God with the lives of other people.

In contrast to pseudoreformists, *visionary* killers, as rare as they may be, genuinely believe in their missions. They hear the voice of the devil or God instructing them to kill. Driven by these delusions, visionary killers tend to be psychotic, confused, and disorganized. Because their killings are impulsive and even frenzied, visionaries rarely remain on the street long enough to become prolific serial killers.

The final category of serial murder includes those who are motivated by the expedience of either profit or protection. The *profit-oriented* serial killer systematically murders as a critical element of the overall plan to dispose of victims to make money (e.g., Sacramento landlady Dorothea Puente murdered 9 elderly tenants to cash their social security checks). By contrast, the protection-oriented killer uses murder to cover up criminal activity (e.g., the Lewington brothers systematically robbed and murdered 10 people throughout Central Ohio).

MYTH 9: SERIAL KILLERS SELECT VICTIMS WHO SOMEHOW RESEMBLE THEIR MOTHERS

Shortly after the capture of Hillside Strangler Kenneth Bianchi, psychiatrists speculated that he tortured and murdered young women as an expression of hatred toward his mother, who had allegedly brutalized him as a youngster (Fox & Levin, 1994). Similarly, the execution of Theodore Bundy gave psychiatrists occasion to suggest that his victims served as surrogates for the real target he sought, his mother.

Although unresolved family conflicts may in some cases be a significant source of frustration, most serial killers have a more opportunistic or pragmatic basis for selecting their victims. Quite simply, they tend to prey on the most vulnerable targets—prostitutes, drug users, hitchhikers, and runaways, as well as older hospital patients (Levin & Fox, 1985). Part of the vulnerability concerns the ease with which these groups can be abducted or overtaken. Children and older persons are defenseless because of physical stature or disability; hitchhikers and prostitutes become vulnerable as soon as they enter the killer's vehicle; hospital patients are vulnerable in their total dependency on their caretakers.

Vulnerability is most acute in the case of prostitutes, which explains their relatively high rate of victimization by serial killers. A sexual sadist can cruise a red-light district, seeking out the woman who best fits his deadly sexual fantasies. When he finds her, she willingly complies with his wishes—until it is too late.

Another aspect of vulnerability is the ease with which the killers can avoid being detected following a murder. Serial killers of our time are often sly and crafty, fully realizing the ease with which they can prey on streetwalkers and escape detection, much less arrest. Because the disappearance of a prostitute is more likely to be considered by the police, at least initially, as a missing person rather than a victim of homicide, the search for the body can be delayed weeks or months. Also, potential witnesses to abductions in red-light districts tend to be unreliable sources of information or distrustful of the police.

Frail older persons, particularly those in hospitals and nursing homes, represent a class of victims that is at the mercy of a different type of serial killer, called "angels of death." Revelations by a Long Island nurse who poisoned his patients in a failed attempt to be a hero by resuscitating them and of two Grand Rapids nurses aides who murdered older patients to form a lovers' pact have horrified even the most jaded observers of crime.

Not only are persons who are old and infirm vulnerable to the misdeeds of their caretakers who may have a particularly warped sense of mercy, but hospital homicides are particularly difficult to detect and solve. Death among older patients is not uncommon, and suspicions are rarely aroused. Furthermore, should a curiously large volume of deaths occur within a short time on a particular nurse's shift, hospital administrators feel in a quandary. Not only are they reluctant to bring scandal and perhaps lawsuits to their own facility without sufficient proof, but most of the potentially incriminating evidence against a suspected employee is long buried with the victim.

MYTH 10: SERIAL KILLERS REALLY WANT TO GET CAUGHT

Despite the notion that serial killers are typically lacking in empathy and remorse, some observers insist that deeply repressed feelings of guilt may subconsciously motivate them to leave telltale clues for the police. Although this premise may be popular in media portrayals, most serial killers go to great lengths to avoid detection, such as carefully destroying crime scene evidence or disposing of their victims' bodies in hard-to-find dump sites.

There is an element of self-selection in defining serial killing. Only those offenders who have sufficient cunning and guile are able to avoid capture long enough to accumulate the number of victims necessary to be classified as serial killers. Most serial killers are careful, clever, and, to use the FBI's typology, organized. Of course, disorganized killers, because of their carelessness, tend to be caught quickly, often before they surpass the serial killer threshold of victim count.

Murders committed by a serial killer are typically difficult to solve because of lack of both motive and physical evidence. Unlike the usual homicide that involves an offender and a victim who know one another, serial murders are almost exclusively committed by strangers. Thus, the usual police strategy of identifying suspects by considering their possible motive, be it jealousy, revenge, or greed, is typically fruitless.

Another conventional approach to investigating homicides involves gathering forensic evidence—fibers, hairs, blood, and prints—from the scene of the crime. In the case of many serial murders, however, this can be rather difficult, if not impossible. The bodies of the victims are often found at desolate roadsides or in makeshift graves, exposed to rain, wind, and snow. Most of the potentially revealing crime scene evidence remains in the unknown killer's house or car.

Another part of the problem is that unlike those shown in the media, many serial killers do not leave unmistakable and unique "signatures" at their crime scenes. As a result, the police may not recognize multiple homicides as the work of the same perpetrator. Moreover, some serial killings, even if consistent in style, traverse jurisdictional boundaries. Thus, "linkage blindness" is a significant barrier to solving many cases of serial murder (Egger, 1984). . . .

FROM MYTH TO REALITY

The study of serial homicide is in its infancy, less than two decades old. The pioneering scholars noted the pervasiveness and inaccuracy of longstanding psychiatric misconceptions regarding the state of mind of the serial killer. More recently, these unfounded images have been supplanted by newer myths, including those concerning the prevalence and apprehension of serial killers.

The mythology of serial killing has developed from a pervasive fascination with a crime about which so little is known. Most of the scholarly literature is based on conjecture, anecdote, and small samples, rather than rigorous and controlled research. The future credibility of this area of study will depend on the ability of criminologists to upgrade the standards of research on serial homicide. Only then will myths about serial murder give way to a reliable foundation of knowledge.

REFERENCES

Egger, S. A. (1984). A working definition of serial murder and the reduction of linkage blindness. *Journal of Police Science and Administration*, 12, 348–357.

Egger, S. A. (1990). *Serial murder: An elusive phenomenon.* Westport, CT: Praeger.

Egger, S. A. (1998). *The killers among us: An examination of serial murder and its investigation.* Upper Saddle River, NJ: Prentice Hall.

Fox, J. A., & Levin, J. (1985, December 1). Serial killers: How statistics mislead us. *Boston Herald*, p. 45.

Fox, J. A., & Levin, J. (1994). *Overkill. Mass murder and serial killing exposed.* New York: Plenum.

Fox, J. A., & Levin, J. (1996). *Killer on campus.* New York: Avon Books.

Hickey, E. W. (1997). *Serial murderers and their victims* (2nd ed.). Belmont, CA: Wadsworth.

Holmes, R. M., & DeBurger, J. (1988). *Serial murder.* Newbury Park, CA: Sage.

Holmes, R. M., & Holmes, S. T. (1998). *Serial murder* (2nd ed.). Thousand Oaks, CA: Sage.

Jenkins, P. (1988). Myth and murder. The serial killer panic of 1983–85. *Criminal Justice Research Bulletin* (No. 3). Huntsville, TX: Sam Houston State University.

Jenkins, P. (1994). *Using murder: The social construction of serial homicide.* New York: Walter de Gruyter.

Levin, J., & Fox, J. A. (1985). *Mass murder: America's growing menace.* New York: Plenum.

Lewis, D. O., Lovely, R., Yeager, C., & Femina, D. D. (1989). Toward a theory of the genesis of violence: A follow-up study of delinquents. *Journal of the American Academy of Child and Adolescent Psychiatry*, 28, 431–436.

Lewis, D. O., Pincus, J. H., Feldman, M., Jackson, L., & Bard, B. (1986). Psychiatric, neurological, and psychoeducational characteristics of 15 death row inmates in the United States. *American Journal of Psychiatry*, 143, 838–845.

Leyton, E. (1986). *Compulsive killers: The story of modern multiple murderers.* New York: New York University Press.

Malamuth, N. M., & Donnerstein, E. (1984). *Pornography and sexual aggression.* Orlando, FL: Academic Press.

Meddis, S. (1987, March 31). FBI: Possible to spot, help serial killers early. *USA Today*, p. 3A.

Norris, J. (1988). *Serial killers: The growing menace.* New York: Doubleday.

Ressler, R. K., Burgess, A. W., & Douglas, J. E. (1988). *Sexual homicide: Patterns and motives.* Lexington, MA: Lexington Books.

Serial killers. (1992, October 18). NOVA. Boston: WGBH-TV.

REVIEW QUESTIONS

1. Identify and discuss five myths about serial killers.
2. Distinguish between mass killers and serial killers.
3. What are the advantages of looking at serial killers sociologically, rather than psychologically or biologically?

Chapter 13

WHAT TRIGGERS SCHOOL SHOOTINGS?

MICHAEL S. KIMMEL
MATTHEW MAHLER

Violence is one of the most urgent issues facing our nation's schools. All over the country, Americans are asking why some young people open fire, apparently randomly, killing or wounding other students and their teachers. Are these teenagers emotionally disturbed? Are they held in the thrall of media-generated violence—in video games, the Internet, rock or rap music? Are their parents to blame?

We begin our inquiry with an analysis of the extant commentary and literature on school violence. We argue that, unfortunately, there are significant lacunae in all of these accounts—the most significant of which is the fact that they all ignore the one factor that cuts across all cases of random school shootings—masculinity. Thus, we argue that any approach to understanding school shootings must take gender seriously—specifically the constellation of adolescent masculinity, homophobia, and violence. . . .

MISSING THE MARK

The concern over school shootings has prompted intense national debate, in recent years, over who or what is to blame. One need not look hard to find any number of "experts" who are willing to weigh in on the issue. Yet despite the legion of political and scientific commentaries on school shootings, these voices have all singularly and spectacularly missed the point. At the vanguard of the debates have been politicians. Some have argued that Goth music, Marilyn Manson, and violent video games are the causes of school shootings. Then-President Clinton argued that it might be the Internet; Newt Gingrich credited the 1960s; and Tom DeLay blamed daycare, the teaching of evolution, and "working mothers who take birth control pills." Political pundits and media commentators also have offered a host of possible explanations, of which one of the more popular answers has been violence in the media. "Parents don't realize that taking four-year-olds to *True Lies*—a fun movie for adults but excessively violent—is poison to their brain," notes Michael Gurian. Alvin Poussaint, a psychiatrist at Harvard Medical School, wrote that

> *in America, violence is considered fun to kids. They play video games where they chop people's heads off and blood gushes and it's fun, it's entertainment. It's like a game. And I think this is the psychology of these kids—this "Let's go out there and kill like on television."*

And Sissela Bok (1999), in her erudite warning on violence, suggests that the Internet and violent video games, which "bring into homes depictions

Source: Michael S. Kimmel and Matthew Mahler, "Adolescent Masculinity, Homophobia, and Violence," *American Behavioral Scientist*, vol. 46 (2003), pp. 1439–1458.

of graphic violence . . . never available to children and young people in the past," undermine kids' resilience and self-control.

For others, the staggering statistics linking youth violence and the availability of guns point to a possible cause. Firearms are the second leading cause of death to children between age 10 and 14 and the eighth leading cause of death to those age 1 to 4. In 1994, 80% of juvenile murderers used a firearm; in 1984, only 50% did. Barry Krisberg, president of the National Council on Crime and Delinquency, argues that both the media and guns are at fault. He says, "The violence in the media and the easy availability of guns are what is driving the slaughter of innocents." Or perhaps, if we are to believe National Rifle Association (NRA) president Charlton Heston, the problem is not that there are too many guns but that there are not enough guns. He argues that had there been armed guards in the schools, the shooting would have ended instantly. These accounts, however, that blame a media purportedly overly saturated by violence and a society infatuated with guns are undercut by two important facts, which are often conveniently forgotten amid the fracas. The first is that whereas the amount of violent media content has ostensibly been increasing, both youth violence, in general, and school violence, in particular, have actually been decreasing since 1980. And second, juvenile violence involving guns has been in decline since 1994 (largely as a result of the decline of the crack epidemic). As Michael Carneal, the boy who shot his classmates in Paducah, Kentucky, said, "I don't know why it happened, but I know it wasn't a movie" (Blank, 1998).

Finally, some have proposed psychological variables, including a history of childhood abuse, absent fathers, dominant mothers, violence in childhood, unstable family environment, or the mothers' fear of their children, as possible explanations. Although these explanations are all theoretically possible, empirically it appears as though none of them holds up. Almost all the shooters came from intact and relatively stable families, with no history of child abuse. If they had psychological problems at all, they were relatively minor. . . .

Most important for our argument is the fact that these studies have all missed gender. They use such broad terminology as "teen violence," "youth violence," "gang violence," "suburban violence," and "violence in the schools" as though girls are equal participants in this violence. Conspicuously absent is any mention of just who these youth or teens are who have committed the violence. They pay little or no attention to the obvious fact that *all the school shootings were committed by boys*—masculinity is the single greatest risk factor in school violence. . . .

But the analytic blindness of these studies runs deeper than gender. We can identify two different waves of school violence since 1980. In the first, from 1982 to 1991, the majority of all the school shootings were nonrandom (i.e., the victims were specifically targeted by the perpetrators). Most were in urban, inner-city schools and involved students of color. Virtually all involved handguns, all were sparked by disputes over girlfriends or drugs, and all were committed by boys.

These cases have not entirely disappeared, but they have declined dramatically. Since 1992, only 1 of the random school shootings occurred in inner-city schools (it was committed by a black student), whereas the remaining 22 have been committed by white students in suburban schools. Virtually all involved rifles, not handguns—a symbolic shift from urban to rural weaponry. However, once again, all shootings were committed by boys.

WHO SHOOTS AND WHY?

Still, most students—white or non-white, male or female—are not violent, schools are predominantly safe, and school shootings are aberrations. As a public, we seem concerned with school shootings because its story is not "when children kill" but specifically when suburban white boys kill. To illustrate the distribution of shootings across the country, we have mapped all cases of random school shootings since 1982. There were five cases documented between 1982 and 1991; there have been 23 cases since 1992. School shootings do not occur uniformly or evenly in the United States, which makes one skeptical of uniform cultural explanations such as violent video games, musical tastes, Internet, television, and movies. School shootings are decidedly not a national trend. Of 28 school shootings between 1982 and 2001, all but 1 were in rural or suburban schools. All but 2 were committed by a white boy or boys. . . .

We undertook an analysis of secondary media reports on *random school shootings from 1982 to 2001*. Using the shooters' names as our search terms, we gathered articles from six major media sources—the three major weekly news magazines: *Time*, *Newsweek*, and *U.S. News and World Report* (in order from greatest circulation to least); and three major daily newspapers: *USA Today*, *The New York Times*, and the *Los Angeles Times*. In conducting our analysis, we found a striking pattern from the stories about the boys who committed the violence: Nearly all had stories of being constantly bullied, beat up, and, most significantly for this analysis, "gay-baited." Nearly all had stories of being mercilessly and constantly teased, picked on, and threatened. And most strikingly, it was *not* because they were gay (at least there is no evidence to suggest that any of them were gay) but because they were *different* from the other boys—shy, bookish, honor students, artistic, musical, theatrical, nonathletic, "geekish," or weird.

In a recent interview, the eminent gender theorist Eminem poignantly illustrated the role of "gay-baiting" in peer interactions. In his view, calling someone a "faggot" is not a slur on his sexuality but on his gender. He says,

> *The lowest degrading thing that you can say to a man . . . is to call him a faggot and try to take away his manhood. . . . "Faggot" to me doesn't necessarily mean gay people. "Faggot" to me just means taking away your manhood.*

In this rationalization, Eminem, perhaps unwittingly, speaks to the central connection between gender and sexuality and particularly to the association of gender nonconformity with homosexuality. Here, homophobia is far less about the irrational fears of gay people, or the fears that one might actually be gay or have gay tendencies, and more the fears that *heterosexuals* have that others might *(mis)perceive them as gay* (Kimmel, 1994). Research has indicated that homophobia is one of the organizing principles of heterosexual masculinity, a constitutive element in its construction. And as an organizing principle of masculinity, homophobia—the terror that others will see one as gay, as a failed man—underlies a significant amount of men's behavior, including their relationships with other men, women, and violence. One could say that homophobia is the hate that makes men straight.

There is much at stake for boys and, as a result, they engage in a variety of evasive strategies to make sure that no one gets the wrong idea about them (and their manhood). These range from the seemingly comic (although telling), such as two young boys occupying three movie seats by placing their coats on the seat between them, to the truly tragic, such as engaging in homophobic violence, bullying, menacing other boys, masochistic or sadistic games and rituals, excessive risk taking (drunk or aggressive driving), and even sexual predation and assault. The impact of homophobia is felt not only by gay and lesbian students but also by heterosexuals who are targeted by their peers for constant harassment, bullying, and gay-baiting. In many cases, gay-baiting is "misdirected" at heterosexual youth who may be somewhat gender nonconforming. This fact is clearly evidenced in many of the accounts we have gathered of the shootings.

For example, young Andy Williams, recently sentenced to 50 years to life in prison for shooting and killing two classmates in Santee, California, and wounding several others was described as "shy" and was "constantly picked on" by others in school. Like many of the others, bullies stole his clothes, his money, and his food, beat him up regularly, and locked him in his locker, among other daily taunts and humiliations. One boy's father baited him and called him a "queer" because he was overweight. . . .

In the videotape made the night before the shootings at Columbine High School, the site of the nation's most infamous school shooting, would-be killer Eric Harris says, "People constantly make fun of my face, my hair, my shirts." His fellow-killer Dylan Klebold adds, "I'm going to kill you all. You've been giving us shit for years." What Klebold said he had been receiving for years apparently included constant gay-baiting, being called "queer," "faggot," "homo," being pushed into lockers, grabbed in hallways, and mimicked and ridiculed with homophobic slurs. For some boys, high school is a constant homophobic gauntlet and they may respond by becoming withdrawn and sullen, using drugs or alcohol, becoming depressed or suicidal, or acting out in a blaze of overcompensating violent "glory."

The prevalence of this homophobic bullying, teasing, and violence is staggering. According to the Gay, Lesbian, Straight Education Network, 97% of students in public high school in Massachusetts reported regularly hearing homophobic remarks from their peers in 1993; 53% reported hearing anti-gay remarks by school staff (Bronski, 1999). The recent report *Hatred in the Hallways* paints a bleak picture of anti-gay harassment [and emphasizes how] gender performance—acting masculine—is perceived as a code for heterosexuality (Human Rights Watch, 2001). . . .

Let us be completely clear: Our hypotheses are decidedly *not* that gay and lesbian youth are more likely to open fire on their fellow students. In fact, from all available evidence, *none* of the school shooters was gay. But that is our organizing hypothesis: Homophobia—being constantly threatened and bullied *as if you are gay* as well as the homophobic desire to make sure that others know that you are a "real man"—plays a pivotal role in these school shootings.

WHY BOYS AND NOT GIRLS?

Historically, no industrial society other than the United States has developed such a violent "boy culture," as historian E. Anthony Rotundo (1993) calls it in his book *American Manhood.* It is here where young boys, as late as the 1940s, actually carried a little chip of wood on their shoulders daring others to knock it off so that they might have a fight. It is astonishing to think that "carrying a chip on your shoulder" is literally true—a test of manhood for adolescent boys. And it is here in the United States where experts actually *prescribed* fighting for young boys' healthy masculine development. The celebrated psychologist G. Stanley Hall, who invented the term "adolescence," believed that a nonfighting boy was a "nonentity" and that it was "better even an occasional nose dented by a fist . . . than stagnation, general cynicism and censoriousness, bodily and psychic cowardice" (cited in Stearns, 1994). His disciple, J. Adams Puffer (1912), was even bold enough to suggest in his successful parental advice book *The Boy and His Gang* that it is not unreasonable for a boy to fight up to six times a week and maybe even more depending on the circumstances: "There are times when every boy must defend his own rights if he is not to become a coward and lose the road to independence and true manhood" (cited in Kimmel, 1996).

It is interesting to note that in a recently thwarted school shooting in New Bedford, Massachusetts, it was a young woman, Amylee Bowman, 17, who could not go through with the plot and decided to reveal the details to the authorities. Eric McKeehan, 17, one of the coconspirators, was described in media accounts as constantly angry, especially at being slighted by other students. The mother of a second boy accused in the plot said, "Eric has a temper. He says what's on his mind. He's been known to hit walls and lockers, but what teenage boy hasn't?" (Heslam & Richardson, 2001).

Indeed, what teenage boy hasn't? Eminem had that part right. Calling someone a "faggot" means questioning his manhood. And in this culture, when someone questions our manhood, we do not just get mad, we get even.

WHY WHITE BOYS?

. . . All American men contend with a singular hegemonic vision of masculinity, a particular definition that is held up as the model against which we all measure ourselves. We thus come to know what it means to be a man in our culture by setting our definitions in opposition to a set of subordinated "others"—racial minorities, sexual minorities, and above all, women. As the sociologist Erving Goffman (1963) once wrote,

> *In an important sense there is only one complete unblushing male in America: a young, married, white, heterosexual, father, of college education, fully employed, of good complexion, weight, and height, and a decent record in sports. . . . Any male who fails to qualify in any one of these ways is likely to view himself—during moments at least—as unworthy, incomplete, and inferior.*

It is crucial to listen to those last few words. When we feel that we do not measure up we are likely to feel unworthy, incomplete, and inferior. It is here, from this place of unworthiness, incompleteness, and inferiority, that boys begin their efforts to prove themselves as men. And it is here where violence has its connections to masculinity. As James Gilligan (1966) says in his book *Violence*, violence has its origins in "the fear of shame and ridicule, and the overbearing need to prevent others from laughing at oneself by making them weep instead." Shame, inadequacy, vulnerability—all threaten the self; violence, meanwhile, is restorative, compensatory. . . .

Most important for our current discussion, though, is the fact that failure to see race while looking at gender will cause us to miss the real story. We know that African American boys face a multitude of challenges in schools—racial stereotypes, formal and informal tracking systems, low expectations, and underachievement. But the one thing they do not do is plan and execute random and arbitrary mass shootings. And this is particularly interesting because the classroom and academic achievement have [less attraction] for African American girls and African American boys. In their fascinating ethnographies of two inner-city public high schools, both Signithia Fordham (1996) and Ann Ferguson (2000) discuss these differences. When African American girls do well in school, their friends accuse them of "acting White." But when African American boys do well in school, their friends accuse them of "acting like girls." [Thus, simply by not doing well in school, the boys can easily feel masculine and no need to prove their manhood by committing school violence.]

WHY THESE PARTICULAR BOYS AND NOT OTHERS WHO HAVE HAD SIMILAR EXPERIENCES?

Walk down any hallway in any middle school or high school in America and the single most common put-down that is heard is "That's so gay." It is deployed constantly, casually, unconsciously. Boys hear it if they try out for the school band or orchestra, if they are shy or small, physically weak and unathletic, if they are smart, wear glasses, or work hard in school. They hear it if they are seen to like girls too much or if they are too much "like" girls. They hear it if their body language, their clothing, or their musical preferences do not conform to the norms of their peers. And they hear it not as an assessment of their present or future sexual orientation but as a commentary on their masculinity.

But not all boys who are targeted like that open fire on their classmates and teachers. In fact, very few do. So how is it that some boys—many boys, in fact—resist? As Pedro Noguera (2001) writes in "The Trouble with Black Boys," "We know much less about resilience, perseverance, and the coping strategies employed by individuals whose lives are surrounded by hardships, than we do about those who succumb and become victims of their environment." What is the constellation of factors that facilitate resistance?

Perhaps there is what Robert Brooks, of Harvard Medical School, calls the "charismatic adult" who makes a substantial difference in the life of the child. Most often this is one or the other parent, but it can also be a teacher or some other influential figure in the life of the boy. Perhaps the boy develops an alternative substantive pole around which to organize competence. Gay-baiting suggests that he is a failure at the one thing he knows he wants to be and is expected to be—a man. If there is something else that he does well—a private passion, music, art—someplace where he feels valued—he can develop a pocket of resistance.

Similarly, the structures of his interactions also can make a decisive difference. A male friend, particularly one who is not also a target but one who seems to be successful at masculinity, can validate the boy's sense of himself as a man. But equally important may be the role of a female friend, a potential if not actual "girlfriend." Five of the school shooters had what they felt was serious girl trouble, especially rejection. Luke Woodham was crushed when his girlfriend broke up with him. "I didn't eat, I didn't sleep. It destroyed me," he testified at trial. She was apparently his primary target and was killed. Michael Carneal may have had a crush on one of his victims. Mitchell Johnson was upset that his girlfriend had broken up with him.

Although all the shooters have been boys, that does not mean that girls are inconsequential in boys' social worlds. It may be that the boys who are able to best resist the torments of incessant gay-baiting and bullying are those who have some girls among their friends, and perhaps even a girlfriend, that is, girls who can also validate their sense of masculinity (which other boys do as well) as well as their heterosexuality (which boys alone cannot do). If masculinity is largely a homosocial performance, then at least one male peer, who is himself successful, must approve of the performance. The successful demonstration of *heterosexual* masculinity requires not only the successful performance for other men but also some forms of "sexual" success with women.

These sorts of [social experiences—support from a charismatic adult, competence in something, and male or female friendship, or the lack of these]—will enable us to understand both what led some boys to commit these terrible acts and what enables other boys to develop the resources of resistance to daily homophobic bullying.

CONCLUSION

In a brilliant passage in *Asylums*, Erving Goffman (1961) touched on the interplay between repression and resistance:

> *Without something to belong to, we have no stable self, and yet total commitment and attachment to any social unit implies a kind of selflessness. Our sense of being a person can come from being drawn into a wider social unit; our sense of selfhood can arise through the little ways in which we resist the pull. Our status is backed by the solid buildings of the world, while our sense of personal identity often resides in the cracks.*

It is our task, as researchers concerned with gender and education, to understand how those social forces shape and mold young men's identities and to explore [their resources for] resistance, where they might carve out for themselves a masculinity that is authentic, solid, and confident.

REFERENCES

Blank, J. 1998, December. "The kid no one noticed." *U.S. News and World Report*, p. 27.

Bok, S. 1999. *Mayhem: Violence as Public Entertainment.* Cambridge, MA: Perseus. 16–18.

Bronski, M. 1999, July. "Littleton, movies and gay kids." *Z Magazine.*

Ferguson, A. 2000. *Bad Boys: Public Schools in the Making of Black Masculinity.* Ann Arbor: University of Michigan Press.

Fordham, S. 1996. *Blacked Out: Dilemmas of Race, Identity, and Success at Capital High.* Chicago: University of Chicago Press.

Gilligan, J. 1996. *Violence.* New York: Vintage.

Goffman, E. 1961. *Asylums.* New York: Vintage.

Goffman, E. 1963. *Stigma: Notes on the Management of Spoiled Identity.* Englewood Cliffs, NJ: Prentice Hall.

Heslam, J., and F. Richardson. 2001, November 26. "Suspect labeled outcast, estranged from family." *Boston Herald,* p. 6.

Human Rights Watch. 2001. *Hatred in the Hallways: Violence and Discrimination against Lesbian, Gay, Bisexual, and Transgender Students in the U.S.* New York: Author.

Kimmel, M. 1994. "Masculinity as homophobia: Fear, shame and silence in the construction of gender identity." Pp. 119–141 in H. Brod and M. Kaufman (Eds.), *Theorizing Masculinities.* Newbury Park, CA: Sage.

Kimmel, M. 1996. *Manhood in America: A Cultural History.* New York: Free Press.

Noguera, P. 2001. "The trouble with black boys." *Harvard Journal of African American Public Policy,* 7 (Summer), 23–46.

Puffer, J. A. 1912. *The Boy and His Gang.* Boston: Houghton.

Rotundo, E. A. 1993. *American Manhood.* New York: Basic Books.

Stearns, P. 1994. *American Cool.* New York: New York University Press.

REVIEW QUESTIONS

1. Why do Kimmel and Mahler argue that terms such as "teen violence" are too broad?
2. What do most of the school shootings after 1992 have in common?
3. Do you agree with the premise of this article? Why or why not?

CHAPTER 14

"I HOPE SOMEONE MURDERS YOUR MOTHER!": EXTREME SUPPORT FOR THE DEATH PENALTY

MARGARET VANDIVER
DAVID J. GIACOPASSI
PETER R. GATHJE

In the spring of 2000, the wife of a well-known Tennessee anti-death-penalty activist came home from a busy day at work. When the phone rang, she expected the call to be from her husband, who was involved in a campaign to prevent an execution scheduled for the next day. Instead, the caller was an anonymous stranger who bombarded her with a volley of abuse and obscenities for her husband's winning a stay of execution. We will here present our study of such extreme support for the death penalty.

PUBLIC OPINION ON CAPITAL PUNISHMENT

American support for the death penalty was overwhelmingly high during the 1980s and much of the 1990s. Polls taken in 1999 indicated as many as 80% of Americans supporting the death penalty. More recent surveys, in 2001, have shown a decline in the support of capital punishment. But they still revealed a significantly high level of support, ranging from 60% to 67% (Bohm, 1999; Jones, 2001).

Research has suggested that opinion about capital punishment is not entirely rational. Death penalty proponents, for example, often insist that they would continue to support capital punishment even if it did not lower the murder rate, and, similarly, opponents often maintain that they would continue to oppose the death penalty even if it were an effective deterrent. Also, many Americans still support capital punishment even though they are aware of problems in the administration of capital punishment, such as those stemming from racial and economic inequities. Emotion apparently plays a role in opinion on capital punishment. In one study on the supporters of capital punishment, for example, 34% agreed that the death of certain murderers "would give me a sense of personal satisfaction," and 79% agreed with the statement, "Sometimes I have felt a sense of personal outrage when a convicted murderer was sentenced to a penalty less than death" (Ellsworth and Ross, 1983; Ellsworth and Gross, 1997).

METHODS OF STUDY

Our study here focuses on the state of Tennessee in the year before and after its first execution in

Source: Margaret Vandiver, David J. Giacopassi, and Peter R. Gathje, " 'I Hope Someone Murders Your Mother!': An Exploration of Extreme Support for the Death Penalty," *Deviant Behavior*, vol. 23 (2002), pp. 385–415.

40 years. On April 19, 2000, Tennessee executed Robert Glen Coe for the 1979 rape and murder of Cary Ann Medlin, an eight-year-old child. Coe's case and appeals, expressions of public support for and opposition to his execution, and the death penalty as a general issue received massive publicity in the state's media before the execution. A second very high profile death penalty case in Tennessee, that of Philip Workman, kept the issue before the public in the year following Coe's execution.

We used a variety of sources to gain information on extreme support for capital punishment. Participant observation by us at a weekly peaceful demonstration against capital punishment on a busy street corner in Memphis provided an ample supply of anecdotal information about extreme support for the death penalty. We were further able to observe the reactions of thousands of people to the demonstrators as at least one of us participated in the hour and a half demonstration every week since October 1999.

We also analyzed in the state's two major newspapers for three months all the news stories, editorials, and letters to the editor relevant to Coe's execution and the general issue of capital punishment. In addition, letters to the editors in two other newspapers in the area where the murder took place were reviewed for five months. We further analyzed numerous published books, articles, and newspaper accounts of executions in other states. We then interviewed six individuals who were actively involved in the Coe or Workman cases. These individuals included lawyers, paralegals, spiritual advisers to the condemned or their families, and heads of abolitionist organizations. Briefer interviews were conducted with seven people who had spent a significant amount of time at the public demonstrations against capital punishment. All of those people we interviewed included both males and females ranging in age from college students to retired persons. Nearly all were white; only one was African American. We found what extreme supporters of the death penalty are alike, though they represent a very small minority of those who support capital punishment.

HOSTILITY TOWARD THE CONDEMNED

Condemned prisoners are an obvious and socially acceptable target for expressions of rejection, rage, and the desire for vengeance. Having been formally adjudicated as unfit to live, the condemned could hardly expect any sympathy from their condemners. Thus extreme supporters of the death penalty feel free to openly express their desire to hurt the prisoners as well as their enjoyment of the execution of the prisoners.

An important element in condemning certain people involves denying their humanity. Not surprisingly, then, a frequent theme in statements of support for executions is the assertion that condemned prisoners are not human but instead are animals. See, for example, the following comments about the condemned man Robert Glen Coe, which appeared in the Tennessee newspapers:

> ". . . monster" (from *Jackson Sun*, March 26, 2000)
>
> "He is not human . . . crazed animal" (*Jackson Sun*, March 26, 2000)
>
> ". . . senseless, exorbitant legal fees . . . to keep this animal alive" (*Commercial Appeal*, March 27, 2000)
>
> ". . . get the vermin out of the system . . ." (*Commercial Appeal*, March 27, 2000)
>
> ". . . rattlesnake" (*Jackson Sun*, March 30, 2000)
>
> ". . . animal . . . slime . . . Executing Coe . . . is no more than taking out the trash" (*Jackson Sun*, April 9, 2000)
>
> "Step on him as you would a cockroach." (*Commercial Appeal*, April 15, 2000)

There were other expressions of hostility toward the condemned. At the site of the first Tennessee execution in forty years, one pro-death penalty demonstrator held a sign reading, "Let's get this party started right now." A year later when another Tennessee inmate came within an hour of execution, one demonstrator's sign said, "I hope he cries like a girl." In addition to the continuing presence of demonstrators at prisons, the witnessing of public executions by massive crowds in earlier times seems to have given way in today's electronic age to viewers of live news coverage. At the time of Tennessee's first execution, which occurred at one in the morning, the people in Middle Tennessee who watched the execution coverage were about twice as many as those who normally watched TV at that hour.

For some extreme supporters of capital punishment, the relatively quick and painless methods of executing prisoners are not enough to satisfy the desire to inflict pain. They would like the prisoner to experience the ultimate degree of physical and mental suffering. One supporter of the death penalty expressed his desire to peel all the prisoner's skin off his body, reattach it with glue, and then rape the prisoner with a nail-studded baseball bat before finally killing him. Another supporter of the death penalty told researcher Kimberly Cook (1998):

> *You know how they produce gizzards as delicacies? They cage the birds in this cement box and force feed them until they die in their own waste. I saw that on TV one time and thought that's a pretty awful way to go and immediately thought that would be a good way to execute criminals. They need to feel pain, the way they're killed now, they don't know what suffering is, they don't know what pain is. So, this would make sure they feel pain. After all, think of the pain their victims must have felt.*

HOSTILITY TOWARD OPPONENTS OF THE DEATH PENALTY

Each Wednesday afternoon in 1999 a half dozen to 25 people met at a busy street corner in Memphis during rush hour to demonstrate against the death penalty. They merely held signs expressing their views, standing quietly for about an hour and a half. Once, according to a newspaper account, the following incident took place:

> *A young man in a dress shirt and tie slowly veered his Ford Taurus to the curb. He leaned over to lower the passenger-side window. Prof. Philip J. "Max" Maloney, whose sign said, "Resist the Culture of Death," didn't quite hear when the motorist yelled, "I hope your mother is killed by an ax murderer!" As the car stopped, Maloney stooped to the open window and said, "Pardon me?" Pardon denied: The driver spat at Maloney and sped away (Bailey, 1999).*

A good day for the demonstrators on the street corner would involve only a few shouted Bible verses and curses from the death penalty supporters, punctuated by an occasional obscene gesture. But some passersby in cars would pull over and yell insult at the demonstrators. The degree of anger exhibited by some death penalty supporters was startling and even a bit frightening. One of us was confronted by an enraged man who identified himself as a Christian, yelled Bible verses, and accused her of supporting bestiality. A passing driver once told a 78-year-old demonstrator: "I'm going to set my dog on you."

Such encounters could occur even when death penalty opponents were not engaged in demonstrations. A Nashville woman who had appeared on local television opposing executions told us of an incident that occurred as she was taking a walk by herself. A car with four young white men drove by, and one of the men yelled, "There's that mother fucking bitch that loves child killers!" and either spat or threw liquid at her.

Some of the ugliest expressions of extreme support for capital punishment took the form of anonymous communications. A number of persons we interviewed reported receiving anonymous letters or phone messages. A typical example is the following handwritten note, received by a woman after she had published an abolitionist letter in a local newspaper: "You stupid ass, you & your kind are the reason we have the murder of great people. Go to Hell & you pay to feed & take care of these animals."

DESIRE FOR VIOLENCE

Some of the extreme supporters of capital punishment entertained the wish that the opponent of capital punishment be murdered. An example is the man we cited above as shouting to a death penalty supporter on the street corner: "I hope your mother is killed by an ax murderer!" There are other examples. A female opponent in Nashville told us of receiving an anonymous call at home from someone expressing the wish that if she the activist had a child, she would be raped and murdered. Another anonymous phone message was left on the answering machine of an abolitionist organization. It first accused the abolitionists of being atheists, and then went on to say:

> *Sometimes I wish there was more psychopathic mass murderers that'd just drive by on [the location of the abolitionist weekly demonstration] and blast some of you crazy tree-hugging fruits. . . . You make me sick.*

WHY THE EXTREME SUPPORT?

Why the extreme support for the death penalty? A few contributing factors may be at work.

The Power of Punishment to Unite

Social scientists have long noted that punishment serves to unite the punishers. Emile Durkheim (1949), for example, believed that "crime brings together upright consciences and concentrates them." In effect, one of the functions of crime is to unite the community in opposition to the deviant act and the deviant person and, through this unified opposition, to reaffirm the moral boundaries of society, to clearly differentiate good from evil.

But when consensus regarding methods of punitive justice begins to fray, if not unravel, as manifested by death penalty protesters, some people would react with concern and, perhaps, dismay and anger. Among these people those with extreme support for the death penalty consequently regard opposition to capital punishment as endorsement of the offenders' crimes or at least minimization of harm from the crime. Thus the extreme supporters accuse death penalty abolitionists of being unsympathetic to murder victims and indifferent to the horrendous crime. The abolitionists and other death penalty protesters are effectively seen as undermining the legitimate authority or weakening the ties that unite the society against those criminal forces which are perceived as threatening the conventional, fundamental values.

The Religious Factor

As demonstrators, we have observed the frequency of religious references made by those who shouted at us, as when someone in a passing car yelled, "Praise God for executions!" Certain Christian beliefs seem to lend support for the death penalty, which in turn gives impetus to extreme support for the death penalty. One key belief is that God is a vengeful judge, and the state is a legitimate agent of God's vengeance. Expressions of this belief can be found in newspapers. After Coe's execution, for example, a headline in a Memphis paper read: "God authorized death penalty, Baptists declare." Given such a religious conviction, individuals who oppose the death penalty are perceived as not only misguided in terms of a social policy, but also against the will of God. Thus one letter writer stated, "[God] demanded the death penalty for murder in the book of Genesis, and there is no evidence that He changed His mind in the New Testament. Any assertion to the contrary constitutes a very precarious stance. . . ."

The Brutalizing Effect

It has long been found in criminology that publicized executions may have the *brutalizing effect* on potential killers, indirectly encouraging them to kill (Bowers, 1988). This is because the state in executing a convicted murderer is effectively legitimizing the use of violence against a terrible person like the killer. More generally, the state in effect sends the message that it is all right to resort to violence to deal with a difficult problem with somebody. Such a message may have affected those with extreme support for the death penalty, by making them react in a violent way to those who protest against the death penalty.

CONCLUSION

As a result of participating in weekly anti-capital-punishment demonstrations, we observed numerous angry reactions and even threatening behavior against the peaceful demonstrators. These reactions ranged from impulsive acts (cursing and gesturing at demonstrators) to well-planned activities (letters to the editor or phone messages expressing a desire to see the protestors or their families suffer terrible fates). To determine if the angry reactions were a local phenomenon, we conducted interviews and collected anecdotes from anti-capital-punishment activists locally and from around the country and reviewed letters to the editor, phone and email messages sent to abolitionists, and accounts of celebratory crowds gathered for executions. We conclude that extreme support of capital punishment exists everywhere in the United States although it involves only a very small percentage of the death penalty supporters.

REFERENCES

Bailey, T. 1999, October 28. "Death penalty weightier in streets than in pews." *The Commercial Appeal*, A1.

Bohm, R. M. 1999. *Deathquest: An Introduction to the Theory and Practice of Capital Punishment in the United States.* Cincinnati: Anderson Publishing Co.

Bowers, W. J. 1988. "The Effect of Executions Is Brutalization, Not Deterrence." Pp. 49–89 in *Challenging Capital Punishment: Legal and Social Science Approaches*, edited by K. C. Haas and J. A. Inciardi. Newbury Park: Sage Publications.

Cook, K. J. 1998. *Divided Passions: Public Opinions on Abortion and the Death Penalty.* Boston: Northeastern University Press.

Durkheim, E. 1949. *The Division of Labor in Society* (G. Simpson, Trans.). Glencoe, IL: Free Press. (Original work published in 1893.)

Ellsworth, P. C., and L. Ross. 1983. "A Close Examination of the Views of Abolitionists and Retentionists." *Crime and Delinquency* 29:116–169.

Ellsworth, P. C., and S. R. Gross. 1997. "Hardening Of The Attitudes: Americans' Views Of The Death Penalty." Pp. 90–115 in *The Death Penalty in America: Current Controversies*, edited by H. A. Bedau. Oxford: Oxford University Press.

Jones, J. M. 2001, March. "Two-Thirds of Americans Support the Death Penalty." *The Gallup Poll Monthly* no. 426:5–8.

REVIEW QUESTIONS

1. What is the "brutalizing effect"?
2. What factors, according to the article, lead to extreme support of the death penalty?
3. Do you support the death penalty? Defend your answer.

PART FIVE

INTIMATE VIOLENCE

In 2008, three students from a high school in New Jersey were charged with sexually assaulting a 16-year-old special education student at one of their homes. One suspect was 18 years old and the other two were 16. The older youngster, Romal Roberts, invited the girl to come into his house. For the next four hours or so, Roberts and his two friends forced her to perform sex on them and abused her with a broomstick. According to an acquaintance, Roberts was a "stand-up kid who played video games and wanted to go to college." A neighbor described him as "a polite teenager who would shovel snow for them."[1]

Sexual violence against women is relatively common in the United States. The average chance of women being raped is at least 1 in 10. More significant, the overwhelming majority of these women know their offenders, just like the victim in New Jersey knew the young men who sexually assaulted her. In this part, we learn about various forms of intimate violence inflicted on victims by individuals known to them. In the first article, "Tenured and Battered," Madeline Bates shows how a highly educated woman like herself, a college professor, can be abused by her husband. In the second article, "Intimate Stalking: Characteristics and Consequences," Jennifer Dunn discusses how some men stalk their former girlfriends or wives and how these women react. In the third selection, "Child-to-Mother Violence," Debra Jackson reveals how and why some adolescents assault their mothers. In the fourth reading, "How Child Molesters Explain Their Deviance," Louanne Lawson determines from certain qualitative studies that child molesters see their deviance as having to do with their social isolation, their interest in sex with children, and their justification of the sex as proper.

[1]Kareem Fahim and Nate Schweber, "Three Youths in Montclair Are Charged in Sex Attack," *New York Times*, March 12, 2008, p. A3.

CHAPTER 15

TENURED AND BATTERED

MADELINE BATES

I received my bachelor's, master's, and doctoral degrees from elite institutions. When I went on the job market I received three tenure-track job offers from top colleges, one of which was my first choice. Two years into the perfect job, I fell in love, got married, and ultimately gave birth to several healthy children. I learned how to teach and how to publish, and was *tenured.*

So, if I'm so smart, why did I remain married to a batterer for 12 years?

As it turns out, domestic violence happens to all types of women—regardless of IQ. Before we married, my husband seemed to be the perfect man—kind, gentle, romantic, admiring of me and my academic successes. Three weeks after we married, when I learned that I was pregnant, the battering began. I was baffled that this man, who seemed so perfect during our engagement, was sometimes so cruel.

So, I characterized those sporadic attacks on me as outliers in the data set. And because our relationship followed the typical cycle of domestic violence, with the blowup phases always followed by the honeymoon phases, I persuaded myself that there was sufficient evidence to support my belief that my husband was a good man.

I couldn't see, or wouldn't see, that I was misusing my professional training as a social scientist to perpetuate my denial.

As the years passed, the cycles gradually changed—so gradually that it took me some time to recognize that the pattern had changed. The blowups had become more frequent, more violent, and lasted longer. I needed to invent a new hypothesis to rationalize what was happening.

Being an academic I am used to having a great deal of control over my work life. I'm in control in my classroom. I choose the courses I want to teach, I determine the texts I will assign and how students' work will be evaluated. I choose the research topics I work on and the journals I submit my work to, etc. If I was being so marginalized at home, I theorized it was because I was doing something wrong.

Because my husband was now criticizing me almost constantly, it seemed that I had a plausible theory to fit the data. If only I did a better job taking care of the children; if only I kept the house cleaner and less cluttered; if only I spent more time attending to my husband's needs rather than grading papers or reading journal articles; if only I took care of the children by myself for a few years before my tenure decision and supported him while he went to graduate school in another city, he would be happier—and less violent. I did all of those things.

But I should have known better than to form hypotheses about a subject without first doing a literature review. After reading some of the domestic-violence literature, I learned that no matter how much I tried to comply with my husband's demands, it would never be enough. He would just find something else to be angry about.

Source: Madeline Bates, "Tenured and Battered," *Chronicle of Higher Education*, September 9, 2005, pp. C1–C4.

Trying to work productively during 12 years in which my home life became fraught with danger was difficult. How do you maintain the focus necessary to teach, grade, do research, and write when you are recovering from the most recent attack, or trying to avoid the one you know is coming?

Despite the stress of trying to construct a track record that would merit tenure and to maintain the facade of a happy home life, I found that work was cathartic. My students were so engaging that during classes I would actually forget about the terror at home. Publications, excellent teaching evaluations, and work on important internal college issues gave me reasons to feel good about myself, and the strength to carry on.

After my husband completed his graduate studies and moved back in with us, he began a very highly paid job that he enjoyed, as well as a new cycle of violence—one in which he was battering our children as well as me. When I tried to intervene to protect the children, my husband just became more violent. I knew that I needed to act, but wasn't sure what to do.

Why didn't I just leave? Because leaving a violent marriage is extremely complicated, particularly if you have children. Research shows that batterers are most dangerous (e.g., most likely to kill) when their wives/partners leave. If I left my husband, without the children, I believed that he would hurt them intentionally as a means to hurt me. I also believed that my husband would, out of spite, engage me in a protracted custody battle—which he could afford given his much larger salary.

I considered leaving, taking the children with me, and going into hiding from my husband. That would have required leaving academe for lower-skilled, lower-wage work, assuming false identities, and living on the run.

Desperate to find a way out, I met with a lawyer. She advised me to go to the local magistrate and file a request for a temporary restraining order that would require my husband to temporarily abstain from all contact with me or with our children. It would also require him to vacate our home until after a hearing that would be scheduled a week later. My lawyer also explained that I could be granted temporary custody of my children and that I could file for divorce and begin proceedings to gain permanent custody and obtain child support.

Certain that I would have an expensive custody battle in front of me, I decided that I would max out my credit cards if necessary and borrow money from every member of my family if I had to. I was willing to waive all rights to child support and give my husband the majority of our financial assets, if he would just walk away. Supporting the children and myself on just my salary would cause a significant reduction in our standard of living, but we could still be comfortable.

Shortly after noon, I arrived at the magistrate's office to file a request for a temporary restraining order. The clerk gave me a legal notepad and pen and told me to write down the facts of my case which would be presented to the magistrate that afternoon for a ruling.

I have made many written arguments in my life as a scholar. But in terms of what was at stake, it was clear to me that this was the most important argument I would ever have to make. Nine pages later I returned the notepad to the clerk.

"Why did you write so much?" he chastised me.

"Because this is what happened," I said.

"Nobody ever writes this much," said the clerk. "I don't think the magistrate will read it."

I thought about all the times I have harangued students for writing overly long essays. Was I using the shotgun approach, hoping that if I put enough information down on the page, something I wrote would resonate with the magistrate? Definitely not. I wasn't backing down this time.

"These are all of the relevant facts," I said. "Please ask the magistrate to read it all."

Because my husband was still at work and I knew that it would not be safe for me or the children to come home that evening, my third stop that day was at my house. I grabbed enough clothes for a week, financial documents, and my laptop computer. As I walked out of my house, I looked back and wondered when or under what circumstances I would be able to return.

Later that day, the magistrate granted me the restraining order. Luckily I was on sabbatical at the time and I had good friends who invited me and my children to come stay with them that night and for as many nights thereafter as we needed to stay.

I found out the next morning that a sheriff's deputy had delivered the restraining order to my husband at around 9 P.M. According to the medical examiner, my husband shot himself in the head sometime around 1 A.M.

Now I am a widow and a single mom. Since my husband's death I have told a few friends that he was a batterer, but not many. While I need the emotional support my friends offer, it would only hurt my husband's family to know the truth. So I am careful whom I tell.

As soon as I learned that my husband had died, I made just one phone call, to my dean, to tell him what had happened. One of the good things about being part of a small community is that the news of my husband's suicide spread quickly throughout the campus and the town. Every night, for more than a month, someone brought us dinner. Colleagues, trustees, students, and their parents endowed an educational fund for my children.

Balancing work and family involves a new set of challenges. Every meeting on the weekends or in the evenings and every professional conference requires lining up a babysitter. Getting my children to and from their after-school activities is also a logistical challenge—as is supervising homework, while simultaneously getting dinner on the table. But those challenges don't feel at all daunting compared to the challenges of being married to a violent man.

I have put my academic skills to good use, studying the literature on domestic violence and searching the Internet to find support groups for me and for my children. I am convinced now that there was nothing else I could have done to produce a better outcome to what was a tragic marriage.

I give myself credit for ultimately making choices that saved my life and the lives of my children. I am no longer afraid or embarrassed to ask for help when I need it. Unlike many who experience domestic violence, I am lucky to have the financial security that tenure brings. And finally, I am no longer afraid to drive home at the end of the day.

REVIEW QUESTIONS

1. Why did Bates stay married to a batterer for 12 years?
2. According to Bates, how did she view her marginalization at home?
3. What new challenges does Bates face as a single mom?

CHAPTER 16

INTIMATE STALKING: CHARACTERISTICS AND CONSEQUENCES

JENNIFER L. DUNN

Suppose you were a woman who had broken up with her boyfriend or left her husband. Then he stalked you so persistently that your life turned into hell. Would you ever return to make up with him or at least let him meet with you or talk to you on the phone? You would most likely say "No way!" as common sense would suggest. But I have found from my research just the opposite: most stalking victims comply in one way or another with the wishes and demands of their intimate stalkers.

In the late 1990s I spent two years in a large metropolitan area in the West studying the police files on some 130 women whose former husbands, boyfriends or other intimates had been charged with stalking them. I also participated as an observer in the monthly meetings of a support group of stalking survivors. I finally conducted intensive interviews with 13 stalking victims, which lasted anywhere from 90 minutes in one sitting to several hours over an extended time period. These women ranged in age from 16 to 73, with the average age being 31. They came from a variety of income levels. Of the two largest groups, one had a household income of less than $35,000 a year and another $41,200 to $52,300. Slightly less than half of all the victims were African-American or Hispanic while slightly more than half were whites. There were no Asian-American victims, although Asian Americans made up nearly 9 percent of the population in the area.

CHARACTERISTICS OF STALKING

To understand how stalking victims respond to their victimizers, we may first need to know the characteristics of stalking, which can determine the victim's responses. The characteristics of stalking are what the offenders do to the victims. At least four characteristics emerged from my research. They involved the stalker *courting, surveilling, threatening, and inflicting violence* on the victim.

Courtship

Often the stalker tells his victim he still loves her and begs her to return to him. He acts as if he is engaged in a normal romantic relationship. He would thus try to give the victim flowers and cards and gifts, leave messages of love on her answering machine, or show off his best self in face-to-face interactions with her. Such behaviors appeared in about one third of the stalking cases in my research. In one typical case, a man was charged with setting fire to his ex-wife's apartment and yet he wrote her the following note:

Source: Jennifer L. Dunn, *Courting Disaster: Intimate Stalking, Culture, and Criminal Justice.* New York: Aldine de Gruyter, © 2002.

> *My heart cries every day for my sweetheart . . . I knew I was losing you, my wife, my friend, my world and there was nothing I could do to stop it . . . and all the things I did, I did for you and because I loved you . . . You've done me wrong and no matter what I will always love you.*

As in previous research by other sociologists, many women who are leaving a violent relationship are vulnerable to this deviant form of courtship. They find themselves torn between wanting to permanently leave their former intimates and feeling pulled toward returning to them. As a result, some would agree to meet and talk with their stalkers while others would resume the relationship.

Surveillance

Many stalkers make incessant attempts to continue interaction with their former intimates. The stalker most frequently shows up at his victim's home and repeatedly telephones her. He would also contact her family or employer in an attempt to find her, drive by her home, spy on her by sitting somewhere and watching her, or even tap her phone or videotape her. The following is a typical example as narrated by a victim:

> *Ever since we separated, it's been getting really bad. It got to the point where I was forced to get a restraining order because he has been constantly following me, spying on me, calling at my place of employment, and giving me a lot of problems. Even after I obtained the restraining order, when I go home from work, I find him near my house watching me. When I get up in the morning, I see him right across from my house in his pickup. He calls me at my work and follows me everywhere I go.*

Surveillance such as this happened to victims in over half of the cases that I analyzed. It takes a heavy toll on the victim, flooding her daily with enormous anxiety. As one victim said, "I look over my shoulder wherever I go. I am in a constant state of hypervigilance . . . A ringing phone causes me to jump . . . sometimes I wonder if I will ever have a real life again. Even walking to the mailbox can be filled with anxiety."

Threats

About half of the stalking victims in my study had received threats from their former husbands or boyfriends. Threats can be verbal or nonverbal. The most common verbalizations are death threats, threats to hurt the victim or her family, threatening suicide, and threats to kidnap, kill, or hurt her children. Common examples of these verbal threats are "I will kill you," "I'll cut you to pieces," and "I own you, I'm going to destroy you, and I'm not going to stop until I can piss on your grave." On the other hand, nonverbal threats come from physical violence directed toward inanimate objects, such as breaking into the victim's home, vandalizing her home or car, and stealing her property. Such behaviors convey the message to the victim that she too can be beaten up.

Whether verbal or nonverbal, the threat usually has a devastating impact on the victim. One of my interviewees, for example, suffered tremendously after her ex-boyfriend threatened to kill her. She appeared gaunt and hollow-eyed, had a frantic demeanor, and warily observed everything around her like a frightened kitten. She couldn't sit still, was ever watchful, and seeing her that way was heart-wrenching for me.

Violence

In over half of the case files that I studied, the victims had suffered physical assault at the hands of their former husbands or boyfriends after leaving the relationship. Most of these women had endured the same violence *before* breaking up with their intimates. The violence may take different forms. It includes forcibly blocking the victim from leaving a place or calling for help, threatening her with a weapon, sexually assaulting her, kidnapping her or her children, beating her, and killing her pets or other animals. The following is a very common example:

> *[The stalker] has been bothering me for some time. Tonight, [he] saw me in my car and chased me to a friend's apartment. He grabbed me by the hair and knocked me to the floor, while on the floor he attempted to hit me about the face. I blocked most of the blows with my hands and arms. When he saw that he could not hit me very well with his hands, he kicked me very hard on the left thigh.*

In some cases the violence is much more brutal, though less common. One of the women I studied, for example, was repeatedly tied up, raped, sodomized, and beaten in what her ex-husband called "the punishment for leaving."

CONSEQUENCES OF STALKING

Being stalked may produce a variety of consequences. The victim may try to hide, get help, give in, or fight back. But to get away from the stalker is difficult, costly, and often impossible, while help from the police can be very hard to get. Most important, the victim is likely to be buffeted with the emotions of love, frustration, fear, and ambivalence, which tend to come from being subjected to the four characteristics of stalking. The courtship from the stalker is likely to stir up the residual emotion of love for the former intimate. The surveillance is likely to generate frustration. The threats and violence are likely to arouse fear. As the positive emotion of love clashes the negative feelings of fear and frustration, ambivalence is likely to appear. But the raw feelings of fear and frustration must be more powerful than the fading emotion of love. Consequently, it is mostly the fear that causes almost all of the victims in my study to *comply* with their stalkers' wishes and demands for continued interaction at some time during the staking process. And it is mostly the frustration that galvanizes fewer victims to resist their stalkers by fighting back.

Compliance

Compliance may appear in many different forms and degrees. It may involve accepting phone calls from a former intimate, continuing to interact face-to-face with him, letting him into the house, meeting him somewhere, going someplace with him, visiting him in jail, agreeing not to call the police, asking the police not to arrest him, requesting that the case against him be dismissed, continuing to have sex, returning to the relationship, and recanting the incriminating statements against him made earlier to police. While a few cases of compliance involve having sex or going back to live with the stalker, most are relatively minor such as agreeing to have a talk with the man. A typical example of such minor compliances as reported by a police officer follows:

> *The defendant would drive by her residence daily numerous times, drive by her place of employment daily . . . and drive by her bank while she is banking. Numerous times he has approached her in her employer's parking lot, held on to her arm when she attempted to walk away and he forced her to speak with him. Sometimes the victim would go with him to talk or have coffee . . . When questioned why she went with him. She replied, "It was easier than all the fighting, I thought maybe if I talked to him I could get him to leave me alone."*

In many cases like this, the victim assumes that her compliance would cause the stalker to leave her alone but it is usually to no avail. Apparently, the man is simply too attached to her, having invested too much of his emotion in her that he feels he owns her. Thus, even drastic measures taken to stop him from stalking her may not work. As one victim said, "The restraining order hasn't worked. He won't leave me alone. He has already been arrested for stalking me. He refuses to stay away from me. I've moved six times in one year trying to get away from him, but he just keeps moving wherever I am. I have moved at least 10 times trying to get away from him . . . Nothing seems to work."

Resistance

Being stalked can anger the victim so much that she will put up a resistance against the offender. In most cases the victim does relatively minor things such as hanging up on her former husband or boyfriend when he calls or refusing to allow him entrance into her home. In some cases the victim tells the stalker clearly and loudly that he must end the relationship and all further contact with her. Other women take a step further by obtaining a restraining order from the court against the former husband or boyfriend. Here is an example of victim resistance as described by a woman:

> *About the middle of July, [he] came to my apartment and started yelling and calling me names. He was saying that he knew I was sleeping with someone and that he was going to kill both of us. I kept yelling at him to just go away. He was pounding and kicking the front door, but I would not open the door. I called 911 and told them what he was doing . . . Today [when I got home] . . . as soon as I pulled into the parking lot, [he] was here. He started yelling at me and calling me a bitch . . . I yelled at him to stop and to just leave me alone. I ran into the apartment and closed the door. He ran up and started pounding and kicking on the door and yelling at me. I yelled through the door that I was going to call the Sheriff.*

CONCLUSION

Virtually all of the stalking victims comply with their offender's desires, succumbing to his demands at some point during the course of the stalking. Resistance is less common but it is not unusual. At least one fifth of the victims in the police files that I analyzed had argued with their stalking husbands or boyfriends. Another one fifth had yelled and sworn at them. Finally, one quarter of the victims had physically struggled or fought with their stalkers. All these add up to some 65 percent of all the victims, a majority, who engaged in some resistance against the stalker. It may thus be concluded that compliance occurs much more often than resistance, but most victims do not engage in compliance alone, as at least 65 percent of them also occasionally resort to resistance.

REVIEW QUESTIONS

1. How does Dunn understand resistance in the context of stalking?
2. What are the four phases of stalking, according to the article?
3. Now that you better understand the situation of the stalking victim, what advice would you give her?

CHAPTER 17

CHILD-TO-MOTHER VIOLENCE

DEBRA JACKSON

Violence is recognized as a major social problem, and represents a growing challenge to health and social service providers. However, aspects of violence remain poorly understood. Family violence is increasingly common (McAllister 2000) and, though it undoubtedly has an extensive history, is a relatively new area of interest to researchers, a fact that reflects the lack of recognition (until recently) of the home and family as areas of social and historical significance (Family Violence Educational Taskforce (FVET) 1991). Though the word "family" is becoming increasingly contested, in Western cultures it most often means a heterosexual two-generational nuclear family, and is characterized by a deep-seated sense of privacy in the home, and intimate emotional attachments between children and their parents (FVET 1991, p. 42).

Harbin & Madden (1979, p. 1288) first identified "battered parents syndrome" as a distinct form of family violence. They described it as comprising "actual physical assaults or verbal and non-verbal threats of physical harm" (Harbin & Madden 1979, p. 1288). Parental abuse is even more hidden and invisible than other forms of family violence (Pelletier & Coutu 1992), and because of the hidden nature of the phenomenon it is difficult to determine incidence or frequency with any degree of certainty. Estimates vary, with Pelletier & Coutu (1992) suggesting it affects up to 18% of two-parent families, while the incidence in single-parent families is said to be as high as 29% (Livingston 1985). Sheehan (1997) presents a sample of 60 families living with adolescent violence; of the 60, 25 were single-parent families, 25 were two-parent families, nine were in stepfamilies and one was living with grandparents.

Using National Survey of Youth data collected in 1972, Agnew & Huguley (1989) estimated that between 9.2 and 11.7% of all adolescents had assaulted their parents at least once in a previous three-year period. Data gathered in the late 1970s suggested that severe violence (to parents) was perpetrated by 3% of all adolescents (Cornell & Gelles 1982). In using the term "severe violence" Cornell & Gelles (1982) were referring to kicking, punching, hitting with an object, beating up, or threatening with, or use of, a knife or gun.

Despite the difficulty in obtaining precise figures about incidence and prevalence of child-to-parent violence, it is clear from the available evidence that it is a feature of family life for a significant number of people, yet the literature also suggests that published figures do not reflect actual incidences (Emery 1989). The evidence indicates that families themselves act to keep this problem hidden. Charles (1986) stated that even when asked directly, there is often an initial denial from parents concerning abuse from children, and Pelletier & Coutu (1992, p. 6) asserted that "most assaulted parents will go to considerable efforts to hide the problem."

Source: Debra Jackson, "Broadening Constructions of Family Violence: Mothers' Perspectives of Aggression from Their Children," *Child and Family Social Work*, vol. 8 (2003), pp. 321–329.

The silence that surrounds the issue generally is also seen in the literature. Adolescent violence has not attracted the same level of researcher interest as other forms of family violence, which has been overwhelmingly constructed as elder abuse, violence between adult partners/spouses, or child abuse. The literature tends to position adolescent violence under the rubric of delinquency rather than family violence. Downey (1997) suggests that this effectively means that child-to-parent or adolescent violence toward parents is less likely to be subject to feminist or other scrutiny than it would be were it located within the discourse of family violence. Furthermore, this positioning means that any interventions are situated in the legal/justice system, with little support available to families through health and social services.

It is also noteworthy that the extant literature looks at violence from children to their parents, rather than to mothers specifically. Thus child-to-mother violence remains ill recognized and poorly understood. A search of the literature reveals a gap in terms of the experiential aspects of adolescent child-to-mother violence and abuse.

THE STUDY

This paper is drawn from a larger study that aimed to: develop understandings of experiential aspects of motherhood; develop holistic understandings of women's perceptions of the influence of their mothering role on their own lives and health; and explore aspects of motherhood that were experienced by women as being particularly challenging and stressful. In the primary study, 20 women with children aged 17 years and over were recruited using snowball sampling, and took part in conversational-style interviews. Researcher interest in the phenomenon of child-to-mother violence was sparked when analysis of the data revealed that six of the 20 participants reported experiencing some level of violence from their adolescent children. Though recruits were not asked about family violence specifically, it became apparent that it was a distressing aspect of mothering for these six participants, and it is these women whose narrative is the focus of this paper.

This paper aims to explore the phenomenon of child-to-mother violence from the perspectives of the six participants who raised it as an issue. The specific objectives of this paper are to:

1. Present insights into mothers' lived experiences of child-to-mother violence.
2. Describe the types of child-to-mother violence experienced by these women.
3. Extend knowledge to help raise awareness about child-to-mother violence.
4. Directions for further research.

METHODS

Philosophical Underpinnings of the Study

Because of its focus on the concerns and experiences of a group of women, this exploratory--descriptive study was informed by feminist insights. Feminism has a central concern with recognizing the inherent value of women's ways of being, thinking and doing (Reinharz 1992; Tong 1998). Feminist research principles identified by Cook & Fonow (1986) helped to guide the project. These incorporate the need for continuous recognition of gender as basic to all social life (including the conduct of research); recognition of consciousness-raising as an integral aspect of methodology; acceptance of inter-subjectivity and personal knowing as legitimate sources of knowledge; acknowledgement of ethical responsibilities in research; and understanding of the transformative and empowering aspects of feminist research (Cook & Fonow 1986).

Recruitment and Procedure

Snowball sampling was used to recruit women into the primary study. This is a process where initial informants are recruited, and then are asked to use their networks to recruit additional participants (Jackson et al. 2003). In this study three initial informants were recruited through circulation of study information to e-mail networks and notice boards in health facilities. These three informants then assisted in recruitment through their own social networks.

Following recruitment into the study, procedures of informed consent and the collection of basic demographic data, women were given a triggering statement: "Can you think back over your years as a mother and tell me some stories about the most challenging, as well as the most positive, aspects of your mothering journey?" This statement proved to be effective in generating discussion, and though a series of additional triggers were prepared, these were not generally necessary. Each of the conversational-style interviews lasted for between two and four hours, with the majority being 150–180 minutes in duration. Following the interview, participants were asked if they would be willing to take part in a process of member checking (Webb 1992; Sandelowski 1993) and three women indicated they would be interested in checking emerging understandings at a later date. These three were followed up, but one was not available to participate at this time so subsequently two of the women took part in member checking procedures.

The interviews were audiotaped and transcribed verbatim. Following transcription, tapes were listened to again, while closely reading the transcripts, thus ensuring narrative–transcription accuracy. Narrative was included in this particular aspect of the study if it revealed any experiences of child-to-mother violence, and if it identified maternal fear of her child as an issue that had impinged on the mother/child relationship.

Analysis of Data

Narrative analysis was informed by the work of Anderson & Jack (1991), who advise against superficial listening, because doing so reduces the likelihood of seeing things in new ways, therefore limiting interpretive potential. Rather, they suggest three ways of listening that can guide the analytical process. These are:

- attention to moral self-evaluative statements, which make the relationships between self-concept and accepted cultural norms visible;
- attention to meta-statements, or points in the interview where the participant makes some sort of reflective statement; and
- attention to the logic, internal consistency and the inter-relationship of themes in the narrative (Anderson & Jack 1991).

Using these as a guide, narrative was analyzed and clustered into themes which characterized the experience for the participants.

Ethics Approval

Ethics approval was granted by the University of Western Sydney Institutional Ethics Committee. Pseudonyms are used to ensure participant confidentiality.

Participants

Of the six participants in this part of the study, four were Australian-born and two were born in Britain. They were well educated, with three holding Bachelor's degrees, two holding technical qualifications and one holding a trade certificate. At the time of the study five of the women were engaged in either part time or full time employment outside the home, and the remaining participant was engaged in full time household duties. Two of the women were sole parents, and four were still married to the father of their children. Of the sole parents, both had at one time been married to the father of their children. Of the married women, one reported that her husband resided away from the family home for long periods. Thus, he was often not available to give immediate support to her. The participant women were mothers of two or three children, who ranged in age from 18 to 24 years. Five of the women had female as well as male children, while one woman had male children only. Five of the participants still had at least one child living with them at the time of the study. All women were resident in Australia at the time of the study.

FINDINGS

The interviews revealed that fear and violence had become a feature of mothering for these women. All the young people who perpetrated the violence were male children. They were aged between 14 and 16 when the hostility became overt and threatening, and at the time all were children who were grappling with substance abuse issues. The women felt that the physical size of their sons meant that they were ineffectual in dealing with acts of violence from these children. There were long-standing issues related to family violence in one of the five families—the children of that marriage had grown up frequently witnessing acts of hostility and violence between their parents. The other five participants reported that they had not experienced any family violence before the child becoming violent in the home.

At least initially, all participants had kept their experiences of violence hidden, and expressed feelings of shame and distress which precluded them from disclosing to relatives or friends. Two of the women did eventually actively seek out assistance and support from their extended families which culminated in the young person being accommodated outside the family home; however, both these women had experienced considerable distress before taking this step. Though the women in partnered relationships disclosed to partners, they were unable to get adequate support within the family unit, either because of the partner's lengthy absences from the family home or because the family were unable to effectively modify the young person's behavior. In hindsight, all the women felt they could have benefited from supportive professional intervention, but they stated that they had not known where or how to go about getting help. They were unprepared for this type of violence and hadn't heard of it before experiencing it themselves.

The violence uncovered in the narratives can be grouped into three themes. These are: It was only a matter of time: feeling intimidated and under threat; He just punched me: physical violence from child to mother; and other men in the house: violence directed to the mothers by friends and associates of their children. Detailed findings are presented under these themes.

It Was Only a Matter of Time: Feeling Intimidated and Under Threat

This theme describes the mothers becoming aware of feeling fearful and concerned about their personal safety. This fear and concern was generated by the changes in the relationships they had with one of their children. The women described the nature of their relationships with their children shifting from their previously affectionate and relatively uncomplicated states to becoming strained, fragile and fraught with tension.

All of the women found this new dimension to their mothering frightening and unexpected. Gina and Anita were sole parents and both described feeling particularly vulnerable when dealing with their sons when they were aggressive, because they didn't have the immediate moral support of a male partner. They felt that they needed to create a safe and private place for themselves within their homes. Both disclosed that they took steps to secure their bedrooms as a safe space. Anita said that she didn't feel safe in her bed unless she was physically locked in her room.

> *"It was only a matter of time before he hit me. I could feel it building up. I had started locking myself into my room at night. He was very big and intimidating. I got scared that I would wake up one night and find him and his friends standing over me for money. So I started locking myself in my bedroom [pause] and I didn't like living like that." (Anita)*

Increasing attempts at parental control and discipline were also associated with the fear and intimidation that the women described. All agreed that the discipline of children had become increasingly difficult as the children grew older, and one participant described it as a daily battle to get her son to go to school and stay out of trouble. Participants described the difficulties associated with maintaining discipline and administering punishment for unacceptable behavior.

> *"He used to steal my car. I grounded him. But I'd go to the shop for a loaf of bread and he'd disappear. And how do you deal with that? You can't lock them in their rooms, and he was six foot tall and very strong." (Gina)*

The women raised the physical size and strength of these sons as factors in their attempts at discipline. The clear subtext was that they felt they could not exert any real control over these adolescents. These six mothers all described feeling frightened of their adolescent children and they used words such as *menacing, threatening, intimidating, belligerent, hostile and abusive* to describe their children at certain times.

> *"He's hostile and aggressive. When he wants money he comes and demands it and won't take no for an answer. He is over six foot tall and he frightens me. He is very threatening. He doesn't need to say anything threatening—his whole attitude is threatening." (Lilian)*

Concern that they could not let the violence escalate further to become physical led two of the participants to relinquish the care of their sons to other relatives. Anita was a sole parent, and she felt unable to continue to live with her son while she felt so fearful of him. After an 18-month period in which the relationship had become more and more fraught, Anita took the difficult step of relinquishment.

> *"It couldn't go on like that. I knew that if he crossed that line and hurt me physically [pause] I knew that our relationship would be broken beyond repair and I knew he would wind up hating himself. So I had to make sure that it didn't happen." (Anita)*

He Just Punched Me: Physical Violence from Child to Mother

For four of the mothers, this non-physical intimidation escalated and became physically abusive. Of the six participants, two (Lilian and Gina) also reported their sons being physically abusive to other family members. The nature of the abuse varied from pushing and shoving through to striking and punching. Jacqui noticed her son becoming uncaring and generally rougher toward her.

> *"It was his change in personality, it made him incredibly angry and he was very tough to have around. He never actually punched me . . . but when he was angry he would push me and shove me and generally be physically rough with me. He would do things like elbow me out of the way if I walked past him, whereas before he would have moved aside for me." (Jacqui)*

Participants linked the physical violence to the child's drug use. Incidents such as refusing to give the child money or attempts to keep them in the home were considered by the women to be precipitating factors in the episodes of violence. Narelle felt that her son didn't intend to perpetrate violence towards her. Rather, she felt he couldn't control his anger. She identified his pattern of substance misuse as harmful to him, and believed that it had impaired his problem-solving faculties:

> *"When he doesn't get his own way or when he doesn't like something he has these outbursts. He's got no impulse control. Someone says something that upsets him or makes him angry . . . he reacts and reacts verbally and reacts physically—he lashes out and hits me." (Narelle)*

Felicity recalls the day that her son struck out and punched her. The boy was already under the scrutiny of the judicial system and his mother was trying to keep him home to avoid the possibility of further difficulties.

> *"The day that it happened we had been arguing over him going out. His father was at work and he [son] was grounded, but he wanted to go out. I had said no, and then things got more heated and I put myself between him and the front door. He was 17 at the time, a big, well built kid and he just*

> *punched me [pause]. It was terrible, all the fight went out of me and I just fell over, I was so shocked and crying. We both were shocked. But that's when we all knew that something had to be done. If there is one thing that I regret it is that day. It did us both a lot of damage." (Felicity)*

Though Felicity had experienced months of disruption and unrest through the actions of this son, she was completely unprepared for the violence her son directed at her. By putting herself between him and the front door, Felicity believed she would stop him going out. She didn't consider the possibility that he would knock her down to get past her. Though her son had been intimidating and menacing for some time, Felicity had no previous experience with overt physical violence. On the other hand, Lilian disclosed that there had been a long history of spousal violence directed at her by her husband and that her children had grown up witnessing this. Lilian's son had developed an established pattern of abuse against her and other family members:

> *"Many times he's pushed and shoved me, swore at me, a couple of times he's hit me, he's ripped my clothes another time. He flies off the handle so easily and gets completely out of control. There's nothing you can say or do to calm him down. When he's stoned he gets super irritable and you can never tell what he'll do. He's scary. I won't be alone in the house with him because I never know when these outbursts will be triggered." (Lilian)*

Lilian remained very distressed at her son's treatment of her and other family members, and about the direction his life had taken generally. Though she had more of an accepting attitude towards family violence than the other participants, her conceptualization of family violence was as spousal/partner violence. She found child-to-mother violence to be extremely distressing.

Other Men in the House: Violence Directed to the Mothers by Friends and Associates of Their Children

In addition to family violence from the children themselves, participants reported feeling threatened and vulnerable in their interactions with associates of their children. The six participants reported having to cope with potentially frightening situations such as arriving home to find their houses filled with people. Anita describes regularly waking up in the night to find several intoxicated men in her home, and then having to somehow get them out.

> *"In the middle of the night suddenly I'd be awake to find my son had come home with six or seven mates. All drunk or stoned. It happened nearly every week. Sometimes Friday and Saturday night in the same week, and it scared me. I didn't know them and I felt like he was always putting us [Anita and her other children] in danger." (Anita)*

As discussed earlier in this paper, one of Anita's fears was that she would awake at night to find herself being stood over by her son and his friends, and this fear (as well as the intimidation directed at her by her son) was the catalyst for her decision to lock herself into her bedroom at nights. Participants felt that they were put at risk by their sons' lifestyles, and they frequently had to cope with distressing events taking place in their homes. This meant that the women were reluctant to leave their family homes, and all reported that they modified their usual activities to avoid leaving their homes unattended, as much as was possible. Gina had tried to set boundaries for her son and to get him to respect the family home, but she was not successful. One day she went out to lunch and came home to find

> *". . . there was a girl with alcoholic poisoning in my house, they'd locked the doors and smoked a few joints. There were two or three other big blokes in the house and the girl was 15 or 16 or something. The girl was lying in her own vomit and urine because she'd had so much to drink. I had to get the doctor because I thought she was going to die." (Gina)*

In addition to her distress over these events, Gina also had to face a backlash from the neighbors, who distanced themselves from her and her family because of her son's behavior, and situations such as that related above. Participants also described being deliberately subjected to scare campaigns by their children's associates. These generally occurred either when their children tried to break away from their associates or when their children owed money to associates. Four of the six participants reported receiving unpleasant and intimidating telephone calls at different times that were attributed to their children's activities. Anita, Gina and Narelle also experienced physical intrusion into their homes from associates of their sons. For Narelle, the threatening behavior from his associates continued well after her son had left the family home, and she eventually had to seek a court order to put a stop to it.

DISCUSSION

Some of the characteristics noted by Harbin & Madden (1979) were seen in the present sample. These included the fact that all children lived at home with their parents at the time of the violence, all were economically dependent on parents, the abusive episodes were repetitive and took place in the home, and some of the adolescents had also been violent towards other family members, as well as people outside the home. Among other characteristics noted by Harbin & Madden (1979) that were seen in this current sample were adolescents who were a lot physically larger and stronger than parents, and/or were the only male in the home, lying to protect the adolescent, avoidance of confrontation with the adolescent because it was feared that it would provoke a violent outburst, denial of the seriousness of the problem, and a lack of contact with professional helpers.

Previous exposure to domestic violence is posited as being possibly significant to the incidence of parental abuse. However, in this current study only one of the six participants revealed any history of family violence, in the form of spousal violence. Though the impact on adolescents who have witnessed family violence is not fully understood, Hastie (1998) raises the possibility that parental violence perpetrated by adolescents may be part of a violence continuum that includes violence in a range of intimate relationships. Child-to-mother violence is most often associated with male children (Charles 1986), and all participants in this study experienced violence from adolescent males. Jenkins (1999) identifies son-to-mother violence as being the most common form of parental abuse he has encountered in his therapeutic practice. However, it has been observed in females, though Harbin & Madden (1979) suggested it occurs in lesser numbers with daughters.

All participants in this current study linked their child's violence/aggression to drug-taking activities. Charles (1986) identifies delinquent behavior as a factor in some incidents of parental abuse, and substance abuse is undoubtedly associated with delinquent behavior. Harbin & Madden (1979) did not observe drugs as a major issue in their sample, but other evidence (Sheehan 1997; Bonnar 1999) does support the idea that substance use may be associated with child-to-parent violence in some situations. Though they acknowledge that acts of violence are rarely able to be attributed directly to ingestion of substances, Pelletier & Coutu (1992) point out that use of drugs and alcohol is known to be a factor in other forms of family violence, and they raise the possibility of a relationship existing between adolescent aggression and substance use.

Pelletier & Coutu (1992, p. 8) suggest that substance abuse can indirectly contribute to adolescent violence "not by directly altering the adolescent's behavior but by triggering concerns and stress for the parents," and propose that this then becomes a source of conflict, and thus violence ensues. In this current study, participants suggested that drug-related activity such as adolescents demanding money, or mothers attempting to restrict the adolescent's movements outside the home could precipitate menacing, violent behavior. This finding is in keeping with other findings that suggest the episodes of violence were commonly precipitated by a dispute that could be triggered by parents attempting to curb the young person (Pelletier & Coutu 1992), or by youthful demands for money (Harbin & Madden 1979; Evans & Warren-Sohlberg 1988).

Shame is identified by the women in this study as one of the factors that affected their perceived ability to disclose. Hastie (1998) claims there are many other reasons for the failure of families to disclose parental abuse including: the perception that society does not recognize that parental abuse even exists, and where it does so, it often blames the parent for it; fear of reprisal from the child if they report the abuse; and unwillingness of parents to contribute to labeling of their children and themselves as bad. It is also suggested that the failure of health and welfare personnel to recognize the existence of parental abuse is one of the main reasons for underreporting (Hastie 1998).

It is likely that committing violent acts against his/her mother would cause a young person to experience negative feelings—feelings such as shame, guilt and self-loathing. The awareness of this further complicated the mothers' situations, because the participants at all times remained very concerned about the welfare of their children. In this study, all of the young perpetrators of the violence were already experiencing other problems. The women felt that they were the adults, and so the onus was on them to stop the violence and abuse. However, this was easier said than done.

SPECIAL COMPLEXITIES PERTAINING TO CHILD-TO-MOTHER VIOLENCE

Family violence is known to be a very complex issue, and research has been conducted to elucidate some of its complexities, such as the development of detrimental behavioral patterns, and why the problem defies simple resolution (Shea et al. 1997). There is a well-established link between economic and/or psychological dependence and domestic violence (McAllister 2000), and in partner/spouse abuse situations, victims report complex and confusing feelings of simultaneous love and hatred for perpetrators (Cody 1996). Issues related to child-to-mother violence are more complex still. Child-to-mother violence occurs within a context of intensely intimate and longstanding emotional, familial and caring bonds. Participants were linked to their children by blood and none considered it an option to sever the relationships. In fact, the mothers remained committed to restoring and retaining loving, positive relationships with these young people.

Participants in this study were thrust into a situation of tension and conflict. They experienced conflict between their deeply held and culturally sanctioned beliefs of mother–child love as being an unconditional, permanent love, and other (previously unconflicting) beliefs, that grown children should protect, rather than show aggression to, their parents. The young people in this current study were all under 18 at the time the violence started. This meant that the women still felt a heavy burden of maternal responsibility towards their children.

Though the mothers were aware that they could have the adolescent (perpetrator) declared uncontrollable and have them put into the care of the state, none saw this as a valid option. They were not prepared to withdraw the nurturing and unconditional love and support that is culturally expected from mothers to their children. Even though two of the participants arranged alternative accommodation and care for their children during the worst of the crisis, both these mothers ensured their children were in loving family environments, and continued to provide support for them.

Most of the women strongly believed that women should not have to live with family violence or abuse. Lilian was the exception to this. She held the view that family violence (which she constructed as spousal violence) was a fact of life, and she was the only participant who had a history of family violence in the home. However, child-to-mother violence was completely outside her frame of reference and was extremely distressing to her.

Some of the mothers felt that somehow they were to blame, that it was their failure as mothers that had led to the violence in the first place. Like other victims of family violence (such as battered wives), their distress at the violence itself, and the stigma and shame they felt, made it very difficult for these mothers to seek support, either informally or from health or welfare agencies. This was complicated by the invisibility of this issue and their complete unpreparedness for this violence.

LIMITATIONS TO THE STUDY

Methodological limitations mean the findings from this study are unable to be generalized to the wider population. The main limitation of this particular study is that it is a study of Western Caucasian middle class women. Experiences relating to child-to-mother violence may be different for women of cultural or other minority groups. The women who participated in this study were well educated, and none were affected by extreme poverty. Poverty limits the options available to people when they are trying to problem solve, and therefore would almost certainly complicate aspects of the mothering experience.

CONCLUSION

While generalizability is not claimed, this study provides credible and convincing accounts of women's experiences of child-to-mother violence. Therefore these findings are of interest to those concerned with adolescent, family and women's health. Health and community workers have the potential to be effective in supporting people living with family violence. First, however, there has to be an awareness that this form of violence exists. Child-to-mother violence needs to be reconceptualized to be seen as a form of family violence, rather than being positioned as an aspect of delinquency. Only then will it become visible. Increased visibility of child-to-mother violence will lead to increased awareness and opportunities for support, thus reducing the shame and isolation felt by those living in its shadow.

REFERENCES

Agnew, R., & Huguley, S. (1989) Adolescent violence toward parents. *Journal of Marriage and the Family*, 5, 699–711.

Anderson, K., & Jack, D. (1991) Learning to listen: interview techniques and analysis. In: *Women's Words: Feminist Practice of Oral History* (eds. D. Gluck & D. Patai), pp. 11–26. Routledge, New York.

Bonnar, M. (1999) Impact on mothers. In: *Adolescent Violence Towards Parents. Notes from the Seminar held on 4 June 1999 at Way Hall* (ed. M. Bradford), pp. 5–7. Department of Human Services, Adelaide.

Charles, A. V. (1986) Physically abused parents. *Journal of Family Violence*, 1, 343–355.

Cody, A. (1996) Helping the vulnerable or condoning control with the family: where is nursing? *Journal of Advanced Nursing*, 23, 882–886.

Cook, J., & Fonow, M. (1986) Knowledge and women's interests: issues of epistemology and methodology in feminist sociological research. *Sociological Inquiry*, 56, 69–93.

Cornell, C., & Gelles, R. (1982) Adolescent to parent violence. *Urban and Social Change Review*, 15, 8–14.

Downey, L. (1997) Adolescent violence: a systematic and feminist perspective. *Australian and New Zealand Journal of Family Therapy*, 18, 70–79.

Emery, R. (1989) Family violence. *American Psychologist*, 44, 321–328.

Evans, E., & Warren-Sohlberg, L. (1988) A pattern analysis of adolescent abusive behaviour toward parents. *Journal of Adolescent Research*, 3, 201–216.

Family Violence Educational Taskforce (1991) *Family Violence: Everybody's Business, Somebody's Life.* The Federation Press, Sydney.

Harbin, H., & Madden, D. (1979) Battered parents: a new syndrome. *American Journal of Psychiatry*, 136, 1288–1291.

Hastie, C. (1998) Parental abuse and its links to domestic violence. In: *Proceedings of the 2nd National Conference on Children, Young People and*

Domestic Violence, pp. 29–31. Domestic Violence Resource Centre, Brisbane.

Jackson, D., Daly, J., & Chang, E. (2003) Approaches in qualitative research. In: *Nursing Research: Methods, Critical Appraisal and Utilization*, 2nd edn. (eds. Z. Schneider, D. Elliott, G. Lo-Biondo-Wood & J. Haber), pp. 139–153. Mosby, Sydney.

Jenkins, A. (1999) Therapeutic perspective. In: *Adolescent Violence Towards Parents: Notes from the Seminar held on 4 June 1999 at Way Hall* (ed. M. Bradford), pp. 7–12. Department of Human Services, Adelaide.

Livingston, L. (1985) *Children's Violence to Single Mothers.* University of Illinois, Urbana.

McAllister, M. (2000) Domestic violence: a life span approach to assessment and intervention. *Lippincott's Primary Care Practice*, 4, 174–189.

Pelletier, D., & Coutu, S. (1992) Substance abuse and family violence in adolescents. *Canada's Mental Health*, 40, 6–12.

Reinharz, S. (1992) *Feminist Methods in Social Research.* Oxford University Press, New York.

Sandelowski, M. (1993) Rigor or rigor mortis: the problem of rigor in qualitative research revisited. *Advances in Nursing Sciences*, 16, 1–8.

Shea, C., Mahoney, M., & Lacey, J. (1997) Breaking through the barriers to domestic violence intervention. *American Journal of Nursing*, 97, 26–33.

Sheehan, M. (1997) Adolescent violence—strategies, outcomes and dilemmas in working with young people and their families. *Australian and New Zealand Journal of Family Therapy*, 18, 80–91.

Tong, R. (1998) *Feminist Thought: A More Comprehensive Introduction*, 2nd edn. Westview Publications, Boulder.

Webb, C. (1992) The use of the first person in academic writing: Objectivity, language and gatekeeping. *Journal of Advanced Nursing, 18*, 416–423.

REVIEW QUESTIONS

1. How does Debra Jackson's article differ from other domestic violence research?
2. What role did the friends and associates of the children play in the mothers' safety concerns?
3. What were some of the limitations to Debra Jackson's study?

Chapter 18

HOW CHILD MOLESTERS EXPLAIN THEIR DEVIANCE

LOUANNE LAWSON

Adult sexual contact with children is bewildering to most of us. However, if forensic nurses are to provide evidence-based care for both victims and those accused or convicted of committing crimes, an understanding of the offender's, as well as the victim's, perspective is essential. Victims of child sexual abuse have received considerable attention, but the perspective of those who have molested children is not as well understood. Attempts to describe, explain, predict, and, ultimately, prevent the behavior have been based primarily on clinical impressions or measurement of factors thought to be associated with sexual offending. There have been theoretical efforts to explain deviant sexual behavior, but no synthesis of empirical studies of sex offending from the offender's perspective has been published to date. It is important to understand the offender's frame of reference because this can be used to help victims integrate their experiences (Gilgun & Conner, 1989), guide treatment development and evaluation (Pribyl, 1998; Scheela, 1995, 1996), and suggest new avenues for research. This article therefore reviews descriptions of sex offending as a first step toward understanding child sexual abuse from the offender's perspective.

METHOD

Qualitative English language studies of sex offending published between 1982 and 2001 were selected for review. In these studies, offenders were defined as child sexual abusers whose actions had come to the attention of the criminal justice or child protective services systems. Studies were identified through searches of the Cumulative Index of Nursing and Allied Health Literature (CINAHL), Medline, and PsycInfo. Using this approach, ten studies were identified initially, then five additional studies were identified by examining reference lists, tables of contents, and conference proceedings.

Study Participants

The participants in the studies were men and women who were either in prison or in outpatient treatment at the time of the study. Data were gathered primarily by open-ended interviews and analyzed using grounded theory or phenomenological methods. There were 453 participants, almost all men, in the 13 studies that reported sample sizes. Their victims were both male and female; they had molested children who were family members, as well as children who lived outside their families. In the ten studies that reported the age of the participants, the average age was 37.7. . . .

Data Analysis

The "selective reading approach" (van Manen, 1990) was used to identify phrases the investiga-

Source: Louanne Lawson, "Isolation, Gratification, Justification: Offenders' Explanations of Child Molesting," *Issues in Mental Health Nursing*, vol. 24 (2003), pp. 695–705.

tors used to describe offenders' thoughts, behaviors, and relationships. Offenders can be expected to distort their statements in an attempt to bias an interviewer's opinion (Conte, Wolf, & Smith, 1989). Further, the study participants were imprisoned or in treatment, so their descriptions may have been influenced by incarceration or by the processes of treatment, including challenges by peers and therapists, insights gained in the process of telling their stories, and information they had learned during therapy. However, dysfunctional cognitions, transparent rationalizations, and obfuscations are important in illustrating the offender's perspective, and showing how offenders explain what they have done.

Thematic statements emerged from the offenders' descriptions and were consolidated in memo form and then sent to the authors of the original studies to review for accuracy and completeness. When suggestions and corrections were returned, they were incorporated into the review.

RESULTS

Three themes—isolation, gratification, and justification—emerged during the review. Offenders reported that they were isolated from their families and peers (Gilgun & Connor, 1990) and had unmet needs for parental affection and affirmation (Ivey & Simpson, 1998). They also described how they isolated their victims from routine sources of social support and made the children feel at least partially responsible for their victimization (Christiansen & Blake, 1990; de Young, 1982). Offenders' sexual fantasies reflected their desire to engage children in sexual behavior (Rokach, Nutbrown, & Nexhipi, 1988) and they thought they were entitled to gratify their sexual appetites (Gilgun & Connor, 1989). They had created relationships of varying levels of intimacy (Gilgun, 1994) but misperceived the victim's responses to their sexual behavior (Phelan, 1995). They justified their actions by using excuses (de Young, 1982; Phelan, 1995) and cognitive distortions (Hartley, 2001; Neidigh & Krop, 1992) and by redefining their behavior as an expression of love and mutuality (Gilgun, 1995). Further elaboration on each of the three themes follows.

Isolation

Isolation was associated with the offenders' early childhood and current family and social relationships (Gilgun & Connor, 1990; Ivey & Simpson, 1998) as well as the processes by which they separated children from their protective social networks (Christiansen & Blake, 1990). Offenders had felt ignored and neglected by preoccupied parents and had been exposed to limited modeling of healthy intimacy. They saw their mothers as rejecting and critical and their fathers as cold, distant, and authoritarian. As a result, the transitions from childhood through adolescence to adulthood were said to be "impossible" (Ivey & Simpson, 1998). Their sense of lovableness was damaged in childhood; in adolescence they were loners who were isolated from their age-mates. Some described burdensome responsibility for siblings that limited their social opportunities. They experienced shame about their sexual fantasies and had no close friends to help them integrate the fantasies in a pro-social manner. One man said, "I felt I was oversexed and there was something wrong with me having a sexual fantasy" (Gilgun & Connor, 1990).

The isolation that began in childhood and adolescence continued into adulthood. One man said, "I felt lonely even after I was married. We were together but I was still alone, which I guess the biggest part of that is my fault because I wouldn't open up" (Gilgun & Connor, 1990). Sexual invasiveness was seen as a way to assuage feelings of isolation, however briefly. One of the participants said, "I wanted to be close to somebody." Adult sexuality reminded them of being in the humiliating role of inadequate, unlovable child, so they tried to meet their needs for emotional and physical intimacy through sexual contact with children (Ivey & Simpson, 1998). Children's emotional responsiveness contrasted with adult judgmentalness and rejection, giving the offender a sense of masculinity and emotional potency.

Offenders' sense of isolation was reflected in the ways in which they separated victims from their supportive social environment in order to engage the child in sexual activity (Christiansen & Blake, 1990). Incestuous fathers carefully planned their attempts to develop trust with their daughters. Efforts included presents of candy, food, money, and clothing. The men treated their daughters with favoritism, revealing their own loneliness and their hope that their daughters could alleviate that loneliness. The girls were given preferential treatment, but it was clear that reciprocity was expected. The fathers alienated their daughters from their mothers, their siblings, and their friends by placing them in this favored relationship and by interfering with relationships outside the family. Ordinary boundaries surrounding bathing, dressing, bathroom behavior, and sexually explicit conversation were violated in favor of adding a sexual component to the child's environment. The fathers engaged the girls in increasingly intimate sexual acts. They selected the time and place for the sexual acts to occur and used bribes, threats, and punishment to maintain the relationship. Secrecy was enforced by nonverbal communication, including threatening looks and glares. Christiansen and Blake (1990) concluded that "incest is a gradual, deliberate, and predictable entanglement."

Victims were made to feel at least partially responsible for their victimization (Gilgun & Connor, 1989). Offenders turned children into the gatekeepers of their own victimization, saying that they would only do the things the child allowed. When a child attempted to exercise this pseudo-authority, the offenders retreated to adult prerogative. They manipulated and tricked the child by misrepresenting sexual mores, bargaining, and misusing their authority, further isolating the child from sources of protection and support.

Gratification

Sexual activity with children felt good to the offenders and was the main reason they gave for initiating and maintaining the behavior. Both adult and adolescent onset offenders were obsessed with sexual desire and felt entitled to satisfy their appetites, regardless of the harm they were causing. At least one offender reported fantasizing about multiple paraphilias including sadism and voyeurism in addition to his sexual abuse of children (Rokach, Nutbrown, & Nexhipi, 1988). For some offenders, the focus was on orgasm; for others, planning and controlling the interaction and playing with the child were equally important (Gilgun & Connor, 1989). Offenders who began molesting as adults rather than as adolescents indicated that sexual interest in children was activated during the first abusive incident (Ivey & Simpson, 1998), without, however, explaining how this sequence of events occurred. They were so obsessed with meeting their sexual needs that they ignored all other aspects of the victim's experiences. One participant said, "I was hooked on something and I had to have it. If I couldn't get it I was like a mad person" (Ivey & Simpson, 1998).

Intense sexual pleasure was an important, but not exclusive, component of the relationships offenders created with their victims. Relationships differed depending on the degree of emotional intimacy the offender felt with the child; offenders were avengers, takers, controllers, conquerors, playmates, lovers, and soul-mates (Gilgun, 1994). Avengers intended to harm the child or someone who loved the child. Takers saw the child as a commodity to be used. Controllers bargained with the child for sexual favors. Conquerors used age-sensitive ploys to engage the children in sexual relationships. Playmates regressed to a child-like state and created play activities in order to meet their own emotional needs. Lovers were infatuated with their victims. They described a deep sense of closeness and commitment, seeing the relationship as the single most important personal relationship in their lives. Soul-mates lost themselves in the child by identifying with and sexualizing their perceived loneliness and isolation. The offenders said they thought that their victims either enjoyed the sexual contact or the children were asleep and therefore unaware of the activity (Phelan, 1995). Timing, touch, and eye contact were all calculated so as not to elicit an overt negative response on the part of the child; all of the children's responses were interpreted as either tacit or explicit permission to continue.

Along with sexual entitlement and emotional intimacy, offenders reported that dissatisfaction with their lives, a need to express anger or affection, low self-esteem, or the need for affirmation influenced their abusive behavior (Gilgun & Connor, 1989; Hartley, 2001, Ivey & Simpson, 1998). They reported three main cognitive and behavioral pathways for gratifying their sexual appetites (Hudson, Ward, & McCormack, 1999; Ward, Fon, Hudson, & McCormack 1998; Ward, Louden, Hudson, & Marshall, 1995). These pathways reflected the offender's preoffense mood, the type of planning that took place, the perceived quality of the relationship, the postoffense self-evaluation, and resolutions to either continue or discontinue abusive behavior (Hudson, Ward, & McCormack, 1999).

Some offenders were in a positive mood prior to the offense and explicitly planned the interaction. They thought that the victim enjoyed the activity and that both wanted the sexual interaction to continue. Among other offenders, the preoffense mood was described as depression or loneliness. Planning was explicit. There was a feeling of intensity during the interaction, either positive ("I was feeling really good, very excited") or negative ("I am going to take someone else down with me") (Hudson, Ward, & McCormack, 1999). Following the abuse they experienced regret or felt disgusted with themselves and intended to avoid offending in the future. Still other offenders reported a negative preoffense mood. Their planning was covert, rather than explicit; that is, they denied that they intended for the offense to take place, and once it did, they felt bad about it: "I cried afterward about what I had done" (Hudson, Ward, & McCormack, 1999), resolving never to do it again.

Justification

Offenders justified their behavior in a variety of ways. Some made excuses (Pollock & Hasmall, 1991), while others used cognitive distortions (Hartley, 1998; Neidigh & Krop, 1992) or redefined their actions as love and mutuality (Gilgun, 1995). Offenders were unresponsive to the child's attempts to stop and enforced the secrecy surrounding the incest by instilling fear.

Offenders used excuses to deny responsibility for their actions and to defend themselves from aversive self-awareness. Excuses included psychologically mitigating factors such as denial of fact ("the boy's lying"), denial of responsibility ("the kid came on to me"), denial of sexual intent ("I was just being affectionate"), denial of wrongfulness ("she liked it"), or denial of self-determination ("my wife wouldn't sleep with me" or "I was sexually abused as a child") (Pollock & Hasmall, 1991, p. 57). Figure 18.1 illustrates the Excuse Syntax.

These excuses were similar to some of the cognitive distortions identified by Neidigh and Krop (1992). The distortions were related to the characteristics or behavior of the child ("she is flirting and teasing me, she wants me to do it") or the prerogative of the offender ("children are supposed to do what I want and serve my needs"). Some offenders claimed that the child's responses encouraged them ("she didn't say no or tell, so it must be okay with her") or that their actions were not harmful for the child ("she is asleep so she will never know what I am doing") (Neidigh & Krop, 1992).

Other offenders thought that society would tolerate a certain amount of sexual interest in children as long as the child was not engaged in sexual intercourse (Hartley, 2001). They exploited or exacerbated existing parent–child relationship problems and assumed that they could talk themselves out of trouble if the abuse was discovered. They were particularly emboldened if they could blame the child for initiating the contact, especially if the child delayed disclosure or appeared interested in the activity. They reduced their sense of responsibility for the activity by insisting that they never forced a child to engage in sexual behavior.

Incest offenders reconciled their abusive behaviors with their moral beliefs by redefining the incest in terms of love and mutuality (Gilgun, 1995). Love was expressed as sexualized affection. Some offenders believed themselves to be in a mutually satisfying love affair, rather than an

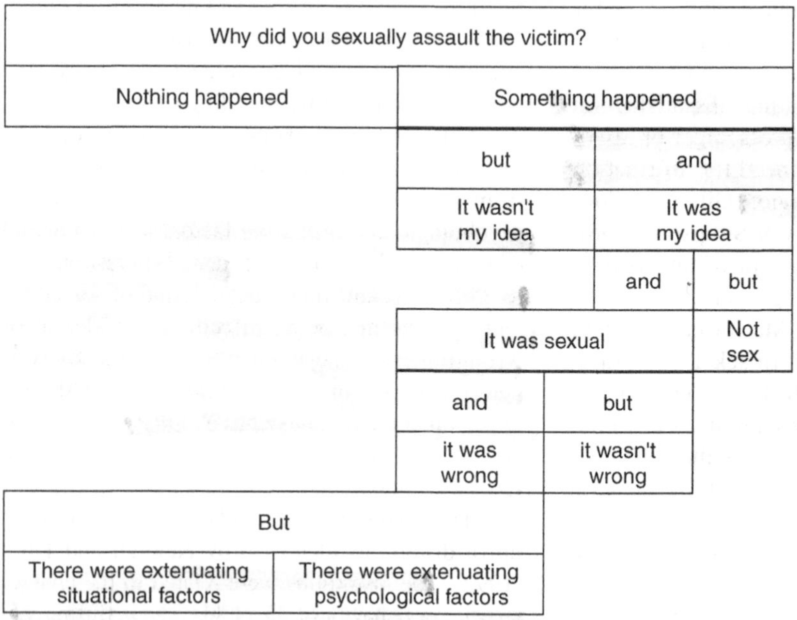

FIGURE 18.1 The Excuse Syntax
Used by permission (Pollock & Hasmall, 1991)

incestuous relationship; they treated the relationship as if the participants were equal in status. There were nonsexual components to the relationship, including playfulness and affection, and some offenders had fantasies of starting a new life with the child somewhere else. It was important to them that the child felt a connection to the offender, as well as for the offender to feel connected with the child. However, offenders were primarily concerned with physical satisfaction, which took precedence over any claim the children had on behalf of their own humanity. Rather than seeing children as needing special protection because of their young age, relative lack of sophistication, and limited experience, offenders exploited the power imbalance between adults and children to meet their own needs for intimacy.

CONCLUSION

Isolation, gratification, and justification are familiar themes for victims, clinicians, and researchers. Child sexual abuse thrives in an atmosphere of secrecy and miscommunication. With their own words, these offenders confirmed [that they] saw the relationship [with children] as a way to gratify their sexual appetites. They felt justified in exploiting the difference in status between themselves and children and they distorted their relationships, their moral beliefs, and even their own thought processes to continue that justification.

REFERENCES

Christiansen, J. R., & Blake, R. H. (1990). The grooming process in father–daughter incest. In A. L. Horton, B. L. Johnson, L. M. Roundy, & D. Williams (Eds.), *The incest perpetrator: A family member no one wants to treat* (pp. 88–98). Newbury Park, CA: Sage.

Conte, J. R., Wolf, S., & Smith, T. (1989). What sexual offenders tell us about prevention strategies. *Child Abuse & Neglect*, 13, 293–301.

de Young, M. (1982). *The sexual victimization of children.* Jefferson, NC: McFarland.

Gilgun, J. F. (1994). Avengers, conquerors, playmates, and lovers: Roles played by child sexual abuse perpetrators. *Families in Society: Journal of Contemporary Human Services*, 75, 467–479.

Gilgun, J. F. (1995). We shared something special: The moral discourse of incest perpetrators. *Journal of Marriage & the Family*, 57, 265–281.

Gilgun, J. F., & Connor, T. M. (1989). How perpetrators view child sexual abuse. *Social Work*, 34, 249–251.

Gilgun, J. F., & Connor, T. M. (1990). Isolation and the adult male perpetrator of child sexual abuse: Clinical concerns. In A. L. Horton, B. L. Johnson, L. M. Roundy, & D. Williams (Eds.), *The incest perpetrator: A family member no one wants to treat* (pp. 74–87). Newbury Park: Sage.

Hartley, C. C. (1998). How incest offenders overcome internal inhibitions through the use of cognitions and cognitive distortions. *Journal of Interpersonal Violence*, 13(1), 25–39.

Hartley, C. C. (2001). Incest offenders' perceptions of their motives to sexually offend within their past and current life context. *Journal of Interpersonal Violence*, 16(5), 459–475.

Hartman, C. R., & Burgess, A. W. (1988). Information processing of trauma: Case application of a model. *Journal of Interpersonal Violence*, 3(4), 443–457.

Hudson, S. M., Ward, T., & McCormack, J. C. (1999). Offense pathways in sexual offenders. *Journal of Interpersonal Violence*, 14(8), 779–798.

Ivey, G., & Simpson, P. (1998). The psychological life of pedophiles: A phenomenological study. *South African Journal of Psychology*, 28(1), 15–20.

Neidigh, L., & Krop, H. (1992). Cognitive distortions among child sexual offenders. *Journal of Sex Education & Therapy*, 18, 208–215.

Phelan, P. (1995). Incest and its meaning: The perspectives of fathers and daughters. *Child Abuse & Neglect*, 19(1), 7–24.

Pollock, N. L., & Hasmall, J. M. (1991). The excuses of child molesters. *Behavioral Sciences & the Law*, 9(1), 53–59.

Pribyl, D. S. (1998). The child sex offender's perspective on treatment and related factors. *Dissertation Abstracts International: Section B: The Sciences & Engineering*, 58(10-B), 5653.

Rokach, A., Nutbrown, V., & Nexhipi, G. (1988). Content analysis of erotic imagery: Sex offenders and non-sex offenders. *International Journal of Offender Therapy and Comparative Criminology*, 32(2), 107–122.

Russell, D. H. (1986). *The secret trauma.* New York: Basic.

Scheela, R. A. (1995). Remodeling as metaphor: Sex offenders' perceptions of the treatment process. *Issues in Mental Health Nursing*, 16, 493–504.

Scheela, R. A. (1996). Use of remodelling in the treatment of sex offenders. *Nursing Times*, 92(4), 34–36.

Van Manen, M. (1990). *Researching lived experience: Human science for an action sensitive pedagogy.* London: State University of New York Press.

Ward, T., Fon, C., Hudson, S. M., & McCormack, J. C. (1998). A descriptive model of dysfunctional cognitions in child molesters. *Journal of Interpersonal Violence*, 13(1), 129–155.

Ward, T., Louden, K., Hudson, S. M., & Marshall, W. L. (1995). A descriptive model of the offense chain for child molesters. *Journal of Interpersonal Violence*, 10, 452–472.

REVIEW QUESTIONS

1. What does Lawson mean when she states: "Child sexual abuse thrives in an atmosphere of secrecy and miscommunication"?
2. Identify the way the offenders justified their behavior.
3. How do the "justifications" the offenders use relate to Sykes and Matza's techniques of neutralization?

PART SIX

SELF-DESTRUCTIVE DEVIANCE

Bob Antonioni, a 48-year-old attorney, has struggled with depression for nearly a decade. In public, he appeared normal, appearing in court on behalf of his clients. But in private, he was irritable and short-tempered and became easily frustrated by small things, such as having difficulty deciding which television show to watch with his girlfriend. Often in his office he would get so exhausted by noon that he would come home and collapse on the couch, where he would stay for the rest of the day. When he decided to seek help, he kept it a secret from his friends and family. He stealthily saw a therapist, and he had his prescriptions for antidepressants filled at a pharmacy 20 miles away.[1]

Like Antonioni, millions of Americans suffer from depression. It is a self-destructive deviance, hurting oneself rather than others. Here we take a close look at various forms of self-destructive deviance. In the first article, "The Desire for Death," Thomas Joiner explains how suicide results from the perception that one is a burden to others and does not belong to any group. In the second article, "Self Injurers: A 'Lonely Crowd,' " Patricia Adler and Peter Adler offer a portrait of the lonely world of self-injurers, who cut, burn, or brand themselves without support of fellow deviants. In the third piece, "Being Sane in Insane Places," David Rosenhan reports a participant-observation study that shows how difficult it is for psychiatrists to tell the "sane" from the "insane" and describes how a person is treated differently once he or she is determined to be "insane." In the fourth article, "The Emergence of Hyperactive Adults as Abnormal," Peter Conrad and Deborah Potter show how the medical diagnosis of hyperactivity in children has been expanded to adults.

[1]Julie Scelfo, "Men and Depression: Facing Darkness," *Newsweek*, February 26, 2007, pp. 43–49.

CHAPTER 19

THE DESIRE FOR DEATH

THOMAS JOINER

I phoned my mother recently, and among the updates about her grandchildren and the family, she said, "Do you remember my friends Kevin and Julie?" I said I did. "Do you remember their son Steve? He was just a year younger than you." I said I thought I might, vaguely. "Well, they just had awful, *awful* news on Steve. He hanged himself last week, just after his girlfriend left for work." I asked the usual questions about Steve's state of mind before his death ("happy as far as anyone knew," my mom said) and his circumstances (happy with his girlfriend though struggling to find a career, according to my mom).

There was a painful subtext to the conversation—my dad, her husband, died by suicide too, years ago. We didn't really need to speak the subtext; it was clear already, and it amounted to a one-word question—"Why?" Why did my dad do that? Why did Steve do that?

Later that night I searched for Steve's name on the Internet, and found his obituary as well as a kind of virtual guest book where people could express condolences and memories. There was no mention of work or career anywhere, though there was this: "Steve was recently re-baptized as a Christian and was a member of Springview Church, and he had found great joy in his renewed faith."

Great joy in faith, and yet dead by suicide in his thirties? My dad was also very religious and involved in his church, yet dead by suicide in his fifties.

The desire for life—life-sustaining desire—can't be about faith and religion only, or else Steve and my dad would be alive. What is it about, then? Career success does not really constitute a satisfying answer either. For one thing, plenty of people who do not have particularly satisfying careers never consider suicide; for another, a lot of people who die by suicide appear to have had successful careers. Six weeks before my dad's death, he made a very large amount of money in a stock deal. A child of the 1930s, my dad had worked toward a deal like that most of his life. He might have said that that was his life's desire, along with his faith and family; his death six weeks later shows that somehow he was mistaken.

How was he mistaken, though? Many prominent psychologists and others have considered psychological needs as a way to understand human motivation and human nature. Several lists of needs exist, and a premise associated with them is that people are highly motivated to meet these needs. When they do, the theory goes, well-being and health are achieved. Of course, the flipside to this is that frustrated needs can lead to an array of problems.

Perhaps the most famous work on this topic is that of Henry Murray, who identified twenty such needs, including autonomy, nurturance, play, understanding, dominance, and achievement, among others. Shneidman, heavily influenced by Murray, highlights these needs as well,

Source: Excerpted from Thomas Joiner, *Why People Die by Suicide.* Cambridge, MA: Harvard University Press, 2005.

postulating that the thwarting of them leads to psychache and thus to suicidality. These theorists might have guessed that though my dad belonged to a church and had career success, something was still missing—some of his fundamental needs were still not being met.

But which needs? Exactly how many are there, and are some more important than others? Models including as many as twenty needs pose a problem for a model of suicide based on needs. Given that there are so many needs and thus so many people with one or more thwarted needs, how to understand that very, very few of these people attempt suicide, and fewer still die by suicide.

Murray was aware of this problem. He wrote, "In many cases the succorance drive is subsidiary to the *need for affiliation* (a basic tendency, whose aim is to establish and maintain friendly relationships with others)." I am intrigued that Murray believed the need for affiliation was a superordinate need, because as I have noted already and will expand on in this chapter, I do too, and more to the point, I believe that the thwarting of this need is a main component of the desire for death.

Shneidman, writing specifically of suicide, stated, "For practical purposes, most suicides tend to fall into one of five clusters of psychological needs. They reflect different kinds of psychological pain." The five are thwarted love, ruptured relationships, assaulted self-image, fractured control, and excessive anger related to frustrated needs for dominance.

My solution to this problem is to assert two bedrock needs, the fulfillment of which satisfies most others and can compensate for frustration of other needs. The thwarting of both of these needs constitutes the desire for death. Shneidman's five failed needs are important, but they are collapsible into the two major categories of thwarted belongingness (i.e., thwarted love, ruptured relationships) and perceived burdensomeness (assaulted self-image, fractured control, anger related to frustrated dominance).

Regarding the first bedrock need, belongingness, the need to belong involves a "combination of frequent interaction plus persistent caring." Thus, there are two components of a fully satisfied need to belong: interactions with others and a feeling of being cared about. In order to meet the need to belong, the interactions an individual has must be frequent and positive. Interactions within a stable relationship will more fully satisfy the need to belong than interactions with a changing cast of relationship partners (i.e., higher levels of stability). The need to belong will be only partially met if an individual feels cared about but does not have face-to-face interactions with the relationship partner (i.e., greater proximity). The model of suicidal behavior developed here asserts that an unmet need to belong is a contributor to suicidal desire: suicidal individuals may experience interactions that do not satisfy their need to belong (e.g., relationships that are unpleasant, unstable, infrequent, or without proximity) or may not feel connected to others and cared about.

I would argue that the other bedrock need is effectiveness or a sense of competence. When this need is thwarted, when one perceives oneself as ineffective, it is painful indeed. To perceive oneself as so ineffective that loved ones are threatened and burdened is even worse, so much so that the desire for death could be generated. The perspective taken here proposes that feelings of ineffectiveness contribute to the desire for suicide, and moreover, that feeling ineffective to the degree that others are burdened is among the strongest sources of all for the desire for suicide.

Those who view themselves as a burden on others have a negative self-image, feel out of control of their lives, and possess a range of negative emotions stemming from the sense that their incapacity spills over to affect others besides themselves.

THWARTED EFFECTIVENESS: THE SENSE THAT ONE IS A BURDEN

If you let yourself down, the experience is not pleasant, but it is contained—it affects just you. If you let your group down, you experience all the negative aspects of letting yourself down (because you are part of the group), but you also experience the sense that your ineffectiveness is not contained, that it negatively affects others.

To take a relatively trivial example, I returned to playing soccer recently, after a layoff of a couple of weeks because of injury and travel commitments. I didn't play very well. I was tentative because I was a little concerned about reinjury, and I was not energetic, because I was out of shape after the layoff. I was disappointed in myself and had the sense that my teammates felt that way about me too. Not pleasant.

So why didn't I just quit? And why didn't my teammates want me to quit? The main reason, I think, is that my teammates and I remember that I have a track record of holding my own, of contributing to the team. Relatedly, everyone understands or at least hopes that my injury-related tentativeness and my layoff-induced lack of stamina are remediable—I can recover from both with time and training.

But what if I judged that my failings were not remediable, that I was a burden to my team and would be permanently? And what if I thought my teammates felt the same way? Under such conditions, I might very well quit the team. In this scenario, I have perceived myself to be a burden on others and, lacking the remedy of time and training, am left with quitting the team as my only solution.

I believe this example, though trivial, is analogous to the non-trivial, life-and-death psychological processes of people seriously contemplating suicide. They perceive themselves to be ineffective or incompetent, but it's not just that. They also perceive that their ineffectiveness affects others, too. Finally, they perceive that this ineffectiveness that negatively affects everyone is stable and permanent, forcing a choice between continued perceptions of burdening others and escalating feelings of shame, on the one hand, or death on the other hand.

When I refer to "perceived burdensomeness," I would like to emphasize the term *perceived.* People who are contemplating suicide *perceive* themselves a burden, and *perceive* that this state is permanent and stable, with death as a solution to the problem. It is very important to point out that their perceptions are mistaken. Indeed, that their perceptions are mistaken is the basis for the psychotherapeutic treatment of suicidal symptoms. Any perception, mistaken or not, can influence behavior. My contention is that perceived burdensomeness, though mistaken, influences suicidal behavior.

The specific role of perceived burdensomeness in suicidal behavior is clear in some cultures. There have been reports that among the Yuit Eskimos of St. Lawrence Island, for example, those who become too sick, infirm, or old may threaten the group's survival; in the past, the explicit and socially sanctioned solution to this problem was ritual suicide. Reportedly, the ritual was graphic, often involving the family members' participation in the shooting or hanging of the victim. There is some question as to the veracity of this specific example, but the general pattern has been noted many times in Eskimo cultures. Arguably, this represents an example of anecdotal evidence being quite persuasive—cultures have sanctioned ritual suicide specifically in response to burdensomeness. Another example is ancient Ceos, where the law obliged all inhabitants over sixty years of age to die by drinking hemlock to make room for the next generation (a law that apparently was enforced only in times of famine).

Similarly, among the ancient Scythians, it was a great honor to die by suicide when one was too old to continue in and contribute to their nomadic lifestyle. Quintus Curtius, who described the Scythians, said: "Among them exists a sort of wild and bestial men to whom they give the name of sages. The anticipation of the time of death is a glory in their eyes, and they have themselves burned alive as soon as age or sickness begins to trouble them."

In 2004, as reported on the news website Ananova.com, an elderly Malaysian couple died by suicide by jumping from the fifteenth floor of their apartment building specifically because they did not want to be a burden on their family. Their suicide note read, "If we had waited for our death due to sickness, we would have caused much inconvenience to all of you." Ritual murder of widows among the Lusi people in New Guinea has been described as essentially suicidal: "A Lusi widow would rather die than be dependent on her children; Lusi widowers are not viewed as a burden on their kin and are not ritually killed by their kin."

Examples like this illustrate that perceived burdensomeness could play a role in suicidal behavior and also shows the link . . . between perceived burdensomeness and Durkheim's concept of altruistic suicide. For Durkheim, altruistic suicides occur when people are so integrated into social groups that individuality fades, and they become willing to sacrifice themselves to the group's interests. My account also emphasizes self-sacrifice in context of the perception that others will benefit, but I do not think this usually occurs when people are especially connected to a group—in fact quite the contrary, as will be expanded on in the next section on failed belongingness.

Returning for now to the concept of perceived burdensomeness, some material from suicide notes also illustrates its potential role in suicidal behavior. A seventy-year-old man wrote "Survival of the fittest. Adios—unfit." The closing line from musician Kurt Cobain's suicide note (addressed to his wife Courtney regarding their daughter Frances) provides anecdotal evidence that perceived burdensomeness is implicated in suicide: "Please keep going Courtney for Frances for her life which will be so much happier without me." A suicide note left by a teenage girl who died by electrocution read, "I have just been a very bad person, but now you are all rid of me."

Shneidman summarized several other examples from suicide notes: "Life is unmanageable. I'm like a helpless 12 year old" (from a 74-year-old widowed woman who died by self-cutting); "The failures and frustrations overwhelm me" (from a 49-year-old married man who died by self-inflicted gunshot wound).

Perhaps the clearest example cited by Shneidman is from a woman's suicide notes to her ex-husband and her daughters. To her ex-husband, she writes, "[the girls] need two happy people, not a sick, mixed-up mother. There will be a little money to help with the extras—it had better go that way than for more pills and more doctor bills." To her daughters, she writes, "Try to forgive me for what I've done—your father would be so much better for you. It will be harder for you for awhile—but so much easier in the long run—I'm getting you all mixed up."

Another example: "I started to list the people who wouldn't mind if I wasn't around. I clearly wasn't a good wife for my ex-husband. He wouldn't miss me. And I never felt that comfortable in my role as a mom—didn't feel like I was a good mom necessarily . . . It's like I'll be a burden off their backs. Clearly their lives will be enhanced because I'm not around. At that point, I honestly felt I was doing them a favor."

Perceived Burdensomeness Contributes to Suicidality

To my knowledge, five studies have been framed as direct tests of the possibility that perceived burdensomeness is involved in serious suicidal behavior; all five affirm the connection. One study was conducted to test DeCatanzaro's model of self-preservation and self-destruction. Arguing from a sociobiological or evolutionary standpoint, this model posits that staying alive actually may reduce inclusive fitness for an individual if the individual is low in reproductive potential and if the individual's continuing to live poses such a burden to close kin that it costs them opportunities for reproduction. One upshot of this view is that suicidal behavior may have been selected in the course of evolution—a controversial point to which I return later.

To test this model, Brown and colleagues conducted a questionnaire study of college students and found the predicted correlation between feeling a burden on kin and suicidality. Burdensomeness stood out as a unique and specific predictor of suicide-related symptoms even when other variables, such as the individual's reproductive potential, were accounted for.

My students and I also conducted empirical tests of the association between perceived burdensomeness and suicidal behavior. We trained raters to evaluate actual suicide notes regarding the following dimensions: perceived burdensomeness, hopelessness, and generalized emotional pain. The raters read each note and then made three separate ratings on a 1-to-5 scale of the amount of perceived burdensomeness, hopelessness, and generalized emotional pain conveyed by the note.

Unknown to the raters, half of the notes were from people who died by suicide, and half were from people who attempted suicide and survived. The goal of the study was to compare perceived burdensomeness versus Shneidman's emphasis on emotional pain versus Beck's emphasis on hopelessness. In statistical analyses, the notes from those who died by suicide contained more perceived burdensomeness than notes from attempters; no effects were found regarding hopelessness and emotional pain. This study's relatively stringent comparison of notes from those who died by suicide to notes from those who attempted and survived (which distinction was unknown to raters), with perceived burdensomeness emerging as the only unique predictor of death by suicide, added to our confidence in the results.

Moreover, a second study from this same paper on a separate collection of notes took a similar approach, except that all notes were from those who died by suicide, and perceived burdensomeness, hopelessness, and generalized emotional pain were used as predictors of lethality of suicide method (e.g., self-inflicted gunshot wound was viewed as relatively more lethal than overdose). Here again, perceived burdensomeness was a significant predictor of lethality, whereas hopelessness and generalized emotional pain were not. The convergence of the two studies made the findings more persuasive.

A survey on reproductive behavior, quality of family contacts, and suicidal ideation on several hundred community participants as well as on five high-suicide-risk groups (e.g., general psychiatric patients and incarcerated psychiatric patients) found that perceived burdensomeness toward family and social isolation were especially correlated with suicidal ideation. It is important to note that these two variables correspond to two of the three main aspects of the present model, burdensomeness and lack of belonging.

My students and I recently completed a study on perceived burdensomeness and suicidality among 343 adult outpatients of the Florida State University Psychology Clinic. Areas of diagnosis for these patients were represented in the following proportions: 39 percent mood disorder, 14.6 percent anxiety disorder, 6 percent substance use disorder, 12.2 percent personality disorder, 9 percent adjustment disorder, and 18 percent other disorders.

We hypothesized that perceived burdensomeness would directly relate to both past number of suicide attempts and an index of current suicidal symptoms, and furthermore, that this relationship would exist even when accounting for known risk factors such as personality disorder status, depressive symptoms, and hopelessness. . . . We also wanted to see if there was a special connection between perceived burdensomeness and suicidality. So, for purposes of comparison, the associations of hopelessness to suicide indices (controlling for personality disorder status, depressive symptoms, and perceived burdensomeness) were examined. Our reasoning was that if perceived burdensomeness is important in suicidality, its associations to suicidality should be as rigorous as those regarding the documented risk factor of hopelessness.

Here, as in other studies, the connection of perceived burdensomeness to suicidality was supported. Specifically, there was an association between measures of perceived burdensomeness and suicidality and this association persisted even when a host of other variables was accounted for (specifically, age, gender, hopelessness, depressive symptoms, and personality disorder status). Furthermore, the link between perceived burdensomeness and suicidality was at least as strong as that between hopelessness and suicidality.

The concept of perceived burdensomeness is fairly easy to understand as applied to adults—the image of the failed breadwinner imagining his family will be better off without him is tragic but not hard to conceive. But what about perceived burdensomeness as applied to younger people, including children? Young people do die by suicide, and so if perceived burdensomeness plays a role in suicide in general, it should be applicable to youth too. In fact, researchers have studied burdensomeness and suicidality in youth in their work on the "expendable child." These authors hypothesized that suicidal adolescents would be rated higher on a measure of expendability than would be a psychiatric control group. The expendability measure specifically included a sense of being a burden on one's family. Results conformed to predictions: Suicidal youth scored higher on the expendability measure than did a psychiatric comparison group.

Studies of youth like this one suggest that the concept of burdensomeness may affect a broad range of ages. Related to feeling a burden on one's family, suicide attempts among children have been linked to perceived inability to meet parental demands. Again, the emphasis on the term *perceived* bears repeating, the facile explanation that parents are responsible for their children's death by suicide because of high demands is hardly worth considering. However, the explanation that people who perceive themselves as not measuring up and as being a burden are prone to suicidal behavior is more serious and is supported by numerous research studies.

The potential importance of perceived burdensomeness emerged in a study of low-income, abused African-American women. This study identified protective and risk factors that differentiated suicide attempters from those who had never made an attempt. Protective factors associated with nonattempter status included self-efficacy as well as effectiveness in obtaining material resources. In the current framework, these results could be viewed as suggesting that those who feel effective in general, as well as effective in providing material resources in particular, are buffered from feeling a burden and thus at relatively low risk for suicidality.

Data on suicide in the Netherlands in the early twentieth century are in accord with a role for perceived burdensomeness as well. A higher suicide rate in rural as compared to urban areas was noted and was attributed to "the peculiar conditions of the Dutch farming system under which the aged find themselves a burden," an experience not shared by older Dutch people in the cities.

THWARTED CONNECTEDNESS: THE SENSE THAT ONE DOES NOT BELONG

William James, in *The Principles of Psychology* (1890), wrote, "No more fiendish punishment could be devised, were such a thing physically possible, than that one should be turned loose in society and remain absolutely unnoticed by all the members thereof. If no one turned around when we entered, answered when we spoke, or minded what we did, but if every person we met 'cut us dead,' and acted as if we were non-existent things, a kind of rage and impotent despair would before long well up in us, from which the cruelest bodily torture would be a relief." I think James's use of the phrase "cut us dead" is telling, as is the insight that bodily torture can, under some circumstances, be a relief.

My view is that this need to belong is so powerful that, when satisfied, it can prevent suicide even when perceived burdensomeness and the acquired ability to enact lethal self-injury are in place. By the same token, when the need is thwarted, risk for suicide is increased. This perspective, incidentally, is similar to that of Durkheim, who proposed that suicide results, in part, from failure of social integration.

Some of the Stoic philosophers were proponents of rational suicide, but even they could not overcome the need to belong. For example, Seneca said, "Does life please you? Live on. Does it not? Go from whence you came. No vast wound is necessary; a mere puncture will secure your liberty. It is a bad thing (you say) to be under the necessity of living; but there is no necessity in the case. Thanks be to the gods, nobody can be compelled to live." But when Seneca became seriously ill and desired suicide, he could not carry through, specifically because he could not bear to think of how his father would react. His connection to his father prevented his suicide. . . . Notably, Seneca later died by suicide, but well after his father's death.

This same sentiment is often expressed in suicide risk assessments. When asked about the likelihood of suicide, many patients respond that though they have thought of suicide, their connection to a loved one makes it impossible (e.g., "I couldn't do that to so-and-so"). This is of course no guarantee that someone will not attempt suicide, but, as noted below, this clinical anecdote has some empirical support. Women with numerous children may be less prone to suicide than women with no or few children, for example.

Shneidman's Ariel recalled that on the day of her self-immolation "I had various friends that I did know and it just seemed like they really just didn't have time for me." Just before her self-immolation, Ariel described going to her friends' house to return a borrowed toaster; she wrote, "I remember just walking in and walking through the house and by this time I was sobbing again. And not one word was said to me by these people . . . And I just walked through the house, put the toaster on the kitchen table and walked right out. And nobody touched my arm, nobody asked what's wrong, nobody even gestured, and it upset me even more that this was sort of the end."

In his 2003 *New Yorker* article on suicide at the Golden Gate Bridge, Tad Friend quoted psychiatrist Jerome Motto on the suicide that affected him most. Motto said, "I went to this guy's apartment afterward with the assistant medical examiner. The guy was in his thirties, lived alone, pretty bare apartment. He'd written a note and left it on his bureau. It said, 'I'm going to walk to the bridge. If one person smiles at me on the way, I will not jump.' "

Shneidman noted several other poignant examples of failed belongingness in suicide: "I haven't the love I want so bad there is nothing left" (from a forty-five-year-old married woman who died by overdose); "I really thought that you and little Joe were going to come back into my life but you didn't" (from a twenty-year-old married man who died by hanging); "I just cannot live without you. I might as well be dead . . . I have this empty feeling inside me that is killing me . . . When you left me I died inside" (from a thirty-one-year-old separated man who died by hanging).

On January 5, 2002, fifteen-year-old Charles Bishop stole a small single-engine plane and crashed it into the Bank of America building in Tampa, Florida. An article from the June 14, 2004 *Tampa Bay Online* described the final report on the boy's death (classified as a suicide). The last line of the article read, "Bishop's mother said he had no neighborhood friends, and she had not met any of his friends from school."

The empirical literature also affirms a connection between failed belongingness and feeling suicidal. In the sections below, this work is summarized, starting with research on the general connection between depressive symptoms (one of which is suicidality) and experiences of disconnection from others.

Behavioral Features of Depression Indicating Low Social Connection

Connection to others can be seen in basic behavior, like eye contact and harmony between one person's and another's facial expressions or gestures. Several studies have demonstrated that depressed people engage in less eye contact than do nondepressed people. Similar findings have emerged with regard to nonverbal gestures. For example, as compared to others, depressed people may engage in less head-nodding during conversation; head-nodding is a gesture affirming connection that communication partners find rewarding. Depressed and suicidal people have trouble engaging in the subtle back-and-forth dance of nonverbal communication—they often do not return eye contact, do not display animated facial expression in reactions to others, and do not use gestures like head-nodding that others find affirming and engaging.

Research on Social Isolation, Disconnection, and Suicidal Behavior

In the last section on perceived burdensomeness, I noted that relatively few studies had empirically assessed the connection between burdensomeness and suicidality, though all studies were supportive of the link. The situation is different with regard to failed belongingness: The fact that those who die by suicide experience isolation and withdrawal before their deaths is among the clearest in all the literature on suicide.

An intriguing example involves language use by poets who died by suicide compared to nonsuicidal poets as the poets' deaths neared. These researchers used the Linguistic Inquiry and Word Count . . . to analyze text into its components—for example, tendency to use action verbs, words denoting negative emotion, and so on. Their results suggested escalating interpersonal disconnection in the suicidal poets but not the poets who died by other means. Specifically, as the suicidal poets' deaths approached, their use of interpersonal pronouns (e.g., "we") decreased noticeably. Similarly, Shneidman reports on a young man who had survived a self-inflicted gunshot wound and later wrote, "Those around me were as shadows, bare apparitions, but I was not actually conscious of them, only aware of myself and my plight. Death swallowed me long before I pulled the trigger. I was locked within myself."

Conner and colleagues assessed men with alcohol dependence who died by suicide. Among the risk factors for completed suicide were living alone and loss of a partner within the last month or two before death. Similarly, a comparison of those who died by suicide and those who died by other means revealed that those who died by suicide were more likely to have been recently separated and living alone. Significant others of people who had recently attempted suicide pointed to loneliness in the patients as an important factor in their suicide attempt.

A study of African-American women examined reasons for the association between types of childhood maltreatment and suicidal behavior. Of various factors examined, alienation (defined as inability to establish basic trust and achieve stable and satisfying relationships) was the most robust, fully explaining the link between all forms of childhood maltreatment and later suicidal behavior.

Marital Status, Parenting, and Suicidality

As the studies on social isolation might suggest, nonmarried status is a demographic risk factor for suicide. The majority of deaths by suicide among Native Americans of the Apache, Navajo, and Pueblo tribes, for instance, were of single people. Statistics indicate the following suicide rates in the United States in 1999: divorced—32.7 per 100,000; widowed—19.7 per 100,000; single—17.8 per 100,000; married—10.6 per 100,000. These national statistics are of course open to many interpretations, but they are consistent with the view that belongingness (as indicated by married status) is a suicide buffer, whereas thwarted belongingness (as indicated by nonmarried status) is a risk for death by suicide. This is particularly evident with regard to divorce (which confers a threefold increase in risk relative to married status). In context of the model proposed here, it is tempting to speculate that suicide rates among divorced people are particularly high because divorce can affect both basic feelings of effectiveness (e.g., feeling a failure as a spouse) and basic feelings of connectedness (losing social contact not only with a spouse, but potentially with the spouse's family, with children, and with friends previously shared with the spouse).

These statistics on marital status converge with a literature inspired by Durkheim's emphasis on failures of social integration as a source for suicide. For example, a study of suicidality and family and parental functioning in over 4,000 high school students in Iceland concluded that those adolescents who were well integrated into their families thereby derived protection from suicide; the indices related to family integration (cf. belongingness) wielded stronger influence on suicidality than did indices related to how the parents were functioning.

With regard to connections with children, there is evidence that having large numbers of children protects against suicide. In a study of nearly a million women in Norway, over 1,000 died by suicide during a fifteen-year follow-up. Women with six or more children had one-fifth the risk of death by suicide as compared to other women. The suicide rates in Canada's provinces are associated with birth rates, such that more births correspond with fewer suicides, consistent with the possibility that ties to new children buffer against suicidality. In a very persuasive study on this point on over 18,000 Danish people who died by suicide and over 370,000 matched controls, having children, especially young children, was protective against suicide, even when accounting for powerful suicide-related variables like marital status and psychiatric disorder. To my knowledge, no studies like this have been conducted specifically on fathers, parenthood, and suicide.

The result on mothers, parenthood, and suicide may even extend to pregnancy. Marzuk and colleagues examined the autopsy reports for all women who died by suicide in New York City from 1990 to 1993 and compared them to overall mortality statistics in age- and race-matched women in New York during the same time period. During the study, there were 315 women who died by suicide in New York City, six of whom were pregnant, which was one-third the number that was expected given New York City female population rates. These researchers concluded that pregnancy conferred protection from suicide; I would suggest that the protective influence involved feelings of connection to the baby, as well as feeling needed by the baby and thus not a burden.

Pregnancy, by itself, is no solution to longstanding feelings of disconnection and perceived burdensomeness, however. In fact, consistent with this assertion, my colleagues and I found that initially pessimistic teenagers reported low depression while pregnant (perhaps because of the belief that connection to the baby and the baby's father would solve ongoing problems), but reported high depression postpartum (perhaps because, in addition to the usual physiological and psychological challenges of childbirth, the idea that motherhood would solve ongoing problems was not confirmed).

If failed belongingness is implicated in suicidality, one might predict that twins enjoy some protection from suicide, given the belongingness inherent in twinship. If fact, there is evidence to support this prediction. Using population-based register data from Denmark, researchers found that twins have a reduced risk of suicide. The suicide rate among the more than 21,000 twins, as compared to non-twins, was 26 percent lower for men and 31 percent lower for women. Some studies have found mental illness to be slightly more common among twins than among singletons. Twins' belongingness may offset the risk for suicide conferred by slightly higher rates of mental disorders.

The loss of a parent relatively early in life appears to confer risk for suicide later in life. In Eskimos in the Bering Strait region, the majority of a sample of suicide attempters had lost a parent during childhood. Close to half of a sample of famous people who died by suicide experienced loss of a parent before age eighteen. Researchers compared the records of patients with borderline personality disorder who had died by suicide to living control patients with borderline personality (a stringent comparison, because some proportion of the living control patients were at elevated risk for later suicide by virtue of their borderline personality disorder diagnosis). The suicide group experienced childhood losses such as death of a parent more frequently than the control group. There are of course alternative explanations to the link between early separation from a parent and later suicidality in the child (especially if the parent's death was by suicide, in which case genetics would be implicated), but a diminished sense of belongingness from losing a parent is one viable viewpoint.

Immigration and Suicide

Like separations from parents, separations from a "mother country," according to a belongingness view, might be associated with heightened suicidality. The very high rate of suicide in Buenos Aires, Argentina in the late 1800s was attributed to massive immigration, with a high rate of suicide among foreign-born males. In a study of nearly lethal suicide attempts by 153 people and 513 matched controls, participants were asked about changing residence over the past year. Changing residence in the past year was associated with a nearly lethal suicide attempt, as were specific dimensions related to the move, such as distance and difficulty staying in touch. All of these aspects of moving are associated with a sense of disconnection.

National Tragedies and Suicide

In times of acute national crisis, people pull together, and belongingness should thus increase. According to my model, then, national crises, despite their negative aspects, should nevertheless suppress suicide rates. There are data to support this view, at least regarding three salient national tragedies in the United States. First, suicide rates in response to the assassination of President John F. Kennedy were investigated. In the twenty-nine U.S. cities included in the report, *no* suicides were reported during November 22–30, 1963. By contrast, several suicides occurred during November 22–30 of years before and after 1963. Second, in the two weeks preceding the Challenger disaster in 1986, there were 1,212 suicides in the United States; in the two weeks following the disaster, there were 1,099. Third, although detailed suicide rates are not readily available for the period following the terrorist attacks of September 11, 2001, calls to 1-800-SUICIDE, a national toll-free suicide crisis hotline, plummeted from an average of around 600 calls per day to around 300 per day—an all-time low—in the days following the attacks.

An additional documented phenomenon that conforms to this pattern is decreased suicide rates during times of war. Regarding war, in their classic study, Dublin and Bunzel stated, "Contrary to what might be expected, times of disorganization and chaos such as prevail during a war apparently do not increase that personal disintegration which leads to a larger number of self-inflicted deaths. It would seem that the all-engrossing, unaccustomed activities and the enlargement of interests to include more than the ordinary petty concerns of a limited circle of family and friends absorb people's entire attention and prevent them from morbid brooding over individual troubles and disappointments . . . There is no time during war to indulge in personal or imaginary worries." They go on to document relatively low rates of suicide during the American Civil War and the Franco–Prussian War.

Statistical bulletins put out by Metropolitan Life Insurance Company in the 1940s also show low suicide rates during World War II. A bulletin from 1942 states, "The death rate from suicides among the policyholders of the Metropolitan Life Insurance Co. for 1942 is practically the same as for 1941 and is with one exception the lowest on record. Likewise, 1941 suicide rates in England were 15%, in Germany 30% below the 1939 level. Wartime drop in suicide rates is a general phenomenon observable even in neutral nations. The phenomenon is ascribed to economic forces and such psychological forces as forgetting one's petty difficulties and finding a new purpose in rallying to the defense of one's country."

A postwar bulletin put out in 1946 read, "The downward trend characterizing the suicide death rate in this country during the war was abruptly reversed following V-E Day." Thus, nationally absorbing incidents, whether they are tragedies or wars, tend to suppress suicide rates, probably because they pull people together. In the case of war, the pulling-together effect appears to fade as the war ends.

Does Being a Sports Fan Have Anything to Do with Suicide?

The camaraderie and sense of belongingness from being a fan of sports teams can be considerable, especially under conditions of success (as many who have lived in university towns have observed when the university wins a national championship). It is interesting to consider, then, whether teams' success affects suicide rates; from the present perspective, it might, in that increased belongingness should be associated with lower suicide rates.

Believe it or not, some studies suggest a connection between sports teams' performance and suicide rates. One study assessed the suicide rates as they related to success of professional sports teams in twenty U.S. metropolitan areas from 1971 to 1990. Results showed that the team making the playoffs and winning a championship both were related to a decline in the local suicide rate. Another study examined the association between a soccer team's defeat (high-profile defeats of Nottingham Forest in 1991 and 1992) and deliberate self-poisoning. The accident and emergency records of a university hospital were examined, and results indicated an excess of deliberate self-poisoning incidents during the time frames following the defeats. A third study postulated that a long run by hockey's Montreal Canadiens in the Stanley Cup playoffs is a time when people in Quebec experience increased informal interpersonal contact, and that this would serve to suppress the suicide rate in the area. By contrast, when the Canadiens are eliminated early on, the study hypothesized that interpersonal contact (belongingness) would be relatively less, and the suicide rate might increase. One of the study's clearer results was an increase in the suicide rate in young men in Quebec when the Canadiens were eliminated from the playoffs early on.

It appears that sports teams' poor performance can affect suicide rates. Can good performance do so as well? My students and I recently conducted three studies to see if sports-related "pulling together" is associated with lower suicide rates. In the first study, the suicide rates in Franklin County (Columbus), Ohio, and Alachua County (Gainesville), Florida were correlated with the final national ranking of the local college football teams—the Ohio State Buckeyes and the Florida Gators, respectively. These teams are of substantial concern to the local population. Given the effect that these teams' success has on their communities, we expected that there may be an association between the teams' final national ranking (which is known by early January of a given year) and the suicide rate in that year. In fact, we found that suicide rates in both Franklin County and Alachua County were associated with national rankings of the college teams, such that better rankings were related to lower suicide rates.

In the second of our three studies, we made a prediction regarding the "Miracle on Ice," when the U.S. Olympic hockey team upset the Russians, the world's dominant hockey team at the time. This occurred on February 22, 1980. It is fair to say that the 1980 U.S. Olympic hockey team's surprising victory over the dominant USSR team captured the country's attention. In fact, twenty-two years later, the players were the final torchbearers for the Salt Lake Winter Games, and there was a 2004 movie about the team entitled *Miracle*. The victory itself was amazing, but its resonance was heightened by the geopolitical climate at the time. On February 22, 1980—the date of the "Miracle on Ice"—the Iran hostage crisis was in its 111th day, and the Soviet Union's invasion of Afghanistan was approximately thirty days old. The victory, both in and of itself and because of its symbolic qualities, clearly exerted a "pulling together" effect on people in the United States. We therefore expected that the U.S. suicide rate might be particularly low on February 22, 1980 as compared to other February 22nds before and after. In fact it was—fewer suicides occurred on the day of the "Miracle on Ice" than on any other February 22 in the 1970s and 1980s.

These first two studies, as well as the previous literature on sports phenomena and suicide, leave open the possibility that suicide rates are lower at times of success not because of pulling together, but because of a sense of increased efficacy, vicariously obtained through the team's success. The studies on national disasters are not compatible with this possibility; nevertheless, in our third study, we were able to address it directly in the domain of sports by examining the number of suicides occurring in the United States on Super Bowl Sunday, as compared to suicides occurring the Sunday before and after. Though approximately a third of the U.S. population watches the Super Bowl, the majority are not devoted fans of either of the teams in a given Super Bowl; thus the "vicarious efficacy" explanation would not be a convincing explanation for any Super Bowl effect. We predicted that suicide rates on Super Bowl Sundays would be lower than on comparison Sundays, but only from the mid-1980s on, when the Super Bowl was firmly entrenched in the national consciousness as an occasion for social gathering (not just for men, but for women too, in part because of the advertising and spectacle associated with the game—a phenomenon that took hold in the early- to mid-1980s). This was precisely what we found.

Although none of these three studies alone provides conclusive evidence that sports-related "pulling together" increases belongingness and thus leads to reduced suicide rates, taken as a whole these studies provide converging evidence that is consistent with the hypothesis. This is particularly true when it is considered together with the diverse and converging lines of evidence (on twins, parents, poets, Faulkner, etc.) relating low belongingness and suicidality.

Fans of teams that have not won championships in decades may be wondering where they fit in here. A prominent example involves fans of the Chicago Cubs (though having grown up in Atlanta, I would point out that I can count major Atlanta sports championships on one finger, whereas people in Chicago have fared far better). Would I predict high suicide rates in Chicago because of the Cubs? My answer is no, and again, it has to do with belongingness. There is a kind of camaraderie inherent in the Cubs' plight, and Cubs fans have pulled together, much as people do for serious tragedies. Another interesting example, of course, is the Boston Red Sox. Like the Cubs, their fans were long-suffering . . . until the fall of 2004, that is, when the Red Sox won the World Series. When detailed suicide data are available for this period in Boston, it will be very interesting to see whether the success of the Red Sox suppressed local suicide rates.

According to the model described here, serious suicidal behavior requires the desire for death. The desire for death is composed of two psychological states—perceived burdensomeness and failed belongingness. On belongingness, recall the example of the man who left a note in his apartment that said, "I'm going to walk to the bridge. If one person smiles at me on the way, I will not jump." The man jumped to his death. On burdensomeness, recall the study that genuine attempts are often characterized by a desire to make others better off, whereas nonsuicidal self-injury is often characterized by desire to express anger or punish oneself. Examples like these support the direct involvement of failed belongingness and perceived burdensomeness in the desire for death. Either of these states, in isolation, is not sufficient to instill the desire for death. When these states co-occur, however, the desire for death is produced; if combined with the acquired ability to enact lethal self-injury, the desire for death can lead to a serious suicide attempt or to death by suicide.

REVIEW QUESTIONS

1. Discuss the five clusters of psychological needs that suicides tend to fall into.
2. What effects does marital status have on suicide rates?
3. What does Joiner mean by the concept "suicide buffer"?

Chapter 20

SELF-INJURERS: A "LONELY CROWD"

PATRICIA A. ADLER
PETER ADLER

Some deviants commit their acts as loners, without the support of fellow deviants. A good example is the newly emerging self-injurers, people who purposely damage some part of their bodies. These people do not know other individuals who participate in their form of deviance, or if they do, they generally do not congregate with them and do not discuss their deviance together. This relative isolation requires the lonely deviants to violate social norms on their own, without the help and support of others. They must decide to do their deviance by themselves and figure out on their own how to do it. Without the company of others, they lack the benefits of a deviant subculture from which to draw rationalizations and justifications that can neutralize the deviancy of their acts. Of all forms of deviants, self-injurers as solitary deviants seem most entrenched in the conventional culture through which they are forced to view their deviant acts with guilt and shame.

To take a closer look at this lonely crowd of self-injurers, we did a study on people who cut, burned, or branded themselves, with self-cutters being the majority. In our research, we conducted in-depth interviews with 25 self-injurers between 2001 and 2004. Participants ranged in age from 16 to 35, who had mostly, but not entirely, stopped injuring themselves. Most self-injury occurred when the subjects were in middle and high school, with only a smattering of them continuing past that age. Nearly three-quarters of the people we interviewed were women, and all were white. Subjects were gathered through a convenience sample of individuals who heard, usually on one of our campuses, that we were interested in talking with people about their self-injury. Those who were interested came forward and contacted us via email, asking for an interview. All of the interviews were conducted on campus in our faculty offices, and many were with college students, friends of students, university employees, or local high school students. Though self-selected for this research, our subjects likely represent the majority of self-injurers, who perform relatively minor, moderate rather than severe forms of body modification on themselves (Conterio and Lader, 1998; Favazza, 1996; Favazza and Conterio, 1989; Harris, 2000; Strong, 1998).

Not all of the self-injurers we interviewed were completely loners. Some cut, branded, burned, or electroshocked themselves in the company of others. The social dynamics and meanings of this kind of self-injury were dramatically different from those in the loner group. In this paper, we focus only on the loners, who comprised nearly 80 percent of our sample.

CHARACTERISTICS OF LONELY DEVIANCE

The people we studied injured themselves for a variety of reasons, including depression, malaise, alienation, and rebellion. For them, especially the younger ones, self-injury provided a form of comfort that assisted them during a stressful

Source: "Self-Injurers as Loners," by Patricia A. Adler and Peter Adler. © 2004 by Patricia A. Adler and Peter Adler. Reprinted by permission of the authors.

period of their lives. But once they became self-injurers, they entered a world of solitary deviance with certain characteristics.

Creating Deviant Meanings

As loners, self-injurers were on their own in creating meanings and rationalizations that could legitimate their deviance. Other deviants often draw on their experiences as members of their deviant subculture, as well as the larger conventional culture of their society, to support their deviant activities. Consider, for example, convicted rapists. Past research has shown how they rationalized their crime (Stevens, 1999; Scully and Marolla, 1984). They denied the violent and coercive nature of their acts and suggested instead that their victims precipitated or desired the incidents. Rapists also drew on the cultural myths about women being men's property, for example, to justify their possessive aggression against their victims. But self-injurers had a much more difficult time giving similar social meanings and legitimacy to their acts because their deviance was, especially initially, undefined and unclear. See how Natalie, a 19-year-old college sophomore, struggled to make sense of her self-injury:

> *I guess at first I didn't think much about it. I knew that it was a source of relief for me, and that was all that mattered to me. And, of course, over time when it becomes more of an issue, and people start noticing it, and other people maybe start commenting on it. And then I had to start thinking more about it and what I was really doing and the consequences and what it meant. And I guess just the way that I thought about it was, at first, I was glad that I was able to do it because it made me feel better.*

After some time they developed their own, personally acceptable, views of their deviance. Some people focused on their neatness, that they were able to do it without making a mess. For others, control was the issue; they could control where their hurt would be. A common thing that many self-injurers shared was their relationship to the pain. Dana, a 19-year-old college sophomore, talked about her pain:

> *The thing with emotional pain—you can't see it! It's all inside. I keep it bottled up inside ninety percent of the time, and people can never, like, quantify emotional pain because it's all inside. And so I try to put a picture to that. That's how much I hurt, I did that to myself. Those cuts, that pain, came from inside here.*

Kyle, a 20-year-old junior, described how he would say to himself when he was ready to begin an episode of branding, "It's time for some pain."

Social Isolation

The deviance of self-injurers as loners was personal. They thus viewed their behavior as private, not to be shared with others. Other deviants, such as embezzlers or pharmacist drug addicts, had no special feeling of personal intensity about committing their deviant acts. But self-injurers, like many sexual asphyxiates, needed the focus and concentration of being alone while they were engaged in their deviance. It was all about them, and they were focused completely on themselves while in the act. It would detract from whatever social benefits such as social support they could get out of the experience if they did it in the company of others. Dana discussed the feeling she had about her self-absorption:

> *When I hurt like that, I get really self-involved. I get my blinders on. I'm all about me, and don't disturb me . . . so that if someone was cutting themselves in my house, even though I do it, I'd be uncomfortable. It's my thing, you know? I'm in control.*

When presented with the opportunity to interact with other self-injurers, many cutters passed it over. While some knew other self-injurers, or were introduced to the idea by knowing others who self-injured, they generally did not want to form a subculture or support group of self-injurers. When approached in high school by a classmate who tried to bond with her over their cutting, Mandy, an 18-year-old college freshman, rejected these overtures:

> *It scared me, I think, more than anything, because I didn't want to be the person she depended on be-*

> *cause I didn't feel ready for that. I still wouldn't, even if she came to me today and said that she needed something. I would be like, "I'm sorry."*

One of the primary reasons people self-injured was that they were lonely and depressed. Episodes of self-injury tended to occur when people were away from the company of friends and family, often in the afternoons after school or at night. They had time to sit around and reflect, while they felt bad. In thinking back on high school, many people noted it as a period in their lives where they spent a lot of time alone. Ironically, when they self-injured to avert their feelings of loneliness and depression, they felt more lonely and depressed. This often occurred when they held themselves back from being with people in situations where their scars would be noticeable. For example, Janice did not want to let the scars on her legs show among her classmates in the gym. As a result, she flunked physical education, for which she endured the ignorant jeers of her classmates, which in turn intensified her sense of loneliness and depression.

Practical Problems

Lacking a deviant subculture, self-injurers often found themselves on their own in coping with the practical problems posed by their deviance. Many of them worried about how to deal with them. Here is how Dana expressed her worry:

> *The practical side to it—how am I going to explain these cuts all over myself in the summer, to my friends? Am I going to go to a job interview with a big scar or a cut on my arm? And that really freaked me out—I don't want anyone to know, no one can know, no!*

Many self-injurers were unable to anticipate what people might say to them or ask them, and had no ready response when confronted by others. This was not a great problem prior to 1996 when self-injury was relatively rare. People could easily explain away their scars with almost any ridiculous answer and nobody questioned them. This all changed after 1996, when self-injury began to be more widely recognized and people became more suspicious. Longer-term cutters, whose parents had become aware of their behavior, were watched very carefully and often quizzed about their scars. This led them to move their cutting away from their hands and arms to less visible bodily locations such as their stomachs and the inside of their thighs.

In other forms of loner behavior such as sexual asphyxia, participants often shared their knowledge with a non-participant who assisted them in their deviance and also helped them keep it secret. By contrast, self-injurers seemed to lack this type of social support. Cutters and burners sometimes told their closest friends or boyfriends about their behavior, but these others usually tried to get them to desist, rather than aiding them.

Conventional Socialization

According to Best and Luckenbill (1982), loners who are deviants are socialized by conventional society, not by fellow deviants, and yet they choose deviance. They choose deviance, not because they want to contradict their socialization, but because they face situations where conventional courses of action are unattractive or unsatisfactory. In choosing deviance, then, they feel torn between what they should do as expected by society and what they want to do as desired by themselves. More positively, they feel simultaneously attracted to the conventional norms of society and their own deviant activity. Such ambivalence prevailed among the self-injurers in our study. As Dana described it,

> *It's not, and I'm not, like, and I never really argue with myself, like, I really want to cut myself but I shouldn't, you know? If I really want to, I do, because it's not all the time, so when it does, I just do it because I'm desperate to feel better, so it's never like, I never, I'm never at war with how I should deal with it, like "Oh, I really want to do it, where's the knife," and my other side being like, "Dana, don't do that." It's always like, one or the other. If I have the urge, I will.*

Without the support of fellow deviants, loners are under greater influence of conventional society than are other people who belong to a deviant group. This may explain why people who self-injured often condemned their own behavior and felt guilty for engaging in it. This is how Lisa, a 20-year-old college sophomore, talked about her deviance: "Oh yeah. I was ashamed of myself because it's disgusting and it's not normal . . . it's just bad to do, I think, to yourself."

Lacking the support of fellow deviants, thereby falling under the greater sway of conventional society, can also deter loners from carrying out their deviance to extremes. If they wanted to rebel, for example, they would not want to rebel too far. Thus, like most loners, one self-injuring young woman in our research found an intermediate point for balancing the strain between conventionality and deviancy. She burned herself occasionally, but never so much that it would make it impossible for her to enjoy social respectability and other benefits of conventional society. Like most other self-injurers, she effectively kept one foot firmly anchored in legitimacy while she dabbled in deviance, able to return anytime she wished to a conventional lifestyle without unduly damaging her "normal" identity.

CONCLUSION

As loners, self-injurers represent the least organizationally sophisticated form of deviant association. They are on their own without fellow deviants either assisting them in their deviant acts or keeping them company in their private moments when they are not engaged in deviance. In fact, they miss a wide gamut of other benefits that typically accrue to members of most other, nonsolitary deviant groups. These benefits may include the basic rudiments of deviant camaraderie, the social support from like-minded people, the guidance of deviant norms and values, an ideology that legitimizes their deviant acts, information providing practical, legal, and medical advice, and subcultural jargon and stories that enrich the deviant experience. By becoming absorbed in their deviance, self-injurers who are already lonely in the first place continue to find themselves lonely.

REFERENCES

Best, Joel, and David F. Luckenbill. 1982. *Organizing Deviance.* Englewood Cliffs, NJ: Prentice Hall.

Conterio, Karen, and Wendy Lader. 1998. *Bodily Harm: The Breakthrough Treatment Program for Self-Injurers.* New York: Hyperion.

Favazza, Armand R., and Karen Conterio. 1989. "Female Habitual Self-Mutilators." *Acta Psychiatrica Scandinavica* 79(3):283–289.

Favazza, Armand R. 1996. *Bodies Under Siege: Self-Mutilation and Body Modification in Culture and Psychiatry*, 2nd ed. Baltimore: Johns Hopkins University Press.

Harris, Jennifer. 2000. "Self Harm: Cutting the Bad Out of Me." *Qualitative Health Research* March 10(2):164–173.

Scully, Diana, and Joseph Marolla. 1984. "Convicted Rapists' Vocabulary of Motive: Excuses and Justifications." *Social Problems* 31(5):530–544.

Stevens, Dennis J. 1999. *Inside the Mind of a Serial Rapist.* San Francisco: Austin & Winfield.

Strong, Marilee. 1998. *A Bright Red Scream: Self-Mutilation and the Language of Pain.* New York: Penguin Putnam.

REVIEW QUESTIONS

1. According to Best and Luckenbill, why do people choose deviance as a course of action?
2. How can self-cutting lead to more self-cutting?
3. What types of deviants, other than those in the article, can be classified as "loners"? Explain your response.

CHAPTER 21

BEING SANE IN INSANE PLACES

DAVID L. ROSENHAN

If sanity and insanity exist, how shall we know them?

The question is nether capricious nor itself insane. However much we may be personally convinced that we can tell the normal from the abnormal, the evidence is simply not compelling. It is commonplace, for example, to read about murder trials wherein eminent psychiatrists for the defense are contradicted by equally eminent psychiatrists for the prosecution on the matter of the defendant's sanity. More generally, there are a great deal of conflicting data on the reliability, utility, and meaning of such terms as "sanity," "insanity," "mental illness," and "schizophrenia." Finally, as early as 1934, Benedict suggested that normality and abnormality are not universal. What is viewed as normal in one culture may be seen as quite aberrant in another. Thus, notions of normality and abnormality may not be quite as accurate as people believe they are.

To raise questions regarding normality and abnormality is in no way to question the fact that some behaviors are deviant or odd. Murder is deviant. So, too, are hallucinations. Nor does raising such questions deny the existence of the personal anguish that is often associated with "mental illness." Anxiety and depression exist. Psychological suffering exists. But normality and abnormality, sanity and insanity, and the diagnoses that flow from them, may be less substantive than many believe them to be.

At its heart, the question of whether the sane can be distinguished from the insane . . . is a simple matter: do the salient characteristics that lead to diagnoses reside in the patients themselves or in the environments and contexts in which observers find them?

Gains can be made in deciding which of these is more nearly accurate by getting normal people . . . admitted to psychiatric hospitals and then determining whether they were discovered to be sane and, if so, how. If the sanity of such pseudopatients were always detected, there would be *prima facie* evidence that a sane individual can be distinguished from the insane context in which he is found. Normality . . . is distinct enough that it can be recognized wherever it occurs, for it is carried within the person. If, on the other hand, the sanity of the pseudopatients were never discovered, serious difficulties would arise for those who support traditional modes of psychiatric diagnosis.

This article describes such an experiment. Eight sane people [including the author] gained secret admission to 12 different hospitals. Their diagnostic experiences constitute the data of the first part of this article; the remainder is devoted to a description of their experiences in psychiatric institutions.

PSEUDOPATIENTS AND THEIR SETTINGS

The eight pseudopatients were a varied group. One was a psychology graduate student in his

Source: David L. Rosenhan, "On Being Sane in Insane Places," *Science*, vol. 179 (January 19, 1973), pp. 250–258.

20s. The remaining seven were older and "established." Among them were three psychologists, a pediatrician, a psychiatrist, a painter, and a housewife. Three pseudopatients were women, five were men.

The settings were similarly varied. In order to generalize the findings, admission into a variety of hospitals was sought. The 12 hospitals in the sample were located in five different states on the East and West coasts. Some were old and shabby, some were quite new. Some were research-oriented, others not. Some had good staff–patient ratios, others were quite understaffed. Only one was a strictly private hospital. All of the others were supported by state or federal funds or, in one instance, by university funds.

After calling the hospital for an appointment, the pseudopatient arrived at the admissions office complaining that he had been hearing voices. Asked what the voices said, he replied that they were often unclear, but as far as he could tell they said "empty," "hollow," and "thud." The voices were unfamiliar and were of the same sex as the pseudopatient. The choice of these symptoms was occasioned by their apparent similarity to existential symptoms. Such symptoms are alleged to arise from painful concerns about the perceived meaninglessness of one's life. It is as if the hallucinating person were saying, "My life is empty and hollow." The choice of these symptoms was also determined by the *absence* of a single report of existential psychoses in the literature. . . .

Immediately upon admission to this psychiatric ward, the pseudopatient ceased simulating *any* symptoms of abnormality.

. . . [T]he pseudopatient behaved on the ward as he "normally" behaved. The pseudopatient spoke to patients and staff as he might ordinarily. Because there is uncommonly little to do on a psychiatric ward, he attempted to engage others in conversation. When asked by staff how he was feeling, he indicated that he was fine, that he no longer experienced symptoms. He responded to instructions from attendants, to calls for medication (which was not swallowed), and to dining-hall instructors. Beyond such activities as were available to him on the admissions ward, he spent his time writing down his observations about the ward, its patients, and the staff. Initially these notes were written "secretly," but as it soon became clear that no one much cared, they were subsequently written on standard tablets of paper in such public places as the dayroom. No secret was made of these activities.

The pseudopatient, very much as a true psychiatric patient, entered a hospital with no foreknowledge of when he would be discharged. Each was told that he would have to get out by his own devices, essentially by convincing the staff that he was sane. The psychological stresses associated with hospitalization were considerable, and all but one of the pseudopatients desired to be discharged almost immediately after being admitted. They were, therefore, motivated not only to behave sanely, but to be paragons of cooperation.

THE NORMAL ARE NOT DETECTABLY SANE

Despite their public "show" of sanity, the pseudopatients were never detected. Admitted, except in one case, with a diagnosis of schizophrenia, each was discharged with a diagnosis of schizophrenia "in remission." The label "in remission" should in no way be dismissed as a formality, for at no time during any hospitalization had any question been raised about any pseudopatient's simulation. Nor are there any indications in the hospital records that the pseudopatient's status was suspect. Rather, the evidence is strong that, once labeled schizophrenic, the pseudopatient was stuck with that label. If the pseudopatient was to be discharged, he must naturally be "in remission"; but he was not sane, nor, in the institution's view, had he ever been sane.

The uniform failure to recognize sanity cannot be attributed to the quality of the hospitals, for, although there were considerable variations among them, several are considered excellent. Nor can it be alleged that there was simply not enough time to observe the pseudopatients.

Length of hospitalization ranged from 7 to 52 days, with an average of 19 days.

Finally, it cannot be said that the failure to recognize the pseudopatients' sanity was due to the fact that they were not behaving sanely. While there was clearly some tension present in all of them, their daily visitors could detect no serious behavioral consequences—nor, indeed, could other patients. It was quite common for the patients to "detect" the pseudopatients' sanity. During the first three hospitalizations, when accurate counts were kept, 35 of a total of 118 patients on the admissions ward voiced their suspicions, some vigorously. "You're not crazy. You're a journalist, or a professor [referring to the continual note-taking]. You're checking up on the hospital." While most of the patients were reassured by the pseudopatient's insistence that he had been sick before he came in but was fine now, some continued to believe that the pseudopatient was sane throughout his hospitalization. The fact that the patients often recognized normality when staff did not raises important questions.

THE STICKINESS OF PSYCHODIAGNOSTIC LABELS

Beyond the tendency to call the healthy sick—a tendency that accounts better for diagnostic behavior on admission than it does for such behavior after a lengthy period of exposure—the data speak to the massive role of labeling in psychiatric assessment. Having once been labeled schizophrenic, there is nothing the pseudopatient can do to overcome the tag. The tag profoundly colors others' perceptions of him and his behavior. . . .

All pseudopatients took extensive notes publicly. Under ordinary circumstances, such behavior would have raised questions in the minds of observers, as, in fact, it did among patients. Indeed, it seemed so certain that the notes would elicit suspicion that elaborate precautions were taken to remove them from the ward each day. But the precautions proved needless. The closest any staff member came to questioning these notes occurred when one pseudopatient asked his physician what kind of medication he was receiving and began to write down the response. "You needn't write it," he was told gently. "If you have trouble remembering, just ask me again."

If no questions were asked of the pseudopatients, how was their writing interpreted? Nursing records for three patients indicate that the writing was seen as an aspect of their pathological behavior. "Patient engages in writing behavior" was the daily nursing comment on one of the pseudopatients who was never questioned about his writing. Given that the patient is in the hospital, he must be psychologically disturbed. And given that he is disturbed, continuous writing must be a behavioral manifestation of that disturbance, perhaps a subset of the compulsive behaviors that are sometimes correlated with schizophrenia.

The notes kept by pseudopatients are full of patient behaviors that were misinterpreted by well-intentioned staff. Often enough, a patient would go "berserk" because he had, wittingly or unwittingly, been mistreated by, say, an attendant. A nurse coming upon the scene would rarely inquire even cursorily into the environmental stimuli of the patient's behavior. Rather, she assumed that his upset derived from pathology, not from his present interactions with other staff members. Occasionally, the staff might assume that the patient's family (especially when they had recently visited) or other patients had stimulated the outburst. But never were the staff found to assume that one of themselves or the structure of the hospital had anything to do with a patient's behavior.

A psychiatric label has a life and an influence of its own. Once the impression has been formed that the patient is schizophrenic, the expectation is that he will continue to be schizophrenic. When a sufficient amount of time has passed, during which the patient has done nothing bizarre, he is considered to be in remission and available for discharge. But the label endures beyond discharge, with the unconfirmed expectation that he will behave as a schizophrenic again.

POWERLESSNESS AND DEPERSONALIZATION

Eye contact and verbal contact reflect concern and individuation; their absence, avoidance and depersonalization. The data I have presented do not do justice to the rich daily encounters that grew up around matters of depersonalization and avoidance. I have records of patients who were beaten by staff for the sin of having initiated verbal contact. During my own experience, for example, one patient was beaten in the presence of other patients for having approached an attendant and told him, "I like you." Occasionally, punishment meted out to patients for misdemeanors seemed so excessive that it could not be justified by the most radical interpretations of psychiatric canon. Nevertheless, they appeared to go unquestioned. Tempers were often short. A patient who had not heard a call for medication would be roundly excoriated, and the morning attendants would often wake patients with, "Come on, you m——f——s, out of bed!"

Neither anecdotal nor "hard" data can convey the overwhelming sense of powerlessness which invades the individual as he is continually exposed to the depersonalization of the psychiatric hospital. It hardly matters *which* psychiatric hospital—the excellent public ones and the very plush private hospital were better than the rural and shabby ones in this regard, but, again, the features that psychiatric hospitals had in common overwhelmed by far their apparent differences.

Powerlessness was evident everywhere. The patient is deprived of many of his legal rights by dint of his psychiatric commitment. He is shorn of credibility by virtue of his psychiatric label. His freedom of movement is restricted. He cannot initiate contact with the staff, but may only respond to such overtures as they make. Personal privacy is minimal. Patient quarters and possessions can be entered and examined by any staff member, for whatever reason. His personal history and anguish is available to any staff member . . . who chooses to read his folder, regardless of their therapeutic relationship to him. His personal hygiene and waste evacuation are often monitored. The water closets may have no doors.

A nurse unbuttoned her uniform to adjust her brassiere in the presence of an entire ward of viewing men. One did not have the sense that she was being seductive. Rather, she didn't notice us. A group of staff persons might point to a patient in the dayroom and discuss him animatedly, as if he were not there. . . .

THE CONSEQUENCES OF LABELING AND DEPERSONALIZATION

. . . [W]e tend to invent "knowledge" and assume that we understand more than we actually do. We seem unable to acknowledge that we simply don't know. The needs for diagnosis and remediation of behavioral and emotional problems are enormous. But rather than acknowledge that we are just embarking on understanding, we continue to label patients "schizophrenic," "manic-depressive," and "insane," as if in those words we had captured the essence of understanding. The facts of the matter are that we have known for a long time that diagnoses are often not useful or reliable, but we have nevertheless continued to use them. We now know that we cannot distinguish insanity from sanity. It is depressing to consider how that information will be used.

Not merely depressing, but frightening. How many people, one wonders, are sane but not recognized as such in our psychiatric institutions? How many have been needlessly stripped of their privileges of citizenship, from the right to vote and drive to that of handling their own accounts? How many have feigned insanity in order to avoid the criminal consequences of their behavior, and, conversely, how many would rather stand trial than live interminably in a psychiatric hospital—but are wrongly thought to be mentally ill? How many have been stigmatized by well-intentioned, but nevertheless erroneous, diagnoses?

Finally, how many patients might be "sane" outside the psychiatric hospital but seem insane in it—not because craziness resides in them, as it were, but because they are responding to a bizarre setting, one that may be unique to institutions which harbor nether people? Goffman calls the process of socialization to such institutions "mortification"—an apt metaphor that includes the processes of depersonalization that have been described here. And while it is impossible to know whether the pseudopatients' responses to these processes are characteristic of all inmates—they were, after all, not real patients—it is difficult to believe that these processes of socialization to a psychiatric hospital provide useful attitudes or habits of response for living in the "real world."

SUMMARY AND CONCLUSIONS

It is clear that we cannot distinguish the sane from the insane in psychiatric hospitals. The hospital itself imposes a special environment in which the meanings of behavior can easily be misunderstood. The consequences to patients hospitalized in such an environment—the powerlessness [and] depersonalization . . .—seem undoubtedly countertherapeutic.

I do not, even now, understand this problem well enough to perceive solutions. But two matters seem to have some promise. The first concerns the proliferation of community mental health facilities, of crisis intervention centers, of the human potential movement, and of behavior therapies that, for all of their own problems, tend to avoid psychiatric labels, to focus on specific problems and behaviors, and to retain the individual in a relatively non-pejorative environment. Clearly, to the extent that we refrain from sending the distressed to insane places, our impressions of them are less likely to be distorted. (The risk of distorted perceptions, it seems to me, is always present, since we are much more sensitive to an individual's behaviors and verbalizations than we are to the subtle contextual stimuli that often promote them. At issue here is a ma tude. And, as I have shown, the magnitu tortion is exceedingly high in the extreme cont that is a psychiatric hospital.)

The second matter that might prove promising speaks to the need to increase the sensitivity of mental health workers and researchers to the *Catch 22* position of psychiatric patient. Simply reading materials in this area will be of help to some such workers and researchers. For others, directly experiencing the impact of psychiatric hospitalization will be of enormous use. Clearly, further research into the social psychology of such total institutions will both facilitate treatment and deepen understanding.

I and the other pseudopatients in the psychiatric setting had distinctly negative reactions. We do not pretend to describe the subjective experiences of true patients. Theirs may be different from ours, particularly with the passage of time and the necessary process of adaptation to one's environment. But we can and do speak to the relatively more objective indices of treatment within the hospital. It could be a mistake, and a very unfortunate one, to consider that what happened to us derived from malice or stupidity on the part of the staff. Quite the contrary, our overwhelming impression of them was of people who really cared, who were committed and who were uncommonly intelligent. Where they failed, as they sometimes did painfully, it would be more accurate to attribute those failures to the environment in which they, too, found themselves than to personal callousness. Their perceptions and behavior were controlled by the situation, rather than being motivated by a malicious disposition. In a more benign environment, one that was less attached to global diagnosis, their behaviors and judgments might have been more benign and effective.

REVIEW QUESTIONS

1. What effects does a psychiatric label have on a person?

2. How was powerlessness evident in the psychiatric hospitals?

3. What ethical concerns arise from Rosenhan's experiment?

CHAPTER 22

THE EMERGENCE OF HYPERACTIVE ADULTS AS ABNORMAL

PETER CONRAD
DEBORAH POTTER

Over the past thirty years there has been keen sociological interest in the medicalization of deviance and social problems. By now, there are dozens of case examples of medicalization and a body of literature has accumulated that has loosely been called "medicalization theory" (see Williams and Calnan 1996). At this point, it is important to build on this corpus of knowledge to better understand different aspects of medicalization. Medicalization is, by definition, about the extension of medical jurisdiction or the expansion of medical boundaries. In different situations, medical professionals, political reformers, lay activists, or social movements have promoted boundary expansion. Most medicalization studies focus on how nonmedical problems become defined as medical problems, usually as illnesses or disorders. But there has been less examination of how medicalized categories themselves can be subjects of expansion, thus, engendering further medicalization. . . .

This paper [focuses] on the emergence of the diagnosis of Attention Deficit-Hyperactivity Disorder (ADHD) in adults in the 1990s. How did hyperactivity, which was deemed largely a disorder of childhood, become adult ADHD? This research follows on Conrad's study of the medicalization of hyperactivity published in the 1970s (Conrad 1975, 1976). Our interest here, however, is also to investigate this case as an example of how medicalized categories, once established, can expand to become broader and more inclusive. . . . After reviewing the state of childhood hyperactivity as a medicalized diagnosis in the 1970s, we trace the emergence of "adult hyperactives" among those whose childhood symptoms persisted into adulthood, and then examine how this was transformed into the category "ADHD adults." We show how lay, professional, and media claims helped establish the expanded diagnosis. We identify particular aspects of the social context that contributed to the rise of adult ADHD.

HYPERACTIVITY IN THE 1970S

The most significant criterion for diagnosis [of ADHD] was a child's behavior, especially at school. The emphasis in identification was on hyperactive and disruptive behaviors (Conrad 1976). The major treatments for hyperactivity were stimulant medications, especially Ritalin. During the 1960s, the disorder became increasingly well known, due, in part, to publicity it received concerning controversies about drug treatment. By the middle 1970s, it had become the most common childhood psychiatric problem (Gross and Wilson 1974) and special clinics to identify and treat the disorder were established,

Source: Peter Conrad and Deborah Potter, "From Hyperactive Children to ADHD Adults: Observations on the Expansion of Medical Categories," *Social Problems*, vol. 47, no. 4 (2000), pp. 559–582.

although most children were diagnosed by their pediatrician or primary care physician.

THE EMERGENCE OF "ADULT HYPERACTIVES"

Beginning in the late 1970s, several cohort studies were published which followed children who had been originally diagnosed with hyperactivity a decade or more earlier and traced their development into adulthood. These studies established that for some hyperactive children, the symptoms persisted into adolescence and even into adulthood. Thus emerged the notion of what we call "adult hyperactives," hyperactive children who did not "outgrow" their symptoms and still manifested some problems as adults.

In [1987], two publications aimed at lay readers heralded a new category of "ADHD Adults"—adults who had not been diagnosed as children, but had suffered from symptoms. Although later claims would be made by those who could not trace their suffering to their youth, these early claims were made either by or for those who, retrospectively, could identify signs of ADHD in their childhood.

In 1987, Paul Wender, a longtime hyperactivity researcher, published a book that examined hyperactivity throughout the life span. Although the book was entitled, *The Hyperactive Child, Adolescent and Adult*, only one chapter described adults with ADHD symptoms. Nonetheless, the book targeted a lay audience and would be cited frequently in subsequent years.

The same year, Frank Wolkenberg (1987), a free-lance photographer and picture editor, wrote a first-person account in the *New York Times Magazine* about his discovery that he had ADHD despite his apparently successful life. When he sought treatment for depression and suicidal ideation, he was diagnosed with ADHD by a psychologist whose specialty was learning disorders. Wolkenberg then began reinterpreting several clues from early in his life (e.g., impulsivity, distractibility, disorganization, and emotional volatility) as signs of the disorder. This highly visible testimony of someone not previously diagnosed with ADHD as a child put the idea of "ADHD Adults" into the public realm. No one had diagnosed him as hyperactive as a child, yet now, he was attributing "seemingly inexplicable failures . . . all unnecessary and many inexcusable" to ADHD. He suggested it was a neurobiological dysfunction "of genetic origin," thus attributing his life problems to a chemical imbalance.

As the notion of ADHD in adulthood was filtering into the public, the psychiatric profession was also turning attention to this new problem. Clinics for adults with ADHD were established at Wayne State University in 1989 and two years later at the University of Massachusetts in Worcester (Jaffe 1995).

In 1990, Dr. Alan Zametkin of the National Institute of Mental Health and several of his colleagues published an often-cited article in the *New England Journal of Medicine*. Using positron-emission tomography (PET) scanning to measure brain metabolism, Zametkin demonstrated different levels of brain activity in individuals with ADHD compared to those without the disorder, providing new evidence for a biologic basis for ADHD. Because of the risks inherent in research involving radiologic images, the researchers used adult subjects who both had childhood histories of hyperactivity and were biological parents of hyperactive children. Although not their intention, Zametkin's work became one of the key professional sources cited by others to demonstrate the presence of ADHD in adults (e.g., Bartlett 1990; and *Newsweek*, December 3, 1990), since it appeared to bolster claims that ADHD could persist into or develop during adulthood. While the study made national headlines, additional follow-up studies which did not confirm the strength of the initial study's findings, received no widespread publicity from the professional and lay press.

Adult ADHD in the Public Sphere

By the early 1990s, several books written for a popular audience looking specifically at ADHD adults were published. Psychologist Lynn Weiss (1992) identified her adult subjects as those who were diagnosable with ADHD, not merely grown-up hyperactive children having remnants of the symptoms carried over from an earlier condition. Another popular book quickly followed with the provocative title of, *You Mean I'm Not Lazy, Stupid or Crazy?!* (Kelly and Ramundo 1993), emphasizing the shift in responsibility that being diagnosed with adult ADHD can bring. Thom Hartmann (1994), writing in a somewhat esoteric, but essentially sociobiological frame, associated ADHD with an evolutionary adaptation to the social environment. He likened those with ADHD to hunters (who are nomadic, scanning the environment for sustenance, seeking of sensation, reacting quickly and decisively) adapting to a more modern farming community (which requires greater stability and focus). This hypothesis, by its nature, supports the notion of ADHD adults.

Further support came from the television news media reports on the spread of ADHD in adults. Major news shows put their own spin on the prevalence of the disorder. For example, on "20/20," Catherine Crier attributed ADHD to a "biologic disorder of the brain" in adults (September 2, 1994). Dr. Timothy Johnson on "Good Morning America" (March 28, 1994) was quoted as saying that experts estimate as many as 10 million adult Americans may have ADHD. The new face of the disorder was not limited to hyperactive children grown-up, but included a new group of "ADHD adults" who came to reinterpret their current and previous behavioral problems in light of an ADHD diagnosis.

The message was reiterated in popular magazines. A feature article in *Newsweek*, for example, described a 38-year-old security guard who held more than 128 jobs since leaving college after being enrolled in the academic institution for 13 years (Cowley and Ramo 1993). He finally "received a diagnosis that changed his life" at the adult ADHD clinic at the University of Massachusetts in Worcester. Similarly, an article in *Ladies' Home Journal* (Stich 1993) described a husband who would continually be fired from job after job, constantly interrupted his wife, and forgot details of conversations. Then "Two years ago, the Pearsons discovered there was a medical reason for Chuck's problems. After their son was diagnosed with attention deficit disorder (ADD) . . . they learned Chuck also had the condition" (Stich 1993). The article does not mention the fact that Chuck, who was diagnosed at age 54, also went on to found the Adult Attention Deficit Foundation, which acts as a clearinghouse for information about adult ADHD (Wallis, 1994).

Adult ADHD was given a great boost in 1994 with the publication of a best-selling book *Driven to Distraction* by Edward Hallowell and John Ratey (1994), two psychiatrists with prestigious organizational affiliations. Hallowell offered his own experience as the springboard for the book: although successful as a medical student, and later as a practicing psychiatrist, he came to believe he had ADHD. Ratey also stated he had ADHD. The book has become a crucial touchstone among the lay public. . . . Both remain very active in promoting their work in public circles. Their affiliation with Harvard Medical School gave them some academic legitimacy, but they came to the area of ADHD adults more as professional advocates than as scientific researchers. In a sense, they are moral entrepreneurs for the adult diagnosis (Leffers 1997).

The cover of July 18, 1994, *Time* magazine issued a clarion call for ADHD adults: "Disorganized? Distracted? Discombobulated? Doctors Say You Might Have ATTENTION DEFICIT DISORDER. It's not just kids who have it." The 9-page article disseminated the criteria and possibilities of ADHD in adults to a wide audience, including speculations that Ben Franklin, Winston Churchill, Albert Einstein, and Bill Clinton may have had the disorder (Wallis 1994).

Diagnostic Institutionalization

By 1994, DSM-IV [the official guide to psychiatric diagnoses] reflected the growing consensus that adults could be diagnosed with ADHD, provided they had exhibited symptoms as children before the age of seven. Two (out of the five) diagnostic criteria were clearly relevant to adults. First, DSM-IV required that "some impairment must occur in at least 2 settings." While for children, these settings usually mean school and home, the range of settings may be greater for adults and include home, school, work, and other vocational or recreational settings. Secondly and related, "there must be clear evidence of interference with developmentally appropriate social, academic, or occupational functioning." The inclusion of work environments in the criteria section of the manual reflected the central and relatively uncontroversial position that the diagnosis of ADHD in adults now occupied.

The new definition allowed for more variations of symptomatic behavior across and within settings. "It is very unusual for an individual to display the same level of dysfunction in all settings or within the same setting at all times" (APA 1994). Adults who might be quite successful at work, but highly inattentive in particular interpersonal relationships and recreational activities, could now be diagnosed with ADHD. As the more expansive criteria in DSM-IV gained acceptance among mental health professionals, some advocated eliminating the requirement that adults be able to retrospectively reconstruct a history of ADHD (Barkley and Biederman 1997). This would permit even greater expansion of the adult ADHD category. Reports from the American Medical Association (AMA) and the National Institutes of Health (NIH) supported an expanded ADHD diagnosis. In 1997, the Council on Scientific Affairs of the AMA issued recommendations for treating ADHD. . . .

[SELF-DIAGNOSIS]

One of the starkest contrasts to the earlier history of ADHD with children is the vast amount of self-diagnosis of ADHD among adults. Virtually all children were referred by parents or schools to physicians (Conrad 1976). Among adults self-referrals are the norm, and many patients come to physicians apparently seeking an ADHD diagnosis. Frequently, adults who encounter a description of the disorder, sense that "this is me" and go on to seek professional confirmation of their new identity. Another common path to self-diagnosis occurs when parents bring a child to a physician for treatment and remark, "I was the same when I was a kid . . ." and thus, begin to see themselves and their own difficulties through the lens of ADHD. While this trend appears to have been precipitated by some of the popular press, it continues with legitimization provided by support groups designed for adults with ADHD such as Ch.A.D.D.

Anecdotes in the popular literature suggest that adults who self-diagnose may recognize the condition in a popular media article or book. Hallowell and Ratey (1994) tell of one woman who noted, "My husband showed me this article in the paper." Comments on Internet sites state directly that it was one of the books on adult ADHD that led individuals to physicians for a diagnosis. Diller (1997) relates that one of his patients came to self-diagnosis after reading *Driven to Distraction*. Diller points out that, while the physician who is presented with such a self-diagnosed patient may have difficulty establishing the existence of symptoms in their childhood (as opposed to a checklist of symptoms absorbed through reading), the self-diagnosis, itself, becomes an element that the professional diagnosis must take into account. One psychiatrist wrote a colleague, "Adult ADHD has now become the foremost *self-diagnosed* condition in my practice. I fear that the condition allows a patient to find a biological cause that is not always reasonable, for job failure, divorce, poor motivation, lack of success, and chronic depression" (Shaffer 1994).

Diagnosis-seeking behavior is an integral feature of the emergence of Adult ADHD. This kind of self-labeling, information exchange, and pursuit of diagnosis fuels the social engine medicalizing certain adult troubles. Without it, the spread of Adult ADHD would be seriously limited. . . .

THE SOCIAL CONTEXT FOR THE RISE OF ADULT ADHD

To the best of our knowledge, there were no breakthrough epidemiological or clinical studies that identified a population of adults as having ADHD who were not previously diagnosed in childhood. Yet it is clear that "adult ADHD" has become a more common and accepted diagnosis in recent years. What would bring adults to physicians seeking such a diagnosis and what spurs physicians to treat them? Several social factors appear to have contributed to the diagnostic expansion.

The Prozac Era

Since the introduction of chlorpromazine in 1955, there has been a psychopharmacological revolution in psychiatry. Psychoactive medications played a major role in deinstitutionalization and became regular parts of physicians' treatment protocols for various life problems, especially anxiety (e.g., Valium). American psychiatrists preferred drugs that would be useful in office psychiatry, rather than medications limited to inpatient populations (Healy 1997).

In 1987, Prozac (fluoxetine) was introduced as a new type of medication to treat depression. This drug is a selective serotonin reuptake inhibitor that directly affected a different group of neurotransmitters with fewer unpleasant side effects than previous types of antidepressants. This drug quickly became a phenomenon in itself, and led to a whole new class of drugs for treating psychiatric and life problems. Peter Kramer's book, *Listening to Prozac* (1993) and the subsequent news media coverage (e.g., cover stories in *Newsweek* and *New York* magazines, and dozens of TV and radio appearances), piqued the public interest in this new drug. Prozac was increasingly depicted as a medication that was a psychic energizer and that could make people feel, in Kramer's terms, "better than well." Prozac was not seen as a medication only for the seriously disturbed, but was a formulation that could improve the lives of people with minor disturbances and distresses.

The introduction and popularity of Prozac (and a series of related medications) created a context whereby taking medications for life problems was more acceptable. Prozac was seen as a drug that was appropriate for a range of psychic difficulties, and whose use could even make an OK life better. It led numerous people to redefine their life woes in terms of mild depression and seek treatment. A person did not have to be severely disturbed to benefit from Prozac. Similarly, Ritalin was now available to adults who had not been diagnosed as hyperactive in childhood, but who were now redefining their life difficulties as related to "inattention," "impulsivity," and "restlessness."

Genetics

Genetics is the rising paradigm in medicine and an increasing number of human problems are being attributed to genetic associations, markers, or causes (Conrad 1999). Some experts have long believed that there is a genetic component to ADHD and its predecessor, hyperactivity, but to date, evidence is only suggestive, even though the claims of inheritance date back at least 25 years. . . . [But] the greater the medical and public acceptance of a genetic component of ADHD, the more adult ADHD becomes a social reality. If the disorder is genetic, then it is deemed an intrinsic characteristic of people with the gene. This supports the notion that ADHD is a lifelong disorder, and the position that adults could have the disorder, even though they were never diagnosed as children.

The Rise of Managed Care

Managed care affects all aspects of medicine, including psychiatry. Health insurance imposes strict limits on the amount of psychotherapy for individual patients. Psychiatrists, now, must make use of utilization review, participate in medication management, consultation, or administering "carve-out programs" (Domino, et al. 1998). Mental health advocates and some researchers argue that, under managed care, there is a growing reliance upon various forms of prescription therapies to treat all types of psychiatric and life problems (Johnson 1998). A recent study found that managed care might fuel growth in the pharmaceutical industry (Murray and Deardorff 1998). Undoubtedly, there are now greater incentives for psychiatrists and other physicians to treat all potential mental health problems with medication, rather with than some form of talking or psychotherapy. Managed care tends to replace psychiatrists with primary care physicians who are less versed in "talking therapies" (Stoudemire 1996), and, thereby, increasing the potential for relying on medication for treatment. . . . [T]here is some evidence that ADHD children are treated with stimulant medications to the exclusion of other "talking therapies" (Woolraich et al. 1990). It is likely there are similar trends with adult ADHD. . . .

CONCLUSION

Adult ADHD offers a clear example of how a medicalized category can expand to include a wider range of troubles within its definition. ADHD's expansion was, primarily, accomplished by refocusing the diagnosis on inattention, rather than hyperactivity, and stretching the age criteria. This allowed for the inclusion of an entire population of people and their problems that were excluded by the original conception of hyperactive children. . . .

But in terms of diagnostic expansion, the ADHD case is not unique. We can point to other cases where medicalized categories, which were originally developed and legitimated for one set of problems, were extended or refrained to include a broader range of problems. Several examples come to mind. Post-Traumatic Stress Disorder (PTSD) was originally conceived of as a disorder of returning Vietnam war veterans who suffered from the after effects of brutal combat experience (e.g., with flashbacks, sleep problems, intense anxiety, etc.). But in recent years, PTSD has been applied to rape and incest survivors, disaster victims, and witnesses to violence. Alcoholism was medicalized, in large part, due to the efforts of AA, but the medicalization has expanded to include adult children of alcoholics, enablers, and especially "codependency" (Irvine 1999). Child abuse, which was originally limited to battering, has expanded to include sexual abuse and neglect, and to lesser extent, child pornography and exploitation and, to a degree, spawned the larger domain of domestic violence (including woman battering and elder abuse). In 1972, multiple personality disorder was a rare diagnosis (estimated at less than a dozen cases in 50 years); by 1992, thousands of multiples were diagnosed (Hacking 1995).

REFERENCES

American Psychiatric Association, The Committee on Nomenclature and Statistics. 1994. *DSM-IV. Diagnostic and Statistical Manual of Mental Disorders*, Fourth Edition. Washington, DC: American Psychiatric Association.

Barkley, Russell A., and Joseph Biederman. 1997. "Toward a broader definition of the age-of-onset criterion for Attention-Deficit Hyperactive Disorder." *Journal of the American Academy of Child and Adolescent Psychiatry* 36:1204–1210.

Bartlett, K. 1990. "Attention deficit: Scientists move toward understanding of brain disorder once thought limited to children." *Houston Chronicle* (December 2):6G.

Conrad, Peter. 1975. "The discovery of Hyperkinesis: Notes on the medicalization of deviant behavior." *Social Problems* 23:12–21.

———. 1976. *Identifying Hyperactive Children: The Medicalization of Deviant Behavior.* Lexington, MA: D.C. Heath.

———. 1999. "A mirage of genes." *Sociology of Health and Illness* 21:228–241.

Cowley, Geoffrey, and Joshua Cooper Ramo. 1993. "The not-young and the restless." *Newsweek* (July 26):48–49.

Diller, Lawrence H. 1997. *Running on Ritalin.* New York: Bantam Books.

Gross, Mortimer B., and William E. Wilson. 1974. *Minimum Brain Dysfunction.* New York: Brunner Mazel.

Hacking, Ian. 1995. *Rewriting the Soul: Multiple Personality and the Sciences of Memory.* Princeton, NJ: Princeton University Press.

Hallowell, Edward M., and John J. Ratey. 1994. *Driven to Distraction.* New York: Pantheon Books.

Hartmann, Thom. 1994. *Attention Deficit Disorder: A Different Perception.* New York. Underwood Books.

Healy, David. 1997. *The Anti-Depressant Era.* Cambridge, MA: Harvard University Press.

Irvine, Leslie. 1999. *Codependent Forevermore: The Invention of Self in a Twelve Step Group.* Chicago: University of Chicago Press.

Jaffe, Paul. 1995. "History and overview of adulthood ADD." In *A Comprehensive Guide to Attention Deficit Disorder in Adults: Research, Diagnosis, and Treatment,* Kathleen G. Nadeau, ed. New York: Brunner/Mazel: 3–17.

Johnson, Dale L. 1998. "Are mental health services losing out in the U.S. under managed care?" *Pharmaco Economics* 14:597–601.

Kelly, Kate, and Peggy Ramundo. 1993. *You Mean I'm Not Lazy, Stupid, or Crazy?! A Self-Help Book for Adults with Attention Deficit Disorder.* Cincinnati: Tyrell and Jerem Press.

Kramer, Peter. 1993. *Listening to Prozac.* New York: Penguin.

Leffers, Jeanne Mahoney. 1997. *The Social Construction of a New Diagnostic Category: Attention Deficit Disorder in Adults (Medicalization).* Unpublished Ph.D. dissertation, Brown University.

Murray, M. D., and F. W. Deardorff. 1998. "Does managed care fuel pharmaceutical industry growth?" *Pharmaco Economics* 14:341–348.

Newsweek. 1990. "A new view on hyperactivity." (December 3):61.

Shaffer, David. 1994. "Attention Deficit Hyperactivity Disorder in adults." *American Journal of Psychiatry* 151:633–638.

Stich, Sally. 1993. "Why can't your husband sit still?" *Ladies Home Journal* (September):74, 77.

Stoudemire, A. 1996. "Psychiatry in medical practice: Implications for the education of primary care physicians in the era of managed care. Part I." *Psychosomatics* 37:502–508.

Wallis, Claudia. 1994. "Life in overdrive." *Time* (July 18):43–50.

Weiss, Lynn. 1992. *Attention Deficit Disorder in Adults: Practical Help for Sufferers and Their Spouses.* Dallas: Taylor Press.

Williams, Simon J., and Michael Calnan. 1996. "The 'Limits' of Medicalization: Modern Medicine and the Lay Populace in 'Late Modernity'." *Social Science and Medicine* 42:1609–1620.

Wolkenberg, Frank. 1987. "Out of a darkness." *New York Times* (October 11):62, 66, 68–70, 82–83.

Woolraich, Mark L., Scott Lindgren, A. Stromquist, R. Milich, C. Davis, and D. Watson. 1990. "Stimulant medication use by primary care physicians in the treatment of Attention Deficit Hyperactivity Disorder." *Pediatrics* 86:95–101.

REVIEW QUESTIONS

1. How is adult ADHD a "clear example of how a medicalized category can expand to include a wider range of troubles within its definition"?
2. Give another example of the expansion of a medicalized category to include a wider range of troubles.
3. Does the ADHD label truly represent deviancy, or is it a means of escaping other negative labels?

PART SEVEN

VICTIMS OF STIGMA

A gay couple, Gary and Greg, both in their 30s, are known to neighbors simply as "the guys" in a small, fairly conservative town in central Pennsylvania. They call each other "honey" in the stores, and their straight friends call them "uncle" and "uncle." At their offices, their straight coworkers seem more familiar with gay issues than the gay couple themselves. As Gary says, "They realize we have the same worries they do. Now in tax season, they'll say, "That sucks, you can't put Greg on your return." All this friendliness shown by straights to Gary and Greg in a conservative town represents a significant progress in attitudes toward gays in the United States. Now, for the first time in U.S. history, only a minority (46 percent) of Americans consider homosexuality a sin. But at the same time a majority (57 percent) are still opposed to gay marriage, and more than thirty-two states have passed new laws banning same-sex marriages.[1] In this new century, then, U.S. society still has a long way to go toward treating gays the same as straights.

The continuing rejection of gays suggests that homosexuality is still a social stigma, something a person has or does that others see as bad in some way. A stigma is practically the same as deviance, so many deviances can be considered stigmas. It is a stigma to be a prostitute, a mental patient, a suicide, a child abuser, a murderer, a rapist, and so on. Some of these stigmas are justifiable. Murderers, rapists, and other nasty criminals, for example, deserve to get what is coming to them. But most stigmas are unjustifiable because people such as gays and lesbians, suicides, mental patients, the obese, and the tattooed do not hurt others yet are stigmatized—punished as victims of stigma. Here we focus on people who file for bankruptcy, obese individuals, rural lesbians, and mentally challenged persons—all of whom are victims of unjustifiable stigma.

In the first article, "Managing the Stigma of Personal Bankruptcy," Deborah Thorne and Leon Anderson discuss the various ways of dealing with the stigma of bankruptcy. In the second article, "The Stigma of Obesity," Erich Goode explains why the obese are stigmatized in U.S. society and how this stigmatization affects the victims. In the third piece, "What Is It Like to Be a Rural Lesbian?" Margaret Cooper discusses the experiences of being lesbian as a child and adult living in rural areas. In the fourth selection, " 'You're Not a Retard, You're Just Wise,' " Steven Taylor shows why people labeled "retarded" by others may not see themselves that way.

[1]John Leland, "Shades of Gay," *Newsweek*, March 20, 2002, pp. 46–49; Richard Corliss, "How the West Was Won Over," *Time*, January 30, 2006, pp. 60–63.

CHAPTER 23

MANAGING THE STIGMA OF PERSONAL BANKRUPTCY

DEBORAH THORNE
LEON ANDERSON

Over the past 20 years, despite an oft-touted strong economy, there has been a four-fold increase in the number of petitions filed for personal bankruptcy. In 1984, 291,532 petitions were filed; by 2004, that number had ballooned to 1,567,846 (Administrative Office of the U.S. Courts, 2005). Many explanations for the increase have been asserted, the most frequent of which is that bankruptcy has shed its stigma and become little more than a financial planning tool for opportunistic filers. Representative Asa Hutchinson (1999), an avid supporter of the recent bankruptcy reform, claimed that, "Having lost its social stigma, bankruptcy 'convenience' filings have become a tool to avoid financial obligations rather than a measure of last resort." This sentiment was echoed by Alan Greenspan, then Chairman of the Federal Reserve, when he stated, "Personal bankruptcies are soaring because Americans have lost their sense of shame" (quoted in Zywicki, 2005). The message from advocates of bankruptcy reform was loud and clear: yesterday's morally responsible consumer had transformed into today's *Homo oeconomicus*. Prodded by lobbying efforts and large campaign contributions from the credit card industry, Congress and President Bush concluded that the most efficient way to simultaneously restore fiscal integrity and reduce the number of filings was to restrict access to the bankruptcy altogether. Thus, in spring of 2005, Congress passed and President Bush signed the Bankruptcy Abuse Prevention and Consumer Protection Act. As he signed the bill into law, Mr. Bush stated: "Too many people have abused the bankruptcy laws" and with a stroke of his pen, he was "restoring integrity to the bankruptcy process" (2005). Interestingly, debtors were labeled deadbeats and laws were passed to make it difficult to file for bankruptcy, but all this happened without any input from debtors themselves or valid empirical evidence about the stigma associated with filing.

Here we provide in-depth empirical data gathered directly from bankrupt debtors to assess their experiences of stigmatization. Further, to accurately represent the concerns expressed by our informants, we center our analysis on a discussion of the stigma management strategies they invoked to mitigate the shame and social disapprobation they experienced as a result of their bankruptcies.

RESEARCH METHODS

To address the kinds of issues we have just described, we analyze direct testimony from debtors who filed for Chapter 7 personal bankruptcy in 1999 in the Eastern District of Washington state. The first author conducted face-to-face interviews with 37 individuals from 19 married couples who

Source: Deborah Thorne and Leon Anderson, "Managing the Stigma of Personal Bankruptcy," *Sociological Focus*, vol. 39 (May 2006), pp. 77–97.

had filed joint petitions for personal bankruptcy. (A total of 38 interviews should have been completed. However, at the last minute, the husband of one couple hid upstairs because, as his wife said, he was ashamed of their bankruptcy.) Originally, the names of ninety debtor couples, whose Chapter 7 cases had closed between April and July 1999, were randomly selected from the website of the Eastern District of Washington State, United States Bankruptcy Court. Each couple received a letter that described the research and explained that they would be contacted to request an interview. Phones were disconnected or letters were undeliverable for 48 (53 percent) of the potential respondent couples. Stanley and Girth (1971) reported similar difficulties when they attempted to contact bankrupt debtors; over two-thirds of their letters requesting interviews were returned and marked as "undeliverable." The remaining 42 couples were contacted, and 15 (36 percent) declined to participate. In total, 27 couples agreed to interviews. Eight of these couples were excluded because they had either moved, were too ill to participate within the research time frame, or had separated or divorced.

The decision to interview both members of marital couples was based on two considerations. First, marital couples are jointly responsible for most financial obligations. Consequently, the legal act of filing is almost always made as a couple. Second, many of the core research questions for this study concerned the effects of bankruptcy on marital relationships and were thus addressed most appropriately by interviewing both partners. One objective of the original research was to explore the effects of debt and bankruptcy on couples' relationships. To insure that husbands and wives were forthcoming with their assessments and that they described their experiences without bias, men and women were interviewed separately.

The interviews were conducted within three months of the couples' bankruptcy filings, and, with only one exception, took place in couples' homes. Whenever possible, husbands and wives were interviewed separately—in only two instances did a spouse refuse to leave while the other was interviewed. On average, the interviews lasted an hour and a half; a few lasted over three hours. The semi-structured interviews loosely followed an interview guide (Lofland et al., 2005) that consisted of a list of general topics and questions covering a range of bankruptcy-related experiences. These topics included the nature of the respondents' debts and the conditions under which they had accrued; how debtors reached the decision to declare bankruptcy; how their insolvency and ultimate bankruptcy influenced their personal, marital, and family lives; how they felt about their decision to file; and their experiences with the legal and bureaucratic processes associated with bankruptcy. Beyond these general themes, the interviewer encouraged debtors to explore other topics that emerged during the interview process, thus maximizing receptiveness to "developing meanings" that might either render the original questions irrelevant or reveal the importance of new ones (Warren, 2002).

Attentive to "how the meaning-making process unfolds in the interview" (Holstein and Gubrium, 2002), the interviewer designed the interview as a dynamic conversation during which she and the respondents constructed the experience of bankruptcy. To facilitate open sharing, she presented herself as nonjudgmental and sympathetic, as well as knowledgeable about bankruptcy (e.g., she used specific terms associated with bankruptcy filing). As a result, the interviews offered bankrupt debtors an opportunity for what Schneider and Conrad (1980) have referred to as "therapeutic disclosure"—cathartic sharing of painful experiences with a sympathetic listener. This put debtors at ease and led them to share aspects of their experience that they said they had concealed from others.

The conversational format of the interviews allowed comments about stigma and stigma management to surface in a variety of contexts, normally without specific prompting. For example, debtors voiced feelings of stigma or embarrassment when they were asked to describe how they felt about their decision to file, their first visit to the bankruptcy attorney, or their attendance at the Section 341 hearing. For others, their assertions of stigma came as unexpected interjections, statements that were outside the immediate topic of conversation, as in the case of a woman who abruptly shifted from a description of the repossession of their vehicles to her generalized feelings of shame about filing: "It was the most embarrassing experience, to file bankruptcy, because [we believed that] we've got to pay our debts, even if it takes forever." Interestingly, the two debtors who did not spontaneously offer comments regarding stigma, and who were therefore prompted to discuss the issue, were the only respondents in the study who said they felt little or no shame or embarrassment. Thus, all 35 debtors who reported feelings of shame broached the subject independently in the course of more general conversation and without any direction from the interviewer.

The interviews were audiotaped, transcribed and then combed for general themes, which served as the basis for initial data coding. Stigma immediately emerged as a key theme. The data files containing general themes were further examined to determine analytically significant subcategories, with the stigma theme ultimately being coded into various subcategories, including those that form the basis of this article.

SAMPLE CHARACTERISTICS

Like most intensive interview studies, the sample for this research was relatively small. Nonetheless, it was demographically quite diverse and consistent in many respects with other bankruptcy studies. The debtors ranged in age from their mid-20s to their early-80s. The modal level of education among primary petitioners (husbands) was as follows: 58 percent graduated high school, 16 percent had some college, another 16 percent earned a bachelor's degree, and 10.5 percent had either a graduate or professional degree. Family size ranged from two members (couples with no children in the home) to six—a couple whose two adult daughters and their two children were living with them. Mean family size was 3.6. Annual income at time of filing ranged from $13,000 to $58,560; median income was $29,832. Unsecured debt at time of filing ranged from $9,800 to $66,500; median debt was $28,900. The most frequently acknowledged cause of bankruptcy was employment problems: 68 percent of debtors claimed either a job loss or a general decline in income as a major reason for filing. Medical expenses and credit card debt were also frequently mentioned. For families with young children, the cost of raising them and providing daycare was also a major factor in their bankruptcies.

BANKRUPTCY

There are five chapters, or kinds, of bankruptcy: Chapter 7, 9, 11, 12, and 13. Families and individuals typically file either a Chapter 7 or Chapter 13 bankruptcy—the other three chapters are generally the domains of corporations, railroads, municipalities, and farmers. Nationally, 95.5 percent of bankruptcies are either Chapter 7 or Chapter 13; just over 70 percent of these are Chapter 7s. All debtors interviewed in this study filed Chapter 7 bankruptcies.

Barring any problems, a petition for Chapter 7 bankruptcy is typically approved within a couple months of filing the paperwork with the courts, at which time unsecured debts (for example, credit card and medical debt) are discharged. Translated, these debts are erased, and the debtor is no longer expected to repay them. Some unsecured debts, such as student loans, taxes, alimony, and child support, are non-dischargeable and the debtor remains responsible for them. A debtor may reaffirm a secured debt on which there is collateral, such as a car loan. This means that in exchange for continued payments, the debtor is allowed to keep the property. Filing the Chapter 7 petition and paperwork with the courts costs a debtor approximately $200; if an attorney is retained, the debtor can expect to pay another $500–700 in attorney's fees. Bankruptcies remain on the credit report for 10 years, and eight years must pass before a subsequent bankruptcy can be filed.

THE EXISTENCE OF STIGMA

As the earlier quote by Congressmen Hutchinson illustrates, there is a common assumption that bankruptcy, which was once tightly laced with stigma, is now embraced by debtors as a purely rational economic decision, nothing more than a "convenient financial planning tool." In glaring contrast to this assumption, debtors who had been through the process insisted that filing for personal bankruptcy was, more than anything else, especially stigmatizing. Specifically, 95 percent of the debtors (all but two) in the study stated that they felt shame and stigmatization as they negotiated the bankruptcy process. For example, when a young mother of two was asked to discuss the disadvantages of filing, she responded: "The disadvantage was just the humiliation." Another respondent, a man in his early 60s who had retired from the U.S. Postal Service, told of how he had kept their bankruptcy from family members because, "I thought of it as a mark against my name . . . I just felt it had to be private. It was too embarrassing. . . . I feel like I failed. You know, to go bankrupt, that's a sign of failure." When asked if he would ever recommend bankruptcy to a friend who was struggling with debt, he said, "I guess I would if there was no way [to pay their bills]. But it isn't that easy. I still feel ashamed about the whole thing."

Comments from the debtors further revealed that their negative perceptions of bankruptcy were nothing new and had been with them for much of their lives, often as a result of socialization by older members of their families. Debtors insisted that they had been raised to believe that "only terrible people," or "only bad people and misfits" file for bankruptcy. One man in his early-30s was determined to avoid bankruptcy at all costs because he remembered hearing his mother saying, "Those damn bastards [people in bankruptcy], all they do is fucking rip off the system and get away with it. I hate them." Another man, who was in his early-80s, insisted that he had been raised knowing that "bankruptcy was one of those things that no one should do"—no surprise given that his grandfather had been a bankruptcy trustee. The contempt for those who file for bankruptcy appears to span generations.

Once the subject of stigma was broached, it was as though the flood gates opened. Indeed, this topic resonated with debtors like no other, generating by far the most pages of transcription. Debtors became increasingly talkative, and provided unprecedented richness and detail. Not only did debtors have much to say, but they were also particularly animated and emotional—many cursed, while others broke into tears.

To avoid the stigma of bankruptcy altogether, the majority of debtors reported that they postponed filing for months and even years after recognizing that their debts were unmanageable. Several couples unsuccessfully attempted to solve their financial problems by making large withdrawals from retirement accounts or borrowing against insurance annuities. Others turned their homes and vehicles back to lenders in last-ditch, and eventually futile, attempts to manage their debt loads. As these efforts met with failure and financial pressures mounted, some marriages were strained to the breaking point. Several debtors sunk into serious self-described depression, and two female respondents reported that they considered suicide as a means to escape the pressures and worries associated with insolvency. Both expressed hope that their life insurance would be adequate to cover their family's debts.

Despite their best efforts and reluctance, however, the couples in our study did file for bankruptcy. While this certainly relieved them from major financial obligations and harassment by bill collectors, it simultaneously placed them in the awkward and uncomfortable position of having engaged in an act that they, their families, and American society at large, disparage. This dilemma and their efforts to manage it served as a focal point of attention for almost all of the bankrupt debtors we interviewed. Consistent with the broader studies on stigma, we found that bankrupt debtors managed or dealt with the stigma in three ways: (1) concealment, (2) avoidance, and (3) deviance avowal.

Concealment

Declaration of bankruptcy is a public act, and petitioners cannot restrict the many venues through which their bankruptcies are publicly declared. The legal records section of most city newspapers reports the names of people who have filed for personal bankruptcy. Further, anyone can visit the courthouse and request a copy of any bankruptcy petition that was filed in that district. For those with access to the internet, debtors' petitions from around the nation are available on-line for a minimal charge. Finally, there are companies, such as Bankruptcy News, that notify residents about neighbors who have filed for bankruptcy. For a price, the company will provide the resident with the bankrupt neighbor's name, Social Security number, list of creditors and amount owed to each—all information that was provided by the debtor to the court.

Such public disclosure notwithstanding, roughly 80 percent of debtors made a concerted effort to keep the news of their bankruptcy contained and particularly to minimize its disclosure to individuals or groups who they felt presented potential risks. Similar to the formerly hospitalized mental patients studied by Nancy Herman (1993), bankrupt debtors engaged in "selective concealment," most frequently from parents, employers and co-workers.

Debtors perceived parents and in-laws as the most critical individuals from whom to hide information. Consequently, three-quarters of those debtors who reported feelings of stigma and whose parents were living worked to keep the bankruptcy from them. For example, the previously quoted man whose mother had described those who file as "bastards who rip off the system" was adamant that she would never learn of his bankruptcy. When asked if he had mentioned either his financial problems or his bankruptcy to her, he virtually erupted:

> *OH HELL NO! No, no, no way, no way! Nope. And she won't ever know. Never. Never. . . . She'd be like, "Argh, you piece of shit. Why did you do that?" . . . I was afraid, you know, and I, my mom has no clue and I think it would just crush her. Because she has a view of me. . . . I'm her success. I am such a success to her because, despite having really been in trouble and all these awful things that went on, here I am. I'm married and I have two kids and I'm making it. Yeah, I'm getting my Ph.D.*

This debtor went on to say that he and his wife had also been very careful to keep his siblings in the dark—lest they accidentally or injudiciously share the news with their mother.

Even debtors whose parents had themselves been through bankruptcy, and who might therefore be supportive, worked to conceal their bankruptcies. A woman in her late-twenties started to sob uncontrollably when asked if her parents, who had gone bankrupt themselves, knew about her situation. She explained that she had not told her mom because she was afraid of her reaction: "She'd be very disappointed. The worst part about this is that I can't tell people. . . . I haven't told my friends or family. No one knows. . . . Please, be proud of me, Mom."

Virtually every debtor whose parents were still living tried to withhold knowledge of the bankruptcy from them. Older debtors whose parents had passed away commented that "if they knew, they'd spin in their graves." One woman, whose father was visiting when the researcher arrived for the interview, nearly pushed the interviewer off the front steps out of fear (as she explained later) that if her father saw the researcher, he would ask disconcerting questions and potentially learn of the bankruptcy.

In addition to concealing the bankruptcy from parents, well over half of debtors who were employed said that they had tried to conceal the bankruptcy from their employers and/or co-workers. While fear of disappointment dominated debtors' concerns with parents finding out, a fear of scorn and criticism prevailed in relation to those with whom they worked. Such fear of disdain was captured by one woman who explained that she had done everything possible to keep the bankruptcy from her employer because,

> *My boss is terribly critical about welfare mothers, people who file bankruptcy, people that have the subsidized medical program, any kind of anybody that doesn't do things on their own. Very vocal, very critical. . . . I just didn't need it. . . . And he's very, I wouldn't say he'd get in your face and say, "You're a loser," but he's very, very judgmental.*

Another female debtor worried that a specific coworker, the accounts receivable clerk, would find out. When customers were late with payment or filed for bankruptcy, it was the job of the coworker to place a lien against any property, and the debtor witnessed her contempt for people who were behind on their bills and feared the same derisive comments would be directed toward her.

> *She says things like "Loser," and she comes up with [derogatory] names [for the clients with delinquent accounts]. She's just, she doesn't call it to their faces, but when she hangs up the phone with this person, or if she gets a note, "Oh great, another bankruptcy hearing I've got to go to and try and cut some more money out of these people." And you just think to yourself, "Shit, I'm not like that, though. Really." You know, it wasn't like I set out and said, "OK, in six years I'm going to file bankruptcy." . . . And the people that take care of credit and stuff like that [at work], they're always harsh on those people. But I'm thinking, "Shit, I don't want them to know about this."*

Despite their best efforts at concealment, it was inevitable that some debtors' parents and coworkers would read about the bankruptcies in the local newspapers. Being confronted by someone from whom they had tried to withhold the information was particularly mortifying for debtors, since they then had to face interrogation about not only their bankruptcies, but about their attempts to hide the information as well. A debtor in her late-30s who worked as bookkeeper at an auto parts store, for instance, related her most difficult experience:

> *The most horrible thing in the whole world is, we didn't tell our parents, both sets of parents. . . . But my mom read it in the paper and called me. I just about died. They happened to be out of town when it was printed. It just happened that way. . . . I was glad that they were going to be out of town when it came out. But then they read the papers, all of the back ones [back issues] and she called me and said, "Why didn't you tell me?" Yeah, like I'm going to call and brag!*

Anxiety over the possibility of such accidental disclosure loomed large in interviewees' experiences. The woman just quoted and her husband, for instance, had also kept it from his parents and she shared that she was "terrified" that they too might read it in the newspaper.

Avoidance

The preceding section documents bankrupt debtors' efforts to conceal information from intimates. Fear of stigmatization also led them to avoid situations that might lead to embarrassing or degrading interactions with non-intimates who would have particular reason to uncover their economic troubles and failures. In fact, bankrupt debtors had typically learned techniques of avoidance earlier in their debt histories. As they slid into bankruptcy and became delinquent with payments, they often found themselves pursued by bill collectors. Contact with bill collectors often represented many debtors' first direct experience with the stigmatization of insolvency. In her classic work on emotional labor, Hochschild (1983) studied how flight attendants and bill collectors perform their jobs. She concluded that the emotional labor performed by flight attendants generally served to make customers feel good about themselves and "enhance the customer's status." In contrast, during the final stages of collection, bill collectors worked to humiliate debtors by suggesting that they were "lazy and of low moral character" which served to "deflate the customer's status." Moreover, to insure that collectors did not sympathize with debtors, and thereby reduce the likelihood of collection, the landscape of the collectors' workplace was peppered with descriptions of the debtor as "loafer" and "cheat."

Only four of the nineteen couples escaped collection calls—they filed what credit card lenders describe as "no advanced warning" or "surprise" bankruptcies. Essentially, these couples remained current with all their bills until the time at which they concluded they were fighting a losing battle. At this point, rather than become delinquent on payments, something they described as irresponsible, they filed. However, the debtors who did receive collection calls attested to collectors' abilities to successfully shame and intimidate them. One debtor, a woman in her late-thirties who had managed her family's bills, said:

> *It was to the point where I couldn't stand to be in the house. I was scared to come home because I didn't want to be faced with the phone calls and the letters. You don't want to go to the mailbox and you don't want to answer the phone. Because all I can say is, "I sent you this much on this date and I'll send you more when I can." . . . I was scared the phone was going to ring. To hear it ring was just horrible. . . . You feel trapped in your own home, you feel trapped.*

Fifteen couples experienced threatening and demeaning collection calls and letters on an almost daily basis. In the face of unrelenting harassment, almost 90 percent of debtors developed strategies—such as the use of caller ID—for avoiding interaction with bill collectors. One advantage of filing for bankruptcy was that bill collectors were legally required to end all collection attempts. For most debtors, this meant that harassing phone calls stopped. However, many debtors worried about the potential for other embarrassing encounters, and began avoiding family, friends, and other associates who might learn of their bankruptcies. One debtor, who had filed for bankruptcy while running a horse-boarding facility, explained that she and her family would no longer visit their long-time family dentist because she had included his bills in their bankruptcy and was too embarrassed to face him again: "He's such a nice man and he does nice work for us. . . . and I had to file bankruptcy on him. So now I'll probably never use him again."

At a more extreme level, an embarrassed husband hid upstairs while his wife was interviewed. During the interview, the wife recounted how she too had withdrawn after filing bankruptcy in an attempt to limit possible humiliation:

> *I just kind of hid for a while. I mean, literally, yes, hid. From family. . . . I didn't call people. I didn't visit anybody. Because you have to figure that somebody's gonna see something in the newspaper, and you know, the next time I talk to them, they'll bring it up. . . . But if you wait long enough, they'll forget about it completely.*

Deviance Avowal

The stigma management strategies discussed so far are based on attempts to evade the stigmatizing label of bankruptcy. Debtors postponed filing, concealed the information, and avoided interactions with those whom they worried might confront them with their negative status. But it was not always possible to hide the bankruptcy. As debtors' status evolved from "discreditable" to "discredited," the stigma management strategies they employed also changed. The most prevalent efforts to manage discredited identity involved deviance avowal (Turner, 1972): debtors acknowledged the wrongfulness of bankruptcy in general but did not see their own bankruptcy as really wrongful. Deviance avowal, then, enabled individuals to cope with stigma by arguing that their particular cases were unique, definitely not the same as the experience of the typical deviant person. Three varieties of deviance avowal were particularly evident among debtors in this study: (1) distancing, (2) excuses and justifications, and (3) transcendence. As their following descriptions of these three stigma management strategies suggest, the debtors do not see themselves or their own bankruptcy as really deviant.

DISTANCING

Discourse about poverty has long been framed in terms of conceptions of the deserving and undeserving poor. The non-poor often employ this distinction to differentiate the poor who are worthy of charity and state support from those who should be denied such support. The distinction has also been used by the poor themselves to manage the stigma of poverty by distancing themselves from images of the unworthy poor and presenting themselves as among those whose poverty is not a reflection of their moral character. So, for instance, Snow and Anderson (1993) found that a significant number of the homeless engaged in "associational distancing" as a form of identity talk to distinguish themselves from other homeless individuals who they felt rightly deserved to be stigmatized. Schwalbe et al. have described such distinctions among the worthy and unworthy, in which potentially stigmatized individuals sharply differentiate themselves from images of unworthy peers, as "defensive othering" (2000).

Associational distancing was extremely common among the debtors in this study. They went to considerable lengths to distinguish their "legitimate" reasons for declaring bankruptcy from the otherwise illegitimate and morally objectionable actions and rationales of other bankrupt debtors. Interviewees often used the term "deadbeats" to describe illegitimate debtors, whom they depicted as having various negative characteristics, including frivolous spending habits, intentionally accrued insurmountable debts, and an inability to learn from their financial mistakes. Three particular stereotypes were drawn upon consistently for this purpose: the extravagant bankrupt, the credit card bankrupt, and the repeat filer.

Distancing from the "Extravagant Bankrupt"

The image of the extravagant bankrupt created by interviewees described debtors who reveled in inappropriately luxurious lifestyles and engaged in profligate spending patterns, only to jettison their debt when it caught up with them. Twenty-nine of the debtors (78 percent) asserted that they knew of someone who fit this negative stereotype, from which they were quick to distance themselves. Fancy cars and expensive vacations were repeatedly used to symbolize a bankruptcy of extravagance. One debtor, who had grown up in a family of Nascar drivers, said he knew someone who "had over $200,000 in credit, went hog-wild, Caribbean cruise. . . . And then filed for bankruptcy and dumped it all. . . . I mean he just used and abused everything." In contrast, he described himself as a "poor slob just trying to get by, just trying to live, versus work the system, you know, file this fancy and extravagant stuff and bail out on it."

Another debtor, a stay-at-home mother of three, juxtaposed her "bankruptcy of necessity" with that of the extravagant bankrupt who charged lavish vacations and home furnishings.

> *We haven't gotten carried away. . . . Most people I talked to, you know, they've charged stereos, they've went on vacations. You know, we weren't afforded that luxury. This [bankruptcy] was all accumulated debt out of necessity. . . . I guess I felt better because, like I said, we didn't go to Tahiti and we didn't drive up major credit cards. It was all debt of necessity.*

Many of the debtors described expensive cars as prime examples of the irresponsible purchases of extravagant bankrupts. In contrast, and as proof of their own frugality, many pointed to their old, but paid-for, cars. One couple, who drove 100 miles every day to work and back, led the researcher outside to show her their numerous old cars, most of which were kept for spare parts. Gesturing at the cars, the wife said, "It's not like we've been doing wasteful things. I mean, *look at our cars*. They all have over 200,000 miles on them."

In their distancing efforts, debtors painted a picture of the stereotypical extravagant bankrupt while insisting that their pre-bankruptcy consumption patterns were conservative and based on necessities. A retired debtor with a Master's degree in education put this succinctly: "Now, if we'd gone out and bought clothes and good times, then I can see why . . . why you need help. You have a problem. We don't have [that] problem."

Distancing from the "Credit Card Bankrupt"

While the stereotype of the extravagant bankrupt emphasized opulent spending, the image of the credit card bankrupt focused attention primarily on fiscal immaturity and a lack of self-control. Faced with easily available "plastic money," credit card bankrupts were portrayed by those we interviewed as having a juvenile tendency to deny the trouble they were getting into until it was too late. Credit card bankrupts' inability to manage their spending provided many debtors with a handy stereotype of what they themselves were not. Over 70 percent of the debtors asserted that they had tried to be conscientious in their credit card charges—even though many of these debtors also discharged considerable credit card balances in their bankruptcies.

Debtors who distanced themselves from credit card bankrupts were quick to point out what they believed was a clear distinction between the kinds of legitimate debt that forced them into bankruptcy, especially medical bills, and the credit card bankrupt irresponsible debts. One couple in their early-30s, for instance, was adamant that they felt no shame whatsoever from their bankruptcy. The husband had fought stomach cancer and their daughter had been born with severe medical problems. They were without health insurance, and their medical bills were exorbitant. Consequently, they filed what they both described as a "medical bankruptcy." They contrasted their bankruptcy with a "credit card bankruptcy" and argued that the two should even be treated differently by the courts. "I think there should be rules for different circumstances," the husband said. "Like medical conditions, something you can't avoid. That's different than going out and maxing out your credit card, and 'I don't want to pay for it.' . . . I think people should be responsible for their debt."

Even debtors who had amassed significant consumer debt of other varieties argued that they were unlike the much-disparaged credit card bankrupts. A debtor for whom the catalysts for the bankruptcy were two large car loans and her husband's unstable employment insisted that their bankruptcy was unique in that it did not include any credit card debt, an observation that, she emphasized, their attorney corroborated.

> *I didn't mind losing all my cars [two of their vehicles were repossessed], but what I was filing bankruptcy on was NOT credit cards. . . . It was NOT a credit card bankruptcy. . . . I NEVER turned a credit card over to bankruptcy, ever. We've never done that. So, we look at it as that wasn't our problem. . . . And even Linda [their bankruptcy attorney] said, "This is not a normal bankruptcy. Normally you see a lot of credit card [debt]."*

While those who did not have credit card debt could readily distance themselves from credit card bankrupts, most debtors did indeed discharge substantial credit card balances. Yet even these debtors typically distanced themselves from the stereotypical credit card bankrupt. Most of them insisted that although they had discharged credit card debt, their charges—unlike those that characterized credit card bankrupts—were for essential needs rather than luxuries or incidentals. For example, one father of three detailed how unemployment left him no choice but to use credit cards, and explained that the things he charged were necessities. "A lot of that debt came from being laid off and when the job's not there anymore, I mean, there was times we actually lived off the credit card, you know, to buy food and stuff. I mean . . . we used them to exist." Another debtor, whose employer unexpectedly reduced his hours, said that he and his wife had taken cash withdrawals from their credit cards to make their mortgage payments and to buy groceries. He defended their use of credit while condemning the actions of credit card bankrupts: "It's not like I bought a computer or anything like that. I mean, we never took that kind of money and did that kind of shit with it. So that's why we always felt so angry with people who did, because we really felt like we were innocent." In all, 61 percent of the debtors who discharged credit card debt made a point to describe their charges as necessities, as opposed to the trivial or indulgent purchases made by "credit card junkies."

Distancing from the "Repeat Filer"

The final stereotype from which debtors worked to distance themselves was that of the "repeat filer." While research reveals that only a small minority of those who declare Chapter 7 bankruptcy do so more than once, debtors frequently mentioned "repeat filers," whom they believed were prevalent among bankrupts. One woman, who worked as a baker, put the matter succinctly: "You know, I'm sure there is a lot of people out there who make a career out of racking up bills every six years and filing bankruptcy and starting all over again." Discussions of repeat filers were often laced with resentment, in part because these "deadbeats" increased the potential stigma for everyone, legitimate and illegitimate filers alike. As a woman in her mid-20s, who had sold her home, a vehicle, and a boat in a futile attempt to avoid bankruptcy, stated:

> *Those people shouldn't get the third and fourth chance. . . . It pisses me off because, you know, we're playing by the rules. We've given some things up, we've made some sacrifices and we are paying for it. . . . And there's people out there that are just raping it [the bankruptcy system] and make it hard for everyone else and that's what's happening. The government is going to make it hard for everybody [via bankruptcy law reform]. . . . If people don't accept it as legitimate, then no one's going to respect it.*

To distance themselves from the repeat filer stereotype, three-quarters of the debtors asserted that they would never set foot in bankruptcy court again. Some stoically stated this as fact, while others became quite heated when discussing the possibility. A father of two young boys shouted in defiance when the issue was broached. "HELL NO!" He elaborated:

> *I'd kill myself first. Damned right. I ain't doing it. I told my wife, "We will not do it again." No way, because that would mean that we've learned nothing. . . . Damn it, man, we're not gonna go through that again. No way. No way. I don't care if we lose a job or whatever. We will live poor.*

Not only did the majority of debtors insist that they would never file again, but they also shared an explanation for why they would not do so that clearly separated them from repeat filers: Bankruptcy had taught them a critical, albeit painful, life lesson. For example, a woman who was forced into early retirement because of multiple chemical sensitivities that began when her workplace was sprayed with pesticides, insisted: "We would do anything in our power to not do it again. It isn't stigma. It's more personal worth. Because if you do this, you should learn and examine why in the hell you got in this position when you didn't believe in it."

In all their distancing activities, the debtors suggested that illegitimacy and irresponsibility were prevalent among those who declare bankruptcy, but they asserted that they themselves were relatively exceptional in not fitting the stereotypical profiles. They were neither extravagant in their spending nor profligate in racking up credit card debt, and they learned from their mistakes. In the case of "learning from their mistakes," they not only distanced themselves from less legitimate bankruptcy filers, but also imbued their struggles with a deeper purpose of personal growth and hard-won maturity.

EXCUSES AND JUSTIFICATIONS

Excuses are statements made by individuals that they had no control over whether or not to engage in the problematic behavior. Justifications, in contrast, involve an acknowledgment that one consciously chose to engage in the action, but only under mitigating circumstances that render one's behavior understandable and acceptable. The debtors consistently provided both excuses and justifications to lessen the negative implications of their bankruptcies.

Excuses

Excuses soften the moral breach through what Sykes and Matza (1957) refer to as a "denial of responsibility." The two most common ways in which debtors denied responsibility for their bankruptcies were "scapegoating" and "appeals to accidents."

Scapegoating involves a claim that the real responsibility for the action in question lies with someone other than the individual under scrutiny. Many debtors accused lenders of being the ones responsible for their bankruptcies. One man, who argued that he could accept partial responsibility for his situation, nonetheless went on to blame credit card lenders for irresponsibly setting debtors up for a fall: "At the same time, they shouldn't have been giving us so many damned [credit] cards either. Why the hell do they give people so many cards?" A homeowner insisted that she and her husband were pushed into bankruptcy by a mortgage lender who encouraged them to refinance their home several times, to the point that the mortgage payment was beyond what they could afford. Yet another woman blamed her bankruptcy on behind-the-scenes machinations by her mortgage company: "The mortgage company started foreclosure procedures on us and we weren't even aware of it. So that's what put us into bankruptcy. We had to come up with $5000 . . . which in turn made us fall behind on a lot of our bills, so we had to file bankruptcy."

The other type of excuse, "appeals to accidents," included two categories of unexpected events that catapulted debtors into filing. The first was an unanticipated loss of employment. Several debtors lamented that they had lost jobs through no fault of their own—with devastating results. A man who had lost his job of 20-plus years at a saw mill in Oregon, for instance, stated: "I wasn't responsible for my situation, you know. I've worked hard all my life. I've done, did what I was supposed to do. I had my entire life yanked out from under me. I had no control over it." Another debtor, a woman whose husband had lost four jobs in three years because of downsizing and employers' business bankruptcies, argued that their bankruptcy was due in large part to "the lack of stability of jobs. . . . It's the profession that he's in [auto parts sales] and it's happened all our lives." Her husband elaborated:

> *Money was so good back then [in the early 1990s]. We were making a lot of money and we were catching up on everything and then it [the economy] just did a one-eighty. Everything they promised that wouldn't happen with workers did happen. They cut the pay down, reduced the hours. . . . It's just harder and harder to keep it [a job].*

Debtors who had faced serious illness and injury also invoked "appeals to accidents" to explain their bankruptcies. The couple who confronted his cancer and their daughter's birth deformities used medical expenses to entirely excuse their bankruptcy. The aforementioned debtor who retired because of chemical sensitivities in her workplace recalled how the combination of illness and debt pushed her to the brink of suicide. She insisted that if she had not been forced to retire, they would never have filed for bankruptcy and instead would still be paying at least the minimum on their credit cards.

Justifications

In contrast to excuses, individuals who rely on justifications argue that the decision to engage in the questionable behavior was in fact a legitimate decision based on other considerations or circumstances. In doing so, they posit that the behavior has "a positive value in the face of a claim to the contrary" (Scott and Lyman, 1968). Two types of justifications were particularly common among debtors: "appeals to higher loyalties" and "condemnation of the condemners."

Appeals to higher loyalties are assertions that a greater good was served by one's action. Citing the unbearable stresses of struggling with insolvency, some debtors invoked self-care as a greater good. In the words of one debtor, a woman who was on disability, "There was enough pressure to kill you. And I don't care what kind of person you are or what you want to do, there's a time when you have to look at the reality, and the reality is, no matter how long you pay [on the credit cards], you can't do it. There's no way. And it's not worth killing yourself over."

Yet others framed their bankruptcies in more altruistic terms, especially in claiming that they filed in order to meet familial responsibilities. For example, when a father of two in his late-20s was asked how he felt when he finally decided to file, he stressed his concern for his children: "I didn't like it. Because that's not the way it's supposed to be done. You're supposed to pay your debts. But also I felt relieved knowing that my house is safe [protected from foreclosure] and I can feed my kids." Another young father pointed to a grocery shopping experience with his two young sons that pushed him and his wife to file.

> *The point that really did it for me . . . we were in the store and we hadn't been grocery shopping for a while, because we couldn't [afford it] . . . trying to get by on macaroni and cheese, and our oldest son was like a little kid in a candy shop. He was so excited. . . . And when his reaction, both him and my youngest son, their reactions . . . they were so infused with life, you know, it was like, "Oh my god, man." I know, myself, I was like, "Fuck, I have really failed these guys man, I mean, I can't, why did I wait so long? Why? God, we gotta deal with this. Somehow we gotta get out of this."*

TRANSCENDENCE

The final form of deviance avowal observed among the debtors is what Warren (1980) has referred to as "transcendence." In her discussion of ways in which individuals seek "destigmatization," Warren notes that some stigmatized individuals attempt to "transcend" or "rise above their condition by means of some persistent type of action [that] displays a 'better' self." Consistent with Warren's conceptualization, several bankrupt debtors attempted transcendence by engaging in actions in the present, or proclaiming intended future actions, that would lift them above their stigmatized identity.

One notable means of transcendence involved a commitment to repay some of the debts from which debtors had been legally relieved. According to court records examined by researchers with the 2001 wave of the Consumer Bankruptcy Project, "One in four families signs on to pay off debts they no longer owe after filing for bankruptcy" (Warren and Tyagi, 2003). Consistent with Zelizer's (1994) analysis of the "social meaning of money," the debts earmarked as critical for repayment were those that reflected valued social relationships. Specifically, debtors in our study focused on repaying creditors with whom they had close personal or professional relationships. So, for example, the previously quoted woman who ran a horse boarding facility explained, "I had some veterinary bills also. I see that as a personal service and a friendship there, so you really hate to file on something like that. . . . [So] I'm still paying them, because, you know, there's a personal stigma that goes along with it too." Another woman, a mother of three who worked as a waitress, also mentioned that she felt an obligation to repay her veterinarian. "I didn't want to include my vet [in the bankruptcy], and I didn't want to have to include my dentist. That was personal and that definitely, I thought, was so wrong that eventually I want to pay those people back, when we can. I will not pay back a credit card company, but I will pay my vet and my dentist."

Yet other debtors sought to transcend the "bankrupt" identity by using the knowledge they had gained through their financial travails to help others avoid similar problems. In their efforts to teach others, debtors demonstrated that they themselves had from their mistakes" and desired to use their hard-won understanding to benefit others. One debtor, whose two granddaughters were living with her and her husband, described how she was teaching her oldest granddaughter to manage credit cards and the associated debt: "She [the granddaughter] will pay it [the credit card] off, then she'll run it up again. And I say to her, 'uh uh, no. That's not the way to go. If you can't pay cash, then . . . don't buy.' She doesn't like to pay the interest, because, see, this is what I've been teaching them. The interest will eat you up." Another debtor, a young woman in her late-20s, recounted that she and her husband had offered to help their friends learn how to work from a budget: "I mean, my husband and I are advocates of budgets. Some of our friends are having problems, and we're like, 'This is how you do a budget. Come on over and we'll teach you how to do it; it's real simple.' "

Finally, a number of debtors made proclamations of intended transcendence. Many insisted that despite futures that might well be plagued by unstable income and new debts, they would do almost anything to avoid a subsequent bankruptcy. As a man in his early-40s who laid cable for a living put it, "I would just give up everything. I would sell the house. Everything." Others said they would sacrifice their marriages before they would file again. And in the most extreme case, quoted previously, a man asserted, "I'd kill myself first. . . . We're not gonna go through that again. No way."

CONCLUSION

Drawing upon data from a study of married couples who filed for bankruptcy, we have accomplished two things. First, we have challenged the popular argument that contemporary Americans do not experience bankruptcy as stigmatizing. Second, we have demonstrated the means through which bankrupt debtors manage this stigma. While our limited sample size constrains our ability to broadly generalize our findings, we have nonetheless presented the only in-depth U.S. data reported to date that directly address the issue of bankruptcy stigma and bankruptcy stigma management.

Our findings are clear. Feelings of stigmatization were a pervasive feature of our informants' bankruptcy experiences. Thirty-five of the thirty-seven individuals in our study stated—frequently, often emphatically, and in a variety of ways—that they felt shame and stigmatization as they negotiated the bankruptcy process. Significantly, these comments emerged without specific prodding from the interviewer regarding stigmatization. Further, our informants exhibited many classic techniques documented in previous sociological studies for managing stigma. They strived to conceal their spoiled identities, especially from particularly significant others. Fearing embarrassment, they avoided interactions with those who might know of their recent failings. And when put in a position of having to openly face their spoiled identities in the context of the research interview, they distanced themselves from stereotypical images of illegitimate bankruptcy filers, provided excuses and justifications for their own bankruptcies, and described their attempts at activities that would enable them, at least partially, to transcend their stigmatized identities.

Given the stigma of filing bankruptcy, why do people still do it? Our respondents gave a resoundingly uniform explanation for their decisions to declare bankruptcy: dire economic necessity. Faced with some combination of huge medical and/or other debts, unrelenting pressures from creditors, an inability to provide for basic family needs, and a loss or reduction in income, our respondents believed that bankruptcy was their only realistic option. This is not a calculus based in business acumen, but rather a calculus of economic desperation. Their statements are consistent with a substantial body of macro-level data which demonstrates that increased bankruptcy rates stem from employment instability, rising costs for housing and health care, and deregulation of the consumer credit industry (see Himmelstein et al., 2005; Sullivan, Warren and Westbrook, 2000; Warren and Tyagi, 2003). This being the case, from a pragmatic standpoint, it seems likely that social policies aimed toward moderating job and income losses, decreasing the high expenses of illness and injury, regulating the interest and fees charged by the lending industry, and reducing levels of personal indebtedness would do far more to lower bankruptcy filing rates than would heightened levels of stigmatization.

REFERENCES

Administrative Office of the U.S. Courts. 2005. "News Releases." Retrieved September 1, 2005 (http://www.uscourts.gov/Press_Release/index.html).

Herman, Nancy. 1993. "Return to Sender: Reintegrative Stigma-management Strategies of Ex-psychiatric Patients." *Journal of Contemporary Ethnography* 22:295–330.

Himmelstein, David, Elizabeth Warren, Deborah Thorne, and Steffie Woolhandler. 2005. "Illness and Injury as Contributors to Bankruptcy." *Health Affairs*, Web Exclusive. Retrieved February 2, 2005 (http://content.healthaffairs.org/cgi/content/full/hlthaff.w5.63/DC1).

Hochschild, Arlie Russell. 1983. *The Managed Heart: Commercialization of Human Feeling.* Los Angeles, CA: University of California Press.

Holstein, James A., and Jaber F. Gubrium. 2002. "Active Interviewing." Pp. 112–126 in *Qualitative Research Methods*, edited by D. Weinberg. Malden, MA: Blackwell Publishers.

Hutchinson, Asa. 1999. "Bankruptcy Reform." Federal Document Clearing House, Inc., Congressional Press Releases. April 20.

Lofland, John, David Snow, Leon Anderson, and Lyn Lofland. 2005. *Analyzing Social Settings.* 4th ed. Belmont, CA: Wadsworth.

Manning, Robert D. 2000. *Credit Card Nation: The Consequences of America's Addiction to Credit.* New York: Basic Books.

Schneider, Joseph W., and Peter Conrad. 1980. "In the Closet with Illness: Epilepsy, Stigma Potential, and Information Control." *Social Problems* 28: 32–44.

Schwalbe, Michael, Sandra Godwin, Daphne Holden, Douglas Schrock, Shealy Thompson, and Michele Wolkomir. 2000. "Generic Processes in the Reproduction of Inequality: An Interactionist Analysis." *Social Forces* 79:419–452.

Scott, Marvin B., and Stanford M. Lyman. 1968. "Accounts." *American Sociological Review* 33:46–62.

Snow, David A., and Leon Anderson. 1993. *Down on Their Luck: A Study of Homeless Street People.* Berkeley, CA: University of California Press.

Stanley, David T., and Marjorie Girth. 1971. *Bankruptcy: Problem, Process, Reform.* Washington, D.C.: The Brookings Institution.

Sullivan, Teresa A., Elizabeth Warren, and Jay Lawrence Westbrook. 2000. *The Fragile Middle Class: Americans in Debt.* New Haven, CT: Yale University Press.

Sykes, Gresham M., and David Matza. 1957. "Techniques of Neutralization: A Theory of Delinquency." *American Sociological Review* 22:664–670.

Turner, Ralph H. 1972. "Deviance Avowal as Neutralization of Commitment." *Social Problems* 19: 308–321.

Warren, Carol A. B. 1980. "Destigmatization of Identity: From Deviant to Charismatic." *Qualitative Sociology* 3:59–72.

Warren, Carol A. B. 2002. "Qualitative Interviewing." Pp. 83–101 in *Handbook of Interview Research: Context & Method*, edited by J. F. Gubrium and J. A. Holstein. Thousand Oaks, CA: Sage Publications.

Warren, Elizabeth, and Amelia Warren Tyagi. 2003. *The Two-Income Trap: Why Middle-Class Mothers and Fathers Are Going Broke.* New York: Basic Books.

Zelizer, Viviana A. 1994. *The Social Meaning of Money: Pin Money, Paychecks, Poor Relief, and Other Currencies.* New York: Basic Books.

Zywicki, Todd J. 2005. "Institutions, Incentives, and Consumer Bankruptcy Reform." George Mason University School of Law, Working Paper 05-07. Retrieved July 15, 2005 (http://www.gmu.edu/departments/law/faculty/papers/wpDetail.php?wpID=285).

REVIEW QUESTIONS

1. Does the enormous increase of personal bankruptcy today suggest that "Americans have lost their sense of shame" as many government officials believe? Defend your answer.
2. How do people who feel stigmatized for filing bankruptcy deal with the stigma?
3. Do you find the bankrupt debtors' excuses and justifications for filing bankruptcy convincing? Why or why not?

CHAPTER 24

THE STIGMA OF OBESITY

ERICH GOODE

Bertha was a massive woman. She weighed well over 400 pounds. Still, people enjoyed her company, and she had an active social life. One Friday night, Bertha and several of her friends stopped in a local Burger and Shake for a quick snack. Bertha disliked fast-food restaurants with good reason: Their seats were inadequate for her size. But, she was a good sport and wanted to be agreeable, so she raised no objection to the choice of an eating establishment. Bertha squeezed her huge body into the booth and enjoyed a shake and burger. A typical Friday night crowd stood waiting for tables, so Bertha and her companions finished their snack and began to vacate the booth so that others could dine. But Bertha's worst fears were realized: She was so tightly jammed in between the table and the chair that she was stuck.

Bertha began struggling to get out of the booth, without success. Her friends pulled her, pushed her, and twisted her—all to no avail. She was trapped. Soon, all eyes in the Burger and Shake were focused on the hapless Bertha and her plight. Onlookers began laughing at her. Snickers escalated to belly laughs, and the restaurant fairly rocked with raucous laughter and cruel, taunting remarks. "Christ, is she fat!" "What's the matter, honey—one burger too many?" "Look at the trapped whale!" "How could anyone get that fat!" Bertha's struggles became frenzied; she began sweating profusely. Every movement became an act of desperation to free herself from her deeply humiliating situation. Finally, in a mighty heave, Bertha tore the entire booth from its bolts and she stood in the middle of the floor of the Burger and Shake, locked into the booth as if it had been a barrel. The crowd loved it, and shrieked with laughter that intensified in volume and stridency, as Bertha staggered helplessly, squatting in the center of the room.

One of Bertha's friends ran to his car, grabbed a hammer and a wrench, came back in, and began smashing at the booth. He broke it into pieces that fell to the floor, freeing the woman from her torture chamber. Bertha lumbered and pushed her way through the laughing, leering crowd, and ran to her car, hot tears in her eyes and burning shame in her throat. The friend who freed her limply placed the pieces of the chair and table onto the counter. The employees, now irritated, demanded that he pay for the damaged booth, but he and Bertha's other companions simply left the restaurant.

After that incident, Bertha rarely left her house. Two months later, she died of heart failure. She was 31 years old.

THE OBESE AND THE THIN IDEAL

In contemporary America, obesity is stigmatized. Fat people are considered less worthy human beings than thin people are. They receive less of the good things that life has to offer, and more of the bad. Men and women of average weight tend to look down on the obese, feel superior to them,

Source: Erich Goode, "The Stigma of Obesity," in Erich Goode, ed., *Social Deviance*. Boston: Allyn and Bacon, 1996, pp. 332–340. Reproduced by permission of Pearson Education, Inc.

reward them less, punish them, make fun of them. The obese are often an object of derision and harassment for their weight. What is more, thin people will feel that this treatment is just, that the obese deserve it, indeed, that it is even something of a humanitarian gesture, since such humiliation will supposedly inspire them to lose weight. The stigma of obesity is so intense and so pervasive that eventually the obese will come to see themselves as deserving of it, too.

The obese, in the words of one observer, "are a genuine minority, with all the attributes that a corrosive social atmosphere lends to such groups: poor self-image, heightened sensitivity, passivity, and withdrawal, a sense of isolation and rejection." They are subject to relentless discrimination, they are the butt of denigrating jokes, they suffer from persecution; it would not be an exaggeration to say that they attract cruelty from the thin majority. Moreover, their friends and family rarely give the kind of support and understanding they need to deal with this cruelty; in fact, it is often friends and family who are themselves meting out the cruel treatment. The social climate has become "so completely permeated with anti-fat prejudice that the fat themselves have been infected by it. They hate other fat people, hate themselves when they are fat, and will risk anything—even their lives—in an attempt to get thin. . . . Anti-fat bigotry . . . is a psychic net in which the overweight are entangled every moment of their lives" (Louderback, 1970). The obese typically accept the denigration thin society dishes out to them because they feel, for the most part, that they deserve it. And they do not defend other fat people who are being criticized because they are a mirror of themselves; they mirror their own defects—the very defects that are so repugnant to them. Unlike the members of most other minorities, they don't fight back; in fact, they feel that they can't fight back. Racial, ethnic, and religious minorities can isolate themselves to a degree from majority prejudices; the obese cannot. The chances are, most of the people they meet will be average size, and they live in a physical world built for individuals with much smaller bodies. The only possibilities seem to be to brace themselves—to cower under the onslaught of abuse—or to retreat and attempt to minimize the day-to-day disgrace.

Our hostility toward overweight runs up and down the scale, from the grossly obese to men and women of average weight. If the hugely obese are persecuted mightily for their weight, the slightly overweight are simply persecuted proportionally less—they are not exempt. We live in a weight-obsessed society. It is impossible to escape nagging reminders of our ideal weight. Standing at the checkout counter in a supermarket, we are confronted by an array of magazines; each with its own special diet designed to eliminate those flabby pounds. Television programs and even more so, advertising, display actresses and models who are considerably slimmer than average, setting up an almost impossibly thin ideal for the viewing public. If we were to gain ten pounds, our friends would all notice it, view the gain with negative feelings, and only the most tactful would not comment on it.

These exacting weight standards not surprisingly fall more severely on the shoulders of women than on men's. In a survey of the 33,000 readers of *Glamour* who responded to a questionnaire placed in the August 1983 issue of the magazine, 75 percent said that they were "too fat," even though only one-quarter were overweight according to the stringent 1959 Metropolitan Life Insurance Company's height-weight tables. . . . Still more surprising, 45 percent who were *under* weight according to Metropolitan's figures felt that they were "too fat." Only 6 percent of the respondents felt "very happy" about their bodies; only 15 percent described their bodies as "just right." When looking at their nude bodies in the mirror, 32 percent said that they felt "anxious," 12 percent felt "depressed," and 5 percent felt "repulsed."

Evidence suggests that the standards for the ideal female form have gotten slimmer over the years. Women whose figures would have been comfortably embraced by the norm a generation or more ago are now regarded as overweight, even fat. The model for the White Rock Girl, inspired by the ancient Greek goddess Psyche, was 5′4″ tall in 1894 and she weighed 140; her measurements were 37″-27″-38″. Over the years, the woman who was selected to depict the "White Rock Girl" has gotten taller, slimmer, and she has weighed less. In 1947, she was 5′6″, weighed 125 pounds, and measured 35″-25″-35″. And today, she's 5′8″, weighs 118, and measures 35″-24″-34″. Commenting on this trend, in an advertising flyer the executives of White Rock explain: "Over the years the Psyche image has become longer legged, slimmer hipped, and streamlined. Today—when purity is so important—she continues to symbolize the purity of all White Rock products." The equation of slenderness with purity is a revealing comment on today's obsession with thinness: Weighing a few pounds over some mythical ideal is to live in an "impure" condition. Interestingly, today's American woman averages 5′4″ and weighs 140 pounds, the same size as 1894's White Rock Girl.

Advertising models represent one kind of ideal; they tend to be extremely thin. . . . Fashion models typically border on the anorexic, and women who take them as role models to be emulated are subjecting themselves to an almost unattainable standard. It would be inaccurate to argue that all American women aspire to look like a fashion model, and it would be inaccurate to assert that women in all media are emaciated. Still, it is entirely accurate to say that the ideal woman's figure as depicted in the media is growing slimmer over the years. Even in settings where women were once fairly voluptuous, today's version has slimmed down significantly.

Prior to 1970, contestants in Miss America pageants weighed 88 percent of the average for American women their age; after 1970 this declined somewhat are 85 percent. More important, before 1970 pageant *winners* weighed the same as the other contestants; after 1970, however, winners weighed significantly *less* than the contestants who didn't win—82.5 percent of the average for American women as a whole. Similarly, the weight of women who posed for *Playboy* centerfolds also declined between 1959 and 1978. Centerfolds for 1959 were 91 percent of the weight for an average American woman in her 20s; this declined to 84 percent in 1978.

The increasingly slim standards of feminine beauty represent the most desirable point on a scale. The opposite end of this scale represents undesirable territory—obesity. If American women have been evaluated by standards of physical desirability that have shifted from slim to slimmer over the years, it is reasonable to assume that during this same period it has become less and less socially acceptable to be fat. In tribal and peasant societies, corpulence was associated with affluence. An abundant body represented a corresponding material abundance. In a society in which having enough to eat is a mark of distinction, heaviness will draw a measure of respect. This is true not only for oneself but also for one's spouse or spouses, and one's children as well. With the coming of mature industrialization, however, nutritional adequacy becomes sufficiently widespread as to cease being a sign of distinction; slenderness rather than corpulence comes to be adopted as the prevailing esthetic standard among the affluent (Powdermaker, 1960; Cahnman, 1968, pp. 287–288). In fact, what we have seen is a gradual adoption of the slim standard of attractiveness in all economic classes for both men and women, but much more strongly and stringently for women. And while more firmly entrenched in the upper socioeconomic classes, the slim ideal has permeated all levels of society.

STIGMATIZATION AND ITS CONSEQUENCES

Not only is obesity unfashionable and considered unesthetic to the thin majority, it is also regarded as "morally reprehensible," a "social disgrace" (Cahnman, 1968). Fat people are *set apart* from men and women of average size; they are isolated from "normal" society (Millman, 1980). Today, being obese bears something of a stigma. In the words of sociologist Erving Goffman, the stigmatized are "disqualified from full social acceptance." They have been reduced "from a whole and usual person to a tainted, discounted one." The bearer of stigma is a "blemished person . . . to be avoided, especially in public places." The individual with a stigma is seen as "not quite human" (Goffman, 1963).

Over the centuries, the word *stigma* has had two meanings—one good and the second, very bad. Among the ancient Greeks, a stigma was a brand on the body of a person, symbolizing that the bearer was in the service of the temple. In medieval Christianity, *stigmata* were marks resembling the wounds and scars on the body of Jesus, indicating that the bearer was an especially holy individual. [On the other hand,] in ancient times criminals and slaves were branded to identify their inferior status; the brand was a stigma. Lepers were said to bear the stigma of their loathsome disease. As it is currently used, stigma refers to a stain or reproach on one's character or reputation, or a symbol or sign of this inferiority or defect. Anything that causes someone to look down upon, condemn, denigrate or ignore another can be said to be *stigmatizing*.

A stigmatizing trait is rarely isolated. Hardly anyone who possesses one such characteristic is thought to have only one. A single sin will be regarded as housing a multitude of others as well, to be the "tip of the iceberg." The one stigmatizing trait is presumed to hide "a wide range of imperfections" (Goffman, 1963, p. 5). . . . The one negative trait is a *master status*—everything about the individual is interpreted in light of the single trait. "Possession of one deviant trait may have a generalized symbolic value, so that people automatically assume that its bearer possesses other undesirable traits allegedly associated with it." Thus, the question is raised when confronting someone with a stigma: "What kind of person would break such an important rule?" The answer that is offered is typically: "One who is different from the rest of us, who cannot or will not act as a moral human being and therefore might break other important rules." In short, the stigmatizing characteristic "becomes the controlling one" (Becker, 1963).

To be stigmatized is to possess a *contaminated* identity. Interaction with non-stigmatized individuals will be strained, tainted, awkward, inhibited. While the non-stigmatized may, because of the dictates of polite sociability, attempt to hide their negative feelings toward the stigmatized trait specifically, or the stigmatized individual as a whole, and act normally, they are nonetheless intensely aware of the other's blemish. Likewise, the stigmatized individual remains self-conscious about his or her relations with "normals," believing (often correctly) that the stigma is the exclusive focus of the interaction.

> *I am always worried about how Jane judges me because she is the real beauty queen and the main gang leader. When I am with her, I hold my breath hard so my tummy doesn't bulge and I pull my skirt down so my fat thighs don't show. I tuck in my rear end. I try to look as thin as possible for her. I get so preoccupied with looking good enough to get into her gang that I forget what she's talking to me about. . . . I am so worried about how my body is going over that I can hardly concentrate on what she's saying. She asks me about math and all I am thinking about is how fat I am (Allon, 1976).*

Highly stigmatized individuals, in the face of hostility on the part of the majority to their traits and to themselves as bearers of those traits, walk along one of two paths in reacting to stigma. One is to fight back by forming subcultures or groups of individuals who share the characteristics the majority rejects, and to treat this difference from the majority as a badge of honor—or at least, as no cause for shame. Clearly, the homosexual subculture provides an example of the tendency to ward off majority prejudices and oppression. This path is trod by those who feel that the majority's opinion of them and of the characteristic the majority disvalues is illegitimate or invalid—just plain wrong. Here, the legitimacy of the stigma is rejected. A trait, characteristic, a form of behavior that others look down upon, they say, is no cause for invidiousness. You may put us down, those who travel this path say, but you have no right to do so. What we are or do is every bit as blameless, indeed, honorable, as what you are or do.

The second path the stigmatized take in reacting to stigma from the majority is *internalization.* Here, stigmatized individuals hold the same negative attitudes toward themselves as the majority does. The stigmatized individual is dominated by feelings of self-hatred and self-derogation. Thus, those who are discriminated against are made to understand that they *deserve* it; they come to accept their negative treatment as *just* (Cahnman, 1968). They feel that the majority has a right to stigmatize them. They may despise themselves for being who or what they are, for doing what they do or have done. As we see in testimony from fat people themselves, there is a great deal of evidence to suggest that the obese are more likely to follow the second path than the first. In fact, it might be said that in comparison with the possessors of all stigmatized characteristics or behavior, the obese most strongly agree with the majority's negative judgment of who they are.

WHY THE OBESE ARE STIGMATIZED

Negative feelings on the part of the majority have been directed at a wide range of different groups and categories. Prejudice and racism against minority groups—what Goffman calls "the tribal stigma of race, nation, and religion" (1963)—is one type of stigma. In some all-white settings, Blacks will be stigmatized if they enter them. Likewise, in certain all-black settings, it is the reverse. Anti-Semitism is rife in some social contexts; in them, to be Jewish is to suffer discrimination. At the same time, gentiles will find themselves shunned and ostracized in specific Jewish settings or contexts. For racial, national, and religious groups, stigma may work both ways; what counts is which group has the most power and resources. Although racism, ethnic hostility, and prejudice are fascinating topics, they are not what we are concerned about here.

A second type of trait or characteristic that tends to attract stigma from the majority who does not share it is made up of individuals who possess those "blemishes of individual character," which include having a "weak will, domineering or unnatural passions, treacherous and rigid beliefs, and dishonesty." Behavior or tendencies that, to the majority, manifest these and other "blemishes of individual character" include "mental disorder, imprisonment, addiction, alcoholism, homosexuality, unemployment, suicidal attempts, and radical political behavior" (Goffman, 1963). Sociologists commonly refer to these forms of behavior as behavioral deviance, deviant behavior, or simply deviance. The archaic notion that deviant behavior is abnormal, a product of a disordered, pathological personality, has been abandoned long ago within sociology. People who engage in disapproved behavior tend to be perfectly normal; psychological abnormality has nothing to do with the concept of deviance. In sociology, deviance simply means a departure from an approved norm, especially where this departure tends to be punished, condemned, or stigmatized. Behavioral deviance, then, is a type of stigma.

The third type of trait or characteristic that commonly attracts stigma from the majority includes what Goffman calls "abominations of the body—the various physical deformities" (1963). While not as thoroughly or as strongly rejected or stigmatized as behavioral deviants, possessors of certain physical characteristics are not completely accepted by the majority, either. Many individuals without a physical handicap feel uncomfortable relating to or interacting with someone who has an obvious disability or disfigurement, and this feeling is translated into real-life behavior—most commonly, avoiding contact, especially if it is intimate, with the disabled. While most nondisabled individuals would state that they would or do treat those with a disability "the same" as those without one, the disabled reported that their treatment at the hands of the majority shows this claim to be fictional. In one study, only a small minority of the sample said that they would marry an amputee (18 percent), someone in a wheelchair (7 percent), a blind person (16 percent), or a stutterer (7 percent). While some might object and argue that marriage is a highly individual matter, having little to do with stigma, the same pattern prevailed in other areas of life. Only a shade over half said that they would have a deaf person as a *friend* (53 percent), and for the cerebral palsied, this was under four respondents in ten (38 percent)! Barely half (54 percent) said that they would live in the same *neighborhood* as a retardate (Shears and Jensema, 1969). Clearly, stigma is alive and well for the possessors of undesirable physical characteristics. The fact that they are involuntarily acquired is no protection against their stigmatization. Stigma is ubiquitous; no society exists in which all members are free of invidious feelings toward individuals with certain physical traits.

It is clear that much the same process of stigma occurs with the obese as with other traits, characteristics, and behavior that are regarded by the majority as undesirable. In fact, obesity is unique in at least one respect: It is considered by the "thin" majority as both a physical characteristic, like blindness and disabilities, and a form of behavioral deviance, like prostitution and alcoholism. The obese, unlike the physically disabled, are held *responsible* for their physical condition. Fatness, in the eyes of the nonobese majority, is viewed as both a physical deformity and as a behavioral aberration (Cahnman, 1968; Allon, 1982). Being fat is regarded as a matter of choice; the obese have gotten the way they are because of something they have done.

Overweight individuals "are stigmatized because they are held responsible for their deviant status, presumably lacking self-control and willpower. They are not merely physically deviant as are physically disabled or disfigured persons, but they [also] seem to possess characterological stigma. Fat people are viewed as 'bad' or 'immoral'; supposedly, they do not want to change the error of their ways" (Allon, 1982). Contrary to the strictly disabled, and contrary to individuals belonging to a race different from our own,

> *the obese are presumed to hold their fate in their own hands; if they were only a little less greedy or lazy or yielding to impulse or oblivious of advice, they would restrict excessive food intake, resort to strenuous exercise, and as a consequence of such deliberate action, they would reduce.... While blindness is considered a misfortune, obesity is branded as a defect.... A blind girl will be helped by her agemates, but a heavy girl will be derided. A paraplegic boy will be supported by other boys, but a fat boy will be pushed around. The embarrassing and not infrequently harassing treatment which is meted out to obese teenagers by those around them will not elicit sympathy from onlookers, but a sense of gratification; the idea is that they have got what was coming to them (Cahnman, 1968).*

The obese are overweight, according to the popular view, because they eat immodestly and to excess. They have succumbed to temptation and hedonistic pleasure-seeking, where other, more virtuous and less self-indulgent individuals have resisted. It is, as with behavioral deviance, a matter of a struggle between vice and virtue. The obese must therefore pay for the sin of overindulgence by attracting well-deserved stigma (Cahnman, 1968; Maddox et al., 1968). The obese suffer from what the public sees as inflicted damnation (Allon, 1973; Allon, 1982). In one study of the public's rejection of individuals with certain traits and characteristics, it was found that the stigma of obesity was in between that of physical handicaps, such as blindness, and behavioral deviance, such as homosexuality (Hiller, 1981, 1982). In other words, the public stigmatized the obese more than possessors of involuntarily acquired undesirable traits, but less than individuals who engage in unpopular, unconventional behavior.

This introduces a *moral* dimension to obesity that is lacking in other physical characteristics. A trait such as being blind or deaf that is seen as beyond the individual's control, for which he or she is held to be not responsible, is seen as a misfortune. In contrast, character flaws are regarded in a much harsher light. Obesity is seen as the outward manifestation of an undesirable character; it therefore invites retribution, in much of the public's eyes.

So powerfully stigmatized has obesity become that, in a *New York Times* editorial (Rosenthal, 1981), one observer argues that obesity has replaced sex and death as our "Contemporary pornography." We attach some degree of shame and guilt to eating. Our society is made up of "modern puritans" who tell one another "how repugnant it is to be fat"; "what's really disgusting . . . is not sex, but fat." We are all so humorless, "so relentless, so determined to punish the overweight. . . . Not only are the overweight the most stigmatized group in the United States, but fat people are expected to participate in their own degradation by agreeing with others who taunt them."

REFERENCES

Allon, Natalie. 1973. The stigma of overweight in everyday life. In G. A. Bray (ed.), *Obesity in Perspective.* Washington, D.C.: U.S. Government Printing Office, pp. 83–102.

Allon, Natalie. 1976. *Urban Life Styles.* Dubuque, Iowa: W. C. Brown.

Allon, Natalie. 1982. The stigma of overweight in everyday life. In Benjamin B. Wolman (ed.), *Psychological Aspects of Obesity: A Handbook.* New York: Van Nostrand Reinhold, pp. 130–174.

Becker, Howard S. 1963. *Outsiders: Studies in the Sociology of Deviance.* New York: Free Press.

Cahnman, Werner J. 1968. The stigma of obesity. *The Sociological Quarterly*, 9 (Summer), 283–299.

Garner, David M., Paul E. Garfinkel, D. Schwartz, and M. Thompson. 1980. Cultural expectations of thinness in women. *Psychological Reports*, 47, 483–491.

Goffman, Erving. 1963. *Stigma: Notes on the Management of Spoiled Identity.* Englewood Cliffs, N.J.: Prentice-Hall/Spectrum.

Hiller, Dana V. 1981. The salience of overweight in personality characterization. *Journal of Psychology*, 108, 233–240.

Hiller, Dana V. 1982. Overweight as master status: A replication. *Journal of Psychology*, 110, 107–113.

Louderback, Llewellyn. 1970. *Fat Power. Whatever You Weigh Is Right.* New York: Hawthorn Books.

Maddox, George L., Kurt W. Back, and Veronica Liederman. 1968. Overweight as social deviance and disability. *Journal of Health and Social Behavior*, 9 (December 1968), 287–298.

Millman, Marxia. 1980. *Such a Pretty Face: Being Fat in America.* New York: W. W. Norton.

Powdermaker, Hortense. 1960. An anthropological approach to the problem of obesity. *Bulletin of the New York Academy of Medicine*, 36, 286–295.

Shears, L. M., and C. J. Jensma. 1969. Social acceptability of anomalous persons. *Exceptional Children*, 35(1), 91–96.

REVIEW QUESTIONS

1. What makes the obese different from other minorities?
2. What are some of the consequences the obese encounter because they are stigmatized?
3. Do you agree or disagree that obese people are stigmatized? Cite examples to support your position.

Chapter 25

WHAT IS IT LIKE TO BE A RURAL LESBIAN?

MARGARET COOPER

Since 1990 I have conducted personal interviews, engaged in participant observations, obtained completed online questionnaires, and accessed women through Internet message boards. My sample now contains over one hundred women. For this article, I focus on rural lesbians living primarily in the South and Midwest. They range in age from 18 to 66. Here I present data on their experiences as lesbians in their childhood, adolescence, and adulthood.

CHILDHOOD

Many of these rural lesbians said that they as children had rejected the traditional feminine gender role. They provided various reasons. To Kate, her reason was attraction to girls. She had consequently tried to present a "macho" appearance of herself to attract girls since she was seven years old. She explained it this way:

> *I used to think, as a kid, that you had to be masculine to get a woman . . . that women liked masculinity and men liked femininity. So I tried to convince every girl on the block that I was a boy. I even took a male name. And, of course, it made perfect sense to me. I never understood why other kids' parents were freaking out about it.*

Another lesbian, Pat, rejected femininity because it "is all sex-oriented. It's the dumb housewife image. If you look at it, that's just the way it is."

Rejection of the traditional femininity appeared in three ways: (1) taking the role of the male, (2) being a "tomboy," and (3) avoiding feminine dress and play. In taking the male role, Anita fantasized being the male hero James Bond or Matt Dillon and never a heroine on the screen. Sally talked about how "I always dressed like a little boy even though I had tons of dresses!" Rhonda said that she "always played the boy . . . always!"

As for being "tomboys," Melissa's description of herself being one was something that many other lesbians could relate to:

> *Until kindergarten, I was femme all the way, dresses with matching purses and shoes, dolls, everyone's little princess . . . then I discovered toughskin jeans, Converse sneakers, GI Joes, AFX racetracks, Matchbox cars . . . I was just a little tomboy from then on, had severe crushes on my teachers that were women from the first grade on and would stay after school often to help them out. Today I am still tomboyish, plain Jane, I don't wear makeup . . .*

Many of the women talked about their disdain for feminine dress and play. Carole had said she would "rather take a beating than put on a dress." Barbara told me that she "wanted to burn the Barbie dolls" that her mother gave her. Karen stated, "I always *hated* playing with dolls and I wanted to go play with my brother . . . I always

Source: Written specifically for this reader.

wanted the toys he got for Christmas like the model cars." In one way or another, the women talked about "playing with boys" and even preferring male company over female company in recreational activities.

ADOLESCENCE

During the childhood years, the rejection of the female role was relatively risk-free. This began to change in adolescence. In my studies, I have discovered at least three types of adolescent lesbians: (1) girls who accepted female identities but sought to redefine their own definitions of femininity, (2) girls who wanted children and adopted a feminine persona to attract males as potential husbands and fathers, and (3) girls who adopted a "mannish" appearance as a sort of lesbian "rite of passage."

Many of those who sought to redefine their own definitions of femininity opted for nontraditional outlooks. Some entered the military or sports activities. One woman in another study described how she wore feminine attire to a sports banquet:

> *If I would have worn what I wanted to wear, it would have been like, dress slacks and a button-up shirt, and I would have matched all the (male) varsity coaches. I would have been more like the guys in the room. I knew that everyone else was going to wear a skirt. I would feel like I would be a sore thumb sticking out. I would feel like everyone in the room would be like, "Oh, there's the lesbian!" (Abes and Jones, 2004)*

Amelia talked about wanting children desperately and how her whole appearance changed to a more feminine one her senior year in high school. She began wearing makeup and feminine clothes, knowing that she must to do so to attract a husband so she could have a child:

> *I let my hair grow and I started fixing it, using rollers and experimenting with makeup. I did it to try to find someone to have kids with, to appeal to a man. I tried to look "girly" rather than the way I always had before. It made my mom real happy.*

Some women who maintained or presented a masculine identity as teens described it as a "rite of passage." As Pat said,

> *I went through that stage when I had to play a dyke. Yeah, I had to ride a motorcycle and wear men's pants, men's clothes, and I didn't wear women's stuff at all. I even wore men's underwear, you know. You go through this phase. And it's one of those things.*

In a way, "it can be liberating," another woman said, "to so blatantly not have to be 'girly.' " Others described the adoption of a masculine identity not only as a "rite of passage" but as "helpful in keeping guys away."

ADULTHOOD

"Nothing but a Lesbian"

In rural areas, many women who maintained the butch appearance were "outed" or identified as lesbians by others and consequently lost the respect of their community. Thus many of these women had chosen to leave their rural hometowns. Those who chose to stay often had a tough life. A butch appearance is synonymous with "lesbian" in the eyes of many of the small town residents. As one of these residents said to a lesbian professor, "Once I knew you were gay, that's all I could see about you. You weren't an excellent teacher. You weren't a nice person. You weren't a good friend. You were just a lesbian. And no matter what you said or did, that's all I could see." Another professor in another study had a worse experience from being seen as "nothing but a lesbian." She wrote about what happened to her when she criticized her university for its lack of access to benefits for partners of gay and lesbian employees:

> *Overnight I was publicly identified as "lesbian," despite never having made that claim myself, and was presumed and constructed as "other" and as "deviant." Overnight I went from "a young and promising new kid on the block" to, in the words of perhaps the most prominent feminist academic*

> *on the campus, "a political ass who wouldn't get tenure anywhere in North America." I was marginalized in my department, I got hate mail, students confronted me in classes and were sometimes downright hostile, and I got death threats on my answering machine. . . . I was the only "out" lesbian faculty member. I was out on a limb and they were sawing it off. (Bryson, 2002)*

The Typical Rural Lesbian

The typical rural lesbian in my study was not someone like a widely admired, seemingly problem-free celebrity such as Melissa Etheridge or Rosie O'Donnell. Instead, she might be a young mother, a grandmother in her fifties, or married for some thirty years to a man but having or desiring a female partner. She might struggle with guilt, with the dread of losing her children, with the fear of being disrespected, condemned, rejected, or ostracized by her church and community. Generally, she felt like she was not having a real life because she was living a lie.

One such woman, Liz, had had a female lover for twelve years although she had been married to a man for many more. She now had several grandchildren. With multiple health problems and surgeries, she felt she must have her husband's insurance. Although her female lover had a good pension and insurance, Liz would not have access to those under the law. So she remained with Richard and saw Anne when she could. Liz was caught in a catch-22, though. She stayed with Richard, in part because of her health problems and his insurance, yet due to the stress of living a double life, her health had worsened, both mentally and physically.

So why did Liz and many other rural lesbians marry in the first place? Among their most often cited reasons were feeling the need to fit in, being religious, wanting to please the family, the internalization of homophobia, and the desire to become a mother. But some rural lesbians did not realize or accept the lesbian identity until after they were married. As one of them said, "After a lot of self exploration, I realized I had always been a lesbian, just too blind and too Catholic to see it." Another said, "I didn't start pursuing the gay life until age 41. I didn't struggle with my feelings in my teens and twenties. I was a Catholic girl, so I did what good girls did. I got married and had a child. As I look back over my life, I realize I was always a lesbian, in spite of being married."

Of all the obstacles to realizing their lesbian identity, the homophobia in their rural areas seemed to exert the most powerful influence over their lives. Obviously, as lesbians, those women felt like outsiders, rejected or ostracized by the straight community. But less obvious was the fact that the rural lesbians often acquired the societal homophobia so as to become homophobic themselves. Such internalized homophobia tended to have a negative impact not only on the lesbians' own emotional wellbeing but also on their relationship with their partners. Amelia, for example, talked about the development of her self-hatred as one aspect of her internalized homophobia:

> *The way people were raised in the rural areas with so much religion in their lives . . . they just believe it's a sin against God and the only way they can deal with it is total denial. It's more than denial. It's worst than denial. They just totally turn inward and hate themselves.*

As for the negative impact of internalized homophobia on lesbian relationships, it can be exemplified by Lynn's experience. Lynn, though a married woman, initiated a relationship with a lesbian at work. Although Lynn would initiate each encounter and send romantic cards and notes, she would immediately feel guilty after each lesbian contact. She would berate her partner, calling her "disgusting and immoral." Lynn would tell her, "I'm straight and you're a lesbian. I'm Mrs. John Smith. I don't even associate with people like you." Part of Lynn's reasoning behind calling her partner a lesbian while she was "straight" was that her partner refrained from wearing makeup, dressed casually with cowboy boots, and did not try to pass as a heterosexual. Lynn, on the other hand, worked very hard to promote her own femininity, to the extent that she spent a great deal of money on hair, nails, clothes, and cosmetics. She would often tell her partner that "God intended for you to be a woman," which meant to her that her partner must "dress like one" and wear makeup. After failing to make her partner appear feminine, Lynn eventually left her for "another woman" who looked as feminine as herself.

In the World of Work

Many rural lesbians were afraid of coming out. A major reason was fear of losing their jobs or becoming a target of harassment at the workplace. Some of the women, like school teachers Jane and Jeanne, were fired after they were outed. More commonly, the women were harassed in one way or another, made to feel uncomfortable in their work environment. As one woman said,

> *I was harassed on the best job I ever had. They did everything they could to be rid of me. I was going to be fired for something that was a setup and I left. Of course, I was told by insiders later that it was because I was gay and had the nerve to be more open about it with some people. What's more, people thought I was gay because of the way I dressed. They were afraid some group like the ACLU would come down on them if they were upfront about it, so instead, I was harassed about every ridiculous thing until I finally said, "enough," and left.*

Often the harassment was based on the stereotypical notion that the lesbians looked "like a man" or "not feminine enough." One woman was asked by a coworker how she was "ever going to be successful" because she didn't "dress in a feminine way." Her supervisor even wrote in her performance evaluation that she "needed to acquire a professional dress" and then noted that "this employee is too progressive for this area and needs to move." Another woman's supervisor implied that "we both know you couldn't get a job anywhere else" due to her attire not being feminine enough. Some women feared that they might be segregated to manual labor positions for which a more masculine style of dress was considered appropriate.

In the Circle of Family

Many rural lesbians were afraid to "come out" to their families. So they tended to remain in the closet. Some did come out and suffered a terrible consequence from it, as Maggie and her partner did:

> *My girlfriend and I came out to our parents over the weekend. It went pretty much the way we thought it would. . . . We are dead to them and they will never talk to us again. . . . My girlfriend still lived with her family. When she told them her mom slapped her a couple of times and threw her out and her stuff on the front yard. . . . The hardest thing is knowing that our parents will never accept us. . . . But we don't feel we can live a lie to appease them.*

Many other rural lesbians didn't dare come out for fear of hurting their parents. But they did every now and then think of telling them, debating with themselves how and when they would ever be able to tell their families, with different consequences. In the case of Carrie, she still could not tell her parents. As she said, "I'm a twenty-year-old lesbian. I've been putting off telling my parents I am a lesbian for almost three years. I can never find the right moment. I have no idea how to tell them." But in the case of Brittney, she finally told her parents this way: "Mom, Dad, I know you guys love me no matter what. Don't get mad at what I'm about to tell you . . . I am GAY." Her mother turned out to be accepting, ironically revealing that she had already known it for three years. Her dad also said he loved her but advised her not to bring her girlfriend home. "He said he doesn't want me to be talked about like Aunt Mary," Brittney said. Nowadays many parents support their lesbian daughters but some still reject them as did the parents of Maggie and her partner mentioned above.

The Hazard of Being Lesbian

The issue of safety is a concern for almost all rural lesbians. Many people may still remember the killing of Matthew Shepard, a young gay college student, or Barry Winchell, a young Ft.

Campbell soldier, both murdered because they were gay. However, most hate crimes against gays across the country are not reported or known to the general public. Most of the women in this study had seen or experienced antigay incidents, afraid for their own safety if they were outed in the community. They often spoke of buying guns, pit bulls, and security systems to protect themselves. As one of them, Brenda, said,

> *I had rifles pulled on me one night because I was with a girl. They were total strangers; I've never seen them before in my life. They stuck their guns in the window of my car. Oh, they said plenty [mostly preaching about the sin of lesbianism]. I just couldn't do anything. And there I was with my lesbian friend. They talked for maybe thirty minutes or so with their rifles in our faces.*

Experiences such as this were fairly typical for the rural lesbians in my study. Through the years I have heard from them many stories about straights vandalizing their cars or assaulting them.

CONCLUSION

This study has found that lesbians in the rural areas go through certain experiences from their childhood through their adolescence and into their adulthood. The experiences involve showing an inclination in childhood to be "tomboys," to enjoy playing with boys, and to reject femininity and its traditional forms of dress and play. When going through adolescence, some of the rural lesbians reject the feminine role and assume a "mannish" appearance but others try to embrace and exhibit the traditional femininity. In adulthood, many of these rural women stay in the closet and those who do come out usually suffer harassment and other homophobic mistreatments by the straight community.

REFERENCES

Abes, Elisa S., and Susan R. Jones. 2004. "Meaning-Making Capacity and the Dynamics of Lesbian College Students' Multiple Dimension of Identity." *Journal of College Student Development*, 45(6):612–633.

Bryson, Mary. 2002. "Me/no lesbian: The Trouble with 'Troubling Lesbian Identities.' " *Qualitative Studies in Education*, 13(3):373–380.

REVIEW QUESTIONS

1. What is internalized homophobia, and how does it affect lesbians?
2. Identify some of the reasons that lesbians don't "come out" in rural communities.
3. Why do many rural lesbians marry?

CHAPTER 26

"YOU'RE NOT A RETARD, YOU'RE JUST WISE"

STEVEN J. TAYLOR

This is a study of the social meaning of disability and construction of social identity in a family I will refer to as the Dukes. The immediate family consists of four members—Bill and Winnie and their two children, Sammy and Cindy—but has grown since I started my study to include Cindy's husband and her four young children. The Dukes are part of a much larger network of extended family members and friends. I have been following the Duke family and many of its kin and friends for the past ten years. . . . Bill, Winnie, and their two children have all been diagnosed as mentally retarded or disabled by schools and human service agencies, and a sizeable number of their kin and friends have been similarly diagnosed.

From a sociological or anthropological perspective, disability can be viewed as a social construct (Whyte and Ingstad 1995). Like other forms of social deviance, what we call disabilities—mental retardation, mental illness, Alzheimer's disease, blindness, deafness, mobility impairments—are not objective conditions but concepts that exist in the minds of people who attach those labels to others.

Disability can serve as a master status (Becker 1963; Schur 1971) and can carry with it a stigma. A stigma is not merely a difference but a characteristic that deeply discredits a person's moral character. Numerous studies have demonstrated how people with disabilities are stigmatized and rejected by society. . . .

THE DUKE FAMILY

Bill and Winnie Duke live just outside of Central City, a medium-size city in the Northeast. Bill and Winnie have lived in and around Central City since they were married more than twenty-five years ago.

Bill

Bill, age fifty, describes himself as a "graduate of Empire State School," a state institution originally founded in 1894 as "Empire State Custodial Asylum for Unteachable Idiots." Born in a small rural community outside of Capital City, Bill was placed at the institution as an adolescent.

Bill was placed on "probation" and lived for a period of time in a halfway house in Central City, approximately 150 miles from his family's home. He was officially discharged from the institution in 1971.

Bill is on disability and receives government Social Security and Supplemental Security Income (SSI) benefits. Shortly after his release from the institution, he held several short-term jobs but has not worked in a regular, tax-paying job since the mid-1970s.

Source: Steven J. Taylor, " 'You're Not a Retard, You're Just Wise,' " *Journal of Contemporary Ethnography*, vol. 29 (February 2000), pp. 58–92. © 2000 by Sage Publications, Inc. Reprinted by permission of Sage Publications, Inc.

Winnie

Winnie, age forty-eight, runs the household, manages the family's finances, and negotiates relations with schools, government programs, and human service workers. Winnie acts very much like a typical wife and mother and performs the work associated with women in American families (DeVault 1991). Winnie was born and raised in Central City. She dropped out of school early to help raise her brother and stepbrothers and sisters, but she can read well and prides herself both on her memory and math skills.

Winnie has a speech impediment, which makes her very difficult to understand until one has known her for a while. She also has a host of medical problems. By her account, she had convulsions until she was nine years old and has arthritis, heart problems, and a clubfoot.

When I first met the Dukes, Winnie was on public assistance or welfare but was subsequently deemed eligible for SSI. She also previously received spouse's benefits from Bill's Social Security. She is eligible for vocational rehabilitation because she has "a disability which results in a substantial handicap to employment," according to her Individual Written Rehabilitation Plan, and she has participated in numerous job-training programs. She has worked twice at a large sheltered workshop for the disabled, Federated Industries of Central City. She took these jobs under the threat of losing her welfare benefits. Her last placement there in the early 1990s ended when Federated ran out of work and laid off most of its clients.

Sammy

Sammy, age twenty-seven, was born with cerebral palsy, which is not currently noticeable, a cleft palate, and heart problems. According to Winnie, he has had more than ninety operations for hearing, heart, and other problems. As an infant, he had a tracheotomy and was fed through a tube in his stomach. Winnie proudly recalls how she learned to handle his tracheotomy. Sammy has a severe speech impediment and is extremely difficult to understand when he talks.

Sammy dropped out of school at age sixteen. He was enrolled in a special education program for students with multiple disabilities, and specifically mental retardation and hearing impairments. He receives SSI. Winnie is the representative payee for Sammy's SSI; that is, Sammy's check comes in Winnie's name, and she must periodically report how the funds are spent.

Sammy has never held a regular job, although he worked for a very brief period of time at a garage where his father worked for a month or so "under the table."

Since reaching adulthood, Sammy has lived off and on with his parents, one of his other relatives, or one of his "girlfriends." Whether or not he is living with Winnie and Bill, he has frequent contact with them. Sammy currently lives with his parents, although he says that he is looking for an apartment of his own.

Cindy

Cindy, age twenty-three, has epilepsy and receives SSI. Prior to dropping out of school at age seventeen, she was enrolled in an intensive special education class, and her federally mandated Individual Education Plan (IEP) indicated that she is "mentally retarded–mild" Both Bill and Winnie were proud of how Cindy was doing in school and disappointed when she dropped out.

One summer, while she was in high school, Cindy was placed at the Federated Industries sheltered workshop as part of a job-training program. Through her school program, she had volunteer job placements at fast food restaurants and a human service agency.

Cindy speaks very clearly but seems to have difficulty reading. Cindy has always been shy among strangers but is becoming less so as she grows older.

Since I started studying the Duke family, Cindy has changed from a girl to a young adult, wife, and mother. When Cindy was about seventeen, Bill and Winnie started to worry that she was becoming sexually active. Their fears were not unfounded. She became pregnant, broke up with her boyfriend, and then married a 26-year-old man, Vinnie, shortly afterward. Cindy's first baby, Mikey, was born in spring, 1993, and she has since had three additional babies. After the birth of her last child, Cindy agreed to be sterilized. Cindy and Vinnie's four children, all boys, are enrolled in an early intervention special education program.

Social Relations Among Kin and Friends

Bill and Winnie not only come from sizeable extended families but also have a large and ever-expanding network of friends and acquaintances. The Dukes make friends easily and bring friends of friends, family of friends, and friends of family into their immediate social network.

Social relations within the Duke network are characterized by mutual support, on one hand, and arguments and feuds, on the other. . . . [T]he Dukes and their kin and friends depend on each other for help and assistance; mutual support networks are a means of coping with their marginal economic and social status. The Dukes as well as their relatives and friends take in homeless family members and friends, lend people food or money, and help each other out in other ways.

People within the Dukes's network also regularly complain about and argue with each other or become embroiled in all-out feuds. At any point in time, someone in the network is fighting with someone else. Hardly a month goes by when Bill and Winnie are not involved in a dispute with relatives or friends. Once an argument begins, other family members and friends are likely to be drawn into it.

Feuds can be emotionally charged and vehement but seldom last long. People can be bitter enemies one day and friendly to each other the next. For example, when I first met the Dukes, Lisa and Gary and their three children were staying with them since they were homeless. Bill and Winnie grew tired of Lisa and Gary and threw them out of their house. Within months, however, Lisa and Gary were once again close friends of the Dukes and frequent visitors to their home.

THE STUDY

When I first heard about the Duke family, I was interested in meeting them. Cindy's family support worker, Mary, had casually told me about the family and how each member had a disability. In particular, Bill's reported description of himself as a "graduate of Empire State School" fascinated me. My dissertation was based on an ethnographic study of a ward at Empire State School (Taylor 1977, 1987), and I had previously conducted life histories with former residents of Empire (Bogdan and Taylor 1976, 1994). Everything I knew based on my previous research led me to believe that people would avoid volunteering information about having lived at an institution for the mentally retarded. The longer this study has gone on, the more I have appreciated Gubrium and Holstein's (1990) notion of "listening in order to see."

Mary regularly collected used clothes, old appliances, and household items for the Dukes. I had an old portable TV and some electric heaters and asked Mary if she would arrange for me to drop them off at the Dukes. She agreed to do so, and I met the Duke family in February 1989. I have been studying the Dukes ever since that time.

From 1989 to the beginning of 1992, I recorded approximately 100 sets of field notes comprising more than 1,200 pages. Since that time, although visiting the Dukes less frequently, I have continued to maintain regular contact with them. In recent years, I have visited them four or five times a year and speak with them on the phone monthly, if not more often.

DISABILITY LABELS AND FAMILY CONSTRUCTIONS

Although Bill, Winnie, Sammy, and Cindy, as well as many of their kin and friends, have been labeled as disabled or might be considered disreputable in other ways, they do not attach the same meanings to disability labels as found in the broader society. Within the Duke family and to a large extent within their broader social network, disability labels are interpreted in nonstigmatizing ways. They are largely successful in insulating themselves from the messages received from programs, agencies, and schools . . . that they are handicapped, disabled, mentally retarded, and incompetent.

The disability labels of Bill, Winnie, Sammy, and Cindy are listed on plans, forms, and correspondence the family receives. *Mentally retarded, disabled,* and *handicapped* appear frequently on government paperwork; teachers and government officials have referred to Cindy's and Sammy's "mental problems" and "mental retardation" in discussions with Winnie. Their labels are not a matter of things said behind their backs but are thrown to their faces.

Yet, the Dukes, along with their friends and kin, attach social meanings to such labels that leave their social identities unscathed.

[In the Dukes's own opinion, they have only medical problems. As Winnie said]: "Cindy has medical problems. She has epileptic seizures. . . . Sammy had medical problems when he was born. Bill has medical problems. He has seizures. And I have medical problems. We all have medical problems." Winnie explained that she and Bill were aware of each other's problems when they got married. . . .

Having medical problems is not something to conceal or to be ashamed of. Winnie volunteers this information to outsiders making their first visits to the home. Medical problems seem to represent a nonstigmatizing way of interpreting the messages received from the outside world. In the same way that a person's identity is not affected by having high blood pressure, allergies, or high cholesterol, the construct of medical problems avoids stains on a person's moral character.

Institutionalization

As Edgerton (1993) notes, institutionalization is itself stigmatizing and a biographical fact that people with mental retardation try to hide. The "cure" (being institutionalized) is worse than the "disease" (having an intellectual deficit).

When Bill discusses his institutional experience, he talks as though Empire State School were a reform school rather than an institution for the mentally retarded. According to Bill, Empire helped him "get my head together," and he is proud that he worked his way off "probation." Bill described his history:

> *I was in Empire State School before I was married. I don't mind talking about that. I'm proud of it. I was there twenty-two years. Now I'm celebrating my eighteenth anniversary. I have a nice family, and I'm doing okay.*

On another occasion, Bill commented that it would "straighten out" Sammy and Cindy if they were sent to institutions. Bill points to Sammy:

> *Now it's too bad they don't have places like Empire today. I'll tell you, if you went to Empire, you wouldn't have the problems you have. I'll tell you. It was hard. You had to work hard scrubbing the floors. Then if you did something, they beat you with a stick or put your head in the toilet.*

Retard, Retarded, Moron, Crazy, Weird, Dumb, and Stupid

As in other parts of society, *retard, retarded, moron, crazy, weird, dumb,* and *stupid* are used as general epithets and do not necessarily refer to intellectual deficits. People casually call each other these names. Bill often calls Sammy and Cindy "stupid" and "dumb" when they avoid doing something he has told them to do or when they irritate him. Bill turns the TV from a program to the VCR. Sammy complains, "Don't turn that. I'm watching it." Bill replies, "Stupid, that's almost over." Cindy says something about riding Sammy's bike. Bill says, angrily, "Stupid, there's bikes downstairs. Get one of them." When he is angry with family or friends, he also refers to them as "stupid." Both Bill and Winnie characterize his family as "crazy" and "weird." Bill told me the following story:

BILL: "I'll tell you, my family's crazy. They're all crazy. How's your stomach?"
ME: "Okay, I guess."
BILL: "I mean, do you have a weak stomach?"
ME: "No, go ahead."
BILL: "My sister Pam. . . . Well, she used to make macaroni salad, with cucumbers and everything. It was real good. This one time, I was over at her house, and she asked me if I wanted some macaroni salad, and I said, 'Sure. Yea.' Well. She gave me a dish, and I went to take a bite, and I looked down, and there were maggots in it. I said, 'Pam, there's maggots in there!' She took the macaroni and ate it, maggots and all. I'll tell you. She's crazy."

Although Bill often calls Sammy and Cindy "dumb" and "stupid," both he and Winnie also communicate to their children that they are not mentally deficient. Bill proudly showed me a TV on which Sammy had worked.

> *Everybody says Sammy's dumb, right? They all say he's dumb. Want to see something? (Bill points to a TV in Sammy's room.) I found that in the trash and brought it home. Sammy took the tube out and put another one in it from another TV I had. (Bill turns on the TV.) Look at that. Everybody says he's stupid, but look at that. He's not dumb.*

The title of this article is a quote from Bill. One day when I was visiting the home, Bill was prodding Cindy to sweep the floor. Avoiding the job, Cindy would sweep for a minute or two and then sit down. After being scolded repeatedly by Bill, she laughed and said, "I'm a retard." This is when Bill said, "You're not a retard, you're just wise." Cindy responded, "I'll be a retard if I don't do my homework." Bill's casual response, "You're not a retard, you're just wise," redefined her behavior in terms of being a smart alec and, hence, was normalizing. However, this exchange and other instances when Cindy called herself "stupid" indicate that she was aware of how she had been labeled at school, and this was problematic for her.

The Dukes simply do not internalize disability labels as a master status and, for this reason, avoid the stigma and spoiled identities associated with them. They do not attempt to pass as normal; they see themselves as normal.

SOCIAL IDENTITIES

The Dukes's kin and friends can be identified as disabled or disreputable in the context of schools, government programs, and human service agencies, but they have untainted identities, or images, within the family and social network.

Bill and Winnie describe themselves in terms of their family roles, interests, and skills. For both of them, their family relationships, gender roles, and responsibilities are especially important in the construction of identity. Bill is a husband, father, grandfather, uncle (who is looked up to by some of his nieces and nephews), son, and brother; and Winnie is a wife, mother, grandmother, aunt, daughter, and sister. Bill expresses pride about having a family, and Winnie prides herself on her child-rearing knowledge and skills. Winnie never passes up a chance to give me advice on raising my own children (six and eight years old) and will scold me if she thinks I am doing something wrong. Both Winnie and Bill like to remind me that I am a newlywed compared to them. Their anniversary, Mother's Day, and Father's Day are special holidays for Bill and Winnie and provide an opportunity to celebrate their status as marriage partners and parents.

When it comes to their children, Bill and Winnie have a way of turning labeling and stigmatizing experiences upside down and inside out. Their definitions of their children stand in stark contrast to how they have been defined by schools, government programs, and agencies. Winnie reports that Sammy was an "A-1 student" prior to dropping out. When I asked what Sammy "wants to be," Winnie answered, "A mechanic, maybe an artist."

When she was a full-time special education student, Cindy received constant reminders of her identity as being disabled or mentally retarded.

Her IEP [Individual Educational Plan] mentioned her mental retardation, and Winnie attended what she called "Committee on the Handicapped" meetings on her behalf. Everything about Cindy's school program told her that she was handicapped and mentally retarded. She took a special education bus to and from school and had always been placed in a self-contained special education class. As her comments "I'm a retard" and "I'm stupid" indicated, Cindy was not oblivious to the messages she received from school, and she had to struggle to maintain an identity as a normal teenager. However, Bill and Winnie constructed an image of Cindy being a normal teenager.

Winnie boasted to family members and friends about Cindy's school achievements. One year, Cindy was awarded certificates of attendance and merit for participation in her special education program, and Winnie talked about her "making the honor roll." On the last day of class that year, Cindy's teacher gave out class awards. Cindy received one for "community service" and one for "student council" (three members of her special education class were among the sixty or seventy members of the school's student council). On the way home after Cindy's last day of class, Winnie commented, "That kid's bright. She'll graduate from high school."

For many, if not most, parents, marriage and child rearing would be out of the question for children with Sammy's and Cindy's limitations. For Winnie and Bill, raising a family is regarded as a natural part of growing up for Cindy and Sammy. Both Winnie and Bill are proud grandparents of Cindy's four children and expect Sammy to get married soon.

CONCLUSION

In the Duke family and broader network of extended family members and friends, people with obvious disabilities are not stigmatized, rejected, or necessarily viewed as disabled. Even when people's disabilities are recognized, as in the case of the handicapped, these disabilities do not represent a master status that controls interactions with them. That people can maintain positive identities while being subjected to labeling at the hands of government programs, human service agencies, and schools is no easy accomplishment. The Duke family experience shows that small worlds can exist that do not simply reproduce the broader social contexts in which they are embedded.

Four related factors seem to account for the Dukes's ability to avoid the stigma and stained identities associated with disability. First, the family stands between individual members and programs or agencies and provides a ready set of meanings and interpretations of their experiences. Reiss (1981) describes how families help members organize their experiences of situations in everyday life. According to Reiss, the family permits individuals to "select, highlight, and transform essential aspects of their experience and delete the rest." Culture, including the cultural meanings associated with disability and imparted by agencies, is interpreted in the context of the family's stock of shared knowledge and understandings.

Second, in the case of the Dukes, their family life world is shared and reinforced by an extensive network of kin and friends. Their extended social network appears to be much more influential than in the nuclear families described in much of the literature on family worlds (Hess and Handel 1995; Gubrium and Holstein 1990; Reiss 1981). Within the Dukes's social network, households are not necessarily identical with nuclear families and often are composed of members of different families. Furthermore, households and families within the network have a high degree of contact with one another.

Third, related to their roles within a family, none of the Dukes or members of the network are full-time clients of human service agencies. Institutions and community facilities engulf people in a separate subculture that provides them with scarce opportunities to define themselves as anything other than disabled. Bill's and Cindy's experiences are instructive in this regard. For Bill, the passage of time since being institutionalized has undoubtedly enabled him to establish a positive identity. In a follow-up study of "The Cloak of Competence," Edgerton and Bercovici (1976) found that ex-institutional residents' concern with stigma and passing became far less evident over time. Of all of the members of the Duke family and perhaps the network, Cindy seemed to struggle the most with an identity as a disabled or retarded person while she was in school. This suggests that the more enmeshed one is in disability programs—in Cindy's case, full-time special education classes—the more one has to contend with a negative identity.

Finally, competence is a relative concept (Goode 1994). Although the Dukes and other members of their network may not perform well on standardized tests, in school programs, or in traditional jobs in the mainstream marketplace, they are competent to meet the demands of day-to-day life as they experience it. Bill knows not only the best junking routes but also where to sell junk at the best price. Winnie knows where to turn for help when food is scarce. Sammy learned about junk [cars] from his father. Cindy was very aware and competent to function in stores and other settings within her immediate neighborhood.

Literacy and verbal agility are not requisite survival skills in the daily lives of the Dukes and other members of their social network. People within the network, therefore, are not defined based on such characteristics.

REFERENCES

Becker, H. S. 1963. *Outsiders: Studies in the sociology of deviance.* New York: Free Press.

Bogdan, R., and S. J. Taylor. 1976. The judged, not the judges: An insider's view of mental retardation. *American Psychologist* 31:47–52.

———. 1994. *The social meaning of mental retardation: Two life stories.* New York: Teachers College Press.

DeVault, M. L. 1991. *Feeding the family: The social organization of caring as gendered work.* Chicago: University of Chicago Press.

Edgerton, R. B. 1993. *The cloak of competence revised and updated.* Berkeley: University of California Press.

Edgerton, R. B., and S. Bercovici. 1976. The cloak of competence: Years later. *American Journal of Mental Deficiency* 80:485–497.

Goode, D. 1994. *A world without words: The social construction of children born deaf and blind.* Philadelphia: Temple University Press.

Gubrium, J. F., and J. A. Holstein. 1990. *What is family?* Mountain View, CA: Mayfield.

Hess, R. D., and G. Handel. 1995. *Family worlds: A psychosocial approach to family life.* Lanham, MD: University Press of America.

Reiss, D. 1981. *The family's construction of reality.* Cambridge: Harvard University Press.

Schur, E. M. 1971. *Labeling deviant behavior: Its sociological implications.* New York: Harper & Row.

Taylor, S. J. 1977. The custodians: Attendants and their work at state institutions for the mentally retarded. Unpublished doctoral dissertation.

———. 1987. "They're not like you and me": Institutional attendants' perspectives on residents. *Child & Youth Services* 8:109–125.

Whyte, S. R., and B. Ingstad. 1995. Disability and culture: An overview. In *Disability and culture,* edited by B. Ingstad and S. R. Whyte, 3–32. Berkeley: University of California Press.

REVIEW QUESTIONS

1. What are some consequences for a deviant being medically labeled?
2. What does the title " 'You're Not a Retard, You're just Wise' " tell us about the study?
3. What is the master status of the four members of the Duke family? Justify your response.

PART EIGHT

HETEROSEXUAL DEVIANCE

When she was 13, Kristie ran away from her home in the Southwest. Friends introduced her to a tall, good-looking man who made her feel good by saying she was very smart and sexy. Soon he had persuaded her to prostitute herself on the streets of Las Vegas—and then other cities, such as Los Angeles, Atlanta, and Phoenix. The pimp had other girls working for him, and he would bring them along with Kristie to a city, make them sell sex throughout the night, and then move on. Kristie stopped only when she was arrested at age 15, two years after she had started prostituting herself. During the preceding six months, she estimates, she had had at least 100 customers, but she had stopped counting long before her arrest.[1]

This kind of prostitution, like any other way in which women sell sex to men, is an example of heterosexual deviance. Other examples include women dancing nude for pay in a club or engaging in socially stigmatized sex. Here we take a look at these deviances. In the first article, "The Globalization of Sex Tourism," Nancy Wonders and Raymond Michalowski show how sex tourism has become globalized, flourishing in both developed and developing countries such as the Netherlands and Cuba. In the second reading, "Flawed Theory and Method in Studies of Prostitution," Ronald Weitzer criticizes radical feminists for equating prostitution with violence against women. In the third selection, "Exotic Dancers: 'Where Am I Going to Stop?' " Jennifer Wesley reports from her research how exotic dancers deal with their identity conflict—between how they see themselves inside the strip club and how they see themselves outside of it. In the fourth article, " 'Everyone Knows Who the Sluts Are': How Young Women Get around the Stigma," Jennifer Dunn shows how sexually active college women try to avoid becoming stigmatized as "sluts."

[1]Bay Fang, "Young Lives for Sale," *U.S. News & World Report*, October 24, 2005, pp. 30–34.

Chapter 27

THE GLOBALIZATION OF SEX TOURISM

NANCY A. WONDERS
RAYMOND MICHALOWSKI

The current era of globalization is characterized by unprecedented movement of material, information, finance, and bodies across borders. In this article, we examine how globalization facilitates the growth of sex tourism, as well as the particular character of sex tourism in different locales. As others have already detailed (Opperman 1998), "sex tourism" is a protean term that attempts to capture varieties of leisure travel that have as a part of their purpose the purchase of sexual services. Clearly the concepts of "prostitution" and "tourism" are both central to an analysis of sex tourism, but neither term captures the full meaning of sex tourism. "Sex tourism" highlights the convergence between prostitution and tourism, links the global and the local, and draws attention to both the production and consumption of sexual services. The growth in sex tourism over the last two decades is well established (Kempadoo and Doezema 1998; Opperman 1998). In this article, we focus specifically on how the global forces shaping this growth connect the practice of sex work in two disparate cities with globalized sex tourism. . . .

Research provides compelling evidence that cities are strategic sites for observing the effects of globalization (Sassen 1998, 2000a, 2000b; Sassen and Roost 1997). In our analysis, we detail the way that the global forces shaping the production and consumption of sex tourism impact two very different cities: Amsterdam and Havana. We explore the global connections that link sex work in these two cities with the forces associated with globalized sex tourism. Specifically, we argue that global forces impact sex work in both cities through four mediating institutions: (1) the tourism industry, (2) labor markets, (3) the localized sex industry, and (4) law and policy. As mediating institutions in these cities adjusted to the impact of global forces, they created opportunities for sex tourism to flourish.

It is important to our analysis that Amsterdam and Havana are very different cities. Many argue that global forces are easily discerned in "global cities" like Amsterdam. Global cities are strategically positioned at the center of the global capitalist system as command points, key locations, and marketplaces for leading industries, and major sites of production. . . .

In contrast, Havana is located in Cuba, one of the last self-identified socialist states in the world. Cuba is a developing island nation struggling to find a foothold in the new global capitalist economy that will enable it to grow economically, while preserving its socialist accomplishments in health, education, and social welfare.

Despite their differences, we illustrate that globalization's reach is evident in both Amsterdam and Havana. The specific responses to global forces differ, but comparison between these two

Source: Nancy A. Wonders and Raymond Michalowski, "Bodies, Borders, and Sex Tourism in a Globalized World: A Tale of Two Cities—Amsterdam and Havana," *Social Problems*, vol. 48 (2001), pp. 545–571.

cities reveals the impact of significant global connections on sex work in both locations.

SEX TOURISM IN AMSTERDAM, HOLLAND

In Amsterdam, the commodification of bodies has been perfected to the level of an art form. The red light district resembles the modern open-air shopping mall in the United States. Relatively clean streets, little crime, a neon atmosphere, and windows and windows of women to choose from—every size, shape, and color (though not in equal amounts). The red light district seems designed to be a sex tourist's Mecca. The range of services for the leisure traveler includes sex clubs, sex shows, lingerie and S&M clothing shops, condomories, and a sprinkling of porno stores. But the character of Amsterdam's red light district is different from most other sex tourist locations because it is centered in an historic district between the Oude Kerk (Old Church) and de Waag (an old weighing station)—two of the most spectacular cultural tourist sites in the city—and it is surrounded by an old, well established residential neighborhood. Indeed, walking through the red light district in the daytime is not so different from walking down any other shopping street in the city, though the area takes on a festival atmosphere at night. Crowds of men walk the street, stopping to gaze at the living merchandise in the window. The routine among men is much like the routine observed among women shopping for clothes, with plentiful commentary on the size, shape, color, and cost of the women on display. The smorgasbord of languages rising through the air reveals the international character of those shopping for bodies.

In describing the Amsterdam scene, it is important to make clear that women sex workers are far from passive in the shopping interaction. On quieter evenings and in the daytime, it is common for women to hover near the doorways of their small window booths, hooting and calling at men to "come here!" in a number of different languages. In an odd role reversal, one male friend commented to me after a walk through the district that: "I've never felt so objectified in my life. I felt like a piece of meat walking through there."

The Tourism Industry

. . . It has been well established that tourism, as a global force, has affected all of Western Europe. As Williams and Shaw (1998) note, "Europe dominates international movements of tourists. . . . Between 1950 and 1990, the number of international tourists in Europe increased 16 times." There is strong competition among European countries for international tourists, since they tend to spend more money than domestic tourists; additionally, starting in the 1970s, "international tourism income grew considerably faster than international merchandise trade" making it a market worth pursuing (Williams and Shaw 1998).

[Amsterdam] was among the top ten most popular European cities for tourism throughout the 1990s, currently ranking seventh (Dahles 1998). Amsterdam's positioning as a major tourist destination may be surprising to some. Although the city is filled with tree-studded canals and quaint narrow buildings, it lacks the tourist attractions characteristic of other tourist destinations in Europe; there is no cathedral, tower, or monument to draw visitors to the city. Yet, as one writer has noted, "foreign tourists have been attracted to the Netherlands in increasing numbers" and, within the country, "Amsterdam is overwhelmingly the dominant target for visitors from abroad. 1.7 million foreigners stayed in the city in 1995, one-third of them from outside Europe" (Pinder 1998). Dahles (1998) argues that: "The image of Amsterdam as a tourism destination is based on two major themes. The first is the image of the city as being dominated by the urban town design of the early modern period. . . . The second is the current popular image of Amsterdam, which was formed in the late 60s and is based on a youth culture of sexual liberation and narcotic indulgence." Pinder (1998) agrees with this assessment and adds that, "The city is renowned for the ready availability of soft drugs, and tolerance has also underpinned the rise of sex tourism as a niche market." . . . As tourism directed toward Amsterdam's cultural heritage stagnates, sex tourism plays an increasingly important role in keeping tourism dollars—and related tourism industry jobs—within the city.

The Labor Market

. . . By the late 1970s and 1980s, the reach of globalization became evident within the Netherlands in other ways as well, particularly in Amsterdam. Clearly, one of the most important global forces affecting sex work in the country was migration. Migration to the Netherlands during this period came from several sources. First, there was an influx of migrants from former Dutch colonies, particularly from Suriname and the Caribbean Islands. Additionally, like many other European countries, the Netherlands was affected by a surge of migrant guest workers from the Mediterranean area, most of whom were directed toward employment in undesirable, low-paying service sector jobs. Later in the 1980s and 1990s, another group of migrants arrived, including those escaping economic hardship in South America and Africa and the former Soviet bloc countries. Importantly, most of these migrant populations settled in the major Dutch cities, including Amsterdam. Almost half of the population of Amsterdam now consists of non-native Dutch residents making it, literally, a global city.

The presence of relatively large numbers of migrants within the city plays an important role in shaping local labor markets and the current character of the sex trade. For many female migrants, sex work is virtually the only employment available, particularly given the relatively high unemployment rate for ethnic minorities within the Netherlands. . . . One estimate put the current number of foreign prostitutes to be approximately 60% of all sex workers in the city (Marshall 1993), and a "repeated count by the Amsterdam police in 1994 and 1995 indicated that about 75% of all prostitutes behind windows in the Red Light District, De Wallen, are foreigners and that 80 percent of all foreign prostitutes are in the country illegally" (Bruinsma and Meershoek 1999).

Localized Sex Work

[Over the last two decades there has been] an important shift within the city from a focus on the individual providers of sexual services, "prostitutes," to a focus on the sex "industry." . . . [T]his shift is partly . . . a response to the global forces associated with the production and consumption of sex tourism. This shift is reflected in two areas: (1) organizational changes that reflect the growth of sex tourism as an industry and (2) the globalized character of sex tourists and sex workers.

In her analysis of prostitution policy in Amsterdam, Brants (1998) describes these changes in some detail:

> *As conditions changed and opportunities for making money from the sex industry increased, ever more power became concentrated in the hands of a few not particularly law abiding citizens. Some of the pimps who had once controlled part of traditional window prostitution now also owned highly lucrative sex clubs and sex theaters. Prostitution had become big business with a huge and partly invisible turnover that was reinvested in gambling halls, sex tourism and more sex clubs.*

This concentration of economic interests combined with consumer interest to create several organizations devoted to supporting sex tourism. Interestingly, some Dutch customers developed an organization to support the interests of the clients of prostitution; this organization is called the Men/Women and Prostitution Foundation. Although the number of active members in this organization is small (personal conversation with a member), it is symbolically important in legitimizing the sex industry as an important "industry" serving consumer desires. Members write articles that articulate client interests and the social benefits of prostitution (ten Kate 1995) and collaborate with other organizations interested in greater acceptance of prostitution.

Another organization that facilitates the sex trade is the Prostitute Information Centre (PIC).

The Centre, which is located in the heart of the Red Light District, serves as an information service for both tourists and prostitutes. Run by a former prostitute, the goals of the center are diverse—education around STD and AIDS prevention, information about prices for sex work, courses to prepare newcomers for sex work and information about how and where to sell sexual labor. For the casual tourist, the most amazing aspect of the PIC is its symbolic character and the way that it resembles a cross between a museum and a sex industry Chamber of Commerce, complete with a sample window brothel to tour (for an extra fee of course), copies of the local Sex Guide, and postcards to purchase.

A second global force shaping the sex industry in Amsterdam is the wide variety of sex tourists visiting the city. Currently, the sex industry is amazingly global in character; not just in terms of the providers of sexual services, but also in terms of the consumers. Sex tourists come to Amsterdam from around the world and vary depending, in part, on national holidays. The local *Pleasure Guide* notes, for example, that Italians are common in August. Although Dutch men are common customers, it appears that the Red Light District exists primarily to fulfill the desires of foreign, male, leisure travelers, often executives conducting business in this global city. Unlike tourists, Dutch consumers of the sex trade can frequent the mostly white women in window brothels down less known side streets, or they can utilize the listings in the paper and obtain door-to-door service. It is important to appreciate that foreign tourists do not just pay for sex, they pay for accommodations, to eat at nice restaurants, and to attend cultural events. Indeed, the consumer behavior of sex tourists visiting this city helps to ensure that there will be many organized interests facilitating the continuation of sex tourism within the city.

Public Policy and Law

[Current policy does not appear to be strengthening the hand of sex workers. It appears that the full package of worker's rights are withheld from prostitutes for a variety of reasons.]

The presence of drug-addicted prostitutes makes it difficult for those advocating rights for prostitutes to argue for respectability. Perhaps, more importantly, the large and growing presence of non-native Dutch sex workers leads to local hostility toward sex work. One consequence of Dutch participation in the global economy is the inability of the state to continue to provide the extensive social welfare benefits it has provided to its citizens since the 1960s (de Haan 1997). . . . Restrictive policies are creeping up everywhere, including in the sex industry. At least one motivation for this greater regulation is to restrict migrant women from engaging in sexual labor. As Raymond (1998) points out, "Third World and Eastern European immigrant women in the Netherlands, Germany, and other regulationist countries lower the prostitution market value of local Dutch and German women. The price of immigrant prostitution is so low that local women's prices go down, reducing the pimps' and brothels' cuts. . . ." To the extent that regulation is designed to keep non-native Dutch women out of sex work, it fosters a two-tiered hierarchy of sex work within the city that leads to even greater impoverishment and risk for migrant women.

. . . Significantly, legislation legalizing brothels was approved by the Dutch Parliament and Senate in 1999 (Brewis and Linstead 2000); this is a radical move in the Netherlands, where sex workers were historically only considered "workers" when "self-employed." Until recently, third party involvement in sex work was considered a crime resulting in the oppression and even enslavement of sex workers. Some argue that the legalization of brothels is a first step toward their ultimate regulation, a situation that could improve the working conditions for some sex workers. However, it seems that the focus of regulation is increasingly on improving the "merchandising" environment for the sex industry and for consumers, and reducing disruption to local citizens. Currently local officials are attempting to identify who owns the buildings that house window brothels and sex clubs so that some standards can be imposed on facilities where sex is sold. Brothels that pass government inspection would receive special certification, serving as a kind of quality control for sex tourists (Visser 1997). Regulations are growing and include strange new guidelines that limit how long clients can be tied up during purchased sadomasochistic acts. A new "red light district manager" will facilitate the implementation of the new regulations. To many, including de Rood Draad, the rights of sex workers have taken a back burner. The proliferation of new regulations has caused some to argue that the red light district is becoming "the red tape district" (Reiland 1996).

. . . [I]t is interesting to note current proposals to impose price controls on the sex industry. At first glance, this policy appears to be a move toward protecting the wages of sex workers. However, it also serves primarily as a way to discourage price-cutting by illegal immigrants engaged in the sex trade. . . . This policy is reflective of growing Dutch concern about immigration; like many other European countries under global migration pressures, the Dutch tend to close doors to gainful employment by outsiders rather than open them.

SEX TOURISM IN HAVANA, CUBA

Havana, like so many other places in the Caribbean, is a sensuous and social city. Warm nights, humid sea breezes laden with the complex perfume of flowers, diesel exhaust, and restaurant odors, music everywhere, bodies unencumbered by layers of cold-weather clothing, and a culture of public interaction that brings tourists and locals into easy contact. This is the context for Havana's particular soft-sell sex trade. Since the reemergence of sex tourism in the 1990s, the following scene has become relatively common in Havana's tourist districts: A woman, usually decades younger than the object of her immediate interest, approaches a foreign tourist. Brandishing a cigarette, she asks for a light, or maybe points to her wrist and asks for the time. The opening gambit leads to other questions: Where are you from? Where are you going? For a walk? Would you like me to walk with you? Have you been to such-and-such disco? Would you like me to take you there? If the mark seems interested, the woman turns the subject to sex, describing the pleasures she can give, often with no mention of price unless the man asks. If they agree to go off to a disco or for a drink, the subject of sex may not even be openly discussed. Instead, both the *jinetera* ["hustler"] and her mark proceed as if they are on a date. Who knows? Maybe this one will be around for a few days, a week, even a month, providing steady work and freedom from having to continually find new customers. Whether the liaison lasts for a night or a month, the tourist will leave something to be remembered by—maybe money or a few nice new dresses, perhaps some jewelry—something that makes the sex and the attention provided worth the effort. This is not the hard sell of commodified bodies typical of sex tourism in Amsterdam. This is a more subtle trade. A trade where local, rather than immigrant women, make themselves available as sex partners and companions to privileged men from North America and Europe who can give them access to the currency of globalization, U.S. dollars. . . .

The Tourism Industry

[In the late 1960s, the emergence of relatively] affordable jet service created a new era of Caribbean island vacations. Between 1970 and 1994, the number of stay-over visits to Caribbean islands increased six-fold (Caribbean Tourism Organization 1995). Just as this boom in Caribbean tourism was beginning, the U.S. embargo against Cuba sent Cuban tourism into a steep decline that bottomed out with a mere 15,000 visitors in 1974. From that point forward, however, Cuba began to reorient its development plans to include investments in the tourist industry (Mesa-Lago 1981). Although some development was focused on internal tourism by Cubans, by 1979, foreign tourism had grown to 130,000 stay-over visits. A decade later, 300,000 foreign tourists visited the island, more than in any year prior to the Revolution (Triana 1995). Moreover, only 18 percent of these tourists were from Soviet-bloc countries. Forty percent came from Canada, 15 percent from Western Europe, 15 percent from Latin America, and—despite the embargo—another 12 percent from the United States (Miller and Henthorne 1997).

The most spectacular growth in Cuban tourism came in the 1990s. During this period, the Cuban government intensified its investment in tourism as part of a broader search for development strategies that would enable the country to survive in the face of post-Soviet economic and political forces determined by a now-worldwide capitalist market (Castro 1999). Between 1994 and 1999, Cuba doubled the number of hotel rooms from 23,500 to just under 50,000. This translated into a five-fold increase in the number of stay-over visits from 300,000 in 1989 to an estimated 1.7 million in 2000. Revenue gains were even greater. Between 1990 and 1998, gross revenue from tourism increased seven-fold, from 243 million in 1990 to 1.8 billion, while the share of the country's GDP contributed by tourism grew from 1.1 percent to 6.9 percent. This growth made Cuba . . . a significant force in Caribbean tourism. At 1.8 billion dollars, Cuba's tourism earnings for 1998 were second only to the 2.1 billion tourism dollars earned by the Dominican Republic, and well ahead of the Bahamas and Jamaica, which respectively earned 1.4 billion and 1.1 billion in tourist revenues (Association of Caribbean States 2001).

The Labor Market

[As the socialist world crumbled between 1989 and 1993,] Cuba underwent a dramatic reversal of fortune that forced a radical reorganization of economic life. The disappearance of Cuba's socialist trading partners created what Cuban sociologist Elena Diaz González (1997) characterized as the worst crisis in the history of Cuban socialism. Between 1989 and 1993, the Cuban GDP fell between 35 and 50 percent, importation of Soviet oil declined by 62 percent, overall imports fell by 75 percent, and the domestic manufacture of consumer goods fell by 83 percent (Diaz González 1997; Espinosa 1999).

As Cuba struggled to reconstruct its trade and financial relations to meet the hard-currency demands of the new capitalist world order, many Cubans found themselves facing a significantly altered labor market. As in other former socialist bloc countries, the Cuban government could no longer provide the extensive employment and social-welfare package it once sought to establish as a universal birthright for all Cubans. By 1999, although Cubans continued to benefit from state subsidies in the areas of food, housing, transportation, health-care, and education, many desired goods could increasingly only be purchased in dollar stores for prices roughly equivalent to those found in the United States for the same goods (Michalowski 1998). It was at this very moment that international tourism to Havana began to increase significantly, with a concomitant growth in tourist-sector jobs—jobs where it was possible to earn at least some portion of one's salary in hard currency. As a consequence, a growing number of high school and college students in Havana began orienting themselves toward tourist-sector employment rather than state-sector jobs, while some Habaneros [Havana natives] already employed in professional careers abandoned them to work in tourism as well (Randall 1996).

The impact of expanding tourism in a city with a shrinking state-sector labor market was also cultural. As youth in Havana were increasingly exposed to the growing number of tourist-oriented nightclubs, restaurants, and beachside hotels, and the clothes, jewelry, and the new model rental cars enjoyed by foreign visitors, some began to feel dissatisfied with their own lack of access to these luxuries. Faced with declining returns from routine labor and rising material desires, some Cuban women (and a smaller number of Cuban men) began making themselves sexually available to foreign tourists. By the late 1990s, a sex worker in Havana could earn forty dollars for providing one night of sex and companionship—double the *monthly* salary of a Cuban university professor (Michalowski 1998). While most young Cubans resisted the temptations created by such disparities, enough succumbed to create a pool of available bodies to serve the desires of sex tourists (Diaz González 1997).

Localized Sex Work

[Although the growth of Havana's tourist industry resulted in a subsidiary increase in sex tourism to the island, so far, this sex] trade has not become the province of the organized syndicates—whether legal or illegal—that typically control sex work in many other nations. During her fieldwork in Cuba in 1995, O'Connell Davidson (1996) observed that there was "no network of brothels, no organized system of bar prostitution: in fact, third party involvement in the organization of prostitution is rare. . . . Most women and girls are prostituting themselves independently and have no contractual obligations to a third party."

Even though the practice of prostituting for sex tourists in Havana is largely independent and entrepreneurial, it is nevertheless embedded in a globalized market for sex services. To compete in a worldwide capitalist marketplace, every local industry needs a global market niche. The sale of what Hochschild (1983) termed "emotional labor" to accompany a sexually commodified body is that niche for many of Havana's *jineteras* serving the male tourist trade. For many male sex tourists from Italy, Spain, England, and Canada, the particular attraction of Cuba is their expectation that *jineteras* will treat them not as customers, but as pseudo-boyfriends. This means acting as a dinner "date" in a restaurant or a dance partner at a disco, serving as a local (and seemingly loving) guide on sightseeing tours, or perhaps spending a few days or even weeks at a seaside resort as bedmate, playmate, and companion.

One Italian sex tourist summarized his attraction to Cuban *jineteras* by saying he came to Cuba because "the women here are really sweet. They make you feel like they really care. They are always trying to do whatever makes you feel good, not just sex, but everything else too." A pair of expatriate American men currently living in Costa Rica echoed this sentiment: "The Cuban women don't act like professional whores, 'here's the sex, now give me the money.' They are really kind. They want to spend time with you, be your friend." As experienced sexual tourists, they bemoaned the growth of sex tourism in Costa Rica because it "ruined" Costa Rican sex workers: "Now they act just like whores in the States. They just do it for the money and when it's over, they want to move on to the next customer. It wasn't like that in the 60s when there were hardly any tourists. Then they were really nice like the Cuban women are today. Things will probably change here [in Cuba], too. So we thought we'd enjoy it while it lasts." Another appeal of sex tourism in Havana is its price. In 1999, a sex tourist could spend as little as ten dollars for a quick sexual encounter, and between thirty and forty dollars for a companion for the entire evening. This means that for between one hundred and two hundred dollars a day, including the meals, the tours, and other "gifts," European, Canadian, and American men in Havana can spend days or even weeks in the company of young, seemingly-exotic women who appear to be providing them with loving attention, all at a price they can afford. In this way, for a short time, they can enjoy a level of class privilege available only to wealthier men in their home countries.

There are several other important elements of the emotional simulacra consumed by sex tourists in Havana that draw them there. . . . One is the opportunity that sex tourism in Havana provides for men who are forty, fifty, or older to receive both sex and sexualized companionship from women thirty or more years younger than themselves. This gratifies the Western male sexual ideal of continuing access to the bodies of young women, regardless of one's own age. Another is the appeal of gaining sexual access to the body of the non-white "other." In the racialized world of the North American and European male sexual fantasy, mixed-race Cuban women provide the ideal, the fetishized combination of the imaginary "hot" Latin and the equally imaginary sexually insatiable African. Thus, it is little surprise that the majority of the women visibly searching for clients in the tourist areas of Havana in 1999, were typically of the "cafe" or "carmelita" skin tones signifying this highly desired racialized "other."

Public Policy and Law

[In 1993, the government legalized the possession of foreign currency, and began allowing] citizens to legally exchange dollars for pesos at banks and government-run, street kiosks known as *cadecas*. Between 1992 and 1994, the Cuban government promulgated a number of other legal changes that would indirectly help create an infrastructure for sex tourism in Havana. These included: (1) permitting the private rental of rooms, apartments, and houses; (2) expanding the arena of self-employment; (3) legalizing the establishment of privately-owned restaurants, colloquially known as *paladares*; (4) expanding the licensing of private vehicles as taxi-cabs; and (5) opening "dollar" stores where Cubans could purchase a broad range of items including food, appliances, furniture, clothes, jewelry, and many other items for U.S. currency (Gordon 1997).

Structurally, these changes facilitated sex-tourism in several ways. The legalization of the U.S. dollar meant that sex workers could obtain hard currency payment from foreign clients without violation of currency laws, and the opening of dollar stores meant they could spend their earnings without having to enter into black market exchanges. Legalizing the rental of private rooms and houses created new opportunities for commercial sexual transaction by eliminating the rules that required tourists to stay in hotels, while prohibiting Cubans from visiting foreigners in their hotel rooms. The legalization of private restaurants provided places where sex workers and tourists could meet and spend non-sex time. Meanwhile, the legalization of private taxis became an important conduit through which some cab drivers could help sex tourists find their way to prime locations for meeting sex workers, or work as pimps by directing their fares to specific sex workers.

CONCLUSION

[The contemporary growth and character of sex tourism is intimately linked to significant global forces. These global forces, which include tourism, migration, and commodification, are not just] abstract concepts; they can be observed within grounded contexts as a variety of local mediating institutions respond to global pressures. In the cases of Amsterdam and Havana, our research suggests that global forces have altered particular institutions in these cities in ways that expand the possibilities for sex tourism. Our work supports Sassen's (1998) view of cities as strategic sites for globalization. . . . At a theoretical level, we contend that the global forces of tourism and migration stimulate the production of sex workers, while the increasing commodification of bodies ensures a steady stream of clients who desire to consume sexual services. Within the cities we analyzed, these global forces find concrete expression at the institutional level, specifically in the changing character of the tourism industries, labor markets, sex work, and laws and policies.

As we have described in some detail, in both Amsterdam and Havana, the tourism industry has become a noticeable sector of the local economy as a by-product of efforts by these cities to secure a share of the burgeoning market created by global tourism. This competition is necessitated by a world in which global markets dominate and determine local fortunes for countries and cities. Additionally, in both of the cities we analyzed, labor markets changed in ways that increased the attractiveness and, for some women, the necessity of sex work. This is particularly true among certain populations of women, such as immigrants in

Amsterdam seeking jobs in an environment hostile to migrant workers, or young Cuban women in Havana for whom the globalization has meant that they can earn more dollars and go to more exciting places by selling sex and companionship than they can through more routine employment.

REFERENCES

Association of Caribbean States. 2001. "Statistical database." Available at www.acs-aec.org/Trade/DBase/DBase_eng/dbaseindex_eng.htm.

Brants, Chrisje. 1998. "The fine art of regulated tolerance: Prostitution in Amsterdam." *Journal of Law and Society* 25, 4:6211–6235.

Brewis, Joanna, and Stephen Linstead. 2000. *Sex, Work and Sex Work: Eroticizing Organization.* London: Routledge.

Bruinsma, Gerben J. N., and Guus Meershoek. 1999. "Organized crime and trafficking in women from Eastern Europe in The Netherlands." In *Illegal Immigration and Commercial Sex: The New Slave Trade*, Phil Williams, ed., 105–118. London: Frank Cass.

Caribbean Tourism Organization. 1995. "Statistical report: 1994 edition." Barbados, WI: Caribbean Tourism Organization.

Castro, Fidel. 1999. *Neoliberal Globalization and the Global Economic Crisis.* Havana: Publications Office of the Council of State.

Dahles, Heidi. 1998. "Redefining Amsterdam as a tourist destination." *Annals of Tourism Research* 25:55–69.

de Haan, Willem. 1997. "Minorities, crime and criminal justice in The Netherlands." In *Minorities, Migrants and Crime: Diversity and Similarity across Europe and the United States*, Ineke Haen Marshall, ed., 198–223. Thousand Oaks, CA: Sage.

Diaz González, Elena. 1997. "Introduction." In *Cuba, Impacto de Las Crises en Grupos Vulnerables: Mujer, Familia, Infancia*, Elena Diaz, Tania Carmen Léon, Esperanza Fernández Zegueira, Sofía Perro Mendoza, and María del Carmen Abala Argüeller, eds., 3–8. Habana: Universidad de La Habana.

Espinosa, Luis Eugenio. 1999. "Globalizaci6n y la economia de Cuba." Interview, Havana, January 23.

Gordon, Joy. 1997. "Cuba's entrepreneurial socialism." *The Atlantic Monthly* 279, 1:18–30.

Hochschild, Arlie Russell. 1983. *The Managed Heart: Commercialization of Human Feeling.* Berkeley: University of California Press.

Kempadoo, Kamala, and Jo Doezema, eds. 1998. *Global Sex Workers: Rights, Resistance and Redefinition.* London: Routledge.

Marshall, Ineke Haen. 1993. "Prostitution in the Netherlands: It's just another job!" In *Female Criminality*, Concetta C. Cullive and Chris E. Marshall, eds., 225–248. New York: Garland.

Mesa-Lago, Carmelo. 1981. *The Economy of Socialist Cuba.* Albuquerque: University of New Mexico Press.

Michalowski, Raymond. 1998. "Market spaces and socialist places: Cubans talk about life in the post-Soviet world." Unpublished paper presented at the Latin American Studies Association, Chicago.

Miller, Mark M., and Tony L. Henthorne. 1997. *Investment in the New Cuban Tourist Industry: A Guide to Entrepreneurial Opportunities.* Westport, CT: Quorum Books.

O'Connell Davidson, Julia, and Jacqueline Sanchez Taylor. 1996. "Fantasy islands: Exploring the demand for sex tourism." In *Sun, Sex, and Gold: Tourism and Sex Work in the Caribbean*, Kamala Kempadoo, ed., 37–54. Lanham, MD: Rowman and Littlefield Publishers.

Opperman, Martin. 1998. *Sex Tourism and Prostitution: Aspects of Leisure, Recreation, and Work.* New York: Cognizant Communication Corporation.

Pinder, David. 1998. "Tourism in The Netherlands: Resource development, regional impacts and issues." In *Tourism and Economic Development: European Experiences*, Allan M. Williams and Gareth Shaw, eds., 301–323. New York: John Wiley and Sons.

Randall, Margaret. 1996. "Cuban women and the U.S. blockade." *Sojourner* 22, 3:10–11.

Raymond, Janice G. 1998. "Violence against women: NGO stone-walling in Beijing and elsewhere." *Women's Studies International Forum* 21, 1:1–9.

Reiland, Ralph. 1996. "Amsterdam's taxing issue: Wages of sin." *Insight on the News* (June) 12, 21:29.

Sassen, Saskia. 1998. *Globalization and its Discontents: Essays on the New Mobility of People and Money.* New York: The New Press.

———. 2000a. *Cities in a World Economy.* Thousand Oaks, CA: Pine Forge Press.

———. 2000b. "Women's burden: Counter-geographies of globalization and the feminization of survival." *Journal of International Affairs* 53, 2:503.

Sassen, Saskia, and Frank Roost. 1997. "The city: Strategic site for the global entertainment industry." In *The Tourist City*, Dennis R. Judd and Susan S. Fainstein, eds., 143–154. New Haven, CT: Yale University Press.

ten Kate, Niel. 1995. "Prostitution: a really valuable asset." Paper distributed by the Mr. A. de Graaf Stichting, Amsterdam: The Netherlands.

Triana, Juan C. 1995. "Consolidation of the economic reanimation." *Cuban Foreign Trade* 1:17–24.

Visser, Jan. 1997. "Dutch preparations for a different prostitution policy." Mr. A. de Graaf Foundation: Institute for Prostitution Research. Amsterdam, The Netherlands (January).

Williams, Allan M., and Gareth Shaw. 1998. *Tourism and Economic Development: European Experiences.* New York: John Wiley and Sons.

REVIEW QUESTIONS

1. Compare and contrast how sex tourism emerged in Havana and Amsterdam.
2. What makes Havana's sex tourism market attractive to foreigners?
3. Contrast the stigma/label attached to prostitutes in the United States to those in Havana and Amsterdam

CHAPTER 28

FLAWED THEORY AND METHOD IN STUDIES OF PROSTITUTION

RONALD WEITZER

In no area of the social sciences has ideology contaminated knowledge more pervasively than in writings on the sex industry. Too often in this area, the canons of scientific inquiry are suspended and research deliberately skewed to serve a particular political agenda. Much of this work has been done by writers who regard the sex industry as a despicable institution and who are active in campaigns to abolish it.

In this commentary, I examine several theoretical and methodological flaws in this literature, both generally and with regard to three recent articles in *Violence Against Women*. The articles in question are by Jody Raphael and Deborah Shapiro (2004), Melissa Farley (2004), and Janice Raymond (2004). At least two of the authors (Farley and Raymond) are activists involved in the antiprostitution campaign.

IDEOLOGICAL BLINDERS

The three articles are only the most recent examples in a long line of writings on the sex industry by authors who adopt an extreme version of radical feminist theory—extreme in the sense that it is absolutist, doctrinaire, and unscientific. Exemplifying this approach are the works of Andrea Dworkin (1981, 1997), Catherine MacKinnon (1987, 1989), Kathleen Barry (1995), and Sheila Jeffreys (1997). These writers view prostitution as categorically evil, the epitome of male domination and exploitation of women irrespective of historical time period, societal context, or type of prostitution. The authors of the three articles under review share these views. Prostitution is decried as a human rights violation, "an institution that doles out death and disease" to women (Raymond, 2004) and "a particularly vicious institution of inequality of the sexes" (Farley, 2004). These writers also insist that prostitution is by definition a form of violence against women, whether or not it involves outright physical violence. Violence is endemic and intrinsic to prostitution, categorically and universally. Raymond titles one of her articles "Prostitution as Violence Against Women" (Raymond, 1998) and another "Prostitution is Rape That's Paid For" (Raymond, 1995). Farley states, "Prostitution must be exposed for what it really is: a particularly lethal form of male violence against women" (Farley & Kelly, 2000), and elsewhere she claims that prostitution is sexual harassment, rape, and battering (Farley, 2000). The distinction between "forced" and "voluntary" prostitution is regarded as a myth; some type of coercion and domination is always involved.

The terminology used in these articles, and other writings in this genre, is designed for maximum shock value. Customers are labeled *prostitute users* and *sexual predators* who brutalize

Source: Ronald Weitzer, "Flawed Theory and Method in Studies of Prostitution," *Violence Against Women*, vol. 11, July 2005, pp. 934–949.

women. Farley declares that "the difference between pimps who terrorize women on the street and pimps in business suits who terrorize women in gentlemen's clubs is a difference in class only, not a difference in woman hating" (Farley, 2004). Raphael and Shapiro (2002) proclaim, "These men must be viewed as batterers rather than customers," and Farley (2004) claims that "johns are regularly murderous toward women." Everyone knows that some johns do indeed have violent proclivities and others are serial killers who prey on vulnerable women on the streets (Lowman, 2000), but studies of customers caution against blanket characterizations. Martin Monto, who has studied more than 2,300 arrested customers, has found that most of the men did not accept rape myths or other justifications for violence against women. He concludes that "a relatively small proportion of clients may be responsible for most of the violence against prostitutes" (Monto, 2000) and that is no reason to believe that most customers are violent (Monto, 2004).

Vivid labels are also applied to the workers. Antiprostitution agencies and activists, and the writers featured in this commentary, are adamant that prostitutes be called *prostituted women* or *survivors*. The former clearly indicates that prostitution is something done to women, not something that can be chosen. "Antiprostitution campaigners use the term *prostituted women* instead of *prostitutes*," writes Jeffreys (1997). "This is a deliberate political decision and is meant to symbolize the lack of choice women have over being used in prostitution." It is true that the conventional term *prostitute* is stigmatizing, so I understand why analysts have searched for alternatives. But *survivors* and *prostituted women* are problematic in their own right: The former suggests persons who have escaped something and the latter completely erases women's agency. Women are described as lacking any agency, except when they resist being prostituted or when they decide to leave prostitution. As Farley puts it, "To the extent that any woman is assumed to have freely chosen prostitution, then it follows that enjoyment of domination and rape are in her nature" (Farley & Kelly, 2000). Talk about a non sequitur.

Prostitutes themselves do not necessarily see themselves as people who have been prostituted or as survivors. Many view themselves in more neutral terms. In a study of 294 prostitutes in Miami, for instance, almost all of them "prefer the terms *sex worker* and *working woman* and refer to themselves as such" (Kurtz, Surratt, Inciardi, & Kiley, 2004). Regardless of how the women see themselves, authors who take the extreme radical feminist position reject the idea that prostitution is "sex work," because viewing it as work might legitimize prostitution.

The problems described above are the tip of an iceberg floating in a larger theoretical quagmire. The extreme version of radical feminism underpinning these studies is a flawed theory according to any conventional definition. A good scientific theory is one whose propositions can be verified and falsified through empirical testing. Unfortunately, few of radical feminism's claims about prostitution are amenable to verification or falsification. These claims are presented as self-evident, absolute principles. How would one ever test the platitudes that customers are predators, that prostitution is paid rape, or as Dworkin (1997) puts it, that "when men use women in prostitution, they are expressing a pure hatred for the female body"?

I am not the first scholar to raise these questions. In a sweeping critique, Gayle Rubin (1993) noted that the radical feminist literature on prostitution and pornography is filled with "sloppy definitions, unsupported assertions, and outlandish claims." Such writers deliberately select the "worst available examples" and the most disturbing instances of abuse and present them as representative (Rubin, 1984). Anecdotes are routinely presented as definitive evidence, and counterevidence is completely ignored. This particular literature "violates most of the criteria for meaningful, serious, systematic, scientific thinking" (Goode, 1997). Rubin, Goode, and others are especially troubled by the claims of Dworkin and MacKinnon, but their criticisms apply with equal force to many others who write on the sex industry.

The extreme radical feminist perspective has been criticized for its essentialism and universalism, in particular the contention that victimization and exploitation are inherent, omnipresent, and unalterable—that prostitution has never been and can never be organized in a way that minimizes coercion and inequality and maximizes workers' interests. Some other feminists disagree. As Christine Overall (1992) points out, "It is imaginable that prostitution could always be practiced, as it occasionally is even now, in circumstances of relative safety, security, freedom, hygiene, and personal control." She is not optimistic about this becoming the norm, but does present a contrasting picture to those writers who portray prostitution as a vile institution under any and all circumstances.

METHODOLOGICAL FLAWS

Many studies of prostitution can be faulted on methodological grounds. Some authors fail to describe how and where they contacted research subjects. Others fail to include comparison groups (nonprostitutes matched on demographic characteristics; e.g., age, social class), without which it is impossible to know if the findings reported for a prostitute sample differ significantly from those of nonprostitutes. Those few studies that do include appropriate control groups yield mixed results. Some find significant differences between prostitutes and controls on, for instance, history of childhood victimization, whereas others find no significant differences (Earls & David, 1989; Nadon, Koverola, & Schludermann, 1998). When it comes to victimization in prostitution, studies are "often methodologically flawed and, moreover, contradictory" (Vanwesenbeeck, 2001).

Reliance on unrepresentative samples is widespread. Although random sampling of sex workers and customers is impossible, too often the findings and conclusions drawn from convenience and snowball samples are not properly qualified as nongeneralizable. Victimization studies are a case in point. Street prostitutes appear to experience high rates of violence in the course of their work, but the samples used in most studies consist of people who contacted service agencies, were approached on the street, or were interviewed in jail (James & Meyerding, 1977; McKeganey & Barnard, 1996; Weisberg, 1985). The high victimization rates reported in such studies are thus vulnerable to selection bias: The most desperate segment of the population or those persons who are most frequently or seriously victimized may be especially likely to contact service providers or agree to interviews. Generalizing from prostitutes in custody to the population of prostitutes is also improper, just as with other types of incarcerated offenders. Yet the implications of this sampling bias typically are neglected in the published reports. Moreover, the victimization rates reported are often reproduced in the secondary literature and in newspaper reports without disclosing the sampling technique and its limitations.

To cite just one example of this tendency: Silbert and Pines (1982) studied 200 street prostitutes in San Francisco and reported that 45% had been robbed, 65% had been beaten, and 70% had been raped or had experienced a customer "similarly going beyond the work contract" (a bit vague). The authors hired interviewers who were former prostitutes, had been residents of a treatment facility in the city, and "had been victims of various assaults" when they worked as prostitutes (Silbert & Pines, 1982). Despite the problematic orientation of the interviewers (given their past experiences) and the fact that the prostitutes interviewed were all drawn from the streets and from a single city, this study is one of the most frequently cited sources (by Farley and others) of evidence that violence is rampant in prostitution.

The three articles examined here, therefore, are hardly alone in using flawed methods. But it is not methodological flaws alone that plague these articles; the problem extends to the central conclusions derived from the research. In each case, the procedures used severely compromise the quality of the findings and the larger arguments made by the authors.

Raphael and Shapiro (2004) recruited 12 "survivors of prostitution" to locate and conduct interviews with other prostitutes. The authors give little indication of how the respondents were located, except to say that they were "already known to" the survivors, "women with whom they worked while previously in prostitution, and women referred by those interviewed" (Raphael & Shapiro, 2004). In other words, no attempt was made to sample the broadest range of workers possible; the sample was heavily skewed by the fact that the interviewers were prostitution "survivors" and by the fact that interviewers and respondents were prior associates who may have been like-minded. The authors point out that the interviewers "did not see their own [prior prostitution] experiences as 'work' or a choice," and "because of the bias of the surveyors, it is likely that this sample is more representative of women who do want to leave prostitution" (Raphael & Shapiro, 2002). Even more serious, this bias appears to have colored the entire study:

> *This research project was designed within a framework of prostitution as a form of violence against women and not prostitution as a legitimate industry. . . . The survey questions and administration were likely biased to some degree by working within this framework and by employing surveyors who had left prostitution. (Raphael & Shapiro, 2004)*

It is unclear how either the survey questions or the administration of the survey were biased, because nothing is said about them. Respondents were asked to state how frequently they had experienced 28 types of violence, but the actual survey questions are not presented.

I congratulate Raphael and Shapiro (2004) for acknowledging these methodological problems and biases, something few other writers ever do. But the bottom line is that we can have no confidence in their findings regarding the amount or nature of violence experienced by these women (see below). As Vanwesenbeeck (2001) points out,

> *When researchers have difficulty understanding rational, not to mention positive, reasons for choosing sex work and find it easier to think of prostitutes as victims, it is understandable that the sex workers [interviewed] will stress their victim status and negative motivations for working.*

Biased procedures beget foregone conclusions.

Raymond's (2004) article discusses her two previous studies of sex trafficking—one on trafficking to the United States and the other on trafficking between Indonesia, the Philippines, Thailand, Venezuela, and the United States. Remarkably, nothing is said about the procedures used in either study. All we are told is that interviews were conducted with social service providers, law enforcement officials, and 186 female "victims of sexual exploitation" and trafficking (Raymond, 2004). Raymond provides no information on where she located the women, how she gained access to them, how diverse or representative they are, and whether they saw themselves as victims. Moreover, none of the interview questions is revealed to the reader.

A major objective was to construct a profile of "prostitute users" and gather information on "men's attitudes and treatment of women in prostitution" (Raymond, 2004). Note that she did not interview even one customer. All of the information about "prostitute users" comes from the "prostituted women." And despite the fact that there is a growing body of academic research on customers (e.g., Monto, 2000, 2004), Raymond cites not one academic study published in a scholarly journal. Her findings are instead presented de novo, as if no one else has studied johns. It is a canon of academic research that authors situate their findings in the related scholarly literature to highlight similarities and differences in findings and build on prior work—something that Raymond opted not to do.

Farley's (2004) article is a wide-ranging discussion of a variety of harms in prostitution, rather than a single research study. Her title reflects her central argument: "Bad for the Body, Bad for the Heart: Prostitution Harms Women

Even if Legalized or Decriminalized." To support this conclusion, she draws very selectively from the literature, citing her own work and that of many antiprostitution activists (including Barry, Dworkin, Giobbe, Hughes, Jeffreys, and MacKinnon). Moreover, most of the empirical studies she cites are deeply flawed methodologically. Sampling biases and other procedural problems, in greater or lesser degree, pervade her literature, yet Farley never addresses this problem because that might undermine her sweeping claims.

What about Farley's own research procedures? Much is left opaque. In one study, Farley and Barkan (1998) interviewed street prostitutes in San Francisco. No indication is given of the breadth or diversity of their sample, or the method of approaching people on the street. In another study, Farley, Baral, Kiremire, and Sizgin (1998) interviewed workers in several countries: In Turkey, they interviewed 50 women who were brought to a hospital by the police for the purpose of venereal disease control; in Zambia, they interviewed 117 women at an organization that offers support services to prostitutes; in Thailand, respondents were interviewed on the street, in a beauty parlor, and in an organization offering support services; in South Africa, people were interviewed on the street, in brothels, and at a drop-in center. No information is provided as to how these locations were selected, or whether alternative locations were rejected for some reason. We know that people accessed at agencies providing services are likely to be particularly distressed. Finally, though Farley lists the topics covered in the interviews, none of the actual questions is presented. It is especially important to know the exact wording of questions, especially on this topic, because question wording may skew the answers.

I fully appreciate how difficult it is to conduct research on individuals who are stigmatized and involved in illegal behavior. Gaining access is a chronic challenge, as is any attempt to create samples that are not skewed in a certain direction. But there are numerous studies that are much better designed than the three examined here. Because of the problems sketched above, we can have no confidence in the results of the three studies.

A QUESTION OF VIOLENCE

Because the three authors define prostitution as violence against women, there is really no reason to try to determine how much violence takes place. Violence is intrinsic to the very definition of prostitution, so there can be no prostitution without violence. As indicated above, these writers simply decree that prostitution is violence, a proclamation that is neither verifiable nor falsifiable. How could one prove or disprove it? But, in one of the most revealing passages, Raymond (2004) uses graphic examples to try to prove the prostitution-as-violence claim:

> *To understand how violence is intrinsic to prostitution, it is necessary to understand the sex of prostitution. The sexual service provided in prostitution is most often violent, degrading, and abusive sexual acts, including sex between a buyer and several women; slashing the women with razor blades; tying women to bedposts and lashing them till they bleed; biting women's breasts; burning the women with cigarettes; cutting her arms, legs, and genital areas; and urinating or defecating on women.*

Note the use of horror stories to arouse the reader's disgust and anger, and recall Rubin's (1984) criticism of those who present the worst examples of abuse as typical.

Given that violence is presumed to be inevitable and omnipresent in prostitution, one wonders why these writers spend so much time trying to document its incidence. Perhaps a finding that violence occurs also establishes that it is intrinsic? I now turn to the question of incidence.

Many studies have attempted to estimate the amount of violence involved in prostitution. Unfortunately, we cannot answer this question definitively until we are able to construct a random sample of workers—something that probably can never be done, given that we have no way of knowing the parameters of the population of prostitutes, not to mention the problem of gaining access to and cooperation from them. Absent a random sample, the best that we can hope for are studies that do an exceptional job of sampling people in different geographical locations in different types of prostitution and doing both the sampling and interviewing in a rigorous and impartial manner.

The amount of violence experienced by prostitutes, as presented in the three articles, is much higher (60% to 90%) than what is reported in several other studies (Kurtz et al., 2004; Perkins, 1991; Perkins & Lovejoy, 1996; Whittaker & Hart, 1996). Raymond's (2004) five-country study reports that "almost 80%" of the respondents had been physically harmed, and "more than 60%" had been sexually assaulted by customers, pimps, and traffickers. It is important to keep in mind that these figures come from a segment of the industry that has had particularly harsh experiences: trafficking victims. Thus, the results certainly should not be extrapolated to "prostitution," as Raymond (2004) does: "The reported findings . . . indicate high levels of violation, harm, and trauma, and the fact that prostitution is a form of violence against women."

Farley found that 78% of her sample of street prostitutes in San Francisco had been threatened with a weapon, 82% had been assaulted, and 68% had been raped (Farley & Barkan, 1998). Similarly high figures are reported for four other societies—Thailand, Turkey, South Africa, Zambia—though less so for Thailand (Farley et al., 1998). In two of the societies (South Africa and Turkey), respondents included women in brothels as well as on the street. Although no comparative figures are presented from these two domains, "We found significantly more physical violence in street, as opposed to brothel, prostitution" (Farley et al., 1998). This seems to challenge Farley's claim that violence is omnipresent in prostitution. Another interesting finding is that 44% of the prostitutes interviewed in San Francisco, 38% in South Africa, and 28% in Thailand said that prostitution should be legalized. Farley dismisses these workers' preferences, insisting that legalization would only make their lives worse (Farley et al., 1998).

Raphael and Shapiro (2002, 2004) report similarly high figures for Chicago. For example, 86% of street workers had been slapped, 70% had been punched, 79% had been threatened with a weapon, and 64% had experienced forced sex.

Raphael and Shapiro (2002, 2004) include in their total figures violence committed by the women's intimate partners, which is not prostitution related. (The article is about violence in prostitution, not that occurring outside it.) Including domestic violence in the figures artificially inflates the total amount of violence experienced. Indeed, intimate partners were responsible for much of the total violence against prostitutes: After customers, these partners were the actors most frequently involved in meting out violence. For workers who work out of their own residence, for instance, their partners were responsible for "25%–100% of the violence," depending on the type of violence; for women who work the streets, their intimate partners committed about one fourth of the violence they experienced (Raphael & Shapiro, 2004). These intimate partners were not pimps; the authors present separate figures for pimps.

A related question is whether street and off-street prostitution differ. Street prostitution accounts for approximately one fifth of all prostitution in America; indoor prostitution is much more common, though less visible. A number of writers argue that there are indeed significant differences between these two domains and that studies that lump all workers together into an undifferentiated prostitution category are simplistic (Chapkis, 2000; Weitzer, 2000a). Vanwesenbeeck (2001) is critical of the widespread "failure to adequately differentiate between sex workers. . . . Sex workers are not 'the category' they are often taken to be." Chancer (1993) notes that "prostitutes' experiences, situations, and circumstances differ greatly over the gamut of this highly class-stratified occupation." And Monto (2004) points out that "empirical analyses demonstrate a remarkable diversity of activities that fall under the term prostitution and a remarkable diversity of experiences among participants." Comparative studies tend to find significant, and sometimes huge, differences between street prostitutes and call girls, brothel workers, and escorts in terms of job satisfaction, self-esteem, physical and psychological health, and occupational practices (Exner, Wylie, Leura, & Parrill, 1977; Lever & Dolnick, 2000; Perkins, 1991; Perkins & Lovejoy, 1996; Perkins & Bennett, 1985; Prince, 1986).

Regarding victimization, a number of studies indicate that street prostitutes are substantially more vulnerable to victimization than indoor workers. A British study, for instance, of 115 women who worked on the streets and 125 who worked in saunas or as call girls found that the street prostitutes were more likely than the indoor workers to report that they had ever been robbed (37% vs. 10%); beaten (27% vs. 1%); slapped, punched, or kicked (47% vs. 14%); raped (22% vs. 2%); threatened with a weapon (24% vs. 6%); strangled (20% vs. 6%); stabbed (8% vs. 0%); or kidnapped (20% vs. 2%; Church, Henderson, Bernard, & Hart, 2001). A comparison of street workers and escorts in Canada (Lowman & Fraser, 1995) found similar disparities: for robbery (37% vs. 9%), kidnapping (32% vs. 5%), sexual assault (37% vs. 9%), strangling (31% vs. 5%), being beaten (39% vs. 14%), and attempted murder (10% vs. 0%). Similar differences are found in other studies in Australia, Britain, Canada, and the United States (Perkins, 1991; Perkins & Bennett, 1985; Perkins & Lovejoy, 1996; Prince, 1986; Whittaker & Hart, 1996). None of these studies uses random samples, so there are limits to the conclusions we can draw from them. However, these studies are better designed than the three under review here.

Our three authors attempt to refute the argument that the amount of violence differs significantly between street prostitution and indoor prostitution. Farley (2004) says that violence is "the norm for women in all types of prostitution." Raphael and Shapiro (2004) conclude that in Chicago, "violence was prevalent across both outdoor and indoor prostitution venues," and they issue a "mandate that we not strive to make strict distinctions or demarcations among different prostitution activities in terms of violence." However, we have already established that Raphael and Shapiro admit to having a strong bias that views prostitution as violence against women, and their exprostitute interviewers shared this perspective and thus were hardly objective in selecting interviewees, persons who are likely to have had bad experiences. It is ludicrous to conduct a study measuring the extent of violence suffered by prostitutes when one's orienting framework equates prostitution with violence, and it is not surprising to find high levels of violence, in any prostitution sector, if one's sampling and interviewing strategy is so transparently slanted.

The other, better designed studies cited above do indeed find significant differences in the amount of violence in various indoor versus street settings. No one is arguing that indoor prostitution is free of violence, but based on the available research literature, violence is nowhere near as prevalent as the image presented by Raphael and Shapiro (2004). Even Farley found "significantly" more violence in street prostitution than in brothel prostitution (Farley et al., 1998). Street prostitutes are more vulnerable to victimization than escorts, call girls, and those involved in consensual brothel and massage parlor work.

CONCLUSION

Violence in prostitution is a serious problem. Workers, particularly those on the streets, are vulnerable to assault, robbery, rape, and murder. The best studies provide us with rough estimates of how frequently this violence occurs. Unfortunately, the three articles reviewed here make little contribution to our understanding of this problem.

Although my critique has been restricted to writings on the extreme radical feminist side, elsewhere I have been equally critical of works that celebrate and romanticize prostitution, pornography, and other forms of sex work

(Weitzer, 1991, 2000a, 2000b). Such studies marshall the "best available examples"—typically upscale call girls and escort agency workers—to argue that prostitution is or can be empowering and lucrative. For some workers, this is indeed the case, but these "best examples" are no closer to the norm in prostitution than the "worst examples." Again, prostitution varies significantly by type, and it is disingenuous to generalize from one type to prostitution as a whole.

Finally, though these writers continually refer to "prostitution," it is not clear if their arguments encompass male and transgender, as well as female, workers. Does the radical feminist definition of prostitution as violence, oppression, and human rights abuse apply, generically, to all types of prostitution? If these claims apply only to female prostitution, then these harms are not intrinsic to prostitution. Studies indicate that male workers experience much less violence and exploitation and exercise greater control over working conditions than female and transgender workers (Aggleton, 1999; Valera, Sawyer, & Schiraldi, 2001; Weinberg, Shaver, & Williams, 1999; West 1993). Further investigation of male and transgender prostitution, as well as better designed and ideologically neutral studies of female prostitution, will contribute to a more sophisticated, nuanced, variegated, and comprehensive understanding of contemporary prostitution.

REFERENCES

Aggleton, P. (Ed.). (1999). *Men who sell sex: International perspectives on male prostitution and HIV/AIDS.* Philadelphia: Temple University Press.

Barry, K. (1995). *The prostitution of sexuality.* New York: New York University Press.

Benson, C., & Matthews, R. (1995). Street prostitution: Ten facts in search of a policy. *International Journal of the Sociology of Law*, 23, 395–415.

Chancer, L. (1993). Prostitution, feminist theory, and ambivalence. *Social Text*, 37, 143–171.

Chapkis, W. (2000). Power and control in the commercial sex trade. In R. Weitzer (Ed.), *Sex for sale: Prostitution, pornography, and the sex industry* (pp. 181–201). New York: Routledge.

Church, S., Henderson, M., Barnard, M., & Hart, G. (2001). Violence by clients towards female prostitutes in different work settings. *British Medical Journal*, 322, 524–526.

Dworkin, A. (1981). *Pornography: Men possessing women.* New York: Putnam.

Dworkin, A. (1997). *Life and death.* New York: Free Press.

Earls, C., & David, H. (1989). Male and female prostitution: A review. *Annals of Sex Research*, 2, 5–28.

Exner, J., Wylie, K., Leura, A., & Parrill, T. (1977). Some psychological characteristics of prostitutes. *Journal of Personality Assessment*, 41, 474–485.

Farley, M. (2000). *Prostitution: Factsheet on human rights violations.* San Francisco: Prostitution Research and Education.

Farley, M. (2004). Bad for the body, bad for the heart: Prostitution harms women even if legalized or decriminalized. *Violence Against Women*, 10, 1087–1125.

Farley, M., Baral, I., Kiremire, M., & Sizgin, U. (1998). Prostitution in five countries: Violence and post-traumatic stress disorder. *Feminism and Psychology*, 8, 405–426.

Farley, M., & Barkan, H. (1998). Prostitution, violence, and posttraumatic stress disorder. *Women and Health*, 27, 37–49.

Farley, M., & Kelly, V. (2000). Prostitution. *Women and Criminal Justice*, 11, 20–64.

Foglino, A. (1998, November). Quitting the streets. *Life*, pp. 96–100.

Goode, E. (1997). *Deviant behavior.* Upper Saddle River, NJ: Prentice Hall.

Heyl, B. (1979). Prostitution: An extreme case of sex stratification. In R. Adler & R. Simon (Eds.), *The criminology of deviant women* (pp. 196–210). Boston: Houghton Mifflin.

James, J., & Meyerding, J. (1977). Early sexual experience and prostitution. *American Journal of Psychiatry*, 134, 1381–1385.

Jeffreys, S. (1997). *The idea of prostitution.* North Melbourne, Australia: Spinifex.

Kurtz, S., Surratt, H., Inciardi, L., & Kiley, M. (2004). Sex work and date violence. *Violence Against Women*, 10, 357–385.

Lever, J., & Dolnick, D. (2000). Clients and call girls: Seeking sex and intimacy. In R. Weitzer (Ed.), *Sex for sale: Prostitution, pornography, and the sex industry* (pp. 85–100). New York: Routledge.

Lowman, J. (2000). Violence and the outlaw status of street prostitution in Canada. *Violence Against Women*, 6, 987–1011.

Lowman, J., & Fraser, L. (1995). *Violence against persons who prostitute: The experience in British Columbia.* Ottawa, Canada: Department of Justice.

MacKinnon, C. (1987). *Feminism unmodified.* Cambridge, MA: Harvard University Press.

MacKinnon, C. (1989). *Toward a feminist theory of the state.* Cambridge, MA: Harvard University Press.

McKeganey, N., & Barnard, M. (1996). *Sex work on the streets.* Buckingham, UK: Open University Press.

Monto, M. (2000). Why men seek out prostitutes. In R. Weitzer (Ed.), *Sex for sale: Prostitution, pornography, and the sex industry* (pp. 67–83). New York: Routledge.

Monto, M. (2004). Female prostitution, customers, and violence. *Violence Against Women*, 10, 160–168.

Nadon, S., Koverola, C., & Schludermann, E. (1998). Antecedents to prostitution: Childhood victimization. *Journal of Interpersonal Violence*, 13, 206–221.

Overall, C. (1992). What's wrong with prostitution? Evaluating sex work. *Signs*, 17, 705–724.

Perkins, R. (1991). *Working girls.* Canberra, Australia: Australian Institute of Criminology.

Perkins, R., & Bennett, G. (1985). *Being a prostitute.* London: George Allen and Unwin.

Perkins, R., & Lovejoy, F. (1996). Healthy and unhealthy life styles of female brothel workers and call girls in Sydney. *Australian and New Zealand Journal of Public Health*, 20, 512–516.

Prince, D. (1986). A psychological study of prostitutes in California and Nevada. Unpublished doctoral dissertation, United States International University, San Diego, California.

Raphael, J., & Shapiro, D. (2002). *Sisters speak out: The lives and needs of prostituted women in Chicago.* Chicago: Center for Impact Research.

Raphael, J., & Shapiro, D. (2004). Violence in indoor and outdoor prostitution venues. *Violence Against Women*, 10, 126–139.

Raymond, J. (1995, December 11). Prostitution is rape that's paid for. *Los Angeles Times*, p. B6.

Raymond, J. (1998). Prostitution as violence against women. *Women's Studies International Forum*, 21, 1–9.

Raymond, J. (2004). Prostitution on demand: Legalizing the buyers as sexual consumers. *Violence Against Women*, 10, 1156–1186.

Rubin, G. (1984). Thinking sex: Notes for a radical theory of the politics of sexuality. In C. Vance (Ed.), *Pleasure and danger* (pp. 267–319). Boston: Routledge.

Rubin, G. (1993). Misguided, dangerous, and wrong: An analysis of antipornography politics. In A. Assiter & A. Carol (Eds.), *Bad girls and dirty pictures* (pp. 18–40). London: Pluto.

Silbert, M., & Pines, A. (1982). Victimization of street prostitutes. *Victimology*, 7, 122–133.

Valera, R., Sawyer, R., & Schiraldi, G. (2001). Perceived health needs of inner-city street prostitutes. *American Journal of Health Behavior*, 25, 50–59.

Vanwesenbeeck, I. (2001). Another decade of social scientific work on prostitution. *Annual Review of Sex Research*, 12, 242–289.

Weinberg, M., Shaver, F., & Williams, C. (1999). Gendered prostitution in the San Francisco tenderloin. *Archives of Sexual Behavior*, 28, 503–521.

Weisberg, D. (1985). *Children of the night: A study of adolescent prostitution.* Lexington, MA: Lexington Books.

Weitzer, R. (1991). Prostitutes' rights in the United States: The failure of a movement. *Sociological Quarterly*, 32, 23–41.

Weitzer, R. (2000a). Deficiencies in the sociology of sex work. *Sociology of Crime, Law, and Deviance*, 2, 259–279.

Weitzer, R. (2000b). The politics of prostitution in America. In R. Weitzer (Ed.), *Sex for sale: Prostitution, pornography, and the sex industry* (pp. 159–180). New York: Routledge.

West, D. J. (1993). *Male prostitution.* Binghamton, NY: Haworth.

Whittaker, D., & Hart, G. (1996). Managing risks: The social organization of indoor prostitution. *Sociology of Health and Illness*, 18, 399–414.

REVIEW QUESTIONS

1. Weitzer contends that many radical feminist scholars, writing in the area of prostitution, equate prostitution with violence against women. How do these scholars arrive at this conclusion, and how would you counter their argument, using this article as your source of information?
2. After reading Weitzer's article, has your view toward prostitution changed? Defend your answer.
3. What does this article say to you about some of the research appearing in scholarly journals?

Chapter 29

EXOTIC DANCERS: "WHERE AM I GOING TO STOP?"

JENNIFER K. WESELY

To the general public, exotic dancing is a "deviant" occupation, and there is a certain stigma associated with deviant work. Being stigmatized can cause an identity conflict in people, a conflict between their perception of themselves as a *conventional* person and their perception of themselves as a *deviant* person. Some researchers have suggested that being an exotic dancer is really more of a "role" than an identity (Reid et al., 1994). This means that the stripper sees her performance only as a job—she does not identify herself as a stripper, namely as a deviant, but instead identifies herself as a wife, mother, girlfriend, student, or some other conventional person. So, basically, the exotic dancer does not really experience an identity conflict. But other researchers have argued that it is difficult for many women who work as exotic dancers to avoid being affected by the stigma of the deviant occupation (Sweet and Tewksbury, 2000b). It is natural, then, for exotic dancers to experience an identity conflict, feeling that their new identity as a deviant is assaulting their long-held identity as a conventional person. In the following analysis, I will describe the nature of exotic dancers' identity conflict and the different ways they deal with it.

METHOD

The information for this analysis is derived from qualitative, in-depth interviews with 20 current and former exotic dancers in a southwestern metropolitan area. From March to November 2000, I used a snowball technique to reach subjects by phone or in person at local exotic dance clubs to request, arrange and conduct interviews. Initial contacts were made from a variety of sources, including my college students who knew club managers or who worked as dancers. Once an initial contact was made an interview was requested. Interviews took place at several different private and mutually convenient locations, including my office, the home of the interviewee, or a local restaurant or bar. Lasting an average of two hours, completed interviews were tape-recorded, transcribed, and coded. I also followed up with phone calls, at which time I got clarification about various issues that had arisen during the interview.

The race and ethnicity of the subjects: one Hispanic/Hawaiian, one African American, one African American/Hispanic, two Puerto Rican, one Mexican American, one Filipino/White, one native African, one Costa Rican/Sicilian, and eleven Caucasian. The ages of the women at the time of the interview ranged from 18 to 40, the average age being 26. The ages at which they began dancing spanned 14 to 29, with 19 being the average age. The amount of time they were employed continuously as dancers ranged from 1½ months to 17 years with an average of 5 years. One woman was a college graduate, one was a high school dropout, five had a high school

Source: Jennifer K. Wesely, " 'Where Am I Going to Stop?': Exotic Dancing, Fluid Body Boundaries, and Effects on Identity," *Deviant Behavior*, 24 (2003), pp. 483–503. © 2003. Reproduced by permission of Taylor & Francis, Inc., www.informaworld.com.

education, and the rest had some college credit. At the time of the interview, five were enrolled in college.

In terms of relationships, six women were married, three were engaged, four were in serious heterosexual relationships (two were cohabitating), three were casually dating, and four were single and not dating. Six had children, and six acknowledged having had one or more abortions. As children or teenagers, nine were raped or molested, three by their fathers, and six by someone outside the family. Six stated that they were neglected or emotionally abused by one or both of their parents. As adults, eight had been or were in violent intimate relationships. Pseudonyms are used in this analysis to protect the identities of the interviewees.

FINDINGS

In the following analysis, I will show how exotic dancers come to experience an identity conflict and how they deal with it.

"The Money Makes It Worth It"

Sweet and Tewksbury's (2000a) study of exotic dancers reveals that the need for "early independence" was the most influential factor in choosing an exotic dancing career for the women they interviewed. Early independence refers to the status of young women and girls who leave the home to survive independently, often to escape abuse. I found a similar situation among several of the women I interviewed. They turned to exotic dancing as their alternative to homelessness at a young age. Irene, for example, was homeless for a time, living on roofs and in stairways. Then, she said, "I started dancing at 18, when I was in New York. I had a girlfriend who said I should do it, make a lot of money . . . Once I started doing it there I did it everywhere I went."

Not everyone was motivated by such dire circumstances, but at a relatively young age many felt tremendous pressure to earn enough money to support themselves or family members. Rita had money stolen from her bank account by her mother, leaving her without any financial resources to finish her first semester of college. It was at this point she began dancing. Tasha lived with her divorced mother, and felt responsible when their electricity was turned off and her mother was unable to support them.

But the initial experience of stripping for a living was extremely difficult for many of the women. Apparently, the stigma of being a stripper challenged their self-identity as a conventional person like everyone else. Many dealt with this problem by reminding themselves that they could quickly make a lot of money. As Rita said,

> *When I first started, I came home from work every night for two weeks and cried. Until I fell asleep. And the only way I could fall asleep is that I would count the money . . . That was my first two weeks, and my second two weeks, I cried every night before work. I'd be so upset when I got there, but then you're ok. The money makes it worth it.*

"Where Am I Going to Stop?"

Exotic dancers are immersed in an environment that puts a monetary value on their sexually objectified bodies. The women in the club are thus tempted to use their bodies in ways that will generate the greatest amount of money possible. The lure of money can easily lead exotic dancers to do things for customers that they ordinarily would not do. As Arlene said,

> *In Vegas, when those guys keep bringing out $100 bills, you let them touch you more. I know I did a lot more there than I would here. A lot more. He was touching me all over my back, and I could care less. I was sitting on his lap. I would never do that at The Kingdom [in hometown]. I could care less, it was totally fine, but I would never do that at The Kingdom. If a guy's going to give you that much money, that's the way it is. Which is really sad. I was like, shit, where am I going to stop? And I mean, I do know where I would stop, but . . . That just scares me, the fact, that it was because of the money I did that.*

By saying "where am I going to stop," Arlene suggested that she was tempted by money to be a deviant and to do a lot of deviant things for customers. But at the same time she said, "I do know where I would stop," indicating that she is basically a conventional person and will not do the most deviant, outrageous things for customers. Other women in my study also suggested that there was a limit to how far they would go in pleasing customers. For the sake of money, many exotic dancers might choose to make increasingly intense body contacts with customers but they would draw the line at having sex with customers. In short, the exotic dancers tried to deal with their identity conflict by refraining from going overboard in their work as exotic dancers. In that way, they still could keep their conventional identity largely intact.

"I Don't Think about What I'm Doing"

The exotic dancers in my study often felt confused, upset, enraged, or concerned about their dirty dancing—making all kinds of body contacts with customers. Such deviant work, then, inevitably threatens the dancers' identity as a conventional person. To ward off this threat and hence resolve the identity conflict, the dancers tended to avoid thinking about the deviant, unpleasant aspects of their work. As Arlene said,

> *It's really a lot of stress. It takes a lot out of you. That's why I forget about it and don't think about what I'm doing at work. If I let it bother me when I was at work, I couldn't do it. I mean, if you think about it, you're showing somebody your tits that you've never seen before. One guy gave me $20 for a dance, so I rubbed up and down on him a little bit. If I had a boyfriend, I wouldn't even do that with a boyfriend. It's really weird. If you think about it, it's terrible.*

"It's Just My Body . . . Not Really Who I Am"

The compromises the dancers made about their body contacts with customers can be placed along a continuum. When they began dancing, they had more rigid boundaries, ones that were more in keeping with their conventional identities. They would, for example, simply expose their breasts but not let customers touch them. Over time, they relaxed some of these limits, letting customers briefly touch some parts of their naked bodies. However, as more money was given to them, the dancers offered more and more body contacts with customers until finally they would do practically everything that customers asked for. However, the more the dancers performed to meet the customer's demands, the greater the threat to the dancers' identity as a conventional person. To protect this self-identity, the dancers tended to engage in dissociation, separating their self as a stripper from their true self as a conventional person. As Gina explained,

> *I think of the body as just an outer, just a shell, it's just material, it's not part of who you are, in terms of what moves on . . . Me, it's just my body. You know what I mean? So if a guy grabs me at work, I rationalize myself out of feeling violated. In terms of just, it's just my body. It's not that it doesn't bother me, when somebody touches me or something, but I could get over something like that, I can mentally overcome something like that, I think . . . I always think about: am I selling my body, am I selling my self—that used to be a big moral issue for me while I was dancing. So I think that's got a little bit to do with disassociating. Well, it's ok to sell, for people to look at my body, because that's not really who I am.*

"It Was Hard to Separate Anymore"

For exotic dancers, increased body contacts with customers can be prevented from obliterating their true self, the self that they present to others *outside* the club. As we have just observed, Gina was able to keep her true self intact by dissociating it from her work as a stripper, so that she could continue to live her life as a conventional person like everyone else. But some exotic dancers cannot. Their work as strippers overwhelm their true, conventional self so much that they may take on the sex object persona outside the strip club. As Sheila said, "I wore heels for probably eight months! Yeah, I wore heels all the time. I would dress sexy all the time. I would show off my body all the time. That's who I became. Played a role and kept it going." Or as Julie put it,

> *It was hard to separate anymore. About a year and a half into it, it was hard to separate the stage Julie from the real-life Julie. I'd walk out with my shorts, half my ass hanging out. I had no desire to change the person. It took over. Took over. I'd go to the river, anyone want to see my tits? It took over completely. I couldn't leave it [at the club]. It took over very quickly.*

CONCLUSION

An exotic dancer's success is measured in the amount of money earned for a night's work. To attain cash reward, dancers must capitalize on the sexual objectification of their bodies. Consequently, money and body are linked in a transactional relationship. However, for female exotic dancers, floating just beneath the surface of this transaction is identity conflict, the conflict between how the dancers see themselves inside the strip club and how they see themselves outside.

The exotic dancers in this study tried to deal with their identity conflict in a number of ways. First, to get over the unpleasantness of working as a stripper, especially in the initial phase of their work, the dancers reminded themselves that the money they earned made it worth it. Second, they were tempted by money to perform increasingly outrageous sex acts for customers but managed to put a limit on how far they would go. Third, whenever they felt uncomfortable about the acts they performed for customers, they tried not to think about them. Fourth, some dancers dissociated their work as a stripper from their true self as a conventional person. And fifth, some dancers let their work as strippers overwhelm their lives outside the club so that they acted as if they were still performing in the club.

REFERENCES

Reid, Scott A., Jonathon S. Epstein, and D. E. Benson. 1994. "Role Identity in a Devalued Occupation: The Case of Female Exotic Dancers." *Sociological Focus* 27:1–16.

Sweet, Nova, and Richard Tewksbury. 2000a. "What's a Nice Girl Like You Doing in a Place Like This?": Pathways to a Career in Stripping," *Sociological Spectrum* 20:325–343.

Sweet, Nova, and Richard Tewksbury. 2000b. "Entry, Maintenance, and Departure from a Career in the Sex Industry: Strippers' Experiences of Occupational Costs and Rewards," *Humanity and Society* 24:136–161.

REVIEW QUESTIONS

1. What did the study find were reasons that the women involved chose to engage in exotic dancing?
2. What does "It's just my body . . . not really who I am" mean?
3. What other professions might lead to identity conflict, as experienced by some of the women in the study?

CHAPTER 30

"EVERYONE KNOWS WHO THE SLUTS ARE": HOW YOUNG WOMEN GET AROUND THE STIGMA

JENNIFER L. DUNN

When deviance from a group's expectations is profound, the person who violates the norm can come to have what the sociologist Erving Goffman (1963) called a stigma. People with a stigma have a "spoiled" identity, because we have discovered that they are not who they claim to be or they act in ways contrary to how we think people like them should act. Goffman said that we carry around stereotypes of people, and when people don't match up—when there is a "discrepancy" between what we expect and what we get—we look down on the stigmatized person and treat him or her accordingly (1963). Not only do we demean such persons, but we treat them as unworthy of our respect and regard, and in this way, Goffman said, "we effectively, if often unthinkingly, reduce [their] life chances."

This article is about how becoming sexually active in the wrong ways can be deeply discrediting for young women, and what young women do to avoid or repair the stigma of being a "slut." It is based on interviews of 22 undergraduate women, individually and in an exploratory focus group, who were asked about their reasons for becoming sexually active or for refraining from sexual activity. Even though adolescents face a variety of pressures to have sex, and almost half (48.4 percent) of teenagers between 15 and 17 are sexually active (Risman and Schwartz, 2002), girls in particular are not free to be sexual as often as, or with whomever, they please. Instead, it is common for young women to be ascribed the "slut" identity if they are perceived as becoming active too young, having too many partners, choosing inappropriate partners, or having intercourse under the influence of alcohol or other drugs.

The young women I interviewed constructed their own "image" and "reputation" by telling me about other despised girls; they adamantly did not want themselves to be seen as a "slut." All but one of the women spoke in these terms. "Susan" (all of the names I use are pseudonyms), for example, discussed her feelings after an alcohol-induced "one-night fling" this way:

> *I felt as oh my god what's going to happen to my image . . . before in high school, I was known as Miss Virgin and I dated a lot of guys in high school, but I was never . . . you know how some girls who date a lot of guys in high school are considered a tease? But I know, 'cause I've talked to some of my ex boyfriends, I was never considered a tease. I was just considered a girl who would never put out.*

Susan explained about different types of women, describing the valued image of the respected virgin and contrasting it to the more sexual "tease"—an identity that does not fit the "nice girl" stereotype of virtue and chastity. Susan went

Source: Written specifically for this reader.

on to explain that she was afraid she would be seen as one of the "slutty girls"—that is, "girls who go to parties and then have sex with men they meet there."

Darla was able to describe this other, stigmatized identity in some detail for me. "Sluts" were the girls who were "popular among the guys" for the "wrong reasons," who called men all the time and were sexually aggressive, and who "forced themselves" on men who, she explained, would rather be left alone. Darla had a friend who would do "anything" to get the approval of men:

> *She's the kind of person . . . if she likes someone, she would call them all the time, do everything to get their attention, all the time . . . and it was like she would even have sex with them, just to like, get their attention.*

"I could never be a person who dates casually and has casual sex," Susan told me, a remark that reflected the consensus among the women I interviewed.

Several of the women I interviewed reported feeling "slutty" as a consequence of a decision to have sex outside the context of a committed relationship. None were more profoundly affected than Valerie, who used the language of stigma to describe the experience with multiple partners she had in high school. After she told me about her self-described decision to trade sex for intimacy, I asked her how she felt about that choice. "I'm still trying to get over that," she acknowledged, "because it gave me, like, the slut complex . . . [I thought] that maybe it was just an inherent personality trait, that I was just a slut, that I slept around."

Valerie took the expectations of her peers, and her deviance from their norms, very seriously. It led her to have intensive counseling, and she claimed to be only just beginning to feel recovered at the time of our interview. Goffman describes shame as a "central possibility" for the person who sees the possession of an attribute as "defiling," and Valerie was extremely conscious of how she thought other people saw her (1963). Sally said that at her high school, "everyone knows who the sluts are; it gets around," and she was careful to distinguish herself from these women, who were friends but not the people she chose to spend much time with. When I asked her what she meant by "sluts," she defined them as "people who were easy and just had sex whenever they went on a date."

It appears that pregnancy and sexually transmitted diseases are not the only hazards associated with becoming sexually active. Young women also run the risk of acquiring the stigmatized identity of the "slut." In their concern for their reputations, the women I interviewed seem to invest sex with what Ehrenreich, Hess, and Jacobs (1986) refer to as "old meanings," understandings of sex that predate the sexual revolution, in which amorous sex is approved and casual sex is condemned. Only one of the women I interviewed spoke of her own pleasure in any kind of sex; the majority were far more likely to describe their feelings as shamed or valued, depending on whether they encountered or avoided the stigma attached to their decisions. Even though the sexual revolution has so changed our thinking about sex that sex divorced from love, marriage, or reproduction has arguably "become a mainstream American value" (Risman and Schwartz, 2002), these women still take into account traditional values that censure the uninhibited expression of female sexuality. In this view, sex that is "purely about play and pleasure" (Risman and Schwartz, 2002) is something that "sluts," not girls with "self-respect," engage in. Sex for fun is a deviation from social norms, violating what Goffman (1963) called a "normative expectation" and thus incurring stigma.

Is there any way out of this dilemma? After all, almost all American teenagers are sexually active by the end of their teen years, and our culture is "highly sexualized" (Risman and Schwartz, 2002). How can a young woman follow her desires, or conform to significant historical, cultural, and peer pressures to have sex, yet still preserve her reputation? The contradictory features of this social structural situation present a dilemma. It is a kind of "identity bind"

(Lofland, 1995). How do you face conflicting expectations and still keep from spoiling your image?

The answer, it turns out, is to simultaneously avoid a stigmatized, discredited identity and acquire a valued one by being in a "relationship" —taking on a "coupled" identity by having a boyfriend. Indeed, having a boyfriend was tremendously important to the young women in this study. For example, Felicia described how important it was for her friends to have a relationship: "All my friends have said, 'God, I want a boyfriend.' It's like, I want a boyfriend so I can feel and have that self-esteem, you know, to feel good about myself." Valerie, too, was eloquent in her description of her need to be coupled:

> *I was destroyed on a regular basis, and then I had to build myself up so I could go on with daily living, but daily living felt like an existence, not, not like I was living, just like I was going through the motions. Until I found a man, and then the man kind of made the life thing worthwhile.*

Tessa said that she and her boyfriend had been "joined at the hip," meaning always together. She matter-of-factly described herself as "consumed with him" and as envisioning herself married, saying she would have married him unless she had met someone else. This is how she described being coupled:

> *My whole life just revolved around him, I was always with him. Just completely, any time, any spare time that I had was with him, and there was never time to myself, it was always with him. We were always together. We were married, I mean, that was the way we acted, that was the way people—it was never Tessa, it was always Tessa and Kyle [she laughs]. We were always together.*

For these young women, being in a relationship enables them to be sexually active while at the same time avoiding the stigma of the "slut" identity. By carefully choosing their partners and the circumstances of coitus, they conform to the stereotype that most young people are no longer virgins by their senior year in high school (in fact, only 25 percent of women and 10 percent of men are still virgins at age 20, according to the survey cited by Risman and Schwartz). Thus, it is "normal" to have sex, but deviant to have "casual" sex, especially if you are female (Risman and Schwartz, 2002). The discrepancies in these expectations, and the possible stigma, are avoided by confining sex to "boyfriends." Goffman might say that the girlfriend identity manages to meet the normative expectations to be both virtuous and sexual.

The interviews support this interpretation. In an adolescent subculture these women understand as valuing sexual experience and chastity, they talk about the importance of forming committed monogamous relationships and what they are willing to do in order to achieve the valued identity attached to such relationships. Susan, for example, said that her "bad experiences" with men who did not maintain relationships with her after sexual encounters had taught her to appreciate the importance of a relationship:

> *Well, does this guy really care about me, you know? . . . I think if a person really cares about you, they're not going to even try to sleep with you on the very first night. . . . And I think I've learned more of what types of guys to look for, you know, if I went out on a date and a guy just seemed interested in trying to sleep with me rather than trying to get to know me, then, I would probably never see him again. Because I don't want to get involved with a person that goes from relationship to relationship.*

Corinne has also learned about the same thing from the failed relationships in her life. When she meets a new male, she says, "I can sit back now, because of this incident, and say, what is this person going to offer me? I just go whoa, does he fulfill all this that I want, and if he doesn't, then that's it. I can't waste my time and risk getting hurt." These understandings are completely consistent with the idea that women who have casual sex are "sluts" and are stigmatized for sexual behavior in a way that "girlfriends" are not. They support these women's decisions to form particular types of relationships in order to be sexually active. In today's world:

Teens and adults have sex before, during, and after marriage with a variety of partners over their life course. . . . For most people, a sexual life begins during adolescence and is likely to include all kinds of sexual behaviors, including coitus, before people reach the legal age for drinking alcohol. (Risman and Schwartz, 2002)

In conclusion, as Goffman would have anticipated in 1963 (just prior to the sexual revolution), there are normative expectations for young women today and different ways of violating them, some of which may lead to stigma and, because of it, being treated badly. On the one hand, it is now pretty "normal" for young women to be sexually active even before they graduate from high school. But such women risk being stigmatized as a "slut." On the other hand, young women who remain as virgins even in their senior year may be afraid of being stigmatized as a "tease." Thus many tend to be sexually active but get around the "slut" stigma by seeking out relationships to have sex in them. Even so, there is no guarantee the stigma will be avoided, because after all, "Everyone knows who the sluts are."

REFERENCES

Ehrenreich, B., E. Hess, and G. Jacobs. 1986. *Remaking Love: The Feminization of Sex.* Garden City, New York: Anchor/Doubleday.

Goffman, E. 1963. *Stigma.* New York: Simon and Schuster.

Lofland, L. 1995. Personal communication.

Risman, B., and P. Schwartz. 2002. "After the sexual revolution: Gender politics in teen dating." *Contexts,* 1:16–24.

REVIEW QUESTIONS

1. How do women get around the stigma of being defined as a "slut"?
2. Do you agree or disagree with the statement "Everyone knows who the sluts are"? Defend your answer by providing concrete examples in defense of your position.
3. What is the definition of a "slut" in this article? How might that label change in ten years? Twenty?

PART NINE

SUBSTANCE USE AND ABUSE

On a typical American college campus, serious weekend partying begins on Friday. Asked after midnight, "Why do you drink so much?" most students give a succinct answer. "Stress!" says a business major outside a bar. Watched by a bored bouncer, he staggers away. . . . "Stress," whispers a female student as she leans on a wall to avoid falling. Nearby are two bull-necked young men, one wearing a T-shirt with the slogan "Take Me Drunk, I'm Home" and the other's stating, "From Zero to Horny in 2.5 Beers." They lift up the disoriented and giggling young woman by the ankles over a beer keg. Hanging upside down, she seizes its plastic hose and begins to gulp. . . . "Outrageous, awesome, major stress," says a third student outside a club, helping her too-drunk-to-walk friend get into a car. The friend, hair soaked with beer, promptly hangs out the window, hiccupping for a few seconds and then vomiting. All of these students engage in what is called *binge drinking*, which is often defined by researchers as the consumption of five or more consecutive drinks for men and four or more for women. Binge drinking began to appear on many campuses in the late 1980s and continues in full force today.[1]

Here we focus on the use of illicit and licit drugs. In the first reading, "Binge Drinking on College Campus," Keith Durkin, Scott Wolfe, and Kara Lewis show with research data how well the social bond theory explains binge drinking by college students. In the second article, "Hey, Don't Blame Me . . . Blame the Booze," Robert Peralta shows how men and women use alcohol to excuse their gender-inappropriate behavior, which involves men acting feminine and women acting manly. In the third selection, "OxyContin: A Prescription for Disaster," James Inciardi and Jennifer Goode document how the prescription drug gets diverted to the illegal marketplace and how its increased abuse has led to government efforts to control it. In the fourth piece, "Damn, It Feels Good to be a Gangsta: Selling Drugs on Campus," Rafik Mohamed and Erik Fritsvold portray what drug dealing is like on campus.

[1]Barrett Seaman, *Binge: What Your College Student Won't Tell You.* Hoboken, N.J.: John Wiley & Sons, 2005. Anne Matthew, "The Campus Crime Wave," *New York Times Magazine*, March 7, 1993, p. 41.

Chapter 31

BINGE DRINKING ON COLLEGE CAMPUSES

KEITH F. DURKIN
SCOTT E. WOLFE
KARA LEWIS

Binge drinking, which involves the consumption of large quantities of alcohol in a single drinking episode, has been getting a lot of attention from the media, college administrators, healthcare professionals, and researchers in the behavioral sciences. Most researchers specifically define binge drinking as the consumption of at least five alcoholic drinks in a single sitting for men and four for women. A number of studies have revealed that this behavior is fairly common on college campuses, with a large minority (about 44 percent) of students having engaged in binge drinking during the previous two weeks (Wechsler et al., 1994; 2002b).

Consensus has been growing that binge drinking represents a very serious threat to the well-being of many of today's college students. Compared to other college students, binge drinkers have been found to be more likely to experience negative consequences as a result of their drinking. These include hangovers, blackouts, missing class, doing something they regret later, getting involved in physical fights and other arguments, and having trouble with the police. The tragic alcohol-related deaths of students at several colleges and universities further highlight the potentially fatal consequences of this activity.

Researchers have also found that binge drinkers can produce "secondhand effects" on nondrinking others by hurting them in some ways. These include verbally insulting or abusing the innocent victims, physically assaulting them, damaging the property around them, making unwelcome sexual advances on women, and disturbing others' sleep or studying (Wechsler et al., 2002a).

A number of recent studies have identified certain demographics associated with binge drinking on college campus. Men, for example, are much more likely than women to binge drink. White students are more likely than non-white students to drink excessively. And students who are athletes, fraternity brothers, or sorority sisters are more likely than other students to drink uncontrollably (Wechsler et al., 1994; 1995; NIAAA, 2002). But these demographics are merely correlates, not causes, of binge drinking. They cannot explain, for example, why men are more likely than women, or why some men are more likely than other men, to binge drink. It is thus important to know the causes of binge drinking.

SOCIAL BOND THEORY

A promising source of such knowledge is Travis Hirschi's control theory of deviance, also known as social bond theory. This theory assumes that

Source: Written specifically for this reader.

the motivation for deviant behavior is present in everyone but the motivation will lead to deviance only for some people—but not for others. The difference depends on the degree of bond between the individual and society. If the bond is weak, the individual will likely turn deviant, but if the bond is strong, the individual will likely not (Hirschi, 1969). This theory has been used to explain a wide variety of deviances including alcohol use, juvenile delinquency, marijuana use, and cheating on tests. The theory can also be used to explain binge drinking as a form of deviant behavior.

There are four elements of social bond. The first is *attachment* to others. This refers to the ties that an individual has to significant others such as family members, particularly parents, and friends. The second element of social bond is *commitment* to conformity, which refers to the willingness and determination to be a good student, a hardworking worker, or a religious person. The third element of social bond is *involvement* in conventional activities. This consists of spending long hours doing schoolwork, doing chores, working as a volunteer or for pay, and engaging in some other conventional activities. The fourth, final component of social bond is *belief* in morals, rules, and laws. This is the acceptance of a conventional value system, which can be expressed with respect for authority.

When applied to binge drinking, social bond theory effectively says that attachment to significant others, commitment to conformity, involvement in conventional activities, or belief in morality and other social values discourages people from drinking excessively, but the lack of any one of these four elements of social bond encourages them to have the drinking problem. The present study was designed to find out if this is indeed the case for binge drinking.

METHODOLOGY

Copies of a questionnaire called the First-Year College Student Lifestyle Inventory were administered to a sample of 361 freshmen at a private university in Ohio as part of their orientation activities during the beginning of the school year in September 2003. A similar questionnaire was given to mostly the same students toward the end of the school year in April 2004. However, thirty-six students of the original sample could not be contacted, largely because they had withdrawn from the university. On April 26, 2004, copies of the First-Year College Student Lifestyle Inventory were sent to the remaining 325 students. All students who responded by May 12 were eligible for a drawing to win one of five $50 Visa gift cards. On May 5, an additional copy of the questionnaire and cover letter were sent to all students who had not yet responded to the initial April 26 mailing. We received a total of 158 completed questionnaires in the second phase of data collection for a total response rate of 48.6 percent.

The dependent variable, binge drinking, was measured by asking male students to indicate how many times during the previous two weeks they had guzzled down five or more drinks in a row, and females how many times they had consumed four or more drinks successively. The questionnaire provided respondents with a definition of a drink as "a twelve-ounce beer or wine cooler, a shot of liquor, or a six- to eight-ounce glass of wine."

The questionnaire presented a variety of empirical indicators that reflect the various elements of social bond. The indicators of attachment to significant others, for example, were the statements that "I have a lot of respect for my parents," "My parents and I can talk about my future plans," and "I live with both of my parents." The indicators of the commitment to conformity included "Regular church attendance is important to me," "Prayer is an important part of my daily life," the number of times the subjects attended religious services, "I study hard in school," "Regular class attendance is important to me," and the student's grade point average. The indicators of the involvement in conventional activities were obtained from asking subjects how many hours a week they spent working, studying, and participating in extracurricular activities respectively. Finally, to get the indicators of the belief in morals and rules, the students were asked whether or not they agreed with statements such as "To get ahead you have to do some things which aren't right" and "It is okay to break the rules if you can get away with it." They were also asked if they respected the police, another indicator of the belief in social rules.

RESULTS

At the beginning of the freshman year, 32 percent of the students engaged in binge drinking. These binge drinkers were indeed more likely than other students to have a weaker social bond in terms of each of its four elements. But only in regard to commitment and belief was the difference between binge drinkers and nondrinkers large enough to be statistically significant. The other two elements, attachment and involvement, were not. Table 31.1 shows only the indicators of commitment and belief in which binge drinkers were significantly different from nondrinkers. First, those students who reported attending religious services less than once a month were more likely than other students to binge drink (38.1 percent vs. 24.6 percent). Second, those students with a high school GPA of B or lower were nearly two times more likely to binge drink than their peers with higher GPAs (50 percent vs. 28 percent). Third, students with a lower level of acceptance of conventional beliefs were more likely to binge drink than those with a higher level of moral beliefs (40.7 percent vs. 22.2 percent). Fourth, students with a low level of respect for authority were nearly twice as likely to become binge drinkers than students reporting a greater respect for authority (46.8 percent vs. 24.7 percent).

At the end of the freshman year, 36.1 percent of the students were binge drinkers, a slightly higher percentage than at the beginning of the school year. Binge drinkers differed somewhat from nondrinkers in regard to all the components

Table 31.1 Binge Drinking and Bond Indicators: Start of Freshman Year

	BINGE DRINKER	
SOCIAL BOND INDICATORS	*Yes* (*n* = *113*)	*No* (*n* = *245*)
Commitment Component		
Church Attendance*		
More than once a month	24.6%	75.4%
Less than once a month	38.1%	61.9%
High School Grade Point Average*		
B+ or higher	28.0%	72.0%
B or lower	50.0%	50.0%
Belief Component		
Acceptance of Moral Beliefs*		
High	22.2%	77.8%
Low	40.7%	59.3%
Respect for Authority*		
High	24.7%	75.3%
Low	46.8%	53.2%

*Chi-square value statistically significant at p <.01

of social bond, but the difference in most cases was not large enough to be statistically significant. Only two indicators of commitment did significantly differentiate binge drinkers from nondrinkers, which are presented in Table 31.2. First, students who attended religious services less than once a month were almost twice as likely to binge drink than their peers who attended church more frequently (48.6 percent vs. 25.0 percent). Second, students with a low degree of religious commitment were more likely than other students to be binge drinkers (47.8 percent vs. 27.0 percent).

DISCUSSION

As the results of the present study show, social bond theory receives mixed support as an explanation of binge drinking by college students. On

Table 31.2 Binge Drinking and Bond Indicators: End of Freshman Year

SOCIAL BOND INDICATORS	BINGE DRINKER	
	Yes (*n* = 57)	*No* (*n* = 101)
Commitment Component		
Church Attendance*		
More than once a month	25.0%	75.0%
Less than once a month	48.6%	51.4%
Religious Commitment*		
High	27.0%	73.0%
Low	47.8%	52.2%

*Chi-square value statistically significant at $p < .01$

the one hand, it appears that both the commitment and belief components of the social bond are negatively related to binge drinking. In other words, students who are committed to conformity (as shown by their religious practices and academic achievement) and hold beliefs that support morality and authority are less likely to binge drink than their peers. On the other hand, the attachment and involvement components of social bond appear much less useful in explaining binge drinking. As Leonard and Decker (1994) suggested, the elements of the social bond may work differently for various age groups. While commitment and belief may be important for college students, attachment to parents and involvement in conventional activities (which by definition are approved by authority figures) seem more powerful in preventing delinquency among juveniles.

REFERENCES

Hirschi, Travis. 1969. *Causes of Delinquency.* Berkeley: University of California Press.

Leonard, Kimberly K., and Scott H. Decker. 1994. "The Theory of Social Control: Does It Apply to The Very Young?" *Journal of Criminal Justice* 22: 89–105

NIAAA (National Institute on Alcohol Abuse and Alcoholism). 2002. *High-Risk Drinking in College: What We Know and What We Need to Learn.* Washington, D.C.: Author.

Wechsler, Henry, et al. 1994. "Health and Behavioral Consequences of Binge Drinking in College: A National Survey of Students at 140 Campuses." *Journal of the American Medical Association* 272: 1672–1677.

Wechsler, Henry, et al. 1995. "A Gender Specific Measure of Binge Drinking among College Students." *American Journal of Public Health* 85:982–985.

Wechsler, Henry, et al. 2002a. "Second-Hand Effects of Student Alcohol Use Reported by Neighbors of Colleges: The Role of Alcohol Outlets." *Social Science and Medicine* 55:425–435.

Wechsler, Henry, et al. 2002b. "Trends in College Binge Drinking During a Period of Increased Prevention Efforts." *Journal of American College Health* 50:203–217.

REVIEW QUESTIONS

1. What are the four elements of social bond theory?
2. Did the study in the article support social bond theory? Why or why not?
3. Do you believe that binge drinking "represents a very serious threat" to college students? Defend your answer.

CHAPTER 32

"HEY, DON'T BLAME ME . . . BLAME THE BOOZE"

ROBERT L. PERALTA

It has long been known in sociology that when people commit a deviant act they tend to excuse it in order to get away with it. In excusing a deviant act, they in effect are saying that "it was wrong, but it wasn't my fault" (Scott and Lyman, 1981). If pressed why the deviant act was not their fault, they would insist that it was not actually they who did it but something beyond their control that caused them to do it. In our culture, that something often turns out to be alcohol. Thus, if people have committed a deviant act when they were drunk, they may insist that it was not their fault but the fault of the alcohol. They are in effect saying, "Hey, don't blame me, blame the booze." Getting drunk from liquor is often used as an excuse for many forms of deviant behavior, which may include insulting others, disorderly conduct, assault, fighting, wife beating, child abuse, and so on. The study here, however, focuses on traditionally or stereotypically gender-inappropriate behaviors, which violate the social norms that require men to behave like men and women to behave like women. Examples of gender-inappropriate behaviors include men acting feminine by paying excessive attention to their appearance, wearing jewelry, or sitting ladylike, and women acting masculine by being assertive, aggressive, tough, or emotionless. Gender-inappropriate behavior can also include the practice of homosexuality, because it is regarded as deviant in our society. We will see how alcohol is used to excuse such deviant behaviors.

METHOD

Seventy-eight one-on-one in-depth interviews lasting an average 1.5 hours were conducted with an all-volunteer sample. Informed consent was given for participation and all respondents were assured confidentiality. Participants were from a medium-sized, public university in the mid-Atlantic region of the United States. College class ranking ranged from freshmen to senior status. Participants lived both on and off campus. Seventy-one percent ($N = 55$) of the sample were whites and 26% ($N = 20$) were African Americans. The remaining three percent were Hispanics and Asians. Fifty-three percent ($N = 41$) were male while 47% were female ($N = 37$). Seventy-two percent ($N = 56$) identified themselves as heterosexual, 22% ($N = 17$) as homosexual, and the remaining 6% ($N = 5$) as bisexual.

Attending the target university as an undergraduate was the only eligibility criterion for this study. The majority of participants responded to announcements in sociology and criminology courses and to 10 notices posted in campus areas frequented by students. Flyers and announce-

Source: Prepared specifically for this reader, with portions drawn from the author's article, " 'Alcohol Allows You to Not be Yourself': Toward Structured Understanding of Alcohol Use and Gender Difference Among Gay, Lesbian, and Heterosexual Youth," *Journal of Drug Issues*, vol. 38 (2008), pp. 373–400. Reprinted by permission.

ments called for participation in a "study on experiences with alcohol use among college students."

A semi-structured open-ended interview guide, consisting of 12 guiding questions, was developed and pilot tested by the author. The questions were asked about drinking quantity, frequency, attitudes toward drinking, reasons for drinking, expectations of alcohol use, and the consequences of drinking. The most important questions for this study were: (1) what does drinking and getting drunk mean to you? (2) what have been your experiences with alcohol? (3) what are your expectations of people who get drunk? and (4) what goes through your mind when you see someone drinking or getting drunk?

FINDINGS

Female and male participants discussed how they used alcohol as an excuse for their gender-inappropriate behaviors that our society traditionally regards as deviant in nature. They also describe how alcohol excuses were used by their friends and peers for behaviors considered "bad," "wrong," or "immoral."

Alcohol Excuses by Women

When asked how she felt under the influence of alcohol, Jenny, a white heterosexual, said:

> *[Alcohol] allows you not to be yourself. It is very common, we use it to have an excuse for things that we do . . . like hooking up with a guy or saying something very mean to your friends or doing something very wrong . . . I mean girls are so much more outgoing when drinking. I do things that I wouldn't do sober, like going up to boys to say, "Hi, my name is . . ."*

This account demonstrates the license alcohol gives young women to take risks, be more bold, assertive and, in some cases, more aggressive in their social interaction and pursuit of romantic partners. Alcohol use appeared to offer some protection against shame and stigma for women engaging in these gender-inappropriate behaviors. To these women, alcohol makes their gender-inappropriate behaviors acceptable, although such behaviors are traditionally regarded as deviant. Consider the next account from Julia, a white heterosexual woman, as an example of how young women alter the traditional mode of being feminine in order to suit their needs as unique individuals instead of as "girls" or "women":

> *It is about being more open when people drink, like being able to talk to people you wouldn't talk to. I think that women are much more self-conscious than guys are and so drinking gets rid of that. You don't care what you look like . . . because you are drunk.*

Note how Julia expressed in the preceding quote the defiant idea that the strict norm requiring women to be concerned with their appearance can be momentarily suspended when drinking. Another white heterosexual female student felt the same way, saying ". . . you don't go into the bathroom and like put your make up on when you're drunk. You don't even think about it." Such statements imply that our culture encourages women to be preoccupied with their appearance to ensure that they look beautiful in a feminine way. But in these women's views, drinking makes them feel that they no longer need to worry about the stereotyped gender-appropriate behavior for women.

Alcohol use further allowed women to ignore the judgment of others. Tina, an African American heterosexual, felt that she was able to be freer in what she said when drinking. As she stated, "the liquor makes you a little more free to say whatever you want." Jen and Susan, both white heterosexuals, illustrated this point as well:

Jen: "I think it [alcohol] opens you up a little more . . . you're not as worried about what people are thinking.

Susan: "It's just a sense of false confidence that you get—like you're more open to talk to just anyone . . . I don't care . . . what I'm saying. When I am sober . . . I'm more cautious. There is this sense that a girl should be either

> passive or quiet and when they are drunk . . . they can be loud . . . more outgoing and not care what people think."

Alcohol enabled other female participants to be freer in their sexuality. Liz, a white lesbian, for example, felt that under the influence of alcohol women became less sexually constrained. To Liz, sex became more "enjoyable" with her partner after imbibing alcohol. In her words, sexual "inhibitions" vanished. As she said,

> *We have the best sex when we're drunk. We are much freer when we are drunk. It is easier to do a lot of things when you're drunk . . . than like say sober sex. We can do or say things that might sound pushy or weird if you weren't, um, drunk. When we are sober we think, "oh that was a dumb thing to say" but I can say "oh, I was drunk!" I'm not big on public displays of affection and neither is my girlfriend but after drinking, that changes. If we are in public and drunk, we do stuff that we think would be inappropriate otherwise.*

Above, Liz makes the distinction between "sober sex" and the bodily empowerment of drunken sex, which includes conspicuous displays of assertiveness. For women, the display of bodily empowerment may require drinking in public, as contrasted with men, who do not have to consume alcohol in order to feel physically powerful. Liz also stated that the fear of sounding "pushy" as a woman disappeared with the aid of alcohol consumption. Another white lesbian, Cindy, discussed how alcohol use can lead to sexual promiscuity. She explained how she used alcohol as an excuse to "hook up" with other women. Without the excuse, she said that she would be labeled by others as a "slut" or "whore," while men engaged in similar sexual promiscuity would be considered more positively as "studs" or "players."

The preceding account by Cindy, a lesbian, reveals how the double-standard of sexuality that exists for heterosexual women also applies to women in the lesbian community. But the lesbians ignored the double-standard allowing only men, not women, to be promiscuous by being promiscuous themselves. They could do this while keeping their feminine identity intact, thanks to the use of alcohol. Liz, a lesbian, also pointed out that one of her friends became "very sexual" with men after using alcohol. As Liz said,

> *My friend . . . would get all drunk and when everybody was drunk she would say, "Okay, who wants to fuck me?" And she would come home with like a random guy. If she wants to have sex with guys, it's not like, "you are gay, and you shouldn't be having sex with guys." Drinking helped her do that in my opinion.*

Embedded in this erotic encounter with men is an element of sexual aggression in Liz's lesbian friend, which represented a form of masculine behavior, hence a traditionally gender-inappropriate experience. Like Liz, many men found how "forward" women could be in initiating sexual contact with men when drinking or drunk. As Anthony, a white heterosexual man observed, "Yeah, they will be more flirtatious after drinking. They will be willing to initiate the first touch." Adrian, another heterosexual male who was black, expressed dismay at the forward behavior of an intoxicated young woman:

> *I went to a party and this girl grabbed my privates, right? And she was like, "Yo dude, what is up?" I was like, "look man, you need to go ahead and chill out." And I thought about it and I was like, "No, I can't do it [reciprocate the sexual advancement]."*

The quote above demonstrates how a female displayed a deviant, gender-inappropriate behavior as a result of consuming alcohol. The use of alcohol could thus be an excuse for the deviant display if it did not sit well with peers and others. That's why many women who feared that their deviant act would be seen by others as such used alcohol as an excuse to explain away potential embarrassment.

Most women—and also men—reported that it was possible for women to be assertive because alcohol was involved. The alcohol excuse protected these women from being bombarded with nasty labels (such as "slut," "bitch," "whore," "tramp," and "hoochie") that are imposed on women who behave in a gender-inappropriate behavior by exerting desire, power, control, or aggression while being sober. Even if their gender-inappropriate behavior caused others to give them those negative labels, the use of alcohol enabled them to feel a boost in their self-esteem.

Taken together, these accounts support the idea that the use of alcohol as an excuse for gender-inappropriate behavior minimizes or absolves responsibility for that deviant behavior. The alcohol excuse further enables women to safeguard their gender identity as normal heterosexuals or homosexuals, without suffering any harmful impact from the gender-inappropriate behavior brought on by alcohol.

Alcohol Excuses by Men

Sammy, a white heterosexual, shared his thoughts about writing poetry as a deviant activity that was inappropriate for his gender as a man to engage in. To him, writing poetry was an activity "normally" reserved for women; it was "girl" behavior. As he said,

> *I got really drunk and I said [to my friends]: "Give me a pad and paper." I started writing poetry! I went on and on for like three hours writing poetry. It was ridiculous. It was all about God and all this stuff. The next morning . . . I felt like an idiot [laughter].*

Sammy explained that he would not "normally" engage in such behavior unless he was drunk. He considered poetry writing a "girl" thing primarily because it entailed an expression of emotion. Like Sammy, many other male participants in this study had difficulty expressing emotion unless they consumed alcohol. Through the use of alcohol, then, these men excused themselves for expressing emotion, so that they could maintain their male gender identity. Another white heterosexual, Steve, discussed how getting drunk helped him express his emotion by crying:

> *During this year, some girl rejected me and I got upset. She was like "Oh, I don't want a relationship with you." I really liked the girl . . . I was pretty drunk and I got upset and I just left and I went back to the dorms and cried . . . I would have been alright if I wasn't drunk.*

Thanks to alcohol, Steve was able to cry "like a woman" but maintain his masculine identity because his feminine act of crying did not come from him but from the liquor. Another white heterosexual male, Alex, also suggested how he and his friends benefited the same way from the use of alcohol:

> *When it is just me and my friends hanging out, and we get really liquored up, we've gotten into really deep conversation. We have cried on each other's shoulders . . . we don't have to act tough.*

Some male heterosexuals in this study discussed how the use of alcohol enabled them to engage in homosexual acts, which are socially stereotyped as unmasculine or effeminate in nature. Again, the liquor provided them with an excuse for committing the gender-inappropriate act. Consider, for example, how Sam, an African American heterosexual, and Adam, a white heterosexual, explained their homosexual activities:

Sam: "When people do things when they are drunk, they meant to do it. So they can have the opportunity to do things that they otherwise couldn't do cause it is morally or ethically incorrect. They have an excuse. And most of the time people accept it."

Adam: "There are "straight" people that use alcohol as an excuse [or] as an outlet because they think that it is wrong at some level [to be gay]. I think they do [engage in homosexual activity] and they can say 'oh I was drunk so it's okay' . . . They can say 'I was really drunk and I didn't know what I was doing.' "

Just as heterosexuals engage in gender-inappropriate behavior by having sex with fellow heterosexuals, they may also have sex with homosexuals. Whether their sex partners are heterosexual or homosexual, the homosexual act is socially considered inappropriate. Similarly, it is also inappropriate for gays to have heterosexuals as sex partners, because gays are socially expected to have sex only with fellow homosexuals. To make it easier to engage in this gender-inappropriate activity, however, gays and straights may resort to the use of alcohol. In the following quote, James, a white gay man, recounted his experience with heterosexual sex partners while everybody was drunk:

> *When I was like eighteen and just finally coming to terms with being gay, I had friends that let me hang with them. I had dealt with guys in high school calling me fag. So I had these friends who liked me for me so it was nice finally to have people accept me. Well these friends had a few guy friends that didn't like me much because I was gay. One night we had this knock-out party, we all got . . . drunk. Well these guys suddenly wanted me to perform oral sex with them and I refused of course. Then they wanted to do it to me so I let them. Anyway, they did it after calling me faggot. These guys went down on me and performed oral sex on me . . . I was not shocked at all. I believe they were covering up their true feelings with alcohol use and the like. I believe men do it to cover it up.*

Gender-inappropriate behavior may also involve a man having sex with an unattractive woman unless he is drunk. Such an experience is described in the following quote from Victor, a white heterosexual:

Victor: "I had sex with someone, like a rather big girl. I was drunk and I didn't have like unprotected sex but the bottom line is I had sex with her. I just like totally gave in."

Interviewer: "Is that something you regretted?"

Victor: "Oh my God, yeah . . . really bad. But I was drunk, so it was an accident."

Victor used the alcohol excuse to distance himself from sexual behavior with women deemed inappropriate. Masculine men are presumed to practice sexual acts with appropriate partners that exclude other men or "undesirable" women. Alcohol can thus be used as an excuse for committing the inappropriate act.

Gay men also tend to use alcohol to counteract the stigma of being homosexual, socially considered undesirable in our homophobic society. This may explain why young gay men who are first experiencing the difficult process of "coming out" often resort to drinking as a way of excusing their "deviancy" so as to accept it as a normal part of their lives. As Hector, a white gay man, said,

Hector: ". . . having one or two drinks helped me to loosen up. . .it helps [me be more] comfortable in a situation and open up a little bit more . . ."

Interviewer: "Have you been progressing with your coming out; are you getting more comfortable?"

Hector: "Oh yeah, definitely. I can actually go to a club sober now."

Like the women in this study, the men here use alcohol as an excuse for their gender-inappropriate behavior. Being drunk, in effect, takes away the responsibility for that deviant behavior. The alcohol excuse also enables those men to protect their gender identity as normal heterosexuals or homosexuals, which they are when sober and not engaging in deviant, gender-inappropriate behavior.

REFERENCE

Scott, M. B., & Lyman S. M. (1981). "Accounts." Pp. 343–361 in G. P. Stone & H. A. Farberman (Eds.), *Social psychology through symbolic interaction*, 2d ed. New York: John Wiley.

REVIEW QUESTIONS

1. Discuss at least three situations where *men* can use alcohol to excuse their gender-inappropriate behavior.
2. Discuss at least three situations where *women* can use alcohol to excuse their gender-inappropriate behavior.
3. Could you avoid behaving badly if you are drunk? If so, how? If not, why not?

CHAPTER 33

OXYCONTIN: A PRESCRIPTION FOR DISASTER

JAMES A. INCIARDI
JENNIFER L. GOODE

If anything has been learned about the drug problem in the United States, it is that patterns of drug abuse are continually shifting and changing. Fads and fashions in the drugs of abuse seem to come and go; drugs of choice emerge and then disappear from the American drug scene; and still others are reconstituted, repackaged, recycled, and become permanent parts of the drug-taking and drug-seeking landscape. And as new drugs become visible, there are the concomitant media and political feeding frenzies, followed by calls for a strengthening of the "war on drugs." It happened with heroin in the 1950s, with marijuana and LSD in the 1960s, with Quaalude and PCP in the 1970s, and with methamphetamine, "ice," ecstasy, crack and other forms of cocaine in the 1980s and 1990s. The most recent entry to the drug scene to receive this focused attention is OxyContin—a narcotic painkiller several times more potent than morphine.

Since OxyContin was first introduced to the market in early 1996, it has been hailed as a breakthrough in pain management. The medication is unique in that its time-release formula allows patients to enjoy continuous, long-term relief from moderate to severe pain. For many patients who had suffered for years from chronic pain, it gave them relief from suffering. But during the past three years OxyContin has received a substantial amount of negative attention—not for its medicinal effects, but for its addiction liability and abuse potential.

OXYCONTIN AND OXYCODONE

The active ingredient in OxyContin is "oxycodone," a drug that has been used for the treatment of pain for almost 100 years. Oxycodone is a semi-synthetic narcotic analgesic most often prescribed for moderate to severe pain, chronic pain syndromes, and terminal cancers. When used correctly under a physician's supervision, oxycodone can be highly effective in the management of pain, and there are scores of oxycodone products on the market—in various strengths and forms. Popular brands include Percocet and Percodan; Roxicet and Roxicodone; and Endocet, OxyIR, and Tylox, to name but a few. However, no oxycodone product has generated as much attention as OxyContin.

Produced by the Stamford, Connecticut-based pharmaceutical company, Purdue Pharma L.P., OxyContin is unique because unlike other oxycodone products that typically contain aspirin or acetaminophen to increase or lengthen their potency, OxyContin is a single entity product that can provide up to 12 hours of continuous pain relief. Tablets are available in 10-, 20-, 40-, and 80-milligram doses. The company also introduced a 160-milligram dose in July 2000 for its

Source: James A. Inciardi and Jennifer L. Goode, "OxyContin and Prescription Drug Abuse," *Consumers' Research Magazine*, vol. 86 (July 2003), pp. 17–21.

opioid-tolerant patients, only later to withdraw it from the market amidst controversy over its alleged abuse.

When the clinical trials for OxyContin were reviewed by the Food and Drug Administration, the drug was demonstrated to be an effective analgesic in individuals with chronic, moderate-to-severe pain. Yet it was also judged by the FDA to carry a substantial risk of abuse because of its properties as a narcotic. As a result, OxyContin was approved by the FDA but placed in Schedule II of the Controlled Substances Act (CSA), which is the tightest level of control that can be placed on an approved drug for medical purposes. The placement of OxyContin in Schedule II warned physicians and patients that the drug carried a high potential for abuse and that it needed to be carefully managed, particularly among those at risk for substance abuse. In addition, in the Physicians' Desk Reference and on the drug's package insert, OxyContin carries a boxed warning—more commonly known as the infamous "black box."

Importantly, this "black box," voluntarily inserted in the packaging information by Purdue Pharma in 2001, alerts potential users that taking broken, chewed, or crushed OxyContin tablets leads to rapid release and absorption of a potentially fatal dose of the drug. But, even before the insertion of the "black box," drug abusers had figured out how to compromise OxyContin's controlled-release formula and set off on a powerful high by injecting or snorting dissolved tablets or by crushing and ingesting them.

Despite the numerous controls and warnings required by the FDA, OxyContin has been a major economic success for Purdue Pharma, accounting for some 80% of the company's total business. Prescriptions have risen steadily since the drug's introduction, as the number of prescriptions dispensed increased 20-fold from 1996 through 2000. More than 7.2 million prescriptions were dispensed in 2001 and retail sales totaled more than $1.45 billion, representing a 41% increase in sales between 2000 and 2001 alone. Retail sales increased again in 2002, topping $1.59 billion. In terms of dollar amount, OxyContin now ranks the highest in retail sales of all brand-name controlled substances. Federal regulators, however, are put off by these numbers, and focus on the diversion of OxyContin to illegal markets and reports of OxyContin abuse and overdose deaths.

DIVERSION OF OXYCONTIN

Prescription drug diversion involves the unlawful movement of regulated pharmaceuticals from legal sources to the illegal marketplace, and OxyContin's attractiveness to drug abusers has resulted in its diversion in a number of ways. The major mechanisms include the illegal sale of prescriptions by physicians and pharmacists; "doctor shopping" by individuals who visit numerous physicians to obtain multiple prescriptions; the theft, forgery, or alteration of prescriptions by patients; robberies and thefts from pharmacies and pharmaceutical warehouses; and thefts of samples from physicians' offices as well as thefts of institutional drug supplies by health-care workers. In all likelihood, OxyContin has been diverted through all of these routes.

Diversion has also occurred by means of fraud, particularly through the abuse of medical insurance programs, a phenomenon observed and investigated most often in a number of rural communities. Medicaid fraud, for example, presents an inexpensive mechanism for abusing drugs and oftentimes an easy route to a lucrative enterprise. For example, a Medicaid patient may pay only $3 for a bottle of a hundred 80-milligram OxyContin tablets. In areas where employment and money are scarce resources, the temptation to sell some of the pills for the going "street price" of $1 per milligram provides an opportunity to earn money. In this example, the $3 bottle from the pharmacy can net the patient up to $8,000 on the illegal market.

Just one corrupt physician, pharmacist, health-care worker, or other employee in the health-care field can have a significant impact on the availability of the product as well. For example, before he was arrested in 2002, a Pennsylvania pharmacist had illegally sold hundreds of thousands of painkillers, including OxyContin, over a three-year period. He made $900,000 on his transactions (only to lose it all in the stock market). Although he operated an independent neighborhood pharmacy, he was reportedly the state's third-largest purchaser of OxyContin. Similarly, a number of physicians in Eastern Kentucky were arrested in 2003 for a variety of diversion schemes. One saw as many as 150 patients each day, writing narcotic prescriptions for them after a visit of less than three minutes each. Another traded pain killers for sex with female patients whom he had addicted to narcotics. A third opened an office in a shopping mall where he generated prescriptions—one after another—almost as quickly as he could write them.

How much diversion of OxyContin actually occurs is impossible to calculate, because there is not a single national reporting system on pharmaceutical diversion. Nevertheless, some data are available which at least suggest the extent of OxyContin diversion, relative to other drugs of abuse, including narcotic painkillers. In a 2001 survey of 34 police agencies with pharmaceutical diversion units, for example, a total of 5,802 cases of diversion (of any drug) were reported during the calendar year. The reporting agencies were asked to indicate which drugs were most commonly diverted, and in how many cases each was investigated. The most commonly diverted pharmaceutical drug was hydrocodone (Vicodin, Lortab, and similar narcotic analgesics), noted in 31% of the total cases. This was followed by oxycodone in 12% of the cases, and alprazolam (Xanax) in 6% of the cases. Of the 701 cases involving an oxycodone product, 416 were OxyContin. Overall, OxyContin was represented in only 7% of the drug diversions, a rather small proportion given the attention the drug has received. In addition, the data documented that the diversion of OxyContin was part of a much broader pattern of prescription-drug diversion. That is, in the great majority of cases in which OxyContin had been diverted, a wide spectrum of other drugs were being diverted at the same time.

OXYCONTIN ABUSE: DO THE FIGURES ADD UP?

Although there are several sources of national data on drug abuse that have been operating for decades, the collection of specific data on OxyContin abuse is quite recent. In the Monitoring the Future Survey, a government-sponsored study of drug abuse among high school students and young adults that has been conducted annually since 1975, the collection of information on OxyContin began only in 2002—and this was initiated at the request of Purdue Pharma. The 2002 survey found that 4% of 12th graders, 3% of 10th graders, and 1.3% of 8th graders had used OxyContin at least once during the past year. Interestingly, the use of Vicodin (a brand of hydrocodone) in the past year was at least double that of OxyContin—9.6% for 12th graders, 6.9% for 10th graders, and 2.5% for 8th graders. In the 2001 National Household Survey on Drug Abuse, another government survey conducted annually, only "lifetime use" (at least once in a person's lifetime "to get high") data were collected for OxyContin. For persons ages 12 and over, less than one-half of 1% reported ever using OxyContin to get high.

The Drug Enforcement Administration started actively collecting and analyzing data from medical examiners in an attempt to establish the extent of the OxyContin problem. Medical examiner reports from 2000–2001 from 32 states reflected that 949 deaths were associated with oxycodone, of which almost half (49%) were "likely" related to OxyContin. Because there are a multitude of oxycodone products on the market, it is impossible to determine the specific brand of drug found in a cadaver. Nevertheless, out of the 949 deaths, DEA reported that 146 were "OxyContin verified," while another 318 were "OxyContin likely." To make things even more complicated, the majority of the toxicological analyses reported multiple-drug use, suggesting that the death may have been the result of an overdose induced by a combination of substances, not just oxycodone by itself. When taking all of these factors into consideration, it is very difficult to establish a direct link between OxyContin and cause of death.

AN EMERGING NATIONAL EPIDEMIC?

OxyContin abuse first surfaced in rural Maine during the late 1990s, and soon after spread down the east coast and Ohio Valley, and then into rural Appalachia. Communities in western Virginia, eastern Kentucky, West Virginia, and southern Ohio were especially hard hit, and a number of factors characteristic of these areas seem to correlate with their apparent high rates of abuse. In northern Maine and rural Appalachia, for example, there are aspects of the culture that are markedly different from those in other parts of the country. Many of the communities are quite small and isolated, often situated in the mountains and "hollers" a considerable distance from major towns and highways. As a result, many of the usual street drugs are simply not available. Instead, locals make do with resources already on hand, like prescription drugs. In addition, isolation impacts heavily on options for amenities and entertainment. Many substance-abuse treatment clients in these rural areas have told their counselors that they started using drugs because of boredom.

Many adults in these rural areas tend to suffer from chronic illnesses and pain syndromes, born out of hard lives of manual labor in perilous professions—coal mining, logging, fishing, and other blue-collar industries which often result in serious and debilitating injuries. As a result, a disproportionately high segment of the population lives on strong painkillers. The use of pain pills evolves into a kind of coping mechanism, and the practice of self-medication becomes a way for life for many. As such, the use of narcotic analgesics has become normalized and integrated into the local culture.

Data suggest that the abuse of OxyContin may be escalating in certain areas. For example, the number of patients in Kentucky seeking treatment for oxycodone addiction increased 163% from 1998 to 2000. While OxyContin is not necessarily always the cause, officials there say that it is one of the most widely abused oxycodone products. Crime statistics seems to support the claim, as Kentucky is one of the leading states for OxyContin-related crimes. Between January 2000 and June 2001 alone, 69 of the state's 1,000 pharmacies reported OxyContin-related break-ins.

Drug treatment admissions from several states may also offer evidence to support a growing trend in OxyContin abuse. Programs in Pennsylvania, Kentucky, and Virginia have reported that 50% to 90% of newly admitted patients identified OxyContin as their drug of choice. Figures obtained by DEA from the American Methadone Treatment Association also suggest an increase in the number of patients admitted for OxyContin abuse. Moreover, according to the Maine Office of Substance Abuse, the number of narcotics-related treatment admissions (excluding heroin) increased from 73 in 1995 to 762 in 2001. While OxyContin cannot take all of the blame, officials say it is nonetheless a major contributor and also point out that opiate-based prescription drugs in general outpaced the percentage increases for all other types of drugs in the state. Treatment admissions for these drugs increased 78% from 1998 to 1999 (199 to 355) and another 47% from 1999 through September 2000 (355 to 521), which suggests a possible increase in OxyContin use.

A separate study conducted by Maine's Substance Abuse Services Commission and the Maine Office of Substance Abuse found that treatment admissions for narcotic abuse increased 500% since 1995, and that opiate-related arrests constituted more than 40% of the Maine Drug Enforcement Agency's caseload. The study, commissioned because of the publicity the state received for being one of the first to identify OxyContin abuse, analyzed several aspects of prescription opiate abuse. The study linked the use of narcotics with increased rates of crime, emergency medical treatment, and outbreaks of hepatitis C. While OxyContin was not the only opiate abused in the state at the time, it constituted the centerpiece of the study results published in *Alcoholism & Drug Abuse Weekly*.

Based on these and similar reports in a few other states, it has been suggested in numerous media outlets that the abuse of OxyContin is on the rise, and that its popularity is rapidly spreading beyond the rural East Coast to other parts of the United States. At the same time, however, there is also concern that the media have played an integral role in boosting the drug's popularity.

THE MEDIA FRENZY

Media outlets in Maine began reporting on OxyContin abuse in early 2000. The *Bangor Daily News*, for example, ran several features which included information not only about the properties of the drug, but also about how to compromise its time-release mechanism, the tactics of diversion that people were using to obtain the drug (including Medicaid fraud), and the concerns of the medical profession about the potential for abusing the drug. In addition, numerous examples of alleged OxyContin-related crimes were described in detail.

Media coverage changed dramatically after Kentucky's sensational "Operation OxyFest 2001," when more than 100 law enforcement officers from numerous jurisdictions worked together to arrest 207 OxyContin users and dealers throughout the state. A blitz of national media coverage followed. The Associated Press, *Time*, *Newsweek*, the *New York Times*, and other media giants, as well as local newspapers across the nation, all ran alarming stories about the potentially lethal and dangerous new drug. Much of the initial coverage of OxyContin seemed to follow a similar formula: It started off with the personal tale of a chronically ill patient for whom OxyContin had suddenly made life worth living, followed by a contrasting tale of a lowly, depraved junkie who had become a slave to the drug, all the while littering the piece with both information and misinformation about the drug. Headlines screamed about OxyContin-related crimes, including pharmacy break-ins and terrifying accounts of elderly patients' homes being invaded and raided for the drug. Some stories of robberies appeared in local media outlets, only to be followed by a string of copycat attempts. There were numerous stories of physicians who ran "pill mills" to feed the addiction of their clients, and contrasting stories of other doctors who had been scared off from prescribing the drug. There were numerous reports of pharmacies that had stopped stocking the drug for fear of inviting crime.

It would appear that, although the abuse of OxyContin is indeed real, it is just one of many drugs that are abused by individuals whose drug-taking and drug-seeking behaviors focus on prescription painkillers. It also appears that the media stories may have contributed to shifting OxyContin abuse from a regional problem to a national problem. Clearly, OxyContin abuse is anything but an "epidemic." Nevertheless, all of the attention given to OxyContin has prompted U.S. government involvement. In response to the heightened awareness of OxyContin abuse and diversion, the DEA launched its own comprehensive plan to prevent the illegal distribution of the product. Its broad goals include enforcement and intelligence; regulatory and administrative authority; industry cooperation; and awareness, education and outreach initiatives. Industry cooperation is an integral part of the plan, including encouraging Purdue to adopt a balanced marketing plan. As recently as January 2003, the FDA sent Purdue a letter contending that the company improperly disclosed information on OxyContin's risks, including a "particularly disturbing" ad that ran in the November issue of *JAMA* (the *Journal of the American Medical*

Association). In response, Purdue has pledged that all future advertisements will balance information about the benefits and risks of the product, as required by the federal Food, Drug and Cosmetic Act.

There have also been calls to reformulate the drug, to make it more difficult for abusers to compromise its time-release mechanism. Purdue has pursued alternative formulas, but success has been elusive thus far. Clinical trials found that when naloxone, a narcotic blocker, was added to OxyContin, it sometimes blocked pain relief for patients who ingested the tablets correctly. The company is pursuing an alternate approach by shifting from a tablet to a capsule that contains similar beads of the oxycodone combined with naltrexone, another narcotic blocker. If taken correctly, only the OxyContin beads would dissolve in the system, but if an abuser were to crush the pill, he would crush and activate the naltrexone, therefore masking the drug's effects. The company said complete testing could take as long as five years. Even if this is accomplished, drug abusers are clever people, and will likely compromise the new formulation in due course.

In the meantime, Purdue has launched its own public relations offensive. Among the initiatives, it has created educational and outreach materials, including a series of print and television ads and "Painfully Obvious," a program that provides resources to educate parents, teachers, and students about the dangers of prescription drug abuse.

Despite the bad press and pressure from the government, the success of OxyContin has not faltered. Only time will tell if the success will be short-lived or if the negative attention will slowly start to chip away at product confidence. In the meantime, those who use it correctly will continue to enjoy consistent pain relief, while those who abuse it will surely continue to inflict pain on the company, law enforcement, the community, and themselves.

REVIEW QUESTIONS

1. What is "doctor shopping"?
2. Do Inciardi and Goode believe that OxyContin abuse is an epidemic in the United States? Explain.
3. Name one possible way of fighting OxyContin abuse not mentioned in the article.

Chapter 34

DAMN, IT FEELS GOOD TO BE A GANGSTA: SELLING DRUGS ON CAMPUS

A. RAFIK MOHAMED
ERIK FRITSVOLD

For our undergraduate educations, each of the current authors attended separate, relatively prestigious, private universities, one on the East coast and the other on the West. Like many middle-class, college-bound students, our parents were very much involved in helping us select our respective institutions and structuring our first-year college experiences. Among the many things that our parents were vehement about was that, at some point, we live on campus in the dorms. By living on campus, they felt we would better integrate ourselves into college life and draw more from our college experiences than we would if we commuted to campus. One thing that our parents did not, and could not, prepare us for was the extent to which the relatively privileged college kids with whom we would interact used illicit drugs. To our surprise, these kids were not only mass consumers of drugs, but several of them, who presumably were not hurting for cash, were heavily involved in supplying these drugs to their peers. What we found equally interesting was that all of this illicit drug activity was taking place during the most draconian era in the history of modern U.S. drug policy.

For three years (2001–2004), we studied a brazen yet little known drug network in Southern California. Unlike the more popular images of drug dealers and users that have become mainstays of our society since the Reagan administration launched its drug war and Hollywood began weaving the drug world into popular cinema, this network does not thrive in darkened alleyways and the shadowy entrances of public housing projects. Rather, this enterprise exists, virtually unmediated, on and around the campus of a highly selective tuition-dependent college in Southern California. Those who sell their wares in this network are not scourge from off-campus attempting to exploit the drug demands of affluent youth; instead, these drug dealers and their clients often are the same people recruited by this university because of their family's ability to afford tuition and fees exceeding $30,000 per year.

This paper offers an introduction to the culture of upper-class collegiate drug dealing and is intended only to be exploratory and provide detail in an understudied area. We provide an overview of this particular college-level network in terms of types of drugs sold, frequency of drug sales, and profitability. We also explore the primary motives for drug sales as expressed by the dealers with whom we conducted interviews.

Source: Specifically written for this reader, with portions drawn from the authors' "Damn, It Feels Good to be a Gangsta: The Social Organization of the Illicit Drug Trade Servicing a Private College Campus," *Deviant Behavior*, vol. 27 (2006), pp. 97–125. Reprinted by permission.

And finally, we briefly touch upon their self-images, perceptions of risk, and their attitudes toward the establishment and agencies of formal social control.

Thus far, we have interviewed more than 25 people in three general categories: dealers of illegal drugs at a tuition-dependent southern California university, those who supply drugs to this university and other area colleges, and those with access to the university's disciplinary procedures and insights into how the sanctions for detected dealers are meted out. The dealer community we observed is comprised mostly of current or former college students of upper-middle or upper socioeconomic status, most all of whom are of Anglo descent. We did not choose to interview principally white dealers. We simply encountered very few who were non-white. As is the case with most of the private universities in Southern California, the vast majority of the student body at our study's university is white.

Marijuana was the focal drug for both use and sales among the dealers we interviewed and observed. Studies have shown that marijuana is neither intrinsically or socioculturally a gateway drug for the use of harsher drugs. Based on our findings thus far, the same might be said for drug sales, as there seems to be some exclusivity among drug markets. Most of our dealers were content to exclusively, or almost exclusively, distribute marijuana rather than branch out into drugs believed to be more serious. Marijuana dealers who did sell harsher drugs such as cocaine or ecstasy could best be described as reluctant dabblers—dealers who preferred to deal only in marijuana but dabbled in other drug sales for greater profits, to meet varying consumer demands, or for ego gratification. For most of our dealers, their foray into drug sales began and ended with marijuana.

We found that the drug markets on this college campus, as well as off-campus markets that cater to college students, are unlike those of television lore. There were no gun-toting Rastafarians asking for passwords through the peepholes of steel reinforced doors. Instead, the environments in which drugs were exchanged for money tended to be significantly more casual and social, although they too had their own rules of etiquette. In fact, when asked how he would describe these markets, Brice remarked they were "friendly-like." Appropriately, it was not uncommon for one transaction to take an hour or more to complete. Part of the reason for this is that the buyers were indeed frequently friends of the distributors, and after making a purchase they would sit around, imbibe, and kibitz with one another. Also, not unlike the deli counter at the local supermarket, customers are generally permitted to sample the product before committing to a purchase. Superficially, this seems to serve as a "quality assurance program" of sorts, allowing a customer to see if he is buying what was advertised and if the price being asked is fair. However, these hardly ever turned into negotiation sessions.

A more realistic interpretation of this sampling process is that it is simply part of the marijuana sales ritual that is allowed to occur in closed markets, when the exchange takes place behind closed doors to select customers rather than in an open-air type of setting; it is a learned and an expected part of the marijuana sales protocol in these more privileged sales environments. It also is a display of good faith by both parties involved in the transaction. After the purchase is made, the buyer typically stays around and smokes a bowl of the newly purchased marijuana, offering the seller the first smoke. Stopper describes the transaction like this:

> *You go over their house and you pick up a sack [of marijuana] from them and you feel like, "Oh, I should hang out with them," almost like you had to do them a favor in addition to paying them. There's the unspoken rule that you have to share your first bowl with whoever you are buying it from . . . It was always like, they ask you a couple of questions about how everything was going . . . It was almost like they wanted it to be a more personal relationship as opposed to more formal.*

WHY RICH KIDS DEAL DRUGS

Rational choice models of crime suggest that law-violating behaviors come as the result of a careful cost-benefit analysis on the part of the offender. Extending this notion to the drug trade that exists on private college campuses like that which we studied, the dealer presumably must see more benefits than drawbacks in drug dealing. In conventional drug policy discourse, the most touted benefit to selling drugs is profit. In approaching this research project, the idea of material gains as the principal motivating factor presented itself as one of biggest quandaries because, to state it bluntly, these rich kids did not need the money. This is not to suggest that all of the dealers we interviewed were super-rich kids who could buy anything they wanted. For many, their parents served as gatekeepers to money by providing them with an allowance or limited access to bank accounts. These allowances still afforded them a relatively high standard of living, but, because of restrictions, dealing remained financially useful.

Therefore, although money was an incentive in the choice to sell drugs, the dealers we observed and interviewed were not motivated by economic necessity in the same way that a dealer in a low-income housing project with no hope for legitimate upward social mobility might be. Making money *was* a factor, but, as we found, this money was largely earmarked for illicit and luxury items rather than necessities such as food and clothing. Through the interview process, we were able to identify other and more significant nonmaterial benefits to be gained by dealers exposing themselves to the risks associated with drug sales.

MOTIVE 1: UNDERWRITE COSTS OF PERSONAL DRUG USE

What we found through this study was that most of our dealers smoked a considerable amount of marijuana, and subsequently most of them saw selling "herb" as a means of not having to pay "retail" for a personal marijuana supply, a practice commonly referred to as "selling for head smoke." This user–seller dynamic is consistent with Tewksbury and Mustaine's (1998) finding that college drug dealers tended to use drugs as well as sell them. Coupled with a seemingly endless demand for drugs on the part of fellow students, underwriting the costs of personal drug use was by far the most common explanation given by our dealers for their initial involvement in drug sales to their peers. As Lacoste stated curtly when asked why he sold drugs, "I don't know, I really just do it to smoke, that's the only reason I sell pot. Then you just start selling tons of pot. Then, like now, I get to smoke tons of pot."

Raoul D., another dealer interviewed, echoed the sentiments of Lacoste. However, his circumstances were somewhat unique in that his indoctrination into the drug scene began later in life than many of our other dealers, most of whom began smoking marijuana and using other drugs in high school. Raoul D., a white upper-middle-class male, had never been a drug user because he was a good athlete in high school, was recruited to play football in college, and did not want to jeopardize his athletic and academic future by using drugs. However, as if part of a Hollywood script, Raoul D.'s football career was brought to an abrupt halt when, during his freshman year, he dislocated his shoulder in a football game and was informed by doctors that he could not play anymore. As he described it, he was devastated because football had been his "life for the past seven years." After having his shoulder surgically repaired, doctors prescribed Vicodin for the pain, and he "really enjoyed the feeling it gave him." Since he could no longer play football, he "did not care about doing drugs and harming his athletic ability anymore" so he "started smoking pot with friends." After recognizing that his personal drug habit was costing him about $200 per week, Raoul D. also came to the conclusion that he could buy marijuana in larger quantities than he had in the past, sell the surplus to friends, and ultimately not have to pay anything for the drugs he was using.

MOTIVE 2: UNDERWRITE OTHER INCIDENTAL AND ENTERTAINMENT EXPENSES

Although most dealers interviewed could reasonably be classified as heavy marijuana users, some barely smoked marijuana at all, apparently adhering to what some call the first commandment of drug dealing—never get high off of your own supply. Nonetheless, these dealers typically saw marijuana sales as a means of supplementing their legitimate income (principally allowances from their parents coupled with sporadic part-time jobs) and a way to underwrite some of the other, social–activities-related costs associated with college life. A conversation on this subject with Ashcan well captures this particular motivation:

Q: What would you sell marijuana for?

A: Mostly beer money. And I had some parking tickets to pay and my parents don't really want me to get parking tickets, so it helps out—the extra money—so I didn't have to tell them or anything like that.

Q: You said parking tickets, what else?

A: Well, when I was a freshman, I drank a lot, so you know the alcohol budget was extensive. And just other stuff; you know, shoes, clothes, whatever. I just had money around, so why not?

Q: Did you smoke a lot of pot yourself?

A: Actually, I stopped smoking that much when I started selling it. But, in high school I smoked a lot; and before I was selling I smoked a lot but I kind of didn't really [sell drugs then] for some reason. I never really thought about that.

Q: So, you weren't really dealing drugs to support your own habit?

A: No, I didn't need to. I never really thought marijuana was addictive. So I didn't have a problem quitting.

MOTIVE 3: THE SPIRIT OF CAPITALISM

As Ashcan suggested, for some, the primary motive driving their foray into drug sales was as simple as subsidiary income. Although his and other's careers in drug sales began as an effort to underwrite incidental college expenses, they often blossomed into more profit-oriented enterprises. Often, the choice to expand the drug business came after what could best described as a utilitarian-based market analysis—a case of demands in the marketplace making themselves known and motivating young entrepreneurs, many of whom were already business majors, to assess the market risks and supply the solution to this demand. As Ashcan said later in the same interview:

> *It was an easy way to make money. Because, in the [dorms] . . . my spring semester, a bunch of people got busted and there was nobody dealing and there was a demand. So I thought, what the hell. I wasn't cash strapped or anything like that. I mean, there were a few weeks when I didn't really eat that much 'cause I didn't have that much money left, so it kind of helped to have an extra forty or fifty bucks lying around.*

While Ashcan's financial gains were modest and seemingly restrained by cautiousness and an absence of excessive greed, the same could not be said for other dealers once they got a taste of the profits to be made in drug sales. After his first few weeks as a marijuana dealer, Lacoste realized that he could do more than simply underwrite his own drug use costs; he realized he could also move forward into greater quantities and other, more profitable drugs. He quickly moved from simple marijuana sales into a menu where marijuana was still the cornerstone, but also offered mushrooms, ecstasy, a variety of prescription drugs (including those prescribed to him for ADHD), and what he found to be the most profitable drug to sell, cocaine:

> *Dude, that's the moneymaker . . . the yeyo [cocaine] . . . that's where the money's at. That's fifty dollars a gram. A hundred and fifty an eight ball. Ah, yeah, that's where the money's at. Pick up like a six hundred or seven hundred ounce of yeyo. Yeah, you make tons of money just 'cause it's so expensive.*

According to Lacoste and the others who sold both marijuana and cocaine, the reason cocaine is so profitable stems from its relatively few suppliers and the outrageously high demand for the powder in this "rich kids gone wild" scene. Essentially, the choice to "kick it up a notch," as TV chef Emeril Lagasse might say, was seen as little more than a business challenge—an opportunity to hone the skills that they would employ after leaving the world of college drug dealing and entering that of legitimate business.

MOTIVE 4: EGO GRATIFICATION AND THE PURSUIT OF STATUS

In our interviews, we explicitly asked each dealer to explain why he started selling drugs and why he chose a relatively intimate college campus as the network of distribution. Initial responses to this question, like those given by Lacoste and Raoul D., were typical—why pay for drugs when, through a bit of creative financing, you could get them for free? Responses like Ashcan's also were typical—drug sales subsidized other entertainment and incidental expenses associated with college life. However, as the interviews went on, it seemed that these were only partial, perhaps even exculpatory, less insidious or more palatable justifications. Similar to Patricia Adler's (1985) findings on drug dealers' perceptions of self, we found that indices of more self-expository rationales like ego gratification, popularity, sense of self-importance, and old fashioned greed frequently manifested themselves as important motivating factors for entering or continuing in the drug trade. As Adler noted:

> *Dealers built commitment through the ego gratification they derived from drug trafficking. Their self-images were lodged in the power they wielded over others by withholding or supplying them with drugs (for both business use and personal consumption). Dealers reveled in their social status (Adler, 1985).*

All of the dealers we interviewed exhibited elements of this fourth motive, but none embodied the use of drug sales as an avenue to gain status more than Lacoste. As a freshman from the Midwest at a cliquish school that recruits most of its students from the West coast, Lacoste felt pressure to have an identity on campus. As he describes it, he was "very popular" at his high school and, in short, he sought to be known in college. On a campus already known for its crass materialism, his $50,000 car and designer clothes, while certainly symbols of status, were not enough to separate Lacoste from his peers. Therefore, he turned to drug sales to differentiate himself, achieve an elevated status, and make himself well known (and rather quickly) on a campus that had high student demand for marijuana and other drugs. As he boasted when asked what he got out of selling drugs, "You can give pot to whoever you want, do whatever you want, buy a ton of shit!"

Indicative of the sense of importance and recognition he received from a being a relatively known drug dealer, Lacoste said with swagger in his voice, "If you said, where'd you get pot, where can I get pot? I'm sure my name would be mentioned." What was most interesting about these comments was, when directly asked if drug dealing made him feel powerful, he replied, "Not really." Somewhat disingenuously he continued, "I could be powerful. I could tell somebody to whoop your ass [laughs] and your ass would get whooped. [But] that's not really powerful. Plus, I gave up fighting for Lent." Our perception from these comments, as well as what we inferred from other comments he made, was that he did indeed feel empowered and recognized because he sold drugs and people knew he sold drugs.

MOTIVE 5: SNEAKY THRILLS AND BEING A GANGSTA

In addition to the other material and non-material motivating factors we discuss in this paper, the attraction to drug sales for many of our dealers seems to simply boil down to wannabe gangstaism and the thrill of "getting away with something." As Katz (1988: 52) noted, "It is not the taste for the pizza that leads to the crime; the crime makes the pizza tasty." In other words, rich white college drug dealers are not motivated by material need as much as they are the idea that they can outsmart those in formal positions of authority, both within and outside of the university setting. And, even if they are caught, they are "powerful" enough and have the symbolic capital to survive relatively unscathed. For some, this voluntary risk taking behavior, this process of artificially exposing themselves to risk, also seemed to fill certain voids or personality needs that they have.

Lacoste is an ideal example of both the thrill of the drug game and the desire to be seen as a gangsta. Lacoste housed his drug operation out of his dormitory room and his expensive SUV, which was typically parked on campus, often directly and illegally in front of his residence hall. When asked if he was afraid of campus police officers detecting his illicit activity, Lacoste replied, "They can kiss my ass. They can't touch me. They can't do anything to me . . . I'd rather get caught by [the campus police] than the [real] police. What's [the campus police] going to do, take my weed away?"

Lacoste's "tough guy" attitude seemed to be driven by a sense of stealth and an overwhelming feeling that he was smarter than anyone who might be investigating his activities. Ironically, conversations with several university officials revealed the contrary; they were aware of his drug activity and suspected him to be involved in other crimes on campus, including a rash of thefts that had recently taken place. Lacoste also was confident that, if university officials or those outside the university caught him, the social status of his parents and access to high power attorneys would ultimately protect him from any real negative sanctions . . .

In fact, during an interview with a university administrator about campus drug activities, the administrator brought up Lacoste as an example of the difficulties in dealing with drug crime suspects on campus. To quote this particular source, "He must have some very influential parents." The administrator further suggested that, even though they were confident that he was selling marijuana in the residence halls, because of his parents' status, the probe into his criminal activity was being handled with extreme caution. It seems the university tolerates a certain degree of deviance and even criminality from its more privileged students because it recognizes their centrality in the university's efforts to distinguish itself from its competitors and the role that these students play in compounding the capital necessary for it to attempt to compete at an elite level.

Lacoste's feeling of invincibility and his somewhat arrogant perception of himself as a "criminal" was well displayed in comments he made in-between telephone drug deals brokered from his dorm room:

> *I won't get caught though. There's nowhere to get caught. [And even if he did get caught], I got really good lawyers . . . See, I got these lawyers that are really good. Like real good, like the "dream team" and shit [laughs]. And, I don't know, catch me . . . if you can.*

As Katz (1988) noted, certain criminal behaviors capture a form of deviance "in which getting away with something in celebratory style is more important than keeping anything . . . in particular." As evidenced by the number of students, administrators, and other campus officials who suspected Lacoste's involvement in drug sales, he derived a thrill from being a drug dealer. But the greater thrill for him came from braggadocios celebration of his deviant activity. Certainly, this untouchable attitude was not embraced by all of our dealers, and several moved more cautiously than Lacoste. Overall, however, the sense of being above the law, even if only marginally, was common with the dealers we interviewed.

Among the affluent college set, it seems increasingly popular for some to present themselves as tough, or "street," or gangstas. They seem seduced by the thuggish and virile hip hop icons whose videos play repeatedly on MTV, and whose songs blare from their $10,000 per academic year dorm rooms or bump from their new Lexus trucks as they cruise the main drag on campus. Hip-hop artists who unremittingly brag about drugs, crime, women, and how "money ain't a thang" seem to provide an irresistible impulse for some college kids looking for a "rep." It does not seem to matter that only a few blocks away from the campus setting we examined, authentic "thug life" exists and wannabe posturing can produce undesired consequences if publicly displayed.

Even if only situational, the "thug life" aspect of this fifth motivating factor is perhaps best captured by Houston-based rapper Scarface's proclamation, "Damn, it feels good to be a gangsta." On the campus where we conducted this research, being a gangsta is thrilling, convenient, and likely to generate peer approval. There is added solace in knowing that the chances of getting caught are slim, even if your deviance is on somewhat public display. And there is even greater comfort in knowing that, if you do get caught, you will not bear the full brunt of the law's wrath because of your ascribed status as a young, relatively affluent, white male college student.

CONCLUSION

We feel that each of the five motivations we found through the course of this study for relatively affluent college student involvement in drug sales is compelling and fills a void in the existing literature. However, we think the final two motives—ego gratification and the pursuit of status and the desire to be perceived as a gangsta—are the most interesting because they defy the logic that drives most drug control policies. Essentially, these motives have little or no direct relationship to profit . . . [They] may fall in step with what Lyng (1998) described as the phenomenological aspects of the risk-taking experience. Essentially, some people engage in voluntary risk taking or "crowding the edge" behavior because it gives them a sense of identity and empowerment that, in these cases, is different from that ascribed by their parents' status. In these cases, status and identity are derived from the successful negotiation of risk taking behavior and, more importantly, that this behavior is recognized by peer group members as risky. It is this passive peer acknowledgment and fanfare that drives many ordinary drug-using college kids to venture into the world of drug sales.

REFERENCES

Adler, Patricia. 1985. *Wheeling and Dealing.* New York: Columbia University Press.

Katz, Jack. 1988. *Seductions of Crime.* New York: Basic.

Lyng, Stephen. 1998. "Dangerous Methods: Risk Taking and the Research Process." In *Ethnography at the Edge: Crime, Deviance, and Field Research,* edited by Jeff Ferrell and Mark Hamm. Boston: Northeastern University Press.

Tewksbury, R., and Mustaine, E. E. 1998. "Lifestyles of the Wheelers and Dealers: Drug Dealing Among American College Students," *Journal of Crime and Justice*, 21, pp. 37–56.

REVIEW QUESTIONS

1. Explain how the drug market described in this study differs from that presented by Hollywood.
2. Discuss any of the three motives that attempt to explain why some students sell drugs on campus.
3. How does selling drugs on campus differ from drug-dealing on the street?

PART TEN

INTERNET DEVIANCE

Deborah Majoras recently bought a pair of shoes from a footwear company and paid for it with a credit card. Later, she found that somebody had stolen her credit card number stored in that company's database and had used it to buy all kinds of stuff in her name. At least 1.4 million other Americans have been victimized in this way. The identity thief who robs a databank with a computer runs a much lower risk of getting caught than a traditional robber who holds up a bank with a gun, thanks to the tendency of many banks, credit card companies, and credit bureaus to look the other way. Identity theft is part of the new, wild frontier of deviance today. Like the Wild West of the old frontier days, the Internet is full of various kinds of deviant activities that can be carried out with relative impunity. Just consider how easy it is for online identity thieves to get away with their crime. Far less than one—or nearly zero—percent of identity thefts leads to a conviction. No wonder identity theft is the fastest-growing crime of this century.[1]

Identity theft is an example of Internet deviance, the execution of a deviant act through the use of a computer. Here we will explore the nature of various forms of Internet deviance. In the first article, "Show Me the Money: Online Mistresses and Slaves," Keith Durkin shows how women use the Internet to lure men to give them money. In the second article, "Online Dating: 'I'm Dysfunctional, You're Dysfunctional,' " Andrea Orr delves into the libidinous world of online dating. In the third reading, "Online Boys: Male-for-Male Internet Escorts," Matthew Pruitt reveals how male prostitutes use the Internet to advertise themselves and their services to attract male customers. In the fourth piece, "Cyberbullying: Offenders and Victims," Sameer Hinduja and Justin Patchin analyze the nature of online bullying.

[1]Byron Acohido and Jon Swartz, *Zero Day Threat: The Shocking Truth of How Banks and Credit Bureaus Help Cyber Crooks Steal Your Money and Identity.* New York: Union Square Press, 2008. Steven Levy and Brad Stone, "Grand Theft Identity," *Newsweek*, July 4, 2005, pp. 38–47.

CHAPTER 35

SHOW ME THE MONEY: ONLINE MISTRESSES AND SLAVES

KEITH F. DURKIN

The Internet has created a fertile ground of opportunity for deviant behavior. There has been a vast array of deviant practices surrounding this technological innovation. Hacking, or the unauthorized intrusion into a computer system or network, is an excellent example. Fraud and other deceptive practices are commonplace on the Internet. Some examples include stock manipulation, the misappropriation of credit card information, investment swindles, and on-line auction fraud. White supremacist groups are using the Internet for the dissemination of propaganda as well as the recruitment of new members. Evidence suggests that cyberstalking, sending harassing or threatening electronic communications to other computer users, is becoming a frequent occurrence. Internet gambling is a rapidly growing phenomenon. Also, the illegal sale of prescription drugs, guns, and alcoholic beverages transpires over the Internet. The Internet has further become a major avenue for the exchange and sale of pornographic materials. The purpose of this article is to report on a group of Internet users involved in a practice called money slavery.

The data for this research were gathered over a period of approximately four years. They were collected from homepages, message forums, Yahoo! groups, user profiles, and blogs. Hundreds of hours were spent examining these materials on-line, and approximately 500 pages were printed out for analysis. This topic was discovered accidentally by the author in the course of his ongoing investigation of deviance on the Internet. Specifically, the author found an advertisement from a woman who described herself as a "money mistress" and claimed she was seeking "money slaves." The initial advertisement provided a brief description of the "services" she provided. Popular search engines such a Google and Yahoo! were used to search for key words such as "money slavery" and "money mistress." The subsequent data collection strategy resembled a snowball sample, except it used Internet sites for information referrals, rather than individuals. The examination of a particular money slavery site often yielded links to several others. The current study was completely unobtrusive. At no point in time did the author ever interact with or correspond with any of the participants in the Internet money slavery subculture.

Obviously, the sample is in no way representative of all Internet money slavery sites. Also, many of these websites, discussion forums, and profiles were ephemeral in nature. During the course of this research, many simply disappeared, while others were created. Despite the fluid nature of the Internet, these type of data "can be useful in providing a snapshot of a given subject at a particular point in time" (Hegland and Nelson, 2002). The data in the current study were

Source: Specifically written for this reader, with portions drawn from the author's "Show Me the Money: Cybershrews and On-line Money Masochists," *Deviant Behavior*, vol. 28 (2007), pp. 355–378.

examined in order to identify common themes, characteristics, and tendencies.

MONEY SLAVERY

The phenomenon called "money slavery" involves males giving money or gifts to women they meet on-line in exchange for being degraded, humiliated, or blackmailed. Regarding this practice, one blogger noted:

> *There's often a financial component to any aspect of consensual BDSM play (just browse through the sex ads in your local alt weekly), but in the world of money mistresses, pay pigs and human ATMs, the exchange of cold hard cash for the "privilege" of being abused, dominated, humiliated, and/or ignored is the whole point of the action. (Financial Slavery, 2006).*

A variety of other terms are sometimes used to describe the practice, including *financial servitude, financial rape, wallet rapping, extreme spoiling*, and *financial domination*. The initial contact between participants can be made via the money mistresses' Web pages. Alternately, interested parties can be located through the scores of discussion groups dedicated to this practice, such as "The Real Money Slaves," "Money Slaves 101," "Cash Fetish," and "Money Slaves Fellowship Forum." The females, or money mistresses, frequently place advertisements on the Internet to recruit men. The following are some examples:

> *I am a beautiful 23-year-old college student who loves to humiliate men as they worship me and drain their bank accounts in my honor. I have expensive tastes, and there is no limit to the amount of money I might demand. Whether you are a millionaire, or a regular Joe, rest assured that I can reduce you to poverty. So if you have the balls, which I doubt you do, you can apply to be my money slave simply by making a tribute. When I receive your tribute I will E-mail with my demands.*

> *I am now accepting cash cows that need to be milked. You must submit your mind, soul, body and wallet to me. Arrangements will be made to drain every cent you have. Do you like pain? Humiliation? Are you a sissy maid? I promise I will bring you to your knees and ruin you forever.*

> *Mature Money Domme Helga will wickedly lead you to your own financial ruination or bankruptcy as you become her cash cow, human ATM, pay pig, money slave. Domme Helga is your boss for financial domination, so drain your credit cards now & give Goddess your cash!!!*

Although advertisements from male participants do not appear to be as prevalent, nonetheless some money slaves place ads in hopes of establishing contact with an appropriate money mistress:

> *I'm looking for a superior female who wants to control my entire life, including total control over my finances. I'm earning about $35,000 a year and I'm willing to give it to a real Goddess. The only thing I want is that she treats me like the shit I am. She should be willing to degrade and destroy me completely.*

> *Money pig, 55, white, seeks spoiled PRINCESS between 18 & 25, to e-mail me every Friday (payday), and demand all extra money from my pay check. When SHE receives the money, SHE will e-mail me to remind me what a stupid pig I am and that I am getting absolutely nothing for my money. I prefer a PRINCESS that I can mail cash or money order to. I must see a picture of the PRINCESS, posing wearing high heels. Prefer a PRINCESS with a web site, but not necessary. PRINCESS may also demand that I get a second job, so SHE can have more money.*

The money mistresses request various forms of remuneration from the men to maintain ongoing contact. They commonly require the money slaves to send tributes (normally $25 or $50) to them electronically by credit card or PayPal, or to a P.O. box via cash, check, or money order. Many money mistresses request an "initiation fee" or "introductory tribute" before they will take the men on as money slaves or even respond to an e-mail. Some money mistresses also require their money slaves to pay off a bill of theirs each month, such as rent, car, electric, phone, or gym membership. The women also may request that the men buy items from a computerized "wish list," which links to on-line stores such as Saks Fifth Avenue, Bloomingdales, Neiman Marcus, and Victoria's Secret. A few of the money mistresses claim to be college students and request the men buy their textbooks at Amazon.com or the Barnes and Noble on-line store. In exchange, the women may send e-mail or pictures to the money slaves, or allow the men to view their Web cam or speak with them on the phone or via instant messenger. Evidently some men actually give exorbitant amounts of money to these women. For instance, one woman's website has a copy of a $50,000 wire transfer allegedly from a money slave, as well as copies of credit card receipts totaling $17,000 (all from the same account), which were supposedly for "services" another incurred on her behalf. However, there is little, if any, evidence that any physical meetings ever occur between the money slaves and the money mistresses.

However, some of the money mistresses provide more elaborate services. For instance, some offer a "blackmail service." The man fills out an on-line application with his name, address, and telephone number of his girlfriend, wife, or employer as well as some discrediting personal information about him. The money slave is then required to pay money to avoid having this information revealed to his significant other or employer by the money mistress. Also, some money mistresses claim to provide a "chastity belt" program in which the money slave buys the device and sends her the key. In turn, he is required to pay a fee to have the key returned to him. Furthermore, some women offer outrageously priced goods and services. For example, one money mistress was selling her used panties ($75), locks of her hair ($100), and worn socks ($45) on her website. Another offers phone sex calls for $9.99 a minute. One money slave reported paying $330 for a conversation. Some of the money mistresses also utilize a commercial e-mail service that charges a fee (e.g., $50) when the recipient opens the e-mail.

While the money mistresses appear to be motivated by financial considerations, sexual interests seem to motivate the money slaves. Although physical pain can play an important role in masochism, psychological pain is also important to many masochists. This pain "encompasses feelings of helplessness, subservience, humiliation, and degradation" (Moser and Levitt, 1987). Many money slaves reported being sexually aroused by making payments. In a posting, one money slave stated:

> *I have found the act of paying so amazing that I actually masturbate when I get the credit card bill. I jerk off.*

Another remarked:

> *The act of paying can be a very stimulating experience, at the time I do it, but there is usually some means of manipulative pressure [on the part of the money mistress] by the way of pushing my submissive button. Going on that makes the act of transferring cash feel like a turn on.*

In turn, the money mistresses are obviously aware of the sexual arousal associated with the act of making a payment. Accordingly, they readily acknowledge this in the information they post. The following statements from various money mistresses illustrate this strategy:

> *Feel the excitement build in your pants as your brain tries to resist your uncontrollable urge to give me every cent that you have.*

> *You're back at home surfing the web, reading my site and stroking that pathetic cock of yours. Why not kill all of the pretenses of dating and come visit me weekly, or daily and just pay your damn masturbation tax.*

SOCIAL CONTROL AND MONEY SLAVERY

Social control plays an important part in the phenomenon of money slavery. By its very nature, this practice is ripe with opportunities for fraud, deception, and deceit. For instance, the money mistresses may receive money or gifts from men and not reciprocate by providing them with e-mail responses, chat time, or other services. Additionally, the money mistresses can deceive men by using photos of other women in their profiles or websites. Moreover, it is possible to disguise one's gender on the Internet. Regarding this deceptive practice, one money slave argued:

> *To be misled by a 45-year-old male posing as a bitchy, cocky, arrogant, beautiful 19-year-old girl in order to fool me out of my money because he knows that I wouldn't offer it to him otherwise is FRAUD.*

There is evidence that at least some of these so-called money mistresses and "financial domination" sites are nothing more than an elaborate hoax. For instance, the same exact photo was used on the profiles of at least a half-dozen money mistresses. Also, a professional dominatrix conveyed the following information in a discussion forum dedicated to sadomasochism enthusiasts:

> *(A friend) knew a few guys who had this great idea to hire some models to take a bunch of pictures of them and then create financial slavery sites of these "Dommes." Most of the models had no idea what their pictures were being used for other than an adult site. They were paid their standard fee and sent home.*

A similar statement appeared in a discussion about money slavery on a forum dedicated to webmasters who host adult sites. One male user stated:

> *A couple of years ago when I was in university, I was surfing through Yahoo chat rooms and found a money slaves forum. I sat in there for about an hour and realized what was going on. Then I set up a fake account as a Mistress (using a fake pic) to see if I could get one of the slaves in the channel to send me money. Within about 10 minutes I had a guy sending me $50. This is when the channel was new and I made about $2000 doing it but the slaves started to get wise and ask for proof and such.*

In an effort to protect their interests, money slaves have collectively formed discussion groups such as the "Money Slaves Fellowship Forum" and "Find Fake Money Slaves" to share information on detecting and avoiding frauds. One poster to a forum shared tips on how to make sure a money mistress is "legitimate," including asking for two or three photos and a Web cam view of the woman before sending any money. Another money slave warned his peers:

> *I have seen several posts and ads by someone calling themselves Asha, and the photo that they were using is actually that poor woman, that ex-porno actress, that has AIDS. One group even contains a picture of the "Fake of the Month." Recently, there was a picture of a Madame Jennifer prominently posted. The group's moderator noted "we all appreciate calling out trailer park tricks like this uneducated fake."*

On the other hand, the money mistresses utilize their own social control strategies. Apparently, some of the male participants engage in deceptive practices of their own. For example, some money slaves lie about forthcoming payments in order to obtain services such as Web cam views and chat time. Others may agree to pay a particular bill for a specified period of time and fail to fulfill their part of the arrangement. Some money mistresses publicly post the on-line identities of these men. For instance, one posted a "loser-list" which, by her description, contained "all of the e-mail addresses and Yahoo usernames of all of the men who pay once and are never heard from again." On one discussion forum, the money mistresses have created a "fakers list" consisting of men who have been deceptive about payment. These men, in turn, are banned from accessing certain forums. In a rather extreme form of social control, one money mistress posts chat transcripts, along with the name and e-mail addresses, of non-paying money slaves in a public forum. In one such transcript, the male was engaged in an interactive erotic discussion about his fantasies about his mother and his desire to perform oral sex on another man. Other women have gone as far as posting the names and telephone numbers of non-paying men.

However, social control can also consist of rewarding desirable behaviors. The money mistresses frequently give public acknowledgment to those money slaves who make substantial contributions. On her website, one thanks by name all of the men who pay her bills. On another website, a money mistress announced:

> *Slipjockey is the big donation winner (read: loser) of the day. He spent about $185 on the phone and another $200 on Pay Pal.*

Another money mistress created a special feature on her website called the "Money Slave Wall of Fame" to recognize the top contributor of the month. She noted, for the month of July, the slave of the month was

> *Perky Pee Pee in a landslide!! This pathetic Pee Pee has contributed over $2600 to his adorable Mistress. Way to go! Let's see if we can make it two months in a row. As for the rest of you slackers, you have a lot of work to do.*

ACCOUNTS AND MONEY SLAVERY

Although the activities of the money mistresses are not illegal, these women nonetheless operate on what has been characterized as the "deviant fringe" (Bryant, 1974). Much like strippers and phone sex operators, the money mistresses are likely to be viewed as violating the norms of sexual propriety. Interestingly, some professional dominatrixes who provide services in commercial studios or private residences consider money mistresses to be deviant. For instance, on an Internet forum, one professional dominatrix noted:

> *I have met a few ladies who do this type of domination. They all think it's the cat's meow. I think it's extortion. What is this lady contributing to the betterment of the other person's psychic/well-being? What are they working at—getting rich? I do this because I love it, trust me in the current climate, I would be doing something else if I wanted to make money. I hate to see women such as these use the same title as those of us who work hard at our craft.*

On the other hand, the money slaves have to face a possible stigma associated with making payments to these women or purchasing overpriced goods and services from them. Chances are that many observers would consider these men deviant for willingly allowing themselves to be exploited and victimized, and in some cases targets of outright deception. If their activities were known to conventional others, they would be likely to elicit scorn, mockery, or ridicule.

Scott and Lyman (1968) defined an account as "a linguistic device that is employed whenever an action is subjected to a valuative inquiry." Accounts are a type of exculpatory mechanism used by individuals to explain deviant behavior, and serve as a stigma management technique. They constitute an effort by the individual "to minimize the damage to his or her identity" (Higginson, 1999). Accounts can be given orally or in written form. Accordingly, computer-mediated communications provide an excellent medium for the dissemination and use of accounts. When an individual engages in a job or other type of activity that can "spoil their identity," it is necessary for them to engage in strategies to manage that stigma. The use of accounts is one type of stigma management technique.

The money mistresses seem to offer two types of accounts for their actions and identities. The first is a *claim of entitlement*. This involves the assertion that an individual "deserves" or is "owed" some form of compensation. Claims of entitlement were ubiquitous on the money mistresses' Web pages. The following statements from various money mistresses illustrate the use of this account:

> *I am blonde and beautiful and you will give me anything I want because I am so beautiful. Give me your money. I am a spoiled controlling college bitch that wants and deserves it all. I believe I shouldn't have to work for anything. My wishes should be granted without hesitation or questioning.*

> *I deserve to live in comfort and luxury while little pay pigs like you work all day long only for my well deserved and lavish lifestyle.*

The other technique used by the money mistresses is *denial of victim*. This involves the individual admitting "that his or her act caused an injury, but insists that the injury was deserved"

(Lyman 2001). On websites and various discussion forums the women routinely refer to the money slaves by various pejorative appellations such as pay pigs, money sluts, bitches, and sissies. This may serve to dehumanize those who are being exploited. The following statements made by various money mistresses illustrate the use of this account:

You will be used and abused while I drain your fucking bank account. You will not ask, or beg, for real time, because your sorry pathetic ass is not worthy of real time. I will humiliate you and turn you into the bitch that you want to be. Without me you are nothing, and with me you are still nothing. You are worthless and pathetic and could never please a real woman.

Yes I am laughing at you, you stupid fool! I know you crave to serve me; it gives your pathetic being a purpose in life. But do remember you are nothing but a dick on a stick. A pig that needs a purpose—a reason to get up in the morning and get your pathetic ass to work.

On the other hand, some of the men offered an account that took the form of a *claim of self-fulfillment*. This involves the assertion that the act in question increases self-consciousness or allows the individual to express their true nature (Scott and Lyman, 1968; Weinstein, 1980). For instance, one male posted the following in a discussion forum:

I am a money slave. I really just enjoy giving money to beautiful women and it so happens that some of the women are mistresses which is fine as long as I can give them money. I started giving away money to women in high school. I would try to put money in a purse or send it in the mail.

DISCUSSION

New forms of sexual behavior frequently develop as an adaptive response to technological innovations. Although the practice of paying for sexual fantasy is not new, the phenomenon of money slavery appears to be a novel manifestation of this type of deviance that is predicated on the existence of the Internet. Traditionally, certain commercial establishments and prostitutes have provided services to submissive men. However, the services provided included actual physical interactions. The primary contacts between the money mistresses and money slaves transpire over the Internet. Although subsequent contacts may occur over the telephone or through the mail, there is no evidence of actual physical contact between any of the participants involved in the practice of money slavery.

Online environments are socially constructed. In the world of cyberspace, "a person interacts with other individuals behind a character that he or she creates" (Zhao, 2004). This process can be compared to participating in a costume party. The computer users construct and present an on-line identity that has been referred to as an electronic self or a virtual self. The money mistresses seek to create and present an image of a shrewish, dominant female. An important part of creating an on-line identity is the selection of a screen name. So the money mistresses select names such as "Financial Ruiness Mistress Kelli" and "Queen of Pay Pigs" that makes the identity and intentions clear. Moreover, they often utilize homepages to aid in the construction of their identity. A computer homepage is a personal introduction and the creator of a page assumes or anticipates a certain audience. These homepages reinforce the money mistresses' identities, and attempt to entice money slaves to contact them.

The men involved in this activity appear to derive sexual gratification from both the image of the domineering, shrewish woman, as well as paying money to this type of woman. McClintock (1993) argued that submissive males are particularly "enthralled by verbal representations of desire." In cyberspace, the money slaves are confronted with both verbal and visual representations of a dominant female.

Many observers would consider the activities of money mistresses to be exploitative. Moreover, there is ample evidence that the identities of some of the money mistresses are completely fraudulent (e.g., a male masquerading as a dominant woman). Some scholars have argued that the anonymity of the Internet may encourage anti-normative behavior. It is relatively simple for a person to disassociate himself or herself "from the implications of one's activities" while on-line (Finch, 2002). Moreover, it appears to be easier to defraud people on the Internet compared to real time. For instance, the very nature of websites makes them an ideal platform for the creation of complete fabrications. Regardless of whether they are engaged in fraud or exploitation, the identity of the person behind the money mistress is relatively insulated from the implications of their on-line deviance.

On the other hand, many would consider the behavior of money slaves, such as paying cash "tributes" to the money mistresses, as deviant. Such behavior would be likely to elicit concern, if not scorn and ridicule, from observers. The money slaves appear to be adopting the role of masochist in their online interactions. This type of individual allows him to be victimized and derives satisfaction from the experience of pain and humiliation.

The phenomenon of money slavery appears to epitomize the postmodern condition. In postmodern culture, the line between reality and unreality is blurred. Baudrillard (1994) argued that in contemporary society, humans are constantly "substituting signs of the real for the real." In the context of online sexual expression, "bodies are transformed into symbol alone—representations, images, descriptive codes, words of expectations, appearance, and actions" (Waskul et al., 2004). Yet in postmodern culture, symbols and images have the capacity to eclipse the real. For example, although the various elements of computer mediated interaction lack empirical and objective manifestations in the traditional sense, "they exert real influences that allow people to respond to them as if they are real" (Waskul et al., 2004). Money slavery involves the presentation and consumption of images—images of a shrewish and dominant woman being driven by financial concerns are being consumed by a male with masochist traits. The money mistress is not a "real" person in the traditional sense. It is a character who exists in cyberspace—whose creator may not even be a female! Nonetheless the money slaves appear to react to this character as if it is a real person.

There is a growing body of literature that suggests the use of the Internet for deviant purposes can have negative consequences in the "real time" lives of some computer users. For example, the availability of online casinos and similar outlets can lead to problems of compulsive gambling (Griffiths, 2003). Also, on-line adultery or "cyber affairs" are sometimes a source of marital dissolution (Ferree, 2003; Young et al., 2000). Accordingly, a large number of marriage and family therapists report seeing clients for "cybersex" issues (Goldberg, 2004). Some gay men have used the Internet to engage in a practice called bug chasing, in which they willingly become infected with the HIV virus (Gauthier and Forsyth, 1999). There have also been reports of people who attempted suicide obtaining information about the method they used from the Internet (Alao et al., 1999). Additionally, the medical literature contains an example of an individual who apparently found the inspiration for sexual self-mutilation on the Internet (Summers, 2003).

There are plenty of reasons to suspect that at least some of these money slaves are experiencing negative consequences in their daily lives because of their on-line activities. Some of these men are spending hundreds, if not thousands, of dollars on these money mistresses. They may be forsaking financial obligations, including those to their own family. In on-line discussion forums, some of these men admitted to neglecting to pay personal bills to give money to these women, whereas others indicated they have "maxed out" their credit cards or taking "payday" loans to get money for the money mistresses. Given the increasing number of people seeking counseling for Internet-related issues, therapists are likely to begin encountering male clients who are dealing with the ramifications of "money slavery."

REFERENCES

Alao, Adekola O. et al. (1999). Cybersuicide: The Internet and Suicide. *American Journal of Psychiatry* 156, pp. 1835–1836.

Baudrillard, Jean. (1994). *Simulacra and Simulations.* Ann Arbor: University of Michigan Press.

Bryant, Clifton D. (1974). *Deviant Behavior: Occupational and Organizational Base.* New York: Rand McNally.

Ferree, Marnie C. (2003). Women and the Web: Cybersex Activity and Implications. *Sexual and Relationship Therapy* 18, pp. 385–393.

Financial Slavery, online blog (2006).

Finch, Emily. (2002). What a Tangled Web We Weave: Identity Theft and the Internet. In: Y. Jewkes (ed.), *Dot.cons: Crime, Deviance, and Identity Theft on the Internet*, pp. 86–104. Collompton, England: Willan Publishing.

Gauthier, DeAnn K., and Forsyth, Craig J. (1999). Bareback Sex, Bug Chasers, and the Gift of Death. *Deviant Behavior* 20, pp. 85–100.

Goldberg, Peter D. (2004). *An Exploratory Study about the Impacts that Cybersex Is Having on Families and the Practices of Marriage and Family Services.* Virginia Polytechnic Institute and State University, Falls Church, Virginia. Unpublished Master's Thesis in Human Development/Marriage and Family Therapy.

Griffiths, Mark D. (2003). Internet Gambling: Issues, Concerns, and Recommendations. *Cyberpsychology & Behavior* 6, pp. 557–568.

Hegland, Jane E., and Nelson, Nancy J. (2002). Cross-Dressers in Cyberspace: Exploring the Internet as a Tool for Expressing Gender Identity. *International Journal of Sexuality and Gender Studies* 7, pp. 139–161.

Higginson, Joanna G. (1999). Defining, Excusing, and Justifying Deviance: Teen Mothers' Accounts for Statutory Rape. *Symbolic Interaction* 22, pp. 25–44.

Lyman, Stanford M. (2001). Accounts, Roots and Foundations. In: Clifton D. Bryant and C. D. Bryant (eds.), *Encyclopedia of Criminology and Deviant Behavior, Volume I: Historical, Conceptual, and Theoretical Issues*, pp. 7–13. Philadelphia: Brunner-Routledge.

McClintock, Anne. (1993). Maid to Order: Commercial Fetishism and Gender Power. *Social Text* 11:4, pp. 87–116.

Moser, Charles, and Levitt, Eugene E. (1987). An Exploratory-Descriptive Study of a Sadomasochistically Orientated Sample. *Journal of Sex Research* 22, pp. 322–337.

Scott, Marvin B., and Stanford, Lyman. (1968). Accounts. *American Sociological Review* 31, pp. 46–62.

Summers, Jeffrey A. (2003). A Complication of an Unusual Sexual Practice. *Southern Medical Journal* 96, pp. 716–717.

Waskul, Dennis D., et al. (2004). *Net.SeXXX: Sex, Pornography, and the Internet*, pp. 13–33. New York: Peter Lang.

Weinstein, Raymond M. (1980). Vocabularies of Motive for Illicit Drug Use: An Application of the Accounts Framework. *Sociological Quarterly* 21, pp. 577–593.

Young, Kimberly S., et al. (2000). Online Infidelity: A New Dimension in Couple Relationships with Implications for Evaluation and Treatment. *Sexual Addiction and Compulsivity* 7, pp. 59–74.

Zhao, Shanyang. (2004). Consociated Contemporaries as an Emergent Realm of the Life World: Extending Schutz's Phenomenological Analysis to Cyberspace. *Human Studies* 27, pp. 91–105.

REVIEW QUESTIONS

1. Describe "money slavery," and explain how providers of this service solicit clients.
2. What strategies do money mistresses use to identify fake slaves and how slaves attempt to deceive money mistresses?
3. How do money mistresses justify their participation in this type of deviant activity?

Chapter 36

ONLINE DATING: "I'M DYSFUNCTIONAL, YOU'RE DYSFUNCTIONAL"

ANDREA ORR

Dara is a pretty 57-year-old artist from Seattle who has an earnest smile and an outdoorsy glow. She was widowed years ago and more recently broke up with her boyfriend of six years. She joined an online dating service and spent a good amount of time writing a detailed and nuanced profile saying she liked old silverware, old houses, old jazz, and wanted a committed relationship. Here are three of the men she heard from:

- One who responded with a one liner: "I love it when you talk dirty."
- A never-married pharmaceutical salesman who sounded interesting enough to meet. They went to a Japanese restaurant where she ordered sushi and he proceeded to inform her about the high mercury content in fish. "Then he pulled a packet of fish oil out of his pocket, opened it up and sucked it down," Dara recalled. "It was kind of disgusting."
- A magazine writer whom she liked well enough to date several times. The relationship seemed to be going well until something happened that made her wonder if she could trust him. One night after they had had dinner together, Dara went home and checked her email and saw that she had received new messages from other men in her dating service. Out of curiosity, she went to the Web site to read about them, but because she was still thinking, fondly, of the man she had been out with that evening, she called up his profile. She saw that he was online too, surfing around the same dating site. She took great offense that he would be so uncouth as to return from a date with her and sit right down at the computer to look for other women.

But Dara herself had been looking at other men, had she not? "Not really," she insists. "I had just happened to check my email and then click through to some of the people who had written to me." Although her date's action may have been equally innocent, she said it left her with a queasy feeling. "We were getting closer and closer to a sexual relationship and I was not about to do that with someone who was going to go back home and log on to a dating site." That night she decided to cool it with the online dating, after concluding that even with the extensive pool of candidates the Internet provided, you could still get stuck with a lot of sex maniacs, cheats and people who drank fish oil for dinner. "I think you'd have to be luckier than the odds on the lottery to win at this game," she said one evening, after several months of active but unsuccessful Internet dating.

Source: Excerpted from Andrea Orr, *Meeting, Mating, and Cheating: Sex, Love, and the New World of Online Dating.* Upper Saddle River, NJ: Reuters, 2004.

Henry, the 40-year-old marketing executive from Denver, does not completely disagree. He has used numerous online dating sites on an off for five years but, many flings and evenings of good conversation later, has yet to find the serious relationship he craves. (He quit online dating for a year and a half while seeing a girlfriend he met offline, through friends.) Today, Henry continues to go on Internet dates, but he is skeptical. An intelligent and engaging man, he has no problem indulging mystery women in long email conversations, and he says that with the computer as a buffer, he can control his image and be so charming that he often feels the women falling for him before they have met. But he has found that 100 pages of sweet email nothings do not add up to three minutes of face to face. According to one newspaper advice column, some online Romeos are doing more than just crafting perfect prose. "I persuaded a shy male friend to try Internet dating," the advice seeker wrote. "He posted his profile and photo but never actually wrote to anyone. So I got him to let me take over. Now I am courting three women via email in the guise of a 35-year-old man. I am a woman (but, it turns out, I have a way with the ladies). This now feels a bit less innocent, but if it gets my shy friend together with a nice woman, is it wrong?"

Martin, the 38-year-old entrepreneur from New York City who doesn't like paying to subscribe to an online dating service, still likes the wealth of women it provides. Yet he too sees a downside. "It actually is a little bit harmful to society. The Internet just gives you a wonderful reason to move on, like her nose turns too red when she sneezes. People online date to find fault."

At a time when online dating is more popular than ever, it is simply too early to know if it will last. Can the Internet be expected to revolutionize dating as much as the telephone and the automobile did, or as little as those fly-by-night computer dating services that appeared briefly in the late 1960s? For all the success stories in circulation, is success really happening in substantial numbers, relative to all the millions of people who are trying this? It will be a long time before that kind of data appears. Yet anecdotally, some arguments against Internet dating are beginning to pile up for those who care to look deeper than the vast quantity of potential dates it provides.

Joel Ginsberg is a 40-year-old management consultant in San Francisco who was drawn to the Internet because he found the city's offline gay scene a little bit cold and more than a little bit superficial. "All about how you look and how young you are," he said. He had often heard the argument about the Internet being so good for high-achieving professionals like himself who didn't have a lot of time. Once online, however, he discovered that although he didn't need a 20-year-old with a perfectly cut body, he was somewhat into looks himself, and not happy about the Internet as a medium for showing a person's outer beauty. "People don't use very good quality pictures. I mean, I posted photos where you can see my build, a couple of close-ups and a couple of smiley faces. A lot of people give you something where they are 15 percent of the entire field and you can't see anything."

Ginsberg also found all the promises of the Internet as a time-saving tool for busy people to be untrue. "I just find it extremely time consuming," he argued. "It takes a long time emailing to sort of get a sense of who might be interesting if you are looking through ads. You go back and forth several times before you even decide to have a phone conversation. Then finally you plan a time to meet, and after all that, you know within five seconds if there's any potential. If there is not any potential, it's been a waste of weeks of email."

Of course, lying about one's physical appearance is one of the easiest tricks of the Internet, so much so that jokes have been written around the often gaping discrepancy between what someone says and what they mean. Women who say they are 40-ish, the joke goes, are actually 48; if they say they are average looking they are ugly; if they say they are beautiful they are pathological liars. Men who say they are 40-ish, on the other hand, are "52 and looking for a 25-year-old," while those who say they are average looking have "unusual hair growth on ears and nose." In all seriousness, almost anyone who has spent any amount of time Internet dating has a story of the truth not living up to reality, and apparently vanity knows no age limit. Noah, the 84-year-old from Florida, found that "a few extra pounds" as a term to define body type was "grossly abused" among women in their seventies. (Lest people assume that everyone who posts a photo online picks the skinniest one they can find, this headline recently appeared on one dating site, above the full face of a 26-year-old man: "I've lost 100 pounds since this picture was taken.")

Sometimes the exaggerated physical attributes are harmless enough. Ravi, a 38-year-old attorney in Los Angeles, said that when he first met his wife, she was heavier than he had expected. But then, she told him that she had expected he would have more hair. Today they have two children and laugh about their first impressions.

Henry, throughout his five years of Internet dating, says he has come across brutal honesty as much as he has encountered serious deceit. One man who contacted him confessed right away that he was a pre-surgery transsexual. "I wrote back and said I was sure that it was hard for him to tell people, and that I was glad he told me, but it was just not my bag." Another woman sent Henry a pretty photo that did not look at all like the person he arranged to meet in a bar. "I had to say something like, 'Oh, it's so dark in here. I didn't even recognize you.' "

Bernardo Carducci, a professor of psychology at Indiana University Southeast, does not think the lies are always a laughing matter. Carducci, who is director of the University's Shyness Research Institute and offers workshops to help people overcome their social anxieties, said that the Internet seems to prevent people from moving from superficial conversation to deep honesty, the way they almost inevitably do in the offline world. "Here is the problem with the Internet that I found," said Carducci. "When we asked people how true they were in describing themselves, there was really no relationship between the amount of time they had spent interacting and how honest they were. You might think the more time you spend talking to someone online, the more you could trust them, but we found no relation. Offline, there is a check on that."

Common and predictable as these stories of age, height or weight distortion are, many people say, the most troubling things they have encountered online is a kind of emotional distortion: the way Internet dating has, for better or worse, upset their notion of things like flirting and sexual tension. Damon is a 35-year-old graphic artist in Minneapolis, who, after years of trial and error, had built flirting into a science. "I tended to gravitate to the places where I was forced to have an elevator pitch ready," he said, explaining his preference for picking up women in the grocery store, in front of their cars while they were fumbling for change to feed the meter or at a bus stop. "The thrill of being able to impress them not only in a short space of time but in an unknown space of time, to have to present myself as cute and funny and safe in 30 seconds, was a fun challenge. I'd come up with some way to present sexual undertones, but not overtones, lay out a challenge, then wait." Like any guy, he struck out a lot of the time but sometimes he got a date. Then he went online. The first woman he met slept with him. So did the second. The third, he said, wanted to, but he was not attracted to her. It went on like that until at some point, he thought about trawling for men. Although he always presented himself to the world as a straight guy, he'd had a bisexual phase years ago during college and he decided to explore it again. Again more easy success. At first he felt like he had won the lottery: unlimited gay and straight sex, almost on demand. Then he started to feel uneasy. "Now that I know it's easy sex, it's kind of a turnoff," he said. "I don't really go out with these women, I think how fast I can slay them. Now I do less online dating. It takes the fun out of it and it kills your drive."

If people like Damon are turned off by the lack of challenge, others looking for something more lasting find success much more elusive. Some profess a frustration more profound than that which comes from the bar scene, the church group or the extended circle of friends. As the numbers go up, so too does the number of people you would never want to date, or, who would never want to date you. The deep disillusionment you typically suffer over that occasional bad date is multiplied many times over. You need a thick skin to get through it. Martin, the New York entrepreneur on a budget, says that aside from disliking having to pay for all those dates, just the act of going on so many has forced him to become a cynic. It is not that he is opposed to all the volume. His business school degree taught him to see all life's challenges, including affairs of the heart, in terms of risk and reward, investment and return. "As I look at it, if I just went about my normal life I would only have 10 dates a year. With the Internet, I can easily have 100. Over the course of a decade, that's a thousand people I will meet versus only 100 without the Internet," he explains. The problem is that those improved odds come at a price. "You have to go into all of these dates with the feeling of 'No, this is not going to work out.' If you go in with a No, you protect yourself. It's the only way you can do it."

Moreover, because there are so many people to choose from, chances are that not all of them will be as thoughtful as Dara, who crafted serious, individualized letters to everyone she communicated with. Equally common as her approach is the "shotgun" method of sending out multiple one-liner emails saying something generic like "You sound interesting," or something inappropriate like, "I love it when you talk dirty." Strange as it sounds that anyone would try to jump-start a loving relationship that way, many people, and men in particular, confess that the online format reduces them to just that. The odds of any particular woman writing back, they figure, are so slim that they see little reason to invest any time or thought. Overall, the ratio of men to women on online dating sites remains around 60/40, making for a lopsided system in which women's inboxes get stuffed and many great men, like HotOrNot's James Hong, are ignored.

One person who you'd think could be the poster boy for Internet dating is Vernon Church, a 41-year-old New York City scientist-turned-writer who met his wife, Susanna, through Yahoo Personals four years ago. Susanna came upon Vernon after suffering through just two other bad Internet dates, including one who reminded her of the Unabomber. If three was a charm for her, though, the lucky number for Vernon was much higher. He went out with 99 different women—along the way collecting enough material to write and produce Connections, an off-Broadway play about Internet dating—before finally getting lucky with number 100. The happy ending did not erase the memory of all the bad experiences that preceded it. As a result, Vernon Church is not a huge fan of Internet dating.

"By the time I met Susanna, I decided it was a horrible way to meet people," Church said. "It is a really false social environment." Church's first 99 Internet dates led him to conclude that most people who date online either lied about their physical attributes, had a false sense of intimacy and revealed too much too soon, or just had poor social skills that prevented them from meeting people offline. When he met Susanna, he said, it was not love at first sight. But it was noticeably different from all the others.

"It wasn't horrendously bad," he said.

What was so bad about the first 99? "Well, one said, 'I'm not thin like a model but I work out all the time and I'm always in the gym.' When she showed up she probably had 60 pounds on me. She wasn't particularly fat, just big in a linebacker kind of way. She was so sweet but I felt no attraction. It was kind of an awkward situation."

"Then there was a woman who spent the entire date talking about how she had doubled her salary every year for the past five years. If you are even marginally good at arithmetic, you know she was making tons and tons of money. She was talking about how she was going to buy a $5,000 lamp from a feng shui consultant. And then the check came, and she did not even blink." Church picked up the check.

Some of the popular jokes about Internet dating have also addressed this discrepancy between stated personality traits and actual personality flaws. Women who say they are "emotionally secure," one joke goes, are in fact medicated; those who say they are "passionate" are loud; "poet" is code for depressive schizophrenic and "fun" means annoying. Men who say they are "athletic" really mean that they like to sit on the couch and watch ESPN, and those who say they are thoughtful mean that they "say please when demanding a beer." Somewhere between the first Internet date and the one hundredth, Church reached the same conclusion as Judy Storandt in Oklahoma City. Forget the candlelit dinner dates, and meet for a quick coffee in a bookstore café.

"You can say that the reason people are now on the Internet in droves is that no one has the time to meet people offline. However, I really believe that most people are there because they have some social deficit," says Vernon Church. "The reality is that if you are a reasonably secure human being with some social skills, you meet people." And Church himself? While conceding that he is a "difficult writer type," who is not free of his own social deficits, he says the main reason he tried the Internet was that he held a managerial position at work and was therefore not available to date his subordinates. Whatever the reason people first decide to take the online dating route, he believes that even the most normal, socially adjusted people can be lulled into an unappealing state of inertia. "Without the Internet, if you were pining to meet someone you would, hopefully, get off the couch and go to a party. But the Internet is a totally nonchallenging way to be social."

Delis Alejandro might agree. As a pastoral associate at St. Monica's Catholic Church in Santa Monica, California, she has seen more couples than she can count meet and get married through church functions. Proof, she believes, that even in today's fast-paced world, there are endless opportunities to meet new faces if you only circulate. Alejandro oversees multiple parish groups from a ministry for divorced people to one for gays, another for lapsed Catholics returning to the church, and several programs to reach out to the poor and imprisoned. She says there is a social component to all these activities. "Even if you sign up to help feed the poor, you are partly doing it to meet people."

Nor is everyone so disillusioned with what has come to be widely disparaged as "the bar scene." People who look for dates online commonly say they are tired of the bar scene, which seems to suggest a place full of sleazy people in search of sleazy sex. This could be one of the biggest myths to grow out of the online dating explosion, that attempting to socialize in a bar is foolhardy or passé and that there are no sincere people who also enjoy unwinding in public watering holes. Shoshana Lombardi, a 32-year-old who works in public relations in Washington, D.C., met her husband in a bar several years ago and remains a big advocate of a venue where people can casually mingle with others from their community while dulling their social anxieties with drink. Lombardi's own story of meeting her husband, Chris, is one of coincidence and mysterious intervention by a third party. She was in the bar in the first place only because she and her friend had gone to the wrong address, missing the bigger party they had meant to attend. As it turned out, one of Shoshana's colleagues was one of Chris' roommates and she seemed intent on getting them together. "She said to me, 'I heard you met my roommate, Chris. He told me that he wanted to see you again,' " Shoshana remembers. "Then she told him that I had said I wanted to see him again, even though I hadn't."

They never did learn the motives behind the woman who was not particularly close to either one of them, but the nudging worked. Still, Lombardi says it was definitely "the bar scene" that gave birth to the initial attraction. She had noticed her future husband from across the bar, thinking nothing so serious as "that is the man I will marry some day." What she thought in her Friday night kick-back mode was, "that is a man who looks a lot like Ferris Bueller," or more precisely, Matthew Broderick, who had played him in the 1986 film *Ferris Bueller's Day Off*. Because she was in a bar and had drunk a couple of cocktails, she giddily called across the bar, "Ferris Bueller!

Ferris Bueller!" Finally, he came over to ask why she was screaming at him.

"I have to tell you," says Lombardi, who is only an occasional drinker, "I am a huge proponent of meeting people in bars. Some people think it might not be a place to meet genuine people. But I wouldn't have met my husband if I hadn't been in a bar. And I probably would never have talked to him if I hadn't been drinking."

Such stories of meetings in traditional offline dating venues do prompt the question of whether Internet dating is actually a solution to the impersonal society so many people claim we have become, or just one more isolating factor for a country where individuals are already sequestering themselves in home gyms, home offices or in airtight automobiles while driving solo to the office. Professor Carducci says his own research has located a clear link between technology and social avoidance. "The Internet has not only given us more access and information, it has created a sense of hyperculture," he said. "The speed at which our culture operates is getting faster and faster. As things get faster, people lose patience. In order to be noticed, you have to be more extreme and louder, and that works against a lot of people who get pushed out of the way." Carducci does not see the Internet or Internet dating as the whole problem. He notes that people in their twenties and younger grew up with the Internet and use it, like the telephone, as a logical extension of their social development. And he says many other factors, like the growth in gated communities, are contributing as much as the Internet to the sense of isolation. Trend watcher Faith Popcorn recently came up with the term "cocooning" to describe a social phenomenon in which four million Americans were living in gated communities, 16.6 million had their own private movie theater and more than 10 million were telecommuting. But within these realities, the Internet provides one more way to avoid face time. "When you have thousands of people doing it, there is some probability of success," argues Carducci. "Of course, if you were to approach thousands of people on the street, you could probably find someone to go out with you too."

Which gets back to that story of Vernon Church and his 100 online dates. Might he have found a wife anyway if he had taken such a systematic approach offline? "A wife or two, I'd say," he responded quickly. "Seriously, I suspect it would have taken much less time in real space. Neither person would bother to pursue someone in that context whom they didn't find attractive in the first place. More importantly, in the real world you find the usual amount of neurosis. In contrast, the anonymity of the online environment selects for people who have difficulties with meeting people face to face. That dysfunction can take many forms—inability to communicate, fear of intimacy, narcissistically high standards. On the street, on a good day, you would simply pass those people by, socially speaking. That's not to say that everyone online is socially challenged, just that one finds a larger percentage of people who are."

His explanation might help explain some of the random and odd responses that Sally, a 37-year-old graduate student in Los Angeles, received when her friends persuaded her to try online dating. One frightened her right off the bat when he wrote to say that he had wonderful relationships that were based on "good conflict resolution." Another said, in his introductory letter, that he was very good friends with his ex and had "other friends as well." Yet another sent a nude photo along with separate close-ups of particular body parts. Finally, a fourth suitor sounded nice enough in print, and she gave him her phone number. He called and asked within the first five minutes what she looked like in a bathing suit. A second man who got her phone number made repeated, pleading phone calls over the course of several months, leaving messages like, "I'm tall and fit, and better looking than my photo."

Like Professor Carducci, many psychologists who specialize in social anxiety say they encourage shy and apprehensive patients to use the Internet as a way to meet new people in a relatively nonthreatening environment. They also warn that technology can exacerbate existing problems, enabling very shy people to avoid confronting their fears while giving others license to be rude and inappropriate from behind a screen of anonymity. "Shy people often go to the Internet," said Jonathan Berent, a psychologist based in Great Neck, New York, and the author of *Beyond Shyness*. "The increase in technology is making social avoidance easier than ever before. People have always been able to avoid other people by sitting in a room and watching television or calling phone sex lines, but the Internet raises the bar, creating the impression that they are interacting, but not requiring that they do any of the hard work in terms of dealing with people face to face."

Merri, the New York City journalist who found her husband on her second Internet date, sees it differently. She too had one bad Internet date. "He was a total loser, weirdo, creepy guy," she says. "I was so demoralized and depressed, but I decided to keep doing it." And that perseverance ultimately led her to adopt a more positive take on the online dating jungle. As she sees it, one of the best things about Internet dating is that it lets you move on from your disappointments more quickly. "Everyone knows you have to kiss a lot of frogs to meet your prince, but the Internet speeds up that process," she said. "You can go through nine frogs in two weeks rather than two years."

When Match.com successfully paired up Alex Siegel, a San Jose, California, engineer, and his wife Rochelle, a teachers assistant, it got more than it bargained for: five success stories. After the Siegels married in 1998, Rochelle gave birth to triplet boys, Ethan, Avery and Justin. Could there possibly be a more wholesome online dating success story? Match.com seems to think not. As part of its promotional material, the company distributes an adorable photo of the three toddlers sitting upright in three boat-like plastic laundry baskets, navigating their living room floor. Curiously, though, neither Rochelle nor Alex is the most enthusiastic supporter of online dating. Rochelle, who joined Match.com in 1997, when she was still in college at a California State University and the Internet was a much smaller place, says she probably would not do it again today, because she thinks the Internet has become more frightening as its ranks have grown.

Like his wife, Alex also has measured enthusiasm for online dating. On the plus side, he notes, it is a lot better than the offline dating services he used back in upstate New York when he was a graduate student at Cornell University. "They had this sort of big room full of binders that had the applications of women you would go through to look for one that seemed suitable, and then you would call her," he explained of the offline service Great Expectations. "It was pretty awkward." Alex Siegel had multiple dating service horror stories, including one that was not the fault of the dating service at all, in which he lost part of his leg in a motorcycle accident and seriously injured the woman he had just met earlier that evening. "We never talked again," he said.

Aside from that tragedy, Siegel said, there was no denying that the people who joined dating services, at least in upstate New York, were a motley crew. "There are a lot of people who use dating services because they have to," he said. "I guess either they are very awkward, or they are very weird, or they have some particular hang-up, or something incredibly specific they are looking for." Then, including himself in the group he just described, he added, "I was a computer geek, so I wasn't very good at meeting people." Siegel said that when he began using online services, the pool of people was much larger, the quality better and the system of emailing before you called or met made him a lot more comfortable. "The Internet is better than a normal dating service," he said, before adding one admonition. "You do have to be very careful because there are a lot of fairly dangerous creeps online."

Spoken like an expert. But what did he, a conservative engineer and father of three, know about the creepy men online?

"What they typically do is tell women they are young and handsome and rich, and when they actually meet them, they are not."

And how did he know that?

"Well," Siegel explained. "I've spent a lot of time in chat rooms. And for a little while my brother and I had this game we would play. We would get online and pretend to be 22-year-old beautiful college girls just out looking for a good time and we would see how many guys we could get going at the same time and try to tease them along. It was tremendously easy to get tremendous numbers of people interested in you."

Because Dara, the artist from Seattle, was not a person to give up easily, she finally erased the memory of the fish-oil drinker and the guy who wanted to talk dirty, and went back online. It got better. She widened her search and came upon a man from Portland, Oregon, with whom she shared numerous things from single parenthood to a passion for the arts, and a love of the written word. Their emails back and forth were long and thoughtful, at once intellectual and erotic, and you could just tell that they would hit it off. Theirs was a highbrow correspondence. Just in the process of describing her day-to-day life, Dara quoted a line from one of Shakespeare's more obscure plays. She confessed that while she was passionate about her work, she had never achieved great success, since she was more passionate about her children. He responded with a long confessional of his own, describing the moment of his daughter's birth when his "body was drained of conflict and, like a dam bursting, a flood of emotions, joy relief and love, washed over me." She wrote back to compliment him on the difficult choices he made to sacrifice a promotion at work to spend more time with his two daughters.

Each letter was hundreds and hundreds of words of intelligent prose packed with references to literature, family and loneliness. It was becoming so intimate that Dara was starting to like this man, in ways other than just as a potential date. She even suggested that he might like to meet her son, who lived just outside of Portland. She was getting the feeling that she had found a solid friend, if not a lover. They were really connecting, and after several more revealing letters Dara felt it safe to share the stories of some of her less positive online dating experiences. He wrote back to say that he was sorry she had had some bad experiences, his had all been positive, without exception. She wrote in response that there was no need to apologize, she had just been making conversation. In the midst of a very warm letter that had mentioned holiday plans and sent good wishes for the New Year, she happened to add that she was curious to see whether he was writing to her out of sincere interest, or because he had been unable to meet any women in Portland. If nothing else, they were email buddies at this point and it seemed like a fair question. He did not think so. The final letter Dara received from him was the shortest of any of them, and it was the last. "There's a caustic tone in recent exchanges that I find unsettling," he said, "so I think I'm interested no longer."

REVIEW QUESTIONS

1. Debate the pros and cons of online dating based on your reading of Orr's article.
2. Identify at least three disadvantages of establishing relationships using Internet online dating not identified in Orr's article.
3. How do you feel your family would respond to you when they learned that you found your significant other on the Internet? Why do you believe they would feel that way, and how would you respond to their reaction?

CHAPTER 37

ONLINE BOYS: MALE-FOR-MALE INTERNET ESCORTS

MATTHEW V. PRUITT

Male-for-male prostitution (hereafter, "male prostitution") is known to have existed at least as far back as Ancient Greece and Rome (Boswell 1980; Sanger 1937). The extent to which this and other forms of prostitution have been openly practiced, and the degree to which prostitution has been stigmatized have varied both cross-culturally and over time (Sanger 1937; Davies and Simpson 1990). As homosexuality has become better tolerated in American society, male homosexual prostitution has become more visible to the public. While "call boys" or "escorts" have advertised their services in gay publications for some time (Jay and Young 1977), these forms of prostitution are less visible to the public than street "hustlers" or "rent boys" who openly and directly solicit clients on the streets of America's larger cities (Calhoun 1992). The Internet has provided yet another means for male prostitutes and their clients to find each other, an avenue more discreet than street solicitation and, arguably, more discreet than picking up magazines that list such services. Our knowledge of Internet escorts is sparse (Parsons, Bimbi, and Halkitis 2001; Uy et al. 2004). This study provides a descriptive, exploratory analysis of male escorts who advertise their services on the Internet and compares this data with the extant literature on male prostitution. This research also provides information not currently found in the literature on male prostitution: self-reported penis size, self-described sexual activities listed in Internet escort advertisements, and the extent of the use of face shots (pictures) in advertisements.

DATA, VARIABLES, AND METHODS

This study is a descriptive analysis of advertisements placed on a single large, national, male Internet escort site in the United States. The men who advertise on this site are marketing themselves to other men. The unit of analysis is the individual advertisement. Data were collected over a period of approximately nine months in the year 2000. Ethical issues associated with the research, including consideration of risks to subjects and the methods of collecting, analyzing, and reporting these data were approved and monitored by the Western Kentucky University Human Subjects Review Board. The researcher contacted no escorts, and the escorts used pseudonyms in their ads.

The author found potential sites by entering "male escorts" in several search engines. The website used in this study was chosen over other websites for several reasons. First, in order to make the sample as representative as possible, a site covering all 50 states was selected. Sites serving only particular cities or areas of the country were eliminated from consideration. To the author's knowledge, this is the first study to

Source: Matthew V. Pruitt, "Online Boys: Male-for-Male Internet Escorts," *Sociological Focus*, vol. 38 (August 2005), pp. 189–203.

use a national sample of male Internet escorts. Second, this site was one of the largest on the web at the time of the study. This was determined by a visual inspection of various sites and by counting the number of escorts listed in key states such as California, Florida, and New York. Third, the website used in this study is not limited to certain types of escorts (e.g., "twinks," college boys, fetishes, or specific racial groups) but rather covers males of various races/ethnicities, ages, sexual services, etc. Fourth, many websites did not have as much information from which a database could be constructed. Some of the websites contained only a picture, escort's name, basic stats (height, weight, age), and an e-mail address or phone number. The escorts on the site chosen provided comparatively more information about themselves (e.g., sometimes detailing aspects of their personality or interests, sexual activities in which they engage, availability for travel). This site had a format the escorts used in posting their advertisements (e.g., a spot for mentioning whether they were available for travel, a link to view adult pictures, if provided). The format made the data more consistent than that found on other websites and easier to code. Fifth, the author considered only sites that did not charge to view escort advertisements. These sites are accessible to anyone with an Internet connection; such free sites are, therefore, arguably more public than pay sites. Moreover, some men will not use credit cards to pay to access sites due to both financial considerations and issues of privacy. Additionally, it seemed advisable to choose one broad-based site rather than sample several escort sites, because some escorts advertise on more than one site.

The website selected for study was "www.escorts4you.com." Before being allowed to view escort advertisements, users had to click on an icon acknowledging their agreement to several statements. For example, users were supposed to be of legal age to view such material and not members of any law enforcement agency. Unlike some websites, this site did not require the use of a credit card number or the use of an age-verification service (e.g., AdultCheck) through which people can use credit card numbers to set up login names and passwords to gain entry to some adult websites. Anyone could click on the icon and gain access to the site. (The website has since changed: in March 2005 the website provided links to male-for-male escort sites but no longer had escort advertisements.)

Advertisements for all 1,262 escorts listed on the site were printed, and data were coded from these printouts. The website listed escorts according to the states that they serve. Some of these escorts advertised themselves in more than one state. They were included only once in the dataset. All variables used in this study were derived or constructed from information provided on the printed pages. No escorts (or agencies) were contacted. Although this study of Internet escort advertisements is limited to the data provided by the escorts in their advertisements, one advantage of using advertisements as the unit of analysis is that the sample is not adversely affected by a low response rate associated with subjects declining to participate in the study. A few advertisements are provided as illustration.

> *Christian B.*
> *22 years old, 5′11″, 170#, blonde hair green eyes, extremely defiend [sic], muscular, gymnast build, washboard abs, great pecs, arms and legs, model goodlooks. Versatile Top! I am extremely good looking and well built european american boy with an amazingly defined body. I enjoy what I do, have no attitude and am also well educated. So if you are interested in a singular experience with a very young, hot blonde adonis let's hook up soon. Based in San Francisco, California. Available for Travel! (email address)*

> *Jon*
> *37 years old, 5′7″, 160#, goatee, muscular gym body—44chest, 30waist, light chest hair, 8! thick Top! I am a friendly guy for your pleasure. All scenes from vanilla to kinky, boy or daddy, top. Educated, well travelled, no attitude. Based in West Fort Lauderdale, FL. Available for Travel! (email address)*

Matt
30 years old, 5′11″, 170#, black muscled, masculine, 7.5 UC! Bottom! Goodlooking, easygoing, friendly, adventurous and very horny tight round butt. Based in Chicago, IL. Available for Travel! (phone number) (email address)

David C.
22, 5′9″, 150#, dishwater blond, blue yes [sic], thin, defined, 8×5! Versatile! Based in Chicago, IL. Available for Travel! (email address)

Ronnie
27 years old, 5′11″, 169#, smooth, 7.5–8! Versatile but prefer Top! I'm a hot blk male, looking to service hot inshape white guys in the age range of 21 to 40. I aim to please. Based in Baltimore, MD. Available for Travel! (email address)

Toby
19 years old, 5′9″, 145#, brown hair, green eyes, tan, smooth, 7! Based in Philadelphia, PA. Available for Travel! (phone number) (email)

All variables that are common to the literature on male escorts and that could be coded from the advertisements were entered into the data set. These variables include age, race, sex act, willingness to "bareback," and agency affiliation. Variables that are not commonly found in the literature (and often are not available) are: availability of a face shot, willingness to travel, the provision of e-mail address, voicemail/pager numbers, phone number, the availability of adult pictures of the escort, and, finally, self-reported penis length.

The variables are defined below. "Age" is the escort's age. "Race" is the escort's race/ethnicity (1 = White, 2 = Black, 3 = Hispanic/Latin, 4 = Asian, 5 = mixed race, and 6 = not determinable). When not self-reported, a person who clearly appeared to be of a given racial group was coded as such. If the author did not believe it would be readily apparent to potential customers that a person appeared "White" or "Black" (for instance) to someone looking at his picture (or if no picture were provided), then the escort's race was coded "not determinable." Individuals who self-reported a mixed-race background were coded as such.

The third variable, "sex act," refers to what role (if any) the escort indicates he will take in anal sex (1 = top, 2 = versatile top, 3 = versatile, 4 = versatile bottom, 5 = bottom, 6 = sex act not indicated by escort). "Top" and "Bottom" refer to roles in anal intercourse. "Top" refers to the one who takes the role of "insertor" in anal intercourse. "Bottom" refers to someone who takes the role of an "insertee." "Versatile top" or "versatile bottom" indicate that an escort may take either role in intercourse but prefers or usually takes the role identified after "versatile." "Versatile" refers to one who does not have a strong preference for either role and will generally take either role. Few of the escorts indicated what role they would take with regard to oral sex. While male escorts are generally willing recipients of oral sex, not all male escorts perform oral sex on their clients.

A series of variables are coded as dichotomies (yes, no). The variable "bareback" refers to whether the escort explicitly mentions involvement in "barebacking"—that is, anal intercourse without the use of condoms. "Agency Affiliation" indicates whether or not the escort lists affiliation with an escort agency. "Face" indicates whether or not a face shot (picture) of the escort is provided. "Travel" refers to whether the escort is available for travel. "Email," "voicemail/pager," and "phone" refer to whether or not the escort can be contacted by each of these means. It is not possible to determine whether telephone numbers are associated with mobile phones or landline phones. "Adult" refers to whether or not the escort provides "adult" pictures of himself. On the website used in this study, individuals must have "AdultCheck" service to view these pictures. While some of the pictures show partially clad men in underwear, most show full nudity. Some of the nude images include face shots while others provided only body shots. Finally, ads included the escort's self-reported measure of penis length.

RESULTS

Descriptive statistics for the personal characteristics of male escorts are provided in Table 37.1. The data show that the male escorts in this study range in age from 18 to 50, with a median age of 26.5 and an average age of 27.2. Most escorts are in the middle range of ages (between 23 and 30), with only about 23% of the escorts between the ages of 31 and 50. With regard to racial/ethnic background, 88–89% are White, just over 6% are Black, with the remaining distributed among Hispanic, Asian, and mixed ethnicity.

Table 37.1 also provides information on the range of behaviors associated with "escort activity." Specifically, the table shows that there is considerable variability among these men with regard to the sex acts that they perform. Of those who specified their role, nearly one-half (48.5%) indicate that they are versatile with regard to the sex act, while a quarter (24.3%) indicate that they take the role of the insertor in anal intercourse ("Top"). At the same time, nearly one-fourth of all those providing escort ads did not indicate what role they would take sexually. In addition to the type of role taken sexually, over two-thirds of the escorts (67.8%) reported penis size in their ads. For those reporting, the average self-reported penis length is 8.0 inches, with a range from 5 to 12 inches. Over two-thirds of the men provided a discernible face shot in the ad, and adult pictures of themselves are provided by 54% of the escorts.

There were three modes of contact listed by escorts on the website: email, voicemail/pager, and phone. While most escorts list more than one method of contact, e-mail is the most commonly listed form (98.8%), with phone contact as the second most frequent (55.5%). In addition, approximately three-fourths of the escorts (76%) indicate they are available for travel in order to have a relationship. Only 11.2% of these men mention an affiliation with an escort service.

DISCUSSION

Male-for-male prostitutes and their clients have generally met and arranged prices on the street, in bars, and through call services listed in gay magazines and newspapers. The Internet has provided a new means for male-for-male escorts and their customers to negotiate prices and arrange meetings. In this study, an analysis of advertisements placed on a large, national (United States), male-for-male escort site is conducted to provide a description of these escorts and the services they provide. In the following discussion, results from this study are compared with those of previous studies of male prostitution. This paper also includes data that have not been included in previous studies of male prostitution.

Race/Ethnicity

In their study of New York City Internet escorts, Parsons et al. (2001) have a sample that is 70% White, 14% Latino, 10% Black, and 6% Asian/Pacific Islander. The racial/ethnic breakdown of the data in this study of escorts across the U.S., however, suggests that Whites are disproportionately involved in Internet escorting, and minorities are underrepresented in male Internet prostitution. It is likely that part of the difference found in the current study is associated with the effects of social class (and its interaction with race) on ownership of personal computers and subscription to Internet service providers. In 2000, while 50% of Whites had Internet access, only 36% of Blacks and 44% of Hispanics had Internet access (Lenhart 2000). Data on U.S. households in 2000 show a positive association between household income and Internet access (Lenhart 2000). Additionally, if one were specifically looking for a man of color, one could visit a website that features such men.

Sexual Acts

At least since the time of the Romans, there have been records of the variety of sexual acts that male prostitutes will perform. Boswell (1980) notes that the Romans had terms that were used to distinguish between male prostitutes who took active or passive roles in homosexual acts with

Table 37.1 The Age and Race, Escort Role, Penis Size, Contact Method, and Related Activities Advertised by Men in Internet Male Escort Service Ads
(Maximum n = 1262)

AGE	FREQUENCY	OVERALL PERCENT	VALID PERCENT
18–22	277	21.9%	22.4%
23–26	341	27.0	27.6
27–30	335	26.5	27.1
31–50	283	22.4	22.9
Age not given	26	2.1	
RACE			
White	1105	87.6%	89.0%
Black	76	6.0	6.1
Hispanic/Latino	23	1.8	1.9
Asian	16	1.3	1.3
Mixed	21	1.7	1.7
Unknown	21	1.7	
ESCORT ROLE (SEX ACT)			
Top	232	18.4%	24.3%
Versatile top	93	7.4	9.7
Versatile	463	36.7	48.5
Versatile bottom	74	5.9	7.8
Bottom	92	7.3	9.6
Not Indicated	308	24.4	
PENIS LENGTH			
5.0–5.9 inches	5	0.4%	0.6%
6.0–6.9 inches	75	5.9	8.8
7.0–7.9 inches	328	26.0	38.3
8.0–8.9 inches	308	24.4	36.0
9.0–9.9 inches	111	8.8	13.0
10.0 in. or more	29	2.3	3.4
Not Indicated	406	32.2	
FORM OF CONTACT:			
E-mail	1247	98.8	
Phone	701	55.5	
Voicemail/pager	252	20.0	
AVAILABLE FOR TRAVEL (YES)	959	76.0	
PICTURE PROVIDED (YES)	848	67.2	
AGENCY AFFILIATION (YES)	141	11.2	

other men. Generally straight male prostitutes are less sexually versatile than gay male prostitutes (Allen 1980; Visano 1991). Some straight male hustlers engage in active but not passive anal sex in an effort to protect their sense of masculinity (Visano 1991). While of interest to researchers, the sexual activities of male prostitutes are rarely addressed in the literature that is not directly concerned with transmission of HIV (for an exception, see Allen 1980). A description of the sexual activities in which Internet escorts are involved provides an important contribution to the literature. As is shown in Table 37.1, in the present study, there is considerable variability among the sexual acts in which the men engage. While most of these men (66%) are to some extent versatile, they make distinctions in their advertisements by noting "versatile-top," "versatile," and "versatile-bottom." These distinctions indicate preferences and/or usual roles of the escort. In addition, such distinctions may be important to potential customers. For instance, a customer who hires an escort for the weekend may want someone who prefers, or is accustomed to, being "a top" but would be willing "to bottom" some of the time. Additionally, customers may personally have a stronger sexual attraction to men who generally take a certain role in sexual activities.

Face Shots

A topic that is not addressed in either the literature on male prostitution, or, more specifically, on male Internet prostitution is the extent to which the men use face shots of themselves in advertising. Although research into prostitution need not be concerned with issues of pathology or with attempts to explain what causes an individual to become involved in prostitution, such behavior is sociologically deviant. These men are involved in behaviors (prostitution and homosexual acts) that are both stigmatized and negatively sanctioned by society (Boyer 1989; Browne and Minichiello 1996; Calhoun 1992). Part of the stigma associated with male prostitution in particular and homosexuality in general is the fact that such behavior involves males accepting a passive, devalued, feminine sexual role (Davies and Simpson 1990). Browne and Minichiello argue that in the United States "to distinguish oneself as homosexual is to adopt a devalued form of masculinity" (1996: 47). It is, therefore, interesting to note that fully 67.2% of these men provide face shots of themselves. Additionally, 54% of these men provide adult pictures of themselves. While some of these adult pictures are body-only shots, many include face shots.

From the customer's perspective there are at least three advantages to having face shots available. First, the customer can ensure that the person he is hiring is, indeed, attractive to him, as opposed to having to rely on a print description. Second, having seen a photograph of the escort, the customer can be certain that the person who shows up is the person associated with the advertisement. West (1993) notes that call services in gay publications often use vaguely worded advertisements, sending whichever available escort most closely matches the description in the ad. The advertisement might not be associated with a particular individual, or, if it is, the agency may send someone else, if he is not available. Third, a customer could more easily cancel service if the escort he meets is not the person shown in the picture. The use of a face shot might indirectly benefit escorts as well by helping them gain the client's trust. Trust is an important issue for people desiring to meet others via the Internet, because research has shown that it is common for Internet users to have fictitious profiles (Lamb 1998).

Age

Youthfulness has long been associated with sexual attractiveness of both males and females. In making this point Visano (1991, 207) quotes two blunt lines from Shakespeare: "Age, I do abhor thee. Youth I do adore thee." The societal association of youthfulness with sexual attractiveness and the way sexual appeal structures social interactions makes age a sociologically significant variable in studies of prostitution. On the street, male hustlers often advertise their youthfulness and fit bodies by wearing tight clothing or open shirts (Visano 1991). Online escorts can provide pictures of themselves to serve the same purpose. Research has consistently shown that clients of male prostitutes (like those of female prostitutes) generally favor youthful rather than older prostitutes (Allen 1980; Calhoun and Weaver 1996; Earls and David 1989; McNamara 1994; Visano 1991; West 1993). Prostitution makes the body a commodity, and youthfulness affects how often street hustlers are solicited and the fees they can charge (Visano 1991). Because of the disadvantage associated with aging, older street hustlers "grant 'extras,' charge less money . . . [and are] more tolerant of their clients' misconduct" (Visano 1991: 214). Visano notes that while gay men who have lost the sexual appeal of youth can buy the sexual services of males that they would not be able to acquire otherwise, older clients are often charged higher fees and are more likely to be treated negatively (verbal/physical abuse, rejection) than younger clients. Studies have shown that male prostitutes find sexual activity with younger and more attractive men more pleasurable than having sex with older and less attractive men (Calhoun and Weaver 1996; Visano 1991).

The percentage of men who are 27–30 (27%) and 31–50 (23%) is somewhat surprising, given the age range and distribution that is commonly found in studies of male prostitution. Specifically, the percentage of older males is greater than one would expect given the findings of other research (Allen 1980; Luckenbill 1986; Pleak and Meyer-Bahlburg 1990). . . . The age distribution among these men is, however, in line with a recent study of male prostitutes (street workers, independents, and escort agency employees) by Minichiello et al. (2000). In their study of New York City Internet escorts, Parsons et al. (2001) report a range of 22–47 with a mean of 31.76, which is somewhat older than the ages of the men in this study (mean = 27.23, median = 26.5).

West (1993) writes that an agency manager interviewed in his study preferred hiring younger males due to customer preference; he also notes that escorts themselves mention this preference and the associated "aging-out" of the profession. Allen (1980), McNamara (1994), and Visano (1991) also argue that, as male street prostitutes age, they find it increasingly difficult to sell themselves. There are, however, a few exceptions to keep in mind. First, as Visano indicates, not all gay men prefer younger sexual partners. Second, many of the previous studies of male prostitution have focused primarily or exclusively on street prostitution. Third, West notes that older men (in their 30s) are more likely to advertise involvement in sado-masochistic activity and that youthfulness is not as important to customers seeking fulfillment of such fantasies. Additionally, van der Poel (1992) states that Dutch men who work independently as call boys are able to work past age 30—a time when they would be too old to work on the street or in brothels. Fourth, a lack of older males on the street is not necessarily a measure of customer preference. Older males may find it more stigmatizing to be on the street, may be more likely to be harassed by police working these areas, and have more to lose if arrested for prostitution than younger, especially juvenile, males. One would expect fewer older adults (who, as a rule, would have more to lose) to be involved in prostitution, especially the forms of prostitution that involve public solicitation of clients. Fifth, Davies and Simpson (1990) argue that the capital needed to be involved in escort and masseur prostitution (having phone service and an apartment for in-calls) as opposed to street prostitution favors those who are wealthier and better educated. With Internet prostitution one can add the cost of a computer and an Internet service provider. As stated earlier in the paper, data from 2000 clearly show a positive association between household income and Internet access (Lenhart 2000). Part of the disproportionate involvement of younger males in street prostitution is attributable to these factors. Sixth, Luckenbill (1986) argues that some adolescent street hustlers work the street because they are too young to legally enter bars or be hired by an escort service. Last, of course, while anyone can hang out a shingle, being open for business does not necessarily result in being busy. Future research investigating age differentials in the frequency of both solicitations of male Internet escorts and the fees charged by them is needed to determine the effects of age on this form of prostitution.

Methods of Contact

Minimally, escort prostitution differs from street prostitution in that escorts do not solicit clients in public. Davies and Simpson (1990) argue that this makes them less susceptible than streetwalkers to police entrapment and physical harm. Involvement in Internet prostitution seems to be more closely related to escort/call boy prostitution associated with gay magazines and newspapers than to street or bar hustling. In fact, one would assume that it differs primarily with regard to manner of advertising—Internet advertising as opposed to print ads in gay publications. Among the males in this study, 98.8% could be contacted by e-mail, but only 55.5% could be contacted by phone. This suggests that, while there is some overlap between these groups, there may be some individuals who are solely involved in Internet prostitution. Additionally, providing a phone number does not mean that these men are also listed in gay magazines. Some Internet prostitutes may therefore be a subset of escorts/call boys who do not advertise in gay publications. In a study of agency employees, streetwalkers, and independents, Minichiello et al. (2000) find that 23.4% of the men studied in their sample were involved in more than one form of prostitution. In his study of career mobility among street, bar, and escort prostitutes, Luckenbill (1986) reports that whether or not male prostitutes are involved in other forms of prostitution depends on their knowledge of other types of prostitution and their access to these worlds. This would also be true for males involved in Internet hustling; they must have knowledge of and access to other forms of male prostitution in order to become involved in them. The extent of overlap among males working as Internet prostitutes, street and bar hustlers, and call boys who advertise in gay magazines is a consideration for future research.

Penis Size

The self-reported size of escorts' penises is something that has not been addressed in previous studies of male prostitution. A discussion of escorts' penis size is included because (1) for some customers this attribute is an important determining factor in choosing an escort, and (2) 67.8% of the escorts in this sample include this information in their description of themselves. It is commonly cited that male penises average approximately 6 inches (or fall within the range of 5–7 inches) (Caron 2003). If such estimates are accurate, and if the size reported by these men is true, then these men are, as a group, above average. While approximately ⅓ of the sample do not mention penis size, 65.5% of the men who do discuss this in their advertisements report having penises in excess of 7 inches. As stated before, this information is important for those gay men who are sometimes referred to as "size queens"—men who prefer males with larger-than-average penises. West (1993) reports that, due to customer preferences, an agency manager in his study preferred hiring escorts with large endowments. It is important to note that the data in this study are self-reported. In addition, it is not known how the penis was measured (i.e., measuring the lower side of the penis may give a different length from that obtained by measuring the upper side of the shaft).

Penis size is of sociological significance to the extent that it is, as some have argued, associated with masculinity (Rothschild 2004; Shah and Christopher 2002). Given this association, it is likely that some escorts and clients may perceive those escorts with larger penises as being more masculine, and, to some extent, more desirable. Of course, masculinity also encompasses behavior, demeanor, and interests. While a larger penis may enhance an escort's masculinity, it is not likely that a large penis negates other aspects of a person's identity that are not in alignment with hegemonic masculinity. Moreover, Boyer (1989) reports that for some male prostitutes, involvement in prostitution is itself seen as a reflection of virility. Some gay men, of course, prefer effeminate-acting men.

Furthermore, the body itself can be a representation of masculinity. Halkitis, Green, and Wilton (2004) report that some HIV positive gay men associate masculinity with "buff" bodies and sexual prowess. Halkitis et al. (2004: 37–38) state that "while it may be argued that masculinity is not a monolithic concept and that multiple types of masculinities may function within gay culture . . . In the day-to-day workings of gay life, it is the buff men—the muscular, masculine men—who are the objects of much attention and desire." This preference is reflected in many of the advertisements examined in this study. Claims of possessing "hot" bodies as well as chest and bicep measurements are commonly found in the advertisements.

Agency Affiliation

While West's (1993) study of escorts/masseurs in London gay publications found that many of these men were affiliated with agencies, only 11.2% of the men in this study list affiliation with an escort service. Of course, the absence of such a listing does not guarantee the person is not affiliated with a service. The contact e-mail address or phone number may be that of an escort agency. West notes that some advertisements in British publications appear to be private masseurs but are, in fact, agency employees. While having someone to schedule appointments and answer the phone/e-mail is an advantage of being associated with an agency, a major concern from the escort's perspective would be giving some percentage of one's earnings to the agency. To the extent that clients feel safer choosing an agency-affiliated escort, however, agency affiliation could indirectly benefit escorts. Clients probably assume that the escorts are, at least loosely, screened and monitored by the agency. Luckenbill (1986) finds this to be true, and his study suggests that agencies will drop escorts about whom customers have complained. Luckenbill notes that agencies, desiring profits and repeat customers, do monitor escorts. Additionally, as Luckenbill discusses, escorts also benefit by having the agencies arrange fees, relieving them from having to haggle with customers. Luckenbill also mentions that agencies sometimes screen clients for problematic individuals and the police. This is beneficial to agency-affiliated escorts because clients can be physically abusive or refuse to pay for services (Calhoun and Weaver 1996; West 1993). Escorts assume that agencies will blackball clients who have caused problems.

Barebacking

Research has shown that some gay men are involved in the practice of barebacking—intentional involvement in unsafe anal intercourse (Halkitis 2001; Halkitis and Parsons 2003; Halkitis, Parsons, and Wilton 2003; Suarez and Miller 2001). Furthermore, the Internet is used by some gay men specifically to find others who engage in this behavior (Grov 2004; Halkitis 2001; Halkitis and Parsons 2003; Tewksbury 2003). In the present study, six male escorts advertise involvement in this activity. Four of these men specifically mention the term "barebacking," and two of the men use the abbreviation "bb." Some men do not mention this practice in their advertisements, but they might be willing to engage in it. While advertising involvement in such behavior may attract certain clients, it would also deter others who would perceive these escorts as being of higher risk for HIV.

CONCLUSION

This study has provided a descriptive exploration of male Internet prostitution based on data provided by men on an Internet escort website. Much remains to be learned, and so this study concludes with a list of questions for further research. First, to what extent are the escorts and clients who are involved in Internet prostitution also involved in other forms of prostitution, such as street or bar hustling and call boy services listed in gay magazines? Second, while research by Uy et al. (2004) has examined rates charged for services, how frequently escorts work, and full-time/part-time status of New York City escorts, more research in this area is needed, and a larger, national study would be beneficial. Third, research has shown that male involvement in street prostitution is either the result of "peer introduction" or "situational discovery" (Allen 1980; Calhoun 1992). Is this also true of Internet prostitution? Fourth, has the Internet provided a means for people to become involved in prostitution who would not otherwise have been involved in prostitution either as workers or clients? Fifth, are these men employed in the licit world of work and, if so, in what capacity?

REFERENCES

Allen, Donald M. 1980. "Young Male Prostitutes: A Psychosocial Study." *Archives of Sexual Behavior* 9:399–426.

Boswell, John. 1980. *Christianity, Social Tolerance and Homosexuality.* Chicago, IL: University of Chicago Press.

Boyer, Debra. 1989. "Male Prostitution and Homosexual Identity." *Journal of Homosexuality* 17:151–184.

Browne, Jan, and Victor Minichiello. 1996. "Research Directions in Male Sex Work." *Journal of Homosexuality* 31:29–56.

Calhoun, Thomas C. 1992. "Male Street Hustling: Introduction Processes and Stigma Containment" *Sociological Spectrum* 12:35–52.

Calhoun, Thomas C., and Greg Weaver. 1996. "Rational Decision-Making among Male Street Prostitutes." *Deviant Behavior* 17:209–227.

Caron, Sandra L. 2003. *Sex Matters for College Students: FAQ's in Human Sexuality.* Upper Saddle River, NJ: Pearson Education, Inc.

Davies, Peter, and Paul Simpson. 1990. "On Male Homosexual Prostitution and HIV." Pp. 103–120 in *AIDS: Individual, Cultural and Policy Dimensions*, edited by Peter Aggleton, Peter Davies, and Graham Hart. London: Falmer Press.

Grov, Christian. 2004. "Make Me Your Death Slave: Men Who Have Sex with Men and Use the Internet to Intentionally Spread HIV." *Deviant Behavior* 25:329–349.

Halkitis, Perry N. 2001. "An Exploration of Perceptions of Masculinity among Gay Men Living with HIV." *Journal of Men's Studies* 9:413–429.

Halkitis, Perry N., Kelly A. Green, and Leo Wilton. 2004. "Masculinity, Body Image, and Sexual Behavior in HIV-Seropositive Gay Men: A Two-Phase Formative Behavioral Investigation Using the Internet." *International Journal of Men's Health* 3:27–42.

Halkitis, Perry N., and Jeffrey T. Parsons. 2003. "Intentional Unsafe Sex (Barebacking) among HIV-Positive Gay Men Who Seek Sexual Partners on the Internet." *AIDS CARE* 15:367–378.

Lamb, Michael. 1998. "Cybersex: Research Notes on the Characteristics of Visitors to Online Chat Rooms." *Deviant Behavior* 19:121–135.

Lenhart, Amanda. 2000. "Who's Not Online: 57% of Those without Internet Access Say They Do Not Plan to Log On." Pew Internet and American Life Project. Retrieved June 8, 2005 (http://www.pewinternet.org/pdfs/Pew_Those_Not_Online_Report.pdf).

Luckenbill, David F. 1986. "Deviant Career Mobility: The Case of Male Prostitutes." *Social Problems* 33:283–296.

McNamara, Robert P. 1994. *The Times Square Hustler: Male Prostitution in New York City.* Westport, CT: Praeger Publishers.

Minichiello, Victor, Rodrigo Marino, Jan Browne, Maggie Jamieson, Kirk Peterson, Brad Reuter, and Kenn Robinson. 2000. "Commercial Sex between Men: A Prospective Diary-Based Study." *Journal of Sex Research* 37:151–160.

Parsons, Jeffrey T., David Bimbi, and Perry N. Halkitis. 2001. "Sexual Compulsivity among Gay/Bisexual Male Escorts on the Internet." *Sexual Addiction and Compulsivity* 8:101–112.

Pleak, Richard R. and Heino F. L. Meyer-Bahlburg. 1990. "Sexual Behavior and AIDS Knowledge of Young Male Prostitutes in Manhattan." *The Journal of Sex Research* 27:557–587.

Rothschild, Louis. 2004. "Penis." Pp. 597–600 in *Men*

and Masculinities: A Social, Cultural, and Historical Encyclopedia, edited by Michael S. Kimmel and Amy Aronson. Santa Barbara, CA: ABC-CLIO.

Shah, Jyoti, and N. Christopher. 2002. "Can Shoe Size Predict Penile Length?" *BJU International* 90:586–587.

Suarez, Troy, and Jeffrey Miller. 2001. "Negotiating Risks in Context: A Perspective on Unprotected Anal Intercourse and Barebacking among Men Who Have Sex with Men—Where Do We Go from Here?" *Archives of Sexual Research* 30:287–300.

Tewksbury, Richard. 2003. "Bareback Sex and the Quest for HIV: Assessing the Relationship in Internet Personal Advertisements of Men Who Have Sex with Men." *Deviant Behavior* 24:467–483.

Uy, Jude M., Jeffrey T. Parsons, David S. Bimbi, Juline A. Koken, and Perry N. Halkitis. 2004. "Gay and Bisexual Male Escorts Who Advertise on the Internet: Understanding Reasons for and Effects of Involvement in Commercial Sex." *International Journal of Men's Health* 3:11–26.

Visano, Livy A. 1991. "The Impact of Age on Paid Sexual Encounters." *Journal of Homosexuality* 20:207–226.

West, Donald J. (with Buz de Villiers). 1993. *Male Prostitution.* Binghamton, NY: Harrington Park Press.

REVIEW QUESTIONS

1. How did Pruitt code an escort's race when it was not specifically mentioned in the advertisement? Do you think this is a valid means of identifying a person's race? What do you think is more important to customers—an escort's self-identified racial categorization or the degree to which he appears to be of a given racial group? Explain.
2. What is the sociological significance of the use of face shots by some escorts in their advertisements?
3. Based on your reading of Pruitt's article, what do you consider to be some weaknesses of the methodology used to gather this data?

CHAPTER 38

CYBERBULLYING: OFFENDERS AND VICTIMS

SAMEER HINDUJA
JUSTIN W. PATCHIN

Adolescents at the turn of the twenty-first century are being raised in an Internet-enabled world where blogs, social networking, and instant messaging are competing with face-to-face and telephone communication as the dominant means and methods through which personal interaction takes place. Apart from the obvious benefits of information at one's fingertips, entertainment value, and speed of correspondence, participation online has valuable utility in teaching youth various social and emotional skills that are essential to successfully navigating life. For example, cyberspace provides a venue to learn and refine the ability to exercise self-control, to relate with tolerance and respect to others' viewpoints, to express sentiments in a healthy and normative manner, and to engage in critical thinking and decision making (Berson, 2000). These skills, however, cannot be effectively internalized if the learning environment is unwelcoming or inhospitable to those who venture online. Indeed, if adolescents are uncomfortable or unwilling to explore the Internet and take advantage of all of its positive attributes, they will be sorely lacking in certain developmental qualities that others who do embrace cyberspace will naturally obtain. Although the vast majority of youth have quickly acquired a proclivity for computers and the Internet (NTIA, 2002), a small but growing proportion of kids are being exposed to interpersonal violence, aggression, mistreatment, and harassment—through what has been termed *cyberbullying*.

Cyberbullying has been succinctly defined as "willful and repeated harm inflicted through the medium of electronic text" (Patchin and Hinduja, 2006). The primary means through which it can occur include the Internet-enabled personal computer and cellular phone. Via both, an offender can send hurtful and denigrating messages and content to a victim, to third parties, or to a public forum or environment that many other online users visit. It has been observed that "social change always provides opportunities for the predatory behavior that is characteristic of a small number of people. With the new technologies which support the Internet, those who cannot adjust rapidly, and that is all of us, are at risk from those who can and will deploy technology as a criminal weapon" (Butterfield and Broad, 2002). Cyberbullying is the unfortunate by-product of the union of adolescent aggression and electronic communication, and its growth is giving cause for concern.

The goal of the current research is to provide a foundational piece for the knowledge base associated with aggression and violence on the Internet by analyzing online survey data from approximately 1,400 adolescents in order to iden-

Source: Specifically written for this reader, with portions drawn from the authors' article, "Cyberbullying: An Exploratory Analysis of Factors Related to Offending and Victimization," *Deviant Behavior*, vol. 29 (2008), pp. 129–156.

tify factors associated with cyberbullying victimization and offending. These preliminary portraits will inform both children and adults in supervisory roles of the demographic, situational, and behavioral variables that increase one's risk of belonging to either group. Accordingly, attention can be directed to these areas, and strategies can be devised to reduce the contributive impact of those elements amenable to isolation and response. Future research can then build on the groundwork laid in this study.

There is no shortage of potential offenders or victims of cyberbullying because of the widespread availability of computers and the Internet in the developed world. Nonetheless, it has been difficult to observe and study the phenomenon due to its intangible, non-corporeal nature—much like many other forms of cyberdeviance. According to a 2005 survey by the National Children's Home charity and Tesco Mobile of 770 youth between the ages of 11 and 19, 20% of respondents revealed that they had been bullied via electronic means. Almost three-fourths (73%) stated that they knew the bully, whereas 26% stated that the offender was a stranger. Another interesting finding was that 10% indicated that another person had taken a picture of them via a cellular phone camera, consequently making them feel uncomfortable, embarrassed, or threatened.

METHOD

In this exploratory study, an online survey methodology was utilized to collect data from over 6,800 respondents during December 22, 2004, and January 22, 2005, about their experiences with electronic bullying (as a victim, offender, and witness). The primary benefit in utilizing such a format concerns the ability to reach a wide number of participants at an economical cost. The subject matter itself was appropriate for this methodology, as it concerns a global phenomenon that occurs exclusively online. Because there does not exist a sampling frame with contact information of possible cyberbullying offenders and victims, the best way to seemingly reach such a population was to select a number of Internet sites whose visitors possessed demographic characteristics similar to the study's target population. As such, the survey instrument was linked to several websites that targeted adolescents. Despite this strategy, approximately 43% (n = 2,978) of the total number of respondents were older than 17 years of age and therefore excluded from the current analysis. In addition, efforts were made to target both adolescent boys and girls, yet the vast majority of respondents (82%) were female. The differential response among gender may reflect a response bias, may characterize the distribution of cyberbullying across youth, or may reflect the greater impact that cyberbullying has on young women and their corresponding concern with the behavior. Future research is necessary to determine the extent to which this bias is substantively meaningful. To limit any partialities that may arise from the disproportionate number of female respondents, a random number of girls was drawn from the sample that was approximately equal to the number of male respondents under the age of 18 (male = 680, female = 698). This approach, although not ideal, resulted in a final sample of 1,378 youth respondents that were relatively equal in terms of gender.

FINDINGS

Our sample consisted of 1,378 respondents under the age of 18 distributed approximately evenly across gender. The vast majority were Caucasian or white (80%) and from the United States (74.6%), and the average age of respondents was 14.8. It is also clear from this study that youth are computer literate, spending an average of 18 hours per week online. Over 32% of boys and over 36% of girls have been victims of cyberbullying, whereas about 18% of boys and 16% of girls reported harassing others while online. This was illustrated in some of the open-ended feedback we received; a 14-year-old boy from Canada declared: "Someone sent me numerous emails with like two words in the email like 'you're gay' 'you're dumb'

Girls more likely victim
Boys were instigators

and that kind of stuff. When I am bullied (which is infrequently) I am called homosexual or gay so I'm used to it but it still hurts." Similarly, an 11-year-old girl from California stated: "Kristina, a friend from school, said in an e-mail 'tomorrow—watch your back—we are coming for you.' It made me feel so bad I started to cry. Nobody likes me." These responses underscore the hurtful nature of cyberbullying victimization.

Interestingly, there was no statistically significant difference between boys and girls in terms of their experiences with cyberbullying either as an offender or victim. This is contrary to traditional schoolyard bullying (especially physical bullying), which has largely been a male-dominated affair. The Internet may be the ideal environment in which the more covert forms of bullying commonly employed by girls are effectuated. Youth were most commonly victimized in a chat room or via computer text message, while girls were more likely than boys to report being victimized via e-mail (13% and 9.7%, respectively). Not surprisingly, the patterns in locations of offending are very similar to victimization, with the two most common environments being chat rooms and computer text messages. By way of example, a 13-year-old girl from an unknown location expressed: "It happened on MSN Messenger about a year ago. A girl threatened to kill me. She said she knew my family and where I lived. She'd come at 1 o'clock to kill me. Then she logged off. I called my mom and told her. She said I should try to find out who it was, and if it continued we'd call the police. I sent an email to the girl, telling her I'd call the police. She replied and said she was sorry and she was only kidding. In front of her email address, there was her name! It was a girl in my class." Similarly, a 17-year-old boy from California reported the following:

> *I was talking to someone in a chatroom and they started telling me things. Like was I really that stupid and making fun of me. I told them privately to please stop and they wouldn't. They then told me they were going to harm me and I was scared because I don't know how but they knew where I lived. I am scared sometimes. One time someone made me feel so bad that I wanted to kill myself because I believe those things that they said. My friends calmed me down and told me not to do anything dumb. I dislike it when people spread rumors online about you and it has happened to mostly everyone who chats.*

The next stage of analysis sought to identify variables that are linked to an increased risk of experiencing all forms of cyberbullying. Notably, there were no statistically significant differences in offending or victimization by gender or race. That is, boys and girls and whites and nonwhites were equally as likely to experience cyberbullying as an offender or victim. In accordance with intuition, older youth were more likely to report victimization and offending. The more time respondents spent on the Internet, and the more computer proficient they were, the more likely they experienced cyberbullying. Finally, a number of off-line maladaptive behaviors appear to be related to cyberbullying. Respondents who reported recent school problems, participation in assaultive behaviors, or substance use were more likely than their counterparts to experience cyberbullying, both as an offender and victim. All of these relationships were statistically significant. Additionally, experience with traditional schoolyard bullying was related to an increased risk of experiencing cyberbullying. For example, youth who reported bullying others in real life in the previous six months were more than 2.5 times as likely to report bullying others online. Similarly, youth who were victims of traditional bullying in the previous 6 months were more than 2.5 times as likely to be victims of cyberbullying. These findings suggest that there are characteristics unique to some individuals that place them at an elevated risk to be victims or offenders in multiple contexts.

DISCUSSION

Cyberbullying as a growing phenomenon is receiving much attention by the popular media, and various news outlets are publishing reports, case studies, and stories on the subject matter. Some data on cyberbullying have been collected by information technology research firms and social service agencies, but they have provided us with an underdeveloped picture of the prevalence of this particular form of deviance. Results from the current study revealed a number of important issues that warrant discussion.

First, findings indicate that cyberbullying does not discriminate based on gender or race. The gender finding is surprising as it contradicts a significant body of traditional bullying research that indicates boys are involved in bullying more often than girls. However, research has consistently noted that adolescent girls tend to participate in more indirect forms of bullying, including psychological and emotional harassment (e.g., rumor spreading). Given the fact that the vast majority of cyberbullying behaviors involve these indirect forms of harassment, it makes sense that girls appear equally as likely to be participants. The race finding is not altogether unexpected as studies examining its distribution across traditional bullying offending and victimization are largely inconclusive. That said, it may simply be that certain demographic characteristics such as race and gender are rendered less relevant in an environment where interpersonal communication occurs predominantly through electronic text.

An alternative explanation is that historically less powerful groups may be more powerful (or at least not disadvantaged) when online. Minority groups (irrespective of race or ethnicity), although potentially unpopular on the schoolyard, may not be exposed as marginal on the Internet. Moreover, youth who may not stand up for themselves on the playground may be more likely to do so via computer communications if the perceived likelihood of retaliation is minimized. Targets may be "turning the table" on bullies because of the equalizing characteristics of the Internet and its ability to preempt the relevance of physical intimidation. That is, victims of traditional bullying may seek retribution through technological means (e-mail, instant message, or cellular phone text message) by contacting those aggressors who have harassed them. Some might contend that bullying in the traditional sense requires certain personal or physical traits and qualities that an individual either has or does not have (such as physical prowess or social competence); cyberbullying requires no such personal traits and can be manifested simply through the outward expression of hate.

Second, the current work exposed a link between cyberbullying and traditional schoolyard bullying. Youth who are bullied at or near school are significantly more likely to be a victim of cyberbullying; those who bully off-line also appear to bully online. A 13-year-old girl from Canada related the following experience:

> *The last time I was bullied online, I was on MSN (instant messaging) talking to some people from school. Someone from my class who doesn't like me started talking shit about me to everyone else. And a bunch of people that she had been talking to came and started harassing me. They were talking about how I had bad grades in math and how I bite my fingernails and other stupid stuff like that. They still say stuff about me at school and make things up about me and tell everyone.*

These findings indicate that the factors associated with traditional bullying behaviors might also be associated with cyberbullying. It may simply suggest that computers and the Internet are new tools which can be employed to augment traditional behaviors and activities. Indeed, bullies may just be adapting to technological change and employing a different medium to harass and mistreat. Those predisposed to harass and mistreat their peers perhaps choose to do so regardless of context—in real space or in cyberspace.

Finally, the qualitative details provided by victims also attest to the virulent nature of cyberbullying. Many youth reported being physically threatened ("I was in a chat room and someone threatened to beat me up because we liked the same girl." "I was sent death threats via email from somebody I knew from school"). A 14-year-old girl from Texas stated: "I think it's just as bad as bullying in person, only harder to be detected. They don't know who it is that is bullying them so they have to continue to endure it. I think it's horrible and people should stop bullying." A 17-year-old girl reiterates this point:

> *Bullying online is terrible because it affects the mind more than the body. It makes me feel so annoyed that people can harm others over a computer. People can say things online to make people more scared than if they were being physically threatened. People feel more vulnerable online than they would elsewhere. Bullying online is really bad because it is mental bullying which is sometimes worse then physical bullying, and can cause people to do stupid things. It makes me angry.*

The current work identified certain factors that make some individuals more likely than others to be involved in cyberbullying offending or victimization. What seems to most logically follow in terms of policy solutions is to ensure that those involved in traditional bullying are aware of their susceptibility to the online variety, and to present them with a systematic plan of action to preclude such an outcome. The Internet is replete with safety tips, and various top-ten precautionary lists to instruct adults that have children who are frequently online. In addition, software is available for adults to install on home computers to filter certain content from the eyes of innocent youth. Neither of these measures, however, is exhaustive or inerrant in their goal to prevent victimization. Research by Berson and colleagues (2002), for example, identified the utility of ongoing discussions by parents, caregivers, or teachers with children about the latter's interactions through the computer. In that study, direct supervision or periodic monitoring of adolescents' online activities also proved advantageous in reducing the likelihood of unhealthy social choices on the Internet. Other research has supported such a strategy, and has stressed the importance of positive caregiver-child relationships—which have been shown to decrease the likelihood of online offending (Ybarra and Mitchell, 2004). The onus of responsibility, though, is not solely placed on the shoulders of parents and guardians. Attenuating the problem of cyberbullying will necessarily involve contributions from multiple stakeholders, including counselors, school teachers and administrators, and law enforcement.

REFERENCES

Berson, I. R., Berson, M. J. and Ferron, J. M. (2002). "Emerging Risks of Violence in the Digital Age: Lessons for Educators from an Online Study of Adolescent Girls in the United States," *Journal of School Violence* 1:2, pp. 51–71.

Berson, M. J. (2000). "The Computer Can't See You Blush." *Kappa Delta Pi Record* 36:4, pp. 158–162.

Butterfield, L. and Broad, H. (2002). Children, Young People and the Internet. Accessed June 30, 2005. Available at http://www.netsafe.org.nz/articles/articleschildren.aspx.

NTIA (2002). *A Nation Online: How Americans Are Expanding Their Use of the Internet.* Washington, DC: Author.

Patchin, J. W. and Hinduja, S. (2006). "Bullies Move Beyond Schoolyard: A Preliminary Look at Cyberbullying," *Youth Violence and Juvenile Justice* 4:2, pp. 148–169.

Ybarra, M. L. and Mitchell, J. K. (2004), "Online Aggressor/Targets, Aggressors and Targets: A Comparison of Associated Youth Characteristics," *Journal of Child Psychology and Psychiatry* 45, pp. 1308–1316.

REVIEW QUESTIONS

1. How were the study respondents chosen?
2. What were the major findings of this study?
3. Based on this study, who is likely to become involved in cyberbullying as offenders or victims?

PART ELEVEN

PRIVILEGED DEVIANCE

As the boss of the worldwide conglomerate Tyco, Dennis Kozlowski made tons of money for his corporation and himself. In the 1990s, he went on a frenzied shopping spree, spending more than $60 billion to buy 200 major corporations and hundreds of smaller ones. As a result, Tyco, once a relatively small industrial-parts manufacturer with $3 billion in yearly sales, turned into a global colossus that annually pulled in $36 billion, selling practically everything from diapers to fire alarms. For that feat, Kozlowski rewarded himself with more than $300 million in total compensation for the three years before the good times ended. He further acquired for himself, among other things, three Harley-Davidson motorcycles, a 130-foot sailing yacht, a private plane, and lavish homes in four states. Unfortunately for him, in the summer of 2002 he was charged first with failing to pay $1 million in sales tax on art purchases and then with stealing $150 million from Tyco. In 2005, he was convicted for systematically looting the company and sentenced to serve 8 to 25 years in prison.[1]

Kozlowski's crime may be called *privileged deviance*, a highly profitable deviance that characteristically involves privileged people—the relatively wealthy, powerful, or well educated. Here we take a look at different aspects of privileged deviance. In the first article, "Criminal Telemarketing: A Profession on the Line," Neal Shover and his colleagues analyze how today's criminal telemarketers come from the higher social classes rather than the lower classes as the professional thieves did in the past. In the second article, "The Neutralization of Professional Deviance among Veterinarians," DeAnn Kalich presents her research findings on the various ways veterinarians try to make their deviant behaviors—such as overcharging their clients—appear acceptable, legitimate, or proper. In the third selection, "Societal Causes of Political Corruption," Xiaohui Xin and Thomas Rudel test their theory that official corruption is likely to result from a high poverty rate, a large population, and the lack of democracy. In the fourth reading, "Enron: Organizational Rituals as Deviance," Jason Ulsperger and David Knottnerus analyze how the prevalence of deviance in the former giant corporation was an integral part of its organizational culture.

[1]*Wall Street Journal*, "Tyco Convictions Upheld," November 16, 2007, p. C2; Daniel Eisenberg, "Dennis the Menace," *Time*, June 17, 2002, pp. 46–49; Andrew Hill, "Ex-Tyco Chairman Free on $10m Bail," *FT.com*, September 27, 2002.

CHAPTER 39

CRIMINAL TELEMARKETING: A PROFESSION ON THE LINE

NEAL SHOVER
GLENN S. COFFEY
DICK HOBBS

In 2000, telemarketing sales accounted for $611.7 billion in revenue in the United States, an increase of 167 percent over comparable sales for 1995. Total annual sales from telephone marketing are expected to reach $939.5 billion by the year 2005 (Direct Marketing Association, 2001). The reasons for the rapid growth of telemarketing are understood easily in context of the "general acceleration of everyday life, characterized by increasingly complicated personal and domestic timetables" (Taylor, 1999). The daily schedule no longer permits either the pace or the style of shopping that were commonplace a few decades ago, and the need to coordinate personal schedules and to economize on time now drives many household activities. In the search for convenience, telemarketing sales have gained in popularity.

But criminals also have been quick to exploit the opportunities presented by telemarketing. Although it was nearly unheard of until recent decades, few adults today are unfamiliar with telemarketing fraud. There are countless variations on the basic scheme, but typically a consumer receives a phone call from a high-pressure salesperson who solicits funds or sells products based on untrue assertions or enticing claims. Callers offer an enormous variety of products and services, and often they use names that sound similar to bona fide charities or reputable organizations. Goods or services either are not delivered at all, or they are substantially inferior to what was promised.

RESEARCH SUBJECTS

Most of the data used for this report were gathered in semi-structured personal interviews with 47 telemarketing offenders convicted of federal crimes. Since there are no lists of the names of criminal telemarketers, investigators interested in learning about them and their activities cannot draw random samples for study. Improvisation is required. We began by examining major metropolitan newspapers for the past five years and an assortment of approximately 75 websites that contain information about telemarketing fraud as well as names of convicted offenders. These search processes yielded the names of 308 persons who were convicted of telemarketing fraud in the period 1996 through 2000.

Under terms of an agreement with the Federal Bureau of Prisons, names were submitted to personnel in their Office of Research and Evaluation, who reported to us the institutional locations

Source: Neal Shover, Glenn S. Coffey, and Dick Hobbs, "Crime on the Line: Telemarketing and the Changing Nature of Professional Crime," *British Journal of Criminology*, vol. 43 (2003), pp. 489–505. Reprinted by permission of Oxford University Press.

of those currently incarcerated. Institutional wardens then were made aware that we were interested in interviewing these inmates. The warden or the warden's designate then presented to the inmates our written description of the research and its objectives and then inquired if they were agreeable to meeting with us when we visited the institution. We later traveled to a number of institutions to meet with inmates who responded affirmatively, to describe and explain our research objectives and to interview those who elected to participate in the study. Twenty-five members of the sample were incarcerated when we interviewed them. They were confined in 12 federal prisons, from Oregon to Florida and Massachusetts to Arizona.

To ensure that our sample included ample numbers of persons with diverse telemarketing experiences, we also interviewed 22 offenders under federal probation supervision. We reasoned that their involvement in telemarketing fraud probably was not as lengthy or as serious as was the case with the incarcerated subjects. Fifteen of the probationers were interviewed in Las Vegas, Nevada, and the remaining seven were interviewed in other cities. Las Vegas was an early hotbed of criminal telemarketing, and it continues as home base for many operations.

The interviews explored a range of topics, including subjects' background and criminal history, their employment history, and the nature and circumstances of their initial and subsequent participation in telemarketing fraud. In addition to interviews with convicted telemarketing offenders, we also had access to pre-sentence investigation reports for 37 of the 47 subjects. Examination of these served not only as an independent check on the validity of information elicited during the interviews but also gave us a more complete picture of the subjects' backgrounds, lives and circumstances. Generally, we found the subjects to be forthcoming about their backgrounds although they were less candid when reporting on the extent of their knowledge of criminal operations and the nature of their participation.

CRIMINAL TELEMARKETING

Of all who begin employment in criminal telemarketing, some quickly discover it is not their cup of tea; they dislike it or they do not perform well. Others find the work attractive and rewarding but see it only as a means to other life and career goals. Most, therefore, pursue it only temporarily. Others, however, discover they are good at fraudulent telephone sales, and they are drawn to the income and the lifestyle it can provide. On average, the members of our interview sample were employed in these endeavors for 8.25 years. Their ages when interviewed range from 26 to 69, with a mean of 42.4 years. Their ranks include 38 white males, three African American males, and six white females. Nearly all have been married at least once, and most have children.

Like its legitimate forms, criminal telemarketing is a productive enterprise that requires the coordinated efforts of two or more individuals. To work in it, therefore, is to work in an organizational setting. The size of criminal telemarketing organizations can vary substantially. Some are very small, consisting of only two or three persons, but others are considerably larger. Their permanence and mobility vary also, ranging from those that operate and remain in one locale for a year or more to others that may set up and operate for only a few weeks before moving on. These "rip and tear" operators count on the fact that up to six months' time may pass before law enforcement agencies become aware of and targets them. "Boiler rooms," operations featuring extensive telephone banks and large numbers of sales agents, have become less common in the United States in recent years, largely because of the law-enforcement interest they attract. There is reason to believe, however, that criminal telemarketers increasingly are locating them in countries with weak laws and oversight and operating across international borders.

Larger telemarketing operations commonly take on the characteristics and dynamics of formal organizations; they are hierarchical, with a division of labor, graduated pay and advancement opportunities. Established by individuals with previous experience in fraudulent sales, they generally employ commissioned sales agents to call potential customers, to make the initial pitch, and to weed out the cautious and the steadfastly disinterested.

Experienced telemarketers generally do not call individuals randomly but work instead from "lead lists" (also known as "mooch lists"). These are purchased from any of dozens of businesses that compile and sell information on consumer behavior and expressed preferences. Individuals whose names appear on lead lists typically are distinguished by past demonstrated interest or participation in promotions of one kind or another. When a person is contacted by telephone, the sales agent generally works from a script. Scripts are written materials that lay out both successful sales approaches and responses to whatever reception sales agents meet with from those they reach by phone. Promising contacts are turned over to a "closer," a more experienced and better paid sales agent. "Reloaders" are the most effective closers; much like account executives in legitimate businesses, they maintain contacts with individuals who previously sent money to the company in hopes of persuading them to send more. As one subject told us: "I had it so perfected that I could get these customers to buy again. . . . I made sure they were happy so I could sell them again. It didn't do me—I didn't want the one time, I didn't want the two-timer. I wanted to sell these people ten times."

The products and services offered by criminal telemarketers span a wide gamut. In one scam, subjects identified and located unaware owners of vacant property, led them to believe that buyers for the property could be found easily, and then charged high fees to advertise it. Other schemes we encountered included collection for charities, drug education programs, and sale of "private" stocks. One subject sold inexpensive gemstones with fraudulent certificates of grossly inflated value and authenticity. The stones were sealed in display cases such that purchasers would have difficulty getting them appraised, particularly since they were told that if they broke the seal, the value of the stones would decrease and the certificate of authenticity would become invalid. "Private stocks" are by definition not listed or traded on a stock exchange, but telemarketers are able to entice investors with smooth talk and promising prospectuses. Those who purchase soon discover that the non-existent stocks take a nose-dive, and they lose their investments. A high proportion of the companies represented by our interview subjects promised that those who purchased products from them were odds-on winners of a prize soon to be awarded once other matters were settled. Typically this required the customers to pay fees of one kind or another. Some of our subjects solicited money for nonexistent charities or legitimate organizations they did not represent. In the products they sell, criminal telemarketers clearly are limited only by the human imagination.

BACKGROUNDS AND CAREERS

A substantial body of research into the lives and careers of street criminals has shown that many are products of disadvantaged and disorderly parental homes. We were interested in determining if the homes in which our subjects were reared reveal similar or functionally equivalent criminogenic characteristics. They do not. Overwhelmingly, the members of our sample describe their parents as conventional and hard working and family financial circumstances as secure if not comfortable. Their parental families were traditional in nature, with the father providing the main source of income. Nevertheless, one-half of the mothers also were employed outside the home. Although the fathers' reported occupations ranged from machinist to owner of a chain of retail stores, 32 were business owners or held managerial positions. A substantial proportion of our subjects were exposed to and acquired entrepreneurial perspectives and skills while young. Business ownership appealed to many of them: "You're always pursuing more money, most of us are. We're raised that way, we are in this country. And that's the way I was raised. But I also wanted to do my own thing. I wanted to be in business for myself, I wanted the freedom that came with that." Clearly, telemarketing criminals are not drawn from the demographic pools or locales that stock and replenish the ranks of street criminals. Although we questioned them at length about their early and adolescent years, their responses reveal little that distinguishes them from [conventional] others of similar age and class background. Certainly, the disadvantages and pathologies commonplace in the early lives of most street criminals are in scant evidence here.

If our subjects' early years reveal few clues to their later criminality, there also are few signs that they distinguished themselves in conventional ways. Their educational careers, for example, are unremarkable; eight dropped out of high school, although most graduated. Twenty-one attended college, but on average they invested only two years in the quest for a degree. Five claimed a baccalaureate degree. When invited to reflect upon how they differ from their siblings or peers, many reported they were aware of an interest in money from an early age. One subject told us: "I had certain goals when I was a teenager, you know. And I had a picture of a Mercedes convertible on my bedroom mirror for years." Another said: "You know, I do have a major addiction, and I don't think I'll ever lose it. And I don't think there's any classes [treatment] for it. And it's money, it's Ben Franklin."

None of our subjects said that as children they aspired to a career in telemarketing, either legitimate or criminal. Some had previous sales experience before beginning the work, but most did not. Their introduction to it was both fortuitous and fateful; while still in high school or, more common, while in college, they either responded to attractive ads in the newspaper or were recruited by friends or acquaintances who boasted about the amount of money they were making.

For our subjects, many of whom were foundering on conventional paths, criminal telemarketing was a godsend; it came along at a time when they needed to show that they could make something of themselves. In the words of one of them, it was "a salvation to me as a means of income." New recruits generally start as sales agents, although most of our subjects later worked also as closers and reloaders. Employment mobility is common; individuals move from one firm to another, with some eventually taking managerial positions.

After gaining experience, former managers told us, they were confident they knew enough about the business to strike out on their own. They did so expecting to increase their income substantially. As one put it: "[I]n my mind I believed I was smarter than the owners of these other companies that were making millions of dollars. And I just said, 'I can do this on my own.' " Typically, defectors lure productive personnel from their current employer with promises of more money, and on the way out they are not above plundering the business's files and lead lists: "I downloaded every lead in his file. I took it all. I opened up . . . my own office, took all those people and said 'now, watch me.' "

What about the criminal histories of fraudulent telemarketers? Information elicited in the interviews and a review of information contained in pre-sentence investigation reports shows that 13 of our subjects had previous criminal records, seven for minor offences (e.g., petty theft and possession of marijuana) and six for felonies. Of the latter, three were convicted previously of telemarketing offences. Clearly, many of our subjects are not one-time or accidental violators; they have histories of multiple arrests and convictions. Others have reported similar findings. Thirty percent of 162 sales agents employed by a California-based fraudulent telemarketing firm, for example, had records of at least one criminal offense, and another 16.4 percent had records of alcohol or drug offences (Doocy et al., 2001). For members of our sample who have previous arrests, the age of onset for criminal activity is considerably higher than for street criminals. Our data do show persuasively, however, that many appear to have recurrent trouble with the law and, like street criminals, they are persistent users of alcohol and other drugs.

ATTRACTIONS AND LIFESTYLES

Overwhelmingly, our subjects told us they got into and persisted at telemarketing for "the money." How well does it pay? Only one subject reported earning less than $1,000 weekly, and most said their annual earnings were in the range of $100,000 to $250,000. Five told us their annual earnings exceeded $1 million. The fact that they can make money quickly and [easily] adds to the attractiveness of the work. They find appealing both the flexible hours and the fact that it requires neither extensive training nor advanced education. Few employers impose rigid rules or strictures; generally there are neither dress codes nor uniforms. The work can be done in shorts and a tee shirt (Doocy et al., 2001).

As important as the income it yields and the casual approach to employment it permits, criminal telemarketing appeals to many who persist at it for [professional respectability]. Despite class and parental expectations, most of our subjects had not previously settled upon promising or rewarding occupations. Asked what he "liked about telemarketing," one subject's reply was typical: "Well, obviously, it was the money." Immediately, however, he added that "it gave me a career, [and] to me it was my salvation." As with him, criminal telemarketing enables others to own their own business despite their unimpressive educational background, their limited credentials and the absence of venture capital. . . . [T]elemarketing provides both outward respectability and an income sufficient to maintain the good life.

Other aspects of the work are attractive as well. Characteristically, our subjects believe they are outstanding salespersons. They are supremely confident of their ability to sell over the telephone despite resistance from those they contact. Doing so successfully is a high. One subject told us:

> *You could be selling a $10,000 ticket, you could be selling a $49.95 ticket. And it's the same principle, it's the same rules. It's the same game. I like to win. I like to win in all the games I play, you know. And the money is a reason to be there, and a reason to have that job. But winning is what I want to do. I want to beat everybody else in the office. I want to beat that person I am talking to on the phone.*

Another subject said simply that the work "gives you power." The importance of this [social psychological] dimension of the payoff from fraud has been commented on by others as well (e.g., Duffield and Grabosky, 2001).

Criminal telemarketers generally distinguish between working hard and "working smart." When asked, therefore, how he viewed those who work hard for modest wages, one replied, "I guess somebody's gotta do it." By contrast, work weeks of 20–30 hours are common for them, and even for owners and managers, the need for close oversight of operations decreases substantially once things are up and running. The short work week and their ample income provides considerable latitude in the use of leisure time and in consumption patterns.

The lifestyles of telemarketing participants vary by age and the aspects of the work that employees find most appealing, but ostentatious consumption is common to all. The young, and those attracted to the work and leisure it permits, live life as party (Shover, 1996). Use of cocaine and other illicit drugs is common among this segment of the criminal telemarketing workforce. Heavy gambling is [also] commonplace. One subject said that they "would go out to the casinos and blow two, three, four, five thousand dollars a night. That was nothing—to go spend five grand, you know, every weekend. And wake up broke!"

What we learned about the lifestyles and spending habits of criminal telemarketers differs little from what is known about street criminals and other vocational predators. It also confirms what has been learned about the relationship between easy, unearned income and profligacy. The lifestyles of telemarketers change somewhat as they get older and take on more conventional responsibilities. For older and more experienced telemarketers, the lifestyle centers around home and family and impressing others with signs of their apparent success:

> *I played some golf. [In the summer] water skiing, fishing. I'm real heavy into bass fishing, me and my dad and my brothers. Hunting. Doing things with my wife and kids. I spent a lot of time with them. Evenings, maybe just walking the golf course, or whatever. Watching the sunset.*

Another subject told us that after he moved up in the telemarketing ranks: "My partner and I played, we played a lot of golf. The office was right down from the golf course. We'd go to the golf course and play two or three times a week." Save for the unrestrained hedonism of their lives when young and neophytes at criminal telemarketing, the broad outlines of their occupational careers, particularly for those who went on to form their own businesses, resemble the work careers of more conventional citizens.

LEGITIMATION AND DEFENSE

Doocy et al. (2001) remark that the telemarketing offender they interviewed "conveyed the assured appearance of a most respectable entrepreneur" and "conveyed no hint that what he was doing might not be altogether legitimate." Our subjects are no different. Notwithstanding the fact that all were convicted felons, most reject the labels *criminal* and *crime* as fitting descriptions of them and their activities. They instead employ a range of mitigating explanations and excuses for their offences. Some former business owners told us, for example, that they set out to maintain a legitimate operation, emulated the operations of their previous employers and assumed, therefore, that their activities violated no laws. Others said they are guilty only of expanding their business so rapidly that they could not properly oversee day-to-day operations. Some said that indulgence in alcohol and illicit drugs caused them to become neglectful of or indifferent toward their businesses. Most claimed that the allure of money caused them to "look the other way." Those who owned or managed firms are prone also to blame rogue sales agents for any fraudulent or deceptive activities. As one put it: "The owners are trying to do the right thing. They're just attracting the wrong people. It's the salesmen." Another subject likewise suggested: "I guess I let the business get too big and couldn't watch over all of the agents to prevent what they were doing." For their part, sales agents charge that their owners and managers kept them in the dark about the business and its criminal nature.

Fraud offenders typically derive moral justification for their activities from the fact that their crimes cannot succeed without acquiescence or cooperation from their victims; unlike victims of burglary and robbery, those who fall prey to fraud usually are willing, if halting or confused, participants in their own victimization. Chief among the legitimating and defensive tenets of telemarketing criminals is belief that "the mooch is going to send his money to someone, so it might as well be me" (Sanger, 1999). In other words, "customers" are thought to be so greedy, ignorant, or incapable that it is only a matter of time before they throw away their money on something impossible. The tendency of fraud offenders to see their victims as deserving of what befalls them was noted by Maurer (1940) more than six decades ago, and it remains true of contemporary telemarketing criminals. One of our subjects told us, "They know what they're doing. They're bargaining for something, and when they lose, they realize that they were at fault." There is neither concern nor sympathy for them. Telemarketing criminals . . . maintain that they were not victimizing their customers but engaging in a routine sales transaction, no different than a retail establishment selling a shirt that is marked up 1,000 percent. Telemarketing fraud is therefore construed by its practitioners as perfectly in tune with mainstream commercial interactions: a "subculture of business" (Ditton, 1977).

Ensconced in their outwardly respectable and self-indulgent lifestyles, our subjects professed belief that, so far as the law was concerned, they were risking nothing more severe than a fine, an adverse civil judgment or a requirement they make restitution. They claim that the entire problem more appropriately was a "civil matter" and "should not be in criminal court." As one put it: "If you have people that are not satisfied, we would be happy to give their money back."

CONCLUSION

Traditional professional thieves [of the past] hailed from [the working class] where the young generally do not acquire the human capital requisite to success in the world of well paid and respectable work. The blue-collar skills of an industrial society, however, are not equal to the challenge of exploiting contemporary, increasingly white-collar, criminal opportunities. The post-industrial service-oriented economy instead places a premium on entrepreneurial, interpersonal, communicative, and organizational skills, and it is the children of the middle-class who are most likely to be exposed to and acquire these skills.

The knowledge and skills needed to exploit criminal opportunities vocationally and successfully do not differ greatly from those required for success in the legitimate world. Like the past professional thief, the new and increasingly white-collar vocational predators commit planned violations of the law for profit, but they do so in the style of the middle class. They take on and publicly espouse a belief system that defends against moral condemnation from outsiders, and they are dismissive of both the world of hourly employment and the lives of those confined to it. But while the professional thieves of an earlier era publicly endorsed and were expected to adhere to norms of loyalty and integrity in dealings with one another, criminal telemarketers by contrast are extremely individualistic and self-centered. . . .

Professional thieves of earlier eras found a measure of success in crime despite their humble beginnings or blue-collar roots. The lives they constructed emphasized freedom to live "life as party" by "earning and burning money," to roam without restraint, and to celebrate these achievements with others of similar perspective. The class origins of contemporary garden-variety white-collar criminals are more advantaged, but they live their lives in substantially similar fashion. [Still, unlike the professional thieves of the past, telemarketing criminals] generally do not gravitate to a criminal netherworld or a self-contained criminal fraternity. Nor do they confine their leisure pursuits to others of similar work. . . .

Detached from the underworld, contemporary professional crime has mutated into an overworld in which the bourgeoisie rather than blue-collar culture is sovereign. This helps explain why telemarketing fraudsters, unlike the professional thieves of previous generations, are likely to spend their weekends on the lake, playing golf, or having friends over for a barbeque. Still, they blow their earnings on drugs, gambling, fast living, and conspicuous consumption.

REFERENCES

Direct Marketing Association. 2001. www.the-dma.org.

Ditton, J. 1977. *Part Time Crime.* London: Macmillan.

Doocy, J., D. Shichor, D. Sechrest, and G. Geis. 2001. "Telemarketing Fraud: Who Are the Tricksters and What Makes Them Trick?" *Securities Journal*, 14:7–26.

Duffield, G., and P. Grabosky. 2001. "The Psychology of Fraud," Paper 199. Australian Institute of Criminology.

Maurer, D. W. 1940. *The Big Con.* Indianapolis: Bobbs-Merrill.

Sanger, D. 1999. "Confessions of a Phone-Scam Artist," *Saturday Night*, 114:86–98.

Shover, N. 1996. *Great Pretenders: Pursuits and Careers of Persistent Thieves.* Boulder, CO: Westview.

Taylor, I. 1999. *Crime in Context: A Critical Criminology of Market Societies.* Boulder, CO: Westview.

REVIEW QUESTIONS

1. What did the researchers discover regarding the offenders' backgrounds?
2. What other forms of deviance did criminal telemarketers engage in prior to arrest?
3. Do you believe that fraudulent telemarketing should be a civil or a criminal matter? Defend your answer.

CHAPTER 40

THE NEUTRALIZATION OF PROFESSIONAL DEVIANCE AMONG VETERINARIANS

DEANN M. KALICH

Like other professions that operate as a business enterprise, veterinary medicine is inevitably faced with some opportunities for the commission of deviance, such as the opportunity for overcharging clients or providing substandard service. Will a veterinarian take advantage of these opportunities and go ahead to commit deviance? The answer, according to Sykes and Matza (1957), is likely to be "yes" if the individuals involved are able to *neutralize* the guilt from committing the deviant act, defining deviancy away, that is, normalizing it so as to make it appear acceptable, legitimate, or proper.

According to Sykes and Matza, there are five techniques of neutralization: (1) denial of responsibility, in which the act is justified because the individual had no control over it; (2) denial of injury, in which individuals claim that no one was harmed so nothing deviant or wrong has occurred; (3) denial of the victim, in which the individual argues that whoever is harmed by the deviance deserves the harm; (4) condemnation of condemners, in which the individual claims that those who disapprove of the act are hypocrites who have done much worse; and (5) appeal to higher loyalties, in which the individual's attachments to norms other than those of the larger society hold preeminence.

Coleman (1994) added four more techniques of neutralization, which are common to the culture of white-collar crime. These include (1) denial of the necessity for the law, because the behavior is not inappropriate; (2) defense of necessity, in which economic survival is at stake; (3) claim that "everybody else is doing it" and not penalized for it; and (4) claim of entitlement, in which the individual argues that the benefit is deserved or owed.

The present study is designed to examine which of these nine techniques of neutralization can be found among veterinarians when they engage in questionable behaviors in the practice of their profession.

METHOD

Data were collected during a five-year period via ethnographic fieldwork and in-depth interviews with veterinarians and support staff in a Southern state. The central research informants included five veterinarians in three private practices in a community of about 75,000 population. All were white, ranging in age from 25 to 47.

Beyond these central sources of interview and observational data, I also spent approximately 40 hours during the first year of the project

Source: Based on the author's article, "Professional Lapses: Occupational Deviance and Neutralization Techniques in Veterinary Medical Practice," published under her former name, DeAnn K. Gauthier, in *Deviant Behavior*, vol. 22 (2001), pp. 467–490. © 2001. Reproduced by permission of Taylor & Francis, Inc., www.informaworld.com.

in observation of various clinical rotations occurring during the final year of training for the Doctor of Veterinary Medicine degree. These included rotations for a class of approximately 50 students at the Veterinary School in the Southern state, and about two to five students would serve on each rotation. The students were predominantly white, and ranged in age from 20 to 50. Additionally, in the final year of the study, I conducted a four hour in-depth interview with a former private practitioner and professor at the Veterinary School. He was in his mid-50s and white. That year, I also conducted a two hour in-depth interview with a retired 82-year-old white male veterinarian who had established a lucrative private practice for small animal medicine during the course of his career. Finally, during the second and third years of the study, I engaged in observational research on approximately 30 veterinarians and their support staff at six continuing education seminars. Most were males of various ages between 25 and 60. All were white. In this situation alone, most were unaware of my research role.

Informants were asked about various aspects of veterinarian medicine. These are questions about the unusual and unexpected occurrences in private practice, the techniques of managing unusual occurrences, their perceptions of clients and patients, their opinion on ethical dilemmas facing the veterinary practitioner, their techniques of neutralizing unethical or illegal actions in themselves or others, and so on. In addition to these guided interviews, observations took place within veterinarian school clinics, private practice clinics, and on calls to homes in the practitioner's service areas.

FINDINGS

Virtually all of the subjects indicated that they had engaged in ethically or legally questionable behaviors in the course of doing their jobs. Only one did not self-identify as a rule breaker, but as a friend and colleague to other rule breakers within the veterinary ranks. However, it might be argued that failure to report friends and colleagues for their rule breaking, or failure to cease associating with them, can be interpreted as complicity toward and approval of those behaviors.

When asked for their opinions on ethical dilemmas facing the veterinary practitioner, seven of the nine techniques of neutralization we mentioned earlier were identifiable in their responses. The two that were not present in the subjects' responses were denial of responsibility and denial of the necessity for the law. Most (about 70%) of the responses included the claim of "everybody else is doing it" and the defense of necessity.

DEFENSE OF NECESSITY

This technique was utilized in circumstances involving either (1) billing ploys or (2) substandard care. Billing ploys most commonly recognized by respondents included charging for services not rendered and overcharging for services rendered. Charging for services not rendered may occur when animals die from injury or illness prior to the performance of a planned treatment. For example:

> *A veterinarian answered a late-night emergency call for a dog that had been hit by a car. The vet tried to give care to the animal anyway. Later that evening, the dog died. After consulting with his partner, the vet decided to wait until morning to call the client. The next morning the doctor told her that her dog had "taken a turn for the worse and might not pull through." Afterwards, he explained to me, "What I'm doing is trying to prepare her for what's coming, because if I just tell her the dog is dead, she will freak out and go nuts. This way, she has a little while to get adjusted to the idea." Approximately twenty minutes had passed, when the client called back and told the doctor she wanted him to "go ahead and put it down" (indicating a desire for euthanasia services), and she would come by the clinic later that afternoon to pick up the body. The doctor said "okay," hung up the telephone, and added a charge for euthanasia to her bill. The veterinar-*

ian, when asked why he was charging to kill a dog that was already dead, invoked the defense of necessity for economic survival.

In addition to billing ploys, the defense of necessity was invoked to justify substandard care involving extraneous tests or procedures. Some veterinarians in this study admitted to occasionally charging for tests or blood work that did not take place. Generally, this occurred in cases where a client was aggressively pursuing health care for their already healthy animal. Even though they did not consider the tests necessary, the veterinarians did them anyway for financial gain. As two respondents said:

(1) We probably shouldn't encourage testing or procedures that might not be necessary, but that helps the practice make more money.

(2) Yeah, sure, we run blood tests on every animal that is spayed or neutered, because the tests may identify kidney or liver problems that could complicate the use of anesthesia, and create a higher risk of death during the spay/neuter procedure. Chances are, 99% of the dogs and cats that come in, you're not going to find anything. It's a way to make fifty extra dollars.

EVERYBODY ELSE IS DOING IT

The second main neutralization technique identified in the data is the claim that "everybody else is doing it" and getting away with it. This technique was typically utilized to account for involvement in (1) questionable distribution of drugs and (2) billing ploys concerning price-fixing. Illegal drug sales in veterinary clinics tend to involve anabolic steroids, along with other drugs. All of the respondents in this study believed illegal drug sales to be a common practice, and many admitted to having been approached by clients themselves for this purpose. Those who engaged in the practice believed they were merely going along with a pattern of accepted behavior.

In addition to questionable involvement in drug distribution, this neutralization technique was utilized to justify billing ploys concerning price-fixing. The clinics in this study were involved in illegal business agreements with other clinics in the same town and nearby communities. Periodically, an informal dinner gathering would occur, at which prices for various procedures would be discussed. Here are responses from various veterinarians:

(1) We did this in order to set a level that no one would go under so that regardless of where somebody went, we would be charging them about the same amount.

(2) Everybody does it (price-fixing).

(3) Human doctors do the same thing (price-fixing).

(4) That (price-fixing) isn't wrong. Well, I guess technically it probably is. But to us what is wrong are the veterinarians who won't "play the game," but instead charge less to undercut the rest of us.

DENIAL OF INJURY

The technique of denial of injury was used in order to justify giving substandard care. For example, many of the veterinarians have agreements with the Veterinary School to engage in supervised training of student interns. A fairly routine procedure during the training is to allow interns to practice surgical operations on live animals prior to a planned euthanasia. The veterinarians deny that anyone in this circumstance has really been hurt by the action. The animal is sedated, feels no discomfort, and will be euthanized after the procedure. They argue that this is not the same thing as human experimentation, and should be viewed differently as a result. Furthermore, the client receives the requested service and knows nothing else that may cause psychological guilt or discomfort. Finally, the student veterinarian hones his or her skills at performing a procedure under realistic conditions that soon he or she will be called upon to perform legitimately. If anything, the respondents argue, more individuals are helped by their actions while no one is hurt.

DENIAL OF THE VICTIM

This neutralization technique involves the veterinarians assuming that although they hurt their clients by providing inadequate care or charging for unperformed service, they insist that their clients get what is coming to them. They resort to this kind of neutralization primarily because their client has failed to pay the bill or treated them with disrespect. The following are illustrations from the two vets of why they engaged in denial of the victim:

> *(1) Some people don't pay their bill to us. They think: oh, they make so much money, this little bit won't make any difference. Man, does that piss me off. My partner beat up a couple of them for stuff like that.*

> *(2) I guess she thinks the world owes her something, but we don't. So sometimes we charge for the tests she wants run, but we don't run them in actuality. It just seems to me that people like that, who come in here demanding premium service like that but treating everybody with such disrespect, well, they just sort of deserve what they get . . . what we charge for and don't do.*

CLAIM OF ENTITLEMENT

This neutralization technique helped some veterinarians feel that they were entitled to whatever compensation they charged the client for their services. Such a feeling largely stemmed from the fact that veterinary medicine is not as profitable and prestigious as human medicine. They complained that they worked as hard as, if not harder than, human doctors and yet did not earn as much money. They consequently tried to make up for it by overcharging their clients:

> *(1) A lot of people think vets make a lot of money. But we don't. We make an average of $50–$60,000 a year AFTER we get established, but they think we're loaded up like human doctors, making $160,000 to START! That burns me up sometimes. So if I pad their bill a little, so what? I deserve it.*

> *(2) Listen, either my partner or I are on call for our clients 24 hours a day, 7 days a week. We work holidays. We work on our anniversaries. We work when our kids are having birthday parties. If their dog eats a Vienna sausage or a piece of aluminum foil at three in the morning, I am there for them. No matter how minor the call, I go. So if my emergency fee is high, or if I pad their bill with an unnecessary charge or two, I think I deserve it. Can you imagine what human doctors would charge for that kind of care?*

APPEAL TO HIGHER LOYALTIES

Some ethical dilemmas were resolved through an appeal to higher loyalties. In these circumstances, the veterinarians faced a dilemma that required them to violate the law in order to maintain their loyalty to a more pressing set of norms. The violation of the law often involves charging clients for services not rendered, and the loyalty to a higher norm frequently involves the refusal to kill a healthy or even a sick animal. When clients ask the veterinarians to euthanize their pet because for one reason or another they no longer want to keep it, some vets would find another family to adopt it, lie to the clients that their animal had been put to sleep, and then charge them for the nonperformance of euthanasia. The vets felt the fee justifiable for having saved the animal, which effectively expressed their loyalty to the higher norm that requires helping rather than harming animals. They felt all the more guiltless because they assumed that their clients were glad to pay the fee for they believed their pet had been euthanized. As one of the vets said, "You do services for people, or they *believe* they are getting services, you gotta play the game."

CONDEMNATION OF CONDEMNERS

This technique of neutralization involved some veterinarians condemning as hypocritical those who condemned their deviant behaviors. In this strategy, the vets shifted the focus from their own deviance to others. For example, when people complained that veterinarians charged too much, the vets blamed it on the "free riders," clients that did not pay their bills. When people complained about veterinarian care being unsatisfactory, the vets blamed it on the public for not respecting veterinarians as much as human doctors:

> *You know, human life is worth more, and all that. But just because people don't respect pets as much, by default, they don't respect vets as much either. You see that in everything we do. It's always cutting corners for the client, to save his pocketbook, but supposedly to still try and save his pet as well. Which is fine, to a point. Still, there's that unstated, implicit assumption behind it all: human medicine is first class; but vet medicine is bulk rate. Well, then, you get what you pay for, don't you?*

CONCLUSION

The primary motivation toward deviance among the veterinarians in this study was financial profit, which reflects the attitude of the larger society, in which the pressure for profit is intense. Veterinarians who commit professional deviance do not question the validity of the dominant norms of society or their profession's code of ethics. More specifically, they do not question the societal expectation that they must be honest with their clients and give their patients the best care possible. Also, they do not question the professional code that they "should consider the welfare of the patient for the purpose of relieving suffering and disability while causing minimum of pain or fright" and therefore they should ensure that "benefit to the patient should transcend personal advantage of monetary gain in decisions concerning therapy" (AVMA, 1989). But many veterinarians question the application of those idealistic norms and codes of conduct to their day-to-day practice of their profession.

They in effect fall short of those ideals largely because they are able to neutralize their professional deviance. The techniques of neutralization that encourage them to commit deviance precede their commission of the deviance, serving to make that deviance possible by reframing it as acceptable and appropriate to them. For the veterinarians in this study, the most common neutralization technique was the defense of necessity, followed by the claim that "everybody else is doing it." Why did these two techniques occur much more frequently than the other seven? Does the same pattern take place in other professions? Questions such as these are beyond the scope of the present study. Further research is needed to address them.

REFERENCES

AVMA (American Veterinary Medical Association). 1989. "Principles of Veterinary Medical Ethics (1989 Revision)." P. 24 in 1990 AVMA Directory. Schaumburg, IL: American Veterinary Medical Association.

Coleman, James William. 1994. *The Criminal Elite: The Sociology of White-Collar Crime.* New York: St. Martin's Press.

Sykes, Gresham M., and David Matza. 1957. "Techniques of Neutralization: A Theory of Delinquency." *American Sociological Review* 22: 667–670.

REVIEW QUESTIONS

1. What did some veterinarians in the study do instead of euthanizing unwanted pets?
2. Do you believe allowing student interns to practice surgical operations on animals due to be euthanized, without the consent of the owners, is acceptable? Defend your answer.
3. What are Coleman's four techniques of neutralization?

CHAPTER 41

SOCIETAL CAUSES OF POLITICAL CORRUPTION

XIAOHUI XIN
THOMAS K. RUDEL

Concern with political corruption grew during the 1990s, and members of the international development community intensified their efforts to control it. In 1996, the members of the Organization of American States (OAS) approved the Inter-American Convention Against Corruption. In 1997, the Organization for Economic Cooperation and Development (OECD) created a convention that criminalized bribery abroad by enterprises based in OECD countries. Politicians in some African states undertook a series of administrative reforms aimed at reducing the incidence of corrupt transactions in their governments. The heads of important multilateral lending institutions such as the World Bank and the Inter-American Development Bank made high-profile commitments to combat corruption in development assistance programs (Quick, 2000; Shihata, 2000).

These actions testify to the emergence of a consensus in the development community that pervasive corruption represents both an impediment to sustained economic development and a threat to newly established democratic regimes. Corruption such as government officials expecting to receive huge bribes from business people discourages investment, which in turn serves to stunt the nation's economic growth. Corruption also threatens the legitimacy of newly created democratic governments in the developing world. For these reasons controlling corruption is not an end in itself but a means for reducing its "anti-developmental effects" (Doig and McIvor, 1999).

Motivated by a desire to help reformers curb corruption, social scientists have tried for the last 30 years to understand its causes and provide guides for its control. To produce practical guides, social scientists have conducted many studies to look into the world of corruption, from which there has emerged a body of knowledge about the causes of corruption.

A THEORY OF CORRUPTION

Most recent theories about the causes of corruption have focused on government institutions that house corrupt officials. The theories assume that the organizational features of the presidency, the legislature, the public agencies, and the courts have a marked impact on whether and how often officials engage in corrupt acts. This suggests that simply removing corrupt officials from office will have little long-term effect on rates of corruption. Instead, the organization in which the officials operate must be changed, with its corruption-inducing features removed. Research has found, for example, that officials usually commit corrupt acts when their governmental agency enables

Source: Xiaohui Xin and Thomas K. Rudel, "The Context for Political Corruption: A Cross-National Analysis," *Social Science Quarterly*, vol. 85 (June 2004), pp. 294–309. Reprinted with permission of Blackwell Publishing Ltd.

them to have wide discretion in their actions, little accountability, and considerable monopoly power (Riley, 1998). To effectively curb further corruption, then, requires limiting official discretion, enhancing accountability, and increasing controls over officials.

But an exclusive focus on the immediate organizational circumstances under which officials work may cause reformers to overestimate the effectiveness of their effort to control corruption. In the aftermath of scandals, reformers may succeed in restructuring institutions and reducing the incidence of corruption, but these efforts are unlikely to have a sustained effect on corruption unless they coincide with changes in the larger society that reinforce the reforms. For example, through a concerted and deftly executed campaign during the late 1970s, Justice Efren Plana, the newly appointed head of the Philippine Bureau of Internal Revenue (BIR), dramatically reduced the incidence of corruption in the BIR. However, the larger societal conditions, particularly the continuing economic instability during the 1980s and the traditional acquisitive ethos among public officials, encouraged BIR employees to resume their corrupt practices several years later when Plana left the agency.

In order to understand more comprehensively and thus curb corruption for the long haul, we need to go beyond the immediate milieu of governmental organizations to see what conditions in their surrounding larger society cause or control corruption.

One societal cause of corruption is probably poverty because it creates strong economic incentives for inadequately paid public officials to expect and receive bribes from the citizens. Max Weber (1968) suggested that economic development was a necessary condition for the emergence of bureaucracies governed by rules and regulations that can control corruption. Moreover, only a prosperous economy can generate sufficient tax revenues for governments to pay public officials adequately on a regular basis. If a country is poor, its governments can collect few taxes and subsequently pay its public servants little. Under these circumstances, officials feel compelled to use their power to supplement their incomes through corrupt transactions. And they are able to engage in corruption because of the lack of rules and regulations for controlling corruption.

A second societal cause of corruption seems to be a large population—hence a large state and government. In huge countries it is difficult to oversee potentially corrupt officials given the inevitable problems of coordinating the numerous activities of personnel in multiple parts and levels of government, often in far-flung places. Conversely, smaller countries are easier to surveil. Singapore's small population, for example, makes its anti-corruption agency highly effective in controlling corruption. Not surprisingly, Singapore is one of the least corrupt in the world (Quah, 1989).

A third societal cause of corruption is apparently the lack of a strong modern democracy. In traditional societies the long history of obligations to kins and clans tends to have developed the patrimonial approach to public office, in which officeholders treat their official positions as a family inheritance (Weber, 1968). Ex-officials in the newly independent African nation of Ghana in the 1960s, for example, described their scandal-ridden government as "a sort of Hobbesian jungle in which illicit behavior was justified in the interests of . . . fulfillment of obligations to kinship and other primary ties" (Levine, 1989). But in a more modern society that practices democracy, widespread citizen participation in political processes tends to discourage official corruption. The citizens expect a high standard of conduct from their public officials, and they create political pressures to punish corrupt officials.

Sometimes, though, the reverse effect of democracy can occur. The increase in corrupt activities in the former Soviet-bloc countries during the early 1990s provides the most recent example of how corruption can proliferate even when governments are becoming more democratic. The transition to democracy can weaken or destroy social control, and for this reason it may increase the incidence of corruption. Controls over corruption, in particular, often disintegrate during periods of rapid social change as happened in Russia and those Eastern European countries after the collapse of their communist regimes. But once democracy is taking hold in the long run, corruption can be expected to diminish.

In short, we theorize that there are three societal causes of official corruption: poverty, a large population, and the lack of democracy.

TESTING THE THEORY

To test the theory, we can find data from various sources on the independent variables (poverty, large population, and lack of democracy) and the dependent variable (official corruption). The most important are cross-national surveys that ask people in different countries questions about their local incidence of corruption. In effect, such public opinion provides a measure of perceived corruption. Some of these surveys asked businesspeople to estimate the perceived incidence of corruption in various nations. The most interesting and useful is the survey that Transparency International (TI), a global nongovernmental organization, has been taking every year. TI has developed a cross-national index called the Corruption Perception Index (CPI), which shows which countries are more, or less, corrupt than others. TI analysts construct the index from three types of sources: surveys of international businesspeople who work in several different countries, assessments of the level of corruption by local experts who work for international business consultants, and multi-country surveys of general populations. In each survey a set of questions focuses on corruption. In the World Bank's business environment survey, the interviewer asks whether the respondent had to make "irregular additional payments to government officials." If the answer is "yes," then as a probe, the interviewer asks the respondents if they could have had the situation rectified by appealing to a higher official without paying a bribe to that official (Transparency International, 2001).

Each survey ranks countries according to the incidence of perceived corruption. The data are generally valid and reliable. The information from businesspeople, for example, is highly accurate because they have often had direct, personal experience with corruption. Different sources of data further show a high degree of agreement, between 80 and 90 percent, with expatriates and citizens, for example, typically agreeing about the incidence of corruption in a country. Such agreements suggest that the different sources are measuring the same phenomena and that an index constructed from these sources provides a reliable measure of corruption.

FINDINGS

The data indicate that the frequency of corrupt acts is generally much higher in poor nations. These findings offer empirical support for Weber's argument that economic development discourages corruption because it makes possible the emergence of rational-legal bureaucracies that can control and restrain corruption. But the lack of economic development, hence the lack of rational-legal bureaucracies, encourages corruption. The data also show that the incidence of corruption is higher in larger nations.

The data clearly demonstrate a strong and consistent relationship between poverty and large population, on the one hand, and corruption, on the other. But they show that the relationship between democracy and corruption is relatively weak. Many democratic countries such as those in Western Europe exhibit low levels of corruption. This finding suggests that democracy deters corruption. But the data also suggest the opposite: democracy encourages corruption. In Latin America, for example, the presumably more democratic countries are more corrupt than the less democratic ones. More specifically, there is more extensive corruption in the *less* interventionist or authoritarian regimes such as Paraguay and Nicaragua than in the more interventionist regimes such as Costa Rica, Uruguay, and Chile (Whitehead, 2000).

CONCLUSION

We have seen that societal factors such as the poverty of a country as a whole and the large population of a country as a whole can cause official corruption. To understand corruption, then, we should take into account these larger societal conditions, not just the immediate organizational situations such as considerable discretion, limited accountability, and other features of the agencies where officials work. Understanding both societal conditions and organizational features that are associated with corruption can suggest effective ways of dealing with the problem.

By bringing those two sets of factors into a single, comprehensive theory of corruption, researchers can see how a relatively small organization can tackle the problems of the larger society that cause corruption. Consider, for example, the huge population of a developing country as a cause of its high incidence of corruption. A major reason why a huge population can cause corruption is the lack of surveillance on public officials. Now, in a relatively large developing country that is highly corrupt, a non-governmental organization (NGO), which comprises newly affluent, well-educated, and articulate citizens, can help reduce official corruption throughout the whole country.

In 1991–1992, for instance, a coalition of NGOs in Brazil successfully mounted a campaign to oust the country's president for massive corruption. They did so by articulating the public's discontent, mobilizing the masses for demonstrations, and pressuring congress members to impeach the president, which eventually caused him to resign. As a result, government officials throughout the country became less corrupt (Mische, 1998).

The effects of democratic reforms and democracy itself on the prevalence of corruption remain ambiguous, however. They, and possibly other societal factors, are in need of further research.

REFERENCES

Doig, A., and S. McIvor. 1999. "Corruption and Its Control in the Developmental Context: An Analysis and Selective Review of the Literature." *Third World Quarterly* 20:657–676.

Levine, Victor. 1989. "Supportive Values of the Culture of Corruption in Ghana." Pp. 363–373 in Arnold Heidenheimer et al., eds., *Political Corruption: A Handbook.* New Brunswick, NJ: Transaction Books.

Mische, Ann. 1998. Projecting Democracy: Contexts and Dynamics of Youth Activism in the Brazilian Impeachment Movement. Doctoral Dissertation, New School for Social Research.

Quah, Jon S. T. 1989. "Singapore's Experience in Curbing Corruption." Pp. 841–853 in Arnold Heidenheimer et al., eds., *Political Corruption: A Handbook.* New Brunswick, NJ: Transaction Books.

Quick, Stephen. 2000. "Inter-American Development Bank Initiatives Against Corruption." Pp. 214–218 in Joseph Tulchin and R. H. Espach, eds., *Combating Corruption in Latin America.* Washington, DC: Woodrow Wilson Center Press.

Riley, Stephen P. 1998. "The Political Economy of Anti-Corruption Strategies in Africa." Pp. 129–159 in Mark Robinson, ed., *Corruption and Development.* London: Frank Cass.

Shihata, Ibrahim F. I. 2000. "The Role of the World Bank in Combating Corruption." Pp. 205–209 in Joseph Tulchin and R. Espach, eds., *Combating Corruption in Latin America.* Washington, DC: Woodrow Wilson Center Press.

Transparency International. 2001. Global Corruption Report 2001. Available at http://www.transparency.org.

Weber, Max. 1968. *Economy and Society.* New York: Bedminister Press.

Whitehead, Laurence. 2000. "High-Level Political Corruption in Latin America: A Transitional Phenomenon?" Pp. 107–129 in J. S. Tulchin and R. H. Espach, eds., *Combating Corruption in Latin America.* Washington, DC: Woodrow Wilson Center Press.

REVIEW QUESTIONS

1. According to this article, what are the three possible societal causes of corruption?
2. How do NGOs affect corruption?
3. How accurate do you believe the Corruption Percentage Index is? Defend your answer.

CHAPTER 42

ENRON: ORGANIZATIONAL RITUALS AS DEVIANCE

JASON S. ULSPERGER
J. DAVID KNOTTNERUS

Enron filed for bankruptcy on December 2, 2001. Soon after, 4,000 workers were fired. The company shocked many employees by using voice mail to fire them. Low-level employees were even more shocked when an investigation found that executives, knowing that the Enron stock's price would plunge, had quickly sold their shares at huge profits. Executives and board members prospered enormously while the Enron stock fell like a rock. When the company filed for bankruptcy, its stock price that had once traded as high as $90 per share was trading at only $4. Having invested in the stock with the encouragement of company executives, many employees lost their entire life savings (Bryce, 2002; Fusaro and Miller, 2002; Sloan et al., 2002).

The U.S. Justice Department launched an investigation on January 9, 2002. It focused on the top management in order to dig out individual decisions that might have led to the scandal (Fusaro and Miller, 2002). To understand deviance in corporations such as Enron, however, we should look beyond the actions of just a few individuals, no matter how important and powerful they are. In this article, we will see how those individual actions reflect the nature of the organization that made Enron one of the most corrupt corporations in recent U.S. history.

ORGANIZATIONAL CULTURE AND RITUALS

When a corporation departs from social standards of behavior and engages in deviant activities, the culprit can be found in its organizational culture. The culture consists of the beliefs held by members of the organization that sets it apart from other organizations. The organizational culture of Enron, for example, was the belief that its members must make the corporation prosper by maximizing its profits and expansion in certain ways. This belief was put into action often enough for it to become a ritual of the organization (Knottnerus, 1997). An organizational ritual is basically a repeated set of actions taken for granted by everybody in the organization as normal and proper because the actions reflect the belief that the members have acquired from the organization. Analysis of books, employee documents, government reports, and news media about Enron suggests that deviance lay at the core of the corporation's culture and rituals.

RITUALIZED DEVIANCE AT ENRON

Within Enron were three organization rituals centering on deceit, self-gain, and allegorical depictions. The ritual of deceit involved fraudulent behavior such as cheating on balance sheets,

Source: Written specifically for this reader.

misrepresenting one's self, and providing false information about the company. The ritual of self-gain included actions driven by a desire for immediate gratification from attaining economic or nonmaterial goals such as money or sex. And the ritual of allegorical depiction involved using the characters and imageries from science fiction movies to depict the company and its employees.

The Ritual of Deceit

The ritual of deceit refers to the routine, common practice of concealing or perverting the truth for the purpose of misleading others. This ritual can best be seen from what *The Washington Post* (2002) wrote about how Enron deceived the public by covering up the risk it took that could bankrupt the company:

> *... [I]t seemed likely that Enron had taken too much risk; that it had hidden this risk from shareholders by parking it in secret partnerships; and that senior executives had urged investors to buy stock even when they themselves were selling out.... Enron's executives apparently used the secret partnerships not just to hide risk but also to steal money.... The small group of financiers and insiders that invested in the partnerships reaped returns higher than ordinary shareholders could dream of; one deal paid out 212 percent in just over three months.... The money belonged to Enron's shareholders. They were robbed.*

It may appear from this quote that just a few executives and their friends swindled the investing public. This was not the case, however. The acceptance of deceit ran so deep that the Enron Board of Directors simply disregarded their own company's code of ethics. Turning a blind eye to conflicts of interest, they allowed or encouraged their employees to conduct fraudulent transactions with companies that appeared separate from and independent of Enron but that were actually owned and operated by other Enron employees. One such satellite company was Chewco Investments (Bryce, 2002; Schmidt and Behr, 2002).

In setting up Chewco, Enron's executives and board directors purposely broke two of the company's own Code of Conduct of Business Affairs rules. First, they waived the requirement that they hire someone who is not associated with Enron as the head of Chewco. Instead, they hired an Enron employee, Michael Kopper. Second, they did not acquire enough equity from outside investors to make Chewco an independent company, with the result that Chewco was saddled with an enormous debt transferred from Enron (Fusaro and Miller, 2002). Enron set up many phony companies like Chewco this way in order to dupe shareholders and the public at large into thinking that Enron was an incredibly successful corporation with huge assets and earnings and hardly any debt.

With the top executives, board members, and high-level management setting the moral (or immoral) tone by regularly engaging in deceitful activities, lower-level employees knowingly participated in rituals of deceit as well. They virtually took for granted that it was normal for everybody at Enron to practice deceit. In fact, they seemed to feel that if they wanted to be loyal employees they must be deceitful on behalf of their company. This shows through the common use of the expression "Crooked E" at Enron.

Enron's logo was a bold letter "E" slightly tilted to the side. This logo was known to the employees as the "Crooked E." It thus served to remind the employees that their job was to misrepresent themselves and their company to the clients and the general public, as can be seen from the following description of a new employee's first day at work (Cruver, 2002):

> *I relaxed at my new desk for about half a second when the phone rang. "Cruver! Welcome to the Crooked E!" It was a friend from business school who was calling from fifteen floors above.... The Crooked E? It was true: the Enron logo was the letter E tilted at forty-five degrees, though the tilt was not exactly what he was referring to. That was the first time I had heard the expression, and it made me laugh....*

The Ritual of Self-Gain

The ritual of self-gain at Enron typically appeared in the form of the company showering employees with extremely generous compensations. The employees could expect to receive bonuses that reached as high as 100 percent of a salary, while enjoying a cornucopia of perks, as the following indicates (Barrionuevo, 2001):

> *. . . [T]here were perks: the in-house health club and doctor's office, as well as laundry and car-washing services. Broadband traders say they were issued Palm Pilots and wireless laptops, and the group spent huge sums traveling the globe in search of customers. Top traders and executives went on junkets to the Bahamas, spent hunting weekends in Mexico and accompanied former chief executive officer Jeff Skilling glacier hiking in Patagonia or Land Cruiser racing in Australia. . . . Some downtown nightclubs waived cover charges for Enron employees.*

The ritual of self-gain at Enron involved more than material gain. It also often involved sexual benefits. According to a Wall Street analyst who had covered Enron for years, sexual shenanigans were an important part of its culture (Bryce, 2002). Many employees, for example, frequented strip clubs and strippers. As Raghavan, Kranhold, and Barrionuevo (2002) observe:

> *Sometimes, employees celebrated their deal or trading wins by heading off to a local strip club. Brittany L. Lucas, a dancer at a club called Treasures, recalls a group of about eight Enron men striding in last Summer and announcing they had $10,000 to celebrate with. "Enron guys were known for spending big money and letting you know they worked there," says Ms. Lucas, who says she made $1,200 for herself that weekday afternoon, her best day ever.*

Enron's employees enjoyed the strippers so often and so much that some of the latter became employees at the company themselves.

The Ritual of Allegorical Depictions

The ritual of allegorical depictions involves using some fictional story and characters, such as a science fiction movie and its characters, to represent a real event and people, such as Enron and its employees. Such rituals usually took place on special occasions at Enron. For one sales event, for example, a video was made to feature Ken Lay, Enron's chairman, as Captain Kirk from the Star Trek television series. Lay was shown piloting the Starship Enterprise as if it were Enron, which revealed, among other things, China's Red Square full of Enron logos. The video was obviously meant to brag about a bogus point about Enron, namely, its "successful" quest to expand its power into every corner of the universe. To make this falsehood convincing,

> *The 10-minute tape—made after a time when Enron's stock price was soaring and the company was lauded by many as the nation's most innovative firm—takes the form of a mock segment from ABC's "20/20" newsmagazine. In it, voices impersonating Barbara Walters and Hugh Downs, dubbed over their images, recount how in the year 2020 Enron was elected "the world's first global governing body." A voice impersonating ABC correspondent Sam Donaldson says, there "isn't a person who is alive today who doesn't know and revere Enron" (Friedland, 2002).*

CONCLUSION

Understanding deviance at Enron should not be limited to the actions of a handful of people at the top of the organization. Though government investigators will continue to focus on the shady practices of the chief executive officers at Enron, they may be missing the critical point about the more powerful source of corporate deviance. All members of a corporation, in participating in deviant practices, contribute to the acceptance of questionable behavior. In the case of Enron, those deviant acts appeared in the forms of deceit, self-gain, and allegorical depictions. They took place so frequently that they became part of the corporation's deviant culture. As such, the employees generally regarded those deviant activities as normal, not as deviant at all.

Organizational deviance will continue to be important to address. Consider that Enron is not the only for-profit organization involved in questionable practices over the last few years. Investigations of corrupt practices continue for corporations such as Tyco and WorldCom. As organizations such as these continue to dominate the economic landscape, unethical practices in them will surely continue.

REFERENCES

Barrionuevo, Alexei. 2001. "Your Career Matters: Jobless in a Flash, Enron's Ex-Employees Are Stunned, Bitter, Ashamed." *The Wall Street Journal*, December 11, p. B1.

Bryce, Robert. 2002. *Pipe Dreams: Greed, Ego, and the Death of Enron.* New York: Public Affairs.

Cruver, Brian. 2002. *Anatomy of Greed: The Unshredded Truth from an Enron Insider.* New York: Carroll & Graf Publishers.

Friedland, Jonathan. 2002. "Questioning the Books: In Spoof Video, Former CEO Steers Enron to Places No Firm Has Gone Before." *The Wall Street Journal*, February 4, p. A8.

Fusaro, Peter C., and Ross M. Miller. 2002. *What Went Wrong at Enron.* Hoboken, NJ: John Wiley & Sons, Inc.

Knottnerus, J. David. 1997. "The Theory of Structural Ritualization", pp. 257–79 in *Advances in Group Processes*, 14, edited by Barry Markovsky, Michael J. Lovaglia, and Lisa Troyer. Greenwich, CT: JAI Press.

Raghavan, Anita, Kathryn Kranhold, and Alexei Barrionuevo. 2002. "Full Speed Ahead: How Enron Bosses Created a Culture of Pushing Limits—Fastow and Others Challenged Staff, Badgered Bankers; Porsches, Ferraris Were Big—A Chart 'to Intimidate People.' " *The Wall Street Journal*, August 26, p. A1.

Schmidt, Susan, and Peter Behr. 2002. "Enron Lawyer Says Company Ignored Alarm; Documents Show He Warned Firm About Deals Last May." *The Washington Post*, February 7, p. A1.

Sloan, Allan, et al. 2002. "Who Killed Enron; It's the Scariest type of Scandal: a Total System Failure." *Newsweek*, January 21, p. 18.

Washington Post. 2002. "A Deliberate Scandal." January 27, p. B6.

REVIEW QUESTIONS

1. What is an "organizational ritual"?
2. Identify the three organizational rituals performed by Enron that are mentioned in the article.
3. What type of punishment do you believe is suitable for the crimes committed by the executives and board members of Enron? Explain.

PART TWELVE

UNDERPRIVILEGED DEVIANCE

The street gangs of Central America have spun a web of robberies and killings through Guatemala, El Salvador, Honduras, and even the United States. They are estimated to have as many as 100,000 members, of which about 40 percent are young women. Benky used to be one of these women. Having lived on the streets since she was six years old, she decided to join one of these gangs at the age of 14. To do so, she had to have sex with a dozen or so of her homeboys. She recalls sobbing when the last young man climbed off her. After thus becoming a full-fledged member of the gang, she always did what its leader told her to do, such as robbing buses and killing rival gangs' members.[1]

Benky, along with other gang members, can be said to engage in underprivileged deviance, deviance that typically occurs among underprivileged people, who come from relatively poor and powerless backgrounds. Underprivileged deviance is generally distinguishable from privileged deviance in being less profitable. Here we take a look at various forms of underprivileged deviance. In the first article, "Shoplifters: 'The Devil Made Me Do It,' " Paul Cromwell and Quint Thurman show with research data how shoplifters try to neutralize their deviant behavior with some rationalization or justification. In the second article, "Burglary: The Offender's Perspective," Paul Cromwell reports from his study of thirty burglars how they choose targets, what makes a vulnerable target, and some burglary prevention strategies. In the third reading, "The Immediate Experiences of Carjacking," Bruce Jacobs and his colleagues present what carjackers feel and experience at the moment when they are committing the crime. In the fourth selection, "The Good Thing About Workplace Deviance," Elizabeth Hoffmann finds how cab drivers purposely violate company rules to address problems and concerns that management cannot deal with.

[1]Marc Lacey, "Abuse Trails Central American Girls Into Gangs," *New York Times*, April 11, 2008, p. A1.

CHAPTER 43

SHOPLIFTERS: "THE DEVIL MADE ME DO IT"

PAUL CROMWELL
QUINT THURMAN

A 30-year-old male shoplifter: "You know that cartoon where the guy has a little devil sitting on one shoulder and a little angel on the other? And one is telling him "Go ahead on, do it," and the angel is saying 'No, don't do it.' You know? . . . Sometimes when I'm thinking about boosting something, my angel don't show up."

By blaming the devil for his shoplifting, the man is in effect saying that he is not responsible for his crime. He is, in other words, trying to neutralize, minimize, or expunge the guilt of committing the crime. Nearly five decades ago Gresham Sykes and David Matza (1957) introduced this idea of neutralization to explain juvenile delinquency. Their neutralization theory is an elaboration of Edwin Sutherland's proposition that individuals can learn to become criminal by developing, among other things, the "motives, drives, rationalizations, and attitudes favorable to violations of the law." Sykes and Matza theorized that if people can neutralize their guilt for their deviance with these rationalizations or justifications, such as blaming the devil rather than themselves for shoplifting, then they are likely to engage in deviant activities.

But since Sykes and Matza introduced this theory, there has developed a controversy over their contention that deviants must engage in neutralization *before* committing a deviant act. Some researchers have found that the neutralization usually occurs *after* the deviant act (Minor, 1981; Pogrebin, Poole, and Martinez, 1992). Unfortunately, our research here could not confirm or refute Sykes and Matza's theory that pre-deviance neutralizations cause deviant behavior. The reason is that the people we studied had already committed an offense so that if they engaged in neutralization they obviously did so after rather than before the offense was committed. But our research was able to find out if shoplifters tried to neutralize their offenses and how they went about doing it.

Sykes and Matza (1957) identified five techniques of neutralization commonly offered to justify deviant behavior. They are denial of responsibility, denial of injury, denial of the victim, condemning the condemners, and appeal to higher loyalties. Other, more recent researchers have identified five additional neutralization techniques. These include defense of necessity, metaphor of the ledger, denial of the necessity of the law, the claim that everybody else is doing it, and the claim of entitlement (Klockars, 1974; Minor, 1981; Coleman, 1994). Our research was intended to determine which of those techniques of neutralizations were popular with the adult shoplifters that we studied.

Source: Paul Cromwell and Quint Thurman, " 'The Devil Made Me Do It': Use of Neutralizations by Shoplifters," *Deviant Behavior*, vol. 24 (2003), pp. 535–550.

METHODS

In 1997 and 1998 in Wichita, Kansas, we obtained access to a court-ordered diversion program for adult "first-offenders" charged with theft. Of these offenders, the majority were charged with misdemeanor shoplifting and required to attend an eight-hour therapeutic and education program as a condition for having their record expunged. A new group met each Saturday. The average group had 18 to 20 participants. The participants were encouraged by the program facilitator to discuss with the group the offense that brought them to the diversion program, why they did what they did, and how they felt about it. They were then engaged in a series of educational exercises and role playing activities. We participated in the sessions as observers, recording their stories and experiences and occasionally asking questions. The participants were told that we were researchers studying shoplifting. At the conclusion of each daily session, we approached attendees and asked them if we could interview them. We obtained interviews with 137 subjects from approximately 350 that we approached.

Out of the 137 subjects were 88 men and 49 women. As for their racial backgrounds, 78 were white, 42 African American, and 17 Hispanic. The average age of these people was 26. Although the diversion program was designed for first offenders, over one-half of the participants had been apprehended for shoplifting in the past. Subjects were promised anonymity and were administered a semi-structured, open-ended questionnaire regarding their first shoplifting experiences, arrest or apprehension history, the role of co-offenders in the initial and subsequent shoplifting, reasons for shoplifting, emotional responses about the act and aftermath, attitude toward the victim, and their reasons and justifications for shoplifting. To test their commitment to conventional values, informants were specifically asked the question, "How do you feel about stealing from stores?" And, "Do you think that shoplifting is morally wrong?" Where appropriate, we probed and sought clarification and further information. Extensive field notes were kept and verbatim quotes were recorded whenever possible.

FINDINGS

Nearly all of the subjects tried to neutralize their crime with some rationalization or justification. They presented a total of nine different neutralizations. Only five of the 137 informants failed to engage in neutralization. When asked how they felt about their illegal behavior, three of these subjects responded by admitting their guilt and expressing remorse, while the other two simply stated that they had nothing to say on that issue. As for the other majority of the subjects, many offered more than one neutralization for the same offense. One female respondent, for example, said, "I don't know what comes over me. It's like, you know, is somebody else doing it, not me [Denial of Responsibility]. I'm really a good person. I wouldn't ever do something like that, stealing, you know, but I have to take things sometimes for my kids. They need stuff and I don't have any money to get it [Defense of Necessity]." They frequently responded with a motivation ("I wanted the item and could not afford it") followed by a neutralization ("Stores charge too much for stuff. They could sell things for half what they do and still make a profit. They're just too greedy"). Thus, in many cases, the motivation was linked to an excuse in such a way as to make the excuse a part of the motivation. The subjects were in effect explaining why they did the crime while justifying it at the same time. The following are examples of the nine neutralizations that our informants used when asked how they felt about their shoplifting.

Denial of Responsibility ("I didn't mean it")

Denial of responsibility frees the subjects from experiencing culpability for deviance by allowing them to perceive themselves as victims of their environment. They see themselves as being acted upon rather than acting. They thus attribute their deviant behavior to poor parenting, bad companions, some uncontrollable impulses within them, drug use, or drunkenness. Sykes and Matza (1957) describe the individual resorting to this neutralization as having a "billiard ball conception of himself in which he see himself as helplessly propelled into new situations."

26-year-old female: "I admit that I lift. I do. But, you know, it's not really me—I mean, I don't believe in stealing. I'm a church-going person. It's just that sometimes something takes over me and I can't seem to not do it."

22-year-old female: "I wasn't raised right. You know what I mean? Wasn't nobody to teach me right from wrong. I just ran with a bad group and my mamma didn't ever say nothin' about it. That's how I turned out this way—stealin' and stuff."

20-year-old male: "If it wasn't for the bunch I ran with at school I never would have started taking things. We used to go the mall after school and everybody would have to steal something. If you didn't get anything, everybody called you names—chicken-shit and stuff like that."

Denial of Injury ("I didn't really hurt anybody")

Denial of injury allows the offenders to regard their behavior as having no harmful consequences to the victim. The victim such as a large store, insurance company, or wealthy person may be seen as easily able to afford the loss. Sometimes the crime is semantically recast, referred to in terms that make the offense trivial, such as when auto theft is called joyriding, or vandalism a prank.

19-year-old male: "The stores are big. Make lotsa money. They don't even miss the little bit I get."

28-year-old male: "They write it off their taxes. Probably make a profit off it. So, nobody gets hurt. I get what I need and they come out O.K. too."

20-year-old male: "Them stores make billions. Did you ever hear of Sears going out of business from boosters?"

Denial of the Victim ("They had it coming")

Denial of the victim facilitates deviance when it can be justified as retaliation upon a deserving victim. In the present study, informants frequently reported that the large stores from which they stole deserved to be victimized because they were believed to be charging high prices and making excessive profits at the expense of ordinary people.

48-year-old female: "Stores deserve it. It don't matter if I boost $10,000 from one, they've made 10,000 times that much ripping off people. You could never steal enough to get even. . . . I don't really think I'm doing anything wrong. Just getting my share."

29-year-old female: "Dillons [food store chain] are totally bogus. A little plastic bag of groceries is $30, $25. Probably cost them $5. . . . Whatta they care about me? Why should I care about them? I take what I want. Don't feel guilty a bit. No sir. Not a bit."

49-year-old female: "I have a lot of anger about stores and the way they rip people off. Sometimes I think the consumer has to take things into their own hands."

Condemning the Condemners ("The system is corrupt")

Condemning the condemners projects blame on law-makers and law-enforcers. It shifts the focus from the offender to those who disapprove of the criminal acts. This neutralization views the "system" as crooked and thus unable to justify making and enforcing rules it does not itself live by. Those who condemn the offender's behavior are viewed as hypocritical since many of them are believed to engage in deviant behavior themselves.

18-year-old male: "I've heard of cops and lawyers and judges and all kind of rich dudes boosting. They no better than me. You know what I'm saying."

35-year-old female: "Big stores like J. C. Penney's—when they catch me with something—like two pairs of pants, they tell the police you had like 5 pairs of pants and 2 shirts or something like that. . . . What they do with the other 3 pairs of pants and shirts? Insurance company pays them off and they get richer—they's bigger crooks than me."

22-year-old male: "They thieves too. Just take it a different way. They may be smarter than me—use a computer or something like that—but they just as much a thief as me. Fuck 'em. Cops too. They all thieves. Least, I'm honest about it."

Appeal to Higher Loyalties ("I didn't do it for myself")

Appeal to higher loyalties is called upon to legitimize a deviant act when the act is carried out to serve a nonselfish, noble purpose, such as meeting the demands of one's friends or taking care of the welfare of one's children.

17-year-old female: "I never do it 'cept when I'm with my friends. Everybody be taking stuff and so I do too. You know—to be part of the group. Not to seem like I'm too good for 'em."

28-year-old female: "I like to get nice stuff for my kids, you know. I know it's not O.K., you know what I mean? But, I want my kids to dress nice and stuff."

The Defense of Necessity ("I gotta do this")

The defense of necessity involves reducing guilt with the argument that the offender had no choice under the circumstances but to engage in a deviant act (Coleman, 1998). In the case of shoplifting, the defense of necessity is most often used when the offender considers the crime necessary to help the offender's family. The situation here may be similar to the appeal to higher loyalties except that it may also involve committing deviance for one's own needs such as when the person is suffering from hunger or starvation because of job loss. In other words, the appeal to higher loyalties calls for meeting only other-centered needs, but the defense of necessity encompasses either other-centered needs or self-centered needs or both.

32-year-old female: "I had to take care of three children without help. I'd be willing to steal it to given them what they wanted."

42-year-old male: "I got laid off at Boeing last year and got behind on all my bills and couldn't get credit anywhere. My kids needed school clothes and money for supplies and stuff. We didn't have anything and I don't believe in going on welfare, you know. The first time I took some lunch meat at Dillons (grocery chain) so we'd have supper one night. After that I just started to take whatever we needed that day. I knew it was wrong, but I just didn't have any other choice. My family comes first."

It's So Common ("Everybody does it")

Here the deviants try to neutralize their guilt feelings by reminding themselves that their deviant behavior is extremely common (Coleman, 1998). They apparently assume that if everybody does it and they themselves do not, they will feel like a sucker or a fool.

19-year-old female: "Everybody I know do it. All my friends. My mother and her boyfriend are boosters and my sister is a big-time booster."

17-year-old male: "All my friends do it. When I'm with them it seems crazy not to take something too."

35-year-old female: "I bet you done did it too . . . when you was coming up. Like 12–13 years old. Everybody boosts."

Justification by Comparison ("If I didn't do this, I'd be doing something worse")

We found this "new" neutralization only in our research, not in other sociologists' studies. This particular neutralization involves offenders justifying their actions by comparing their crimes to more serious offenses. With this neutralization, the offenders in effect argue that "I may be bad, but I could be worse."

40-year-old male: "I gotta have $200 every day—day in and day out. I gotta boost a thousand, fifteen hundred dollars worth to get it. I just *do what I gotta do. . . . Do I feel bad about what I do? Not really. If I wasn't boosting, I'd be robbing people and maybe somebody would get hurt or killed."*

37-year-old male: "Looka here. Shoplifting be a little thing. Not a crime really. I do it 'stead of robbing folks or breaking in they house. [Society] oughta be glad I boost, stead of them other things."

19-year-old male: "It's no thing. Not like its 'jacking' people or something. Its just a little lifting."

Postponement ("I'd think about it later")

Here is another neutralization we found in this research only. With this neutralization, the offenders refrain from thinking about the crime that they are going to commit or the crime that they have just committed. Instead, they say that they would deal with it later.

18-year-old male: "I just don't think about it. I mean, if you think about it, it seems wrong, but you can ignore that feeling sometimes. Put it aside and go on about what you gotta do."

18-year-old male: "Dude, I just don't deal with those kinda things when I'm boosting. I might feel bad about it later, you know, but by then it's already over and I can't do anything about it then, you know?"

30-year-old female: "I worry about things like that later."

CONCLUSION

We found widespread use of neutralizations among the shoplifters in our study. We even discovered two neutralizations that had not appeared in any other studies. These two rationalizations are Postponement and Justification by Comparison. But our research method could not resolve the complex issue of whether our informants neutralized *before* committing the crime. If our subjects did so, it could be used to support the conclusion that pre-crime neutralizations may cause criminal behavior. However, what we found was only the rationalizations our subjects offered *after* they had shoplifted. Neither have other researchers been able to find if pre-deviance neutralizations cause deviant behavior.

REFERENCES

Coleman, James W. 1998. *Criminal Elite: Understanding White Collar Crime.* New York: St. Martin's Press.

Klockars, Carl B. 1974. *The Professional Fence.* New York: Free Press.

Minor, William W. 1981. "Techniques of Neutralization: A Reconceptualization and Empirical Examination." *Journal of Research in Crime and Delinquency* (July):295–318.

Pogrebin, M., E. Poole, and A. Martinez. 1992 "Accounts of Professional Misdeeds: The Sexual Exploitation of Clients by Psychotherapists." *Deviant Behavior* 13:229–252.

Sykes, Gresham M., and David Matza. 1957. "Techniques of Neutralization: A Theory of Delinquency." *American Sociological Review* 22(6): 664–670.

REVIEW QUESTIONS

1. What are the five techniques of neutralization, according to Sykes and Matza?
2. What is "justification by comparison"?
3. Do you believe that postponement can be used with other crimes? Support your answer.

CHAPTER 44

BURGLARY: THE OFFENDER'S PERSPECTIVE

PAUL CROMWELL

Burglary is easy, man. I've done about 500 [burglaries] and only been convicted one time.
—Billy, a juvenile burglar

Why am I a burglar? It's easy money. . . . Beats working!
—Robert, a 20-year-old burglar

These burglars are essentially correct in their appraisal of the benefits and risks associated with burglary. Burglary constitutes one of the most prevalent predatory crimes, with an estimated 5.1 million burglary offenses committed in 1990, resulting in monetary losses estimated to be more than $3.4 billion annually. Yet only about one-half of all burglaries are even reported to the police (Bureau of Justice Statistics, 1991). More alarming still, U.S. Department of Justice statistics reveal that less than 15 percent of all reported burglaries are cleared by arrest. Consequently, burglary has been the subject of a great deal of research in the hope that understanding will lead to the development of effective prevention measures and ultimately to reduction in the incidence of burglary (Lynch, 1990).

THEORETICAL PERSPECTIVE

Here I will report findings from a study of burglars and burglary as seen through the perspective of the offenders themselves. The study addresses several issues critical to the understanding of burglary and to the consequent development of burglary prevention and control strategies. Among these are: (1) How do residential burglars choose targets? and (2) What determines a burglar's perception of a particular site as a vulnerable target?

Such issues are based on the theory that the commission of a crime is primarily a product of opportunity. Thus, how burglars choose targets and make other relevant decisions has much to do with the opportunity for carrying out burglary. In fact, several researchers have concluded that the majority of burglaries result from exploitation of opportunity rather than careful, rational planning (Scarr, 1973; Rengert and Wasilchick, 1985, 1989; Cromwell, Olson, and Avary, 1991). The assumptions are that offenders develop a sensitivity to the opportunities in everyday life for illicit gain and that burglars see criminal opportunity in situations where others might not. This "alert opportunism" (Shover, 1971) allows them to rapidly

Source: Written specifically for this reader, with portions drawn from *Breaking and Entering: An Ethnographic Analysis of Burglary* (Newbury Park, CA: Sage, 1991) by Paul Cromwell, James N. Olson, and D'Aunn W. Avary. Reprinted by permission.

recognize and take advantage of potential criminal opportunities. Their unique perspective toward the world results from learning experiences that have sensitized them to events ignored by most. Just as an architect looking at a house notes its functional, technological, and aesthetic qualities, burglars perceive it in terms of its vulnerability to break-in and potential for gain. They do not simply see an open window, but the chance for covert entry and a "fast buck." These perceptual processes are almost automatic and are as much a part of the tools of the burglar as a pry bar or a window jimmy.

METHOD

The Sample

Thirty active burglars in an urban area of 250,000 population in a southwestern state were recruited as research subjects (hereinafter referred to as *informants*) using a snowball sampling procedure. They were promised complete anonymity and a "referral fee" of $50 for each active burglar referred by them and accepted for the study. They were also paid a stipend of $50 for each interview session. The initial three informants were introduced to the researchers by police burglary detectives who had been asked to recommend "burglars who would be candid and cooperate with the study."

The final sample consisted of 27 men and 3 women, of whom 10 were White, 9 Hispanic, and 11 African American. The mean age of these informants was 25 years with the range 16 to 43.

Procedure

The procedure consisted of extensive interviews and "ride alongs," during which informants were asked to reconstruct burglaries they had previously committed and to evaluate sites burglarized by other informants in the study. During these sessions, previously burglarized residences were visited, evaluated, and rated on their attractiveness as burglary targets. Informants were also asked to select sites in the same neighborhood that they considered too risky as targets and to explain why they were less vulnerable than those previously burglarized. At each site informants were asked to rate the "hypothetical" vulnerability of the site to burglary on a scale of 0 to 10. A rating of "0" meant "Under the circumstances that are present now, I would not burglarize this residence." A rating of "10" meant "This is a very attractive and vulnerable target and I would definitely take steps to burglarize it right now." Informants were told that a rating of "5" was an "average" score. At the conclusion of the study, informants had participated in as many as nine sessions and had evaluated up to thirty previously burglarized and high-risk sites. Four hundred sixty previously burglarized and high-risk sites were evaluated. Each session was tape recorded and verbatim transcripts were made.

FINDINGS

Motivation

Almost every informant used some of his or her proceeds from burglary to buy food or clothing and to pay for shelter, transportation, and other licit needs. However, the greatest percentage of proceeds went toward the purchase of drugs and alcohol and for the activity the burglars loosely labeled "partying." In fact, most informants stressed their need for money to fulfill these needs as the primary motivation for their burglaries. Only one informant reported a primary need for money to purchase something other than alcohol or drugs or for partying.

Second in importance was the need for money to maintain a "fast, expensive life." Keeping up appearances was stressed by many as a critical concern. One young burglar reported:

> *The ladies, they like a dude that's got good clothes. You gotta look good and you gotta have bread. Me, I'm always looking good.*

Katz (1988) has noted that young people may find certain property crimes (joyriding, vandalism, burglary, shoplifting) appealing, independent of material gain or esteem from peers.

He categorized these as "sneaky crimes that frequently thrill their practioneers." Similarly, in the present study, almost every informant mentioned excitement and thrills; however, only a few would commit a burglary for that purpose only. Like Reppetto (1974), we concluded that the younger, less experienced burglars were more prone to commit crimes for the thrill and excitement.

Time of Burglary

Rengert and Wasilchick (1985, 1989) found that burglars work during periods when residences are left unguarded. We found the same thing. Our informants stated they preferred to work between 9:00 and 11:00 A.M. and in mid-afternoon. Most organized their working hours around school hours, particularly during the times when parents (usually mothers) took children to school and picked them up after school. Several told us that they waited "until the wife left to take the kids to school or to go shopping." Most stated that they did not do burglaries on Saturday because most people were home then. Only a small number ($n = 3$) of burglars in our study committed burglaries at night. Most preferred to commit their crimes during hours when they expected people to be at work and out of the home. Those who did nighttime burglary usually knew the victims and their schedules or took advantage of people being away from home in the evening.

Inside Information

Burglars often work with "inside men" who have access to potential targets and advise the burglar about things to steal. They may also provide such critical information as times when the owner is away and of weaknesses in security. One female burglar reported that she maintained close contact with several women who worked as maids in affluent sections of the community. She would gain the necessary information from these women and later come back and break into the house, often entering by a door or window left open for her by the accomplice. Others gained information from friends and acquaintances who unwittingly revealed information about potential burglary targets. One told us:

> *I have friends who mow yards for people and work as maids and stuff. When they talk about the people they work for, I keep my ears open. They give me information without knowing it.*

Information about potential targets is frequently gained from "fences." Because many fences have legitimate occupations, they may have knowledge of the existence of valuable property from social or business relationships. They can often provide the burglar with information about the owners' schedules and the security arrangements at the target site.

People involved in a variety of service jobs (repair, carpet cleaning, pizza delivery, lawn maintenance, plumbing, carpentry) enter many homes each day and have the opportunity to assess the quality of potential stolen merchandise and security measures taken by the residents. Burglars will often establish contact with employees of these businesses for purposes of obtaining this "inside" information. One informant said:

> *I know this guy who works for [carpet cleaning business]. He sometimes gives me information on a good place to hit and I split with him.*

Occupancy Probes

Almost all burglars avoid selecting houses that are occupied as targets. Only two informants stated that they would enter a residence they knew was occupied. Therefore, it is important that the burglar develop techniques for probing the potential target site to determine if anyone is at home. The most common probe used by our informants was to send one of the burglars to the door to knock or ring the doorbell. If someone answered, the prober would ask directions to a nearby address or for a nonexistent person, for example, "Is Ray home?" The prospective burglar would apologize and leave when told that he or she had the wrong address. A female informant reported that she carried her two-year-old child to the target residence door, asking for directions to a nearby address. She reported:

> *I ask them for a drink [of water] for the baby. Even when they seem suspicious they almost always let me in to get the baby a drink.*

Several informants reported obtaining the resident's name from the mailbox or a sign over the door. They would then look up the telephone number and call the residence, leaving the phone ringing while they returned to the target home. If they could still hear the phone ringing when they arrived at the house, they were sure it was unoccupied.

Burglar Alarms

In general, burglars agreed that alarms were a definite deterrent to their activities. Other factors being equal, they preferred to locate a target that did not have an alarm instead of taking the additional risk involved in attempting to burglarize a house with an alarm system. More than 90 percent of the informants reported that they would not choose a target with an alarm system. Most were deterred merely by a sign or window sticker stating that the house was protected by an alarm system. As Richard, an experienced burglar, stated:

> *Why take a chance? There's lots of places without alarms. Maybe they're bluffing, maybe they ain't.*

Although several informants boasted about disarming alarms, when pressed for details, almost all admitted that they did not know how to accomplish that task. One informant stated that while she could not disarm a burglar alarm, she was not deterred by an alarm. She stated that once the alarm was tripped, she still had time to complete the burglary and escape before police or private security arrived. She explained that she never took more than 10 minutes to enter, search, and exit a house. She advised:

> *Police take 15 to 20 minutes to respond to an alarm. Security [private security] sometimes gets there a little faster. I'm gone before any of them gets there.*

Locks on Doors and Windows

Past research has been inconsistent regarding the deterrent value of locks on windows and doors. A few studies have reported that burglars consider the type of lock installed at a prospective target site in their target selection decision. Others did not find locks to be a significant factor in the selection process.

The majority of informants in the present study initially stated that locks did not deter them. However, during burglary reconstructions, we discovered that given two potential target sites, all other factors being equal, burglars prefer not to deal with a deadbolt lock. Several told us that they allowed themselves only one or two minutes to effect entry and that a good deadbolt lock slowed them down too much.

The variation in findings regarding security hardware appears related to the burglar's level of expertise and experience. To the extent to which burglars are primarily opportunistic and inexperienced, locks appear to have deterrent value. The opportunistic burglar chooses targets based on their perceived vulnerability to burglary at a given time. Given a large number of potential targets, the burglar tends to select the most vulnerable of the target pool. A target with a good lock and fitted with other security hardware will usually not be perceived to be as vulnerable as one without those items. The professional or "good" burglar chooses targets on the basis of factors other than situational vulnerability and conceives ways in which he or she can overcome impediments to the burglary (such as the target site being fitted with a high-quality deadbolt lock). Thus, to the extent that burglars are skilled and experienced, deadbolt locks have limited utility for crime prevention. However, our findings support the deterrent value of deadbolt locks. Seventy-five percent of the burglaries reconstructed during our research were opportunistic offenses. Many of those burglaries would have been prevented by the presence of a quality deadbolt lock. *It is important to note that nearly one-half of the burglary sites in the present study were entered through open or unlocked windows and doors.*

Dogs

Almost all studies agree that dogs are an effective deterrent to burglary. Although there is some individual variation among burglars, the general rule is to bypass a house with a dog—any dog. Large dogs represent a physical threat to the burglar and small ones are often noisy, attracting attention to a burglar's activities. We found that although many burglars have developed contingency plans to deal with dogs (petting, feeding, or even killing them), most burglars prefer to avoid them. When asked what were considered absolute "no-go" factors, most burglars responded that dogs were second only to occupancy. However, approximately 30 percent of the informants initially discounted the presence of dogs as a deterrent. Yet, during "ride alongs," the sight or sound of a dog at a potential target site almost invariably resulted in a "no-go" decision. As Richard said:

> *I don't mess with no dogs. If they got dogs, I go someplace else.*

Debbie reported that she was concerned primarily with small dogs:

> *Little dogs "yap" too much. They [neighbors] look to see what they are so excited about. I don't like little yapping dogs.*

Opportunity and Burglary

The "professional burglars" among our informants tended to select targets in a purposive manner, analyzing the physical and social characteristics of the environment and choosing targets that they knew from experience were ideally vulnerable. But by far the greater proportion of the informants were opportunistic. The targets they chose appeared particularly vulnerable at the time. Thus, most burglaries in the jurisdiction studies seem to result from the propitious juxtaposition of target, offender, and situation.

Our findings suggest that a burglar's decision to "hit" a target is based primarily on environmental cues that are perceived to have immediate consequences. Most burglars appear to attend only to the present; future events or consequences do not weigh heavily in their risk-versus-gain calculation. Drug-using burglars and juveniles are particularly oriented to this immediate-gain and immediate-risk decision process. Non-drug-using and experienced burglars are probably less likely to attend only to immediate risks and gains. Our informants, though experienced burglars, were all drug users, and tended to have a "here and now" orientation toward the rewards and costs associated with burglary.

Exploiting opportunity characterized the target selection processes in more than 75 percent of the burglaries reconstructed during our research. Even professional burglars among our informants often took advantage of opportunities when they arose. Chance opportunities occasionally presented themselves while the professional was "casing" and "probing" potential burglary targets chosen by more rational means. When these opportunities arose, the professional burglar was as likely as other burglars to take advantage of the situation.

IMPLICATIONS FOR CRIME PREVENTION

This study suggests burglars may be much more opportunistic than previously believed. The opportunistic burglar chooses targets based on their perceived vulnerability to burglary at a given time. Given a large number of potential targets, the burglar tends to select the most vulnerable of the target pool. The burglar does not, however, choose targets on the basis of situational vulnerability alone. He also considers how to overcome impediments to the burglary.

Programs designed to prevent burglary must be based on valid assumptions about burglars and burglary. Measures designed to combat the relatively small population of high-incidence "professional" burglars tend to overemphasize the skill and determination of most burglars. These measures are expensive, complex, and require long-term commitment at many levels. However, the typical burglar is not a calculating professional against whom complex prevention tactics must be employed. In fact, most burglars are young, unskilled, and opportunistic. This suggests that emphasis should be directed at such factors as surveillability, occupancy, and accessibility. More specifically, dogs, good locks, and alarm systems deter most burglars. Methods that give a residence the "illusion of occupancy" (Cromwell, Olson, and Avary, 1990) deter almost all burglars and are maintained with little effort or cost. Our study suggests that these simple steps may be the most cost-efficient and effective means for residents to insulate themselves from victimization by burglars.

REFERENCES

Bureau of Justice Statistics. October 1991. *Criminal Victimization 1990.* Bulletin. Washington, DC: U.S. Department of Justice.

Cromwell, Paul, James N. Olson, and D'Aunn Avary. 1991. *Breaking and Entering: An Ethnographic Analysis of Burglary.* Newbury Park, CA: Sage.

Katz, Jack. 1988. *Seductions of Crime.* New York: Basic Books.

Lynch, James P. 1990. Modeling Target Selection in Burglary: Differentiating Substance from Method. Paper presented at the 1990 annual meeting of the American Society of Criminology, Baltimore, Maryland.

Rengert, G., and J. Wasilchick. 1985. *Suburban Burglary: A Time and a Place for Everything.* Springfield, IL: Charles C. Thomas.

Rengert, G., and J. Wasilchick. 1989. Space, Time and Crime: Ethnographic Insights into Residential Burglary. A report prepared for the National Institute of Justice. (Mimeo).

Reppetto, T. G. 1974. *Residential Crime.* Cambridge, MA: Ballinger.

Scarr, H. A. 1973. *Patterns of Burglary.* Washington, DC: U.S. Government Printing Office.

Shover, Neal. 1971. Burglary as an Occupation. Ph.D. Dissertation, University of Illinois. Ann Arbor, MI: University Microfilms, 1975.

REVIEW QUESTIONS

1. Of what value are "inside men" to someone who wants to engage in burglary?
2. What are some factors that encourage a burglar to pick one house instead of another?
3. How do Cromwell's findings differ from common conceptions of the nature of burglary?

CHAPTER 45

THE IMMEDIATE EXPERIENCES OF CARJACKING

BRUCE A. JACOBS
VOLKAN TOPALLI
RICHARD WRIGHT

This article explores offender decision making in carjacking. How do would-be carjackers move from an unmotivated state to one in which they are committed to taking an occupied motor vehicle by force or threat of force? An adequate answer to this question can only be achieved by focusing on the phenomenological foreground of carjacking: the immediate context in which the decision to offend is made. Background conditions [such as poverty, unemployment, or drug abuse] may help us to understand why some individuals are more likely than others to commit such crimes, but they cannot identify the factors that activate carjackings in the offending moment. . . . But this foreground of offending is embedded in an ongoing socio-cultural context—namely, the urban street culture, which places great emphasis on spontaneity, hedonism, the ostentatious display of wealth, and the maintenance of honor. . . . With this in mind, we aim to provide [a series of immediate] offender decision making in carjacking, drawing on ethnographic interview data from 28 currently active carjackers in St. Louis, Missouri. . . .

BANKROLLING STREET LIFE

The spontaneous hedonism and ostentatious display characteristic of street culture mean that financial need is effectively a constant, fuelled by reckless spending habits and the restless desire for material goods. On the streets, cash is burned as fast as it is made, typically on "party pursuits" like drugs and alcohol or status-enhancing items such as high-end trainers. . . . Those with the ability to do so, whether by legal or illegal means, are accorded respect and high status. Participants unable to sustain these activities are liable to be labeled "scum bums" and excluded from the action. It is easy to appreciate why street offenders regard the lack of money as an immediate threat to their social standing (Wright and Decker, 1994). Seen in this light, PoPo's willingness to commit a carjacking to finance what, to an outsider, might appear to be frivolous pursuits takes on a different meaning:

> *I ran up to her [victim] and said, "Bitch, give me them keys. Drop your bags and get the fuck out of the way." . . . I took her purse and took her goddamn diamond ring . . . went and bought some drink [alcohol] and . . . weed and . . . got my hair did, bought me some tennis shoes and walked the street with that ring.*

[SEIZING EMERGENT OPPORTUNITIES]

Opportunistic carjackings involve little advance planning or casing of targets. The would-be of-

Source: Bruce A. Jacobs, Volkan Topalli, and Richard Wright, "Carjacking, Streetlife, and Offender Motivation." *British Journal of Criminology*, vol. 43 (2003), pp. 673–688. Reprinted by permission of Centre for Crime & Justice Studies (formerly ISTD) and Oxford University Press.

fender "sees a vulnerable target from which to gain some immediate reward, and does not preplan considerations of attack" (Pettiway, 1982). Motivation, target selection, and commission of the offense are merged into one continuous process:

> *[We were] just walking around . . . looking for things to happen . . . to get money. . . . He [victim] just drove up and my cousin was like "Look at that car, man, that's tough. I'm getting that." "Straight up, you want to do it?" He was like, "Yeah." He was all G for it. [Corleone]*

Opportunity dominates carjackings more than it does most other street crimes, because the targets of such offenses are uniquely mobile. A car is there and gone in a matter of seconds, and there often is little or no time for hesitation. Opportunities that are allowed to slip past may be lost forever. This means that would-be carjackers have to be primed to see what they want and strike immediately. . . .

[BEING PART OF A NETWORK]

Dense street networks mean that well-connected offenders sometimes receive inside information about potentially lucrative targets. This allows them to broaden their predatory horizons and target persons not otherwise in their immediate "sampling frame." Here again, such opportunities are likely to be transient, so offenders must be primed to strike. Along these lines, Little Rag's cultivation of a "tipster" ultimately paid off handsomely. "I told him that if he ever sees something," he recalled, "give me a phone [call] and I'd come up over and do it." The informant phoned and Little Rag pounced, netting a nice take in the process ($500 cash, the victim's wallet, jewelry, a stash of crack-cocaine and, of course, the victim's car). Similarly, Goldie was given the location and approximate time when a particular individual would drive his vehicle through the neighborhood. His informants apparently did not want to jack the car themselves, but stood to benefit from its seizure. Using this intelligence, Goldie waited at the appropriate spot and attacked when the moment arrived:

> *He pulled up [to the described location] you know and the light changed just in time. So I just tapped on his window you know and [said], "Can you please spare some change?" Then I put the gun to his head, asked him if he was going to get out or die, you know what I'm saying, "Either one, you going to get out this motherfucker or die?" Boom! Shot him on his leg. He got to screaming and shit hollering, you know what I'm saying, "You shot me! You shot me! You shot me!" like a motherfucker gonna hear him or something. Cars just steady drive past and shit, you know what I'm saying. By this time I opened up the door, "Fuck you!" Forced his ass on up out of there. . . .*

GOING WITH THE FLOW

Street culture is characterized by spontaneity and an openness to illicit action whereby participants can never know for sure what will happen next. This may be part of its attraction for people who live outside the law. The offenders in our sample, like virtually all street criminals, associate with similarly situated others who often have enemies and agendas of their own. This can unexpectedly pull the offenders into carjackings induced by circumstances not of their own making. When this happens, they have little choice but to go with the flow of unfolding events. C-Low, for instance, got caught up in a carjacking when he and a friend, Mackie, became embroiled in a running gun battle. The incident started in a neighborhood dentist's office, where he and Mackie were waiting to have some dental work done. Mackie recently had ripped off a local drug dealer. As fate would have it, the drug dealer, accompanied by two friends, arrived at the same office for his own dental appointment. Recognition was followed by accusations and an angry exchange of threats. The drug dealer's friends pulled out their guns, whereupon C-Low and Mackie rushed out the door. They desperately needed a getaway car. C-Low picks up the story:

> *They started popping at my partner, just started shooting at him. . . . [W]e had no car . . . so we were running . . . and the guy was popping at us. . . . So, there was a lady getting out of her car, and*

[Mackie] stole it.... [S]he had her purse and everything. [Mackie] just came on her blind side, just grabbed her, hit her. She looked, she just looked like she was shocked, she was in a state of shock.... And [we] took her car and we left....

PUNISHING AFFRONTS

"Flossing" was by far the most common instigating affront. To floss means to show off material possessions such as clothes, jewelry, and, of special relevance for our purposes here, cars. In regard to cars, flossing involves cruising slowly through an area in a gaudily fancy vehicle with the stereo pumping out a bass heavy beat, while the driver regards those on foot with a look of disdainful disinterest and invulnerability. While middle-class observers may regard flossing as nothing but a minor annoyance, bothered more by the noise than anything else, the practice is anathema within the context of street culture because it is widely understood as both a putdown and a provocation that says, "I'm better than you." As such, it easily can move potential offenders from an unmotivated state to one in which they are determined to act. On the street, where one's honor must be protected at all cost, no affront is trivial. Esteem is so precarious that it can be undermined by a mere word or glance (Anderson, 1999).

Playboy thus took retaliatory action against a showboating driver who looked at him the wrong way while he was walking home with friends:

People were out there with their windows down or whatever late at night. You know you got your little self on or you flossing. That's considered flossing... you know, you look at a certain person and one of them's like when we was walking, he looked at us.... But a look like, ha, they walking and I'm not [so we jacked him].

Making such crimes easier to contemplate was a widespread belief that would-be victims had probably not obtained their wealth legitimately. It was one thing to show off, it was quite another to show off spoils that were themselves taken from someone else. As Pacman declared, "[A] motherfucker that's rich ... done nothing good to get rich." Snake echoed these sentiments: "[T]hey [victims] got the stuff the same way [as we do]."

"Deserving" victims were not limited exclusively to those who flossed. Other sorts of social wrongs also can activate the desire to inflict punishment. The nature of such wrongs varied from the personal and filial, to the social and subcultural, capable of inspiring vendetta-laden offenses designed to put the violator in his or her proper place. Goldie, for example, claimed that he carjacked one victim in retaliation for a sexual assault against a female friend when he chanced upon him at a local gas station.... In a similar vein, Playboy carjacked a woman at a service station who refused to pay a young child for pumping her gas. Witnessing the incident, Playboy became sufficiently incensed to act. "She don't want [to] pay the little dude," he recounted. "[T]his was a little boy, no older than eight or nine, he just want to make some change to buy some snacks and you don't do people like that. ... [W]hat she did was what she got."

BEING THRILLED

[Crime] is thrilling, the thrill comes from the danger, and that is what entices offenders to break the law. Without the prospect of discovery, arrest, or victim-resistance, the motivation to offend would probably dissipate. Crime, in this view, is a dance with danger and the "rush" comes from facing adversarial circumstances and [overcoming] them through sheer force of will.

Threat of arrest did not appear to be a major issue for the carjackers in our sample, one way or another. Carjackings could be completed in a matter of moments, and as long as police were out of sight, they tended also to be out of mind. Confronting and dominating drivers and passengers was a different story. A number of our respondents clearly relished the prospect of using brute force to get their way. Tall, for instance, described the adrenaline surge that coursed through him as he wrenched one driver from his vehicle. "[I]t's a rush thing ... when you're pulling someone out the car," he said, just a rush come over me. . . . I mean, I feel good." Sleazy-E took obvious pleasure in smashing a recalcitrant victim's head with a bottle. . . . PoPo claimed that she felt compelled to hit her victim during one offense, even though the victim put up no resistance. "[I] had to hit her," she explained, "I had to hit her. . . . I like to be bad. . . . It's just in me."

Instilling panic in victims seemed to be something of a sport for several of the carjackers we interviewed. PoPo thus found amusement in "the way people look at you when they scared and panicky and stuff. . . . It is funny just to see them shaking and pissing all over theyself." Big Mix described the scared reactions of his victims as "hilarious," adding that "you just get a kick out of seeing [them] screaming and hollering." And Nukie loved seeing the "motherfuckers [victims] scared of me . . . especially [when] they [think they are] all tough."

CONCLUSION

What light, then, does our research shed on the motivations that drive carjacking in real-life settings and circumstances? The short answer is that the carjackings committed by the offenders in our sample grow out of their broader participation in urban street culture. Street culture subsumes a number of powerful conduct norms, but the ones most relevant to our argument here include the hedonistic pursuit of sensory stimulation, disdain for conventional living, lack of future orientation, and persistent eschewal of responsibility. Street culture lionizes spontaneity, and dismisses "rationality and long-range planning . . . in favor of enjoying the moment" (Shover and Honaker, 1992). Offenders caught up in the street life typically conduct their affairs as if there will be no tomorrow, confident that the future will take care of itself. On the streets, "every night is Saturday night" (Hodgson, 1997), a philosophy that finds its expression in the pursuit of trendy consumerism and open-ended "partying."

REFERENCES

Anderson, E. 1999. *Code of the Street.* New York: Norton.

Hodgson, J. 1997. *Games Pimps Play.* Toronto: Canadian Scholars' Press.

Pettiway, L. 1982. "Mobility of Robbery and Burglary Offenders: Ghetto and Nonghetto Spaces." *Urban Affairs Quarterly* 18: 255–270.

Shover, N., and D. Honaker. 1992. "The Socially-bounded Decision Making of Persistent Property Offenders." *Howard Journal of Criminal Justice* 31: 276–293.

Wright, R., and S. H. Decker. 1994. *Burglars on the Job.* Boston: Northeastern University Press.

REVIEW QUESTIONS

1. How does being part of a network help carjackers?
2. How does "flossing" become a motivation for some carjackers?
3. The participants in this study often used the money they stole to attain status symbols and to "party." Does this change the nature of the crime in your mind? Justify your answer.

CHAPTER 46

THE GOOD THING ABOUT WORKPLACE DEVIANCE

ELIZABETH A. HOFFMANN

This article explores cab drivers' attempt to address the inadequacy of the cab companies' goals and rules such as those that generate revenue and conflict resolution through formal mechanisms. That attempt involves committing workplace deviance by achieving the cab drivers' own goals of justice and safety through direct, more expeditious self-help. Such workplace deviance appears in two forms: revenge and rescue, performed both by individual cab drivers and by groups. Both types of workplace deviance are useful for strengthening group solidarity, teaching group expectations, and reinforcing group values.

To study the workplace deviance in the taxicab industry, I used open-ended interviews. In some ways, cab driving is an atypical job; cab drivers do not occupy a single designated station, window, or office. Instead, they roam the streets continuously, having contact with a wide variety of people in many different parts of the city. In addition, their income is always uncertain: it can be affected by road conditions, generosity of passengers, weather, skillfulness of dispatchers, personal ability, and luck. Nevertheless, cab driving is also similar to other occupations in many ways. Many problems that cab drivers encounter resemble those of office, retail, or factory workers. Like these workers, cab drivers have conflicts with coworkers, supervisors, and customers, which disrupt their day, cause them stress, and may impact their income.

The cab drivers I interviewed work for two major companies in the taxicab industry of a medium-sized, Midwestern college town. The companies, Coop Cab and Private Taxi, are similar in that they both draw from similar groups of people for workers and are approximately the same size. They both also run their businesses similarly, allowing only single calls (picking up only one party at a time) except for airport runs, and using a commission payment system whereby drivers pay the company a portion of the fares, in contrast to other cab companies where drivers "rent" the cab for a flat fee and then keep all revenue for themselves. Both cab companies have management structures, discipline procedures, and grievance procedures, although Coop Cab is owned collectively, while Private Taxi is privately owned.

METHOD

I conducted 34 interviews. The sample of taxicab drivers is divided between the two companies with 14 people (41%) from Private Taxi and 20 (59%) from Coop Cab. I gained entry by spending time at the cab companies' workers' rooms and offices. I did not post a "sign-up" sheet for in-

Source: Specifically written for this reader, with portions drawn from the author's " 'Revenge' and 'Rescue': Workplace Deviance in the Taxicab Industry," *Sociological Inquiry*, vol. 78 (2008), pp. 270–289. Reprinted by permission of the author.

terviewees to volunteer nor did I ask the cab companies' managements to suggest or assign people to be interviewed. I avoided these two means of gathering interviewees because I was concerned that such methods could produce a pool of subjects that would over-represent characteristics that were important to this study. For example, would-be interviewees who are sufficiently assertive to volunteer could represent the more brash and aggressive of the drivers; conversely, potential interviewees offered by management might be the more docile and obedient drivers. Instead of either of these methods, I, myself, approached workers, explained my study, and asked if I could interview them. Sometimes I interviewed the driver immediately; other times we set a time for me to interview her/him, either on-site or off-site. Later in the interview process, I telephoned ahead to set up interviews with the managers and owners of the businesses, some on-site, some off-site.

In order to address concerns that participating in this study could have harmed participants by asking them to discuss unpleasant issues, I approached each interviewee with respect for their well being. All interviewees signed a consent form which told them that they could stop the interview at any time. In addition, I orally told them that they could discontinue the interview at any point. I also emphasized that they could stop the tape recorder, and still be part of the interview.

FINDINGS

Unlike many other occupations, cab driving allows a great deal of autonomy. Although management structures and rules officially govern the taxicab drivers, while on the road, cab drivers often engage in self-help, deviating from the formal rules. When conflict occurs, whether with a customer or a fellow driver, cab drivers often must "fend for themselves" (Hoffmann, 2003).

A consequence of the mobile nature of the cab driving job is that the driver rarely deals with any one customer on a regular basis. This makes the job both more exciting, with its constant variety, and more dangerous, with more unknowns. Potentially unpleasant situations can range from armed robberies to harassment by drunken passengers to fare-jumpers to harboring persons fleeing the police (Davis, 1959). For these reasons, many taxicab drivers feel that cab driving can be dangerous and unpredictable.

The formal goals for both companies in this study are to generate revenue while incurring the fewest costs possible. Thus, the explicit, specific job of these cab drivers is to transport passengers safely and quickly. Neither company officially encourages the drivers to go out of their way either to aid or to "discipline" others. If a driver encounters a passenger who needs emergency help, both companies' handbooks say that the driver is to call the police or have the dispatcher contact the police. If a passenger misbehaves, the driver is to report the person's name and any additional information, including details of the incident, to the dispatcher on duty who might formally report it to the management or the police. If a driver misbehaves towards a fellow driver, the offended driver is to report that behavior to the dispatcher or manager, either informally or through formal grievance procedures. If a driver is in danger, the driver is to call the police.

In actual practice, however, these formal rules are often insufficient. The cab drivers found that police assistance is often more inconvenient than helpful and that formal procedures usually yield insufficient punishment for misbehaving passengers or co-workers. To address these gaps, the cab drivers often resorted to various forms of workplace deviance, deviating from the formal rules and goals of management in order to address the needs they saw in their everyday work lives.

Sometimes these acts were done alone, as an individual, while other times these acts were carried out by a group and thus became a social event. These acts, whether executed by individuals or groups, represent two types of workplace deviance: revenge and rescue.

Revenge by an Individual

Dispatchers, who assign rides, play an important role for the cab drivers in this city, where most rides are requested by phone, rather than by flagging down a cab. Thus, dispatchers have the power to affect how bored or busy one is (i.e., how much "dead time" one has), the quality of one's passengers, and, most importantly, one's income. If a driver believes that a dispatcher is discriminating against him or her or otherwise mistreating the driver, under the rules of both taxicab companies, that driver may bring a formal grievance against the dispatcher to the cab company management. This, however, is seen as a lengthy and often ineffective process. It also makes the conflict open and public. Instead of adhering to the formal procedures of the cab company, a driver might target the dispatcher for revenge if he or she felt cheated by the dispatcher. For example, John, a young, male cab driver, described how he would punish a dispatcher he felt consistently assigned him low-fare rides and frequent dead time.

> *When there's two drivers calling [on the radio] at the same time, you don't [hear] anything instead of [hearing] one of them. So if you're mad at a dispatcher and you want to get back at him, right, you don't want him to know it's you. So every time they call someone else's cab number, you just push your button on your microphone, and so they get static and it really annoys them for like 20 minutes, and then you stop. So it's a good way to piss off your dispatcher.*

In this way, John was able to anonymously exact revenge on the dispatcher without risking open confrontation.

The companies also had rules about how drivers are to handle problematic passengers. If passengers are simply rude or obnoxious, drivers are to ignore the behavior; however, if passengers damage or dirty the taxicab, then the cab driver is to report the incident to the dispatcher or manager along with as much information about the guilty passengers as possible.

However, drivers found this formal policy to involve a burdensome level of paperwork and delay. Instead of following these workplace rules, the drivers might target passengers for revenge. Most frequently, this involves minor revenge, such as refusing a customer a ride or asking a customer to exit the cab. The following quote from Larry, a middle-aged male driver, illustrates how this driver handles rude would-be passengers.

> *If they come and they rip open my door and they demand a cab ride, they're not gonna get one. Or if they start [littering in my cab], that's my office and I try to keep a nice, clean office. You know, I drive the same cab every night; try to keep it nice for everybody. And the people that get into my car, and disrespect my space, they won't get a cab ride.*

Sometimes other cab drivers are the targets of revenge. A serious infraction in the cab driving industry is misrepresenting one's location when bidding for a call ("long-hooding"). When the dispatcher announces a passenger's pick-up location, various drivers in the area will call in to "bid" on the ride by telling where each is presently located. The dispatcher then gives the fare to the closest driver. However, when a driver long-hoods and lies about his/her true location, s/he will win the ride instead of another driver who is actually closer to the passenger's location. In the following example, Jenny, a former waitress, describes how she gets revenge on fellow drivers who misbehave in this way:

> *Some drivers out there will long-hood it, meaning that there's a destination [e.g.,] at State and Gill, okay. Well they're actually farther away from State and Gill than what they say they are. Let's say they're at Regent and Park, and they're saying, 'I'm at State and Gill.' If they get caught by another driver and then the other driver gets really upset. And sometimes [the other driver] will go and scoop their calls when they get a call, just to get them back. Sometimes you have stuff like that: the tit for tat process.*

Since long-hooding is officially against the rules, a driver could raise a formal grievance against a long-hooding co-worker. However, as the above quote illustrates, the long-hooder might become the object of revenge rather than a formal grievance. This cab driver enacted her revenge on long-hooders by engaging in another form of misbehavior herself, picking up the ride of the other cab driver before the assigned cab driver could reach the passenger.

Revenge by a Group

Sometimes the cab drivers will work together to get revenge on another driver. These acts of revenge can be carefully coordinated among nearly a dozen drivers, as in the example below, or more spontaneous, as in the next detailed quote. Ed, a cab driver for over a decade, described how a number of drivers disciplined a driver whom they believed had been stealing other drivers' calls.

> *You're not supposed to steal other people's calls. There's not really rules about that. But there's sort of etiquette. You just want to be fair to everyone. Because if you start stealing people's calls, then everyone will get mad. Then everyone else will start stealing all your calls. We did this to someone a couple weeks ago who was being a real problem.*
>
> *She's like just nasty and greedy. She just can't see beyond the moment, [e.g.,] if she's driving past, even if she has someone in her car—you just take one person at a time for the most part—if she drives past a spot where someone else's call is, she'll just stop and throw 'em in and drive. Really bad things. And she's always doing it. And so we got frustrated and finally said, well, we'll try and give you a taste of your own medicine.*
>
> *We decided, like for a night, we were going to steal every one of this person's calls, and we did. At the end of the night she'd made $20 in ten hours or something. She was broke, right? So you just sort of do things like that, sort of like teach them a lesson: 'Be good!' you know? [Interviewer: How many of you were doing that?] Probably at least ten people and that was downtown. So if you have ten people downtown, it's a really small area, so you can pretty much always have someone really close to the call. [Interviewer: Do you think she realized what was going on?] Oh, absolutely.*

Just as individual cab drivers targeted dispatchers for revenge when the driver felt mistreated by the dispatcher, sometimes groups of drivers would cooperate to punish a dispatcher who had upset all of them. Jim, a middle-aged man who had been driving cab for 13 years, provides a good example.

> *There have been times when there's a really bad dispatcher and all the drivers don't like this dispatcher and don't want him to be working. And then one day,* everyone *decided that they'd rather not be working than be working with such-and-such dispatcher, so they* all *check in. [Before the bad dispatcher started, the drivers were] really busy, and there's 20, 30 people driving cab. Half an hour later, all the cabs are parked in the lot and everyone's turning in their keys and going home; and that's it. Then [the dispatcher] is stuck for a day until the following shift of drivers comes in.*

Even if "everyone" does not decide to check in and turn in their cabs for the day, having only a few cabs on the road would be stressful for a dispatcher who is trying to cover all the passenger calls. Like the other examples of group revenge, this way of punishing the dispatcher takes a significant amount of coordination and monetary self-sacrifice. Unlike stealing someone's calls, which would increase one's own income, turning in one's cab early would have the opposite effect: reducing the amount of money one would earn that day.

Both the small, annoying revenge and the large-scale coordinated revenge are examples of the cab drivers' workplace deviance to fill in the gaps of the official rules. The managements of both cab companies have formal processes for censuring cab drivers and dispatchers. However, the cab drivers feel that these are time-consuming and less effective. The above examples of workplace deviance illustrate how the cab drivers acted creatively to address workplace needs that were not met by the management's formal procedures.

Rescue by a Group

Drivers will also work together to rescue each other when in need, violating company rules in order to protect drivers from physical or financial harm. These acts of rescue are important aspects of the taxicab culture, whether done by individuals or by many cab drivers together.

One reason cab drivers might be in need of rescue is if their passengers are harassing or intimidating them. For example, Michael, who often worked the day shifts and rush-hours, recounted an incident in which another driver was being threatened by his passenger:

> *One of our drivers had a guy who was being really abusive to his girlfriend in the back of his cab, and then spit on the seat of his cab because he was drunk and being arrogant. And so [the driver] turned around and said, 'If you're gonna do that, I'm gonna have to ask you to get out of my car.' So then the guy was threatening him and was gonna punch him in the head and grabbed him by the coat collar from behind the seat and pulled him back. So the driver got out of the car and grabbed his radio and used this code that we have for that he needs help. And then other drivers just automatically went over there. And they got there faster than the cops.*

Many drivers shared stories in which they were either the rescuer or the rescued and the rescuing cab drivers arrived before the police or instead of the police.

Beatrice, a female driver who often worked the night shift, explained how she and another driver came to the assistance of a cab driver who was being threatened by a mob of drunken students:

> *I can remember once, Kevin was downtown on State Street, and there was a pack of people who wouldn't let this guy drive through. The dispatcher said, 'Are there any cabs close to State and whatever?' I told the dispatcher where I was and the dispatch says, 'Can you go to this location; driver needs assistance.' I just said, yeah, turned to the passenger and explained. I turned the meter off and we agreed on what the price was. I said, 'I'm not gonna take you home right now, I'm gonna help this other driver.' The guy that I was driving was cool because he had heard what the dispatcher had said, too. So I just drove down State Street. Another cab was coming from the opposite direction. When the pack of people there saw that there were two other cabs coming, like, right away, they just dispersed and the guy drove away. It wasn't like anything really happened, but that driver felt the need to ask for other cabs to come. They wouldn't let him through and they were trying to get into his cab. Whether they were going to rob him or pull him out of his cab, whatever, who knows?*

Sometimes simply the presence of more cab drivers will force people to behave. In the above example, Beatrice and the other driver did not get out of their cars, yet by arriving at the scene quickly they were able to rescue the other driver.

These acts of workplace deviance served the goals of the drivers—safety from physical danger and from being robbed—although they violated the of cab companies' official policies and removed drivers (and a mechanic) from the work that they were supposed to be doing. These workers deviated from the formal rules and worked together to create a more efficient, cost-effective solution. Having fellow cab drivers come to one's rescue meant that the driver did not waste time (and, hence, money) filling out paper work with police officers and received a faster rescue, lessening the possibility of lost fares or physical harm to the cab driver.

Rescue by an Individual

While drivers often spoke about rescuing other drivers from passengers, occasionally drivers would rescue a passenger from another passenger. Alexandra, who had been driving cab for over ten years, recounted a recent incident:

> *I had two couples [one couple in the front seat and the other in the back]. The second man tried to rape his wife in my back seat. I was going 55*

[m.p.h.] down the Beltline. All of a sudden I had this woman screaming in the back seat, 'No, no! Stop it! No.' She's screaming and crying. I look in the back seat and see him with her, I see him unzip his pants and he's got his hand on the back of her head and is trying to force her head down on his cock.

I turned on the dome light. They were all rip-roaring drunk. I turned on the dome light and yelled, 'Hey, what the hell is going on back there! What the hell do you think you're trying to do to her?! Stop it right now!' And then the people in the front seat got in the act, saying come on now, knock it off. The woman was just crying and crying. So he came to. I said, 'Zip up your pants!'

When we got to where they were going, I pulled the woman aside and handed her my business card with my name and phone number on it. I made him pay for the cab also, because he was trying to get her to pay for the cab. This guy was scum. I insisted that he or the other man come up with the money so that she'd have some money left in her purse. I wanted to make sure she wasn't giving up her last dime. Then I pulled her aside and told her, 'You don't have to go in there with him or with your party; you don't have to go. You're already drunk; you don't have to get drunker. Free cab ride anywhere in the city, anywhere in the county.' And she said, 'No, no; he's my husband.' That's when I found out they were married. I said, 'That's really sad, but . . . you know . . . in the meantime here's my name and number.'

Alexandra believed that she had a duty to do more than simply drive her passengers safely, her official job goal, but that she should also try to ensure their actual safety. She was willing to give up a future paying fare to drive this woman to safety.

DISCUSSION

This research explores workplace deviance in the taxicab industry. I explore the tension between the cab drivers' goals and those of the cab companies and the resulting rule violations that occur. The main goal of both companies' managements was generating revenue and each had rules about resolving conflicts through formal mechanisms, such as submitting a formal grievance to the management regarding a fellow worker or contacting the police to address trouble or danger on the road. This structure, however, left several gaps: filing formal grievances and police complaints often demanded time by the complainant, during which s/he is not on the road earning money. Additionally, the companies' internal formal procedures were viewed by many as seldom being effective, immediate means to stopping undesirable behavior.

In circumventing and violating the formal workplace structure and rules, the cab drivers worked to further their own goals of justice and safety by resolving disputes through direct, more expeditious self-help. Sometimes these deviant acts were done alone, as individuals, while other times these were group acts, even social events. In either case, the cab drivers embraced deviant behavior, violating their workplace's official rules. But such deviance is good for the cab drivers as an organization.

As Hodson's (1991) research shows, workers in many settings create a great deal of autonomy for themselves, whether or not the particular job inherently facilitates much autonomy. Taxicab driving is thus an occupation with a high level of autonomy. But their workplace deviance—revenge and rescue—further heightens the level of autonomy for the cab drivers. These high levels of autonomy, in turn, may facilitate workplace deviance in two ways. First, the cab drivers' greater autonomy could increase the need for workplace deviance by elevating the need for worker solidarity, and, second, heightened autonomy might increase the cab drivers' ability to engage in workplace deviance.

The deviant acts of revenge and rescue also enhance the taxicab drivers' solidarity with each other. Whether going outside the official rules to help or to punish, the cab drivers' deviant acts enforce the informal group norms of the taxicab driving industry. Hodson (2001) found that two major components of solidarity are the enforcement of group norms and mutual defense. The cab drivers' acts of rescue and revenge serve to defend themselves and each other—whether from financial or physical harm, disrespect, or harassment—and, in doing so, strengthens their solidarity with each other.

CONCLUSION

By analyzing acts of rescue alongside revenge, this study illustrates that workplace deviance can be positive in nature, despite being rule violations. Thus, this study broadens the focus of much scholarship on workplace deviance that concentrates on the destructive or harmful deviance in the workplace.

This research also has a practical value as it implies that management cannot assume that the only employees to disobey rules will be the "bad employees" who are trying to rebel against or harm the company. As we have observed, employees trying to do something helpful may effectively engage in workplace deviance. Therefore, management may do well to avoid regarding as harmful workplace deviance all worker behavior that violates official company policies. Well-intentioned employees might just as likely violate company rules as the rebellious, destructive ones. Indeed, by violating official policies, employees sometimes address problems and concerns that management is unable to ameliorate.

REFERENCES

Davis, Fred. 1959. "The Cabdriver and His Fare: Facets of a Fleeting Relationship." *American Journal of Sociology* 65:158–165.

Hodson, Randy. 1991. "The Active Worker: Compliance and Autonomy at the Workplace." *Journal of Contemporary Ethnography* 20:47–78.

———. 2001. *Dignity at Work.* Cambridge, UK: Cambridge University Press.

Hoffmann, Elizabeth A. 2003. "Legal Consciousness and Dispute Resolution: Different Disputing Behavior at Two Similar Taxicab Companies." *Law & Social Inquiry* 28:691–715.

REVIEW QUESTIONS

1. Explain why cab driving can be dangerous and unpredictable.
2. Discuss two ways in which cab drivers deal with their problems at work.
3. Why does the author conclude that "workplace deviance can be positive in nature"?

PART THIRTEEN

CONTROLLING DEVIANCE

Two days before U.S. troops invaded Iraq in April 2003, Harry Gillway, a small-town Arizona police chief, received a phone call from DynCorp International, a Texas company that recruits police, pilots, and bodyguards for overseas work funded by the American government. Asked if he would like to work in Iraq as a police adviser training Iraqis to help restore order to their own country, Gillway said that he was interested and soon decided to accept the job offer. Seven months later he was in Iraq. He is part of America's attempt to keep order in a chaotic foreign land whose government the United States has overthrown.[1]

What Gillway does is basically the same as what the police in every country do: try to control what the society regards as its deviant population. The control of deviants by the police represents the formal type of social control, as opposed to informal control. Formal control is carried out through surveillance, imprisonment, expulsion, or killing by the government and its law-enforcement agencies, the military, for-profit organizations, and other civilian organizations. Informal control comes from relatives, neighbors, peers, and even strangers through discipline, criticism, ridicule, or dirty looks.

Here we take a look at both the formal and informal control of deviants. In the first article, "What It's Like to be Known as a Sex Offender," Richard Tewksbury and Matthew Lees offer data to show how the registration of sex offenders as a formal social control makes life more difficult for the offenders but does not deter them from committing additional sex offenses. In the second article, "Responses to Workplace Bullying," Joanne Leck and Bella Galperin suggest how the formal social control of anti-bullying policies and practices in an organization fail to produce positive results. In the third piece, "Eating for Two: How Pregnant Women Neutralize Nutritional Deviance," Denise Copeltom finds that our culture's use of informal social control to discourage pregnant women from unhealthy eating practices falls short, leading the culprits to justify their bad eating behavior. In the fourth reading, "A New Way of Fighting the War on Drugs," Erich Goode argues that the best approach for the war on drugs is not formal social control in the form of strict criminal punishment or outright legalization, but rather "harm reduction," reducing drug-related deaths, disease, financial cost, and crime.

[1]Andrew Higgins, "Contract Cops," *Wall Street Journal*, February 2, 2004, pp. A1, A12.

Chapter 47

WHAT IT'S LIKE TO BE KNOWN AS A SEX OFFENDER

RICHARD TEWKSBURY
MATTHEW LEES

The passage of the Jacob Wetterling Crimes Against Children and Sexually Violent Offender Registration Act of 1994 formalized the practice of registering sex offenders in centralized databases. This federal statute led to the creation of state-wide registries that require listings of registrants' demographic information, current residence and a description of each individual's offense(s). It was Megan's Law, however, that is credited with making the information on sex offender registries accessible to the public. Passed in 1996 in response to the murder of a seven-year-old New Jersey girl by a previously convicted sex offender living unmonitored in the victim's community, the purpose of Megan's Law was to make communities aware of the presence of sex offenders in an effort to reduce recidivism. Today, 40 states have sex offender registries. Sex offender registries are well known in society, and nearly 1 million individuals are listed on these Web-based, publicly accessible lists of offenders. While most Americans believe that registries are a valuable tool for preventing crime, relatively little is known about either the true value of registries as tools to protect society or how registries affect the offenders who appear on them.

Research has, however, found that the sex offender registration has brought about numerous, unforeseen collateral consequences, defined by criminologists as the legal and social, often unintended, results that accompany criminal processing and labeling (Levenson, 2008; Levenson and Cotter, 2005; Tewksbury, 2004, 2005). Collateral consequences affect both community residents (whom registries are designed to protect) and also impose consequences for individual, registered offenders. Zevitz and Farkas (2000) report that citizens attending community notification meetings experienced increased levels of anxiety. Obstacles reported by sex offenders include social ostracism, relational and emotional difficulties, harassment, and problems finding housing and employment. It is even possible that these types of consequences may indirectly result in recidivism because of the isolation and frustration likely experienced by offenders.

At the level of the individual offender, survey research has shown that there are negative interpersonal, financial, professional, and psychological effects of sex offender registration. Registered sex offenders are known to frequently move, often as a result of either community pressure or financial difficulties (Mustaine, Tewksbury, and Stengel, 2006). Studies looking at where registered offenders live have consistently shown that while they can be found in any and all types of neighborhoods, in most instances registered sex offenders reside in socially disorganized

Source: Written specifically for this reader, with portions derived from the authors' "Perceptions of Sex Offender Registration: Collateral Consequences and Community Experiences," *Sociological Spectrum*, vol. 26 (2006), pp. 309–334. Reprinted by permission of the author.

communities and neighborhoods that are among the least desirable in communities (Tewksbury and Mustaine, 2006, 2007, 2008).

THE PRESENT STUDY

The present study examines the experiences of registered sex offenders as they live in the community. Our focus is on how registered sex offenders experience the social, emotional, and practical consequences of being publicly labeled as sex offenders.

METHOD

Data for this study were collected by way of one-on-one, personal interviews conducted with 22 offenders listed on the Kentucky Sex Offender Registry (http://kspsor.state.ky.us). The sample is almost exclusively male (95%), primarily white (86%), and has a mean age of 48. The interviewed offenders have been on the registry for an average of just over three years. In the sample, 27% have been convicted of rape, 59% have a sexual abuse conviction, 45% have a conviction for sodomy, and 5% have a conviction for some other sexual offense. Additionally, 41% are currently married, 64% have children (but, only 9% have minor children) and 36% live with a spouse/significant other, 50% live alone, and one individual lives in a substance abuse treatment facility, one with his parents, and one with a friend/roommate.

FINDINGS

There are four primary types of collateral consequences experienced as problems by these registered sex offenders (RSOs). These four varieties of problems are:

- Relationship difficulties
- Employment difficulties
- Harassment
- Stigmatization and persistent feelings of vulnerability

Each of these issues runs through and affects the experiences of registered sex offenders in many ways. While each of these types of experience is common across the sample, there are also variations in how each is experienced by individuals.

Relationship Difficulties

Difficulties in personal and social relationships are among the most common collateral consequences for RSOs. The challenges of relationships center on attempting to overcome or cope with rejection by others. When one's significant other, family, and/or friends learn that one is a "pervert," it is not surprising that relationships suffer. For some RSOs, the difficulties are in the form of creating stressed and strained relationships, while for others their family and friends simply reject them and cut off all contact.

When an RSO suffers a complete loss of some relationships, these are most often with extended family members. Siblings, parents, and children as well as nieces, nephews, aunts, uncles, and cousins have all curtailed contact and interactions with some RSOs. In some instances, these persons limit their interactions with the offender to only occasional, public, and superficial interactions. Travis, explained his loss of family saying,

> *My mom passed away and she cut me out of the will after it happened. My mom didn't—I talked to my mother after the incident happened and I don't know if she didn't believe me or what the story was, but I just know I got cut out of the will because of it. . . . When my mom passed away in May I didn't see one of those people until the funeral. Basically, it's the only time I see them anyways, main events. I don't see nobody personally at all in my family. . . . They don't want to come here. They are welcome, but they don't want to come. So be it.*

Similarly, Arthur, a 53-year-old former family therapist, explained that his family had abandoned him.

> *My family? It's difficult to gauge. They haven't spoken to me since I offended. I haven't had any contact with my family in over 9 years. I have one*

sister and 2 grown sons and not one of them have had any contact with me since I offended. . . . I have no idea what their reaction or response to it has been.

Some RSOs are legally prohibited from seeing or interacting with some of their family members. When one's victim was a family member they typically have conditions of their probation or parole that restrict them from interacting with either the victim or the victim's family. As David, who molested his niece four years earlier, explained,

I can't have contact with the family. I can't have contact with (victim) or my older sister and her kids. . . . Which I can understand, you got to give her time to heal. . . . My probation orders me not to talk to them. She has to understand that too. It's real hard because I do want to talk to her and let her know that I'm sorry and it will never happen again.

Not all relationship losses are due to either rejection of RSOs by others or to legal prohibitions, however. Some RSOs withdraw and interact with only a few select loved ones. This is done as one means of attempting to cope with their own feelings. Jordan, convicted of first-degree sexual abuse and attempted sodomy and out of prison for five years, explained that, "I live kind of private, sheltered. I go to work, I come home. My activities I take out of town . . . I don't do social events." Or, in the words of Travis,

I've distanced myself from other people. When you look at a person you can just see something there . . . I just distance myself. I just don't deal with people. You just stay away. I deal with my family members on a somewhat impersonal level . . . I don't have very many friends. Because, like I said, people just don't understand.

In rare cases, however, RSOs report being pleasantly surprised to not have suffered any significant difficulties or losses of relationships. Andy, a 51-year-old who has been on the registry for 10 months, said that,

The thing that was probably the most shocking was that I did not lose a friend through the experience. I didn't know how friends would be. If anything, I have actually gained friends.

The one type of relationship that all RSOs feel is negatively affected is one with a current or potential significant other. While most RSOs with a long-term significant other report that their spouse/girlfriend is among their most valuable support system members, single men report fearing that they will never develop a serious romantic relationship. Most single RSOs dismiss the idea of dating as unrealistic and "not worth what it might bring to you." As related by Felix, a handsome, 6′ 3″ tall, 25-year-old university senior who lives with his parents,

I don't date. I used to, but now I just don't even really think about it. I still have my friends from high school. But, I don't think that's going to happen. It's just too easy for someone to find out and if I did get involved with someone, how do you tell them? You know they're probably not going to want to stay with you. So, why bother?

Mike, a twice divorced 56-year-old, explained his lack of dating, saying,

I have been in situations where I could have dated or whatever. I avoid it though because of fear of getting too involved with whoever and them not knowing anything about me. . . . Whoever you were with would have this image or thought of you way up here and fall in love with you and then all of the sudden you mention that and the bricks come tumbling down. It's over. Why get yourself in that situation? So that's what I do, I avoid it at all costs.

Relationship difficulties present RSOs with emotional challenges that hinder their reintegration into the community. For those who suffer significant losses of relationships with family members and friends, important support structures are removed from the RSO's world. This feeling of social isolation, coupled with the employment/financial difficulties, fears of harassment and sense of stigmatization (as discussed below), may increase the likelihood of feeling isolated and subsequently increase the chances of the individual reoffending.

Employment Difficulties

Difficulties finding and maintaining employment are common for RSOs. The problems arise both simply from being a convicted sex offender and from having employers and coworkers find out about or know of one's registration.

The relatively few RSOs who are professionals or who were able to maintain their pre-offense employment recognize that they are "lucky" in comparison to other RSOs. Most commonly, individuals report either losing employment or having a series of low-level jobs. Finding a job can be a major challenge that is largely created when potential employers learn of an RSO's status. Chris, a 67-year-old convicted child molester considers himself to have a "good" situation.

> *I think if I were a young man and on the registry and if I had the same kind of crime I did, I think it would be a terrible situation, because of the job situation and so forth. I am retired. But I still need to work a little bit, and I think it's definitely worse now.*

Jon, who moved to the city because he believed it would be easier to find a job than in a small town, said that his parole officer provided him with a list of possible employers, but,

> *They have a list of places that will hire ex-cons. But, if you're an ex-con and a sex offender, they won't. And they tell you straight up. Several places will hire ex-convicts, but all of them say no to sex offenders. All of them.*

This prejudice is not necessarily thought of as a result of being a convicted sex offender, but rather simply being a convicted offender. As explained by Charlie, "The farthest most people get is 'have you been convicted of a felony?' A lot of them when they see that, it ends right there."

Some types of jobs have legal restrictions that prohibit employers from hiring convicted felons. Jobs involving regular handling of money, or those working with children, around drugs and medical supplies, or where licensure is a requirement are all jobs with some legal or licensing restrictions. This can be especially challenging when an individual's pre-offense job becomes unavailable and they are forced to change careers. Travis's experience shows this clearly.

> *I'm an electrician by trade and it's just killed me—I haven't been able to find an electrical job since I got out of prison. And I know it's because of this. You have to tell an employer, and when they find out, it puts a stigma on it or something.*

As a result, many RSOs must take any employment they can find. Typically this means low-paying jobs and those that require little if any special skills. As Paul, a 52-year-old convicted of first-degree rape and sodomy explained, "It's just tough. You're just about going to be stuck with McDonalds, bottom of the ladder type of jobs. That's all you're going to get. I don't care what kind of education you have." For others, the solution is to be self-employed. However, for a convicted offender, who may or may not have business training or marketable job skills, identifying a means of self-employment to support oneself can be a significant challenge in and of itself. Felix, a university student preparing to graduate with a bachelor's degree in business, explained that although he has good grades and has always wanted to go into marketing, he has recently begun his own landscaping business, anticipating that he will be unable to get "a real job" upon graduation. Financial worries are a constant for him and he reports feeling that his college education will have been "probably just a waste of my time and money in the end."

One theme that runs through almost all of the RSOs experiences is a sense of acceptance of their employment difficulties. This is not to say that RSOs believe their challenges are just or fair, but they recognize they are present and are "just another part of what you have to put up with."

Harassment

Without exception, RSOs reported having both anticipated and feared being verbally and physically harassed once their name, photograph, address, and other identifying information appeared on the sex offender registry. While some RSOs simply expected to "get weird looks from people, for everyone to recognize me and shun me," others expected to be regularly assaulted and publicly humiliated.

These fears most often are about expectations of being recognized in public, and subsequently being rejected or publicly proclaimed as a "rapist" or "pedophile." Charlie recalled that while still in prison he anticipated his time after release to actually be more difficult than being incarcerated. As he explained, "I thought it would be more of a hassle than what I've had so far. There was time when I was close to getting out that I was really worried about it." Similarly, Andy says that when he was sentenced, while he felt relieved to be sentenced to probation, he feared a number of problems would accompany registration. He said he feared that he would receive "telephone calls, maybe a physical attack or someone throwing something at the home or leaving signs on the doors—redneck type of violence." While none of these things did occur, he still feels that they could, at any time.

Fears of harassment are common, but almost without exception they were unfounded. A few RSOs did report at least one instance of harassment, but these very rarely involved personal attacks, never involved physical violence, and typically involved having their registry page photocopied and either posted or distributed in their neighborhood.

Harassment does occur on occasion. However, no one has been physically assaulted, no one has been "run out of town," and for almost all RSOs, the anticipation of possible harassment was far worse than what actually happened.

Stigmatization

There is a strong sense of stigmatization expressed by all RSOs. Universally, the RSOs interviewed report feeling that society perceives all sex offenders as highly and equally reprehensible. RSOs believe that in the eyes of the community, all individuals associated with sexual offending are considered heinous, violent, and dangerous. This is in sharp contrast to how sex offenders see themselves. In their eyes, there are "those who really are dangerous and should be locked up" and "low-level guys," but the sex offenders do not see themselves that way. All, however, report feeling publicly labeled, obvious to observers, and generally despised by the general public. Travis explained this perception, saying,

> *They just look at you one way. They aren't looking at the circumstances or what you went through, they don't care. You are just labeled and you are always going to be that and that's the way you're looked at.*

Or, as experienced by Jordan,

> *I hate to be categorized and monitored with all these people who are serial, re-offenders or vicious child predators. I don't put myself in that category with them. I hate to be looked upon as that kind of person because I don't feel I am that kind of person.*

Stigmatization extends beyond the individual offender, with courtesy stigmas (Goffman, 1963) both experienced and perceived by RSOs to be attached to the family members of offenders. Recognition of this introduces its own level of stress and suffering, as RSOs worry about the consequences and labeling of their actions and how this will affect their spouses, children, extended family members, employers, and friends/acquaintances. For some RSOs the concerns and fears for their families, especially their children, outweighs their own experience. In the words of Adam, a 64-year-old widower and former union official with four adult children, "I know that the kids feel like when they turn their backs they're being talked about. That's the part that hurts me more than anything." Or, as explained by Chris, a retired educator with six adult children,

> *I've got a couple of sons who've got similar first names to mine. So, I'm sure it's come up when they've started to examine and look over their records for jobs. So, I'm sure it's been a big pain to them.*

While recognized as a powerful force, offenders also realize that there is essentially nothing they can do to remove, reduce, or control stigmas, for themselves or others.

The other important aspect of RSO's perceptions of stigmatization comes from their feeling that they are symbols or targets of political posturing and "get tough" policies. As sex offenders, not only are they "the lowest of the low," but they also believe that they are "the perfect target for all of these politicians running around wanting to say they're doing something about crime." Preston, a convicted child molester, summed up this feeling, saying, "The problem is that it seems like I committed the crime du jour."

RSOs report that they never escape the label, and it is always present as part of their interactions and daily activities. When asked what she looks forward to in the future, Emily related that, "Even if it's 10 years down the road and it's not in the front of my head any more, it will always be there." In this same vein, Andy, who will be on the registry for the remainder of his life, lamented that,

> *I never dreamed I'd find myself in such a situation. . . . You are stripped and labeled with the ugliest of crimes. . . . I know it's there to remind and punish, but it will always be like a roadblock in the way for those of us who wish to truly rehabilitate and change our lives.*

Directly related to the experience of feeling stigmatized, but by far the most universal experience of RSOs is a persistent and constant feeling of vulnerability. This feeling comes from the belief that they are likely to be recognized in public, and at any moment they could be "outed" as a convicted sex offender. Regardless of where they are or what they do, RSOs report they constantly feel on-guard about being recognized and announced to the world. As Tyler, a 29-year-old convicted rapist and fairly well-known member of the local gay community, explained this feeling: "It's kind of like a low numb pain in a tooth that you haven't had fixed. Some days it doesn't bother you that bad, but then other days it's worse."

Regardless of where they are or what they do, RSOs consistently report never feeling able to forget their status. Few, if any, things in their life are not structured, at least in part, by their being labeled a registered sex offender. At least for the period of their listing on the registry (which for many is the rest of their life), these individuals live with the knowledge and experience. As one RSO said, "It's just a horrible feeling knowing that it's out there and it's public information. And, everybody and anybody can get into it. I hate it."

CONCLUSION

The purpose of this study was to identify what, if any, collateral consequences were experienced as a result of sex offender registration. Through in-depth qualitative interviews, this research sought to gain insights into the extent and nature of collateral consequences as perceived by registered sex offenders. As shown, the experiences of RSOs are negative consequences for employment and relationships, and experiences of harassment, stigmatization, and perceived feelings of vulnerability.

Registered sex offenders report experiencing specific employment difficulties with regard to both getting hired and maintaining a job. Common among registered sex offenders is the belief and experience that employers and society attach especially harsh stigmas to sex offenders. Respondents felt that their status as a "felon" was not as hard to overcome as their "sex offender" label.

Sex offenders also reported important and varied difficulties with their personal relationships. These relationship difficulties reported included rejection and ostracism from family, friends, co-workers, and significant others, most of which RSOs attributed to their status as a registered sex offender. Offenders also perceived negative impacts as a result of registration by feeling more "known" to society. Respondents felt that this public labeling presented serious challenges for both existing romantic and familial relationships as well as for potential future relationships with significant others.

Societal ostracism and prejudice led to labeling that was perceived as very difficult to overcome. Almost without exception, respondents were fearful of the way that being registered would continue to affect their own, and their families', lives.

Registered sex offenders attribute the severe extent and nature of the collateral consequences that they experience to the presence and current structure of the sex offender registry. It is possible that the presence and harsh nature of collateral consequences may ultimately lead to increased recidivism, countering the very goal of sex offender registries. More research is needed to further examine the ways that shaming may influence recidivism and the value of registries in relation to the collateral consequences that they have on registrants, communities, and recidivism.

Convicted sex offenders are subject to registration across the nation. Every year thousands more individuals are added to the rolls and are subject to anyone and everyone in their lives learning of their status. For some registrants the registry/notification process may also inform others of the nature of their offenses; for other registrants simply being known as a registered sex offender will lead others to assume or deduce the details of the offender's publicly despised conduct. And, for yet others the registration process may lead to no positive outcomes. While legislators and policymakers have intended to curtail sex offending through the registration process, available evidence does not suggest such an achievement. Rather, what is supported by research is that sex offender registration has effectively extended and intensified the consequences of a sex offense conviction.

REFERENCES

Goffman, Erving. (1963). *Stigma: Notes on the management of a spoiled identity.* New York: Touchstone Books.

Levenson, J. S. (2008). Collateral consequences of sex offender residence restrictions. *Criminal Justice Studies*, 21(2), 153–166.

Levenson, Jill S., & Cotter, Leo P. (2005). The effect of Megan's Law on sex offender reintegration. *Journal of Contemporary Criminal Justice*, 21(1), 49–66.

Levenson, J. S., Brannon, Y., Fortney, T., & Baker, J. (2007). Public perceptions about sex offenders and community protection policies. *Analyses of Social Issues and Public Policy*, 7(1), 1–25.

MacKenzie, Doris L. (2002). Reducing the criminal activities of known offenders and delinquents: crime prevention in the courts and corrections. Pp. 330–404 in L. W. Sherman, D. C. Farrington, B. C. Welsh, & D. L. MacKenzie. New York: Routledge.

Mustaine, Elizabeth Ehrhardt, Richard Tewksbury, & Kenneth M. Stengel. 2006. Residential location and mobility of registered sex offenders. *American Journal of Criminal Justice*, 30(2), 177–192.

Tewksbury, Richard. (2004). Experiences and attitudes of registered female sex offenders. *Federal Probation*, 68(3), 30–33.

Tewksbury, Richard. (2005). Collateral consequences of sex offender registration. *Journal of Contemporary Criminal Justice*, 21(1), 67–81.

Tewksbury, Richard, & Elizabeth Ehrhardt Mustaine. 2008. Where registered sex offenders live: Community characteristics and proximity to possible victims. *Victims & Offenders*, 3(1), 86–98.

Tewksbury, Richard, & Elizabeth Ehrhardt Mustaine. 2007. Collateral consequences and community reentry for registered sex offenders with child victims: Are the challenges even greater? *Journal of Offender Rehabilitation*, 46(1–2), 113–131.

Tewksbury, Richard, & Elizabeth Ehrhardt Mustaine. 2006. Where to find sex offenders: An examination of residential locations and neighborhood conditions. *Criminal Justice Studies*, 19(1), 61–75.

Welchans, Sarah. 2005. Megan's Law: Evaluations of sexual offender registries. *Criminal Justice Policy Review*, 16(2), 123–140.

Zevitz, Richard G., & Mary Ann Farkas. (2000). Sex offender community notification: Examining the importance of neighborhood meetings. *Behavioral Sciences and the Law*, 18(2–3), 393–408.

REVIEW QUESTIONS

1. How did the authors get their sample?
2. What are "collateral consequences"?
3. What do you consider to be the strengths and weaknesses of this study?

CHAPTER 48

RESPONSES TO WORKPLACE BULLYING

JOANNE D. LECK
BELLA L. GALPERIN

Workplace bullying can be defined as the intentional and repeated unpleasant behavior of an individual onto another, less powerful individual. Bullying includes both verbal and physical behaviors ranging from hurtful teasing to acts of physical aggression. Workplace bullying is theoretically related to other forms of worker mistreatment, such as violence, aggression, abuse, tyranny, incivility, antisocial behavior, and harassment.

Although employees can be bullied by peers, subordinates, and clients, this paper will focus exclusively on bullying by the victim's immediate supervisor, that is, the employee's boss. Bosses can bully their subordinates by intimidating, criticizing, teasing, mimicking, excluding, and belittling them. Bosses can also bully by assigning work that is unpleasant and setting impossible deadlines (Leck, 2004).

PRIOR RESEARCH

Historically, research on bullying has focused on school-age children and schoolyard bullying. In the past two decades, interest and research on workplace bullying has grown rapidly. This is partly due to the organizational and social costs associated with bullying as well as the extensive media attention to tragic events, such as the shooting rampages by disgruntled employees.

Many studies have been conducted to assess the frequency with which employees are bullied in the workplace. Research conducted in Danish workplaces reported that approximately 2 percent of all employees are bullied at work (Hogh and Dofradottir, 2001). Another study reported that 8.8 percent of European business professionals are bullied "once in a while" and 1.6 percent are bullied on a weekly basis (Salin, 2001). Yet another study conducted in the United Kingdom reported that as many as 53 percent of employees felt that they had been bullied at work at some time in their life (Rayner, 1997). A recent Canadian study found that about 16 percent of all subjects reported being bullied by their boss at least on a monthly basis and about 6 percent reported being bullied by their boss at least on a weekly basis (Leck, 2004). Although some of these percentages are relatively small, even small percentages suggest that thousands of workers are victimized by their bosses in Canada and other countries.

Because bullying is intended to do harm, it is not surprising that victims are more likely to be stressed and suffer from stress-related symptoms, such as decreased productivity, decreased satisfaction, and increased absenteeism (Budd, Arvey, and

Source: Prepared specifically for this reader, with portions drawn from the authors' article, "Worker Responses to Bully Bosses," *Canadian Public Policy*, March 2006, pp. 85–97. Reprinted by permission of the author.

Lawless, 1996). As a result, workplace bullying has a direct effect on the organization's bottom line and legal liability. But it is widely believed that there are ways to tackle bullying and thereby decrease both human suffering and negative organizational consequences. For instance, bullying can be prevented by conducting reference checks prior to hiring, establishing codes of conduct, providing assertiveness and sensitivity training, and adopting zero-tolerance policies. Bully bosses can be identified by introducing anonymous hotlines, investigating areas with high turnover and absenteeism, and conducting exit interviews. Workplace bullying can be stopped by disciplining bullies and by giving human resources departments greater power to act on bullies.

PRESENT RESEARCH

In this study, we sought to find out whether workers who have been bullied in the past would respond to some issues of workplace bullying differently than workers who have never been bullied by their boss. To find the answer, we first conducted a quantitative study comparing the responses of bullying victims and nonvictims. Then we conducted a second, qualitative study that entailed interviewing only the victims.

First Study: Sample and Methods

In the first, quantitative study, the sample consisted of 474 students attending evening undergraduate classes at the School of Management of the University of Ottawa. Thirty-six percent of the sample was male, ranging in age from 18 to 60 years and averaging 24.2 years. Approximately 18 percent were unionized, 42 percent worked in the service sector, 30 percent worked in government, and the remaining worked in the health, education, communication, and financial sectors. All subjects worked a minimum of 20 hours per week, and 36 percent worked at least 40 hours per week.

To classify subjects as either victims or nonvictims, subjects were asked to rate the frequency with which their boss bullied them using the following five choices: daily, weekly, monthly, yearly, or never. Although there is some variation in the past research about how frequently the behavior in question has to occur to be considered bullying, most researchers agreed that bullying on a monthly basis constitutes the minimum. We chose to use this standard as well. Therefore, if subjects indicated that they were bullied at least once a month, they were considered to be bully victims. This resulted in a victim sample of 76 (16 percent of the sample). The remaining 398 were classified as nonvictims.

Subjects were also asked to indicate how frequently they were victims of 34 more specific bullying behaviors. These bullying behaviors were compiled from an extensive review of the studies that dealt strictly with bullying. Sample items include: "my boss intimidates me," "my boss physically harms me," and "my boss sets unrealistic or impossible deadlines for work." These, too, were rated either daily, weekly, monthly, yearly, or never. The number of bullying acts a victim was subjected to on a monthly basis was used to measure the frequency of bullying.

To assess how workers perceive their organization's attitude toward bullying, subjects were asked to indicate the extent to which they agreed or disagreed with ten statements describing their organization's response to bullying using a five-point Likert scale (from 1 for "strongly disagree" to 5 for "strongly agree"). Sample statements included "my organization condemns bullying," "it is useless to file complaints," and "bullies are punished for their actions."

To assess how workers perceive the usefulness or effectiveness of anti-bullying practices adopted by their organization, subjects were asked to evaluate the effectiveness of 19 programs, policies, or practices using a five-point Likert scale (1 for "make things a lot better," 2 for "make things somewhat better," 3 for "make no difference," 4 for "make things somewhat worse," and 5 for "make things a lot worse").

To identify how workers would respond to a bully boss, subjects were asked to evaluate the effectiveness of 16 behavioral responses to bullying using a five-point Likert scale (from 1 for "make things a lot better" to 5 for "make things a lot worse").

First Study: Findings

We did find that victims differed significantly from nonvictims on various issues of workplace bullying in the following ways:

1. Victims were more likely than nonvictims to see their organization's attitude toward bullying in negative ways. More specifically, victims were more likely to agree that senior management and the human resources department was indifferent to their complaints, that there was no point in filing complaints, that no actions would be taken, that they would be blamed if they admitted to being bullied, that bullies would not fear repercussions if they victimized another worker, and that bullying was accepted by their organizations. Victims were also less likely to agree that the organization they worked for condemned bullying, that bullies were punished for their actions, and that they felt comfortable filing a complaint. In short, victims were more likely than nonvictims to agree that their organization's overall attitude toward bullying was one that tolerated bullying.
2. Victims were more likely than nonvictims to perceive their organization's anti-bullying policies and practices as ineffective. For example, victims felt significantly less strongly than nonvictims that policies such as zero-tolerance policies and anonymous hotlines were effective (i.e., would make things better). Victims also felt significantly less strongly than nonvictims that telling a bully boss that their behavior is unacceptable was effective.
3. Victims were more likely than nonvictims to deal with bullying in a passive way, whereas nonvictims were more likely to deal with bullying in an active and assertive way. Thus victims indicated that passive strategies such as staying away from work, keeping quiet, and laughing it off were significantly better in dealing with bullying than did nonvictims. Nonvictims, however, indicated that it was significantly better to take an active role in stopping bullying by finding other people who are bullied in order to gather evidence, by putting the bullies on notice that their actions will not be tolerated, by discussing the situation with others (such as lawyer, colleagues, and human resources department), and by fighting back.

Second Study: Sample and Methods

Fifteen subjects were interviewed. All were female, between 21 and 26 years of age, and working full time. Six worked in the financial sector, two in retailing, and seven for the federal government. They were all victims of workplace bullying.

Subjects from the first study were invited to provide their contact information if they wished to participate in a follow-up in-depth interview. Thirty-seven subjects (7.6 percent) indicated that they would like to be interviewed and provided their names and contact information. All thirty-seven had indicated that they had been bullied in the past; none of the nonvictims provided their names for the follow-up interview. Of the 37, 15 were subsequently interviewed. The objective of the interview was to better understand what workers do when bullied by their boss. Subjects were first asked to describe their latest bullying incident. After the description was provided, subjects were asked to describe how they responded to the incident. The interviewer did not interject except to ask prompting questions such as "What did you do next?" and clarifying questions such as "Could you be more specific?" The interviews were tape-recorded and transcribed. Each interview lasted about 20 minutes.

Second Study: Findings

Subjects were first asked to discuss their latest bullying incident, and then to describe how they subsequently responded to their bully boss. The reactions described by the 15 subjects are provided in their own words below:

1. "I kept doing this broken record technique and stating that this was coming sort of unexpectedly and that this was an inappropriate time to discuss it and that I wasn't prepared to talk about it and that if they'd like to schedule another time where we could sit down and talk further about it that I'd be happy to do it."
2. "Well, I focused on doing my job and I was looking for something else because I know that I was in a no-win situation. My motivation originally was that if I could just keep doing things really excellent and achieving the results that they were looking for, I'd have to win them over eventually, but it was just never going to happen."
3. "I would just click into a mode of thinking that this had really nothing to do with me, it had to do with other issues."
4. "I would keep a sense of humor about it. I would picture them like cartoon characters with an axe in their head."
5. "My philosophy is that we are all put here to get along, so find a way to get along. If it means bending or if it means biting your tongue or if it means a lot of things, then do them."
6. "At one point I said that I was going to go smoke because I couldn't take it anymore. I punched the metal door on the way out."
7. "It used to really upset me but it got to the point where now I just don't say anything or I say 'OK' and go on because I know it's not personal."
8. "So what I have to do is that I have to be very careful of the way I say things to him. I have to be very careful because he's always on the defensive and he's always afraid of being attacked and he lies."
9. "And I'm at the point where I can't anymore. I've had several bullying situations and I've tried to settle these situations but it hasn't changed anything. So at the point where I'm at, I prefer to leave."
10. "It was one of these situations where I was really young and foolish and thought I was responsible. So I actually had never told anybody."
11. "If we see her coming down the hall we just pick up the phone and pretend that we're calling someone. Or we say that we are really busy and don't have time to talk about this, you know. Or just hope that someone calls for you at the moment when she walks in the office."
12. "I had spoken about the problem with the general manager and I had explained to her how it was impossible to talk with him. She tried talking with him but the only thing that happened is that he'd act all nice and so she wouldn't understand why the employees were complaining. Now for them we were just complainers."
13. "I've tried going to the manager of human resources but that did nothing. She believed the supervisor. They were supposed to put up meetings and stuff to try to fix the situation, but the employers are nice for a week after and then they go back."
14. "So we look out for each other. If he walks in and starts talking about somebody then another person will make a comment telling him, well you know, 'look, there are friends among us, keep your mouth shut.' "
15. "So my reaction was to yell even louder and to swear at him in front of the clients. He called his assistant so that she could continue to supervise while we went to finish our discussion in his office. We fixed our differences and everything was OK."

We discussed with each other the above statements made by the 15 victims and then we summarized them as follows. Of the 15 interviews, three engaged in a direct behavior (i.e., walk out and punch door, no. 6; told bully to shut up, no. 14; yell even louder, no. 15). Two intended to look for another job (numbers 2 and 9). Two tried (unsuccessfully) to get help from others (i.e., general manager, no. 12; human resources, no. 13). Two attempted to avoid the bullying by either pretending to talk on the phone (no. 11) or postpone the discussion until later (no. 1). Five endured their bully boss by reminding themselves that it wasn't personal (numbers 3 and 7), keeping a sense of humor (no. 4), finding a way to get along (no. 5), and being very careful not to antagonize the bully (no. 8). Finally, one person thought it was their own fault (no. 10).

DISCUSSION AND CONCLUSIONS

The results of this study suggest that victims are less confident in the effectiveness of anti-bullying policies and practices, such as zero-tolerance policies and anonymous hotlines, than are nonvictims. This could mean that even when organizations adopt anti-bullying policies and practices, victims may not use them. Further, it is unclear whether victims would report transgressions to the human relations department, because victims are less likely to feel that outside help would improve their situation. Victims are more likely than nonvictims to stay quiet. Paradoxically, nonvictims are more likely to believe that dealing with a bully boss in a more active and assertive way (e.g., telling them that their actions will not be tolerated) would make the situation better. The results suggest that being bullied may change how workers perceive their organization and its policies, and may change how they would behave if bullied again. Clearly, a new approach to help victims is needed.

But it is understandable why victims may not use their organization's anti-bullying policies and practices. They know that even when anti-bullying practices are adopted, organizations may be reluctant to enforce them, especially if the bully is an otherwise effective and productive employee. Further, because bullies who "get the job done" are often rewarded by promotion, they frequently occupy positions of power and are inherently "fireproof."

Still, bullying occurs too frequently and its costs are too high to be ignored or tolerated. Legislation prohibiting bullying would go a long way in making the workplace safer and more accessible to workers. The results of this research suggest, however, that merely adopting anti-bullying policies is not enough; employers must find ways of assuring those victims that "staying silent" is not the best option as they believe—they should instead be more assertive in dealing with the bully boss.

In fact, employees can be provided with assertiveness training. More opportunities to form teams, alliances, clubs, and friendships can be provided; there is "power in numbers" in organizations. Being able to tell someone can be reiterated, especially to those who may have lost faith in the human relations department. Finally, it might be helpful for employees to know that it is easier to cope with a bully boss by keeping a sense of humor about it as a coping mechanism, empathizing with the bully (e.g., my boss is under pressure), walking away or giving them what they want; at least until the bullying situation is remedied through other means.

REFERENCES

Budd, J. W., R. D. Arvey, and P. Lawless. 1996. "Correlates and Consequences of Workplace Violence," *Journal of Occupational Health Psychology* 1(2):197–210.

Hogh, A., and A. Dofradottir. 2001. "Coping with Bullying in the Workplace," *European Journal of Work and Organizational Psychology* 10(4):485–495.

Leck, J. D. 2004. "Coping with Bully Bosses," *HR Professional* (June–July): 37.

———. 2005. "Violence in the Canadian Workplace," *The Journal of American Academy of Business* 7(2):308–315.

Rayner, C. 1997. "The Incidence of Workplace Bullying," *Journal of Community and Applied Social Psychology* 7:199–208.

Salin, D. 2001. "Prevalence and Forms of Bullying among Business Professionals: A Comparison of Two Different Strategies for Measuring Bullying," *European Journal of Work and Organizational Psychology* 10(4):425–441.

REVIEW QUESTIONS

1. In what ways do victims of workplace bullying differ from nonvictims?
2. How do victims react when they are bullied by their bosses?
3. What do you think organizations should do to improve their anti-bullying policies and practices?

CHAPTER 49

EATING FOR TWO: HOW PREGNANT WOMEN NEUTRALIZE NUTRITIONAL DEVIANCE

DENISE A. COPELTON

Eating is an important social act that is regulated by a variety of social norms (Belasco, 2008; Germov and Williams, 1999). What we eat, when, and how we eat, are socially and culturally determined. Because of the Western cultural links between femininity and body size, many women are acutely aware of nutritional norms and monitor their diets in an attempt to achieve the thin ideal. Dietary norms take on added moral significance in pregnancy, when women's nutritional habits are highly scrutinized by themselves and others because they are "eating for two." Women have been responsible traditionally for "feeding the family" (DeVault, 1996), but pregnant women are held to higher nutritional standards, subject to greater social control, and held morally accountable for fetal health.

Cultures label foods as either "good" and thus "good for you" or "bad" and thus "bad for you." Western cultures equate the kind of foods consumed with the kind of person who consumes it, as in the popular phrase, "you are what you eat." Eating healthy or good foods bestows healthful and morally positive qualities on the individual. But consuming unhealthy or bad foods bestows negative qualities, and can result in moral condemnation by self and others (Lupton, 1996). Because pregnant women are "eating for two," consuming "good" food is linked with "good" mothering, and consuming "bad" food is linked with "bad" mothering (MacIntyre, 1983; Murcott, 1982, 1988).

The mothers-to-be in this study generally believed that eating healthy foods during pregnancy was necessary to be considered a good mother, and they attempted to follow the strict social norms for prenatal nutrition described in detail in popular pregnancy advice books such as *What to Expect When You're Expecting*, *The Pregnancy Diet*, and *What to Eat When You're Expecting*. Because prenatal nutritional guidelines are quite strict (Copelton, 2003), most women fall short. Here I examine the techniques of neutralization 55 white middle-class pregnant women use to sustain identities as good mothers when they fall short of the strict nutritional standards promoted in pregnancy.

Techniques of neutralization are verbal accounts that explain or rationalize norm violations, freeing individuals to engage in deviant behavior without seriously damaging their self-concept (Sykes and Matza, 1957). These take two general forms—justifications and excuses (Scott and Lyman, 1968). With justifications, the individual admits to the behavior, but admits no wrongdoing and challenges the behavior as deviant. Pregnant

Source: Specifically written for this reader, with portions drawn from the author's article, " 'You Are What You Eat': Nutritional Norms, Maternal Deviance, and Neutralization of Women's Prenatal Diets," *Deviant Behavior*, vol. 28 (2007), pp. 467–494. Reprinted by permission of the author.

women who offer justifications for consuming unhealthy foods essentially claim, "Yes, I ate this, but it's really not so bad because . . ." With excuses, one admits that the act was deviant, but maintains that the violation could not be prevented. Pregnant women who offer excuses for eating unhealthy foods maintain, "It's regrettable that I ate this, but it couldn't be helped." Although justifications challenge social norms, excuses support them. In this article I discuss the techniques of neutralization pregnant women use to account for violations of prenatal nutritional norms.

THE MORAL IMPERATIVE TO EAT RIGHT

The larger cultural distinction between good and bad foods was readily apparent in women's accounts of eating during pregnancy. Being pregnant created new and strict dietary norms, even for those women who enjoyed healthy diets before pregnancy. The women I studied reported increasing their consumption of "good" foods (i.e., milk, water, fruits and vegetables, and high protein foods) and limiting their consumption of "bad" foods (i.e., caffeinated or alcoholic beverages, foods high in sodium, sugar, fat, or calories, and fast food). Madelyn made a special effort to "eat the right kind of food" since becoming pregnant, which includes limiting caffeinated beverages and sweets. Fran tried to "get the fruits and vegetables in," while Patricia described herself as a "variety eater" since becoming pregnant: "I'm trying to do a little Brussels sprouts, a little asparagus . . . I try to get a variety of vegetables." Becoming pregnant also meant eating on a regular basis—three meals a day meals plus healthy snacks. Emily noted, "Before [I got pregnant] I'd skip meals and . . . eating wasn't a big priority. I'd grab a sandwich or something fast, but now I'm really conscious of eating regularly and very healthy."

The larger cultural mandate to be a good mother required constant monitoring of one's prenatal diet. Roschelle noted, "I really watch what I'm putting in my mouth." Pauline explained, "I'm more conscious about what I'm eating and at every meal I think: is this good for me, is this good for the baby?" Like Pauline, most questioned whether or not particular foods were good for the developing baby and tended to prioritize fetal health over their own taste preferences. Such selfless altruism is a key component of the good mother ideal constructed in popular culture (Hays, 1996). Orinda explained, "If you are really concerned about the health of your baby, you will eat nutritiously and do whatever it takes to have a healthy child." Doing "whatever it takes" includes eating a nutritious diet, whereas failing to eat nutritiously indicates a lack of concern for fetal health and runs counter to the cultural construct of the good mother.

Deborah's decision to eliminate caffeine provides a vivid illustration of how food choices in pregnancy are linked to the motherly quality of selflessness: "It was going very easy for me . . . and I thought I should have to sacrifice something, you know. So I thought, well, I'll give up my caffeine . . . I didn't smoke before, and I didn't have to cut out drinking or drugs or anything, so this'll be my sacrifice." For Deborah, motherhood entails sacrifice, beginning in pregnancy and continuing after birth, and good mothers make voluntary sacrifices for the good of their children. Because she could not demonstrate altruism for the fetus in other ways (giving up alcohol or drugs), she demonstrates it by sacrificing caffeine. Finally, Veronica spoke for the majority of women in the study when she claimed that healthier eating is a result of being "in tune to the fact that someone else is dependent on you." Thus, most women interpreted the popular phrase "eating for two" to mean eating for one—and that one is the baby. The need to eat right for the baby was a moral imperative that most respondents embraced, but did not always follow.

When pregnant women consume "bad" foods, they are open to charges of maternal deviance for breaking current prenatal nutritional norms. If consuming "good" food during pregnancy is indicative of "good" mothering, then those women who choose instead to consume "bad" food can be seen as placing their own wants and desires above concern for fetal health. They violate the motherly norm of selflessness and risk of being seen as poor mothers. Erika recalled:

> *Every once in a while I just want a pop [soda] with sugar and caffeine in it. And I feel like when you're at the mall or something and you look [visibly pregnant] and you order a Coke, the ladies behind the counter just look at you like, 'What are you doing? You shouldn't be having that. You should be having a bottle of water.' So it's hard because I feel bad about it.*

Like Erika, many respondents felt pressure to conform to nutritional mandates and felt guilty when they consumed foods of questionable nutritional value. Fran noted feeling guilty when she consumed sweets, and invoked the idea of "cheating" on her pregnancy diet. The feelings of guilt women experience from "cheating" during pregnancy are similar to the guilty pleasures of indulging when dieting to lose weight. Some of this guilt is tied to concern over weight gain, but much of it derives from the larger cultural link between good nutrition and good mothering. Hope expressed this most directly when, after noting that she sometimes drank caffeinated soda, confessed, "I feel very guilty. I feel like a bad mom." Because women wanted to see themselves as good mothers, they used neutralization techniques to alleviate guilt and protect their self-concept.

ACCOUNTING FOR NUTRITIONAL DEVIANCE

Not one woman of the 55 I interviewed followed the nutritional advice on diet and nutrition perfectly. Most did what they felt was reasonable and accounted for specific instances of noncompliance. Here I describe the justifications and excuses women offered for their deviant diets.

Denials of Injury

Women used the denial of injury to refute the importance of nutrition by asserting that eating so-called "bad" foods will do no harm (Sykes and Matza, 1957). Women used a variety of evidence to support this claim, including the health of the fetus. They also claimed that despite not following nutritional norms entirely, they have done enough to ensure a healthy pregnancy. Rhonda maintained, "I've changed it enough where, with the vitamins and adding more milk and stuff like that to my diet that I'm getting stuff that I need. The baby's healthy, I'm healthy." Not following the advice perfectly has not appeared to cause harm to herself or her baby, who she argued is active and an appropriate size.

Others discounted particular aspects of nutritional advice by arguing that attending to every detail of their diet will have no discernible impact. Women were especially likely to disregard advice to consume particular portions of food, count servings, or calculate the recommended daily allowance of particular food constituents like iron or calcium. Annette remarked on both her lack of time to measure portions and her inability to do so given that she did not own a kitchen scale:

> *You kind of to some degree have to wing it. I just don't think it's going to make a heck of a lot of difference in the long run. You know, you just do your best to eat fruits, vegetables, protein, stuff like that, and take your prenatal vitamins, and I don't think it's going to matter in the long run if you've had four ounces of tuna that day versus—You know what I mean? [emphasis added]*

Annette does not reject the principles of good nutrition outright; rather, she agrees that pregnant women should do their best to consume a variety of "good" foods. However, she takes issue with the degree of scrutiny necessary to protect fetal health and emphasizes repeatedly that counting ounces is not worth the effort. Joyce argued similarly that small things, like chewing artificially sweetened gum, are not serious threats to fetal health: "The amount of aspartame in one little piece of gum isn't going to make that big of a difference in a pregnancy. It's a small piece of gum." According to these women, adhering to a lesser dietary standard will do no harm.

Fiona was one of the few women to challenge the importance of a strict diet by drawing on genetics: "[Following nutritional advice] does give you a better advantage, but you can't discount all the genetic things that are going on also." According to Fiona, then, because there are other factors at play besides nutrition, not strictly following nutritional norms will do no harm.

Condemning Their Condemners

Pregnant women also used the condemnation of condemners justification (Sykes and Matza, 1957) by attempting to shift attention away from their own deviant behaviors and onto the behaviors of others, thus condemning anyone who might criticize their food choices. By comparing her own eating habits to those of her pregnant coworkers, Emily condemns her would-be-condemners: "They're eating M&M's and crappy food and junk food and stuff . . . I'm not showing a ton and people are like, 'Oh, you're so lucky.' Well, I haven't eaten fast food since I got pregnant. I mean, I'm really doing it right." Emily points out what she has done "right" (cutting out fast food) and what her pregnant coworkers have done wrong (eating candy and junk food). Even though Emily has not eaten perfectly and admits to gaining more weight than recommended, she is able to deflect any potential criticism and injury to her self-concept by pointing to a group of pregnant women who have consumed worse.

Many women noted that following prenatal dietary norms was difficult because of time constraints and other limitations imposed by modern life. Instead of condemning would-be-condemners, pregnant women faulted society at large. The need to consume meals on the go and the lack of time to cook or shop were frequent themes. Irisa blamed today's "fast paced society," for preventing her from "taking time to sit down and cook the perfect little meal. You want something really quick and fast." Fran agreed, adding that it is hard to eat nutritiously "when you're busy and hectic and running here and there . . . or you're tired and don't want to cook and make a mess."

Most women linked these constraints of modern living to the fact that they needed to work full-time to maintain a middle-class lifestyle. Sarah complained that the recommended dietary changes are "just not realistic when you're working," though she concedes they are good recommendations and has tried to follow them. Though Tanya was not currently working at the time of our interview, she linked her reliance on processed foods, which are not recommended in pregnancy diets, to her prior work schedule: "It's easy to throw together somethin' quick and that's what we were used to because I was working nights and my boyfriend worked days . . . It's harder to prepare the food. It takes more time." The types of food available at work also sometimes made it difficult to eat well. Hope, who worked full time at a shopping mall, explained, "You just take for granted when you go to Subway you're not gonna ask for a milk or anything like that. You just . . . you get a beverage." This typically meant a carbonated beverage, mostly high in sugar and also containing caffeine, two items pregnant women are supposed to avoid. Here Hope shifts the focus away from her behaviors and onto the nutritional qualities of the food supply, neutralizing the suggestion that she is not a good mother because she has not completely cut out "bad" foods.

Women also claimed that the dietary norms in pregnancy are too restrictive and impossible to follow. Nadia asserted, "I don't think you can avoid everything . . . I just think you have to eat. So if you're worried about what's in every little—you know, there's too much." Nadia's statement that "there's too much" to worry about is also a subtle critique of nutritional advice itself and represents another instance of the condemnation of condemners. The issue is no longer whether a woman followed nutritional decrees; rather, the issue is their validity and practicality. The claim is that the norms are too stringent, the diet impossible for any reasonable woman to follow. Therefore, pregnant women should not be held responsible when they violate prenatal nutritional norms; the culture that created those norms and the current social arrangements that make it impossible to follow them are to blame.

The Metaphor of the Ledger

Women drew on "the metaphor of the ledger" justification (Klockars, 1974) whenever they used "bad" food as a treat for eating "good" food. They kept a mental list (or ledger) of all foods consumed, believing the good to cancel out the bad. Wendi said of chocolate and other sweets, "I do allow myself probably a little bit. I think, okay, I've done really good this week. It's okay. I try to balance it out in my mind." Helen also emphasized trying to achieve a balance between good and bad foods: "I'm trying to eat decent stuff. I eat the junk too, but I eat good stuff too!" Madelyn said of caffeinated drinks: "I like cappuccino very much, and you're not supposed to drink that much caffeine, so I pretty much cut out pop and allowed myself at least one or two cappuccinos . . . So then I'm still getting what I want, but yet not doing it as much as I used to. So it kinda balances out." Finally, Rebecca noted, "if you're going to gain 35 pounds anyway, you gotta let yourself have a treat every now and again." A treat, whether junk food, sweets, or a caffeinated beverage, is acceptable, in part, because it is unusual—the occasional reward for good behavior.

Self-Fulfillment

With self-fulfillment, the pleasure the deviant act brings (for example, the pleasure of eating sweets) is used to justify it (Scott and Lyman, 1968). Yet it was quite rare for women to justify eating bad foods with claims of self-fulfillment since it goes against the motherly norm of selflessness. When self-fulfillment was used, it was combined with some other technique of neutralization as if to neutralize the justification itself.

It was extremely rare for women to view pregnancy itself as giving them permission to eat nutritionally deficient foods. Rebecca was the only respondent to take this self-fulfilling view. She rationalized her consumption of "bad" foods by highlighting the special circumstances surrounding it—her lactose intolerance prior to pregnancy. When Rebecca became pregnant, she discovered that she could tolerate dairy. Not knowing if this change was permanent, she decided to "live up the dairy products" by drinking whole milk, adding heavy cream and whipped cream to her cereal, making cheesecake with extra cream, and topping it with ice cream. "I love the fat!" she exclaimed, "I really do like cream!" Rebecca rationalized her consumption of full-fat dairy products by emphasizing the calcium they contained. This, paired with her lactose intolerance before pregnancy, more than justified in her mind, the sugar and fat she was also consuming. Though she combines several justifications in accounting for her behavior, she emphasized the pleasure she took in finally being able to enjoy dairy. Nevertheless, the sheer joy of eating was not something most women stressed, as it runs counter to the motherly norm of selflessness.

Appeals to Biology

The only excuse women used to neutralize their deviant prenatal diet was appealing to biological drives (Scott and Lyman 1968), specifically, pregnancy cravings. Cravings are sudden and strong desires for particular foods that are attributed to the pregnancy itself. Cravings are typically for foods lacking in nutritional content, such as those high in fat, calories, or sugar, and represent weakness, or lack of resolve. Kristen exclaimed, "Cookie dough—that's my big weakness!" But cravings are also a tool used to navigate the terrain of "bad" foods in ways that sustain, rather than detract from the good mother ideal. Unlike justifications, cravings do not call nutritional norms into question. But cravings allow women to temporarily "indulge" in foods defined as nutritionally deficient while providing an excuse for such behavior. Cravings thus function to condemn the behavior generally, while simultaneously excusing individual women when they engage in that same behavior.

Many respondents experienced cravings for nutritiously deficient foods they consumed regularly prior to becoming pregnant, but have since tried to eliminate from their pregnancy diet. For example, Tanya tried to eliminate hot dogs because of their high sodium and fat content. She complained, "I miss my hot dogs," and related a recent hot dog craving: "I ate a bite of [my boyfriend's] hot dog the other day 'cause I had to, you know? I just, I had to!" Given the availability of the food, her hot dog craving was too strong to resist. Rhonda, who tried to limit her consumption of junk food, noted that this was difficult when a craving strikes: "When you're kind of craving it you kind of can't help it!" By appealing to biological cravings, women absolve themselves from responsibility for eating "bad" foods, claiming, as Tanya did, that they "had to" or as Rhonda did, that it couldn't be helped. Such passive compliance with biological drives deflects moral condemnation and removes responsibility from their eating behaviors.

Some women craved foods they did not usually eat before becoming pregnant. Greta explained, "I've never been a junk food person but since I've been pregnant I really crave french fries." Annette remarked similarly, "I was never a sweet lover at all before I got pregnant, and now all I want to do is eat candy bars . . . because I crave it for some reason." Both Greta and Annette expressed concern over their new love for "junk food," and claimed that cravings made it difficult to conform to prenatal nutritional norms.

Finally, like the self-fulfillment justification, the claim of biological cravings was not always sufficient to protect women's self-concept, and many women felt guilty when they satisfied their cravings. The cravings excuse was therefore often combined with one or another justification to neutralize remaining guilt. For example, Annette took great pains to explain her craving for Slimfast, a popular weight-loss drink: "I crave Slimfast all the time, which is really strange, and my doctor said that's okay . . . It's chocolate-flavored, but it has like a ton of, you know, vitamins and stuff in it, so it's really not bad for you. It's got a hundred percent of vitamin C and E, and five grams of fiber, and a bunch of protein and stuff." Consuming a weight-loss beverage, one specifically designed as a meal replacement, seems out of sync with nutritional advice that warns against cutting calories and/or skipping meals during pregnancy, and Annette feels compelled to offer a detailed explanation for her Slimfast craving. Though she recognizes chocolate as a "bad" food overall, she redefines the drink as nutritious. Her rationale for drinking it includes its nutritional content, her doctor's seal of approval, and her own biological craving. Thus, she combines an excuse (cravings) with a justification (denial of injury) to create a powerful account that protects her from accusations of maternal deviance and sustains her identification as a good mother despite consuming a beverage that, on first glance, seems nutritionally inappropriate in pregnancy.

CONCLUSION

In this study, I examined how pregnant women respond to nutritional norms. Women's food choices were influenced by both popular nutritional advice and the cultural construct of the good, self-sacrificing mother. Good mothers and mothers-to-be are supposed to be selfless and place the needs of their children above their own. Choosing "healthy" foods and abstaining from "unhealthy" ones indicates a woman's "healthy" acceptance of the norms of expectant mothering.

Despite widespread acceptance of the link between good prenatal nutrition and good mothering, women do not always comply with prenatal nutritional norms. Because every one of the 55 women I interviewed violated some facet of nutritional advice, they risked being discredited as good mothers. To protect their self-image and preserve their definition of the situation (Goffman, 1959), women drew on techniques of neutralization in the form of justifications and excuses. In acknowledging that their lax dietary behavior was regrettable, women who offered excuses for poor food choices legitimize prenatal nutritional norms. For example, in appealing to biological cravings, women offer only passive resistance to prenatal nutritional norms. They are biologically compelled to consume "bad" foods and comply with their uncontrollable cravings. However, women who offered justifications for their deviant diets challenge the legitimacy of dietary norms by either denying that bad foods will harm fetal health, pointing the finger at other women or blaming society at large, or claiming that "good" foods erase the effects of "bad" ones.

That justifications were more common than excuses indicates women's greater willingness to challenge, rather than accept, the legitimacy of prenatal nutritional norms. Yet not all justifications (e.g., self-fulfillment) or excuses (e.g., cravings) were effective in neutralizing charges of maternal deviance and none of them succeeded in alleviating all of women's guilt. The fact that feelings of guilt persisted, despite the variety of neutralization techniques at women's disposal, indicates how deeply internalized these norms are for many women.

REFERENCES

Belasco, Warren. 2008. *Food: The Key Concepts.* New York: Berg.

Bordo, Susan. 1993. *Unbearable Weight: Feminism, Western Culture, and the Body.* Berkeley: University of California Press.

Copelton, Denise A. 2003. "Pregnancy by the Book: Women's Accommodation and Resistance to Medicalized Pregnancy Practices." Ph.D. dissertation, Department of Sociology, Binghamton University, Binghamton, NY.

DeVault, Marjorie. 1996. *Feeding the Family.* Chicago: University of Chicago.

Germov, John, and Lauren Williams. 1999. *A Sociology of Food and Nutrition.* New York: Oxford University.

Goffman, Erving. 1959. *The Presentation of Self in Everyday Life.* New York: Doubleday.

Hays, Sharon. 1996. *The Cultural Contradictions of Motherhood.* New Haven, CT: Yale University.

Klockars, Carl. 1974. *The Professional Fence.* New York: Free Press.

MacIntyre, Sally. 1983. "The Management of Food in Pregnancy." Pp. 57–72 in *The Sociology of Food and Eating*, edited by Anne Murcott. Aldershot: Gower.

Murcott, Anne. 1982. "Menus, Meals and Platefuls: Observations on Advice about Diet in Pregnancy." *International Journal of Sociology and Social Policy* 2(4):1–11.

Murcott, Anne. 1988. "On the Altered Appetites of Pregnancy: Conceptions of Food, Body and Person." *Sociological Review* 36(4):733–764.

Scott, Marvin, and Stanford Lyman. 1968. "Accounts." *American Sociological Review* 33:46–62.

Sykes, Gresham, and David Matza. 1957. "Techniques of Neutralization: A Theory of Delinquency." *American Sociological Review* 22(6):664–670.

REVIEW QUESTIONS

1. Why is it difficult for pregnant women to control their nutritional deviance?
2. How do the women in this study justify their nutritional deviance?
3. How does culture influence eating behavior?

CHAPTER 50

A NEW WAY OF FIGHTING THE WAR ON DRUGS

ERICH GOODE

The explosion of crack cocaine use in the mid-1980s set off a fierce debate in the United States. In the midst of calls to crack down on drug users and suppliers, a formerly politically unpalatable proposal emerged: drug legalization. Advocates argue that enforcing the drug laws has fattened the wallets of drug gangs, increased drug-related violence, corrupted law enforcement, dissuaded drug abusers from seeking medical help, and in the end failed to deter drug use. It is time, these critics claim, to legalize illicit drugs, stop arresting drug users and focus entirely on treatment.

It is true that the "war" approach to controlling drug abuse and its side effects has failed. But the hope that simply legalizing drugs will work is also unrealistic. The optimal strategy is a program focused largely—and pragmatically—on reducing the damage that both drug abuse and the war on drugs inflict on users and society at large.

Legalization proposals vary across a wide spectrum. Some plans call for regulating all psychoactive substances in the same way we currently regulate alcohol. The alcohol model would legalize the possession of any and all drugs, but the government would control how they can be sold. Others endorse dispensing certain substances by prescription to the drug-dependent. The most radical proposals call for no state control whatsoever. This laissez-faire model of full decriminalization is endorsed by libertarians. Other decriminalization approaches are limited to certain drugs—usually marijuana—in small quantities, and to possession, not sale or distribution. Advocates of these various models agree that law enforcement should not and cannot solve the problem of drug abuse. They argue that the current system causes harm, which some form of legalization would alleviate, and that drug use would not skyrocket under legalization.

"Harm reduction"—more a strategy for evaluating policies and their consequences than a specific proposal—is often confused with legalization. Harm reductionists are pragmatic rather than programmatic. They weigh costs and benefits, focus more on the health of the community than on individual rights, tend to be cautious or even pessimistic about some legalization models and argue that policy should be set on a drug-by-drug basis. According to this approach, the goal of drug policy is to reduce death, disease, predatory crime, and other costs, not to attain some idealized outcome.

LEGALIZE IT?

Would any form of drug legalization work better than the war on drugs? In what specific ways might legalization succeed or fail? While most of what is written on drug laws has been polemical, serious researchers have studied the possible con-

Source: Erich Goode, "Legalize It? A Bulletin from the War on Drugs," *Contexts*, vol. 3 (Summer 2004), pp. 19–25.

sequences of changes to the law. Most focus on the practical effects of various policy proposals, leaving the moral issues to philosophers, politicians and pundits. One strategy is to look at the history of drug regulation.

Drug Policy and Drug Use, Past and Present

Journalist Edward Brecher described 19th-century America as "a dope fiend's paradise." For much of the 1800s, few jurisdictions controlled psychoactive substances. During the first half of the century, children were permitted to purchase and drink alcohol, politicians and the military distributed liquor, and work in rural planting fields and urban workshops was usually accompanied by more than one pull at the jug. Tax records indicate that in 1830, per-capita alcohol consumption was more than three times what it is today. As for narcotics, the problem of addiction has hardly improved from the days when these substances were legal. During the 19th century, under a laissez-faire policy, there were at least as many narcotic addicts as there are today. Historians estimate that at the end of the 19th century there were at least 300,000 opiate addicts, most of whom started using drugs to treat medical problems. That amounts to about 3.7 addicts per 1,000 people. Today, about 1 million people are addicted to heroin, which is approximately 3.55 per 1,000 people.

But a comparison between then and now should take into consideration more than numbers alone. Under a more or less laissez-faire 19th-century legal system, few addicts committed crimes to pay for their habit, the criminal-addict subculture was small and violent gangs did not distribute drugs. Today, our laws prohibit and penalize the possession and distribution of nearly all psychoactive substances for recreational purposes—and some for any reason. Each year, we arrest 1.5 million people for drug offenses, and between 300,000 and 400,000 drug offenders reside in state and federal prisons, more than the number of violent offenders. Today, about one-third of state prison inmates and half of federal inmates are serving time for drug crimes. There are more than 15 times as many people in state prisons for drug crimes now than there were in 1980, and the proportion of all state prisoners who are drug offenders has quadrupled. Likewise, federal prisons house four times more drug offenders now than in 1980, and the proportion of all federal prisoners who are drug offenders has doubled. Comparatively, the United States incarcerates more drug offenders (150 per 100,000 people) than the European Union does for all crimes put together (fewer than 100 per 100,000). It seems the social costs of drug use are higher than ever.

Perhaps the fear of arrest and imprisonment discourages potential users from taking up the joint, pipe or needle. Supporters of prohibition consider Reagan's war on drugs a success, because use—especially among adolescents and young adults, which had shot up during the permissive 1960s and 70s—declined significantly and spectacularly during the 1980s. (Ironically, the crack epidemic hit precisely when casual, recreational drug use declined.) Yet, beginning in the early 1990s, rates of recreational drug use increased again among young people. (After 2000, they declined a bit.) Another blow to advocates of a law enforcement approach is that today American schoolchildren are more than twice as likely to use marijuana—and almost four times as likely to use other illicit drugs—as are their European peers. Also, Reagan's drug war failed to curb supply. During his presidency, the purity of the two most dangerous illicit drugs—heroin and cocaine—increased, while their price declined. Methamphetamine, a powerful and once-popular stimulant commonly referred to as "speed," also made a strong comeback. Moreover, "club" drugs such as Ecstasy, GHB, and Rohypnol, which were not on anyone's radar screen a decade ago, are now widespread.

For these reasons, critics of the current system believe that drug prohibition has been a failure. Legalizers believe that enforcement of drug laws has untoward social side-effects. They argue that the prohibitions more than the drugs are responsible for the crime, violence and medical pathology. And they think the solution to the substance abuse problem is legalization. Under close scrutiny, however, the evidence does not always back up their claims.

Lessons from Alcohol Prohibition

Critics of the drug laws often point to national prohibition of alcohol in the United States as evidence that banning illicit substances does not work. Actually, Prohibition (1920–33) offers a complex lesson. Evidence on cirrhosis of the liver and hospital admissions for alcohol-related dementia indicates that alcohol consumption almost certainly declined during Prohibition—mainly among the heaviest drinkers. (Interestingly, these measures of heavy alcohol consumption began to decline before both state and federal prohibitions were imposed.) Tax records indicate that American adults drank an average of two gallons of absolute alcohol per year before Prohibition. During 1934, the first full year after Prohibition was repealed, this figure came to just under one gallon, suggesting that the experience of Prohibition deterred drinking even after it became legal again. The first lesson we learn from Prohibition is that criminalization can work—at least partially—to discourage use.

Deterrence aside, Prohibition proved a costly mistake. It enriched and empowered organized crime, increased murders, generated disrespect for the law, encouraged corruption among government officials, deprived the government of tax revenue and drove people to drink toxic "bootleg" substitutes. The second lesson of Prohibition is that outlawing illicit substances may generate damaging unanticipated consequences.

The fact is, most Americans did not regard alcohol consumption as a sin. When state referenda were held, voters chose to repeal rather than continue Prohibition by 15 million to 4 million votes. Alcohol was a part of the lives of many Americans—something that is untrue today of heroin, cocaine or speed. Hence, Prohibition offers a third lesson: behavior that is in the mainstream of American culture probably cannot be successfully prohibited. But behavior that runs against the grain may be an altogether different matter.

The Lesson of Marijuana Decriminalization

Possessing small amounts of marijuana has been decriminalized—or, to use a term coined by Robert MacCoun and Peter Reuter, "depenalized" —in 12 states. This means that, if apprehended with pot, users cannot be arrested, will not serve jail or prison time, and will have no criminal record. Instead, they may have their stash confiscated and be required to pay a small fine. (Marijuana possession in any quantity—approved scientific research excepted—remains illegal according to federal law.) Surveys as recent as an October 2002 *Time*/CNN poll show that 7 out of 10 Americans favor assessing fines over jail time.

Most policy analysts believe—based on systematic before-and-after comparisons—that removing criminal penalties on small-quantity possession did not open a floodgate of marijuana use in the depenalized states. Year-by-year changes in use in the decriminalized states basically follow the same up-and-down patterns as the nation as a whole. Also, many law enforcement officials feel that decriminalization has saved the states money at relatively little risk to public health.

The Netherlands provides another case study of the consequences of legalizing marijuana. There, anyone beyond the age of 18 can walk into one of roughly 800 "coffee shops" and purchase up to five grams of marijuana or hashish, a bit less than a quarter of an ounce. No "hard" drugs may be sold in these shops, selling to minors is illegal, and blatant advertising is not permitted. Studies of marijuana use in the Netherlands do not provide clear-cut evidence either for or against legalization. On the one hand, use among Dutch youth increased rather dramatically after legalization. In 1984, only 15 percent of 18-to-20-year-olds had ever used marijuana; by 1996, 44 percent had. Similarly, the percentage of youth who had used the drug in the previous month more than doubled from 8 to 18 percent during that period. This evidence seems to support the prohibitionists' argument.

On the other hand, usage rates have increased only modestly during the past decade and appear to be leveling off. According to surveys, rates of Dutch high schoolers using cannabis, although lower than in Ireland, the United Kingdom, and France, are among the highest in Europe. Yet, they are still considerably below the rates for high school students in the United States, where most states continue to criminalize marijuana. Clearly, the *de facto* legalization of cannabis in the Netherlands has not brought about a torrent of marijuana and hashish consumption, and most Dutch citizens and officials favor the current laws. In short, the experiences of the Netherlands and the United States suggest that decriminalization would not produce significantly higher levels of marijuana use. It is entirely possible that, uniquely for marijuana, nearly everyone who wants to use the drug already does so.

The Economics of Drug Use

Legalizers typically argue that we need not worry about decriminalization making drugs cheaper and thus more enticing, because the relationship between the price of drugs and demand for them is weak or nonexistent. Economists, however, find that cost significantly influences demand for drugs. Elasticity—the variation in demand for goods as prices rise and fall—differs considerably from drug to drug. Demand for heroin drops only 0.2 to 0.3 percent for every 1 percent increase in price, but the demand for marijuana drops roughly 1 percent for every 1 percent increase in price. Cigarettes (a 0.4 percent decrease) and alcohol (a 0.7 percent decrease) fall somewhere in between.

Prohibition hugely increases the price of illicit drugs and therefore should discourage use. (Decriminalization retains penalties on distribution, sale and large-quantity possession. Hence, even in the decriminalized states, marijuana remains fairly expensive.) Legalization would lower prices, which would probably reduce the property crimes committed by addicts (their habits would be cheaper), but it would almost certainly increase rates of use. Prohibitionists predict that tens of millions of Americans would take up cocaine or heroin. This worst-case scenario is almost certainly wildly off the mark. Use would increase the most not among current nonusers, but among the heaviest current users. Studies indicate that if these drugs were cheaper and less difficult to acquire, addicts would use them in much greater volume.

When drugs are legal, the government can use taxes to raise prices and discourage use. Current state and federal taxes on legal drugs—alcohol and tobacco—are far too low, at less than 50 cents per drink and 1 dollar per pack of cigarettes, to significantly deter drinking and smoking. Not included in that dollar is the price markup charged by cigarette companies to pay off the $200 billion that they have agreed to pay the states in a legal settlement; in effect, this is taxation by another means. Since most drug-related deaths stem from alcohol (85,000 per year, according to the Centers for Disease Control) and tobacco (440,000 per year), increasing alcohol and cigarette taxes could save lives. Whether through prohibition or taxes, policies that raise costs are a powerful way to depress demand.

Of course, financial cost is not the only way in which prohibition might reduce use. Criminalization imposes other types of costs: the extra time and effort required to get drugs and the risk of incarceration. Proponents of "absolute deterrence" believe that enforcing drug laws yet more firmly can drastically reduce or eliminate illegal drug use by locking up users and dealers and scaring off would-be violators. From that perspective, the war on drugs has been a failure, because it has been insufficiently aggressive. But "stamping out" drug use is a fool's errand. "Stamping out"—or even drastically reducing—drug use is an unrealistic standard by which to judge the effectiveness of the drug laws. No one expects laws penalizing robbery, rape, or murder to "stamp out" those crimes.

"Relative deterrence"—a more moderate position—argues that, while prohibition cannot eliminate it, drug use would be more common in the absence of law enforcement. Imagine if any adult could freely purchase currently illegal drugs in licensed shops or markets, out of a catalogue or over the Internet. Drug use would surely increase. And it would rise significantly under almost any of the more radical forms of proposed legalization. Would such increased drug use be bad? It depends on the drug, and for some drugs, it depends on how the drug is used and who uses it. Apparently, for alcohol, a drink or two a day can actually stimulate good health. But for tobacco, any use is harmful, and the greater the use, the greater the harm. The story is a bit more complicated with heroin and cocaine. The way they are used today is harmful, and while legalization would eliminate some features of that harm, others would remain. Hence, higher levels of use would inevitably mean higher levels of harm.

On the other hand, the more similar a system of "legalization" is to the current system of prohibition, the more the black market would step in to provide an alternative supply of illegal drugs as it does today.

HARM REDUCTION

Today, critics of the war on drugs are less likely to advocate legalization, and more likely to endorse some form of "harm reduction." There is a vast middle ground between strict criminal punishment and outright legalisation. That territory should be explored, harm reductionists argue, to reduce deaths, disease, financial cost and crime. Find out what programs work to reduce harm, they urge, and adopt them. These advocates believe that better results will be achieved by being experimental, pragmatic and empirical.

The United States currently spends three times more money on law enforcement than on treatment and prevention. Harm reduction strategists suggest that we reverse the priority of these expenditures. They also advocate eliminating programs for drug eradication and crop substitution in source countries. Evidence gathered by the RAND Corporation indicates that these programs do not work. In addition, they are financially and politically costly. Tax dollars would be far better spent on more effective ways to combat addiction, such as treatment programs.

Needle exchange programs are another effective approach to reducing harm. They appear to lower rates of HIV transmission. Between 1988 and 1993, HIV rates decreased by 6 percent in major cities with needle exchange programs, and increased by 6 percent in cities without them. Critics of needle exchange have been unable to explain this phenomenon. These programs have been adopted nearly everywhere in the Western world. Yet they reach only 10 percent of intravenous drug users in the United States. In spite of favorable evaluations of the policy by expert panels—including the General Accounting Office and the Institute of Medicine of the National Academy of Sciences—and in spite of positive findings from the dozens of studies done to evaluate these programs, the federal government staunchly opposes needle exchange programs as "encouraging drug abuse." From a harm reduction perspective, such objections are counter-productive because the programs can help control a deadly epidemic.

Researchers have also conducted hundreds of studies of drug treatment. Overwhelmingly, these studies show that treatment works. Drug addicts and abusers who spend time in treatment programs—and the more time spent, the more this is true—tend to reduce their levels of drug abuse, commit less predatory crime, and live longer, healthier lives, than those who do not. Methadone maintenance has been studied particularly carefully. It cuts crime and saves lives. Equating the administration of methadone to heroin addicts with giving vodka to an alcoholic, as some critics do, is semantic hocus-pocus, harm reductionists argue. Even with cheating, enrollees significantly reduce their drug use and its byproducts, such as crime.

As with all policy research, the causal arrows are not always easy to draw, but most analysts are convinced from controlled studies that, over the long run, treatment is considerably more cost-effective than incarceration. Although failure rates are high, treatment programs reduce the total volume of illicit drug use and criminal behavior by roughly one-third to one-half. And a majority of drug abusers significantly reduce or abandon their use of illicit substances after a second, third, fourth, or fifth attempt at treatment—roughly comparable to the repeated failures following treatment for smoking.

Experimental programs that administer injected methadone are underway in the United Kingdom. Oral morphine is being tried in Austria, Australia, Switzerland and the Netherlands. In Germany, programs involving the use of codeine have been tried. Switzerland and the Netherlands have inaugurated injected heroin maintenance programs. Do they work? At this writing, we do not have definitive answers. But, if the goal is reducing harm and not simply drug use, American authorities should also be exploring such avenues.

A CHOICE

The outright legalization of hard drugs is both politically impossible and potentially dangerous for our society. Debating drug legalization is at present little more than cocktail party chatter, what legal scholars Franklin Zimring and Gordon Hawkins refer to as a "sideshow." Public opinion polls show that fewer than 5 percent of Americans support the legalization of hard drugs. The prospects for harm reduction strategies look somewhat better. While these strategies face formidable political obstacles in the United States, they can be adopted pragmatically, one step at a time, in individual locales or jurisdictions. Such programs are being instituted in Western Europe. They should be studied and, if they work, emulated.

Yet even after the facts are in, moral issues cannot be circumvented. Decisions about public policy ultimately rest on morality and ideology, because all programs result in a "mixed bag" of results, some good, some less desirable. How do we weigh the outcomes? Debate over which mixed bag is the least bad can never be resolved on strictly scientific grounds.

Many concerned citizens oppose any program that appears to condone drug use, even if it saves lives, while many proponents of legalization or decriminalization—especially free market libertarians—favor fully decriminalizing drugs, even if that results in higher rates of drug-related fatalities. Still, the sanctity of human life is a rhetorical "ace in the hole" for harm reduction proponents. It is time, they argue, to begin taking steps to save lives.

RECOMMENDED RESOURCES

Goode, Erich. *Between Politics and Reason: The Drug Legalization Debate.* New York: St. Martin's Press, 1997. This book provides an overview of the effect of prohibition and the likely effect of drug legalization.

Goode, Erich. *Drugs in American Society* (6th ed.). New York: McGraw-Hill, forthcoming. This study provides background detail on drug use in the United States.

Inciardi, James A., ed. *The Drug Legalization Debate* (2nd ed.). Thousand Oaks, CA: Sage, 1999. This is a book of essays, pro and con, on the question of legalization.

MacCoun, Robert J., and Peter Reuter. *Drug War Heresies: Learning from other Vices, Times, and Places.* Cambridge, UK: Cambridge University Press, 2001. This is an informative, well-reasoned volume on the consequences of drug policy.

Nadelmann, Ethan. "The Case for Legalization." *The Public Interest* 92 (Summer 1988): 3–31; and "Commonsense Drug Policy." *Foreign Affairs* 77 (January/February 1998):111–126. These two articles reflect how a prominent spokesperson for drug legalization has shifted to a more moderate position of harm reduction.

Project Cork. "Cork Bibliography: Harm Reduction." Online. http://www.projectcork.org/bibliographies/data/Bibliography_HarmReduction.html. A 128-citation bibliography of empirical studies on harm reduction published between January 2002 and September 2003.

Zimring, Franklin E., and Gordon Hawkins. *The Search for Rational Drug Control.* New York: Cambridge University Press, 1992. This is an excellent general framework for understanding the foundations and implications of drug control policy.

REVIEW QUESTIONS

1. How does drug use today differ from that in the nineteenth century?
2. What options are other countries considering or implementing in response to drug problems?
3. Do you believe that drugs should be legalized? Why or why not?

Name Index

Subject Index

P

Q

R